Reciprocity, Evolution, and Decision Games in Network and Data Science

Learn how to analyze and manage evolutionary and sequential user behaviors in modern networks, and how to optimize network performance by using indirect reciprocity, evolutionary games, and sequential decision-making. Understand the latest theory without the need to go through the details of traditional game theory. With practical management tools to regulate user behavior and simulations and experiments with real data sets, this is an ideal tool for graduate students and researchers working in networking, communications, and signal processing.

Yan Chen is a professor at the School of Cyberspace Security, University of Science and Technology of China.

Chih-Yu Wang is an associate research fellow at the Research Center for Information Technology Innovation, Academia Sinica.

Chunxiao Jiang is an associate professor at the School of Information Science and Technology at Tsinghua University.

K. J. Ray Liu is Distinguished University Professor at the University of Maryland, College Park. A highly cited researcher, he is a fellow of the IEEE, the American Association for the Advancement of Science (AAAS), and the National Academy of Inventors. He is the 2021 IEEE president elect. He is a recipient of the IEEE Fourier Award for Signal Processing, the IEEE Leon K. Kirchmayer Graduate Teaching Award, the IEEE Signal Processing Society 2014 Society Award, and the IEEE Signal Processing Society 2009 Technical Achievement Award. He has also co-authored several books, including *Wireless AI* (Cambridge, 2019).

Reciprocity, Evolution, and Decision Games in Network and Data Science

YAN CHEN
University of Science and Technology of China

CHIH-YU WANG
Academia Sinica

CHUNXIAO JIANG
Tsinghua University

K. J. RAY LIU
University of Maryland, College Park

CAMBRIDGE
UNIVERSITY PRESS

University Printing House, Cambridge CB2 8BS, United Kingdom

One Liberty Plaza, 20th Floor, New York, NY 10006, USA

477 Williamstown Road, Port Melbourne, VIC 3207, Australia

314–321, 3rd Floor, Plot 3, Splendor Forum, Jasola District Centre, New Delhi – 110025, India

103 Penang Road, #05–06/07, Visioncrest Commercial, Singapore 238467

Cambridge University Press is part of the University of Cambridge.

It furthers the University's mission by disseminating knowledge in the pursuit of
education, learning, and research at the highest international levels of excellence.

www.cambridge.org
Information on this title: www.cambridge.org/9781108494748
DOI: 10.1017/9781108859783

© 2021 Cambridge University Press

First published 2021

Printed in the United Kingdom by TJ Books Limited, Padstow Cornwall

A catalogue record for this publication is available from the British Library.

ISBN 978-1-108-49474-8 Hardback

Contents

Preface

Human-like behaviors commonly exist in various networks, such as wireless and social networks. Smartphones compete with each other to access wireless networks. Social agents cooperate with each other to provide discount deals on social media, and collaborate with each other to provide answers to various questions on social computing networks. These behaviors could be analyzed using traditional game theory, which has been proven to be a great success over the decades. Nevertheless, existing studies based on traditional game theory have reached their limit when it comes to more realistic settings in modern networks, including repetitive interactions, indirect relationships, information asymmetry, network externality, and so on.

These challenges call for modern game theory, which extends traditional game theory and is inspired by the study of human social behaviors in the social sciences and biological evolution in nature. To resolve the indirect relationship challenge, indirect reciprocity with the key concept "I help you not because you have helped me, but because you have helped others" could be borrowed from the social sciences in order to build up a reputation and social judgment system, while in order to model the evolution of repetitive interactions, we could bring in evolutionary games from evolutionary biology to capture the idea of "survival of the fittest." In this book we discuss how to utilize modern game theory to study behaviors in network and data science, particularly addressing the analysis and prediction of the competitive and/or cooperative behaviors of agents in a complex social and information-related network.

In the wireless networks access problem, for instance, mobile users may access a network at different times with different requirements. Rational users tend to select the best wireless network with the greatest transmission quality. The information regarding the wireless network could be more accurate when these users share their collected information with each other. This advantage potentially leads to cooperative behaviors. However, due to network externality, the more users select the same network, the less access time each user may receive. This suggests that competitive behaviors among users also exist. In addition, each user may be facing different network statuses, since some users may have selected certain networks and some may become inactive and leave the networks – this is known as information asymmetry.

Another example is the information diffusion problem, where users repeatedly decide whether to post information or not on social networks. This information forwarding is often not unconditional. One has to make a decision as to whether or not to share this information based on many factors, such as whether the information is exciting or whether one's friends are interested in it. Moreover, due to their selfish nature, users will act to pursue their own interests, which often conflicts with the system designers' goal. How can system designers create incentives to steer users toward behaving in the way that the system designers desire, especially when the relationship among users is indirect?

These critical characteristics should be addressed as a whole when studying networks. Nevertheless, they are only partly addressed, if not ignored entirely, in the existing studies based on traditional game theory. A full understanding of the process of rational, repetitive, sequential, indirect, information-asymmetric, and dynamic-aware decision-making based on modern game theory is necessary to investigate the potential influence of these networks on the overall system, and proper regulation and management solutions can then be proposed to improve the overall network performance.

The main goal of this book is to summarize the recent progress in both the theoretical analysis and the applications of modern game theory. Three branches of modern game theory – indirect reciprocity, evolutionary games, and sequential decision-making – are presented and studied in this volume. For each branch, a series of game-theoretic frameworks will be introduced, and through the evolution of the frameworks, the critical characteristics of each branch will be captured. Given the foundations in theoretical analysis, practical management tools for regulating the behaviors of users will be discussed. In summary, both in-depth theoretical analysis and data-driven experimental results on various applications will be presented.

In Chapter 1, the fundamental concepts of game theory, which include the basic settings, game models, and corresponding solution concepts and their applications, are introduced. Then, the three main parts of this book (i.e., indirect reciprocity, evolutionary games, and sequential decision-making) are discussed.

In the first part of this book, the first branch of modern game theory – indirect reciprocity – is studied. Chapter 2 introduces the basic model to illustrate the concepts and characteristics of indirect reciprocity. The application to cognitive networks is also highlighted. Chapter 3 studies the application of indirect reciprocity to dynamic channel access with a theoretical analysis of reputation updating policy and stationary reputation distribution. In Chapter 4 an indirect reciprocity game for cooperative wireless communication is presented. Stability analysis based on Markov decision processes is provided in this chapter. Finally, Chapter 5 introduces a new form of indirect reciprocity game for general data fusion problems. Its application for improving the accuracy of dynamic channel access is presented.

In the second part of this book, the second branch of modern game theory – evolutionary games – is studied. In Chapter 6 the basic evolutionary game model for peer-to-peer streaming is presented for studying cooperative behavior. The basic approach for analyzing the evolutionarily stable strategy in this evolutionary game is discussed. In Chapter 7 we extend the evolutionary game to solve the problems of spectrum sensing and access in cognitive radio networks. Chapter 8 introduces an advanced graphical evolutionary game for distributed adaptive networks in signal processing. Chapter 9 introduces the graphical evolutionary game formulation for information diffusion in social networks. The characteristics of information diffusion in different types of networks are studied. The results are also verified with experiments based on real social network data. Finally, in Chapter 10, an extended graphical evolutionary game for information diffusion in heterogeneous social networks is presented. The influence of heterogeneous user types, either known or unknown, is studied theoretically.

In the third part of this book, the third branch of modern game theory – sequential decision-making – is presented. In Chapter 11 the motivation of sequential decision-making is presented using several examples from real-world systems. The important components in sequential decision-making, such as network externality, information asymmetry, and user rationality, are presented and defined. The limitations of the existing approaches, such as social learning, multiarmed bandit problems, and reinforcement learning, are also presented. In Chapter 12 the sequential decisions-making problem is analyzed in a static system. Network externality and the Bayesian learning model are presented to formulate how rational users learn about the uncertain system state through the observed signals shared by others. Chapter 13 analyzes the sequential decision-making problem in a dynamic system. A stochastic game-theoretic model called the Dynamic Chinese Restaurant Game is introduced to consider the uncertainty in both the network externality and the system state. Chapter 14 presents the first extension of the Chinese Restaurant Game, which considers the case in which one agent may make multiple decisions simultaneously in sequential order. The non-Bayesian learning approach is also considered in this extension. In Chapter 15 the signal-based information space is extended to an action-based information space in the Hidden Chinese Restaurant Game to show that actions are as informative as signals in the learning process. This extension prevents extra overheads in signal exchanges and gets rid of the assumption of reliable signal exchange protocols. Chapter 16 presents the wireless access point selection problem as the first application of the Chinese Restaurant Game framework. A mechanism design is presented to regulate the access decisions of rational users in order to improve the overall system performance within the sequential decision-making scenario. In Chapter 17, the second application – the deal selection problem and cross-media learning behavior in social media – is presented. The experimental results in real social media networks verify the rationality assumption of the model. Finally, Chapter 18 presents the third application: rationality analysis of the heterogeneous actions (answer vs. vote) of users in social computing systems. The experimental results based on user behavior data collected from Stack Overflow confirm the correctness of the model.

This book is aimed at graduate students and researchers who work/study electrical engineering or computer science, especially in the area of network and data science. This book can be used as a graduate-level course textbook in courses focused on modern game theory in network and data science. Readers should have prior knowledge of probability and wireless communications.

This book would not have been possible without the contributions of the following people: Biling Zhang, Yang Gao, Yu-Han Yang, and Xuanyu Cao. We also would like to thank them for their technical assistance during the preparation of this book.

1   Basic Game Theory

Game theory is the study of mathematical modeling of strategic interactions among agents. Agents, or players in the game, are usually considered rational (i.e., seeking their own maximum benefit from the game's outcome). The outcomes of the game, or the consequences of the actions of agents, depend on their (strategic) interactions and (nonstrategic) environmental factors. Thus, a rational player should observe, analyze, and predict the actions of other players in the game in order to select the appropriate action that leads to the most desired outcome. In game theory, the main goal is to predict the outcome of the game given the rationality of players and defined environments.

A game is composed of at least the following elements: players, actions, outcomes, and utility functions. Players, which are denoted as $\mathcal{N} = \{1, 2, 3, \dots, N\}$, are the agents who would rationally maximize their utilities in the game. The way for Player i to maximize the corresponding utility is to choose the action a_i from the action set $\mathcal{A}_i$. An action profile $\mathbf{a} = \{a_1, a_2, \dots, a_N\}$ represents the actions that each player may select in the game. When the action profile $\mathbf{a}$ is determined, the outcome of the game can then be derived by the outcome function $O(\mathbf{a})$. Given the outcome, each player may receive a utility according to the utility function $U_i(O(\mathbf{a}))$. In sum, we may describe a game as a tuple $\mathcal{G} = \{\mathcal{N}, \mathcal{A}, \mathcal{U}, O\}$.

1.1   Strategic-Form Games and Nash Equilibrium

The strategic-form game is one of the most basic game structures, where the relation between outcome and action can be represented in a matrix form. A well-known strategic-form game is the prisoner's dilemma. Two players are questioned by the prosecutor regarding the evidence of a crime. They may choose to stay silent or betray the other for a shorter prison sentence. The prisoner's dilemma can be explained with the payoff matrix in Table 1.1. In the matrix, each cell represents the utility received by Players A and B, respectively, if they choose the action profile.

In a strategic-form game, we seek the Nash equilibrium, which represents the expected action profile (i.e., the outcome of the game) if the players are rational.

Table 1.1. Prisoner's dilemma: a strategic-form game

(A B)	Stay Silent	Betray
Stay Silent	$(-1,-1)$	$(-8,0)$
Betray	$(0,-8)$	$(-5,-5)$

DEFINITION 1.1 (Nash equilibrium)   Nash equilibrium is the action profile $\mathbf{a}^* = \{a_1^*, a_2^*, \ldots, a_N^*\} \in \mathcal{A}$ that

$$U_i(O(a_i^*, \mathbf{a}_{-i}^*)) \geq U_i(O(a_i, \mathbf{a}_{-i}^*)), \forall i \in \mathcal{N}, a_i \in \mathcal{A}_i,$$

where a_i is the action of Player i and $\mathbf{a}_{-i}$ is the action profile of all players except Player i.

The concept of the Nash equilibrium states that every player is satisfied with the selected action in the profile given the actions selected by other players in the profile. In other words, no player can receive higher utility by changing their own action. Therefore, rational players have no incentive to change their actions when the game falls into Nash equilibria. Notice that the Nash equilibrium or pure-strategy Nash equilibrium we defined in Definition 1.1 may not always be unique or even may not exist. It is necessary to analyze the existence and uniqueness of Nash equilibria in the defined game model.

In the prisoner's dilemma game illustrated in Table 1.1, readers may observe that, given any action selected by one player, the other player will have higher utility if they choose to betray. Therefore, $\{Betray, Betray\}$ is the unique Nash equilibrium. Given that a Nash equilibrium exists and is unique in the prisoner's dilemma, we could predict that the final outcome of the game, if all players are rational, will be $\{Betray, Betray\}$.

One may notice that the best choice for the players, if they cooperate, would be the $\{Stay\,Silent, Stay\,Silent\}$, for the utility of $(-1, -1)$. Nevertheless, this better outcome is impossible in the prisoner's dilemma, since both players have the incentive to betray for a shorter prison sentence. This rational choice eventually leads them to a worse outcome, which explains why this is a "dilemma." This example suggests that rational decisions in the game may lead to suboptimal outcomes from the perspective of overall system efficiency.

1.2   Extensive-Form Games and Subgame-Perfect Nash Equilibrium

In a strategic-form game, players do not have knowledge of the actions selected by the other players. Such games are suitable for problems involving simultaneous decision-making or if the decisions are privately made. For scenarios in which the actions of players can be observed, either fully or partially, by other players, extensive-form games would be more suitable.

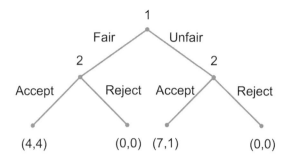

Figure 1.1 Ultimatum game

An extensive-form game can be represented by a game tree, in which the terminal nodes are the outcomes of the game with payoffs to the players, and the rest of the nodes are the decision timings when the players (and/or the nature) may select the actions (and/or external influence) to direct the game toward certain outcomes.

The ultimatum game, which is illustrated in Figure 1.1, is a famous example of an extensive-form game. In the ultimatum game, Player 1 is requested to propose an offer for sharing a cake, while Player 2 can choose to accept or reject the offer. If Player 2 accepts the offer, the cake will be allocated as is. Nevertheless, if Player 2 chooses to reject the offer, neither player will receive the cake.

In this game, we may identify three Nash equilibria according to Definition 1.1:

(1) Player 1 offers to fairly share the cake and Player 2 only accepts when the offer is fair, or $\{Fair, Fair|Accept, Unfair|Reject\}$.
(2) Player 1 offers to unfairly share the cake and Player 2 only accepts when the offer is unfair, or $\{Unfair, Fair|Reject, Unfair|Accept\}$.
(3) Player 1 offers to unfairly share the cake and Player 2 accepts any offer, or $\{Unfair, Fair|Accept, Unfair|Accept\}$.

The first one is the offer that we sometimes see when people are facing the situation similar to Player 2; that is, they will make an ultimatum or threat that they will damage both of them if they are treated unfairly. This is why the game is called the ultimatum game. Nevertheless, although such a claim can be supported by a Nash equilibrium, it may not be a suitable solution concept for the extensive-form game, as it does not consider the fact that Player 2 already knows which action Player 1 has selected at the time of their decision.

The subgame-perfect Nash equilibrium is a refined solution concept for the extensive-form game. A subgame is a subtree of the game tree starting from any node and including all branches following the starting node. A subgame-perfect Nash equilibrium is defined as follows:

DEFINITION 1.2 (Subgame-perfect Nash equilibrium) A Nash equilibrium is a subgame-perfect Nash equilibrium if it is a Nash equilibrium in every subgame.

The concept of the subgame-perfect Nash equilibrium captures the rationality of players when they know the actions of other players beforehand. In the ultimatum game, for instance, Player 2 already knows whether Player 1 has offered a fair share when they choose to accept or not. In both subgames, after Player 1 proposes the offer, the only Nash equilibrium in the subgames would be Player 2 choosing to accept the offer, since rejecting will give Player 2 zero utility. With this refinement, the only subgame-perfect Nash equilibrium would be $\{Unfair, Fair|Accept, Unfair|Accept\}$.

1.3   Incomplete Information: Signal and Bayesian Equilibrium

In some problems, the outcome of the game involves uncertainty. The uncertainty may come from the external factors that could not be observed directly or the private preferences and actions of the players. The exact outcome of the game therefore may not be known at the time of the decision-making. In such a game, rational players must estimate the influence of this uncertainty. Instead of seeking utility maximization, they aim to maximize their expected utility.

Let us consider a game with player set $\mathcal{N}$ and action set $\mathcal{A}$. The game is in a state $\theta \in \Theta$, which is unknown to some or all players. The utility of Player i is given by $U_i(\mathbf{a}, \theta)$, $\mathbf{a} \in \mathcal{C}$, which depends on the action selected by Player i, the actions selected by the other players, and the state θ.

The uncertainty in the state can be estimated if the distribution of the state is known. It can either be known in advance (signaling game) or learned about from the received information (social learning). Let us assume that the probability of the state $\mathbf{p_i}$ (or belief), on state θ over state space Θ is known or derived after strategic thinking. Players then may maximize their expected utilities based on the belief as follows:

$$\mathbf{p_i}(\mathbf{I_i}) = \{p_{i,\theta}|\theta \in \Theta\}, \sum_{\theta \in \Theta} p_{i,\theta}(I_i) = 1,$$

where I_i is the information received by Player i in the game.

$$p_{i,\theta}(I_i) = \frac{Prob(I_i|\theta)}{\sum_{\theta' \in \Theta} Prob(I_i|\theta')}$$

Given this new objective of the players, we may extend the equilibrium concept to a Bayesian Nash equilibrium.

DEFINITION 1.3 (Bayesian Nash equilibrium)   A Bayesian Nash equilibrium is the action profile $\mathbf{a}^*$, where

$$\sum_{\theta \in \Theta} p_{i,\theta}(I_i)U_i(a_i^*, \mathbf{a}_{-i}^*, \theta) \geq \sum_{\theta \in \Theta} p_{i,\theta}(I_i)U_i(a_i, \mathbf{a}_{-i}^*, \theta), \forall i \in \mathcal{N}, a_i \in \mathcal{A}_i.$$

The reputation game is a famous example of a game with incomplete information. In the game we have two firms. Firm 1 is in the market and prefers a monopoly. Firm 2 is new and would like to enter the market. There are two possible types of

Table 1.2. Reputation game

	Stay	Exit
Sane/Prey	(2,5)	(X,0)
Sane/Accommodate	(5,5)	(10,0)
Crazy/Prey	(0,−10)	(0,0)

Firm 1: Sane and Crazy, each with 0.5 probability. Their actions and corresponding utilities are illustrated in the game matrix in Table 1.2.

In such a game, there are two possible Bayesian Nash equilibria, while their existence depends on the value of X.

Pooling equilibrium: When X = 8, both Sane and Crazy Firm 1 will choose to prey. In such a case, Firm 2 has no way to distinguish between these two types. Given the distribution of the type, Firm 2 will choose to exit instead of stay.

Separating equilibrium: When X = 2, Sane Firm 1 will accommodate and Crazy Firm 1 will prey. Firm 2 will stay when seeing accommodate and exit when seeing prey. In this equilibrium, Firm 2 can judge Firm 1's type through the observed action. In other words, Firm 1's action can be treated as a signal to improve the estimation of the unknown types. The rules of signaling in incomplete information will be discussed in detail in Part III.

1.4   Repeated Games and Stochastic Games

The previous game models are based on the assumption that the game will be played only once (i.e., a one-shot game). In practice, agents may face the same problem multiple times, each time with the same or different players. In such a scenario, we may formulate the problem as a repeated game. A repeated game consists of a series of base games in which the players play the same base game sequentially. It can be written as an extensive-form game by expanding the base game in a game tree repeatedly.

There are two kinds of repeated games: finite and infinite repeated games. For finite repeated games, the number of rounds of the base game is finite. This suggests that an ending base game exists, and the game tree in the extensive form is finite. In such a scenario, the game can be analyzed directly within the concept of a subgame-perfect Nash equilibrium. For the other case, where the rounds are infinite, there is no ending game and therefore a subgame-perfect Nash equilibrium cannot be applied directly. The utility of Player i in a repeated game can be written as follows:

$$U_i = \lim_{T \to \infty} \sum_{t=0}^{T} \delta^t u_i(a_i(t), \mathbf{a}_{-i}(t)), \tag{1.1}$$

where $a_i(t)$ and $\mathbf{a}_{-i}(t)$ are the actions selected by Player i and the other players at round t, respectively, and $0 < \delta < 1$ is the discount factor for evaluating the utility in the future to the players in the present.

Taking the prisoner's dilemma as an example, we may consider a repeated version of the prisoner's dilemma, which is called the iterated prisoner's dilemma. When the rounds are finite, it can be easily shown that the original {*Betray, Betray*} equilibrium still holds as the unique Nash equilibrium of the game. Nevertheless, when the rounds are infinite, the equilibrium becomes nonunique as cooperation between players becomes possible. For instance, a tit-for-tat strategy (i.e., stay silent in the first round and then choose the action selected by the opponent in the previous round) is also a Nash equilibrium, since any deviation from such a strategy will lead to {*Betray, Betray*} in every round, while continuing to use the strategy will keep them at {*StaySilent, StaySilent*} and eventually lead to higher utility in the long run. This example suggests that cooperation is likely to emerge in a repeated game. Readers will find more related examples in Part I.

In practice, even if the agent is facing the same problem and applying the same action multiple times, the results could be different due to external uncertainty or randomness in the system. We may capture this characteristic with stochastic games, which are repeated games with uncertainty.

The uncertainty is captured through adding a state $\theta \in \Theta$ to the game. The state is observable by the players but it may change in the next round with the probability described by $P(\theta'|\theta, \mathbf{a})$, which depends on the current state and the action profiles selected by the players. The utility of the players depends on not only the action profile, but also the state. Therefore, the utility of Player i in the stochastic game can be written as follows:

$$U_i = \lim_{T \to \infty} u_i(\theta(0), a_i(0), \mathbf{a}_{-i}(0))$$

$$+ \sum_{t=1}^{T} P(\theta(t)|\theta(t-1), \mathbf{a}(t-1))\delta^t u_i(\theta(t), a_i(t), \mathbf{a}_{-i}(t)). \tag{1.2}$$

Given that the state transitions depend on the previous state and the action profile, the system can be formulated as a Markov decision process when the action profile is given, which helps us to derive the expected utility given certain action profiles. Then, a Bayesian Nash equilibrium can be applied to derive the equilibrium of the game. Readers will find more examples in Parts II and III.

Part I

Indirect Reciprocity

2 Indirect Reciprocity Game in Cognitive Networks

Considering that nodes are commonly subject to different authorities with various goals in cognitive networks, there will be no cooperation among nodes unless they can perform better through cooperation. Therefore, it is important to understand how to stimulate cooperation. However, the majority of the approaches in game-theoretic cooperation stimulation are based on the presumption that the exclusive interaction of each pair of players is constant. Without this, the inimitable Nash equilibrium (NE) would act noncooperatively in the light of the Prisoner's dilemma and the backward induction principle theories. In this chapter, we consider a scenario with a certain number of interactions among players. By using indirect reciprocity game modelling, the main idea is that "*I help you not because you have helped me but because you have helped others.*" To formulate the problem of discovering the optimal action rule and to orientate the optimal action rule, the Markov decision process (MDP) is used and a modified value iteration algorithm is utilized, respectively. Based on the example of the packet forwarding game, we show that by forwarding the number of packets with an equal reputation degree to the receiver at an appropriate cost-to-gain ratio, the evolutionarily stable strategy (ESS) is formed.

2.1 Introduction

Varying network conditions that can be adapted dynamically are the elements of the cognitive network aimed at optimizing end-to-end performance through learning and reasoning [1]. Inside this network, it can be seen that nodes are intelligent and capable of observing, learning, and optimizing. Considering that nodes are generally subject to different authorities with different goals, cooperative behaviors cannot be taken for granted, such as mutually unconditionally forwarding packets. An important problem in cognitive networks lies in the process of stimulating cooperation among selfish nodes owing to the fact that nodes only achieve mutual cooperation under conditions in which their own performance can be improved.

In order to stimulate node cooperation for different cognitive networks such as ad hoc networks [2,3] and peer-to-peer networks [4,5], several methods have been put forward, and one is to use payment-based methods among selfish nodes [6,7]. Although satisfying cooperation stimulation results can be achieved using these methods, potential applications are restricted significantly by the requirement of central billing services or tamper-proof hardware.

Within selfish nodes, using reputation-based methods under essential monitoring is another way of stimulating cooperation [8–10]. "Watchdog" is one of the mechanisms used to identify misbehaving nodes, and another is called "pathrater," which aims at deflecting the traffic around misbehaving nodes [11]. The main shortcoming of these two methods is that the misbehaving nodes would not trigger punishment, leading to there being no incentive for the cooperation of nodes. In order to solve this, reputation-based mechanisms were proposed by Buchegger and Boudec [12] and Michiardi and Molva [13] to enforce node cooperation. In their approaches, mutual behaviors can be observed by nodes and information can be stored and distributed locally in reputation reports. Based on observations, the misbehaving nodes are isolated through denying the forwarding of packets to them. Nevertheless, there is no evidence that such approaches are optimal theoretically.

Recently, efforts have been made to analyze cooperation mathematically in cognitive networks using game theory [14–17]. A generous TIT-FOR-TAT strategy was proposed by Srinivasan et al. [18], while Urpi et al. [19] came up with Bayesian games. Based on game theory and graph theory, in [20] equilibrium conditions of packet forwarding strategies were investigated through considering the network topology. The authors in [21] proposed a game theoretic framework in autonomous, mobile, ad hoc networks to analyze cooperation stimulation and security jointly. It has turned out that for a two-player packet forwarding game, the help provided by the special cheat-proof NE for each node cannot surpass that provided by their opponent.

However, the assumption of a game between a pair of players being directly played infinite times is the basis of many extant game theoretical frameworks. The truth is that to improve performance due to mobility or changes of environment, partners would need to be updated periodically, which is to say that any pair of players ought to play only finite times, while the termination time is either mutually understood or can be estimated by each player. Under this circumstance, the only optimal strategy is to play noncooperatively all the time according to the well-known Prisoner's dilemma and backward induction principle [22]. This result mainly comes from the implicit assumption of direct reciprocity in most games, in which the history of the way in which the opponent treats the player defines their action. Distinctly, in this situation, due to the fact that the behavior cannot be assessed by other players except their opponents, there is no impetus for any player to play cooperatively.

The evaluations from the opponents and other observers ought to be taken into account to stimulate the players' incentives to play cooperatively, which the notion of "indirect reciprocity" can lead to. As a main mechanism, indirect reciprocity for the evolution of human cooperation is very important. It has drawn much attention in the field of evolutionary biology and social science recently [23,24]. And for indirect reciprocity, the key concept is "*I help you not because you have helped me but because you have helped others.*" In the following section, the process of utilizing indirect reciprocity game modeling in order to stimulate the cooperation of selfish nodes in the scenario where interactions among players are finite is going to be discussed.

2.2 The System Model

Figure 2.1 shows that there is a cognitive network with an adequately huge population of nodes. Short interactions instead of persistent associations between anonymous partners are dominant because of the changes and/or mobility of the environment. For each time slot, a portion of players in the population are chosen to form pairs in order to forward packets. For each pair, a player behaves as a receiver and the other as a transmitter. Let $\mathbf{A} = \{0, 1, \ldots, L\}$ denote the action set that the transmitter might choose, where the action $i \in \mathbf{A}$ is that the transmitter forwards i packets to the receiver.

In the easiest model with $L = 1$, the receiver can acquire a gain g at a cost c to the transmitter. It often ought to be presumed that no transmissions are going to appear, or that the gain g exceeds the cost c. In this case both players get $g - c$, which is better than the gain obtained by defecting, namely 0 under the condition that both players collaborate and forward one packet to the other. However, the highest payoff g would be earned by a unilateral defector, while the oppressed cooperator would pay

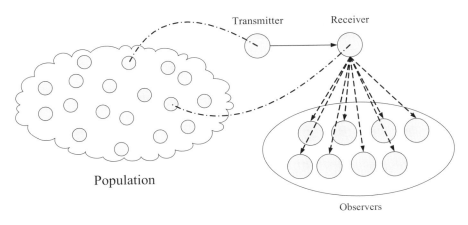

Figure 2.1 System model. A receiver and transmitter are randomly sampled from the population during every interaction. Then, the transmitter would forward a certain amount of packets to the receiver based on the receiver's and their own reputations. After the transmission, the transmitter's reputation would be updated by the receiver and the observers. Finally, the transmitter's reputation from the observers and the receiver would be propagated to the entire population through a noisy gossip channel.

the cost c and get nothing. A model of the well-known Prisoner's dilemma game is yielded according to the payoff system, and the inimitable NE shows the defecting feature (i.e., both players do not forward the packet to each other). In addition, even if the game is played for limited times, with backward deduction, the NE still remains the same. The use of direct reciprocity, where the action of a transmitter taken toward a receiver is only determined by the history of how the receiver treats them, thus causes such a noncooperative optimal strategy. Under a certain pattern, all transmitters have no impetus to forward packets, since their behaviors would only be evaluated by their corresponding receivers instead of other players.

Under this circumstance, indirect reciprocity game modeling is applied to stimulate cooperation. The establishment of the notion of reputation is the evaluation of the history of the players' actions because of the intrinsic concept, "*I help you not because you have helped me but because you have helped others*," and this is a key concept in the indirect reciprocity game. It is assumed that the reputation is quantized to $L + 1$ levels, with "L" as the best reputation and "0" as the worst reputation for simplifying the analysis. In other words, $\mathbf{T} = \{0, 1, \ldots, L\}$ can be written for the reputation set. The results can be easily broadened on the condition that the reputation set has a different size compared with the action set. Furthermore, we assume that the reputation of an individual is acknowledged by everyone and no private opinions are allowed. However, errors may occur in assigning reputation. In each interaction, based on the receiver's and transmitter's own reputations, the transmitter decides their action, which is the number of packets to forward to the receiver. After each interaction, the reputation of the recipient would not alter, whereas the transmitter's reputation is overhauled by the observers and the recipient first, which at that point is proliferated to the full population through the noisy gossip channel. Each participant (including both the receiver and transmitter) leaves the population with the probability $1 - \delta$ or goes back to the population with the probability δ. The parameter δ can be treated as a discounting factor for the future. A new individual enters with equal probability $\frac{1}{L+1}$ and owns an initial reputation selected randomly from the reputation set when a player leaves the population.

2.2.1   Social Norms

$\mathbf{Q}$, the social norm, is a matrix to update players' instant reputations, which can be instantly acquired by a transmitter by taking an action. In the social norm, each element $Q_{i,j}$ denotes the instant reputation assigned to a transmitter that has taken the action i toward a receiver whose reputation is j. In order to preserve generality, it is assumed that the same norm is shared by all players in the population. Though only the reputation of the receiver and the action of the transmitter can decide the instant reputation, it can be found in the coming analysis that the transmitter's reputation is also affected by the final reputation updating rule.

Because the cardinalities of both the reputation set and the action set are $L+1$, there are $(L + 1)^{(L+1)\times(L+1)}$ possible social norms. According to the instinct that denying the forwarding of packets to a receiver with a bad reputation or the forwarding of packets to a receiver with a good reputation ought to generate a good reputation, the instant reputation $Q_{i,j}$ is defined as follows:

$$Q_{i,j} = L - |i - j|, \tag{2.1}$$

which means that the social norm is

$$\mathbf{Q} = \begin{pmatrix} L & L-1 & \cdots & 1 & 0 \\ L-1 & L & \cdots & \vdots & 1 \\ \vdots & L-1 & \ddots & L-1 & \vdots \\ 1 & \vdots & \cdots & L & L-1 \\ 0 & 1 & \cdots & L-1 & L \end{pmatrix}. \tag{2.2}$$

For the special case when $L = 1$, the 2×2 social norm can be written as

$$\mathbf{Q}^{2\times2} = \begin{pmatrix} 1 & 0 \\ 0 & 1 \end{pmatrix}, \tag{2.3}$$

in which "1" is a good reputation and "0" is a bad reputation.

The social norm in (2.3) proves that by denying the forwarding of packets to the receiver with a bad reputation or the forwarding of packets to the receiver with a good reputation, the transmitter can gain a good immediate reputation. Meanwhile, a bad immediate reputation would be obtained by the transmitter if they deny the forwarding of packets to the receiver with a good reputation and vice versa.

2.2.2 Action Rules

a, the action rule, is the transmitter's action table, in which the ith row and j^{th} column element $a_{i,j}$ represents the transmitter's action with their own reputation being i and the corresponding receiver's reputation being j. Because the cardinalities of both the reputation set and the action set are $L + 1$, there exist $(L + 1)^{(L+1)\times(L+1)}$ possible action rules. **a***, the optimal action rule, ought to be the one that maximizes the payoff function, which is going to be discussed in the following section.

2.3 Optimal Action Rule

2.3.1 Reputation Updating Policy

In the indirect reciprocity game, reputation is the main concept [24]. The similar notion of trust is mainly based on direct reciprocity [25]. Players screen the social interactions inside their group and offer others assistance to gain a reputation for being a helpful player. Therefore, the actions of the player are the key step for updating reputation in indirect reciprocity game modeling. A reputation updating policy on the basis of the transmitter's actions, the reputation of the receiver, and the reputation of the transmitter are going to be discussed in this section.

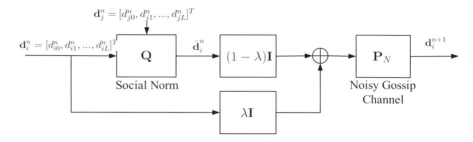

Figure 2.2 Reputation updating policy.

In order to capture all likelihoods of the transmitter's reputation and the crucial behavior regarding the transmitter's reputation, each player is assigned a reputation distribution. We set $\mathbf{d} = [d_0, d_1, \ldots, d_L]^T$ as the reputation distribution for a certain player, and the likelihood of the player being assigned reputation i is d_i.

Figure 2.2 shows the reputation updating policy. It is supposed that at time index n, a transmitter with a reputation distribution $\mathbf{d}_i^n$ matches to a receiver with a reputation distribution $\mathbf{d}_j^n$. Through a certain action, an immediate reputation $\hat{\mathbf{d}}_i^n$ is assigned to the transmitter according to the social norm. After that, the transmitter's reputation distribution would be updated by the observers and the receiver by combining the transmitter's original and immediate reputations linearly, in which the weight λ can be seen as a discounting factor of the past reputation. In the end, observers and receivers are going to propagate the reputations of transmitters among the population through a noisy gossip channel.

In a simple example, it is assumed that the reputation distribution of the transmitter is $\mathbf{d}_i^n = \mathbf{e}_i$ and the reputation distribution of the receiver is $\mathbf{d}_j^n = \mathbf{e}_j$. $\mathbf{e}_i$ and $\mathbf{e}_j$ represent the standard basis vectors. Assuming $\mathbf{e}_{Q_{a_{i,j},j}}$ to be the transmitter's immediate reputation, the action that the transmitter takes regarding the receiver would be $a_{i,j}$. Based on the reputation updating policy in Figure 2.2, after the transmission, the reputation distribution of the transmitter would be

$$\mathbf{d}_i^{n+1} = \mathbf{P}_N\big(\lambda \mathbf{e}_i + (1 - \lambda)\mathbf{e}_{Q_{a_{i,j},j}}\big), \tag{2.4}$$

where $\mathbf{P}_N$ is the transition matrix of the noisy channel. Despite the loss of generality,[1] $\mathbf{P}_N$ is defined as

$$\mathbf{P}_N = \begin{pmatrix} 1 - \mu & \mu/L & \ldots & \mu/L & \mu/L \\ \mu/L & 1 - \mu & \ldots & \vdots & \mu/L \\ \vdots & \mu/L & \ddots & \mu/L & \vdots \\ \mu/L & \vdots & \ldots & 1 - \mu & \mu/L \\ \mu/L & \mu/L & \ldots & \mu/L & 1 - \mu \end{pmatrix}, \tag{2.5}$$

where $\mu \in [0, 0.5]$ is a constant.

---

[1] Note that the analysis is also applicable to $\mathbf{P}_N$ with other forms.

The $\mathbf{d}_i^{n+1}$ in (2.4) is the transmitter's updated reputation distribution after the transmitter with an original reputation $\mathbf{e}_i$ takes an action $a_{i,j}$ toward the receiver with a reputation $\mathbf{e}_j$. Because the updated reputation distribution is going to appear in the later analysis aimed at finding the optimal action rule, it is indicated as a specific symbol $\tilde{\mathbf{d}}_{i \to j}$, i.e.,

$$\tilde{\mathbf{d}}_{i \to j} = \mathbf{P}_N \left(\lambda \mathbf{e}_i + (1 - \lambda) \mathbf{e}_{Q_{a_{i,j},j}} \right). \tag{2.6}$$

For the general case that $\mathbf{d}_i^n \neq \mathbf{e}_i$ and/or $\mathbf{d}_j^n \neq \mathbf{e}_j$, based on (2.4), the updated reputation distributions of transmitters cannot be simply expressed owing to the fact that when an action rule is given, combining the receiver's and the transmitter's reputations differently might result in the same immediate reputation. Under this circumstance, the immediate reputation can be found firstly by

$$\hat{\mathbf{d}}_i^n(k) = \sum_p \sum_{q: \, Q_{a_{p,q},q} = k} \mathbf{d}_i^n(p) \mathbf{d}_j^n(q). \tag{2.7}$$

After that, on the basis of Figure 2.2, the updated reputation distribution of the transmitter can be calculated by

$$\mathbf{d}_i^{n+1} = \mathbf{P}_N \left(\lambda \mathbf{d}_i^n + (1 - \lambda) \hat{\mathbf{d}}_i^n \right). \tag{2.8}$$

2.3.2   Stationary Reputation Distribution

Let $\mathbf{x} = [x_0, x_1, \ldots, x_L]^T$ represent the entire population's reputation distribution and let x_i represent the part of the population with the reputation i. As every pair of transmitters and receivers is selected from the population, when the transmitter with reputation i is given, the possibility of matching the receiver with reputation k is x_k. According to the protocol in Figure 2.2, the transmitter's reputation is updated after the transmission. Hence, the evolution of $\mathbf{x}$ can be defined by the following differential equation

$$\frac{d\mathbf{x}}{dt} = \mathbf{x}^{new} - \mathbf{x}, \tag{2.9}$$

in which $\mathbf{x}^{new}$ is the new reputation distribution of the entire population, which can be computed by

$$\mathbf{x}^{new} = \mathbf{P}_N \left(\lambda \mathbf{I} + (1 - \lambda) \mathbf{P}_T \right) \mathbf{x}, \tag{2.10}$$

with the ith row and j^{th} column elements of the matrix $\mathbf{P}_T$ being defined as

$$\mathbf{P}_T(j,i) = \sum_{k: \, Q_{a_{i,k}^\star, k} = j} x_k. \tag{2.11}$$

Based on (2.9), (2.10), and (2.11), the stationary reputation distribution $\mathbf{x}^\star$ is the solution of the following equation

$$\mathbf{P}_N \left(\lambda \mathbf{I} + (1 - \lambda) \mathbf{P}_T \right) \mathbf{x}^\star = \mathbf{x}^\star. \tag{2.12}$$

Algorithm 1: Finding a stationary reputation distribution using gradient descent.

---

(1) Given the optimal action $a_{i,j}^\star, \forall i, \forall j$, the tolerance $\eta_0 = 0.01$, the index $t = 0$, and step size $\alpha = 0.1$, initialize $\mathbf{x} = [x_0, x_1, \ldots, x_L]^T$ with $\mathbf{x}^0 = [x_0^0, x_1^0, \ldots, x_L^0]^T$, set $\epsilon = 1$, and let $\mathbf{F}(\mathbf{x}) = \mathbf{P}_N (\lambda \mathbf{I} + (1 - \lambda)\mathbf{P}_T(\mathbf{x})) \mathbf{x} - \mathbf{x}$.

(2) While $\epsilon > \eta_0$

- Compute the updating vector $\Delta \mathbf{x}^{t+1}$ using $\Delta \mathbf{x}^{t+1} = -\alpha \times \nabla \mathbf{F}(\mathbf{x}^t) \times \mathbf{F}(\mathbf{x}^t)$.

- Update $\mathbf{x}^{t+1}$ by $\mathbf{x}^{t+1} = \mathbf{x}^t + \Delta \mathbf{x}^{t+1}$.

- Normalize $\mathbf{x}^{t+1}$ using $\mathbf{x}^{t+1} = \frac{\mathbf{x}^{t+1}}{||\mathbf{x}^{t+1}||_2}$.

- Update the parameter ϵ by $\epsilon = ||\mathbf{x}^{t+1} - \mathbf{x}^t||_2$.

- Update the index $t = t + 1$.

End.

(3) The stationary reputation distribution is $\mathbf{x}^\star = \mathbf{x}^t$.

(2.11) and (2.12) show that through the solving of the nonlinear equation in (2.12) with the given optimal action $\mathbf{a}^\star$, the stationary reputation distribution would be found. Furthermore, Algorithm 1 proposes a gradient descent algorithm for finding the stationary reputation distribution given the optimal action rule.

2.3.3   Payoff Function

We assume that the cost of forwarding a packet is a constant, c, and the total cost to the transmitter with reputation i taking action $a_{i,j}$ toward a receiver with reputation j is given by

$$C(a_{i,j}) = a_{i,j}c. \tag{2.13}$$

Correspondingly, if the gain of receiving a packet is a constant, g, the total gain of the receiver with reputation i can be calculated by

$$G(a_{j,i}) = a_{j,i}g, \tag{2.14}$$

where $a_{j,i}$ denotes the action of the corresponding transmitter with reputation j.

$W_{i,j}$ denotes the maximum payoff that a player, who has current reputation i and has been matched to a player with reputation j, can get from this interaction in future. Intuitively, when the player with reputation i is a transmitter, the long-term payoff that they can expect through taking action $a_{i,j}$ is

$$f_1(a_{i,j}) = -a_{i,j}c + \delta \sum_k \sum_l \tilde{\mathbf{d}}_{i \to j}(k)\mathbf{x}^\star(l)W_{k,l}, \tag{2.15}$$

in which the immediate cost to the transmitter when taking action $a_{i,j}$ is in the first term $a_{i,j}c$, and the benefit they can expect in the future with a discounting factor δ is in the second term $\sum_k \sum_l \tilde{\mathbf{d}}_{i \to j}(k)\mathbf{x}^\star(l)W_{k,l}$. According to (2.6), changes from $\mathbf{e}_i$ to $\tilde{\mathbf{d}}_{i \to j}$ will happen in the transmitter's reputation distribution by taking action $a_{i,j}$. With probability $\tilde{\mathbf{d}}_{i \to j}(k)\mathbf{x}^\star(l)$, the transmitter's reputation is k and their opponent's reputation is l owing to the fact that their opponent in the next round is sampled from the population randomly with a stationary reputation distribution $\mathbf{x}^\star$.

If the player with reputation i is a receiver, the long-term payoff that they would expect is

$$f_2 = a_{j,i}^\star g + \delta \sum_l x_l^\star W_{i,l}, \tag{2.16}$$

in which the first term $a_{j,i}^\star g$ is the immediate gain that they would have when the transmitter takes the optimal action $a_{j,i}^\star$. The second term $\sum_l x_l^\star W_{i,l}$ is the benefit they can expect in the future with a discounting element δ. As a receiver, their reputation does not alter after the transmission. With possibility $\mathbf{x}^\star(l)$, the receiver's reputation is i and their opponent's reputation is l because their opponent in the coming round is stochastically sampled from the population with a stationary reputation distribution $\mathbf{x}^\star$.

Within every interaction, the player serves as either a receiver or a transmitter with an equal possibility $\frac{1}{2}$. Thus, the Bellman equation of $W_{i,j}$ could be written as

$$W_{i,j} = \max_{a_{i,j}} \left[\frac{1}{2} \left(-a_{i,j}c + \delta \sum_k \sum_l \tilde{\mathbf{d}}_{i \to j}(k)\mathbf{x}^\star(l)W_{k,l} \right) \right.$$
$$\left. + \frac{1}{2} \left(a_{j,i}^\star g + \delta \sum_l \mathbf{x}^\star(l)W_{i,l} \right) \right], \tag{2.17}$$

and the optimal action $a_{i,j}^\star$ would be calculated by

$$a_{i,j}^\star = \arg\max_{a_{i,j}} W_{i,j}$$
$$= \arg\max_{a_{i,j}} \left[\frac{1}{2} \left(-a_{i,j}c + \delta \sum_k \sum_l \tilde{\mathbf{d}}_{i \to j}(k)\mathbf{x}^\star(l)W_{k,l} \right) \right]. \tag{2.18}$$

From (2.17) and (2.18), it can be found that the optimal action rule, in which the state is the reputation pair (i, j), the action is $a_{i,j}$, the transition possibility is determined by $\tilde{\mathbf{d}}_{i \to j}$ and $\mathbf{x}^\star$, and the reward is determined by c and g, is a MDP. Thus, we can find the optimal action by solving (2.18) through dynamic programming according to the given stationary reputation distribution. As is shown in Algorithm 2, a modified value iteration algorithm is utilized to find the optimal action with the given stationary reputation distribution.

2.3.4   Optimal Action Using an Alternative Algorithm

Through Algorithm 1, we can determine the stationary reputation distribution with the given optimal action. With the given stationary reputation distribution, the optimal action can be obtained through Algorithm 2. Accordingly, the stationary reputation distribution and the optimal action alternatively can be obtained by iteratively fixing one and solving the other. Algorithm 3 summarizes the processes in detail. Note that the convergence speed of Algorithm 3 is mostly determined by the initial action

---

Algorithm 2 : Modified value iteration for optimal action selection given a stationary reputation distribution.

---

(1) Given the stationary reputation $\mathbf{x}^\star$ and tolerance $\eta_0 = 0.01$, initialize $a_{i,j}^\star$ with $a_{i,j}^0$ $\forall i$ $\forall j$ and set $\epsilon_1 = 1$ and $\epsilon_2 = 1$.

(2) While $\epsilon_1 > \eta_0$

- Set $\epsilon_2 = 1$.
- Initialize $W_{i,j} = 0$ $\forall i$ $\forall j$.
- While $\epsilon_2 > \eta_0$

  - Compute $\tilde{\mathbf{d}}_{i \to j}$ using $\tilde{\mathbf{d}}_{i \to j} = \mathbf{P}_N\left(\lambda \mathbf{e}_i + (1-\lambda)\mathbf{e}_{Q_{a_{i,j},j}}\right)$.
  - Compute $\hat{W}_{i,j}$ using $\hat{W}_{i,j} = \max_{a_{i,j}}\left[\frac{1}{2}\left(-a_{i,j}c + \delta \sum_k \sum_l \tilde{\mathbf{d}}_{i \to j}(k)\mathbf{x}^\star(l)W_{k,l}\right)\right.$
    $\left. + \frac{1}{2}\left(a_{j,i}^\star g + \delta \sum_l \mathbf{x}^\star(l)W_{i,l}\right)\right]$.
  - Compute $\hat{a}_{i,j}$ using $\hat{a}_{i,j} = \arg\max_{a_{i,j}}\left[\frac{1}{2}\left(-a_{i,j}c + \delta \sum_k \sum_l \tilde{\mathbf{d}}_{i \to j}(k)\mathbf{x}^\star(l)W_{k,l}\right)\right]$.
  - Update the parameter ϵ_2 by $\epsilon_2 = ||\hat{\mathbf{W}} - \mathbf{W}||_2$.
  - Update $\mathbf{W}$ by $\mathbf{W} = \hat{\mathbf{W}}$.
  - End.

- Update the parameter ϵ_1 by $\epsilon_1 = ||\hat{\mathbf{a}} - \mathbf{a}^\star||_2$.
- Update $\mathbf{a}^\star$ by $\mathbf{a}^\star = \hat{\mathbf{a}}$.

  End.

(3) The optimal action is $\mathbf{a}^\star$.

Algorithm 3 : An alternative algorithm for finding a stationary reputation distribution and an optimal action.

---

(1) Given the tolerance $\eta_0 = 0.01$, initialize $\mathbf{a}^\star$ with $\mathbf{a}^0$ and set $\epsilon = 1$.

(2) While $\epsilon > \eta_0$

- Given the optimal action $\mathbf{a}^\star$, find the stationary reputation distribution $\mathbf{x}^\star$ using Algorithm 1.
- Given the stationary reputation distribution $\mathbf{x}^\star$, find the optimal action $\hat{\mathbf{a}}^\star$ using Algorithm 2.
- Update the parameter ϵ by $\epsilon = ||\hat{\mathbf{a}}^\star - \mathbf{a}^\star||_2$.
- Update $\mathbf{a}^\star$ by $\mathbf{a}^\star = \hat{\mathbf{a}}^\star$.

  End.

(3) The stationary reputation distribution is $\mathbf{x}^\star$ and the optimal action is $\mathbf{a}^\star$.

---

rule $\mathbf{a}^0$. However, the algorithm is going to converge due to the limited number of possible action rules. Furthermore, the evolutionary stability of any action rule can be tested by setting the tested action rule as the initial action rule and checking whether it can converge in one iteration with Algorithm 3.

2.4   Action Spreading Due to Natural Selection

On the basis of Algorithm 3, the stationary reputation distribution and the optimal action rule can be found. However, in the analysis above, the perturbation effect is not included, through which players might employ a nonoptimal action rule because of incorrect (noisy) parameters and/or an uncertain system. It is necessary to evaluate the stability of the optimal action rule in which perturbation effects are present. Here, the concept of an evolutionarily stable strategy (ESS) is adopted [26], which is "a strategy that, if all members of the population adopt it, no mutant strategy would occupy the population under the influence of natural selection." Next, the way in which action rules spread over a population by natural selection is going to be discussed, specifically the following two action spreading algorithms: the action spreading algorithm that the replicator dynamic equation adopts [26] and the action spreading algorithm that the Wright–Fisher model adopts [27]. The optimal action rule's stability derived from Algorithm 3 through the simulations will then be examined.

We set M as the number of action rules, and $\mathbf{a}_1, \mathbf{a}_2, \ldots, \mathbf{a}_M$ are used in the population. Let p_i^t represent the percentage of the population in which action rule $\mathbf{a}_i$ at time t is used. Then, $\sum_{i=1}^M p_i^t = 1$. Let U_i^t represent the average payoff utilizing action rule $\mathbf{a}_i$ at time t.

2.4.1 Action Spreading Algorithm Using the Wright–Fisher Model

Regarding reproduction in population genetics, the Wright–Fisher model is the most popular stochastic model [27]. It assumes that the odds of an individual using a certain strategy are proportional to the expected payoff of the population adopting that strategy. The Wright–Fisher model is utilized here in order to describe the way in which action rules spread over a population because of the model's capacity to simply capture the essence of the biology involved.

Let y_i be the possibility of an individual adopting action $\mathbf{a}_i$, then $\sum_{i=1}^M y_i = 1$. Based on the Wright–Fisher model and the assumption that y_i is proportional to the total payoff of the users adopting $\mathbf{a}_i$, y_i can be computed by

$$y_i = \frac{p_i^t U_i^t}{\sum_{j=1}^M p_j^t U_j^t}, \tag{2.19}$$

where the numerator $p_i^t U_i^t$ is the total payoff when the users adopt action $\mathbf{a}_i$ and the denominator $\sum_{j=1}^M p_j^t U_j^t$ is the total payoff for the whole population, which is the normalization term that ensures $\sum_{i=1}^M y_i = 1$.

On the basis of the presumption that the scale of the population is large enough, the proportion of the population exhibiting action $\mathbf{a}_i$ is equivalent to the odds of an individual adopting $\mathbf{a}_i$. Accordingly, the action spreading equation could be denoted as

$$p_i^{t+1} = \frac{p_i^t U_i^t}{\sum_{j=1}^M p_j^t U_j^t}. \tag{2.20}$$

2.4.2 Action Spreading Algorithm Using the Replicator Dynamic Equation

In evolutionary game theory, the replicator dynamic equation is adopted to broadly characterize population evolution [26]. Intuitively, the population share using any one strategy is going to increase at a rate that is proportional to the difference between the expected payoff of the whole population and the expected payoff of the population using that strategy under the condition that a certain strategy leads to a higher payoff than average. In order to model the evolution of the proportion of the population adopting a specific action rule, we use the replicator dynamic equation. This means that the evolution of p_i is given by the subsequent equation

$$\frac{dp_i}{dt} = \eta \left(U_i - \sum_{j=1}^{M} p_j U_j \right) p_i, \tag{2.21}$$

where η is a scale coefficient determining evolution's speed.

Through discretizing the replicator dynamic equation in (2.21), the action spreading equation is

$$p_i^{t+1} = p_i^t + \eta \left(U_i^t - \sum_{j=1}^{M} p_j^t U_j^t \right) p_i^t$$

$$= p_i^t \left[1 + \eta \left(U_i^t - \sum_{j=1}^{M} p_j^t U_j^t \right) \right]. \tag{2.22}$$

2.5   Evolutionarily Stable Strategy and Simulations

In this chapter, the packet forwarding game is simulated to evaluate Algorithm 3. A fixed-size population with $N = 1,000$ is studied. An initial reputation is assigned to every new player and is aimlessly selected from $\{0, 1, \ldots, L\}$ with equivalent probability $\frac{1}{L+1}$. Every player follows one of $(L + 1)^{(L+1) \times (L+1)}$ possible action rules, and all players within the population share the fixed social norm in (2.2). There are exactly 20 interactions with other random individuals for every player before any elementary steps of action updating, and those players serve as receiver and transmitter 10 times on average, respectively. As is shown in Figure 2.2, the transmitter's reputation would be updated according to the reputation updating policy after the interaction. It is assumed that each player within the population approves the reputation that is engendered by the reputation updating policy and does not consider private lists of reputations. Then, the possibility that each player, both the receiver and transmitter, goes back to the population is δ, and the possibility that they leave the population is $1 - \delta$ after 20 interactions. New individuals enter the population to maintain the total population once any players leave. A new player's initial reputation is aimlessly chosen from $\{0, 1, \ldots, L\}$ with equal probability $\frac{1}{L+1}$. Furthermore, all players within the population that is formed by both the new players who enter and the old players who stay would choose their new action rules based on the payoff history in the entire population. Two possible actions are considered: (1) the actions that spread according to the replicator dynamic equation, which is labeled "**RDE**" and (2) the actions that spread according to the Wright–Fisher model, which is labeled "**WFM**." All players' payoffs will be be reset to 0 after updating the action rule, which is to say that older players' payoffs do not accumulate. For the following simulations, the parameters λ, δ, and μ are set as 0.50, 0.90, and 0.95, respectively. The parameter η, representing the speed of evolution in the **RDE**, is controlled and set as 0.1.

2.5.1 Binary Reputation Scenario

The binary reputation scenario where $L = 1$ is evaluated to gain further insight. It is assumed that the cost per unit is 0.1 and the gain per unit is 1 (i.e., $g = 1$ and $c = 0.1$). Based on Algorithm 3, with given different preliminary conditions, there are three pairs of stationary reputation distribution $\mathbf{x}^\star$ and the optimal action rule $\mathbf{a}^\star$:

$$\mathbf{x}_1^\star = \begin{pmatrix} 0.5 \\ 0.5 \end{pmatrix}, \quad \mathbf{a}_1^\star = \begin{pmatrix} 0 & 0 \\ 0 & 0 \end{pmatrix}. \tag{2.23}$$

$$\mathbf{x}_2^\star = \begin{pmatrix} 0.0909 \\ 0.9091 \end{pmatrix}, \quad \mathbf{a}_2^\star = \begin{pmatrix} 0 & 1 \\ 0 & 1 \end{pmatrix}. \tag{2.24}$$

$$\mathbf{x}_3^\star = \begin{pmatrix} 0.9091 \\ 0.0909 \end{pmatrix}, \quad \mathbf{a}_3^\star = \begin{pmatrix} 1 & 0 \\ 1 & 0 \end{pmatrix}. \tag{2.25}$$

The transmitter is going to forward no packets to the receiver despite their own reputation and the corresponding reputation of the receiver by using $(\mathbf{x}_1^\star, \mathbf{a}_1^\star)$. This is a rather improper strategy because no cooperation would happen and the payoff for every player is zero when using it. $(\mathbf{x}_2^\star, \mathbf{a}_2^\star)$ and $(\mathbf{x}_3^\star, \mathbf{a}_3^\star)$ are symmetric pairs. With $(\mathbf{x}_2^\star, \mathbf{a}_2^\star)$, packets would always be forwarded to receivers with a good reputation, while the transmitter would always forward packets to receivers with a bad reputation when using $(\mathbf{x}_3^\star, \mathbf{a}_3^\star)$. It can also be seen that the pair $(\mathbf{x}_2^\star, \mathbf{a}_2^\star)$ brings about a population with over 90% of players having a good reputation, while $(\mathbf{x}_3^\star, \mathbf{a}_3^\star)$ brings about a population with over 90% of players having a bad reputation. So, $(\mathbf{x}_2^\star, \mathbf{a}_2^\star)$ is preferred owing to the fact that it results in a "good" society in which over 90% of the population has a good reputation.

Next, the evolutionary stability of $(\mathbf{x}_2^\star, \mathbf{a}_2^\star)$ is evaluated. In the simulation, as is shown in (2.24), the initial frequency of the optimal action rule $\mathbf{a}^\star$ is set as 0.6, while the initial frequencies of the other action rules are chosen aimlessly. A new player's initial reputation is chosen from $\{0, 1\}$ randomly with equal possibility $\frac{1}{2}$. Figure 2.3(a) shows the evolutionary results of the population with reputation level $L = 1$. In Figure 2.3(a), it can be seen that for both **RDE** and **WFM**, the reputation distribution converges to the stationary reputation distribution $\mathbf{x}_2^\star$. The convergence speed of **RDE** is a little bit slower than for **WFM**, because in **RDE** a small speed-controlling parameter $\eta = 0.1$ is applied.

The evolutionary results of the population utilizing the action rule $\mathbf{a}_2^\star$ are shown in Figure 2.3(b). We can see that the action rule $\mathbf{a}_2^\star$ would be spread over the entire population for both **RDE** and **WFM**. No player is going to deviate once the whole population adopts $\mathbf{a}_2^\star$. Thus, under this circumstance, the action rule $\mathbf{a}_2^\star$ is an ESS [26].

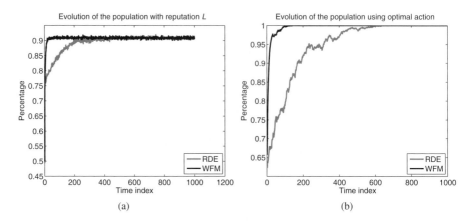

Figure 2.3 The population evolution when $L = 1$, $g = 1$, and $c = 0.1$: (a) the percentage of the population with reputation $L = 1$; (b) the percentage of the population using the optimal action shown in (2.24).

In (2.17), a conclusion can be drawn that the values of g and c determine the optimal action rule. Furthermore, each player would like to cooperate with the others if $g \gg c$, because the potential gain of cooperation would surpass the cost of immediate cooperation in this situation. However, if $c \gg g$, no players would tend to cooperate owing to the fact that the potential gain would be less than the cost. Therefore, a critical cost-to-gain ratio γ should exist such that the optimal action rule $\mathbf{a}_2^\star$ is steady if $c < \gamma g$, and it is not steady otherwise.

By varying g and c and setting $\mathbf{a}_2^\star$ as initial action rule $\mathbf{a}^0$ in Algorithm 3, we can see that if $\frac{c}{g} \leq 0.582$, the optimal action rule is $\mathbf{a}_2^\star$ through applying Algorithm 3; if $\frac{c}{g} > 0.582$, the optimal action rule turns into $\mathbf{a}_1^\star$. Hence, the critical cost-to-gain ratio γ is equal to 0.582 under this circumstance, and this means that the stable region for $\mathbf{a}_2^\star$ is the shaded region shown in Figure 2.4.

To verify the statement above, the stability of $\mathbf{a}_2^\star$ when $c = 0.6$ and $g = 1$ is evaluated, and in Figure 2.5, the corresponding evolutionary results are shown. Figure 2.5(b) shows that when $\frac{c}{g} = 0.6 > 0.582$, for both **RDE** and **WFM**, the population's percentage adopting action rule $\mathbf{a}_2^\star$ does not converge to 1. Thus, there is no stability for $\mathbf{a}_2^\star$ under this circumstance. Accordingly, it can be seen from Figure 2.5(a) that the reputation distribution does not converge to $\mathbf{x}_2^\star$ under this circumstance.

2.5.2   Multilevel Reputation Scenario

For the multilevel reputation scenario in which $L \geq 2$, it is difficult to find all of the possible pairs of the optimal action rule $\mathbf{a}^\star$ and stationary reputation distribution $\mathbf{x}^\star$ due to the large dimensions of the action space $((L + 1)^{(L+1) \times (L+1)})$. However, according

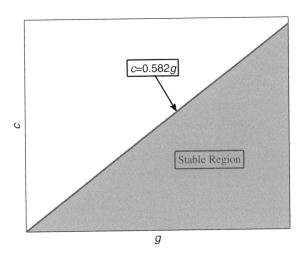

Figure 2.4 The stable region for the optimal action rule shown in (2.24) when $L = 1$.

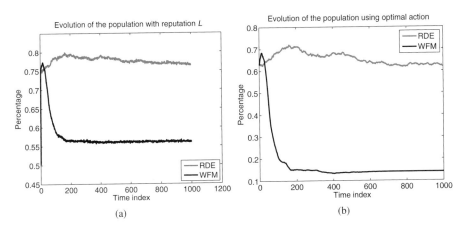

Figure 2.5 The population evolution when $L = 1$, $g = 1$, and $c = 0.6$: (a) the percentage of the population with reputation $L = 1$; (b) the percentage of the population using the optimal action shown in (2.24).

to the results in the binary reputation scenario, it can be inferred that forwarding i packets to the receiver with reputation i is one probable optimal action rule $\mathbf{a}_0^\star$; in other words, $\mathbf{a}_0^\star$ could be given as follows:

$$\mathbf{a}_0^\star = \begin{pmatrix} 0 & 1 & \cdots & L \\ 0 & 1 & \cdots & L \\ \vdots & \vdots & \vdots & \vdots \\ 0 & 1 & \cdots & L \end{pmatrix}. \tag{2.26}$$

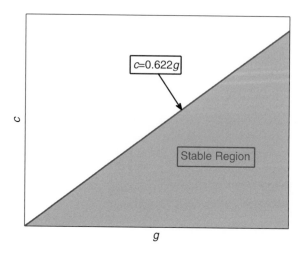

Figure 2.6 The stable region for the optimal action rule shown in (2.26) when $L = 4$.

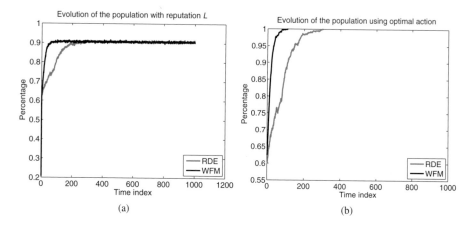

Figure 2.7 The population evolution when $L = 4$, $g = 1$, and $c = 0.5$: (a) the percentage of the population with reputation $L = 4$; (b) the percentage of the population using the optimal action shown in (2.26).

Based on Algorithm 1, the corresponding stationary reputation distribution $\mathbf{x}_0^\star$ can be found. As for the special case with $L = 4$, $\mathbf{x}_0^\star$ is

$$\mathbf{x}_0^\star = \left(\begin{array}{ccccc} 0.0235 & 0.0235 & 0.0235 & 0.0235 & 0.906 \end{array}\right)^T. \tag{2.27}$$

Then, the stable region for the optimal action rule $\mathbf{a}_0^\star$ can be acquired in a similar fashion. It is expected that if $\frac{c}{g} \leq 0.622$, the optimal action rule obtained from Algorithm 3 would still be $\mathbf{a}_0^\star$ when $\mathbf{a}_0^\star$ is set as the initial action rule $\mathbf{a}^0$ in Algorithm 3, and the optimal action rule would change if $\frac{c}{g} > 0.622$. Hence, the critical cost-to-gain ratio γ under this circumstance is equivalent to 0.622, and a conclusion can be drawn that the stable region for $\mathbf{a}_0^\star$ is the shaded region shown in Figure 2.6.

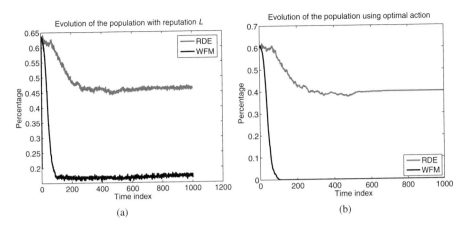

Figure 2.8 The population evolution when $L = 4$, $g = 1$, and $c = 0.7$: (a) the percentage of the population with reputation $L = 4$; (b) the percentage of the population using the optimal action shown in (2.26).

The statement above is then verified through simulating the packet forwarding game with two different cost-to-gain ratio settings. One setting is $g = 1$ and $c = 0.7$ $\left(\text{i.e., } \frac{c}{g} = 0.7 > 0.622\right)$ and the other is $g = 1$ and $c = 0.5$ $\left(\text{i.e., } \frac{c}{g} = 0.5 < 0.622\right)$. Figure 2.7 shows the evolutionary results for the latter setting, and it can be seen that the optimal action rule $\mathbf{a}_0^\star$ spreads over the entire population and the reputation distribution converges to $\mathbf{x}_0^\star$ for both **WFM** and **RDE** when the cost-to-gain ratio is set to be $\frac{c}{g} = 0.5 < 0.622$, verifying that $\mathbf{a}_0^\star$ is an ESS under this circumstance.

As is shown in Figure 2.8, the evolutionary results of the former cost-to-gain ratio setting are different, from which it can be found that under the condition of the cost-to-gain ratio being set as $\frac{c}{g} = 0.7 > 0.622$, the action rule $\mathbf{a}_0^\star$ does not spread over the entire population and the reputation distribution does not converge to $\mathbf{x}_0^\star$ for both **RDE** and **WFM**. Thus, $\mathbf{a}_0^\star$ is not stable under this circumstance.

2.6   Conclusion

In this chapter, a cooperation stimulation scheme for cognitive networks with indirect reciprocity game modeling, which differs from the existing game-theoretic methods and does not depend on the presumption that interactions in any pair of players are infinite, is discussed. It is shown from the simulation results that the action rule of forwarding i packets to the receiver with reputation level i is an ESS with an appropriate cost-to-gain ratio. The optimal action rule would spread over the whole population very rapidly by natural selection, even when starting from 60% of the population using the optimal action rule. Once the optimal action rule is undertaken by the whole population, there would be no deviating players. Furthermore, a "good" society would be created through such an ESS, in which over 90% of the population enjoys a good reputation.

References

[1] R. W. Thomas, D. H. Friend, L. A. Dasilva, and A. B. Mackenzie, "Cognitive networks: adaptation and learning to achieve end-to-end performance objectives," *IEEE Communications Magazine*, vol. 44, pp. 51–57, 2006.

[2] L. Buttyán and J. P. Hubaux, "Enforcing service availability in mobile ad-hoc networks," in *Proc. ACM MobiHoc*, 2000.

[3] S. Zhong, J. Chen, and Y. R. Yang, "Sprite: A simple, cheat-proof, credit-based system for mobile ad-hoc networks," in *Proc. IEEE INFOCOM*, 2003.

[4] V. Vishumurthy, S. Chandrakumar, and E. Sirer, "Karma: A secure economic framework for peer-to-peer resource sharing," in *Proc. 2003 Workshop on Economics of Peer-to-Peer Systems*, 2003.

[5] P. Golle, K. Leyton-Brown, and I. Mironov, "Incentive for sharing in peer-to-peer networks," in *Proc. ACM Conference on Electronic Commerce*, 2001.

[6] S. Zhong, L. Li, Y. G. Liu, and Y. R. Yang, "On designing incentive-compatible routing and forwarding protocols in wireless ad-hoc networks – an integrated approach using game theoretical and cryptographic techniques," in *Proc. ACM MobiCom*, 2005.

[7] L. Anderegg and S. Eidenbenz, "Ad hoc-VCG: A truthful and cost-efficient routing protocol for mobile ad hoc networks with selfish agents," in *Proc. ACM MobiCom*, 2003.

[8] W. Yu and K. J. R. Liu, "Attack-resistant cooperation stimulation in autonomous ad hoc networks," *IEEE Journal on Selected Areas in Communications*, vol. 23, pp. 2260–2271, 2005.

[9] S. Marti and H. Garcia-Molina, "Limited reputation sharing in P2P systems," in *Proc. 5th ACM Conference on Electronic Commerce*, 2004.

[10] M. Gupta, P. Judge, and M. Ammar, "A reputation system for peer-to-peer networks," in *Proc. ACM 13th International Workshop on Network and Operating Systems Support for Digital Audio and Video*, 2003.

[11] S. Marti, T. J. Giuli, K. Lai, and M. Baker, "Mitigating routing misbehavior in mobile ad hoc networks," in *Proc. ACM MobiCom*, 2000.

[12] S. Buchegger and J. Y. L. Boudec, "Performance analysis of the confidant protocol," in *Proc. ACM MobiHoc*, 2002.

[13] P. Michiardi and R. Molva, "Core: A collaborative reputation mechanism to enforce node cooperation in mobile ad hoc networks," in *Proc. IFIP-Communications and Multimedia Security Conference*, 2002.

[14] P. Michiardi and R. Molva, "A game theoretical approach to evaluate cooperation enforcement mechanisms in mobile ad hoc networks," in *Proc. Workshop Modeling and Optimization in Mobile, Ad Hoc and Wireless Networks (WiOPT'03)*, 2003.

[15] J. Crowcroft, R. Gibbens, F. Kelly, and S. Ostring, "Modeling incentives for collaboration in mobile ad hoc networks," in *Proc. Workshop Modeling and Optimization in Mobile, Ad Hoc and Wireless Networks (WiOPT'03)*, 2003.

[16] W. S. Lin, H. V. Zhao, and K. J. R. Liu, "Incentive cooperation strategies for peer-to-peer live multimedia streaming social networks," *IEEE Transactions on Multimedia, Special Issues on Community and Media Computing*, vol. 11, pp. 396–412, 2009.

[17] M. Xiao and D. Xiao, "Understanding peer behavior and designing incentive mechanism in peer-to-peer networks: An analytical model based on game theory," in *Proc. International Conference on Algorithms and Architectures for Parallel Processing (ICA3PP)*, 2007.

[18] V. Srinivasan, P. Nuggehalli, C. F. Chiasserini, and R. R. Rao, "Cooperation in wireless ad hoc networks," in *Proc. IEEE INFOCOM*, 2003.

[19] A. Urpi, M. Bonuccelli, and S. Giordano, "Modeling cooperation in mobile ad hoc networks: A formal description of selfishness," in *Proc. Workshop Modeling and Optimization in Mobile, Ad Hoc and Wireless Networks (WiOPT'03)*, 2003.

[20] M. Felegyhazi, J.-P. Hubaux, and L. Buttyan, "Nash equilibria of packet forwarding strategies in wireless ad hoc networks," *IEEE Transactions on Mobile Computing*, vol. 5, pp. 463–476, 2006.

[21] W. Yu and K. J. R. Liu, "Game theoretic analysis of cooperation stimulation and security in autonomous mobile ad hoc networks," *IEEE Transactions on Mobile Computing*, vol. 6, pp. 507–521, 2007.

[22] M. J. Osborne and A. Rubinste, *A Course in Game Theory*. MIT Press, 1994.

[23] M. A. Nowak and K. Sigmund, "Evolution of indirect reciprocity," *Nature*, vol. 437, pp. 1291–1298, 2005.

[24] H. Ohtsuki, Y. Iwasa, and M. A. Nowak, "Indirect reciprocity provides only a narrow margin for efficiency for costly punishment," *Nature*, vol. 457, pp. 79–82, 2009.

[25] Y. Sun, W. Yu, Z. Han, and K. J. R. Liu, "Information theoretic framework of trust modelling and evaluation for ad hoc networks," *IEEE Journal of Selected Areas in Communications, Special Issue on Security in Wireless Ad Hoc Networks*, vol. 24, pp. 305–317, 2006.

[26] J. M. Smith, *Evolution and the Theory of Games*. Cambridge University Press, 1982.

[27] R. Fisher, *The Genetical Theory of Natural Selection*. Clarendon Press, 1930.

3 Indirect Reciprocity Game for Dynamic Channel Access

Besides improving primary users' (PUs') quality of service (QoS) within dynamic spectrum access (DSA) networks, cooperation is also a vital approach to utilizing spectrum resources efficiently. However, secondary users (SUs) might not behave as cooperatively as the PUs would hope due to their selfish nature. Therefore, it is crucial to employ methods for stimulating SUs to play cooperatively. In this chapter, a reputation-based spectrum access framework is going to be discussed, within which an indirect reciprocity game is applied for modeling cooperation stimulation. In this game, the SUs choose the method of helping PUs relay information to gain reputation, and a certain amount of vacant licensed channels can be accessed by them in the future based on the result. The optimal action rule can be obtained through formulating the decision-making of the SUs to be a Markov decision process (MDP), and according to the rule, if the channel is not in an outage, the SU will apply their maximum strength to help the PU relay data. Thus, spectrum utilization efficiency as well as the PU's QoS can be improved. Furthermore, the uniqueness of the stationary reputation distribution is proved, and the conditions under which the optimal action rule is evolutionarily stable are theoretically derived.

3.1 Introduction

Recently, it has been reported that a huge quantity of the radio spectrum authorized by the Federal Communications Commission (FCC) to licensed users, also known as PUs, remains underutilized [1]. The DSA technique of sharing and accessing the licensed spectrum for a short time drew much attention owing to the fact that it can significantly improve the efficiency of spectrum utilization. Furthermore, unlicensed users, also called SUs, can be allowed to access the spectrum by using this technique [2–4].

There are several spectrum access approaches in the literature. Spectrum sharing is one of those approaches, and it is used in researching the allocation of vacant spectra in which PUs are sensed as inactive [5–8]. The authors in [5] gave an introduction to a cognitive multiple-access protocol. In order to forward their packets to improve the PUs' QoS, SUs sense and exploit idle channels to cooperate with the PUs in the cognitive multiple-access protocol, while the authors in [6–8] paid much attention to designing spectrum-sharing rules for SUs aiming at sharing the vacant channels to forward packets efficiently and fairly. As for SUs, another method of using the licensed spectrum is through spectrum trading [9,10], spectrum leasing [11,12], or spectrum auctioning [13,14]. In [9], a trading mechanism in which the spectrum with a suitable cost and/or quality is adopted by SUs and prices and/or qualities for their idle spectra is set by PUs was modeled as a market. Instead of getting virtual currency, within spectrum leasing [11,12], PUs require SUs to cooperate through leasing a portion of the spectrum to them in order to improve the QoS of PUs, while the right to access the licensed spectrum is obtained by SUs.

In DSA networks, stimulating the cooperation of SUs is a vital issue. SUs may not cooperate if they cannot benefit from cooperation because of different service providers and different objectives. As a full-fledged mathematical tool for researching the interactions among rational users [15], game theory, has been utilized to analyze the cooperative behaviors among nodes within DSA networks [11,12,16–21]. However, based on the direct reciprocity model [11,12] and repeated games [19], there is a fundamental assumption that the games among a group of nodes are played infinite times in the majority of the existing game-theoretic frameworks for DSA networks. In reality, this assumption is not true owing to the fact that, based on the changes or the mobility of the environment, players should frequently change partners, which means always playing noncooperatively is the only optimal strategy. Moreover, players might cheat despite having an agreement to cooperate when there is no punishment for cheating. For example, in systems such as [12], less power might be required to relay than had been promised after obtaining the opportunity of using the spectrum because there is no evaluation and supervision of the actions of SUs.

Two other categories of cooperation stimulation schemes are reputation-based schemes and payment-based schemes. Reputation-based cooperation stimulation schemes are widely used within P2P networks [22,23] and ad-hoc networks [24,25]. In [22], a reputation-based system in which peers got resources in proportion to their reputation and obtained reputations through their contributions was proposed by Tassiulas and Satsiou. The authors presented the idea that rational peers looking for maximal utility with the least possible contribution tend to cooperate under this reputation system. However, there are few reputation-based mechanisms for DSA networks, and there is no theoretical analysis of reputation for stimulating cooperation within DSA networks. Payment-based schemes have been used to enforce cooperation within DSA networks, such as auctions [26–28] and virtual currencies [29]. In [29], the authors proposed a payment mechanism enabling SUs and PUs to pay charges to each other, so as to instigate cooperation among multiple SUs and multiple PUs. In [28], an auction-based protocol was proposed to embolden PUs to free up a portion of their spectrum resources to SUs in exchange for help from the SUs with relaying their signals to their destinations. Their potential applications have been hugely restricted due to the requirement of central billing services or tamper-proof hardware, even if promising results could be realized using these schemes.

Recently, indirect reciprocity has attracted much attention in the field of evolutionary biology and social science [30,31]. According to indirect reciprocity, interactions between each pair of recipients and donors are short term. Within the interaction, the donor's help to the recipient could be seen as an indirect expression of gratitude, formulated as, "*I help you not because you have helped me but because you have helped others.*" In [32], it is argued by Chen and Liu that in order to stimulate cooperation among cognitive nodes, the indirect reciprocity game is a fresh paradigm. However, the framework in [32] is so general that it cannot be implemented in DSA networks directly for two reasons. The first one is that the cooperation between a secondary system and a primary system is asymmetric. For example, SUs provide power while PUs provide spectrum. The second reason is that, unlike other cognitive networks in which players are homogeneous, cooperation in DSA networks is more frequent between a secondary system and a primary system, in which the PU acts as a leader and the SU behaves as a follower in most cases. Therefore, it is necessary to design the resource allocation carefully within DSA networks in order not to impact overall system performance.

In this chapter, in order to solve the problem of the efficient allocation of channels, we are going to discuss a spectrum access framework by incorporating indirect reciprocity in order to stimulate the cooperation of SUs through an incentive mechanism.

3.2   System Model

According to Figure 3.1, PUs are far away from the base station (BS) within the system, thus it is considered that PUs are experiencing low achievable rates, and some SUs between the BS and the PUs are looking to use the licensed spectrum. It is also clear that cooperative communications are capable of upgrading communication

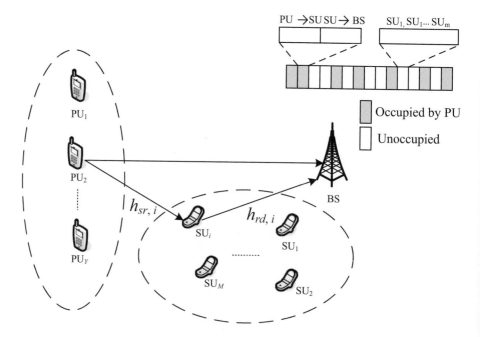

Figure 3.1 The system model.

performance to a large extent [33]. To enhance the PU's QoS (e.g., throughput or achievable rate), on the basis of the relay selection strategy in [34], one of the SUs can be chosen by the BS as a relay if SUs have more helpful channel conditions compared with the PU. There is no competition among SUs since their selection is only determined by the channel condition. In this chapter, the uplink transmission case will be addressed, in which the SUs serve as the relays, the BS as the destination, and the PUs as the source nodes. The channels between an SU and the BS, a PU and the BS, and a PU and an SU are abbreviated as R-D channels, S-D channels, and S-R channels, respectively.

A selected SU needs to decide whether to help the PU relay the information and the extent to which it is going to help. Although every cooperation protocol can adopt this scheme, it is assumed that the Decode-and-Forward (DF) protocol is used by SUs for relaying the signals of PUs, and there are two time slots: the chosen SU relays the PU's information in the second time slot and the PU transmits in the first time slot. The reputation of the chosen SU would be updated by the BS after the transmission. Then the BS would give the right to access a certain amount of vacant channels according to their reputation when the SU applies.

The discussion above has shown that the concept of indirect reciprocity states that the BS helps certain SUs because SUs have helped PUs.

3.2.1 Action

In the model, the power level of an SU is represented by action $a \in \mathcal{A}$ for relaying the data of a PU, in which $\mathcal{A} = \{1, \ldots, N\}$ is the action set that an SU is capable of choosing for its own action once it is selected as a relay. In the action set $\mathcal{A}$, "1" means that an SU runs zero power to the relay (e.g., cooperation would be denied by the SU), while "N" denotes that an SU relays a PU's data with its maximum power P_{max} (e.g., the best effort is made by an SU to cooperate).

The reputation it has earned and the condition of the source–relay–destination channel must be taken into consideration by the SU while making decisions. $a_{i,j} \in \mathcal{A}$ is adopted to describe the action that is performed by an SU with reputation i, $i \in \{1, \ldots, N\}$, under the condition of taking the source–relay–destination channel as j, $j \in \{1, \ldots, N\}$. It is assumed that both the source–relay–destination channel quality and the SU's reputation are quantized to N levels.

3.2.2 Social Norm: How to Assign Reputation

A matrix of social norm $\mathbf{\Omega}$ is adopted to assign the immediate reputation of each player. Within a social norm $\mathbf{\Omega}$, the element $\Omega_{i,j}$ is the reputation assigned to an SU after taking an action i on the basis of the source–relay–destination channel quality j. It is assumed that the same social norm is shared by all SUs in the system.

Accordng to the DF protocol, the signal-to-noise ratio (SNR) at the BS could be calculated as [33]

$$SNR_{DF} = \frac{P_r |h_{rd}|^2}{\sigma_n^2}, \tag{3.1}$$

where the variance of additive white Gaussian noise in the R-D channel is σ_n^2, the relay power is P_r, and the channel coefficient of the R-D channel is h_{rd}.

From (3.1), it can be seen that the more power an SU uses, the higher the SNR the BS would achieve. Therefore, $\Omega_{i,j}$ is defined as

$$\Omega_{i,j} = \begin{cases} 1, & j = 1, \\ i, & j \neq 1, \end{cases} \tag{3.2}$$

and the corresponding social norm is

$$\Omega = \begin{pmatrix} 1 & 1 & \cdots & 1 \\ 1 & 2 & \cdots & 2 \\ \vdots & \vdots & \ddots & \vdots \\ 1 & N & \cdots & N \end{pmatrix}. \tag{3.3}$$

The design of the social norm (3.3) aims to embolden an SU to use a higher power for relaying the PU's signal through the assignment of an SU with a greater reputation once the channel is not in an outage.

3.2.3   Power Level and Relay Power

According to the social norm, the reputation of an SU on the basis of its action would be assigned by the BS (e.g., according to the relay power level it used). The method to quantize the relay power to N levels in light of the outage probability is going to be discussed in the following. Other QoS measurements such as bit error rate (BER) could be analyzed similarly. Based on [35], for the repetition-coding DF protocol, the maximum average mutual information is

$$I_{DF} = \frac{1}{2}\min\{\log_2(1 + SNR_{sr}|h_{sr}|^2), \log_2(1 + SNR_{sd}|h_{sd}|^2 + SNR_{rd}|h_{rd}|^2)\}, \tag{3.4}$$

where $SNR_{sd} = SNR_{sr} = P_s/\sigma_n^2$, $SNR_{rd} = P_r/\sigma_n^2$, and P_s is the PU's transmission power. Here, σ_n^2 is assumed to be the same for all S-D, S-R, and R-D channels.

Presume that all S-D, S-R, and R-D channels are Rayleigh fading channels in which the channel coefficient is complex Gaussian (i.e., $h_{sr} \sim \mathcal{CN}(0, \sigma_{sr}^2)$, $h_{rd} \sim \mathcal{CN}(0, \sigma_{rd}^2)$, and $h_{sd} \sim \mathcal{CN}(0, \sigma_{sd}^2)$). Then, with the transmission rate threshold R, the outage probability at the BS with the DF relay protocol can be derived as follows [35]:

$$p^{out} = \begin{cases} 1 - \left[\left(\frac{\lambda_v}{\lambda_v - \lambda_u}\right)\exp(-\lambda_u\omega) + \left(\frac{\lambda_u}{\lambda_u - \lambda_v}\right)\exp(-\lambda_v\omega)\right], & \lambda_u \neq \lambda_v, \\ 1 - (1 + \lambda\omega)\exp(-\lambda\omega), & \lambda_u = \lambda_v = \lambda, \end{cases} \tag{3.5}$$

where $\lambda_u = SNR_{sd}\sigma_{sd}^2$, $\lambda_v = SNR_{rd}\sigma_{rd}^2$, and $\omega = 2^{2R} - 1$.

Since p^{out} is a monotonic function of P_r, if the required outage probability interval $[p_{min}^{out}, p_{max}^{out}]$ is quantized to $N - 2$ levels $\mathcal{P}^{out} = \{p_1^{out}, p_2^{out}, \ldots, p_{N-2}^{out}\}$ with

$p_1^{out} = p_{max}^{out}$ and $p_{N-2}^{out} = p_{min}^{out}$, then $\forall p_i^{out} \in \mathcal{P}^{out}$, the power an SU should use can be attained as

$$P_{r_{i+1}} = F^{-1}(p_i^{out}), \tag{3.6}$$

where F^{-1} is the inverse function of p^{out} in (3.5).

When $p^{out} > p_{max}^{out}$, it can be quantized as the first level and set $P_{r_1} = 0$, and for $p^{out} < p_{min}^{out}$, we quantize it to the Nth level and set $P_{r_N} = P_{max}$. In this way, the N power levels as well as their corresponding transmission powers are successfully obtained.

3.2.4 Channel Quality Distribution

The source–relay–destination channel's quality is also quantized to N levels (i.e., $1, 2, \ldots, N$). Here, the channel that has encountered an outage is represented by level "1," while levels from level "2" to level "N" stand for different channel qualities (i.e., level "N" is the best channel quality). The way of acquiring such N levels of channel quality and the channel quality distribution $\mathbf{q} = [q_1, q_2, \ldots, q_N]$ with the kth element q_k, $k \in \{1, 2, \ldots, N\}$, which is the channel quality's probability at level k, will be discussed later.

The relay selection strategy determines the channel quality distribution. Here, an SU with the "best" source–relay–destination channel is going to be chosen in light of the relay selection strategy in [34]. Or, the relay metric of SU_i, h_i, is denoted as

$$h_i = \frac{2\beta_1 \beta_2 |h_{sr,i}|^2 |h_{rd,i}|^2}{\beta_1 |h_{rd,i}|^2 + \beta_2 |h_{sr,i}|^2}, \tag{3.7}$$

where β_1 and β_2 are two parameters defined in (5) of [34]. Then in the secondary system, the SU with the maximum metric $h^* = \max_i h_i$ is the one with the "best" source–relay–destination channel.

We presume that within the secondary system, there are M SUs, and the R-D channel for all SUs and the S-R channel are independent, identical distribution Rayleigh fade channels with complex Gaussian channel coefficients (i.e., $h_{rd,i} \sim \mathcal{CN}(0, \sigma_{rd}^2)$, $\forall i \in \{1, 2, \ldots, M\}$, and $h_{sr,i} \sim \mathcal{CN}(0, \sigma_{sr}^2)$). Under this circumstance, according to [34], we could derive the probability distribution function (PDF) of h^*. Finally, N levels of channel quality can be obtained by dividing the domain of h^* into N intervals, and the channel quality distribution $\mathbf{q}$ can be obtained through integrating the PDF of h^* over each interval.

3.3 Theoretical Analysis

3.3.1 Reputation Updating Policy

An SU would be assigned with a reputation after relaying, and based on this reputation, the usage of vacant channels can be applied in the future. A reputation updating

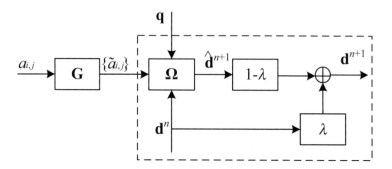

Figure 3.2 Reputation updating policy.

policy is utilized to form SU reputations using the social norm, which can be seen in Figure 3.2. Unlike the reputation updating policy in [32] with reputation propagation, this model does not have a reputation propagation error owing to the fact that the reputation is assigned by and stored in the BS. Nevertheless, the SUs' reputation updating may be influenced by the noise in channels between the BS and SUs because such noise might impact the SUs' actions and so influence the BS's detection accuracy. Consequently, in this reputation updating policy, $\mathbf{G}$ is defined as the power detection transition matrix for illustrating the impact of R-D channels on SUs' actions, which will be discussed latter.

In order to occupy the range of possibilities of SU reputation after the action $a_{i,j}$ is taken, the SU is assigned with a reputation distribution $\mathbf{d}(a_{i,j}) = [d_1(a_{i,j}), d_2(a_{i,j}), \ldots, d_N(a_{i,j})]^T$, where $d_k(a_{i,j})$, $k \in \{1, 2, \ldots, N\}$ is the probability of the SU being assigned with reputation k. There is no chance for the BS to learn the power level that an SU used precisely because of the channel noise. Under such a circumstance, $a_{i,j}$ might be detected incorrectly as $\tilde{a}_{i,j}$. Therefore, an SU that runs action $a_{i,j}$ at time index $n + 1$ is going to be assigned an immediate reputation $\hat{\mathbf{d}}^{n+1} = \mathbf{d}(\tilde{a}_{i,j})$ based on the social norm. Finally, the BS updates the SU's reputation distribution at time index $n + 1$, $\mathbf{d}^{n+1}(a_{i,j})$ by combining the immediate reputation distribution $\hat{\mathbf{d}}^{n+1}$ linearly with a weight λ and the SU's original reputation distribution $\mathbf{d}^n$. Under this condition, the weight λ can be regarded as a past reputation's discount element.

In a simple circumstance, taking an SU's original reputation distribution as the standard basis vector $\mathbf{e}_i$, based on the reputation updating policy in Figure 3.2, after the SU takes action $a_{i,j}$, its reputation distribution $\mathbf{d}(a_{i,j})$ can be updated as

$$\mathbf{d}(a_{i,j}) = (1 - \lambda) \sum_{l=1}^{N} [\mathbf{e}_{\Omega_{l,j}} \cdot G_{a_{i,j},l}] + \lambda \mathbf{e}_i, \tag{3.8}$$

where $G_{a_{i,j},l}$ is the probability of the SU's action $a_{i,j}$ being detected as l. $\Omega_{l,j}$ is the immediate reputation that is assigned to the SU when the SU taking an action l with channel quality j is observed by the BS.

3.3.2 Power Detection and Power Detection Transition Matrix

Set $x_i, i = 1, 2, \ldots L$, as the signals modulated with frequency shift keying, amplitude shift keying, or phase shift keying and broadcast by a PU in L frames. After being relayed by an SU with the DF protocol, the signals obtained by the BS are

$$y_i = \sqrt{P_r} h_{rd} \hat{x}_i + n_i, \quad i = 1, 2, \ldots, L, \tag{3.9}$$

where $\hat{x}_i$ is the signal decoded by the SU, $E\left(\hat{x}_i^2\right) = \sigma_x^2$, and n_i is channel noise. The value of $\hat{x}_i$ can be obtained after coherent demodulation and can be matched with the constellation map, and based on this value, the BS is capable of further estimating the relay power that the SU used.

Presume that both the relay power that the SU used and the channel state information of the R-D channel do not change in L frames. To estimate this more accurately, the BS combines L received signals $y_i, i = 1, 2, \ldots, L$, using maximal ratio combining (MRC) and gets

$$z = \sqrt{P_r} |h_{rd}|^2 ||\mathbf{x}||^2 + h_{rd}^* \mathbf{x}^H \mathbf{n}, \tag{3.10}$$

where h_{rd}^* is the complex conjugate of h_{rd}, $\mathbf{x} = [x_1, x_2, \ldots, x_L]$, and $\mathbf{n} = [n_1, n_2, \ldots, n_L]$.

It can be seen from (3.10) that z follows a Gaussian distribution with the mean $E[z] = L \sqrt{P_r} \sigma_{rd}^2 \sigma_x^2$ and variance $Var[z] = L \sigma_{rd}^2 \sigma_x^2 \sigma_n^2$. Thus, as for every N possible power levels (i.e., $P_{r_i} \in \mathcal{P}_r = \{P_{r_i}, i = 1, 2, \ldots N\}$), let $B_i = \sqrt{P_{r_i}}$, $B_i \in \mathcal{B} = \{B_i, i = 1, 2, \ldots N\}$, and there will be

$$z_i \sim \mathcal{N}(L \sigma_{rd}^2 \sigma_x^2 B_i, \ L \sigma_{rd}^2 \sigma_x^2 \sigma_n^2) = \mathcal{N}(\mu_i, \sigma^2), \tag{3.11}$$

where $\mu_i = L \sigma_{rd}^2 \sigma_x^2 B_i$ and $\sigma^2 = L \sigma_{rd}^2 \sigma_x^2 \sigma_n^2$.

With the optimal thresholds that are $v_i = \frac{\mu_i + \mu_{i+1}}{2}, i = 1, 2, \ldots N - 1$, since all z_is are Gaussian, the power detection probabilities will be $P_d(B_j | B_i)$, $\forall i, j$. These probabilities are adopted to construct the power detection transition matrix $\mathbf{G}$ as follows:

$$G_{i,j} = \begin{cases} P_d(B_j | B_i) = 1 - Q\left(\frac{\mu_1 + \mu_2 - 2\mu_i}{2\sigma}\right), & j = 1, \\ P_d(B_j | B_i) = Q\left(\frac{\mu_{j-1} + \mu_j - 2\mu_i}{2\sigma}\right) - Q\left(\frac{\mu_j + \mu_{j+1} - 2\mu_i}{2\sigma}\right), & 1 < j < N, \\ P_d(B_j | B_i) = Q\left(\frac{\mu_{N-1} + \mu_N - 2\mu_i}{2\sigma}\right), & j = N, \end{cases} \tag{3.12}$$

where $G_{i,j} \in \mathbf{G}$ is the probability of an SU using power level i to relay while being disclosed as power level j, and Q is a Q-function that is defined as $Q(x) = \frac{1}{\sqrt{2\pi}} \int_x^\infty \exp\left(-\frac{u^2}{2}\right) du$.

There are two nice properties in the power detection transition matrix $\mathbf{G}$ in (3.12) that are described below in and Lemmas 3.1 and 3.2, and they are going to be adopted in the later analysis.

LEMMA 3.1 $G_{N,j} < G_{i,j}, \forall 1 \leq i < N$ and $1 \leq j < i$.

Proof • If $j = 1, \forall\, i < N$, we have

$$G_{N,1} - G_{i,1} = Q\left(\frac{\mu_1 + \mu_2 - 2\mu_i}{2\sigma}\right) - Q\left(\frac{\mu_1 + \mu_2 - 2\mu_N}{2\sigma}\right). \qquad (3.13)$$

Since $\mu_1 < \mu_2 < \cdots < \mu_N$, then $\frac{\mu_1+\mu_2-2\mu_i}{2\sigma} > \frac{\mu_1+\mu_2-2\mu_N}{2\sigma}$. Since $Q(x)$ is monotonically decreasing in x, we have

$$G_{N,1} - G_{i,1} = Q\left(\frac{\mu_1 + \mu_2 - 2\mu_i}{2\sigma}\right) - Q\left(\frac{\mu_1 + \mu_2 - 2\mu_N}{2\sigma}\right) < 0. \quad (3.14)$$

• If $1 < j < i, \forall\, i < N$, we have

$$G_{N,j} - G_{i,j} = Q\left(\frac{\mu_{j-1} + \mu_j - 2\mu_N}{2\sigma}\right) - Q\left(\frac{\mu_j + \mu_{j+1} - 2\mu_N}{2\sigma}\right)$$

$$- Q\left(\frac{\mu_{j-1} + \mu_j - 2\mu_i}{2\sigma}\right) + Q\left(\frac{\mu_j + \mu_{j+1} - 2\mu_i}{2\sigma}\right). \quad (3.15)$$

Let $a_1 = \frac{\mu_{j-1}+\mu_j-2\mu_N}{2\sigma}$, $a_2 = \frac{\mu_j+\mu_{j+1}-2\mu_N}{2\sigma}$, $a_3 = \frac{\mu_{j-1}+\mu_j-2\mu_i}{2\sigma}$, and $a_4 = \frac{\mu_j+\mu_{j+1}-2\mu_i}{2\sigma}$. Note $a_1 < a_2 < a_3 < a_4 < 0$ and $a_3 - a_1 = a_4 - a_2$. From the characteristic of the Q-function, we can obtain that $Q(a_1) - Q(a_3) < Q(a_2) - Q(a_4)$. Hence

$$G_{N,j} - G_{i,j} = Q(a_1) - Q(a_2) - Q(a_3) + Q(a_4) < 0. \qquad (3.16)$$

In all, $G_{N,j} < G_{i,j}, \forall\, 1 \le i < N$ and $1 \le j < i$.

LEMMA 3.2 $G_{j,j} > G_{i,j}, \forall\, 1 \le i, j \le N$ and $i \ne j$.

Proof • If $j = 1, \forall i \ne j$, we have

$$\begin{aligned}
G_{1,1} - G_{i,1} &= 1 - Q\left(\frac{\mu_1+\mu_2-2\mu_1}{2\sigma}\right) - 1 + Q\left(\frac{\mu_1+\mu_2-2\mu_i}{2\sigma}\right) \\
&= Q\left(\frac{\mu_1+\mu_2-2\mu_i}{2\sigma}\right) - Q\left(\frac{\mu_1+\mu_2-2\mu_1}{2\sigma}\right).
\end{aligned}$$

Since $\frac{\mu_1+\mu_2-2\mu_i}{2\sigma} < \frac{\mu_1+\mu_2-2\mu_1}{2\sigma}$, we have

$$G_{1,1} - G_{i,1} = Q\left(\frac{\mu_1 + \mu_2 - 2\mu_i}{2\sigma}\right) - Q\left(\frac{\mu_1 + \mu_2 - 2\mu_1}{2\sigma}\right) > 0. \quad (3.17)$$

• If $1 < j < N, \forall i \ne j$, we have

$$\begin{aligned}
G_{j,j} - G_{i,j} &= Q\left(\frac{\mu_{j-1}+\mu_j-2\mu_j}{2\sigma}\right) - Q\left(\frac{\mu_j+\mu_{j+1}-2\mu_j}{2\sigma}\right) \\
&\quad - Q\left(\frac{\mu_{j-1}+\mu_j-2\mu_i}{2\sigma}\right) + Q\left(\frac{\mu_j+\mu_{j+1}-2\mu_i}{2\sigma}\right).
\end{aligned} \qquad (3.18)$$

Let $b_1 = \frac{\mu_{j-1}+\mu_j-2\mu_j}{2\sigma}$, $b_2 = \frac{\mu_j+\mu_{j+1}-2\mu_j}{2\sigma}$, $b_3 = \frac{\mu_{j-1}+\mu_j-2\mu_i}{2\sigma}$, and $b_4 = \frac{\mu_j+\mu_{j+1}-2\mu_i}{2\sigma}$. Then we have $b_3 - b_1 = b_4 - b_2$.

If $i > j, b_3 < b_1 < b_4 < 0 < b_2$, then $Q(b_4) - Q(b_2) > Q(b_3) - Q(b_1)$, and we have

$$G_{j,j} - G_{i,j} = Q(b_1) - Q(b_2) - Q(b_3) + Q(b_4) > 0. \tag{3.19}$$

If $i < j, b_1 < 0 < b_3$, and $0 < b_2 < b_4$, then $Q(b_1) - Q(b_3) > Q(b_2) - Q(b_4)$, and we have

$$G_{j,j} - G_{i,j} = Q(b_1) - Q(b_2) - Q(b_3) + Q(b_4) > 0. \tag{3.20}$$

- If $j = N, \forall i \neq j$

$$G_{N,N} - G_{i,N} = Q\left(\frac{\mu_{N-1} + \mu_N - 2\mu_N}{2\sigma}\right) - Q\left(\frac{\mu_{N-1} + \mu_N - 2\mu_i}{2\sigma}\right). \tag{3.21}$$

Since $\frac{\mu_{N-1} + \mu_N - 2\mu_N}{2\sigma} < \frac{\mu_{N-1} + \mu_N - 2\mu_i}{2\sigma}$, we have

$$G_{N,N} - G_{i,N} = Q\left(\frac{\mu_{N-1} + \mu_N - 2\mu_N}{2\sigma}\right) - Q\left(\frac{\mu_{N-1} + \mu_N - 2\mu_i}{2\sigma}\right) > 0. \tag{3.22}$$

To summarize, $\forall\, 1 \leq i, j \leq N$ and $i \neq j$, we have $G_{j,j} > G_{i,j}$ (i.e., the diagonal entry of matrix G is the maximum element in its column).

3.3.3 Stationary Reputation Distribution

Let $\eta = [\eta_1, \eta_2, \ldots, \eta_N]$ be the whole population's reputation distribution, where η_i, $i \in \{1, 2, \ldots, N\}$, is the portion of the population with reputation i. The reputation of the SU is developed based on the reputation updating policy after the transmission, and the whole population's new reputation distribution η^{new} is computed by

$$\eta^{new} = (1 - \lambda)\eta\mathbf{P}_t + \lambda\eta, \tag{3.23}$$

where $\mathbf{P}_t$ is the reputation transition matrix. Every element $P_{t_{i,j}}$ in $\mathbf{P}_t$ represents the probability of reputation i changing into j after an action is taken by the SU. Recalling that $q_k, k \in \{1, 2, \ldots, N\}$, is the probability of the channel quality being at the level k, on the basis of Figure 3.2, $P_{t_{i,j}}$ can be calculated by

$$P_{t_{i,j}} = \sum_{k,l:\Omega_{l,k}=j} G_{a_{i,k}^*,l} q_k, \tag{3.24}$$

where $a_{i,k}^*$ is the optimal action for an SU with reputation i under channel condition k.

The new reputation distribution η^{new} ought to correspond with η in the steady state (i.e., $\eta^{new} = \eta$). Consequently, the stationary reputation distribution η^*, if it exists, has to be the solution to the following equation:

$$(1 - \lambda)\eta^*\mathbf{P}_t + \lambda\eta^* = \eta^*, \tag{3.25}$$

which is equivalent to

$$\eta^* \mathbf{P}_t = \eta^*. \tag{3.26}$$

It is going to be shown that there is an exclusive stationary reputation distribution in the following Theorem 3.3.

THEOREM 3.3   *The stationary reputation distribution is* $\mathbf{P}_t$*'s eigenvector with the corresponding eigenvalue 1. An extraordinary stationary reputation distribution of the entire population with any given optimal action rule exists.*

Proof   For any given optimal action rule $a^*_{i,j}$, we have

$$P_{t_{i,j}} = \sum_{k,l:\Omega_{l,k}=j} G_{a^*_{i,k},l} q_k > 0, \qquad \forall i,j. \tag{3.27}$$

Furthermore, $\sum_j P_{t_{i,j}} = 1$. Thus, $\mathbf{P}_t$ is a stochastic matrix with strictly positive entries. Based on the Perron–Frobenius theorem [36,37], there is a unique eigenvector of $\mathbf{P}_t$ equal to eigenvalue 1. Such an eigenvector is the stationary reputation distribution.

3.3.4   Payoff Function and Equilibrium of the Indirect Reciprocity Game

Intuitively, an SU will only cooperate when cooperation can bring benefits. Through assisting in relaying the PU's data, the SU is going to incur a cost due to power consumption (i.e., the power level $a_{i,j}$). Here, a linear cost function is assumed as follows:

$$C(a_{i,j}) = c(a_{i,j} - 1), \tag{3.28}$$

where c is the price per unit power level.

However, on the basis of its newest reputation after relaying, the SU can gain benefits from the allocation of certain vacant channels in the future. We suppose that there are Y channels and p is the probability of a channel being unoccupied. Meanwhile, $N_v = pY$ is the forecasted amount of vacant channels. In the model, the BS allocates the vacant channels to all M SUs in a proportionally fair manner. Under this circumstance, the number of vacant channels $t(a_{i,j})$ that an SU is going to be allocated after it takes action $a_{i,j}$ is

$$t(a_{i,j}) = N_t \frac{\sum_{n=1}^{N} n \cdot d_n(a_{i,j}) - 1}{\sum_{n=1}^{N} n \cdot \eta^*_n - 1}, \tag{3.29}$$

where $N_t = N_c N_v / M$ and N_c is the number of SUs one channel is allowed to accommodate, $\sum_{n=1}^{N} n \cdot d_n(a_{i,j})$ is the SU's expected reputation, and $\sum_{n=1}^{N} n \cdot \eta^*_n$ is the expected reputation of the entire system. Note that with η^* the entire population's stationary reputation distribution and the influence of other users' reputations have been incorporated into $t(a_{i,j})$. Suppose the gain from accessing one channel is a constant g, then the total gain of an SU taking action $a_{i,j}$ is

$$T(a_{i,j}) = P_v gt(a_{i,j}), \tag{3.30}$$

where $P_v = 1 - (1 - p)^Y$ is the probability of the BS having vacant channels.

We set $\mathbf{W} = (W_{i,j}|i = 1, 2, \ldots, N, \; j = 1, 2, \ldots, N)$, where $W_{i,j}$ denotes the maximum payoff of an SU. With the current reputation i, after taking action $a_{i,j}$ under channel condition j, the SU could obtain not only the immediate benefit but also the long-term benefit in the future. Then we can get

$$W_{i,j} = \max_{a_{i,j} \in \mathcal{A}} -c(a_{i,j} - 1) + P_v gt(a_{i,j}) + \gamma \sum_k \sum_l d_k(a_{i,j}) q_l W_{k,l}. \tag{3.31}$$

The first term in (3.31) represents the immediate cost that an SU incurs by taking action $a_{i,j}$ as denoted in (3.28), the second term is the immediate gain it might obtain with a certain probability as denoted in (3.30), and the last term is the long-term benefit it receives in the future with a discount factor γ. We can see from the definition of $W_{i,j}$ that an SU's maximum payoff is related to its own reputation and channel condition, as well as other players' actions due to $t(a_{i,j})$ defined in (3.29).

Note that (3.31) is a Bellman equation of $W_{i,j}$ [38], so the MDP is the process of seeking the optimal action rule $a_{i,j}^*$. A modified value iteration algorithm is adopted for solving the MDP, and the details of the algorithm are listed in Algorithm 4. According to Algorithm 4, all other SUs have adopted optimal actions when finding $a_{i,j}^*$ for a specific SU. In this case, $a_{i,j}^*$ is the Nash equilibrium based on the definition in [15].

Algorithm 4: Find the optimal action using value iteration.

(1) Given the tolerance $\varepsilon = 0.01$, set $\varepsilon_1 = 1$ and initialize a^* with a^0.

(2) While $\varepsilon_1 > \varepsilon$

- Set $\varepsilon_2 = 1$.
- Initialize $W_{i,j} = 0, \forall i, \forall j$.
- While $\varepsilon_2 > \varepsilon$

  - Compute reputation distribution $\mathbf{d}(a_{i,j})$ using (3.8).
  - Find the stationary reputation distribution $\hat{\eta}^*$ using (3.26) and Theorem 3.3.
  - Calculate the number of vacant channels $t(a_{i,j})$ using (3.29).
  - Obtain $\hat{W}_{i,j}$ based on the stationary reputation distribution $\hat{\eta}^*$ using (3.31).
  - Find the optimal action $\hat{a}_{i,j}^* = \arg \max_{a_{i,j}} \hat{W}_{i,j}$.
  - Update the parameter ε_2 by $\varepsilon_2 = ||\hat{W}_{i,j} - W_{i,j}||^2$.
  - Update $W_{i,j}$ with $W_{i,j} = \hat{W}_{i,j}$.
  - End.

- Update the parameter ε_1 by $\varepsilon_1 = ||\hat{a}^* - a^*||^2$.
- Update a^* with $a^* = \hat{a}^*$.

  End.

Through adjusting the primary conditions in Algorithm 4, two possible optimal actions can be found as follows:

$$a_1^* = \begin{pmatrix} 1 & 1 & \cdots & 1 \\ 1 & 1 & \cdots & 1 \\ \vdots & \vdots & \ddots & \vdots \\ 1 & 1 & \cdots & 1 \end{pmatrix} \quad \text{and} \quad a_2^* = \begin{pmatrix} 1 & N & \cdots & N \\ 1 & N & \cdots & N \\ \vdots & \vdots & \ddots & \vdots \\ 1 & N & \cdots & N \end{pmatrix}. \tag{3.32}$$

Recall that "1" signifies that an SU adopts no power to relay and that the first optimal action a_1^* is a noncooperative equilibrium in which SUs would not act as relays regardless of the channel qualities and their own reputations. Clearly, a_1^* is a bad strategy because SUs always deny cooperation with such a strategy, leading to zero payoffs. The second optimal action a_2^* is the expected equilibrium in which SUs always relay PUs' data with their maximum power except when an outage is encountered by the source–relay–destination channels.

With the optimal action rule a_2^* in (3.32), there is an important property in the payoff function $W_{i,j}$ in (3.31), which is explained in Lemma 3.4 and will be used in the later analysis.

LEMMA 3.4   *Given the optimal action rule a_2^* and the corresponding stationary reputation distribution $\eta^* = [\eta_1^*, \eta_2^*, \ldots, \eta_N^*]$, we have*

$$[W_{i,:} - W_{k,:}]\mathbf{q}^T = W_{i,j} - W_{k,j} = \frac{P_v g \lambda N_t}{\bar{\eta}(1 - \gamma\lambda)}(i - k), \tag{3.33}$$

where $\bar{\eta} = \sum_{n=1}^{N} n \cdot \eta_n^* - 1$, $\mathbf{q} = [q_1, q_2, \ldots, q_N]$, and $W_{k,:} = [W_{k,1}, W_{k,2}, \ldots, W_{k,N}]$.

Proof   For any $a_{i,j}^*$ and the corresponding stationary reputation distribution $\eta^* = [\eta_1^*, \eta_2^*, \ldots, \eta_N^*]$, we have

$$W_{i,j} = -c(a_{i,j}^* - 1) + P_v g t(a_{i,j}^*) + \gamma \sum_k \sum_l d_k(a_{i,j}^*) q_l W_{k,l}. \tag{3.34}$$

- If $j = 1$, $a_{i,j}^* = 1, \forall i$, we have

$$\mathbf{d}(a_{i,j}^*) = \mathbf{d}(1) = (1 - \lambda)\sum_{l=1}^{N} \mathbf{e}_1 \cdot G_{1,l} + \lambda \mathbf{e}_i = (1 - \lambda)\mathbf{e}_1 + \lambda \mathbf{e}_i, \tag{3.35}$$

and

$$t(a_{i,j}^*) = N_t \frac{\sum_{n=1}^{N} n \cdot d_n(a_{i,j}^*) - 1}{\sum_{n=1}^{N} n \cdot \eta_n^* - 1} = \frac{(i - 1)\lambda N_t}{\bar{\eta}}. \tag{3.36}$$

Then, by substituting (3.35) and (3.36) into (3.34), we have

$$W_{i,j} = P_v g \frac{(i - 1)\lambda N_t}{\bar{\eta}} + \gamma(1 - \lambda)W_{1,:}\mathbf{q}^T + \gamma\lambda W_{i,:}\mathbf{q}^T. \tag{3.37}$$

According to (3.37), we have

$$W_{i,j} - W_{k,j} = P_v g \frac{\lambda N_t}{\bar{\eta}}(i - k) + \gamma\lambda\left[W_{i,:} - W_{k,:}\right]\mathbf{q}^T. \tag{3.38}$$

- If $j \neq 1, a^*_{i,j} = N, \forall i, j$, we have

$$\mathbf{d}(a^*_{i,j}) = \mathbf{d}(N) = (1 - \lambda)\left[\sum_{l=1}^{N} \mathbf{e}_{\Omega_{l,j}} \cdot G_{N,l}\right] + \lambda \mathbf{e}_i$$

$$= (1 - \lambda)G_{N,:} + \lambda \mathbf{e}_i, \qquad (3.39)$$

where $G_{N,:} = [G_{N,1}, G_{N,2}, \ldots, G_{N,N}]$, and

$$t(a^*_{i,j}) = t(N) = N_t \frac{(1 - \lambda)\left(\sum_{n=1}^{N} n \cdot G_{N,n} - 1\right) + \lambda(i - 1)}{\bar{\eta}}. \qquad (3.40)$$

Then, by substituting (3.39) and (3.40) into (3.34), we have

$$W_{i,j} = -c(N - 1) + P_v g \frac{(i - 1)\lambda N_t}{\bar{\eta}} + \frac{P_v g N_t (1 - \lambda)}{\bar{\eta}}\left(\sum_{n=1}^{N} n G_{N,n} - 1\right)$$

$$+ \gamma(1 - \lambda)\sum_{k=1}^{N} G_{N,k} W_{k,:} \mathbf{q}^T + \gamma \lambda W_{i,:} \mathbf{q}^T. \qquad (3.41)$$

According to (3.41), we have

$$W_{i,j} - W_{k,j} = P_v g \frac{\lambda N_t}{\bar{\eta}}(i - k) + \gamma \lambda [W_{i,:} - W_{k,:}]\mathbf{q}^T. \qquad (3.42)$$

From (3.38) and (3.42), it can be seen that $W_{i,j} - W_{k,j}$ does not rely on j, which signifies that entries in the vector $W_{i,:} - W_{k,:}$ are the same. Under such a circumstance, let $W_{i,j} - W_{k,j} = x$, then we get

$$x = P_v g \frac{\lambda N_t}{\bar{\eta}}(i - k) + \gamma \lambda x. \qquad (3.43)$$

Therefore, we can obtain

$$\left[W_{i,:} - W_{k,:}\right]\mathbf{q}^T = W_{i,j} - W_{k,j} = \frac{P_v g \lambda N_t}{\bar{\eta}(1 - \gamma \lambda)}(i - k). \qquad (3.44)$$

3.3.5   Stability of the Optimal Action Rule

An evolutionarily stable strategy (ESS) [39] is defined as "a strategy that if all members of the population adopt it, under the influence of natural selection, no mutant strategies could invade the population." On the basis of [40], an optimal strategy a^* is an ESS if and only if, $\forall a \neq a^*$, a^* satisfies

- the equilibrium condition: $U_i(a, a^*) \leq U_i(a^*, a^*)$; and
- the stability condition: if $U_i(a, a^*) = U_i(a^*, a^*)$, $U_i(a, a) < U_i(a^*, a)$,

where U_i is the payoff function of player i in the game.

In order to acquire the stable condition for the optimal action a^*_2, firstly, let us represent $\boldsymbol{\delta}(a_{i,j}) = (G_{N,:} - G_{a_{i,j},:}) - (\mathbf{e}_N - \mathbf{e}_{a_{i,j}}) = [\delta_1(a_{i,j}), \delta_2(a_{i,j}), \ldots, \delta_N(a_{i,j})]$ as the gap vector between $G_{N,:} - G_{a_{i,j},:}$ and $\mathbf{e}_N - \mathbf{e}_{a_{i,j}}$. Secondly, let us characterize four nice properties of $\delta(a_{i,j})$, which are illustrated in Lemmas 3.5–3.8 for later analysis.

LEMMA 3.5   *The sum of all of the elements in $\delta(a_{i,j})$ is zero.*

Proof   From the definition of $\delta(a_{i,j})$, we have

$$\sum_i \delta_i(a_{i,j}) = \sum_i ((G_{N,i} - G_{a_{i,j},i}) - (e_{N,i} - e_{a_{i,j},i})) = 0. \qquad (3.45)$$

LEMMA 3.6   *The $a_{i,j}^{th}$ element is the first positive element in $\delta(a_{i,j})$ and the Nth element is the last negative element.*

Proof   From Lemmas 3.1 and 3.2, it can be seen that $\forall j \leq a_{i,j} < N$, $G_{N,j} - G_{a_{i,j},j} < 0$, which means that all of the first $a_{i,j}$ elements in vector $G_{N,:} - G_{a_{i,j},:}$ are negative. It can also be seen that the Nth element in vector $G_{N,:} - G_{a_{i,j},:}$ is positive and no larger than 1. After $G_{N,:} - G_{a_{i,j},:}$ subtracts $\mathbf{e}_N - \mathbf{e}_{a_{i,j}}$ and yields $\delta(a_{i,j})$, the $a_{i,j}^{th}$ element in $\delta(a_{i,j})$ becomes positive, the Nth element becomes negative, and other elements remain unchanged, as in vector $G_{N,:} - G_{a_{i,j},:}$. Therefore, the $a_{i,j}^{th}$ entry in $\delta(a_{i,j})$ is the first positive element, while the Nth entry is the last negative one.

LEMMA 3.7   *Let $\xi = [1, 2, \ldots, N]$, then $\delta(a_{i,j})\xi^T > (a_{i,j} - N)(1 - G_{a_{i,j},a_{i,j}} + \sum_{k=a_{i,j}}^{N-1} G_{N,k})$.*

Proof   Let $S_+ = \{k | \delta_k > 0, \delta_k \in \delta(a_{i,j}), k = 1, 2, \ldots, N\}$ and $S_- = \{k | \delta_k < 0, \delta_k \in \delta(a_{i,j}), k = 1, 2, \ldots, N\}$. Then $\delta(a_{i,j})\xi^T$ can be calculated as follows:

$$\delta(a_{i,j})\xi^T = \sum_{k \in S_+} k\delta_k + \sum_{k \in S_-} k\delta_k > \sum_{k \in S_+} a_{i,j}\delta_k + \sum_{k \in S_-} N\delta_k,$$

$$= (a_{i,j} - N)\sum_{k \in S_+} \delta_k > (a_{i,j} - N)\left(\delta_{a_{i,j}} + \sum_{k=a_{i,j}+1}^{N-1} G_{N,k}\right),$$

$$= (a_{i,j} - N)\left(1 - G_{a_{i,j},a_{i,j}} + \sum_{k=a_{i,j}}^{N-1} G_{N,k}\right), \qquad (3.46)$$

where the first inequality and the second equality come from Lemmas 3.6 and 3.5, respectively. The second inequality is from the fact that $\forall k \in S_+ \backslash a_{i,j}, G_{N,k} > \delta_k$ and $a_{i,j} < N$.

LEMMA 3.8 $\delta(a_{i,j})\mathbf{W}\mathbf{q}^T > \frac{P_v g \lambda N_t}{\bar{\eta}(1-\gamma\lambda)}(a_{i,j} - N)(1 - G_{a_{i,j},a_{i,j}} + \sum_{k=a_{i,j}}^{N-1} G_{N,k})$.

Proof   Every positive element $\delta_k, k \in S_+$, is capable of being decomposed into n_k parts as each part has a common value with the negative element in $\delta(a_{i,j})$. Let S_-^k be the set of subscripts of those negative elements with the same value of n_k parts of δ_k, then $\delta(a_{i,j})\mathbf{W}\mathbf{q}^T$ can be computed as follows:

$$\delta(a_{i,j})\mathbf{W}\mathbf{q}^T = \sum_{k \in S_+} \sum_{m \in S_-^k} |\delta_m|(\mathbf{e}_k - \mathbf{e}_m)\mathbf{W}\mathbf{q}^T,$$

$$= \frac{P_v g \lambda N_t}{\bar{\eta}(1-\gamma\lambda)}\left(\sum_{k \in S_+} k \sum_{m \in S_-^k} |\delta_m| - \sum_{k \in S_+} \sum_{m \in S_-^k} |\delta_m|m \right),$$

$$> \frac{P_v g \lambda N_t}{\bar{\eta}(1-\gamma\lambda)}\left(a_{i,j} \sum_{k \in S_+} \sum_{m \in S_-^k} |\delta_m| - N \sum_{k \in S_+} \sum_{m \in S_-^k} |\delta_m| \right),$$

$$= \frac{P_v g \lambda N_t}{\bar{\eta}(1-\gamma\lambda)}(a_{i,j} - N) \sum_{k \in S_+} \delta_k,$$

$$> \frac{P_v g \lambda N_t}{\bar{\eta}(1-\gamma\lambda)}(a_{i,j} - N)\left(1 - G_{a_{i,j},a_{i,j}} + \sum_{j=a_{i,j}}^{N-1} G_{N,j} \right), \quad (3.47)$$

where the first inequality is from Lemma 3.6, the last equality is from Lemma 3.5, and the last inequality is from the fact that $\forall k \in S_+ \backslash a_{i,j}, G_{N,k} > \delta_k$ and $a_{i,j} < N$.

Next, let $F(a_{i,j}, a^*)$ be the payoff that an SU is capable of acquiring when it deviates to action $a_{i,j}$ for one iteration while others always adopt the optimal action $a_{i,j}^*$, i.e.,

$$F(a_{i,j}, a^*) = -c(a_{i,j} - 1) + P_v gt(a_{i,j}) + \gamma \sum_k \sum_l d_k(a_{i,j})q_l W_{k,l}. \quad (3.48)$$

Then, based on the definition of an ESS and the one-shot deviation principle for an MDP [41], a^* is an ESS if the following inequality holds:

$$F(a_{i,j}^*, a^*) > F(a_{i,j}, a^*), \quad \forall a_{i,j}. \quad (3.49)$$

According to (3.49), the stable condition for optimal action a_2^* as illustrated in Theorem 3.9 can be derived.

THEOREM 3.9   *The optimal action a_2^* is an ESS if the cost-to-gain ratio c/g satisfies*
$$0 < c/g < \frac{P_v N_t(1-\lambda)}{\bar{\eta}(1-\gamma\lambda)}\left(\min_{a_{i,j} \in \mathcal{A}} G_{a_{i,j},a_{i,j}} + G_{N,N} - 1 \right).$$

Proof   (1) If $j = 1, a_{i,j}^* = 1, \forall i$. Then $\forall a_{i,j} \neq a_{i,j}^*$, we have

$$\mathbf{d}(a_{i,j}) = (1-\lambda) \sum_{l=1}^{N} \mathbf{e}_{\Omega_{l,1}} \cdot G_{a_{i,j},l} + \lambda \mathbf{e}_i = (1-\lambda)\mathbf{e}_1 + \lambda\mathbf{e}_i, \quad (3.50)$$

and

$$t(a_{i,j}) = N_t \frac{\sum_{n=1}^{N} n \cdot d_n(a_{i,j}) - 1}{\sum_{n=1}^{N} n \cdot \eta_n^* - 1} = \frac{(i-1)\lambda N_t}{\bar{\eta}}. \tag{3.51}$$

By substituting (3.35), (3.36), (3.50), and (3.51) into (3.48), we have

$$F(a_{i,j}^*, a^*) - F(a_{i,j}, a^*) = -c(a_{i,j}^* - a_{i,j}). \tag{3.52}$$

Since $a_{i,j}^* - a_{i,j} < 0$, for (3.49) to be held, it should have

$$c > 0. \tag{3.53}$$

(2) If $j \neq 1$, $a_{i,j}^* = N$, $\forall i$. Then $\forall a_{i,j} \neq a_{i,j}^*$, we have

$$\mathbf{d}(a_{i,j}) = (1-\lambda)\sum_{l=1}^{N} \mathbf{e}_{\Omega_{l,j}} \cdot G_{a_{i,j},l} + \lambda \mathbf{e}_i = (1-\lambda)G_{a_{i,j},:} + \lambda \mathbf{e}_i, \tag{3.54}$$

and

$$t(a_{i,j}) = N_t \frac{\sum_{n=1}^{N} n \cdot d_n(a_{i,j}) - 1}{\sum_{n=1}^{N} n \cdot \eta_n^* - 1} = N_t \frac{(1-\lambda)\left(\sum_{n=1}^{N} n \cdot G_{a_{i,j},n} - 1\right) + \lambda(i-1)}{\bar{\eta}}. \tag{3.55}$$

Since $\delta(a_{i,j}) = (G_{N,:} - G_{a_{i,j},:}) - (\mathbf{e}_N - \mathbf{e}_{a_{i,j}})$, by substituting (3.39), (3.40), (3.54), and (3.55) into (3.48), we have

$$F(a_{i,j}^*, a^*) - F(a_{i,j}, a^*)$$

$$= -c(N - a_{i,j}) + P_v g \frac{N_t(1-\lambda)}{\bar{\eta}}(\mathbf{e}_N - \mathbf{e}_{a_{i,j}})\xi^T$$

$$+ \gamma(1-\lambda)(\mathbf{e}_N - \mathbf{e}_{a_{i,j}})\mathbf{W}\mathbf{q}^T + P_v g \frac{N_t(1-\lambda)}{\bar{\eta}}\delta(a_{i,j})\xi^T + \gamma(1-\lambda)\delta(a_{i,j})\mathbf{W}\mathbf{q}^T,$$

$$> -c(N - a_{i,j}) + P_v g \frac{N_t(1-\lambda)}{\bar{\eta}}(N - a_{i,j}) + \gamma(1-\lambda)\frac{P_v g \lambda N_t}{\bar{\eta}(1-\gamma\lambda)}(N - a_{i,j})$$

$$+ P_v g \frac{N_t(1-\lambda)}{\bar{\eta}}\left(1 - G_{a_{i,j},a_{i,j}} + \sum_{k=a_{i,j}}^{N-1} G_{N,k}\right)(a_{i,j} - N)$$

$$+ \gamma(1-\lambda)\frac{P_v g \lambda N_t}{\bar{\eta}(1-\gamma\lambda)}\left(1 - G_{a_{i,j},a_{i,j}} + \sum_{k=a_{i,j}}^{N-1} G_{N,k}\right)(a_{i,j} - N),$$

$$= -c(N - a_{i,j}) + \frac{P_v g N_t(1-\lambda)}{\bar{\eta}(1-\gamma\lambda)}\left(G_{a_{i,j},a_{i,j}} - \sum_{k=a_{i,j}}^{N-1} G_{N,k}\right)(N - a_{i,j}), \tag{3.56}$$

where the inequality above adopts the results of Lemmas 3.7 and 3.8.

Since $1 \leq a_{i,j} < N$, $\forall a_{i,j}$, for (3.49) to be held, it should have

$$c < \frac{P_v g N_t (1-\lambda)}{\bar{\eta}(1-\gamma\lambda)} \left(G_{a_{i,j},a_{i,j}} - \sum_{k=a_{i,j}}^{N-1} G_{N,k} \right). \tag{3.57}$$

According to (3.53) and (3.57), the sufficient condition for a_2^* to be an ESS is

$$0 < c/g < \frac{P_v N_t (1-\lambda)}{\bar{\eta}(1-\gamma\lambda)} \left(\min_{a_{i,j} \in \mathcal{A}} G_{a_{i,j},a_{i,j}} + G_{N,N} - 1 \right). \tag{3.58}$$

It can be seen from Theorem 3.9 that in a society where a large number of the SUs acquire a good reputation (i.e., $\bar{\eta} \approx N - 1$), the BS shows acceptable power detection accuracy $\left(e.g., \min_{a_{i,j} \in \mathcal{A}} G_{a_{i,j},a_{i,j}} = 0.9 \right)$, the vacant channel probability of the PU system is high enough (e.g., $P_v = 0.8$), there is a large possibility of the SUs continuing to stay in the system (e.g., $\gamma = 0.9$), there is a suitable weight on the past reputation (e.g., $\lambda = 0.5$), and a great many SUs could be accommodated in the vacant channels (e.g., $N_t = 0.8$), then c/g acquires a reasonable upper bound (e.g., 0.13 with $N = 5$ power levels). In such a scenario, it is easy to satisfy the condition for the optimal action a_2^* being an ESS in a practical system.

3.4   Simulation

Within this section, first, the evolutionary stability of the optimal action a_2^* as described in (3.32) is examined. Then, the effectiveness of the method discussed in this chapter is evaluated by comparing it with the state-of-the-art DSA methods. Finally, the characteristics of different social norms are studied and their performances also compared.

3.4.1   Evolutionary Stability of Optimal Action a_2^*

In order to assess the evolutionary stability of optimal action a_2^*, a scenario including $Y = 500$ PUs and $M = 1,000$ SUs is studied. In the beginning, every SU is assigned an initial reputation aimlessly chosen from $\{1, 2, \dots, N\}$ with equal probability $\frac{1}{N}$, and every SU chooses the action it would take. Not all SUs would take the optimal action because of the perturbation effect that is caused by the noisy parameters and/or the uncertainty of the system. In the simulation, 60% of SUs would make a choice to adopt the optimal action shown in (3.32), while the rest choose other action rules aimlessly. Other parameters (i.e., vacant channel probability p, discount factor λ, and the number of SUs allowed to approach a channel simultaneously N_c) are set to be 0.8, 0.5, and 1.0, respectively.

Each SU performs the action it has chosen 10 times under different R-D channel conditions before updating the action. After performing the same action 10 times, an average payoff and a new reputation would be acquired by the SU on the basis

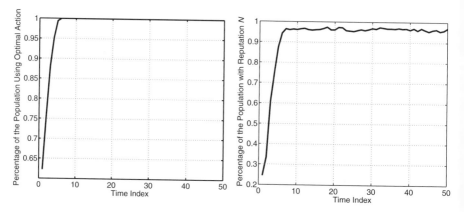

Figure 3.3 The percentage of the population using optimal action a_2^* shown in (3.32).

Figure 3.4 The percentage of the population with reputation $N = 4$ under the social norm in (3.3).

of the reputation updating policy illustrated in Figure 3.2. It is assumed that in the system all SUs obey a fixed social norm shown in (3.3) and agree on the reputation that is generated by the reputation updating policy. Then the SU has probabilities of $\gamma = 0.97$ and $1 - \gamma$ to stay in or leave the system, respectively. In order to keep the total population constant, a new SU will access the system once an SU leaves. The newcomer's initial reputation is aimlessly selected from $\{1, 2, \ldots, N\}$ with equal probability $\frac{1}{N}$. All of the SUs need to choose their actions, no matter if they remain in the system or simply access the system. Here, the Wright–Fisher model [42], by far the most popular stochastic model for reproduction in population genetics, is adopted to investigate the SUs' methods of updating their actions. Based on the Wright–Fisher model, the population's percentage using action a_i at time index $t + 1$, y_i^{t+1} is proportional to the users' total payoff using a_i in time index t, i.e.,

$$y_i^{t+1} = \frac{y_i^t U_i^t}{\sum_{i=1}^{M} y_i^t U_i^t}, \qquad (3.59)$$

where U_i^t is the users' total payoff using a_i at time index t.

The evolutionary results of the population's percentage using the optimal action are shown in Figure 3.3. From Figure 3.3 it can be seen that within 10 iterations the optimal action a_2^* disseminates over the whole system, and once it has been adopted by the entire population, no player will deviate from it, verifying that under the simulation conditions, the optimal action a_2^* is an ESS. Consequently, the population's percentage with the reputation N converges within 10 iterations, as is illustrated in Figure 3.4, proving that action a_2^* is a desired strategy owing to the fact that it leads to a "good" society where most of the SUs have a good reputation.

Based on the results obtained above, we next only take the performance of the system is into consideration within the steady stage, and so most of the SUs have the highest reputation.

3.4.2   System Performance

The performance of a DSA network with one BS, a single PU, and multiple SUs is considered. It is assumed that the PU and BS locate at coordinates (0,0) and (1,0), respectively. Five SUs are aimlessly located in a circle centered at coordinates (0.5,0) with a radius of 0.25. An SU's receiver is randomly located in a circle centered at the corresponding SU with a radius of between 0.10 and 0.25.

The channels are complex Gaussian channels with average power gains $\sigma_{sd}^2 = 1$, $\sigma_{sr,i}^2 = 1/d_{sr}^\theta$, $\sigma_{rd,i}^2 = 1/d_{rd}^\theta$, and $\sigma_{ss,i}^2 = 1/d_{ss}^\theta$. The path loss factor θ is set to be 4, and d_{sr}, d_{rd}, and d_{ss} represent the distances between the PU and the selected SU, the selected SU and the BS, and the SU and its receiver accordingly. The maximum transmission power of the PU and SUs is $P_s = P_{r_i} = 10$, and the SNR is $P_s/\sigma_n = 10\,\text{dB}$.

By comparing the indirect reciprocity game-theoretic scheme with two other existing schemes, the system performance in terms of outage probability and total throughput is evaluated. The first approach is "NCPC," where SUs do not cooperate with PU and all SUs can only access unoccupied channels aimlessly and transmit their own data through a noncooperative power control game. The second method is spectrum leasing, as proposed in [12]. Under the Stackelberg game-theoretic framework, the PU leases a fraction of its spectrum to a group of SUs, and this is a direct reciprocity-based scheme. After relaying, in order to obtain their own data transmission within the leased time slot, this group of SUs would compete with each other. However, only the problem of the methods of utilizing channels occupied by a PU has been addressed in [12]. For a fair comparison, it is assumed that all SUs access those vacant channels randomly and transmit their own data through a noncooperative power control game. This scheme is denoted as "SL-NCPC." Within SL-NCPC, the SUs that have the best performance will be selected. Note that in the spectrum leasing approach in [12], after gaining the chance to use the spectrum, the SU may use less power to relay owing to the fact that no evaluation nor supervision of its action exists. However, here we presume that all SUs are honest and utilize the power that they have promised.

Within the primary simulation, the achievable end-to-end throughput of PU versus vacant channel probability p for different schemes is evaluated, and within the scheme, there is only one SU selected as a relay on the basis of the relay selection strategy in [34]. It is assumed that the signals broadcast by PUs are modulated with binary phase shift keying. Due to the selected SU using the same channel as the PU for relaying data, the way of allocating the transmission time between the selected SU and the PU ought to be considered. Here, two strategies are taken into consideration: the first is "IR-Equal," in which one time frame is fairly divided into two time slots, and the second is "IR-Unequal," in which the length of time slot, α, allocated to a PU's transmission is given by the following strategy. Let $R_{sr} = \log_2(1 + SNR_{sr}|h_{sr}|^2)$, $R_{rd} = \log_2(1 + SNR_{rd}|h_{rd}|^2)$, and $R_{sd} = \log_2(1 + SNR_{sd}|h_{sd}|^2)$ signify the achievable rates of the S-R, R-D, and S-D channels, respectively. To make the performance better, α is adopted in a way that the rate at the relay is equal to that at the BS (i.e., $\alpha = R_{rd}/(R_{sr} + R_{sd} - R_{rd})$).

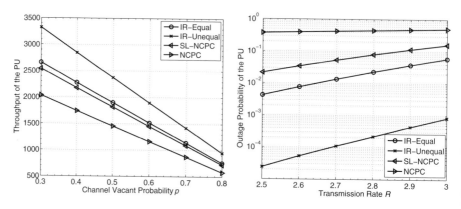

Figure 3.5 Throughput of the PU under the social norm in (3.3).

Figure 3.6 Outage probability of the PU under the social norm in (3.3).

Figure 3.5 shows the results of the first simulation, from which we can see that the performance of NCPC is the worst owing to the fact that no cooperation between the SUs and the PU exists and the PU is only capable of acquiring its throughput via direct transmission without any QoS improvement. The throughput of the PU could be improved by SL-NCPC through cooperation with SUs using spectrum leasing. However, because of their selfish nature, only part of their transmission power of SUs will be used to relay data as the spectrum leasing game is played, leading to inefficient cooperation. The PU's throughput is capable of being greatly improved through the indirect reciprocity game-theoretic method, where the selected SU is motivated to utilize its full power to relay the PU's data. Furthermore, from Figure 3.5 it can be seen that with the IR-Unequal time slot allocation, the scheme's performance could be further developed. In addition, as the vacant channel probability decreases (i.e., the performance gap between different schemes would increase if there is more information for the PU to transmit, indicating the greater significance of cooperation stimulation), the heavier the PU's load could be.

In terms of outage probability, the PU system's performance is also studied. In Figure 3.6, it can be seen that when $R = 2.5$, the outage probability of the PU with NCPC is as high as 0.5 without cooperation. If there is cooperation, the outage probability in SL-NCPC could fall to around 10^{-2}. Thus, the PU system is capable of achieving the lowest outage probability with the cooperation stimulation framework discussed in this chapter.

In the third simulation, the throughput of all SUs versus vacant channel probability is evaluated, as is shown in Figure 3.7. In the scheme discussed in this chapter, for each channel only one SU is allowed to access the channel as SUs apply for vacant channel usage. There are two methods for the BS to select the SU: one is "IR-RA," which chooses the SU aimlessly, and the other is "IR-Best," which chooses the SU with the best channel gain. Figure 3.7 shows that the throughput of all SUs with the scheme discussed in this chapter is up to 45% larger than that with NCPC

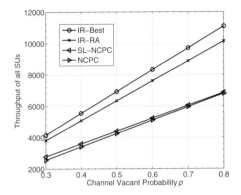

Figure 3.7 Throughput of all SUs under the social norm in (3.3).

and SL-NCPC. The main reason for this is that only one SU is assigned to access one channel in this scheme. Under this circumstance, the interference introduced by multiple SUs' transmissions over one channel within NCPC and SL-NCPC could be avoided. In Figure 3.7, it can also be seen that all SUs' throughput increases with the vacant channel probability due to the greater opportunities for SUs to access the vacant channel.

3.4.3   Different Social Norms

The first social norm, defined as $\boldsymbol{\Omega}_1$, is the one in (3.3). Recall that $\boldsymbol{\Omega}_1$ is set to help an SU relay the PU's signal utilizing greater power by assigning it a higher reputation when the channel is not in an outage. To avoid blindly penalizing SUs with poor channel quality, we consider a revised social norm, $\boldsymbol{\Omega}_2$, as follows where the reputation is assigned only on the basis of the SU's action:

$$\boldsymbol{\Omega}_2 = \begin{pmatrix} 1 & 1 & \cdots & 1 \\ 2 & 2 & \cdots & 2 \\ \vdots & \vdots & \ddots & \vdots \\ N & N & \cdots & N \end{pmatrix}. \tag{3.60}$$

To prevent the use of inordinate transmission power for relaying, the social norm $\boldsymbol{\Omega}_3$ is considered

$$\boldsymbol{\Omega}_3 = \begin{pmatrix} 1 & 1 & \cdots & 1 \\ 2 & 2 & \cdots & 2 \\ \vdots & \vdots & \ddots & \vdots \\ N-2 & N-2 & \cdots & N-2 \\ N & N & \cdots & N \\ N & N & \cdots & N \end{pmatrix}. \tag{3.61}$$

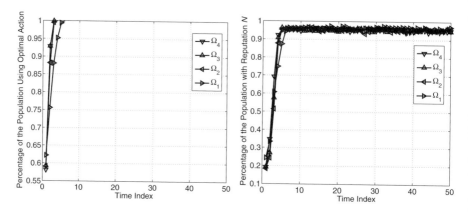

Figure 3.8 The percentage of the population using the optimal action shown in (3.63) with different social norms.

Figure 3.9 The percentage of the population with reputation $N = 5$ with different social norms.

The channel quality-dependent social norm Ω_4 is another social norm we study, and it is defined as follows:

$$\Omega_4 = \begin{pmatrix} 1 & 1 & 1 & \cdots & 1 & 1 \\ 1 & 2 & 3 & \cdots & N-1 & N \\ \vdots & \vdots & \vdots & \ddots & \vdots & \vdots \\ N-2 & N-1 & N & \cdots & N & N \\ N-1 & N & N & \cdots & N & N \end{pmatrix}. \tag{3.62}$$

On the one hand, even when relaying with maximum power, an SU that has a bad channel condition might not be able to get a good reputation with Ω_4. On the other hand, a low power level could lead to a high reputation if the channel condition is good enough.

With Algorithm 4, the optimal action rules for SUs with Ω_i, $i = 2, 3, 4$, can be derived as follows:

$$a^*_{\Omega_2} = \begin{pmatrix} N & \cdots & N \\ N & \cdots & N \\ \vdots & \ddots & \vdots \\ N & \cdots & N \end{pmatrix}, \quad a^*_{\Omega_3} = \begin{pmatrix} N-1 & \cdots & N-1 \\ N-1 & \cdots & N-1 \\ \vdots & \ddots & \vdots \\ N-1 & \cdots & N-1 \end{pmatrix}$$

$$\text{and} \quad a^*_{\Omega_4} = \begin{pmatrix} N & N & N-1 & \cdots & 2 \\ N & N & N-1 & \cdots & 2 \\ \vdots & \vdots & \vdots & \ddots & \vdots \\ N & N & N-1 & \cdots & 2 \end{pmatrix}. \tag{3.63}$$

Then, the evolutionary stability of the optimal action rules given in (3.63) is examined. From the simulation results shown in Figures 3.8 and 3.9, it can be seen that both the percentage of the population with reputation N and the optimal actions converge within 10 iterations, verifying that all of the optimal action rules are ESSs.

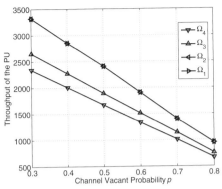

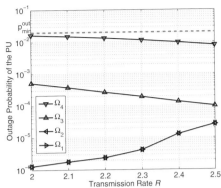

Figure 3.10 Throughput of the PU with different social norms.

Figure 3.11 Outage probability of the PU with different social norms.

Finally, we compare the system performance through different social norms. In the following, it is assumed that the IR-Unequal strategy is utilized and the PU's QoS requirement is set as $p_{min}^{out} = 0.02$ and $p_{max}^{out} = 0.2$.

Firstly, the end-to-end throughput of the PU versus the vacant channel probability is evaluated. According to Figure 3.10, the PU has the highest throughput with Ω_1 and Ω_2 since under both of these social norms SUs use their maximum power for relaying. With Ω_3, SUs decrease their relay power to the second highest power level because it is not crucial for them to utilize their entire power to earn the highest reputation, which leads to a degradation of the PU's throughput. With Ω_4, SUs adjust their power levels according to the channel conditions. They will further lower their power levels because most selected SUs' channel quality is good enough, and thus the PU gains the lowest throughput.

Figure 3.11 shows the simulation results of the PU's outage probability versus the transmission rate threshold. It proves that the PU could meet the QoS requirement with the help of SUs with Ω_4, and its outage probability is capable of being further developed with Ω_3. This phenomenon is mostly because this social norm's power level is quantized according to the average channel condition, while the selected SU always has a better channel condition. In addition, the PU could obtain the lowest outage probability with Ω_1 and Ω_2 through experiencing the largest relay power.

In the last simulation, the performance of the secondary system is studied. In view of the fact that given a specific vacant channel probability, all SUs' throughputs will be the same, here only the total energy consumption of all SUs versus the transmission rate threshold with the vacant channel probability being $p = 0.55$ is compared. From Figure 3.12 it can be seen that SUs need to spend most of their energy on relaying with social norms Ω_1 and Ω_2 to gain the same throughput. They can save at least 26% of the energy with Ω_3, and even 90% with Ω_4.

Moreover, Figures 3.8–3.12 show that there is almost no difference of performance between Ω_1 and Ω_2 because of the rare probability of the selected SU's channel quality falling to the lowest channel quality level, and it is difficult for reputation assignment to make a distinct difference.

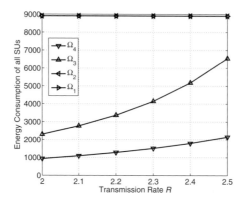

Figure 3.12 Energy consumption of all SUs with different social norms.

Thus, among the four social norms, Ω_1 and Ω_2 are preferable to the PU because they are capable of bringing about better performance, while Ω_4 makes the SUs the most effective. Furthermore, Ω_4 is more difficult for a real system to realize than Ω_1, Ω_2, and Ω_3, since Ω_4 requires fine quantization of the relay power and channel quality and an accurate relationship among them.

3.5   Conclusion

In this chapter, a novel spectrum access scheme is discussed for utilizing channels efficiently on the basis of indirect reciprocity game modeling. The SUs are stimulated by reputation to adopt the optimal strategy of the indirect reciprocity model (i.e., maximal power to help PUs relay data when the channel is not in an outage), resulting in the improvement of PUs' QoS. By using theoretical analysis, the cost-to-gain ratio is derived under which an optimal strategy is stable. The results of the simulation show that the optimal strategy would lead to a "good" society in which most of the SUs obtain the highest reputation. Compared with the state-of-the-art direct reciprocity-based spectrum access schemes, the scheme discussed in this chapter achieves much better performance.

References

[1] Federal Communications Commission, *Spectrum Policy Task Force Report*. FCC Document ET Docket, 2002.

[2] S. Haykin, "Cognitive radio: brain-empowered wireless communications," *IEEE Journal of Selected Areas in Communications*, vol. 23, pp. 201–220, 2005.

[3] J. M. Peha, "Approaches to spectrum sharing," *IEEE Communications Magazine*, vol. 43, pp. 10–12, 2005.

[4] B. Wang and K. J. R. Liu, "Advances in cognitive radios: A survey," *IEEE Journal of Selected Topics in Signal Processing*, vol. 5, pp. 5–23, 2011.

[5] A. K. Sadek, K. J. R. Liu, and A. Ephremides, "Cognitive multiple access via cooperation: protocol design and performance analysis," *IEEE Transactions on Information Theory*, vol. 53, pp. 3677–3695, 2007.

[6] R. Etkin, A. Parekh, and D. Tse, "Spectrum sharing for unlicensed bands," *IEEE J. Select. Areas in Commun.*, vol. 25, pp. 517–528, Apr. 2007.

[7] L. Cao and H. Zheng, "Distributed rule-regulated spectrum sharing," *IEEE Journal of Selected Areas in Communications*, vol. 26, pp. 130–145, 2008.

[8] B. Wang, Z. Ji, K. J. R. Liu, and T. Clancy, "Primary-prioritized Markov approach for efficient and fair dynamic spectrum allocation," *IEEE Transactions on Wireless Communications*, vol. 8, pp. 1854–1865, 2009.

[9] D. Niyato, E. Hossain, and Z. Han, "Dynamics of multiple-seller and multiple-buyer spectrum trading in cognitive radio networks: A game-theoretic modeling approach," *IEEE Transactions on Mobile Computing*, vol. 8, pp. 1009–1022, 2009.

[10] S. Sengupta and M. Chatterjee, "An economic framework for dynamic spectrum access and service pricing," *IEEE/ACM Transactions on Networking*, vol. 17, pp. 1200–1213, 2009.

[11] G. E. Howayek and S. K. Jayaweera, "Distributed dynamic spectrum leasing (D-DSL) for spectrum sharing over multiple primary channels," *IEEE Transactions on Wireless Communications*, vol. 10, pp. 55–60, 2011.

[12] O. Simeone, I. Stanojev, S. Savazzi, Y. Bar-Ness, U. Spagnolini, and R. Pickholtz, "Spectrum leasing to cooperating secondary ad hoc networks," *IEEE Journal of Selected Areas in Communications*, vol. 26, pp. 1–11, 2008.

[13] X. Zhou and H. Zheng, "Trust: A general framework for truthful double spectrum auctions," *Proc. IEEE INFOCOM*, pp. 999–1007, 2009.

[14] Y. Wu, B. Wang, K. J. R. Liu, and T. Clancy, "A scalable collusion-resistant multi-winner cognitive spectrum auction game," *IEEE Transactions on Communications*, vol. 57, pp. 3805–3816, 2009.

[15] M. J. Osborne and A. Rubinste, *A Course in Game Theory*. MIT Press, 1994.

[16] Z. Ji and K. J. R. Liu, "Dynamic spectrum sharing: A game theoretical overview," *IEEE Communications Magazine*, vol. 45, pp. 88–94, 2007.

[17] K. J. R. Liu and B. Wang, *Cognitive Radio Networking and Security: A Game-Theoretic View*. Cambridge University Press, 2010.

[18] B. Wang, Y. Wu, Z. Ji, K. J. R. Liu, and T. C. Clancy, "Game theoretical mechanism design methods: suppressing cheating in cognitive radio networks," *IEEE Signal Processing Magazine, Special Issue on Signal Processing for Cognitive Radio Networks*, vol. 25, pp. 74–84, 2008.

[19] Y. Wu, B. Wang, K. J. R. Liu, and T. C. Clancy, "Repeated open spectrum sharing game with cheat-proof strategies," *IEEE Transactions on Wireless Communications*, vol. 8, pp. 1922–1933, 2009.

[20] Y. Tan, S. Sengupta, and K. P. Subbalakshmi, "Analysis of coordinated denial-of-service attacks in IEEE 802.22 networks," *IEEE Journal of Selected Areas in Communications*, vol. 29, pp. 890–902, 2011.

[21] Y. Tan, S. Sengupta, and K. Subbalakshmi, "Competitive spectrum trading in dynamic spectrum access markets: A price war," *Proc. GLOBECOM*, 2010.

[22] A. Satsiou and L. Tassiulas, "Reputation-based resource allocation in P2P systems of rational users," *IEEE Transactions on Parallel and Distributed Systems*, vol. 21, pp. 466–479, 2010.

[23] Y. Zhang and Y. Fang, "A fine-grained reputation system for reliable service selection in peer-to-peer networks," *IEEE Transactions on Parallel and Distributed Systems*, vol. 18, pp. 1134–1145, 2007.

[24] S. Vassilaras, D. Vogiatzis, and G. S. Yovanof, "Security and cooperation in clustered mobile ad hoc networks eith centralized supervision," *IEEE Journal of Selected Areas in Communications*, vol. 24, pp. 329–342, 2006.

[25] S. Buchegger and J.-Y. L. Boudec, "Self-policing mobile ad hoc networks by reputation systems," *IEEE Communications Magazine*, vol. 43, pp. 101–107, 2005.

[26] Z. Ji and K. J. R. Liu, "Multi-stage pricing game for collusion-resistant dynamic spectrum allocation," *IEEE Journal of Selected Areas in Communications, Special Issue on Cognitive Radio: Theory and Applications*, vol. 26, pp. 182–191, 2008.

[27] Y. Chen, Y. Wu, B. Wang, and K. J. R. Liu, "Spectrum auction games for multimedia streaming over cognitive radio networks," *IEEE Transactions on Communications*, vol. 58, pp. 2381–2390, 2010.

[28] S. K. Jayaweera, M. Bkassiny, and K. A. Avery, "Asymmetric cooperative communications based spectrum leasing via auctions in cognitive radio networks," *IEEE Transactions on Wireless Communications*, vol. 10, pp. 2716–2724, 2011.

[29] D. Li, Y. Xu, X. Wang, and M. Guizani, "Coalitional game theoretic approach for secondary spectrum access in cooperative cognitive radio networks," *IEEE Transactions on Wireless Communications*, vol. 10, pp. 844–856, 2011.

[30] H. Ohtsuki, Y. Iwasa, and M. A. Nowak, "Indirect reciprocity provides only a narrow margin for efficiency for costly punishment," *Nature*, vol. 457, pp. 79–82, 2009.

[31] M. A. Nowak and K. Sigmund, "Evolution of indirect reciprocity," *Nature*, vol. 437, pp. 1291–1298, 2005.

[32] Y. Chen and K. J. R. Liu, "Indirect reciprocity game modelling for cooperation stimulation in cognitive networks," *IEEE Transactions on Communications*, vol. 59, pp. 159–168, 2011.

[33] H. V. Zhao, W. S. Lin, and K. J. R. Liu, *Behavior Dynamics in Media-Sharing Social Networks*. Cambridge University Press, 2011.

[34] A. S. Ibrahim, A. K. Sadek, W. Su, and K. J. R. Liu, "Cooperative communications with relay selection: when to cooperate and whom to cooperate with?" *IEEE Transactions on Wireless Communications*, vol. 7, pp. 2814–2827, 2008.

[35] J. Laneman, D. Tse, and G. Wornell, "Cooperative diversity in wireless networks: efficient protocols and outage behavior," *IEEE Transactions on Information Theory*, vol. 50, pp. 3062–3080, 2004.

[36] P. Oskar, "Zur theorie der matrices," *Mathematische Annalen*, vol. 64, pp. 248–263, 1907.

[37] G. Frobenius, "Ueber matrizen aus nicht negativen elementen," *Sitzungsberichte der Königlich Preussischen Akademie der Wissenschaften*, vol. 26, pp. 456–477, 1912.

[38] D. P. Bertsekas, *Dynamic Programming: Deterministic and Stochastic Models*. Prentice Hall, 1987.

[39] J. M. Smith, *Evolution and the Theory of Games*. Cambridge University Press, 1982.

[40] Y. Chen, B. Wang, W. S. Lin, Y. Wu, and K. J. R. Liu, "Cooperative peer-to-peer streaming: An evolutionary game-theoretic approach," *IEEE Transactions on Circuits and Systems for Video Technology*, vol. 20, pp. 1346–1357, 2010.

[41] D. Blackwell, "Discounted dynamic programming," *Annals of Mathematical Statistics*, vol. 36, pp. 226–235, 1965.

[42] R. Fisher, *The Genetical Theory of Natural Selection*. Clarendon Press, 1930.

4 Multiuser Indirect Reciprocity Game for Cooperative Communications

The willingness of users helps determine the viability of cooperative communications to a great extent. However, in future wireless networks, unless the act is capable of improving their own utility, users would not help relay information to others because they are rational and may be pursuing different objectives. Thus, it is of great importance to study incentive issues when designing cooperative communication systems. In this chapter, a cooperation stimulation scheme for multiuser cooperative communications using the indirect reciprocity game will be discussed. With the introduced notion of social norms and reputation, rational users that care for their future utility are inclined to cooperate. Unlike the existing reputation-based schemes that mostly depend on experimental verification, the effectiveness of the scheme is demonstrated in two steps. First, steady-state analysis of the game will be conducted. This shows that when the cost-to-gain ratio is below a certain threshold, cooperation with users who have a good reputation can be sustained as an equilibrium. It is then shown that the equilibria discovered in the steady-state analysis are stable and can be reached with appropriate initial conditions through modeling the action spreading through transient states as an evolutionary game. Furthermore, energy detection for dealing with users' possible cheating behaviors and their influence on the indirect reciprocity game are introduced.

4.1 Introduction

A transmission paradigm that is promising for future wireless networks is cooperative communications [1]. Through the cooperation of relays, it is possible to improve the performance, capacity, and speed of communication, decrease battery consumption, prolong network lifetime, increase the stable region and throughput for multiple access schemes, broaden the transmission coverage area, and bring about cooperation trade-offs beyond source–channel coding for multimedia communications.

Nevertheless, users are by default assumed to be unconditionally altruistic and willing to provide support regardless of their own utility in most existing works, and this is unrealistic in wireless networks in which they are intelligent, rational, and often do not pursue the same objective. Intelligent decisions based on their own preferences would be made. Furthermore, users will not tend to help and only act selfishly as "free riders" because relaying others' information could consume valuable resources such as power and frequency. Under this circumstance, cooperative communication protocols would not accomplish good social outcomes unless they consider incentive issues. Thus, designing effective incentive schemes that are capable of stimulating cooperation among selfish users has aroused interest.

Three classes of schemes [2], including payment-based, direct reciprocity-based, and reputation-based schemes, have been proposed in the literature for stimulating cooperative behaviors within communication networks of selfish and rational users. Payment-based schemes have generally been adopted in order to stimulate cooperation for peer-to-peer networks [3,4] and wireless ad hoc networks [5–7]. The problem of cooperation stimulation has been researched within multiuser cooperative communication networks [8], in which a two-level Stackelberg game was utilized to address the incentive, relay selection, and resource allocation problems in a distributed manner. In [9], the authors studied the pricing game within scenarios in which channel state information (CSI) was held confidentially. However, some tamper-proof hardware and services are required by payment-based schemes, and this is impractical for many applications.

Direct reciprocity-based schemes depend on the repeated prisoner's dilemma model and are also capable of being employed to maintain cooperation [10,11]. In [12], a set of optimal cooperation strategies for users within the ad hoc networks were derived using optimality criteria, such as cheat-proofing, Pareto optimality, and fairness. In [13], the problem of cooperation stimulation was researched for mobile ad hoc networks within situations in which imperfect and noisy observations exist. However, there is a generally incorrect assumption for multiuser cooperative communications in direct reciprocity-based schemes that infinite interactions can occur between a pair of users. Actually, different relay nodes would be chosen by source nodes at each time to achieve a higher order of spatial diversity and better performance, instead of having a fixed relay.

Reputation-based schemes are also sufficient for cooperation stimulation [14,15]. In [16], a local reputation system was initially set up on the basis of the shared history among the neighborhood of nodes, which was then used to identify and punish noncooperative nodes. The work in [17] enforced cooperation with a global reputation mechanism. However, there is no theoretical justification for the effectiveness of these reputation-based schemes.

In this chapter, as a key concept for illustrating the evolution of human cooperation, the indirect reciprocity game is employed to stimulate cooperation among selfish users within a multiuser cooperative communication network. It was first studied under the name of "third-party altruism" in 1971 [18] and then drew wide attention in the fields of evolutionary biology [19,20] and economics [21]. It is based on the idea that cooperation is capable of leading to a good reputation and the expectation of being rewarded by others in the future within a reputation and social judgment system. Furthermore, according to indirect reciprocity game modeling, the use of reputation in stimulating cooperation can be justified theoretically.

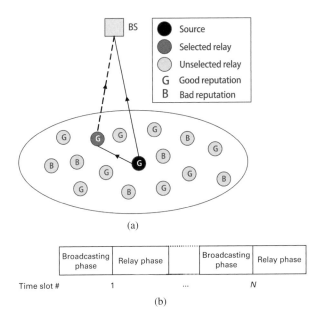

(a)

(b)

Figure 4.1 Multiuser cooperative communication system: (a) system model, (b) time frame structure. BS = base station.

4.2 System Model

In this section, the physical layer model utilizing the relay selection and the amplify-and-forward (AF) cooperation protocol are presented. The incentive scheme using the indirect reciprocity game and its overheads are presented.

4.2.1 Physical Layer Model with Relay Selection

In Figure 4.1(a), a time division multiple access (TDMA)-based multiuser cooperative communication network is considered in which N nodes numbered $1, 2, \ldots, N$ have their own information to be transmitted to a base station (BS) d. Without loss of generality, the information will be transmitted by nodes in packets that, in practice, contain many symbols. We assume that nodes are rational in the sense that they would act to maximize their own utility. In this chapter, "user," "node," and "player" are used interchangeably.

As is shown in Figure 4.1(b), time is divided into time frames and each frame is further divided into N time slots. The AF protocol is employed in the system model: only one prescribed node at each time slot is authorized to transmit, and all the remaining $N - 1$ nodes could serve as potential relays. Accordingly, there are two phases in every time slot. In Phase 1, the information of the source node is broadcast to the BS and all other nodes. Presuming that node i acts as the source node, then the received signals $y_{i,d}^{(1)}$ and $y_{i,j}^{(1)}$ at the BS and node j, respectively, could be defined as

$$y_{i,d}^{(1)} = \sqrt{P_s}h_{i,d}x_i + n_{i,d}, \tag{4.1}$$

$$y_{i,j}^{(1)} = \sqrt{P_s}h_{i,j}x_i + n_{i,j}, \tag{4.2}$$

where P_s is the transmitted power at the source node, x_i is the transmitted symbol with unit energy, $h_{i,d}$ and $h_{i,j}$ are channel coefficients from user i to the BS and user j, respectively, and $n_{i,d}$ and $n_{i,j}$ are additive noise. Generally, the additive noise is modeled for all links as independent and identically distributed zero-mean, complex Gaussian random variables with variance N_0. Furthermore, we consider the homogeneous channel condition, in which we model channel coefficients $h_{i,d}$ and $h_{i,j}$ as zero-mean, complex Gaussian random variables with variance σ_1^2 and σ_2^2, respectively, for all $i,j \in \{1,2,\ldots N\}$. In addition, the quasi-static channel is assumed in the system model, and this means that channel conditions would not change at every time slot and would not alter independently from one time slot to another.

In Phase 2, a relay node is chosen to strengthen the received signal and send it to the destination with transmitted power P_r. The received signal at the destination in Phase 2 could be calculated by

$$y_{j,d}^{(2)} = \frac{\sqrt{P_r P_s}h_{i,j}h_{j,d}}{\sqrt{P_s|h_{i,j}|^2 + N_0}}x_i + \frac{\sqrt{P_r}h_{j,d}}{\sqrt{P_s|h_{i,j}|^2 + N_0}}n_{i,j} + n_{j,d}. \tag{4.3}$$

On the basis of (4.3), the relayed signal-to-noise ratio (SNR) could be calculated through relaying node j for source node i as

$$\Gamma_{i,j,d} = \frac{P_r P_s |h_{i,j}|^2 |h_{j,d}|^2}{P_r|h_{j,d}|^2 N_0 + P_s|h_{i,j}|^2 N_0 + N_0^2}. \tag{4.4}$$

Two relay selection schemes based on the availability of CSI are adopted. For one, the BS obtains the global CSI (e.g., the BS is capable of collecting the CSI of all potential relays from the feedback channel) and optimal relay selection (ORS) is employed where the relay node that could bring the best relayed SNR would be chosen to support the source node. Then source nodes could obtain the full spatial diversity under the condition that the relay nodes make the choice regarding cooperation [22,23]. For the other scheme, if the global CSI is not recognized by the BS, a random relay selection (RRS) is employed where the BS would aimlessly select one node as the relay from all potential relays with the same probability and the selected relay would consider whether it is going to help based on a certain action rule that maximizes its own payoff, and its decision would be given back to the BS. If it makes a choice to help, then the received SNR increment at the BS after maximal-ratio combining (MRC) could be written as

$$\Gamma_i^c = \begin{cases} \max\limits_{j \neq i} \Gamma_{i,j,d} & \text{for ORS,} \\ \Gamma_{i,j,d} & \text{for RRS if node } j \text{ is selected.} \end{cases} \tag{4.5}$$

Table 4.1. Social norm.

k \ i,j	GG	GB	BG	BB
C	1	λ	$1-\lambda$	0
D	λ	1	0	$1-\lambda$

Notice that for RRS, after the relay selection, the BS is able to obtain the required CSI of MRC with channel estimations. If the selected relay node does not choose to help, then it is assumed that during that phase the source node would not resend its packet and the system would remain idle.

4.2.2   Incentive Schemes Based on the Indirect Reciprocity Game

For stimulating the selected relay node to cooperate, an incentive scheme based on the indirect reciprocity game in which social norms and reputation are two key concepts is employed. In particular, at the end of each time slot, a reputation score is assigned to every user to reflect the social assessment of this user. A binary reputation score is adopted in which users are capable of obtaining either bad or good reputations signified by B and G, respectively. A binary reputation score could be adequate for sustaining cooperation among rational users, thus more complicated reputation scores are not adopted here. As a function utilized for updating reputation, the social norm specifies what new reputation users would get based on their current reputation and performed actions. In the system model, only the reputation of the selected relay node would be updated, while those of the source node and unselected relays remain unchanged. In the rest of this chapter, "relay" or "relay node" will be used to signify the selected relay node unless otherwise specified. Furthermore, the BS maintains the reputation information of all users, and the reputation updates will be performed here.

The social norm Q is designed as a function of the relay's present reputation, the source node's reputation, and the relay's action as

$$Q : \{G, B\} \times \{G, B\} \times \{C, D\} \mapsto [0, 1], \tag{4.6}$$

where cooperation and defection of the relay are represented by C and D, respectively. The social norm's value is designed to be the probability of assigning a good reputation to the relay. More precisely, for any $i, j \in \{G, B\}$ and $k \in \{C, D\}$, $Q(i, j, k)$ signifies the probability of obtaining a good reputation at the end of this time slot for the relay that has reputation i currently and chooses action k toward the source node with reputation j. Table 4.1 shows the values of the social norm, where $\lambda \in [0, 1]$ is a parameter that holds the current reputation's weight in determining the new reputation. When λ becomes smaller, the relay's new reputation would be less relevant to its current reputation but more relevant to the immediate reputation regulated by the relay's action and the source's reputation.

Algorithm 5: Indirect reciprocity game in one time frame.

---

(1) The BS notifies users of the reputation distribution of the population.

(2) Users decide their action rules based on the social norm and reputation distribution.

(3) For time slots $i = 1, 2, \ldots, N$

- User i broadcasts to the BS and other users.
- The BS selects one relay node using ORS or RRS and notifies the selected relay of the source node's reputation.
- The selected relay decides whether to cooperate according to their action rule and reports their decision to the BS.
- The selected relay amplifies and forwards signals for the source if they choose to cooperate or remains silence if not.
- The BS updates the selected relay's reputation.

An action rule, $\mathbf{a} = [\, a_{G,G} \quad a_{G,B} \quad a_{B,G} \quad a_{B,B} \,]^T$, is an action table of the relay in which element $a_{i,j}$ represents the probability of cooperation when the relay's reputation is i and the source's reputation is j. For the particular circumstance of pure action rules, only values of 0 or 1 can be taken by elements in the action table. According to the network's reputation distribution and the social norm, every user in the system model chooses its action rule when each time frame begins.

The indirect reciprocity game for one time frame is summarized in Algorithm 5.

4.2.3   Overheads of the Scheme

In this section, the overheads of the scheme discussed in this chapter will be briefly analyzed. The key overhead that is introduced by relay selection is an effort paid for channel estimations. Two additional channel estimations have to be performed within each time slot when RRS is employed, aiming at obtaining the CSI between the selected relay and the BS and that between the selected relay and the source, leading to a complexity of $\mathcal{O}(1)$, which has the same order as the traditional TDMA scheme. And if ORS is employed, the CSI between all potential relays and the BS and that between all potential relays and the source has to be estimated, resulting in a complexity of $\mathcal{O}(N)$.

Furthermore, the BS has to first notify the selected relay node of the source node's reputation score at each time slot, then update the selected relay's reputation in the end. By only considering binary reputation scores, each reputation score can be represented efficiently with one bit. Therefore, compared with users' packet' sizes, the two bits per time slot for the overheads of communications and reputation updating are almost negligible.

4.2.4   Payoff Functions

In each time slot, if the relay declines the request, both relay and source would get a payoff of zero; if it cooperates, the source node would obtain $\mathcal{G}$ while the relay would experience the cost C. Owing to the fact that users are unaware of the channel as they determine their action rules, payoff functions ought to be measured with an average sense. Within this chapter, the cost as a linear function of transmitted power is chosen, and it is signified as

$$C = P_r c, \tag{4.7}$$

where c is the cost per unit power. We design the gain function to be a linear function of the averaged SNR increment as

$$\mathcal{G} = E_h[\Gamma_i^c] \cdot g, \tag{4.8}$$

where g is the gain per unit SNR increment. In the calculation, the expectation is taken over the joint distribution of all channel coefficients and the user i is assumed to be the source node. Note that other forms of payoff functions could also be considered in the same manner and work within the framework of this chapter.

PROPOSITION 4.1   In view of the channel models and assuming $P_s/N_0 \gg 1$ and $P_r/N_0 \gg 1$, the gain function could be evaluated by

$$\mathcal{G} \approx \begin{cases} \dfrac{P_r P_s \sigma_1^2 \sigma_2^2 g}{P_r \sigma_1^2 N_0 + P_s \sigma_2^2 N_0} \displaystyle\sum_{n=1}^{N-1} \dfrac{1}{n} & \text{for ORS}, \\[4mm] \dfrac{P_r P_s \sigma_1^2 \sigma_2^2 g}{P_r \sigma_1^2 N_0 + P_s \sigma_2^2 N_0} & \text{for RRS}. \end{cases} \tag{4.9}$$

Proof   For ORS, let $Y = \max\limits_{j \neq i} \dfrac{P_r P_s |h_{i,j}|^2 |h_{j,d}|^2}{P_r |h_{j,d}|^2 N_0 + P_s |h_{i,j}|^2 N_0}$. Based on [16,23], the cumulative distribution function (CDF) of Y could be defined as

$$P_Y(y) = \left[1 - 2y\sqrt{\beta_1 \beta_2} e^{-y(\beta_1+\beta_2)} K_1(2y\sqrt{\beta_1 \beta_2})\right]^{N-1}, \tag{4.10}$$

where $\beta_1 = N_0/P_r \sigma_1^2$, $\beta_2 = N_0/P_s \sigma_2^2$, and $K_1(x)$ is the first-order modified Bessel functions of the second kind, defined in (9.6.22) in [24]. Furthermore, because $Y \geq 0$, the expectation of Y could be calculated as

$$E[Y] = \int_0^\infty [1 - P_Y(y)] dy,$$

$$= \sum_{n=1}^{N-1} \binom{N-1}{n} (-1)^{n-1} \int_0^\infty \left(2y\sqrt{\beta_1 \beta_2}\right)^n e^{-y(\beta_1+\beta_2)n} \cdot \left(K_1(2y\sqrt{\beta_1 \beta_2})\right)^n dy,$$

$$\tag{4.11}$$

$$\approx \frac{1}{\beta_1 + \beta_2} \sum_{n=1}^{N-1} \binom{N-1}{n} \frac{(-1)^{n-1}}{n}, \tag{4.12}$$

$$= \frac{1}{\beta_1 + \beta_2} \sum_{n=1}^{N-1} \frac{1}{n}. \tag{4.13}$$

From (4.11) and (4.12) we approximated $K_1(x)$ as given in (9.6.9) in [24] by $K_1(x) \approx 1/x$, and (4.13) is obtained using the identity in (0.155, 4) in [25]. Finally, when $P_s/N_0 \gg 1$ and $P_s/N_0 \gg 1$, the ORS can be defined as

$$\mathcal{G} \approx E[Y] \cdot g \approx \frac{P_r P_s \sigma_1^2 \sigma_2^2 g}{P_r \sigma_1^2 N_0 + P_s \sigma_2^2 N_0} \sum_{n=1}^{N-1} \frac{1}{n}. \tag{4.14}$$

Owing to the fact that the estimate of $\mathcal{G}$ under RRS is capable of being signified as a particular case of that under ORS with $N - 1 = 1$, the results for RRS follow precisely from (4.14).

Within the modeling, the gain could be estimated by (4.9) or experiments conducted at the BS. The cost-to-gain ratio of the game is represented as $\rho = \frac{C}{\mathcal{G}}$, which can significantly influence user behaviors. Intuitively, if ρ is smaller, users are more likely to cooperate. In this section, we restrict this to $0 < \rho < 1$.

4.3   Steady-State Analysis Using Markov Decision Processes

4.3.1   Stationary Reputation Distribution

In indirect reciprocity games, reputation is a key concept, and thus the reputation distribution among the entire population is a significant aspect of the network state within the game modeling. First, we derive the reputation distribution updating rule. Then, the stationary reputation distribution is determined and the steady state of the game is defined.

Let x_t stand for the probability of a user having a good reputation at time frame t. Presuming all users in the network employ an action rule $\mathbf{a}$, we have

$$x_{t+1} = x_t[x_t d_{G,G} + (1 - x_t)d_{G,B}] + (1 - x_t)[x_t d_{B,G} + (1 - x_t)d_{B,B}],$$

$$= (d_{G,G} - d_{G,B} - d_{B,G} + d_{B,B})x_t^2 + (d_{G,B} + d_{B,G} - 2d_{B,B})x_t + d_{B,B},$$

$$\overset{\Delta}{=} f_{\mathbf{a}}(x_t), \tag{4.15}$$

where $d_{i,j}$ with $i, j \in \{G, B\}$ is the reputation updating probability that represents the probability that the relay would gain a good reputation after one interaction, with its source's reputation j and its current reputation i. Based on the social norm in Table 4.1, $d_{i,j}$ can be computed as follows:

$$d_{i,j} = a_{i,j} Q(i, j, C) + (1 - a_{i,j}) Q(i, j, D). \tag{4.16}$$

Obviously, $d_{i,j}$ is a function of the action $a_{i,j}$, and for simplicity, $d_{i,j}$ is used instead of $d_{i,j}(a_{i,j})$. In view of Table 4.1 and (4.16), it can be defined as

$$\begin{cases} d_{G,G} &= a_{G,G}(1 - \lambda) + \lambda, \\ d_{G,B} &= -a_{G,B}(1 - \lambda) + 1, \\ d_{B,G} &= a_{B,G}(1 - \lambda), \\ d_{B,B} &= -a_{B,B}(1 - \lambda) + (1 - \lambda). \end{cases} \tag{4.17}$$

According to the reputation distribution updating rule in (4.15), the stationary reputation distribution is studied and the following proposition is obtained.

PROPOSITION 4.2 For any action rule $\mathbf{a}$, a stationary reputation distribution exists, and it is the solution to the following equation:

$$x_{\mathbf{a}} = f_{\mathbf{a}}(x_{\mathbf{a}}). \tag{4.18}$$

Proof First, based on (4.15), the stationary reputation distribution $x_{\mathbf{a}}$ given action rule $\mathbf{a}$, if it exits, must be the solution to (4.18). Next, in order to demonstrate the stationary reputation distribution's existence, it ought to be verified that (4.18) obtains a solution in the interval $[0, 1]$. Let $\tilde{f}_{\mathbf{a}}(x) = f_{\mathbf{a}}(x) - x$. We have $\tilde{f}_{\mathbf{a}}(0) = d_{B,B} \geq 0$ and $\tilde{f}_{\mathbf{a}}(1) = d_{G,G} - 1 \leq 0$. Since (4.18) is a quadratic equation, a solution in the interval $[0, 1]$ must exist.

It can be seen from Proposition 4.2 that, if an action rule $\mathbf{a}$ is employed by all users, a stationary reputation would be achieved and the game would be stable, leading to the steady state of the indirect reciprocity game defined as follows.

DEFINITION 4.3 (Steady state) $(\mathbf{a}, x_{\mathbf{a}})$ is a steady state of the indirect reciprocity game if $\mathbf{a}$ is an action rule employed by all users and $x_{\mathbf{a}}$ is the corresponding stationary reputation distribution.

4.3.2 Long-Term Expected Payoffs at Steady States

It is assumed that the indirect reciprocity game is in a steady state $(\mathbf{a}, x_{\mathbf{a}})$ (i.e., action rule $\mathbf{a}$ is chosen by all players and the reputation distribution remains stable at $x_{\mathbf{a}}$). Let $v_{i,j}$ with $i, j \in \{G, B\}$ denote the expected payoff that a player with reputation i matched with a player with reputation j is capable of obtaining from this interaction in the future. For one aspect, if the player acts as the relay, then the long-term expected payoff is defined as

$$u^r_{i,j}(a_{i,j}) = -Ca_{i,j} + \delta \big[d_{i,j} x_{\mathbf{a}} v_{G,G} + d_{i,j}(1 - x_{\mathbf{a}}) v_{G,B} $$
$$+ (1 - d_{i,j}) x_{\mathbf{a}} v_{B,G} + (1 - d_{i,j})(1 - x_{\mathbf{a}}) v_{B,B} \big], \tag{4.19}$$

where the first term denotes the cost incurred in the present interaction and the second stands for the future payoff discounted by a discounting factor $\delta \in (0, 1)$. However, if the player acts as the source, then the long-term expected payoff could be denoted as

$$u_{i,j}^s(a_{j,i}) = \mathcal{G}a_{j,i} + \delta \left[x_{\mathbf{a}} v_{i,G} + (1 - x_{\mathbf{a}}) v_{i,B} \right]. \tag{4.20}$$

Note that only the relay's reputation would be updated. Furthermore, based on a similar presumption, the probabilities of being the source or the relay for a user are $\frac{1}{N}$ and $\frac{N-1}{N} \frac{1}{N-1} = \frac{1}{N}$, respectively. Hence, once the user is taking part in the interaction, it ought to act as either the relay or the source with equal probability $1/2$. Then we can obtain the long-term expected payoff at the steady state as

$$v_{i,j} = \frac{1}{2} u_{i,j}^r(a_{i,j}) + \frac{1}{2} u_{i,j}^s(a_{j,i}). \tag{4.21}$$

Substituting (4.19) and (4.20) into (4.21), we have

$$v_{i,j} = \frac{1}{2} \left\{ -Ca_{i,j} + \delta \left[d_{i,j} x_{\mathbf{a}} v_{G,G} + d_{i,j}(1 - x_{\mathbf{a}}) v_{G,B} + (1 - d_{i,j}) x_{\mathbf{a}} v_{B,G} \right. \right.$$
$$\left. \left. + (1 - d_{i,j})(1 - x_{\mathbf{a}}) v_{B,B} \right] \right\} + \frac{1}{2} \left\{ \mathcal{G}a_{j,i} + \delta [x_{\mathbf{a}} v_{i,G} + (1 - x_{\mathbf{a}}) v_{i,B}] \right\} \tag{4.22}$$

Let $\mathbf{V} = [\ v_{G,G} \quad v_{G,B} \quad v_{B,G} \quad v_{B,B} \ ]^T$ stand for the long-term expected payoff vector. Then we can derive the following proposition.

PROPOSITION 4.4   Within the indirect reciprocity game, the long-term expected payoff vector in a steady state $(\mathbf{a}, x_{\mathbf{a}})$ could be defined as

$$\mathbf{V} = \left(\mathbf{I} - \frac{\delta}{2} \mathbf{H_a} \right)^{-1} \mathbf{b_a}, \tag{4.23}$$

where $\mathbf{H_a}$ is signified in (4.24), $\mathbf{b_a}$ is defined in (4.25), and $\mathbf{I}$ is a 4×4 identity matrix.

$$\mathbf{H_a} = \begin{bmatrix} (1 + d_{G,G}) x_{\mathbf{a}} & (1 + d_{G,G})(1 - x_{\mathbf{a}}) & (1 - d_{G,G}) x_{\mathbf{a}} & (1 - d_{G,G})(1 - x_{\mathbf{a}}) \\ (1 + d_{G,B}) x_{\mathbf{a}} & (1 + d_{G,B})(1 - x_{\mathbf{a}}) & (1 - d_{G,B}) x_{\mathbf{a}} & (1 - d_{G,B})(1 - x_{\mathbf{a}}) \\ d_{B,G} x_{\mathbf{a}} & d_{B,G}(1 - x_{\mathbf{a}}) & (2 - d_{B,G}) x_{\mathbf{a}} & (2 - d_{B,G})(1 - x_{\mathbf{a}}) \\ d_{B,B} x_{\mathbf{a}} & d_{B,B}(1 - x_{\mathbf{a}}) & (2 - d_{B,B}) x_{\mathbf{a}} & (2 - d_{B,B})(1 - x_{\mathbf{a}}) \end{bmatrix}, \tag{4.24}$$

$$\mathbf{b_a} = \frac{1}{2} \left[(\mathcal{G} - C)a_{G,G} \quad \mathcal{G}a_{B,G} - Ca_{G,B} \quad \mathcal{G}a_{G,B} - Ca_{B,G} \quad (\mathcal{G} - C)a_{B,B} \right]^T, \tag{4.25}$$

Proof   By rearranging (4.22) into the matrix form, we have

$$\left(\mathbf{I} - \frac{\delta}{2} \mathbf{H_a} \right) \mathbf{V} = \mathbf{b_a}. \tag{4.26}$$

To prove (4.23), it suffices to show that the matrix $\left(\mathbf{I} - \frac{\delta}{2} \mathbf{H_a} \right)$ is invertible. Since the row sum of $\frac{1}{2} \mathbf{H_a}$ is 1 for every row and $0 < \delta < 1$ by the Gerschgorin theorem and the definition of a spectral radius in [26], we have

$$\mu \left(\frac{\delta}{2} \mathbf{H_a} \right) < 1, \tag{4.27}$$

where $\mu(\cdot)$ signifies the spectral radius. Then, corollary C.4 in [27] establishes the invertibility of $\left(\mathbf{I} - \frac{\delta}{2} \mathbf{H_a} \right)$.

4.3.3 Equilibrium Steady State

According to the above analysis, every player's utility relies on other players' actions. Consequently, every player, as a rational decision-maker, would condition their action on the actions of others. For instance, in the social norm in Table 4.1, the relay node would obtain a good reputation through choosing cooperation instead of defection when the source node has a good reputation. Under this circumstance, if players with a good reputation are favored by other players' action rules, then the relay node would choose to help in the current time slot, since they will benefit from others' help in the future; however, if that phenomenon happens with a very low probability, then the relay node might choose not to help due to the costly cooperation.

In order to study these interactions theoretically, first, we define a new concept of equilibrium steady state. Then, through modeling the problem of finding the optimal action rule at the steady state as a Markov decision process (MDP), we characterize all equilibrium steady states of the indirect reciprocity game mathematically.

DEFINITION 4.5 (Equilibrium steady state) $(\mathbf{a}, x_{\mathbf{a}})$ is an equilibrium steady state of the indirect reciprocity game if:

(1) $(\mathbf{a}, x_{\mathbf{a}})$ is a steady state.
(2) $\mathbf{a}$ is the best response of any user given that the reputation distribution is $x_{\mathbf{a}}$ and all other users are adopting action rule $\mathbf{a}$ (i.e., the system is in steady state $(\mathbf{a}, x_{\mathbf{a}})$).

According to this, it can be seen that any unilateral deviations will not benefit users in an equilibrium steady state. Furthermore, in order to discover the best response of users in this steady state, determining whether a steady state is an equilibrium could be modeled as an MDP. Within this MDP formulation, the action is action rule $\mathbf{a}$, the state is the reputation pair (i, j), the transition probability is determined by $\{d_{i,j}\}$, and the reward function is determined by the steady state $(\mathbf{a}, x_{\mathbf{a}})$, $\mathcal{C}$, and $\mathcal{G}$. In addition, the MDP is stationary [27] because the reward function and the transition probability remain unchanged for a given steady state.

Based on the MDP formulation, the optimality equation can be written as

$$v_{i,j} = \max_{\hat{a}_{i,j}} \left[\frac{1}{2} u^r_{i,j}(\hat{a}_{i,j}) + \frac{1}{2} u^s_{i,j}(a_{j,i}) \right]. \tag{4.28}$$

To solve this numerically, we can use the value iteration algorithm [27]. Within this chapter, we will analyze the equilibrium steady states theoretically by exploring the structure of this problem instead of solving the problem numerically. Notice that the formulated MDP varies in different steady states, and the problem of finding all equilibria is quite hard since there are infinite steady states. The latter proposition, which successfully reduces the potential equilibria that are of practical interest to the set of three steady states, is derived to make the problem tractable.

PROPOSITION 4.6   In the indirect reciprocity game, if $(\mathbf{a}, x_\mathbf{a})$ is an equilibrium steady state for more than one possible ρ, it must be one of the following steady states:

(1) $(\mathbf{a_1}, x_{\mathbf{a}_1})$ with $\mathbf{a_1} = [\ 0\quad 0\quad 0\quad 0\ ]^T$ and $x_{\mathbf{a}_1} = 1/2$.
(2) $(\mathbf{a_2}, x_{\mathbf{a}_2})$ with $\mathbf{a_2} = [\ 1\quad 0\quad 1\quad 0\ ]^T$ and $x_{\mathbf{a}_2} = 1$.
(3) $(\mathbf{a_3}, x_{\mathbf{a}_3})$ with $\mathbf{a_3} = [\ 0\quad 1\quad 0\quad 1\ ]^T$ and $x_{\mathbf{a}_3} = 0$.

Proof   Any single user has no incentive to deviate from the specified action rule for one interaction, which is the essential condition for a steady state to be an equilibrium. This can be mathematically defined as

$$\frac{1}{2}u_{i,j}^r(a_{i,j}) + \frac{1}{2}u_{i,j}^s(a_{j,i}) \geq \frac{1}{2}u_{i,j}^r(\hat{a}_{i,j}) + \frac{1}{2}u_{i,j}^s(a_{j,i}) \qquad (4.29)$$

for all $i, j \in \{G, B\}$ and $\hat{a}_{i,j} \in [0,1]$. In (4.29), $\{a_{i,j}\}$ is the steady-state action rule that is employed by all other players and $\{\hat{a}_{i,j}\}$ is an alternative action rule for the player. The second terms on both sides are identical because only the relay's actions would influence the payoffs. Furthermore, since only one-shot deviation is considered, the long-term expected payoffs starting from the next interaction remain unchanged. After substituting (4.19) into (4.29), it can be rewritten as

$$\mathcal{C}(\hat{a}_{i,j} - a_{i,j}) \geq \delta\left[\Delta d_{i,j}x_\mathbf{a}v_{G,G} + \Delta d_{i,j}(1-x_\mathbf{a})v_{G,B}\right.$$
$$\left. - \Delta d_{i,j}x_\mathbf{a}v_{B,G} - \Delta d_{i,j}(1-x_\mathbf{a})v_{B,B}\right], \qquad (4.30)$$

where $\Delta d_{i,j} = \hat{d}_{i,j} - d_{i,j}$ and $\hat{d}_{i,j}$ is the reputation updating probability of a user using action rule $\hat{a}_{i,j}$. Through substituting (4.17) into (4.30) and rearranging the equations, we have

$$[\mathcal{C} - \delta(1-\lambda)\mathbf{r}^T\mathbf{V}](\hat{a}_{G,G} - a_{G,G}) \geq 0, \forall \hat{a}_{G,G} \in [0,1]. \qquad (4.31)$$

$$[\mathcal{C} + \delta(1-\lambda)\mathbf{r}^T\mathbf{V}](\hat{a}_{G,B} - a_{G,B}) \geq 0, \forall \hat{a}_{G,B} \in [0,1]. \qquad (4.32)$$

$$[\mathcal{C} - \delta(1-\lambda)\mathbf{r}^T\mathbf{V}](\hat{a}_{B,G} - a_{B,G}) \geq 0, \forall \hat{a}_{B,G} \in [0,1]. \qquad (4.33)$$

$$[\mathcal{C} + \delta(1-\lambda)\mathbf{r}^T\mathbf{V}](\hat{a}_{B,B} - a_{B,B}) \geq 0, \forall \hat{a}_{B,B} \in [0,1]. \qquad (4.34)$$

In (4.31)–(4.34), $\mathbf{V}$ is the long-term expected payoff vector that could be computed by (4.23) and $\mathbf{r} = [\ x_\mathbf{a}\quad 1-x_\mathbf{a}\quad -x_\mathbf{a}\quad -1+x_\mathbf{a}\ ]^T$.

Two coefficient terms, $[\mathcal{C} + \delta(1-\lambda)\mathbf{r}^T\mathbf{V}]$ and $[\mathcal{C} - \delta(1-\lambda)\mathbf{r}^T\mathbf{V}]$, are critical here in evaluating the steady state. According to (4.23), we can see that $\mathcal{C} + \delta(1-\lambda)\mathbf{r}^T\mathbf{V} = 0$ and $\mathcal{C} - \delta(1-\lambda)\mathbf{r}^T\mathbf{V} = 0$ are two linear equations of ρ, and each of them is capable of obtaining at most one solution. Hence, if a steady state is an equilibrium for more than one possible ρ, it must satisfy (4.31) and (4.33) when $\mathcal{C} - \delta(1-\lambda)\mathbf{r}^T\mathbf{V} \neq 0$ holds and (4.32) and (4.34) when $\mathcal{C} + \delta(1-\lambda)\mathbf{r}^T\mathbf{V} \neq 0$ holds.

If $[\mathcal{C} - \delta(1-\lambda)\mathbf{r}^T\mathbf{V}] > 0$, then (4.31) and (4.33) are valid, and we must have $a_{G,G} = 0$ and $a_{B,G} = 0$. However, if $[\mathcal{C} - \delta(1-\lambda)\mathbf{r}^T\mathbf{V}] < 0$, (4.31) and (4.33) will lead to $a_{G,G} = 1$ and $a_{B,G} = 1$. Likewise, from (4.32) and (4.34), we would get $a_{G,B} = 0$ and $a_{B,B} = 0$ if $[\mathcal{C} + \delta(1 - \lambda)\mathbf{r}^T \mathbf{V}] > 0$, as well as $a_{G,B} = 1$ and $a_{B,B} = 1$ if $[\mathcal{C} + \delta(1 - \lambda)\mathbf{r}^T \mathbf{V}] < 0$. Moreover, since $[\mathcal{C} - \delta(1 - \lambda)\mathbf{r}^T \mathbf{V}] < 0$ and $[\mathcal{C} + \delta(1 - \lambda)\mathbf{r}^T \mathbf{V}] < 0$ cannot be satisfied simultaneously, there are only three potential equilibrium action rules. The corresponding reputation distributions can then be calculated respectively based on Proposition 4.2.

According to the results in Proposition 4.6, there are two classes of steady states in the indirect reciprocity game. Within the first class, three steady states exist that have the potential to be equilibria for a set of ρ and are resistant to one-shot deviations. In the second class are all of the remaining steady states that either can only be an equilibrium for a specific cost-to-gain ratio or cannot be equilibria. Nevertheless, this kind of equilibrium is of no practical interest because it is not robust to the estimation errors of system parameters that are highly likely within a multiuser wireless network scenario. Accordingly, only three steady states, instead of infinite steady states, need to be analyzed in order to research the indirect reciprocity game's practical equilibria.

Then, we solve the optimality equations for the three steady states to represent the conditions under which they are equilibria. The following theorem summarizes the main results.

THEOREM 4.7   *In the indirect reciprocity game, there are three equilibrium steady states, which can be given as follows:*

(1) $(\mathbf{a_1}, x_{\mathbf{a_1}})$ *is an equilibrium for all* $0 < \rho < 1$.

(2) $(\mathbf{a_2}, x_{\mathbf{a_2}})$ *is an equilibrium if* $0 < \rho \leq \frac{\delta(1-\lambda)}{2-\delta-\lambda\delta}$.

(3) $(\mathbf{a_3}, x_{\mathbf{a_3}})$ *is an equilibrium if* $0 < \rho \leq \frac{\delta(1-\lambda)}{2-\delta-\lambda\delta}$.

$$v_{i,j}(\hat{\mathbf{a}}, \mathbf{a}) = -\frac{1}{2}\mathcal{C}a_{i,j} + \frac{1}{2}\delta\big[\hat{d}_{i,j}x_{\mathbf{a}}v_{G,G}(\hat{\mathbf{a}}, \mathbf{a}) + \hat{d}_{i,j}(1 - x_{\mathbf{a}})v_{G,B}(\hat{\mathbf{a}}, \mathbf{a})$$

$$+ (1 - \hat{d}_{i,j})x_{\mathbf{a}}v_{B,G}(\hat{\mathbf{a}}, \mathbf{a}) + (1 - \hat{d}_{i,j})(1 - x_{\mathbf{a}})v_{B,B}(\hat{\mathbf{a}}, \mathbf{a})\big] + \frac{1}{2}\mathcal{G}a_{j,i}$$

$$+ \frac{1}{2}\delta\big[x_{\mathbf{a}}v_{i,G}(\hat{\mathbf{a}}, \mathbf{a}) + (1 - x_{\mathbf{a}})v_{i,B}(\hat{\mathbf{a}}, \mathbf{a})\big] \qquad \forall i, j \in \{G, B\}.$$

$$(4.35)$$

Proof   Since the formulated MDP for each steady state is stationary, it suffices to find the optimal action rule by considering only stationary action rules according to theorem 6.2.7 in [27]. At a steady state $(\mathbf{a}, x_{\mathbf{a}})$, we could define the long-term expected payoff that one user choosing action rule $\hat{\mathbf{a}}$ gains while others are adopting action rule $\mathbf{a}$ as in (4.35).

The matrix form of (4.35) can be given as

$$\mathbf{V}(\hat{\mathbf{a}}, \mathbf{a}) = \frac{\delta}{2}\mathbf{H}_{\hat{\mathbf{a}}}\mathbf{V}(\hat{\mathbf{a}}, \mathbf{a}) + \mathbf{b}(\hat{\mathbf{a}}, \mathbf{a}), \qquad (4.36)$$

where $\mathbf{H_{\hat{a}}}$ is signified in (4.24). The subscript emphasizes its dependence on action rule $\hat{a}$ and $\mathbf{b}(\hat{a}, \mathbf{a}) = \frac{1}{2}\mathcal{G}[\ a_{G,G}\quad a_{B,G}\quad a_{G,B}\quad a_{B,B}\ ]^T - \frac{1}{2}\mathcal{C}\hat{a}$. Applying the results in Proposition 4.4, we have

$$\mathbf{V}(\hat{a}, \mathbf{a}) = \left(\mathbf{I} - \frac{\delta}{2}\mathbf{H_{\hat{a}}}\right)^{-1}\mathbf{b}(\hat{a}, \mathbf{a}). \tag{4.37}$$

Furthermore, the essential and sufficient condition for the steady state $(\mathbf{a}, x_\mathbf{a})$ to be an equilibrium could be given as

$$\mathbf{V}(\mathbf{a}, \mathbf{a}) \geq \mathbf{V}(\hat{a}, \mathbf{a}) \tag{4.38}$$

for all $\hat{a} = [\ \hat{a}_{G,G}\quad \hat{a}_{G,B}\quad \hat{a}_{B,G}\quad \hat{a}_{B,B}\ ] \in [0, 1].^4$

In the following, we solve (4.38) according to (4.37) for each of the three steady states in Theorem 4.7, respectively.

(1) When $\mathbf{a} = [\ 0\quad 0\quad 0\quad 0\ ]^T$ and $x_\mathbf{a} = 1/2$, we have $\mathbf{V}(\mathbf{a}, \mathbf{a}) = \mathbf{0}$ and $\mathbf{b}(\hat{a}, \mathbf{a}) = -\frac{1}{2}\mathcal{C}\hat{a}$. Hence, (4.38) is equal to

$$\mathcal{C}\left(\mathbf{I} - \frac{\delta}{2}\mathbf{H_{\hat{a}}}\right)^{-1}\hat{a} \geq \mathbf{0}. \tag{4.39}$$

Because all elements in matrix $\mathbf{H_{\hat{a}}}$ and vector $\hat{a}$ are nonnegative, we have $(\mathbf{H_{\hat{a}}})^n\hat{a} \geq \mathbf{0}$ for all integers n and all action rules $\hat{a}$. Then, applying the identity $\left(\mathbf{I} - \frac{\delta}{2}\mathbf{H_{\hat{a}}}\right)^{-1} = \sum_{n=0}^{\infty}\left(\frac{\delta}{2}\mathbf{H_{\hat{a}}}\right)^n$, it can be seen that (4.39) holds for all $0 < \rho < 1$. Thus, $(\mathbf{a}, x_\mathbf{a})$ is an equilibrium steady state for all $0 < \rho < 1$.

(2) When $\mathbf{a} = [\ 1\quad 0\quad 1\quad 0\ ]^T$ and $x_\mathbf{a} = 1$, according to (4.37), we can have

$$v_{G,G}(\hat{a}, \mathbf{a}) = \frac{2(1-\delta)(\mathcal{G} - \mathcal{C}\hat{a}_{G,G}) + \delta(1-\lambda)(\mathcal{G} - \mathcal{C})\hat{a}_{B,G}}{2(1-\delta)(2 - \delta(1+\lambda + (1-\lambda)(\hat{a}_{G,G} - \hat{a}_{B,G})))},$$

$$v_{G,B}(\hat{a}, \mathbf{a}) = \frac{\psi_1 + \psi_2\hat{a}_{G,G} + \psi_3\hat{a}_{G,B} + \psi_4\hat{a}_{B,G}}{2(1-\delta)(2 - \delta(1+\lambda + (1-\lambda)(\hat{a}_{G,G} - \hat{a}_{B,G})))},$$

$$v_{B,G}(\hat{a}, \mathbf{a}) = \frac{(\delta(1-\lambda)\mathcal{G} - (2 - \delta - \delta\lambda)\mathcal{C})\hat{a}_{B,G}}{2(1-\delta)(2 - \delta(1+\lambda + (1-\lambda)(\hat{a}_{G,G} - \hat{a}_{B,G})))},$$

$$v_{B,B}(\hat{a}, \mathbf{a}) = \frac{\delta(1-\delta)(1-\lambda)(\mathcal{G} - \mathcal{C}\hat{a}_{G,G}) + \psi_5\hat{a}_{B,G} + \psi_3\hat{a}_{B,B}}{2(1-\delta)(2 - \delta(1+\lambda + (1-\lambda)(\hat{a}_{G,G} - \hat{a}_{B,G})))},$$

where

$$\begin{cases} \psi_1 &= \left[2 - \delta(1+\lambda) - \delta^2(1-\lambda)\right]\mathcal{G}, \\ \psi_2 &= -\delta(1-\delta)(2\mathcal{C} + \mathcal{G}(1-\lambda)), \\ \psi_3 &= -(1-\delta)\left[\delta(1-\lambda)\mathcal{G} \right. \\ & \quad \left. + (2 - \delta(1+\lambda + 2(1-\lambda)(\hat{a}_{G,G} - \hat{a}_{B,G})))\mathcal{C}\right], \\ \psi_4 &= \delta(1-\lambda)(\mathcal{G} - \delta\mathcal{C}), \\ \psi_5 &= \delta^2(1-\lambda)\mathcal{G} - \delta(1+\lambda - 2\lambda\delta)\mathcal{C}. \end{cases}$$

Since $\psi_3 < 0$ and the denominator $2(1-\delta)(2 - \delta(1+\lambda + (1-\lambda)(\hat{a}_{G,G} - \hat{a}_{B,G}))) > 0$, when $\hat{a}_{G,B} = 0$ and $\hat{a}_{B,B} = 0$, the long-term expected payoffs are maximized. Then, fixing $\hat{a}_{G,B} = 0$ and $\hat{a}_{B,B} = 0$ and maximizing the long-term expected payoffs with respect to $\hat{a}_{G,G} \in [0, 1]$ and $\hat{a}_{B,G} \in [0, 1]$, we can show that the payoff functions are maximized at the boundary point where $\hat{a}_{G,G} = 1$ and $\hat{a}_{B,G} = 1$ when $\rho = \frac{\mathcal{C}}{\mathcal{G}} \le \frac{\delta(1-\lambda)}{2-\delta-\lambda\delta}$.

(3) The steady state with $\mathbf{a} = [\ 0 \quad 1 \quad 0 \quad 1\ ]^T$ and $x_\mathbf{a} = 0$ is symmetric with the steady state in (2). Hence, the same result could be proved in a similar manner as in (2).

According to Theorem 4.7, there are three equilibria in the indirect reciprocity game in practice. In the first equilibrium, there is no cooperation between users in which a reputation distribution with half of the population having a good reputation can be lead to. Within the second, only users with good reputations would be cooperated with, and all of the population has a good reputation. Within the third, users only cooperate with those who have a bad reputation and all of the population has a bad reputation. In fact, the latter two steady states are mutually symmetric states of the game, leading to full cooperation with different interpretations of reputation scores. Furthermore, the results in Theorem 4.7 show that cooperation could be enforced by the indirect reciprocity game if the cost-to-gain ratio is less than a certain threshold.

4.4 Evolutionary Modeling of the Indirect Reciprocity Game

4.4.1 Evolutionary Dynamics of the Indirect Reciprocity Game

Before reaching the steady state, the indirect reciprocity game is profoundly dynamic. All users are doubtful about the network state and the actions of others because the entire population's reputation distribution and the actions adopted by users change continually. In such transient states, users would try different strategies in each game and learn from them using the methodology of understand-by-building to improve their utility. Moreover, the probability of a certain pure action rule being adapted as the network state evolves owing to the fact that a mixed action rule is a probability distribution over pure action rules. This kind of evolutionary process could be modeled by replicator dynamics within evolutionary game theory. Specifically, let $p_\mathbf{a}$ denote the probability of using pure action rule $\mathbf{a} \in \mathbf{A}^D$, where $\mathbf{A}^D$ signifies the set of all pure action rules. Then, with replicator dynamics, the evolution of $p_\mathbf{a}$ could be calculated as

$$\frac{dp_\mathbf{a}}{dt} = \eta \left(U_\mathbf{a} - \sum_{\mathbf{a} \in \mathbf{A}^D} p_\mathbf{a} U_\mathbf{a} \right) p_\mathbf{a}, \tag{4.40}$$

where $U_\mathbf{a}$ is the average payoff of users using action rule $\mathbf{a}$ and η is a scale element controlling the evolution's speed. After discretizing the replicator dynamic equation in (4.40), we can get

$$p_\mathbf{a}^{t+1} = \left[1 + \eta \left(U_\mathbf{a} - \sum_{\mathbf{a} \in \mathbf{A}^D} p_\mathbf{a} U_\mathbf{a} \right) \right] p_\mathbf{a}^t. \tag{4.41}$$

4.4.2   Evolutionarily Stable Strategy

If and only if an action rule is an evolutionarily stable strategy (ESS) [28], it is asymptotically stable regarding the replicator dynamics, and this is an equilibrium concept that is universally used in evolutionary game theory. Let $\pi(\mathbf{a}, \hat{\mathbf{a}})$ represent a player's payoff who use action rule $\mathbf{a}$ against other players who uses action rule $\hat{\mathbf{a}}$. Then, an ESS could be formally defined as follows.

DEFINITION 4.8   An action rule $\mathbf{a}^*$ is an ESS if and only if, for all $\mathbf{a} \neq \mathbf{a}^*$,

- Equilibrium condition: $\pi(\mathbf{a}, \mathbf{a}^*) \leq \pi(\mathbf{a}^*, \mathbf{a}^*)$;
- Stability condition: if $\pi(\mathbf{a}, \mathbf{a}^*) = \pi(\mathbf{a}^*, \mathbf{a}^*)$, $\pi(\mathbf{a}, \mathbf{a}) < \pi(\mathbf{a}^*, \mathbf{a})$.

Based on the definition of an ESS above, the following theorem can be proposed.

THEOREM 4.9   *In the indirect reciprocity game, we have*

(1)   For all $0 < \rho < 1$, action rule $\mathbf{a}_1$ is an ESS at the steady state $\{\mathbf{a}_1, x_{\mathbf{a}_1}\}$.

(2)   When $\rho < \frac{\delta(1-\lambda)}{2-\delta-\lambda\delta}$, action rule $\mathbf{a}_2$ and $\mathbf{a}_3$ are ESSs at steady states $\{\mathbf{a}_2, x_{\mathbf{a}_2}\}$ and $\{\mathbf{a}_3, x_{\mathbf{a}_3}\}$, respectively.

Proof   It suffices to verify that the equivalent equilibrium is strict for representing whether an action rule is an ESS by the definition of an ESS. When $\mathbf{a} = \mathbf{a}_1$, (4.39) holds for all $0 < \rho < 1$ and all action rules $\hat{\mathbf{a}}$ from the proof of Theorem 4.7. Moreover, since the row sum of matrix $\frac{\delta}{2}\mathbf{H}_{\hat{\mathbf{a}}}$ is $\delta \in (0, 1)$ for each row, the equality in (4.39) holds only if $\hat{\mathbf{a}} = \mathbf{a}$. Hence, $(\mathbf{a}_1, x_{\mathbf{a}_1})$ is a strict equilibrium steady state for all $0 < \rho < 1$. Likewise, for the proof of Theorem 4.7, $(\mathbf{a}_3, x_{\mathbf{a}_3})$ and $(\mathbf{a}_2, x_{\mathbf{a}_2})$ are strict equilibrium steady states when $0 < \rho < \frac{\delta(1-\lambda)}{2-\delta-\lambda\delta}$.

We can know from Theorem 4.9 that the equilibrium steady states found in Theorem 4.7 are also stable when ρ takes values at certain intervals, which means that if this kind of action rule is used by most of the population, under the influence of replicator dynamics, any other action rule will not expand among the population.

4.5   Energy Detection

The indirect reciprocity game that has been discussed so far operates under the assumption that the relay reports its action to the BS. However, the selected relay would cheat if a higher payoff could be gained through cheating than reporting due to their selfish nature. For instance, the relay might inform the BS that it would help but report nothing at the relay phase when the source node has a good reputation, causing system performance to degrade. In order to overcome these limitations, energy detection is introduced at the BS to detect whether the relay forwards the source's signal.

The received signals hypothesis model at the relay phase is

$$H_0 : y(t) = n(t), \tag{4.42}$$

$$H_1 : y(t) = P_r h x(t) + n(t), \tag{4.43}$$

where $x(t)$ is the normalized signal forwarded by the relay, $n(t)$ is the additive white Gaussian noise, h is the channel gain from the relay to the BS, and P_r is the transmitted power of the relay. The detection statistics of the energy detector are represented by the average energy of M observed samples

$$S = \frac{1}{M} \sum_{t=1}^{M} |y(t)|^2. \tag{4.44}$$

Then, the BS could determine whether the relay helped forward signals for the source through comparing a predetermined threshold S_0 with the detection statistics S. We express the probability of false alarm P_F and the probability of detection P_D for a given threshold as

$$P_F = \Pr\{S > S_0 | H_0\}, \tag{4.45}$$

$$P_D = \Pr\{S > S_0 | H_1\}, \tag{4.46}$$

which could be calculated according to the receiver operating characteristic (ROC) curves in [29]. In the following, we consider P_F and P_D as system parameters and analyze their impacts on user behaviors.

With energy detection, the performance degradation caused by cheating can be prevented since the BS would no longer depend on reports from the relay. However, reputation might be assigned incorrectly because of the missing detection and the false alarm information. Hence, after considering the influence of energy detection, the new reputation updating probability $d_{i,j}$ could be given as

$$d_{i,j} = \left[a_{i,j}P_D + (1 - a_{i,j})P_F\right] Q(i,j,C)$$
$$+ \left[a_{i,j}(1 - P_D) + (1 - a_{i,j})(1 - P_F)\right] Q(i,j,D). \tag{4.47}$$

Then, similarly, we study the indirect reciprocity game with energy detection using the same analysis process and we obtain following results.

COROLLARY 4.10   *In the indirect reciprocity game with energy detection, we have*

(1)   The steady state with $\mathbf{a} = [\ 0 \quad 0 \quad 0 \quad 0\ ]^T$ and $x_{\mathbf{a}} = 1/2$ is an equilibrium for all $0 < \rho < 1$.

(2)   When $0 < \rho \leq \frac{\delta(1-\lambda)(P_D-P_F)}{2-\delta-\lambda\delta}$, the steady state with $\mathbf{a} = [\ 1 \quad 0 \quad 1 \quad 0\ ]^T$ and $x_{\mathbf{a}} = \frac{1-P_F}{2-P_D-P_F}$ and the steady state with $\mathbf{a} = [\ 0 \quad 1 \quad 0 \quad 1\ ]^T$ and $x_{\mathbf{a}} = \frac{1-P_D}{2-P_D-P_F}$ are equilibria.

(3)   Action rule $\mathbf{a} = [\ 0 \quad 0 \quad 0 \quad 0\ ]^T$ is an ESS for all $0 < \rho < 1$.

(4)   When $0 < \rho < \frac{\delta(1-\lambda)(P_D-P_F)}{2-\delta-\lambda\delta}$, action rules $\mathbf{a} = [\ 1 \quad 0 \quad 1 \quad 0\ ]^T$ and $\mathbf{a} = [\ 0 \quad 1 \quad 0 \quad 1\ ]^T$ are ESSs.

Proof Following the same procedure as in the proof of Proposition 4.6 and Theorem 4.7, we can verify (1) and (2). Then, we can verify (3) and (4) in a similar manner as within the proof of Theorem 4.9.

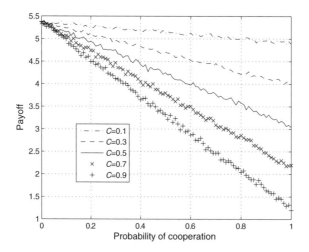

Figure 4.2 The payoff versus the probability of cooperation in systems without incentive schemes.

4.6   Simulation Results

In this section, to evaluate the indirect reciprocity game, we conduct numerical simulations of a fixed-size population with $N = 100$. The discounting factor δ of every user is set as 0.9 and $\mathcal{G} = 1$ in the simulations.

First, we demonstrate the necessity of cooperation stimulation schemes by looking at the circumstance without social norms and reputations. We presume that one particular user decides to cooperate with probability p while all of the others decide to always cooperate, and the first user's payoffs versus p for different cost values are shown in Figure 4.2. In Figure 4.2, the user could always acquire a better payoff through cooperating with a lower probability under all cost values, since cooperation is expensive and no incentive scheme is employed. Accordingly, users would not decide to cooperate and behave as free riders selfishly to maximize their payoffs, resulting in the failure of the cooperative communication system.

Within the second simulation, the performance of the incentive scheme is evaluated, in which λ is set to be 0.5. In Figure 4.3, we first presume that the game begins at steady state $(\mathbf{a}, x_{\mathbf{a}})$ with $x_{\mathbf{a}} = 1$ and $\mathbf{a} = [\ 1\ \ 0\ \ 1\ \ 0\ ]^T$. Then we illustrate the payoffs of a specified user that deviates from action rule $[\ p\ \ 0\ \ p\ \ 0\ ]^T$ within different cost values. It can be seen from Figure 4.3 that, when $C = 0.2$, the user's payoff increases with the probability of cooperation p; when $C = 0.8$, it decreases. This result matches the theoretic derivations in Theorem 4.7 because the threshold $\frac{\delta(1-\lambda)}{2-\delta-\lambda\delta} = 9/13$ is based on the simulation settings.

Figure 4.4 shows the results of the equilibrium steady state of the indirect reciprocity game with energy detection. Within the simulation, P_F and P_D (i.e., the probability of detection and the probability of false alarm) are set to be 0.9 and 0.1, respectively. Based on Corollary 4.10, the cost-to-gain ratio threshold that

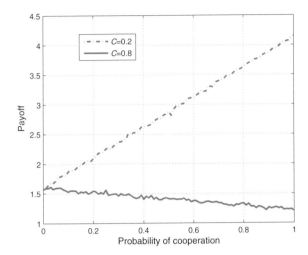

Figure 4.3 Equilibrium evaluation of the game without energy detection.

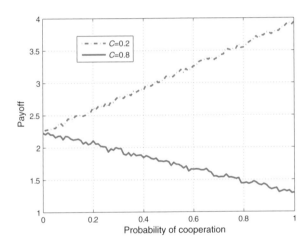

Figure 4.4 Equilibrium evaluation of the game with energy detection.

enables cooperation becomes $\frac{\delta(1-\lambda)(P_D-P_F)}{2-\delta-\lambda\delta} = 36/65$ and the stationary reputation distribution that corresponds to $\mathbf{a} = [\; 1 \quad 0 \quad 1 \quad 0\;]^T$ is $x_{\mathbf{a}} = \frac{1-P_F}{2-P_D-P_F} = 0.9$. For such a steady state, a particular user's payoff that deviates from action rule $[\; p \quad 0 \quad p \quad 0\;]^T$ within different cost values is shown. As expected, we can see from Figure 4.4 that the user would obtain no incentive to deviate from the steady-state action rule when $C = 0.2$, while they would not cooperate when $C = 0.8$.

Then a comparison between the indirect reciprocity game's performance and that of the tit-for-tat incentive mechanism is conducted. The tit-for-tat incentive mechanism is adopted by the BitTorrent file distribution system for stimulating cooperative behaviors among users [10], and the strategy of the specified user is to choose cooperation unless the opponent chooses to defect in the previous round. In Figure 4.5, the utilities

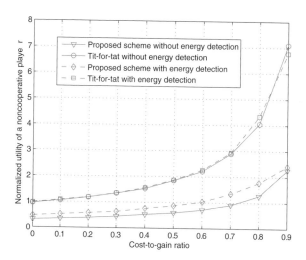

Figure 4.5 Comparison of normalized utilities between the indirect reciprocity game and the tit-for-tat mechanism [10] in the case of unilateral deviations.

of a user using the action of pure defection normalized against those using the desired actions between the two schemes are compared in the situation in which all other users are presumed to use the respective desired actions within these two schemes. We can see that deviating from the desired action to defection is beneficial when the normalized utility is greater than 1. The results show that the scheme discussed in this chapter can enforce cooperation over a much larger range of cost-to-gain ratios than the tit-for-tat mechanism, since the direct reciprocity model that underlies the tit-for-tat incentive mechanism presumes implicitly that the interaction between a pair of users holds for a long time, which is no longer the case within the multiuser cooperative communications scenario.

Then the evolutionary properties of the indirect reciprocity game are studied. The initial probability of applying a specified action rule $\mathbf{a} = [\ 1 \quad 0 \quad 1 \quad 0 \ ]^T$ is set to be 0.6,[1] while the initial probabilities of applying other pure action rules are set equivalently as 0.4/15. The population's initial reputation distribution is set as 1/2. Meanwhile, we adopt $\eta = 0.1$ in the replicator dynamics equation. First, the low-cost case where $\mathcal{C} = 0.2$ is studied. According to Theorem 4.9, the specified action rule is an ESS for both games with and without energy detection. The evolutionary results for the indirect reciprocity game without energy detection are represented in Figure 4.6, in which the game converges to the equilibrium steady state, which is equal to the action rule $\mathbf{a} = [\ 1 \quad 0 \quad 1 \quad 0 \ ]^T$ and remains stable once it has converged. Consequently, the specified action rule for the low-cost case is verified to be an ESS.

---

[1] This simulation is intended to show that the specified action rule $\mathbf{a} = [\ 1 \quad 0 \quad 1 \quad 0 \ ]^T$ is an ESS in the low-cost case and thus is resistant to the invasion of any other action rules. In practice, the BS can guide users to adopt the action rule $\mathbf{a}$ at the very beginning by assigning the initial reputation according to the stationary reputation distribution x_a.

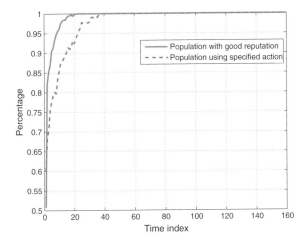

Figure 4.6 Population evolution of the game without energy detection ($C = 0.2$).

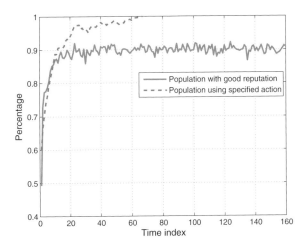

Figure 4.7 Population evolution of the game with energy detection ($C = 0.2$).

Figure 4.7 shows the evolutionary results for the game with energy detection. We can see that the specified action rule spreads over the entire population quickly. In addition, the reputation distribution converges to 0.9 and then remains stable, as is indicated by Corollary 4.10.

Then the high-cost case where we set $C = 0.8$ is studied. Thus, compared with the thresholds, the cost-to-gain ratio ρ is larger for both games with and without energy detection. Accordingly, the ESS is no longer the specified action rule and cooperation cannot be sustained. The evolutionary results under $C = 0.8$ for games with and without energy detection are shown in Figures 4.8 and 4.9, respectively, to verify the theoretical results. From Figures 4.8 and 4.9, the reputation distributions converge to $1/2$ and the probabilities of applying the specified action finally become

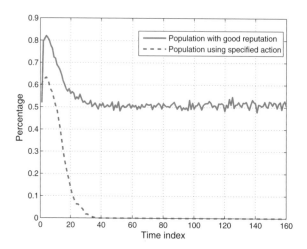

Figure 4.8 Population evolution of the game without energy detection ($C = 0.8$).

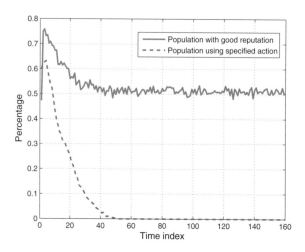

Figure 4.9 Population evolution of the game with energy detection ($C = 0.8$).

zero for both games. This demonstrates that the specified action rule is not an ESS in the high-cost case, which agrees with the results in Theorem 4.9 and Corollary 4.10.

Finally, the scheme discussed in this chapter and the tit-for-tat mechanism are compared from the population evolution perspective. With $C = 0.5$ and the initial probability of adopting the desired action being 0.6 for both schemes, we also set the initial reputation distribution of the population to be $1/2$ for the scheme discussed in this chapter. Moreover, two actions (pure cooperation and pure defection) other than the tit-for-tat strategy are considered for the tit-for-tat mechanism with an initial probability of 0.2, respectively. Figure 4.10 shows the population evolution for the case without energy detection. From Figure 4.10, it can be seen that the desired action, $\mathbf{a} = [\ 1 \quad 0 \quad 1 \quad 0\ ]^T$, in the scheme discussed in this chapter is evolutionarily stable,

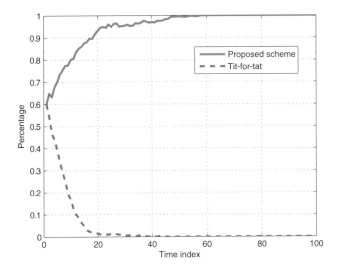

Figure 4.10 Comparison of population evolution between the indirect reciprocity game and the tit-for-tat mechanism [10].

as the tit-for-tat strategy is vulnerable to invasions of other actions, showing that, compared with the direct reciprocity based methods, the indirect reciprocity-game is more suitable. The results regarding energy detection are similar to those shown in Figure 4.10, and therefore they are skipped here.

4.7 Discussion and Conclusion

In this chapter, we discuss a cooperation stimulation scheme for multiuser cooperative communications using the indirect reciprocity game. Based on the concepts of social norms and reputation, the scheme discussed in this chapter can be incorporated within every ORS algorithm to acquire full spatial diversity, since it does not depend on the presumption that the interactions between a pair of users are infinite. Furthermore, unlike experimental verification using existing results, the usage of reputation for stimulating cooperation is justified theoretically. Specifically, cooperation with users who have a good reputation could be maintained as an equilibrium if the cost-to-gain ratio is under a certain threshold. Through modeling the action expansion as an evolutionary game, the action rule of relaying information for users with a good reputation is an ESS in the low-cost case; therefore, it can resist the mutation of any other action rules. Furthermore, energy detection at the BS and its influence on the indirect reciprocity game regarding the potential cheating behaviors of users are also introduced. Simulation results show that the scheme discussed in this chapter works effectively for stimulating cooperation among selfish and rational users.

Different outcomes might be observed with different initial conditions since there are multiple equilibria in the game. For instance, if the network begins under quite bad circumstances, most users would decide not to cooperate at the very beginning, and the game would converge to a noncooperative equilibrium steady state. However, the initial condition requirements are not stringent in order to achieve full cooperation. For example, from the simulation results, we find that the action rule of cooperating with users who have a good reputation will expand over the entire population quickly, leading to a cooperative society even if it is adopted by only 60% of the population at the beginning. Furthermore, in the scheme discussed in this chapter, there is a possible way to ensure that the network begins in good circumstances, which is letting the BS assign the initial reputation to users based on the stationary reputation distribution x_a of the desired action rule a. Through this, an equilibrium is established when all rational users use the action rule a, because (a, x_a) is an equilibrium steady state, and the game could still converge to the desired steady state owing to the fact that it is evolutionarily stable even if other actions are chosen by a small portion of users.

References

[1] K. J. R. Liu, A. Sadek, and A. K. W. Su, *Cooperative Communications and Networking*. Cambridge University Press, 2008.

[2] M. Feldman and J. Chuang, "Overcoming free-riding behavior in peer-to-peer systems," *SIGecom Exchanges*, vol. 5, pp. 41–50, 2005.

[3] P. Golle, K. Leyton-Brown, and I. Mironov, "Incentives for sharing in peer-to-peer networks," *Proc. ACM Symposium on Electronic Commerce, (EC' 01)*, 2001.

[4] V. Vishumurthy, S. Chandrakumar, and E. Sirer, "Karma: A secure economic framework for peer-to-peer resource sharing," in *Proc. 2003 Workshop on Economics of Peer-to-Peer Systems*, 2003.

[5] S. Zhong, J. Chen, and Y. R. Yang, "Sprite: A simple, cheat-proof, credit-based system for mobile ad-hoc networks," in *Proc. IEEE INFOCOM*, 2003.

[6] P. Marbach and Y. Qiu, "Cooperation in wireless ad hoc networks: A market-based approach," *IEEE/ACM Transactions on Networking*, vol. 13, pp. 1325–1338, 2005.

[7] M. Neely, "Optimal pricing in a free market wireless network," in *INFOCOM 2007. 26th IEEE International Conference on Computer Communications. IEEE*, pp. 213–221, 2007.

[8] B. Wang, Z. Han, and K. J. R. Liu, "Distributed relay selection and power control for multiuser cooperative communication networks using Stackelberg game," *IEEE Transactions on Mobile Computing*, vol. 8, pp. 975–990, 2009.

[9] H. Xiao and E. M. Yeh, "Pricing games with incomplete information in parallel relay networks," *Proc. IEEE International Conference on Communications (ICC)*, 2011.

[10] B. Cohen, "Incentives build robustness in BitTorrent," *Proc. 1st Workshop on Economics of Peer-to-Peer Systems*, 2003.

[11] S. Jun and M. Ahamad, "Incentives in BitTorrent induce free riding," in *ACM SIGCOMM Workshop on the Economics of Peer-to-Peer Systems (P2PECON'05)*, 2005.

[12] W. Yu and K. J. R. Liu, "Game theoretic analysis of cooperation and security in autonomous mobile ad hoc networks," *IEEE Transactions on Mobile Computing*, vol. 6, pp. 459–473, 2007.

[13] Z. Ji, W. Yu, and K. J. R. Liu, "A belief evaluation framework in autonomous manets under noisy and imperfect observation: vulnerability analysis and cooperation enforcement," *IEEE Transactions on Mobile Computing*, vol. 9, pp. 1242–1254, 2010.

[14] P. Michiardi and R. Molva, "Core: A collaborative reputation mechanism to enforce node cooperation in mobile ad hoc networks," in *Proc. IFIP-Communications and Multimedia Security Conference*, 2002.

[15] S. D. Kamvar, M. T. Schlosser, and H. Garcia-Molina, "The EigenTrust algorithm for reputation management in P2P networks," in *Proc. 12th International World Wide Web Conference*, pp. 640–651, 2003.

[16] S. Buchegger and J. Y. L. Boudec, "Performance analysis of the confidant protocol," in *Proc. ACM MobiHoc*, 2002.

[17] M. Gupta, P. Judge, and M. Ammar, "A reputation system for peer-to-peer networks," *Proc. ACM NOSSDAV*, 2003.

[18] R. L. Trivers, "The evolution of reciprocal altruism," *Quarterly Review of Biology*, vol. 46, pp. 35–57, 1971.

[19] M. A. Nowak and K. Sigmund, "Evolution of indirect reciprocity," *Nature*, vol. 437, pp. 1291–1298, 2005.

[20] H. Ohtsuki, Y. Iwasa, and M. A. Nowak, "Indirect reciprocity provides only a narrow margin for efficiency for costly punishment," *Nature*, vol. 457, pp. 79–82, 2009.

[21] M. Kandori, "Social norms and community enforcement," *Review of Economic Studies*, vol. 59, pp. 63–80, 1992.

[22] Y. Zhao, R. Adve, and T. Lim, "Improving Amplify-and-Forward relay networks: optimal power allocation versus selection," *Proc. IEEE International Symposium on Information Theory (ISIT 06)*, pp. 1234–1238, 2006.

[23] A. S. Ibrahim, A. K. Sadek, W. Su, and K. J. R. Liu, "Cooperative communications with relay selection: when to cooperate and whom to cooperate with?" *IEEE Transactions on Wireless Communications*, vol. 7, pp. 2814–2827, 2008.

[24] M. Abramowitz and I. A. Stegun, *Handbook of Mathematical Functions with Formulas, Graphs, and Mathematical Tables*, 9th ed. Dover Publications, 1970.

[25] I. S. Gradshteyn and I. M. Ryzhik, *Tables of Integrals, Series, and Products*, 5th ed. Academic Press, 1994.

[26] P. Lancaster and M. Tismenetsky, *The Theory of Matrices: With Applications*, 2nd ed. Academic Press, 1985.

[27] M. L. Puterman, *Markov Decision Processes: Discrete Stochastic Dynamic Programming*. John Wiley & Sons, 1994.

[28] J. W. Weibull, *Evolutionary Game Theory*. MIT Press, 1995.

[29] H. Urkowitz, "Energy detection of unknown deterministic signals," *Proceedings of the IEEE*, vol. 55, pp. 523–531, 1967.

5 Indirect Reciprocity Data Fusion Game and Application to Cooperative Spectrum Sensing

Encouraging sensors to share their data is a crucial issue due to the importance of data sharing in data fusion. In this chapter, we discuss a reputation-based incentive framework in which an indirect reciprocity game is used to model the data sharing stimulation problem. Within this framework, sensors decide on how to report their results to the fusion center (FC) and earn a reputation. On the basis of this reputation, they are capable of gaining benefits in the future. For accuracy of fusion and sensing, reputation distribution is introduced within the game, in which the game's Nash equilibrium (NE) is derived and the corresponding uniqueness is proven theoretically. Furthermore, the scheme is applied to cooperative spectrum sensing. It is shown that with an appropriate cost-to-gain ratio, when the average received energy exceeds a given threshold, the optimal strategy for the secondary users (SUs) is to report; otherwise, they would remain silence. It is also verified that this kind of optimal strategy is a desirable evolutionarily stable strategy (ESS).

5.1   Introduction

Today, in the big data era, with diversified measurement techniques in various domains, information about a system of interest or a phenomenon can be acquired through different types of sensors (as well as data suppliers). In order to extract knowledge for various purposes and analyze information from multiple sensors jointly, concepts of data fusion were developed and corresponding techniques were introduced [1]. The data fusion process's analytic outcomes enable users to acquire a comprehensive view and a more united picture of the system, make more accurate decisions, and answer questions about the system.

Data fusion methodologies were first created for military applications and then evolved into nonmilitary fields such as driver assistance systems [2], cognitive radio networks (CRNs) [3], and smart grids [4]. Numerous algorithms have been proposed to exploit the diversity of multiple sensors effectively, including those based on soft fusion and hard fusion. Within the soft fusion-based algorithms, a quantized version of a local decision statistic such as any suitably sufficient statistics or the log-likelihood ratio would be sent to the FC, while within the hard fusion-based algorithms, a one-bit hard local decision would be sent by every sensor to the FC.

It is verified that the existing fusion algorithms could improve system reliability, but most of them assume that every sensor is altruistic and willing to unconditionally share data for fusion, which may not be true in reality. Actually, if cooperation is not capable of bringing benefits to sensors on account of the extra energy and cost required in collecting and reporting data, the sensors might not choose the cooperation. Accordingly, the fusion algorithms would not run properly due to a lack of sufficient data. Therefore, stimulating different data providers to collaborate and share their data is a crucial topic.

As for cooperation stimulation schemes, reputation-based and payment-based schemes are two most common types. Reputation-based cooperation stimulation schemes have been broadly discussed within wireless data networks [5], ad hoc networks [6], and peer-to-peer (P2P) networks [7] to guarantee trustworthy communications, or in CRNs [8] and wireless sensor networks [9] to guarantee data fusion. However, few reputation-based schemes have been developed in order to stimulate sensors to share their sensing results until recently, and this kind of approach has no theoretical justification yet. Payment-based schemes such as auctions and virtual currencies have been proposed to guarantee participatory sensing [10] within wireless communication systems, file sharing within P2P networks [11], and dynamic spectrum sharing within CRNs [12]. Though these schemes have produced promising results, they are applied with limitations such as central banking server(s) for the sake of security control or the requirement of tamper-proof hardware.

Another way of analyzing the cooperation problem is game theory. Specifically, a number of cooperation schemes on the basis of cooperative game theory such as the coalition game [13,14] and the bargaining game [15,16] have been introduced. The focus of cooperative game-theoretic frameworks is allocating and acquiring net income within an alliance. In cooperative games, players have an interest in maximizing their outcome, though when considering the benefits on both sides, they might want to accept a solution that involve bargaining. Thus, a stimulation mechanism or an enforceable contract is needed to guarantee cooperation. Furthermore, most game-theoretic frameworks are based on the direct reciprocity model in which other players would not evaluate all players' behaviors, but only their opponents' behaviors. According to the backward induction principle and the prisoner's dilemma, two directly participating players would cooperate only when repeating the game infinite times. However, players could alter their partners periodically to obtain better performance due to mobility or changes of environment; thus, for them, playing noncooperatively is the only optimal strategy. In this case, they also need a stimulation mechanism.

Indirect reciprocity has been broadly adopted within social science and evolutionary biology [17,18] and has recently drawn a lot of attention in applications such as energy exchange [19], package forwarding [20] and cooperative transmission [21,22]. Its concept is "*I help you not because you have helped me but because you have helped others*," which means that the current donor could give help to the recipient since it helped others as a donor before. This signifies that the evaluations from both other observers and opponents would be taken into consideration, and this endows players with the incentive to cooperate even though the game would not be replayed limitlessly.

Within the chapter, first, we discuss a framework that achieves successful data fusion through incorporating an incentive mechanism on the basis of indirect reciprocity and stimulating cooperation among sensors that are not required to play with the same group of sensors all of the time. Then, the application to the cooperative spectrum sensing (CSS) system would be discussed.

5.2   Indirect Reciprocity Data Fusion Game

5.2.1   System Model

A data fusion system is considered as shown in Figure 5.1, where there are M sensors sensing and obtaining local observations. It is assumed that the local observations are obtained for classic hypothesis tests. Presume that the hypotheses could be evaluated from the observation of which sensor receives its signal energy (i.e., energy detection). Let $S_m = \frac{1}{N} \sum_{t=1}^{N} |r_m(t)|^2$ denote the signal's average energy that is received by sensor m, where N represents the signal sample' number and $r_m(t)$ represents the sample of observed signals at sensor m's receiver, which could be signified as

$$r_m(t) = \begin{cases} h_m s(t) + n_m(t), & \text{if } H_1, \\ n_m(t), & \text{if } H_0. \end{cases} \tag{5.1}$$

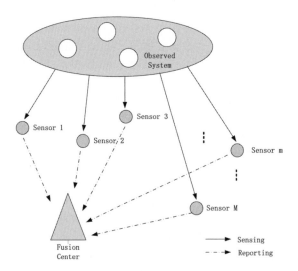

Figure 5.1 The system model.

In (5.1), $s(t)$ represents the signal that shows up at time slot t, $n_m(t)$ represents the additive white Gaussian noise (AWGN), and h_m represents the channel gain. Then compared with the predefined threshold λ, if the observed signal's energy is lower (i.e., $S_m < \lambda$), the sensor m would recognize H_0 as true, otherwise it would recognize H_1 as true.

Within the data fusion system, setting a FC is for fusing data gathered from multiple sensors. If local data would be reported by each sensor truthfully, the outcome, which is the alternative hypothesis or null hypothesis, could be accomplished by the FC [2] more accurately.

5.2.2 Action and Action Rule

Within the data fusion system, for simplicity hard fusion is first taken into consideration, and on the basis of that, sensors are required to report to the FC about their local decisions on the hypotheses instead of their original observations. In such a case, we signify a sensor's action after sensing as $a \in \mathcal{A}$, where $\mathcal{A} = \{1, 2\}$ represents the action set. Within the action set $\mathcal{A}$, "2" stands for a sensor reporting its local decision of judging hypothesis H_1 to be true. If H_0 is true, it decides action "1" through remaining silent to conserve energy.

Note that a sensor could take any action on the basis of the same average received energy level. Given any average received energy level, an action that is taken by a sensor would form the sensor's strategy. To illustrate the sensor's strategies, the concept of an action rule is further introduced.

DEFINITION 5.1 (Action rule)   An action rule is an action vector where the jth element stands for the action that a sensor would take under average received energy level j.

Considering the FC's rule of data fusion (i.e., hard fusion) and the sensor's method of observation (i.e., energy detection), the average energy would only be quantized to two levels (i.e., $\mathcal{L} = \{1, 2\}$, in which $\mathcal{L}$ represents the set of average energy levels). When the average energy that the sensor observes is below the given threshold λ, it is denoted as level 1; when it is equal to or above the given threshold, it is denoted as level 2. Based on Definition 5.1, there are four action rules that a sensor needs to follow: $a^{(1)} = (2, 2), a^{(2)} = (2, 1), a^{(3)} = (1, 2)$, and $a^{(4)} = (1, 1)$, with the action rule set $\mathcal{A}_l = \{(2, 2), (2, 1), (1, 2), (1, 1)\}$. $a^{(l)}, l = 1, 2, 3, 4$, is used to signify the action rule in $\mathcal{A}_l$ for simplicity. The action rule $a^{(1)}$ ($a^{(4)}$) signifies that a sensor would (not) report that it takes hypothesis H_1 to be true regardless of its average received energy level, while the action rule $a^{(2)}$ ($a^{(3)}$) signifies that a sensor would report that it takes hypothesis H_1 to be true only under the condition that its average received energy is at level 2 (level 1).

Furthermore, $a_{i,j} \in \mathcal{A}$ is used to describe the action performed by a sensor with reputation i, $i \in \mathcal{R}$, under average received energy level j, $j \in \mathcal{L}$, when a sensor has to consider the reputation obtained before making the decision. Here, the set of reputation is represented by $\mathcal{R}$.

5.2.3   Social Norm: How to Assign Reputation

A matrix of the social norm $\boldsymbol{\Omega}$ is needed to assign the sensors' immediate reputation value, and we presume that the same norm is shared by all sensors within the system.

Since the FC makes the final decision on the basis of the sensors' local data, the FC is more capable of making a correct decision when the local data are more accurate. Under this circumstance, a sensor that has a high average received energy level is encouraged to send out its local decision indicating H_1 to be true, while the sensor with a low received energy level should remain silent, which is equivalent to reporting H_0 to be true. Through this, the FC can successfully avoid interference and the sensor can save energy as well.

However, the FC that assigns a sensor's reputation based on the social norm does not have a clue as to the sensor's actual average received energy level when the sensor takes the action. Hence, the social norm is signified according to the FC's final decision and the sensor's action instead of the average received energy level of the sensor. Let the FC's final decision be "1" if the FC's fusion result signifies H_0 to be true, and let the final decision be "2" otherwise. Thus, we can define the social norm $\boldsymbol{\Omega}$ as

$$\boldsymbol{\Omega} = [\Omega_{i,j}] = \begin{bmatrix} 2 & 1 \\ 1 & 2 \end{bmatrix}, \tag{5.2}$$

where $\Omega_{i,j}$ represents the reputation value assigned to a sensor that takes action i, while j is the FC's final decision, and the set of a sensor's reputation value is $\mathcal{R} = \{1, 2\}$.

According to the definition of $\boldsymbol{\Omega}$, a sensor would obtain a high reputation value when the FC's final decision is consistent with its action. Otherwise, it would receive a low reputation value. Note that according to the inaccuracy of both the sensor's sensing and the FC's fusion, there is a gap between a sensor's average received energy level and the FC's final decision, which affects the sensors' reputation values and actions. We do not discuss the ways in which a sensor's action may be distorted by the channel in this chapter, since sensors are mostly supposed to transfer their data through a dedicated control channel where the error could be minimized and thus would be made negligible by channel coding such as fountain code or automatic repeat request (ARQ). Readers interested in this subject could refer to [21].

5.2.4   Decision Consistency Matrix

Because the FC believes that it obtains the true hypothesis accurately from the fusion result and can evaluate the sensor's action correctly, the FC assigns a reputation value to a sensor based on the sensor's action and its final decision, as discussed earlier. Nevertheless, a sensor may estimate the hypothesis inaccurately because of the possible false alarm and miss detection within its sensing. Here, the probability of detection

$P_{d,m}$ is adopted to symbolize sensor m's probability of assessing hypothesis H_1 successfully and the probability of false alarm $P_{f,m}$ is adopted to symbolize sensor m's probability of assessing hypothesis H_0 unsuccessfully, i.e.,

$$P_{d,m}(\lambda) = Pr(S_m > \lambda|H_1), \tag{5.3}$$

and

$$P_{f,m}(\lambda) = Pr(S_m > \lambda|H_0). \tag{5.4}$$

Because all of the sensors adopt the common threshold λ, we have $P_{d,m} = P_d$ and $P_{f,m} = P_f$.

As a consequence, we describe the gap between the average energy level of a sensor and the FC's fusion result with the decision consistency matrix $\boldsymbol{D}$ as

$$\boldsymbol{D} = [D_{i,j}] = \begin{bmatrix} D_{1,1} & D_{1,2} \\ D_{2,1} & D_{2,2} \end{bmatrix}, \tag{5.5}$$

where $D_{i,j}$ represents the probability that the sensor's received signal energy is at level i while the FC's fusion result signifies that it ought to be at level j.

Suppose that the FC makes final decisions by the majority rule. Let $P_s(i|k)$ denote the probability that under hypothesis H_k the sensor's received signal energy is at level i, let $P_{fc}(j|i,k)$ be the probability that the FC considers that the sensor's received signal energy ought to be at level j given that the hypothesis is H_k and the sensor's received signal energy is at level i, and let P_0 and P_1 be the probabilities that hypotheses H_0 and H_1 are true, respectively. The level determined by the FC and the sensor's received signal energy level are not independent because the FC makes decisions according to the sensor's reports. Then $D_{1,1}$ can be computed as

$$D_{1,1} = P_{fc}(1|1,0)P_s(1|0)P_0 + P_{fc}(1|1,1)P_s(1|1)P_1,$$

$$= \sum_{k=[\frac{M}{2}]-1}^{M-1} \binom{M-1}{k}[(1-P_f)^{k+1}P_f^{M-k-1}P_0 + (1-P_d)^{k+1}P_d^{M-k-1}P_1]. \tag{5.6}$$

Note that $P_{fc}(1|1,0)$ ($P_{fc}(1|1,1)$) is computed as in (5.6) since there ought to be more than $[\frac{M}{2}] - 1$ other sensors and the received signal energy is at level 1. Similarly, we have $D_{1,2} = \sum_{k=[\frac{M}{2}]+1}^{M-1} \binom{M-1}{k}[P_f^k(1-P_f)^{M-k}P_0 + P_d^k(1-P_d)^{M-k}P_1]$, $D_{2,1} = \sum_{k=[\frac{M}{2}]+1}^{M-1} \binom{M-1}{k}[(1-P_f)^k P_f^{M-k}P_0 + (1-P_d)^k P_d^{M-k}P_1]$, and $D_{2,2} = \sum_{k=[\frac{M}{2}]-1}^{M-1} \binom{M-1}{k}[P_f^{k+1}(1-P_f)^{M-k-1}P_0 + P_d^{k+1}(1-P_d)^{M-k-1}P_1]$. Without loss of generality, we have $D_{1,1} > D_{1,2}$ and $D_{2,2} > D_{2,1}$.

5.2.5 Reputation Updating Policy

We develop a reputation updating policy such as that shown in Figure 5.2 for establishing a sensor's reputation with the social norm. The fusion error of the FC and the imperfect sensing of the sensors are taken into consideration in the reputation updating

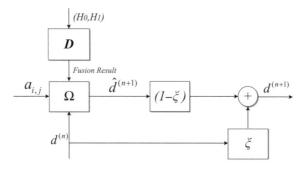

Figure 5.2 The reputation updating model.

model since they both affect the updating of sensors' reputations. Hence, D (discussed previously) is incorporated into the reputation updating policy.

A sensor would not have a certain probability of being assigned a low or high reputation until taking an action due to the FC's fusion error and the influence of sensors' imperfect sensing. To capture this, we select the sensor with a reputation distribution $d = (d_l, d_h)$ with $d_l + d_h = 1$, where d_l and d_h indicate the probabilities of the sensor being assigned a low or high reputation value, respectively.

Within a simple case, a sensor's reputation at time index n is i and its received energy is at level j. After determining and performing action $a_{i,j}$, a sensor's immediate reputation distribution at time index $n + 1$ will be

$$\hat{d}^{(n+1)}(a_{i,j}) = \sum_{l=1}^{2} e_{\Omega_{a_{i,j},j}} \cdot D_{j,l}, \tag{5.7}$$

where the standard basis vector is e_i. Here, $\Omega_{a_{i,j},j}$ denotes the reputation value that is assigned to the sensor after action $a_{i,j}$ is taken under the received energy level j, and $e_{\Omega_{a_{i,j},j}}$ is the equivalent reputation distribution without considering the FC's fusion error and the influence of the sensor's imperfect sensing. However, the sensor's reputation value $\Omega_{a_{i,j},j}$ might be shifted to the high one or the low one with the probability of $D_{j,1}$ and $D_{j,2}$, respectively, under the influence of the sensor's imperfect sensing. Thus, the sensor's immediate reputation distribution is shown in (5.7).

On the basis of the reputation updating policy in Figure 5.2, the FC updates (and then broadcasts) the sensor's reputation distribution at time index $n + 1$ (i.e., $d^{(n+1)}(a_{i,j})$) after collecting all of the information from the sensors through linearly combining the sensor's original reputation distribution $d^{(n)}$ and the immediate reputation distribution $\hat{d}^{(n+1)}$ with a weight ξ as

$$d^{(n+1)}(a_{i,j}) = (1 - \xi)\hat{d}^{(n+1)}(a_{i,j}) + \xi d^{(n)}. \tag{5.8}$$

Here, the weight ξ is regarded as the past reputation's discounting factor.

A sensor may take a certain action in its own interest with the reputation distribution d, and its overall performance can also be evaluated based on d. For example, decisions that contradict the FC's fusion results must have been made by the sensor with a high value of d_l all of the time, meaning that there is a quite bad sensing environment or the sensor is incorrectly reporting decisions. In addition, decisions that are consistent with the FC's fusion results must have been made by a sensor with a high value of d_h all of the time, and this indicates that the sensor is truthfully reporting accurate decisions. Within this case, the FC can know whether a sensor is malicious and thus overcome the cheating behavior through disposing of the information that a malicious sensor has reported.

Suppose that sensor m takes action $a_m \in \mathcal{A}$ as well as acquires reputation distribution $d^{(n)}(a_m)$ at time index n. The entire data fusion system's reputation distribution could be signified as

$$\eta^{(n)}(a_1, \ldots, a_M) = \frac{1}{M} \sum_{m=1}^{M} d^{(n)}(a_m). \tag{5.9}$$

We can see from this that $\eta^{(n)}(a_1, \ldots, a_M)$ involves all of the sensors' actions, and this would be signified as $\eta^{(n)}(\cdot)$ for simplicity.

5.2.6   Payoff Function

First, we give the expected reputation distribution's definition that is applied for demonstrating the reputation distribution for a given action rule, then we represent the sensor's payoff function.

DEFINITION 5.2 (Expected reputation distribution)   For each given action rule a, a sensor's expected reputation distribution is $d(a) = P_{L_1} d(a(1)) + P_{L_2} d(a(2))$, where P_{L_1} (P_{L_2}) is the probability that the sensor's average received energy is at level 1 (level 2).

Based on the reputation updating policy, we can get the expected reputation distribution's updating policy as is shown in Lemma 5.3.

LEMMA 5.3 $\forall a \in \mathcal{A}_l$ and $d^{(n)}$, the sensor's expected reputation distribution at time index $n+1$, is updated as $d^{(n+1)}(a) = (1-\xi)\hat{d}^{(n+1)}(a) + \xi d^{(n)}$, where $d^{(n)}$ is the sensor's reputation distribution at time index n and $\hat{d}^{(n+1)}(a)$, following Definition 5.2, is the sensor's immediate expected reputation distribution with action rule a at time index $n+1$.

Proof   According to (5.8), $\forall a \in \mathcal{A}_l$, and $d^{(n)}$, we respectively have $d^{(n+1)}(a(1)) = (1-\xi)\hat{d}^{(n+1)}(a(1)) + \xi d^{(n)}$ and $d^{(n+1)}(a(2)) = (1-\xi)\hat{d}^{(n+1)}(a(2)) + \xi d^{(n)}$. Then we have $d^{(n+1)}(a) = P_{L_1} d^{(n+1)}(a(1)) + P_{L_2} d^{(n+1)}(a(2)) = (1-\xi)\hat{d}^{(n+1)}(a) + \xi d^{(n)}$.

Under these particular conditions, $d^{(n+1)}(a)$ possesses a very useful property, as is characterized in Lemma 5.4 for later analysis.

LEMMA 5.4 $\forall a \in \mathcal{A}_l$, $d^{(n+1)}(a) = \hat{d}(a)$ represents the steady expected reputation distribution if a is followed all of the time. Here, $\hat{d}(a)$ represents the immediate expected reputation distribution after the sensor follows action rule a.

Proof   If the sensor continues following action rule a at time index n, then, according to Lemma 5.3, its expected reputation at that time index is updated as $d^{(n)}(a) = (1-\xi)\hat{d}^{(n)}(a) + \xi d^{(n-1)}(a)$, where $\hat{d}^{(n)}(a) = (P_{L_1}e_{\Omega_{a(1),L_1}} + P_{L_1}e_{\Omega_{a(1),L_2}} + P_{L_2}e_{\Omega_{a(2),L_1}} + P_{L_2}e_{\Omega_{a(2),L_2}})D$. We notice that $\hat{d}^{(n)}(a)$ is deterministic and independent with n when a is given. Hence, we drop the subscript n in $\hat{d}^{(n)}(a)$ and rewrite it as

$$d^{(n)}(a) = (1-\xi)\hat{d}(a) + \xi d^{(n-1)} = (1-\xi^{n-1})(\hat{d}(a) - d^{(1)}) + d^{(1)}. \qquad (5.10)$$

Since $0 < \xi < 1$, when a is followed all of the time (i.e., $n \to \infty$), we have a steady reputation distribution

$$d^{(n)}(a) = (1-\xi^{n-1})(\hat{d}(a) - d^{(1)}) + d^{(1)} = \hat{d}(a). \qquad (5.11)$$
$$\phantom{d^{(n)}(a)}_{n\to\infty} \phantom{= (1-\xi^{n-1})}_{n\to\infty}$$

In Lemma 5.4, a sensor's expected reputation distribution with a particular action rule is close to the equivalent immediate expected reputation distribution and remains steady if it continues following the action rule. Moreover, the stability of an individual sensor's expected reputation distribution would create a steady reputation distribution for the entire system, which will be shown within Theorem 5.9.

Next, the sensor's payoff function when following a particular action rule at any given time index is to be defined, and we omit the time index's superscript for simplicity.

As is well known, energy must be consumed to report local information, and a sensor pays this cost when taking a certain action. Therefore, a cost function $f_c(a)$ is defined for measuring a sensor's cost after taking action $a \in \mathcal{A}$. By taking action a, a corresponding reputation distribution $d(a)$ would be obtained by the sensor when the particular benefit $f_g(d,\eta)$ could be achieved. It is assumed that $f_g(d,\eta)$ is an increasing function of d while it is a decreasing function of the reputation of the entire population η considering that the resource is allocated fairly. Hence, a sensor's utility function, such as sensor m taking action a_m while other sensors take actions a_{-m}, ought to be

$$W(a_m, a_{-m}) = f_g(d(a_m), \eta(a_m, a_{-m})) - f_c(a_m). \qquad (5.12)$$

Similarly, sensor m's expected utility with action rule $a_m \in \mathcal{A}_l$ while other sensor take action rules a_{-m} is defined by revising (5.12) as

$$W(a_m, a_{-m}) = f_g(d(a_m), \eta(a_m, a_{-m})) - f_c(a_m). \qquad (5.13)$$

From (5.12) and (5.13), it can be seen that a sensor's (expected) utility function is determined both by its action (or action rule) and by other sensors' actions (or action rules) that have been incorporated into the entire population distribution $\eta(\cdot)$. In this case, the interactions among sensors form an indirect reciprocity data fusion game.

5.2.7 Equilibrium of the Indirect Reciprocity Data Fusion Game

In order to discuss the ways in which a sensor chooses the optimal action within the game, we first give the formal definition of an NE, then we derive the NE for the game.

DEFINITION 5.5 (Nash equilibrium)   An NE represents the action rule profile $a^* = \{a_1^*, \ldots, a_M^*\}$ where $\forall m \in \mathcal{M} = \{1, \ldots, M\}$, $a_m^* = \arg\max_{a_m \in \mathcal{A}_l} W(a_m, a_{-m}^*)$. Here, sensor m utilizes the action rule a_m, a_{-m}^* represents all sensors' optimal action rules except sensor m, and $W(a_m, a_{-m}^*)$ represents sensor m's expected utility, which is signified in (5.13).

With the definition, it is shown in Theorem 5.6 that an NE exists.

THEOREM 5.6   *Given the set of action rules $\mathcal{A}_l$ and the set of sensors $\mathcal{M}$, an NE of the game exists (i.e., $a^* = \{a_1^*, \ldots, a_M^*\}$) that satisfies*

$$W(a_m, a_{-m}^*) \geq W(a_m', a_{-m}^*), \quad \forall m \in \mathcal{M}, \tag{5.14}$$

where $a_m' \in \mathcal{A}_l \setminus a_m^*$ and $W(\cdot)$ are signified in (5.13).

Proof   Presuming that the player set $\mathcal{M} = \{1, \ldots, M\}$ and the set of action rules $\mathcal{A}_l$ are finite, in view of [23], an NE of the game exists.

$\forall m \in \mathcal{M}$, given other sensors' optimal action rules as a_{-m}^*, if sensor m's action rule a_m^* satisfies $W(a_m^*, a_{-m}^*) \geq W(a_m', a_{-m}^*)$, where $a_m' \in \mathcal{A}_l \setminus a_m^*$, then we can get $a_m^* = \arg\max_{a_m \in \mathcal{A}_l} W(a_m, a_{-m}^*)$ (i.e., a_m^* is sensor m's best response to a_{-m}^*). In view of Definition 5.5, the action rule profile $a^* = \{a_1^*, a_2^*, \ldots, a_M^*\}$ constructed by a_m^*, $m \in \mathcal{M}$, is the NE of the game.

Notice that the NE might not be unique. For instance, if certain sensors satisfy the equality of (5.14), then every kind of sensor has at least two action rules that are capable of bringing about its maximal expected utility, and each of them would result in a different NE. However, when (5.14) strictly holds for all sensors, the NE is unique.

5.3 Application to Cooperative Spectrum Sensing

Within this section, the application of the indirect reciprocity data fusion game in CSS will be studied, which is utilized to upgrade the sensing accuracy and to counter the hidden terminal problem in CRN. Many aspects of CSS approaches have been studied thoroughly in the literature, where cooperation strategies [14,15,24], sensing schemes for an individual SU [25], and fusion algorithms for the FC [26] have been investigated intensively. However, in practice, SUs are selfish and belong to different organizations. They would not take part in CSS unconditionally, and therefore they do not wholly conform to the assumptions of existing CSS approaches that the spectrum sensing results would be shared by each of the SUs.

Thus, the sensing result sharing problem in CSS could be modeled ideally as an indirect reciprocity data fusion game in which the SUs are represented by the sensors,

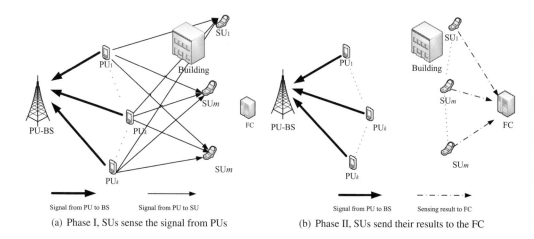

(a) Phase I, SUs sense the signal from PUs   (b) Phase II, SUs send their results to the FC

Figure 5.3   The cooperative sensing system. BS = base station.

the hypothesis is whether the primary users (PUs) are active in the channels, and the FC is a dedicated sever or cognitive radio station [27]. In this game framework, the ways in which the SUs make their decisions on results sharing and how they are stimulated to cooperate are demonstrated.

5.3.1   System Model

As is shown in Figure 5.3, a system consisting of a secondary network and a primary network is considered. Assume that the primary network has K PUs and a licensed channel is owned by each of them. Meanwhile, M SUs within the secondary network are sensing these K channels in order to discover spectrum holes for access opportunities. The entire procedure is divided into two phases so as to implement CSS. Within the first phase, the SUs can sense the signal from the PUs, and their local sensing information would be sent to the FC within the second phase. The FC makes final decisions for them after collecting all of the individual decisions or local sensing results from the SUs. After a certain action is taken, the FC assigns a corresponding reputation value to the SU (i.e., it reports its sensing result to embolden SUs to take part in CSS). Acquiring the usage of vacant channels is possible for the SU in the future based on its reputation.

To detect the PUs, energy detection, which is the most common approach to spectrum sensing without knowing the PUs' prior information, is adopted by the SUs. Let H_1 and H_0 be hypotheses of the PU being present or absent, respectively. Given the energy threshold λ, the SU's probability of detection $P_{d,m}$ and probability of false alarm $P_{f,m}$ could be calculated utilizing (5.3) and (5.4), respectively. Generally, the threshold λ is first determined by the desired false alarm probability, then the probability of detection is computed as $P_{d,m} = 1 - \dfrac{e^{-\sqrt{z}C_m}E(e^{B_m})}{e^{-\sqrt{\lambda}}}$, where the groups of observation samples are represented by z, a constant is represented by C_m, and a limiting distribution is represented by B_m, which are signified in (18) of [28].

In the following section, the game is applied to the CSS system in which at first only one primary channel exists (i.e., $K = 1$), the FC makes the final decision with hard fusion, and the NE of the game and the stable condition of the NE will be derived theoretically. Then, the single-channel scenario, which moves from the hard fusion case to the soft fusion case, will be discussed. Finally, we discuss the ways of applying this scheme to systems in which multiple primary channels exist (i.e., $K > 1$).

5.3.2 Fusion Game for the Single-Channel ($K = 1$) and Hard Fusion Case

The game can be directly applied to the CSS system in which the FC makes the final decision with hard fusion and only one primary channel exists. That is, given the threshold λ, an SU's average energy can be quantized into two levels (i.e., $\mathcal{L} = \{1, 2\}$) and an SU has two options: keeping silent or reporting under each level. Its selection (i.e., its action) then could be signified as $a \in \mathcal{A} = \{1, 2\}$. $a_{i,j} \in \mathcal{A}$ is then adopted to demonstrate the action that is performed by an SU with reputation i under average energy level j. The social norm utilized by the FC to assign an SU's immediate reputation value has been signified as Ω in (5.2). In order to characterize the gap between the SU's actual average energy level and the fusion result, we can obtain the decision consistency matrix D for this CSS scenario by following the definition in (5.5), in which P_1 and P_0 are the prior probabilities of PUs being present and absent, respectively. After that, we adopt the reputation updating policy shown in Figure 5.2. Within the game, every SU is assigned a reputation distribution $d = (d_l, d_h)$, and an SU's reputation distribution with action a at time index $n + 1$ (i.e., $d^{(n+1)}(a)$) is updated by (5.8) according to the policy, while its expected reputation distribution when adopting a certain action rule follows $d^{(n+1)}(a) = (1 - \xi)\hat{d}^{(n+1)}(a) + \xi d^{(n)}$ as verified in Lemma 5.3.

An SU with reputation distribution d could apply for a corresponding number of vacant channels whenever it owns data to forward. Presume that the FC allocates the vacant channels to SUs proportionally, then the access time of the vacant channel allocated to the SU with reputation distribution d would be

$$t(d, \eta) = (1 - P_F)\frac{N_s}{M}\frac{E(d) - 1}{E(\eta) - 1}, \tag{5.15}$$

where the FC's probability of false alarm is represented by $P_F = \sum_{k=\left\lceil\frac{1+M}{2}\right\rceil}^{M}\binom{M}{k}P_f^k(1 - P_f)^{M-k}$, the CSS system's current reputation distribution signified in (5.9) is represented by η, the number of SUs that a vacant channel allows access to is represented by N_s, the average available channels for every SU is represented by $(1 - P_F)\frac{N_s}{M}$, and the expected operation on the reputation distribution is represented by $E(\cdot)$. Let g be the gain in unit access time for vacant channels, then the benefit that the SU achieves is represented by

$$f_g(d, \eta) = gt(d, \eta). \tag{5.16}$$

On the other side, all of the SUs sense the channel, and their sensing results would be reported by some of them. We consider power consumption instead of the cost of sensing when the SU delivers its sensing result to the FC since the former is same for all SUs. Let c be the power's unit price, so the cost function of an SU taking action a is represented by

$$f_c(a) = c(a - 1). \tag{5.17}$$

Then, since the action rule is taken into consideration, the expected utility of SU_m that takes action rule $\boldsymbol{a}_m \in \mathcal{A}_l$ while other SUs take action rules $\boldsymbol{a}_{-m}$ is signified statistically as

$$W(\boldsymbol{a}_m, \boldsymbol{a}_{-m}) = f_g(d(\boldsymbol{a}_m), \eta(\boldsymbol{a}_m, \boldsymbol{a}_{-m})) - f_c(\boldsymbol{a}_m)$$

$$= g(1 - P_F)\frac{N_s}{M}\frac{E(d(\boldsymbol{a}_m)) - 1}{E(\eta(\boldsymbol{a}_m, \boldsymbol{a}_{-m})) - 1} - c(E(\boldsymbol{a}_m) - 1), \tag{5.18}$$

where the SU's expected action is represented by $E(\boldsymbol{a}_m) = P_{L_1}\boldsymbol{a}_m(1) + P_{L_2}\boldsymbol{a}_m(2)$.

According to $W(\cdot)$, the SU's optimal action rule can be derived theoretically. The analytical result is shown in Theorem 5.7, in which the optimal action rule's uniqueness can be seen.

THEOREM 5.7   *The optimal action rule for SUs (i.e., $\boldsymbol{a}^*$) is signified as follows:*

$$\boldsymbol{a}^* = \begin{cases} \boldsymbol{a}^{(2)} = (1, 2), & \text{if } 0 < c/g < (1 - \xi)(1 - P_F)\frac{N_s}{M}\frac{D_{2,2} - D_{2,1}}{E(\eta^*) - 1}, \\ \boldsymbol{a}^{(4)} = (1, 1), & \text{otherwise,} \end{cases} \tag{5.19}$$

where the stationary reputation distribution of the system is represented by η^*.

Proof   Let $\boldsymbol{d}'$ represent the current reputation distribution of an SU and η^* represent the stationary reputation distribution of the system. After following action rule $\boldsymbol{a}$, the SU's immediate reputation distribution and the expected reputation distribution, respectively, ought to be

$$\hat{\boldsymbol{d}}(\boldsymbol{a}) = (P_{L_1}\boldsymbol{e}_{\Omega_{a(1),L_1}} + P_{L_1}\boldsymbol{e}_{\Omega_{a(1),L_2}} + P_{L_2}\boldsymbol{e}_{\Omega_{a(2),L_1}} + P_{L_2}\boldsymbol{e}_{\Omega_{a(2),L_2}})\boldsymbol{D} \tag{5.20}$$

and

$$\boldsymbol{d}(\boldsymbol{a}) = (1 - \xi)\hat{\boldsymbol{d}}(\boldsymbol{a}) + \xi\boldsymbol{d}'. \tag{5.21}$$

Furthermore, the expected action of action rule $\boldsymbol{a}$ is defined as

$$E(\boldsymbol{a}) = P_{L_1}\boldsymbol{a}(1) + P_{L_2}\boldsymbol{a}(2). \tag{5.22}$$

Given other SUs' optimal action rules $\boldsymbol{a}^*_{-1}$ and substituting (5.21) and (5.22) into (5.18), we can obtain the SU's expected utilities for the four action rules (i.e., $W(\boldsymbol{a}^{(1)}, \boldsymbol{a}^*_{-1})$, $W(\boldsymbol{a}^{(2)}, \boldsymbol{a}^*_{-1})$, $W(\boldsymbol{a}^{(3)}, \boldsymbol{a}^*_{-1})$, and $W(\boldsymbol{a}^{(4)}, \boldsymbol{a}^*_{-1})$).

Because $D_{1,1} > D_{1,2}$, we can obtain

$$
W(a^{(2)}, a^*_{-1}) - W(a^{(1)}, a^*_{-1}) = W(a^{(4)}, a^*_{-1}) - W(a^{(3)}, a^*_{-1})
$$

$$
= g(1 - P_F)(1 - \xi)\frac{N_s}{M}\frac{P_{L_1}(D_{1,1} - D_{1,2})}{E(\eta^*) - 1} + cP_{L_1} > 0.
$$

$$(5.23)$$

That is, $W(a^{(2)}, a^*_{-1}) > W(a^{(1)}, a^*_{-1})$ and $W(a^{(4)}, a^*_{-1}) > W(a^{(3)}, a^*_{-1})$.

In order to find the optimal action rule, we have to compare $W(a^{(2)}, a^*_{-1})$ and $W(a^{(4)}, a^*_{-1})$. If $W(a^{(2)}, a^*_{-1}) > W(a^{(4)}, a^*_{-1})$ holds, i.e.,

$$
0 < c/g < (1 - \xi)(1 - P_F)\frac{N_s}{M}\frac{D_{2,2} - D_{2,1}}{E(\eta^*) - 1},
$$

$$(5.24)$$

then the action rule $a^{(2)}$ represents the optimal action rule. Otherwise, the optimal action rule is represented by $a^{(4)}$.

In summary, we have the optimal action rule a^* that is shown in (5.19).

Obviously, the local decisions would not be reported by the SUs with strategy $a^{(4)}$ to the FC under any circumstances, and the FC's performance would degrade since such a strategy is noncooperative. Thus, $a^{(2)}$ is the desired equilibrium that can upgrade the fusion accuracy of FC greatly because SUs report their local decisions on hypothesis H_1 being true only under the circumstance that their average received energy is above the given threshold, otherwise they would remain silent.

In this analysis for finding the optimal action rule, the perturbation effect is not included. Nevertheless, the SUs might use a nonoptimal action rule in practice due to incorrect (noisy) parameters and/or uncertainty in the system. Regarding the perturbation effect, the stability of the optimal action rule has to be evaluated; that is, whether an SU would deviate from the optimal action rule while others follow it all of the time and under what kind of circumstances the SU would keep following the optimal action rule.

The concept of an ESS is adopted to discuss the stable condition for optimal strategy $a^{(2)}$. An ESS could be defined as "a strategy such that, if all members of the population adopt it, then no mutant strategies could invade the population under the influence of natural selection." In view of [29], an optimal strategy a^* represents an ESS only if $\forall a \neq a^*$, a^* satisfies

- Equilibrium condition: $U_m(a, a^*) \leq U_m(a^*, a^*)$, and
- Stability condition: if $U_m(a, a^*) = U_m(a^*, a^*)$, $U_m(a, a) < U_m(a^*, a)$,

where $U_m(a, a^*)$ stands for the utility of SU$_m$'s deviation from the optimal action rule a^* and $U_m(a^*, a^*)$ represents SU$_m$'s utility when action rule a^* is followed by all SUs.

Then, according to the definition of an ESS and the one-shot deviation principle, $a^{(2)}$ represents an ESS if the following inequality holds:

$$
U_m(a^{(2)}, a^{(2)}) > U_m(a, a^{(2)}), \quad \forall a.
$$

$$(5.25)$$

With (5.25), we are capable of deriving the stable condition for $a^{(2)}$ as demonstrated in Theorem 5.8.

THEOREM 5.8   *The optimal action rule $a^{(2)}$ is an ESS if the cost-to-gain ratio c/g satisfies*

$$0 < c/g < (1 - \xi)(1 - P_F)\frac{N_s}{M}\frac{D_{2,2} - D_{2,1}}{E(\eta^*) - 1}. \tag{5.26}$$

Proof   As is shown in Lemma 5.4, if action rule $a^{(2)}$ is followed by all of SUs all of the time, an SU's expected reputation distribution at time index $n + 1$ ought to be

$$d^{(n+1)}(a^{(2)}) = \hat{d}(a^{(2)}). \tag{5.27}$$

But if the SU deviates from action rule $a^{(2)}$ and chooses to follow action rule $a^{(l)}$ at time index $n + 1, i \neq 2$, its expected reputation distribution would be

$$d^{(n+1)}(a^{(l)}) = (1 - \xi)\hat{a}^{(n+1)}(a^{(l)}) + \xi d^{(n)}(a^{(2)}). \tag{5.28}$$

Furthermore, we can obtain

$$E(a^{(l)}) = P_{L_1}a^{(l)}(1) + P_{L_2}a^{(l)}(2). \tag{5.29}$$

Substituting (5.29) and (5.27) into (5.18), we can obtain the SU's utility when the optimal action $a^{(2)}$ is continually followed by it (i.e., $U(a^{(2)}, a^{(2)})$). Substituting (5.29) and (5.28) into (5.18), we can obtain the SU's utility when it deviates from the optimal action rule and chooses action rule $a^{(l)}, i \neq 2$ (i.e., $U(a^{(l)}, a^{(2)})$).

Because $D_{2,2} > D_{2,1}$ and $D_{1,1} > D_{1,2}$, we would obtain $U(a^{(2)}, a^{(2)}) > U(a^{(1)}, a^{(2)})$ and $U(a^{(4)}, a^2) > U(a^{(3)}, a^{(2)})$. In view of (5.25), for $a^{(2)}$ to be an ESS, $U(a^{(2)}, a^{(2)}) > U(a^{(4)}, a^{(2)})$ must be held, which leads to (5.26).

Furthermore, the CSS system has a unique stationary reputation distribution for the entire population, as is stated within Theorem 5.9 when all SUs follow the optimal rule $a^{(2)}$ without deviation all of the time.

THEOREM 5.9   *Within the CSS system where (5.26) is satisfied, there is a unique stationary reputation distribution for the whole population that can be signified as*

$$\eta^* = \eta^{(n)}_{n \to \infty}(a_1, \ldots, a_M)$$

$$= (P_{L1}D_{1,2} + P_{L2}D_{2,1}, P_{L1}D_{1,1} + P_{L2}D_{2,2}), \tag{5.30}$$

and the condition for $a^{(2)}$ being an evolutionarily stable and optimal strategy therefore is

$$0 < c/g < (1 - \xi)(1 - P_F)\frac{N_s}{M}\frac{D_{2,2} - D_{2,1}}{P_{L1}D_{1,1} + P_{L2}D_{2,2}}. \tag{5.31}$$

Proof In view of the definition within (5.9), the entire system's reputation distribution in time index n ought to be

$$\eta^{(n)}(a_1, \ldots, a_M) = \frac{1}{M} \sum_{m=1}^{M} d^{(n)}(a_m). \tag{5.32}$$

If action rule a_m is followed by sensor m all of the time, based on Lemma 5.4, $\eta^{(n)}(\cdot)$ would be

$$\eta^* = \eta^{(n)}_{n \to \infty}(a_1, \ldots, a_M) = \frac{1}{M} \sum_{\substack{m=1 \\ n \to \infty}}^{M} d^{(n)}(a_m)$$

$$= \frac{1}{M} \sum_{m=1}^{M} d^{(n)}_{n \to \infty}(a_m) = \frac{1}{M} \sum_{m=1}^{M} \hat{d}(a_m), \tag{5.33}$$

which is the whole system's stationary and unique reputation distribution.

Within the CSS system where (5.26) is satisfied, action rule $a^{(2)}$ is followed by the SUs all of the time. For this circumstance, we have

$$\eta^* = \frac{1}{M} \sum_{m=1}^{M} \hat{d}(a^{(2)}) = (P_{L1}D_{1,2} + P_{L2}D_{2,1}, P_{L1}D_{1,1} + P_{L2}D_{2,2}). \tag{5.34}$$

From Theorem 5.8 and Theorem 5.7, (5.31) therefore is the condition for $a^{(2)}$ being an evolutionarily stable and optimal strategy.

5.3.3 Fusion Game for the Single-Channel ($K = 1$) and Soft Fusion Case

In the previous section, the game's characteristics were analyzed on the basis of the presumption that the FC applies hard fusion in which only 1 bit is needed for an SU to indicate its detection of the PU. However, the scheme is also adoptable in the scenario in which the FC applies soft fusion. With soft fusion, SUs are required to report their original observed signal strengths regardless of their local decisions. In this section, a soft fusion case analysis is conducted in which only one primary channel ($K = 1$) exists.

Suppose that equal-gain combining (EGC), which is one of the methods for implementing soft fusion, is exploited within this scenario. Thus, the average energy that is collected by the FC from M SUs would be

$$S_{fc} = \frac{1}{M} \left(\sum_{m \in \mathcal{M}_1} S_m + |\mathcal{M}_2| \right), \tag{5.35}$$

where $\mathcal{M}_1$ stands for the set of SUs that report their sensing observations, S_m represents the sensing observation that SU_m reports, and $\mathcal{M}_2$ stands for the set of SUs of keeping silent. For those SUs within $\mathcal{M}_2$, their received energy is supposed to be equal to the average energy of AWGN, which is always set to 1 [30]. Hence, $|\mathcal{M}_2|$ represents the total energy of the SUs within $\mathcal{M}_2$. Then the FC achieves its final decision by comparing S_{fc} to the predefined threshold λ.

The SU's average received energy is quantized into J ($J > 2$) levels in the soft fusion case, unlike that of hard fusion. Level 1 stands for the average received energy of the SU that is lower than the given threshold λ, while levels from 2 to J represent energies that are higher than or equal to the given threshold λ. An SU's action is signified as $a \in \mathcal{A}_s = \{1, \ldots, J\}$ in which the action set is represented by $\mathcal{A}_s$. If an SU intends to indicate that the given threshold λ is higher than its average received energy, it would keep silent and choose action $a = 1$; otherwise, action $a > 1$ would be chosen, reporting the ath-level received energy of the PU to the FC.

Then, the social norm for the soft fusion case is extended from (5.2) as $\mathbf{\Omega}' = [\Omega'_{i,j}]$ with

$$\Omega'_{i,j} = \begin{cases} 2, \text{if } i = j = 1 \text{ or } 1 < i \le J \text{ and } j = 2, \\ 1, \text{otherwise,} \end{cases} \tag{5.36}$$

where $\Omega'_{i,j}$ stands for the reputation value assigned to an SU that takes action i, while j represents the FC's final decision.

Accordingly, the decision consistency matrix is extended from (5.5) as

$$\mathbf{D}_s = [D_{i,j}], \quad i = 1, \ldots J, j = 1, 2. \tag{5.37}$$

Here, level 2 to level J is quantized equally, thus we have $D_{j,1} = D_{j',1}$ and $D_{j,2} = D_{j',2}$ when $j, j' > 1$ and $j \ne j'$. Without loss of generality, we presume that $D_{j,1} > D_{j,2}$ when $j = 1$ and $D_{j,2} > D_{j,1}$ when $j > 1$.

From (5.36), it can be seen that when the SU keeps silent, it is given a high reputation value when the FC finally decides that the PU is not active, or when its average received energy is reported and the FC finally decides that that the PU is active; otherwise, a low reputation value would be given to the SU. Therefore, SUs would be encouraged to join in the CSS and report their sensing results truthfully, which is verified within Theorem 5.10.

THEOREM 5.10 $\boldsymbol{a}^* = (1, 2, \ldots, J)$ *presents the optimal action rule for SUs within the soft fusion case under the condition* $0 < c/g < (1 - \xi)(1 - P_F)\frac{N_s}{M}\frac{D_{2,2} - D_{2,1}}{E(\eta^*) - 1}$.

Proof Let $\boldsymbol{d}'$ stand for an SU's current reputation distribution and η^* stand for the stationary reputation distribution of the system. By contradiction, we assume that another optimal action rule $\boldsymbol{a}' \ne \boldsymbol{a}^*$ exists where there is at least one element that is not equal to that in $\boldsymbol{a}^*$, say $\boldsymbol{a}'(j) \ne \boldsymbol{a}^*(j)$ and $\boldsymbol{a}'(j) = j'$.

If $j = 1$, thus $\boldsymbol{a}'(j) = j' > 1$. The immediate average reputation distribution of the SU ought to be

$$\hat{\boldsymbol{d}}(\boldsymbol{a}'(j)) = \boldsymbol{e}_{\Omega_{j',1}} D_{j,1} + \boldsymbol{e}_{\Omega_{j',2}} D_{j,2} = (D_{1,1}, D_{1,2}). \tag{5.38}$$

Otherwise, the SU's observation could be truthfully reported (i.e., it takes the action $a(j)$). Then its immediate average reputation distribution ought to be

$$\hat{\boldsymbol{d}}(\boldsymbol{a}(j)) = \boldsymbol{e}_{\Omega_{j,1}} D_{j,1} + \boldsymbol{e}_{\Omega_{j,2}} D_{j,2} = (D_{1,2}, D_{1,1}). \tag{5.39}$$

Given other SUs' optimal action rules $\boldsymbol{a}^*_{-1}$ and substituting (5.38), (5.39), and $\boldsymbol{d}'$ into (5.18), respectively, we have the SU's expected utilities of following $\boldsymbol{a}'(j)$ and $\boldsymbol{a}(j)$ as $W(\boldsymbol{a}(j), \boldsymbol{a}^*_{-1})$ and $W(\boldsymbol{a}'(j), \boldsymbol{a}^*_{-1})$, and

$$W(\boldsymbol{a}'(j), \boldsymbol{a}^*_{-1}) - W(\boldsymbol{a}(j), \boldsymbol{a}^*_{-1}) = (1 - \xi)g(1 - P_F) \cdot \frac{N_s}{M} \frac{E(\hat{\boldsymbol{d}}(\boldsymbol{a}'(j))) - E(\hat{\boldsymbol{d}}(\boldsymbol{a}(j)))}{E(\eta^*) - 1}$$

$$- c(\boldsymbol{a}'(j) - \boldsymbol{a}(j)). \tag{5.40}$$

Since $E(\hat{\boldsymbol{d}}(\boldsymbol{a}'(j))) - E(\hat{\boldsymbol{d}}(\boldsymbol{a}(j))) = D_{1,2} - D_{1,1} < 0$ and $\boldsymbol{a}'(j) > \boldsymbol{a}(j)$, we have

$$W(\boldsymbol{a}'(j), \boldsymbol{a}^*_{-1}) - W(\boldsymbol{a}(j), \boldsymbol{a}^*_{-1}) < 0. \tag{5.41}$$

Similarly, if $j > 1$ and $j' > j$, or $j > 1$ and $1 < j' < j$, we have $E(\hat{\boldsymbol{d}}(\boldsymbol{a}'(j))) - E(\hat{\boldsymbol{d}}(\boldsymbol{a}(j))) = 0$ and $c(\boldsymbol{a}'(j) - 1) = c(\boldsymbol{a}(j) - 1)$. Thus, there is $W(\boldsymbol{a}'(j), \boldsymbol{a}^*_{-1}) - W(\boldsymbol{a}(j), \boldsymbol{a}^*_{-1}) = 0$.

Finally, if $j > 1$ and $j' = 1$, there are $\boldsymbol{a}'(j) = j'$ and $\boldsymbol{a}(j) = j$, then we have $\hat{\boldsymbol{d}}(\boldsymbol{a}'(j)) = (D_{j,2}, D_{j,1})$ and $\hat{\boldsymbol{d}}(\boldsymbol{a}(j)) = (D_{j,1}, D_{j,2})$.

Since $E(\hat{\boldsymbol{d}}(\boldsymbol{a}'(j))) - E(\hat{\boldsymbol{d}}(\boldsymbol{a}(j))) < 0$ and $c(\boldsymbol{a}'(j) - 1) - c(\boldsymbol{a}(j) - 1) < 0$, when $0 < c/g < (1 - \xi)(1 - P_F)\frac{N_s}{M} \frac{D_{j,2} - D_{j,1}}{(\boldsymbol{a}'(j) - \boldsymbol{a}(j))(E(\eta^*) - 1)}$, we have $W(\boldsymbol{a}'(j), \boldsymbol{a}^*_{-1}) - W(\boldsymbol{a}(j), \boldsymbol{a}^*_{-1}) < 0$.

Noting $D_{j,2} = D_{2,2}$ and $D_{j,1} = D_{2,1}$ when $j > 2$, we have

$$c/g < (1 - \xi)(1 - P_F)\frac{N_s}{M} \frac{D_{j,2} - D_{j,1}}{(\boldsymbol{a}'(j) - \boldsymbol{a}(j))(E(\eta^*) - 1)}$$

$$< (1 - \xi)(1 - P_F)\frac{N_s}{M} \frac{D_{2,2} - D_{2,1}}{E(\eta^*) - 1}. \tag{5.42}$$

In summary, no such optimal action rule $\boldsymbol{a}' \neq \boldsymbol{a}^*$ exists in which at least one element is not equal to that in $\boldsymbol{a}^*$ for the SU when $0 < c/g < (1 - \xi)(1 - P_F)\frac{N_s}{M}\frac{D_{2,2} - D_{2,1}}{E(\eta^*) - 1}$.

Through deductive analysis, a conclusion is drawn that no such optimal action rule exists in which more than one element is not equal to those in $\boldsymbol{a}^*$. Therefore, $\boldsymbol{a}^* = (1, 2, \ldots, J)$ represents the optimal action rule for SUs within the soft fusion scenario when the condition within (5.42) is satisfied.

5.3.4 Fusion Game for the Multichannel ($K > 1$) Case

In the previous sections, the discussion was focused on the single-channel case (i.e., $K = 1$), which could be easily extended to the multichannel case where $K > 1$.

Within the literature, it is assumed that channels in the primary system are usually independent [31]. Hence, an SU's action only needs to be redefined as $a_{i,j} = (a_{i,j,1}, \ldots a_{i,j,k}, \ldots, a_{i,j,K})$ to apply to the indirect reciprocity scheme, in which $\mathcal{A}_k$ stands for the SU's action set toward channel k and $a_{i,j,k} \in \mathcal{A}_k, 1 \leq k \leq K$, represents the action that the SU would take toward channel k when i represents its reputation and the average received signal energy on channel k is at the jth level.

In order to assign the SU's reputation, the same social norm signified in (5.2) is exploited for the hard fusion scenario or (5.36) for the soft fusion scenario by the FC. For an SU, say SU_m, its reputation distribution of all K channels is signified as $\boldsymbol{d}_m = (\boldsymbol{d}_{m,1}, \dots, \boldsymbol{d}_{m,k}, \dots, \boldsymbol{d}_{m,K})$, with $\boldsymbol{d}_{m,k} = (d_l, d_h)$ being the reputation distribution of channel k.

The reputation updating policy for every channel also follows the one demonstrated within Figure 5.2, with which SU_m's reputation distribution for taking action a for channel k at time index $n+1$ (i.e., $\boldsymbol{d}_{m,k}^{(n+1)}(a)$) could be updated by linearly combining the SU's original reputation distribution $\boldsymbol{d}_{m,k}^{(n)}$ and the immediate reputation distribution $\hat{\boldsymbol{d}}_{m,k}^{(n+1)}(a)$ with a weight ξ as

$$\boldsymbol{d}_{m,k}^{(n+1)}(a) = (1 - \xi)\hat{\boldsymbol{d}}_{m,k}^{(n+1)}(a) + \xi\boldsymbol{d}_{m,k}^{(n)}. \tag{5.43}$$

By following action rule $\boldsymbol{a}_m = (\boldsymbol{a}_{m,1}, \dots, \boldsymbol{a}_{m,k}, \dots, \boldsymbol{a}_{m,K})$, SU_m obtains the expected reputation distribution $\boldsymbol{d}_m = (\boldsymbol{d}_{m,1}(\boldsymbol{a}_{m,1}), \dots \boldsymbol{d}_{m,k}(\boldsymbol{a}_{m,k}), \dots, \boldsymbol{d}_{m,K}(\boldsymbol{a}_{m,K}))$, with which the SU could adopt a corresponding amount of vacant channels whenever there are data to forward. In a fair and proportional manner, the access time of the vacant channel k allocated to the SU according to this channel's reputation distribution (i.e., $\boldsymbol{d}_{m,k}$) would be

$$t(\boldsymbol{d}_{m,k}, \boldsymbol{\eta}_k) = (1 - P_F)\frac{N_s}{M}\frac{E(\boldsymbol{d}_{m,k}) - 1}{E(\boldsymbol{\eta}_k) - 1}. \tag{5.44}$$

The benefit that the SU achieves from K channels therefore is

$$f_g(\boldsymbol{d}_m(\boldsymbol{a}_m), \boldsymbol{\eta}) = \sum_{k=1}^{K} gt(\boldsymbol{d}_{m,k}, \boldsymbol{\eta}_k), \tag{5.45}$$

where $\boldsymbol{\eta} = (\boldsymbol{\eta}_1, \dots, \boldsymbol{\eta}_k, \dots, \boldsymbol{\eta}_K)$ is the reputation distribution of the whole population for K channels and $\boldsymbol{\eta}_k = \boldsymbol{\eta}_k(\boldsymbol{a}_{1,k}, \dots, \boldsymbol{a}_{M,k})$, following (5.9), represents the reputation distribution of channel k.

The SU's cost resulting from following action rule $\boldsymbol{a}_m$ would be

$$f_c(\boldsymbol{a}_m) = \sum_{k=1}^{K} c(E(\boldsymbol{a}_{m,k}) - 1). \tag{5.46}$$

Letting $W(\boldsymbol{a}_m, \boldsymbol{a}_{-m})$ denote an SU's expected utility when action rule $\boldsymbol{a}_m$ is taken while action rules $\boldsymbol{a}_{-m}$ are taken by other SUs, we have

$$W(\boldsymbol{a}_m, \boldsymbol{a}_{-m}) = f_g(\boldsymbol{d}_m(\boldsymbol{a}_m), \boldsymbol{\eta}) - f_c(\boldsymbol{a}_m)$$

$$= \sum_{k=1}^{K} gt(\boldsymbol{d}_{m,k}, \boldsymbol{\eta}_k) - \sum_{k=1}^{K} c(E(\boldsymbol{a}_{m,k}) - 1)$$

$$= \sum_{k=1}^{K} W(\boldsymbol{a}_{m,k}, \boldsymbol{a}_{-m,k}), \tag{5.47}$$

where $W(\boldsymbol{a}_{m,k}, \boldsymbol{a}_{-m,k})$, which is signified within (5.13), is SU_m's expected utility acquired from channel k through following action rule $\boldsymbol{a}_{m,k}$.

Since $W(\boldsymbol{a}_{m,k}, \boldsymbol{a}_{-m,k})$, $k = 1, \ldots, K$, are independent of each other, in order to maximize W, the SU only has to choose the optimal action rule for channel k. In such a circumstance, we have Theorem 5.11.

THEOREM 5.11 $\forall m \in \mathcal{M}$, SU_m's optimal action rule for K channels (i.e., $\boldsymbol{a}_m^* = (a_{m,1}^*, \ldots, a_{m,K}^*)$) is given as

$$W(a_{m,k}^*, \boldsymbol{a}_{-m,k}^*) \geq W(a_{m,k}', \boldsymbol{a}_{-m,k}^*), \quad \forall k \in \{1, \ldots, K\}, \tag{5.48}$$

where $a_{m,k}' \in \mathcal{A}_k \setminus a_{m,k}^*$ and $W(\cdot)$ are signified in (5.13).

Theorem 5.11 is proved in a similar way as Theorem 5.10 for the soft fusion case or as Theorem 5.6 for the hard fusion case.

It can be proved that there is a unique stationary reputation distribution for channel k within the CSS system if $\boldsymbol{a}_k^* = (a_{1,k}^*, \ldots, a_{M,k}^*)$ represents an ESS, as is stated in Lemma 5.12.

LEMMA 5.12 *A unique stationary reputation distribution for channel k within the CSS system exists that is $\eta_k^* = \eta(a_{1,k}^*, \ldots, a_{M,k}^*)$.*

Lemma 5.12 could be verified in a similar way as Theorem 5.9.

5.4 Simulation

Within this section, the efficiency and effectiveness of the scheme discussed in this chapter in the CSS of CRNs will be evaluated. More specifically, the optimal action rule of the game and its evolutionary stability is verified, then the CSS system's performance under the incentive mechanism is evaluated through comparing it with other CSS schemes, and finally we evaluate the extent to which cheating behaviors could overwhelm the scheme when the SUs' sensing results are reported untruthfully.

5.4.1 The Optimal Action Rule and Its Evolutionary Stability

We consider a scenario in which there are $M = 40$ SUs within the secondary system. Then we presume that the PU locates at coordinate $(0,0)$ and the SUs are distributed within a circle centered at coordinates $(1,0)$ with a radius of 0.3. The channels between the SUs and the PU are Rayleigh fading channels in which the channel coefficient is complex Gaussian (i.e., $h_m \sim \mathcal{CN}(0, \sigma_m^2)$ with $\sigma_m^2 = 1/r_m^\theta$, r_m being the distances between SU_m and the PU and the path loss factor θ being set to 4). The PU's transmission power is set as 5, each channel's noise variance is set as $\sigma_n^2 = 1$, and the pattern of the PU's activity is presumed to be $P(H_0) = P(H_1) = 0.5$. The reputation distribution of each SU is initialized as $(0.5, 0.5)$, N_s is 5, and the discount weight ξ is 0.5. The P_f and P_d of the SU are set to 0.1 and 0.9, respectively, and the threshold for energy detection is thereby set to 1.57 as in [30].

First, the SUs' optimal action rule without perturbation effects is verified. Taking hard fusion as an example, we assume that all SUs within the system utilize the social norm signified in (5.2) and agree on the reputation updating policy that is shown in Figure 5.2. The simulation is conducted only on the single-channel case owing to the fact that the performance of the multichannel case is similar, and the results are shown in Figure 5.4.

Note that the critical cost-to-gain ratio is equal to 0.12 according to the simulation setting and (5.31). It can be seen from Figure 5.4 that, in the case of $c/g = 0.1$ (i.e., $c/g < 0.12$), the SU chooses action $a^* = 1$ when the given threshold is higher than its received energy, otherwise it chooses action $a^* = 2$. It is willing to cooperate because the cooperation gain is more than the cost in this case. However, in the case of $c/g = 0.2$ (i.e., $c/g > 0.12$), the SU always chooses action $a^* = 1$ regardless of the energy received because the SU's cooperation gain will be smaller than the cooperation cost in this case, and it thus refuses to participate. In both cases, the curve of the optimal action rules obtained through simulations matches that derived from the theoretical analysis in Theorem 5.7, indicating that the analysis is correct and solid.

Next, the evolutionary stability of the optimal action rule is verified when $c/g = 0.1$, where the cost-to-gain ratio is lower than the critical value and the optimal action rule is $a^{(2)}$.

We assume that only half of the SUs will take the optimal strategy $a^{(2)}$ under the same condition as (5.31), while the others choose strategies $a^{(1)}$, $a^{(3)}$, or $a^{(4)}$ randomly, because not all SUs will take the optimal action at the beginning due to perturbation effects such as noise. It is also assumed that the SU stays in the system with a probability of 95% and leaves the system with a probability of 5%. A new SU enters the system to keep the total population size constant for every SU that leaves. Here, the Wright–Fisher model [32] is adopted to investigate how the SUs update their actions. According to this model, the percentage of the population using action rule $a^{(l)}$ at time index $n + 1$ (i.e., $y_l^{(n+1)}$) is proportional to the total payoff of the users using $a^{(l)}$ at time index n, i.e.,

$$y_l^{(n+1)} = \frac{y_l^{(n)} U_l^{(n)}}{\sum_{l=1}^{4} y_l^{(n)} U_l^{(n)}} \tag{5.49}$$

where $U_l^{(n)}$ is the total payoff of the users using $a^{(l)}$ at time index n.

Figure 5.5 shows the percentage of the population using the optimal strategy $a^{(2)}$ and the percentage of the population with a good reputation. From this, we can see that the optimal strategy spreads over the whole system within 10 iterations, and once it is adopted by the whole population, there would be no mutation that could lead to SUs deviating from this state, which confirms that the optimal strategy $a^{(2)}$ is the ESS under the simulation conditions. It can also be seen that the distribution of the whole population with a good reputation converges within 10 iterations, which proves that strategy $a^{(2)}$ is a desirable strategy since it leads to a "good" society where almost 95% of SUs have a good reputation.

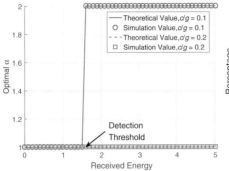 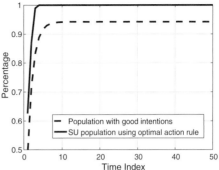

Figure 5.4 The optimal action rules of SUs.

Figure 5.5 The percentage of the SU population when $c/g = 0.1$.

According to the results obtained above, we only evaluate the performance of the system in the steady state where most of SUs take optimal strategy $\boldsymbol{a}^{(2)}$ and have a good reputation.

5.4.2   System Performance

In this section, we will evaluate the performance of the system in terms of the receiver operating characteristic (ROC) curve, total throughput, and fairness. In the first two simulations, we compare the indirect reciprocity-based CSS scheme (IRCS) with three other existing schemes: random spectrum sensing (RCS), CSS [33], and evolutionary CSS (ESSCS) [34]. In the RCS scheme, SUs send their sensing results to the FC in a random way (i.e., reporting and not reporting each with a probability of 0.5), while in the CSS scheme, all of the SUs send their sensing results. In the ESSCS scheme, the probability of an SU taking action $a, (a \in \{1,2\})$ at $t + 1$ can be calculated as

$$P_a(t + 1) = P_a(t) + \triangle[\bar{U}(a, \boldsymbol{a}_{-1}) - \bar{U}(a')]P_a(t), \qquad (5.50)$$

where $\bar{U}(a, \boldsymbol{a}_{-1})$ is the SU's average payoff when taking action a while the other SUs take actions $\boldsymbol{a}_{-1}$ at t, $\bar{U}(a')$ is the SU's average payoff using mixed strategy a' at t, and $\triangle$ is the step size of adjustment.

Unless stated otherwise, the FCs use the soft fusion approach of EGC in these four schemes. The use of hard fusion in the scheme is discussed and denoted as "IRCS-HD" in this chapter to demonstrate the gap in performance between different fusion approaches.

First, we evaluate the performance of the different schemes in terms of ROC and demonstrate the results in Figure 5.6, from which the RCS scheme shows the worst performance among all of the schemes with the same fusion approach, since SUs in the secondary system only share part of their information with the FC. The CSS scheme increases the fusion data in the FC and increases fusion accuracy through the reporting of all SUs. Nevertheless, a portion of the SUs will suffer seriously from

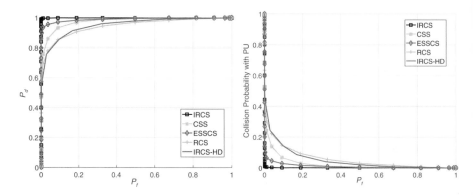

Figure 5.6 The ROC curves of the four different schemes.

Figure 5.7 Collision probability with the PU under the different schemes.

fading or shadow effects due to unstable environment conditions, which cause the SUs to be unable to receive even the primary signal when the PU is active. In such a case, the SUs will send a certain degree of incorrect information to the FC, leading the FC to make wrong judgments. Taking this into consideration, the ESSCS scheme limits the impact of sensing results of poor quality and improves sensing accuracy by decreasing (increasing) the sending probability when the estimated average energy is low (high). In this system, the FC can therefore make the most accurate decisions, since unreliable SUs are completely constrained to silence, and only those with good sensing quality send out their results. From Figure 5.6, we know soft fusion outperforms hard fusion for the same scheme (e.g., IRCS) because it retains more information with which the FC can make more accurate decisions. From the perspective of CRNs, the performance of the above schemes in terms of SUs' collision probability with the PU is provided in Figure 5.7.

Next, we study the performance of the schemes in terms of the total throughput of the secondary system in both the single-channel scenario and the multichannel scenario. In the multichannel scenario, we assume there are five PUs randomly distributed in a circle centered at coordinates $(0,0)$ with a radius of 0.4, each having one channel, while the other settings are the same for these two scenarios. The pattern of each PU's activity is assumed to be $P(H_0) = P(H_1) = 0.5$, and the results are shown in Figure 5.8.

The trends in the two scenarios are similar because an SU will be selected to use the vacant channel with a probability that is proportional to its expected reputation. Moreover, SUs are allocated the vacant channel in a way that can maximize the throughput of the secondary system, which is formulated into a maximum weight bipartite graph matching problem and solved using the Kuhn–Munkres algorithm. In such a case, SUs in the system are motivated to gain a good reputation by sending accurate information, and they gain high throughput in return. However, vacant

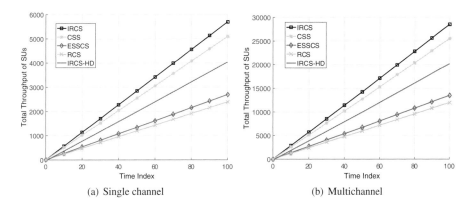

Figure 5.8 The total throughput of SUs.

channels are allocated through auctions in the CSS scheme, where the SU is assigned a channel that is not optimal for the whole system's throughput and can only guarantee the SU's individual transmission rate, while they are randomly allocated to SUs in the RCS and ESSCS schemes. As a result, the throughput of the system with the CSS scheme is lower than that with the scheme discussed in this chapter, and that with the RCS and ESSCS schemes is the lowest. From Figure 5.8 we can also see that soft fusion obtains a better performance than hard fusion from the perspective of throughput.

In the third simulation, we study the fairness issue of the scheme discussed in this chapter. To evaluate fairness performance, we use Jain's fairness index, i.e.,

$$F = \frac{\left(\sum_{m=1}^{M} T_m \right)^2}{M \sum_{m=1}^{M} T_m^2}, \tag{5.51}$$

where T_m is the access time of SU_m. Note that the fairness index varies between 0 and 1, with a larger value meaning more fairness. Figure 5.9 shows that in both the single-channel and multichannel cases Jain's fairness index of the scheme discussed in this chapter approaches 1 and is almost unchanged with increases in the number of SUs, indicating that the scheme can achieve good performance in terms of fairness.

5.4.3 Anticheating

According to the social norm, an SU obtains a high reputation value only when its report is consistent with the decision of the FC (i.e., the decisions of most SUs). In such a case, no SUs have an incentive to cheat if most SUs in the system are honest. However, this may be different in a network where most SUs are malicious.

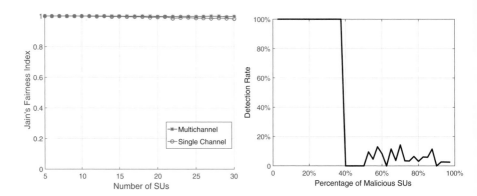

Figure 5.9 Jain's fairness index of the scheme discussed in this chapter.

Figure 5.10 The detection rate of malicious SUs.

Therefore, we will now examine the extent to which the scheme discussed in this chapter can overcome cheating behaviors when the SUs report their sensing results untruthfully.

For those 40 SUs, we change the percentage of malicious SUs from 0% to 100%, and the results of the detection rate of cheating behaviors versus the percentage of malicious SUs are shown in Figure 5.10. From this we can see that the detection rate of cheating behaviors is near 100% when the percentage of malicious SUs is lower than 38%, indicating that the cheating actions of those SUs are successfully limited by the scheme.

5.5   Conclusion

In this chapter, a data sharing incentive scheme based on indirect reciprocity game modeling is discussed, which provides a general framework for analyzing the uniqueness and stationary nature of the reputation distribution as well as the optimal action rule for the sensors in the system. We further discuss the application of the scheme to CSS in CRNs. It is shown that the SUs are stimulated through reputation to use the optimal action rule (i.e., to report the sensing result when the average received energy is above a given threshold, or otherwise to keep silent). The FC's fusion accuracy is greatly improved and at the same time the SU's energy is saved with such an optimal action rule. Furthermore, we derive the cost-to-gain ratio under which such an optimal strategy is stable. The simulation results show that the optimal action rule will lead to a "good" society where most of the SUs have a high reputation. These results also demonstrate that the scheme discussed in this chapter achieves a better ROC and a higher total throughput of the secondary system, as well as displaying a convincing performance in terms of fairness compared with the state-of-the-art direct reciprocity-based CSS schemes. In addition, the cheating actions of malicious SUs can be successfully limited through the scheme discussed in this chapter.

References

[1] D. Lahat, T. Adali, and C. Jutten, "Multimodal data fusion: An overview of methods, challenges, and prospects," *Proceedings of the IEEE*, vol. 103, pp. 1449–1477, 2015.

[2] D. Macii, A. Boni, M. D. Cecco, and D. Petri, "Tutorial 14: multisensor data fusion," *IEEE Instrumentation and Measurement Magazine*, vol. 11, pp. 24–33, 2008.

[3] L. Zhang, G. Ding, Q. Wu, Y. Zou, Z. Han, and J. Wang, "Byzantine attack and defense in cognitive radio networks: A survey," *IEEE Communications Surveys & Tutorials*, vol. 17, pp. 1342–1363, 2013.

[4] Y. Wang, J. Ye, G. Xu, Q. Chen, H. Li, and X. Liu, "Novel hierarchical fault diagnosis approach for smart power grid with information fusion of multidata resources based on fuzzy Petri net," in *IEEE International Conference on Fuzzy Systems (FUZZ-IEEE)*, 2014.

[5] M. Mahmoud and X. Shen, "Credit-based mechanism protecting multi-hop wireless networks from rational and irrational packet drop," in *IEEE GLOBECOM 2010*, 2010.

[6] S. Buchegger and J.-Y. L. Boudec, "Self-policing mobile ad hoc networks by reputation systems," *IEEE Communications Magazine*, vol. 43, pp. 101–107, 2005.

[7] A. Satsiou and L. Tassiulas, "Reputation-based resource allocation in P2P systems of rational users," *IEEE Transactions on Parallel and Distributed Systems*, vol. 21, pp. 466–479, 2010.

[8] F. Gao, W. Yuan, W. Liu, and W. Cheng, "A robust and efficient cooperative spectrum sensing scheme in cognitive radio networks," in *2010 IEEE ICC Workshops*, 2010.

[9] H. Marzi and A. Marzi, "A security model for wireless sensor networks," in *2014 IEEE International Conference on Computational Intelligence and Virtual Environments for Measurement Systems and Applications (CIVEMSA)*, 2014.

[10] Z. Song, E. Ngai, J. Ma, X. Gong, Y. Liu, and W. Wang, "Incentive mechanism for participatory sensing under budget constraints," in *2014 IEEE WCNC*, 2014.

[11] G. Tan and S. A. Jarvis, "A payment-based incentive and service differentiation scheme for peer-to-peer streaming broadcast," *IEEE Transactions on Parallel and Distributed Systems*, vol. 19, pp. 940–953, 2008.

[12] N. Tran, L. Le, S. Ren, Z. Han, and C. Hong, "Joint pricing and load balancing for cognitive spectrum access: non-cooperation vs cooperation," *IEEE JSAC, Special Issue on Cognitive Radios*, vol. 33, pp. 972–985, 2015.

[13] B. Venkat and C. Hota, "Efficient cooperative spectrum sensing in cognitive radio using coalitional game model," *IEEE International Conference on Contemporary Computing in Informatics (IC3I)*, 2014.

[14] W. Wang, B. Kasiri, J. Cai, and A. S. Alfa, "Distributed cooperative multi-channel spectrum sensing based on dynamic coalitional game," in *IEEE GLOBECOM*, 2010.

[15] M. Pan and Y. Fang, "Bargaining based pairwise cooperative spectrum sensing for cognitive radio networks," in *IEEE MILCOM*, 2008.

[16] K. Cao and Z. Yang, "A novel cooperative spectrum sensing method based on cooperative game theory," *Journal of Electronics (China)*, vol. 27, pp. 183–189, 2010.

[17] H. Ohtsuki, Y. Iwasa, and M. A. Nowak, "Indirect reciprocity provides only a narrow margin for efficiency for costly punishment," *Nature*, vol. 457, pp. 79–82, 2009.

[18] M. A. Nowak and K. Sigmund, "Evolution of indirect reciprocity," *Nature*, vol. 437, pp. 1291–1298, 2005.

[19] L. Xiao, Y. Chen, and K. J. R. Liu, "Anti-cheating prosumer energy exchange based on indirect reciprocity," in *IEEE International Conference on Communications*, 2014.

[20] Y. Chen and K. J. R. Liu, "Indirect reciprocity game modelling for cooperation stimulation in cognitive networks," *IEEE Transactions on Communications*, vol. 59, pp. 159–168, 2011.

[21] B. Zhang, Y. Chen, and K. J. R. Liu, "An indirect-reciprocity reputation game for cooperation in dynamic spectrum access networks," *IEEE Transactions on Wireless Communications*, vol. 11, pp. 4328–4341, 2012.

[22] Y. Gao, Y. Chen, and K. Liu, "Cooperation stimulation for multiuser cooperative communications using indirect reciprocity game," *IEEE Transactions on Communications*, vol. 60, pp. 3650–3661, 2012.

[23] T. Wang, L. Song, Z. Han, and W. Saad, "Overlapping coalition formation games for emerging communication networks," *IEEE Network*, vol. 30, pp. 46–53, 2016.

[24] T. Wang, L. Song, Z. Han, and W. Saad, "Distributed cooperative sensing in cognitive radio networks: An overlapping coalition formation approach," *IEEE Transactions on Communications*, vol. 62, pp. 3144–3160, 2014.

[25] C. Jiang, Y. Chen, and K. J. R. Liu, "Multi-channel sensing and access game: Bayesian social learning with negative network externality," *IEEE Transactions on Wireless Communications*, vol. 13, pp. 2176–2188, 2014.

[26] Y. Zhu, W. Wu, D. Li, and L. Ding, "A double-auction-based mechanism to stimulate secondary users for cooperative sensing in cognitive radio networks," *IEEE Transactions on Vehicular Technology*, vol. 64, pp. 3770–3781, 2015.

[27] B. Zhang, Y. Chen, C. Wang, and K. J. R. Liu, "A Chinese restaurant game for learning and decision making in cognitive radio networks," *Computer Networks*, vol. 91, pp. 117–134, 2015.

[28] L. Shen, H. Wang, W. Zhang, and Z. Zhao, "Blind spectrum sensing for cognitive radio channels with noise uncertainty," *IEEE Transactions on Wireless Communications*, vol. 10, pp. 1721–1724, 2011.

[29] Y. Chen, B. Wang, W. S. Lin, Y. Wu, and K. J. R. Liu, "Cooperative peer-to-peer streaming: An evolutionary game-theoretic approach," *IEEE Transactions on Circuits and Systems for Video Technology*, vol. 20, pp. 1346–1357, 2010.

[30] Y. C. Liang, Y. Zeng, E. C. Y. Peh, and A. T. Hoang, "Sensing–throughput tradeoff for cognitive radio networks," *IEEE Transactions on Wireless Communications*, vol. 7, pp. 1326–1337, 2008.

[31] S. Ahmad, M. Liu, T. Javidi, Q. Zhao, and B. Krishnamachari, "Optimality of myopic sensing in multichannel opportunistic access," *IEEE Transactions on Information Theory*, vol. 55, pp. 4040–4050, 2009.

[32] R. Fisher, *The Genetical Theory of Natural Selection*. Clarendon Press, 1930.

[33] J. Rajasekharan and V. Koivunen, "Cooperative game-theoretic approach to spectrum sharing in cognitive radios," *Signal Processing*, vol. 106, pp. 15–29, 2015.

[34] B. Wang, K. J. R. Liu, and T. Clancy, "Evolutionary cooperative spectrum sensing game: how to collaborate?" *IEEE Transactions on Communications*, vol. 58, pp. 890–900, 2010.

Part II

Evolutionary Games

6 Evolutionary Game for Cooperative Peer-to-Peer Streaming

The peer-to-peer (P2P) video streaming systems introduce a large number of unnecessary traversal links causing substantial network inefficiency, although they have achieved promising results. Therefore, we discuss how to enable cooperation among "*group peers*" for addressing this problem and obtaining better streaming performance. Group peers are geographically neighboring peers with large intragroup upload and download bandwidths. Considering the peers' selfish nature, the cooperative streaming problem is formulated as an evolutionary game and the evolutionarily stable strategy (ESS) is introduced for each peer, which is the stable Nash equilibrium (NE) that no one would deviate from. Moreover, a simple and distributed learning algorithm is discussed for the peers aiming at converging to the ESSs, with which each peer decides whether to be a free rider that downloads data from the agents through simply tossing a coin, or whether to be an agent that downloads data from the peers outside the group, in which the probability of getting a head from the coin toss can be obtained from the history of the peer's own past payoffs. The strategy of a peer converges to the ESS, as is shown by the simulation results. Compared with the traditional noncooperative P2P schemes, the discussed cooperative scheme obtains much better performance due to social welfare, video quality (source rate), and probability of real-time streaming.

6.1 Introduction

The applications of "Video over internet protocol (IP)" have become more popular and have attracted millions of Internet users [1,2] with the rapid development of networking technologies, signal processing, and communications. For example, the client–server service model [3,4] is a simple solution to video streaming over the Internet in which the video is streamed directly from a server to clients. However, large-scale video streaming is impractical with the client–server service model since the server's upload bandwidth grows proportionally with a number of clients [5].

Thus, the P2P service model is proposed [6,7] for reducing the workload of the server, in which a peer acts not only as a server to upload data for the other peers within the network, but also as a client to download data from the network. Through this, the peers' upload bandwidth dramatically decreases the workload placed on the server, making large-scale video streaming possible. Several industrial large-scale

P2P video streaming systems have been upgraded recently, including Sopcast [8], Coolstreaming [7], PPLive [9], PPStream [10], and UUSee [11], which studies have shown can support thousands of users simultaneously [12].

P2P video streaming systems, have several drawbacks, although they have achieved promising results. The first drawback is that there are a large number of unnecessary traversal links within a provider's network because each P2P bit on the Verizon network traverses 1,000 miles and takes 5.5 metro-hops on average, as was observed in [13]. The second is that a great deal of cross-Internet service provider (ISP) traffic exists; that is, 50–90% of the existing local pieces within active peers are downloaded externally, as was shown in [14,15]. The third is that the differences in playback time among peers can be as much as 140 seconds [12], and a higher source rate could lead to greater lag. The fourth is that the assumption of most of the current P2P systems that all peers are willing to contribute their resources might not be true owing to the fact that P2P systems are self-organizing networks and the peers are selfish by nature [16,17]. Note that selfish peers would act as free riders if doing so is capable of improving their utility.

Within the literature, many approaches have been proposed in order to overcome these drawbacks. For example, Madhyastha et al. [18] and Karagiannis et al. [14] proposed to adopt locality-aware P2P schemes for reducing the download time by reducing unnecessary traversal links within and cross ISPs. Purandare and Guha [19] came up with an alliance-based peering scheme for improving the quality of service (QoS) and reducing the playback time lag. Xie et al. [13] came up with a provider portal for P2P applications (P4P) architecture that supports cooperative traffic control between network providers and applications. Moreover, reputation schemes [20,21] and payment mechanisms [22,23] have been proposed for stimulating selfish peers to contribute their resources, in which peers pay points for receiving data and earn points through forwarding data to others. However, the scalability of this kind of reputation-based mechanism or payment is often hindered by their need for the centralized architecture.

As a mathematical tool for analyzing the strategic interactions among multiple decision-makers, game theory has recently attracted much attention within multimedia social networking [24] and cognitive networking [25]. Many multimedia signal processing problems adopt game theory, such as multimedia communications [26] and video coding [27]. Within P2P networks, peers make intelligent decisions on their strategies of requesting and forwarding packets according to their own demands and the actions of other peers. Furthermore, the peers have no incentive to contribute their resources to others since they are rational and naturally selfish. Therefore, the intelligent interactions and behaviors of selfish peers are studied within P2P networks from a game-theoretic perspective [16,28], and a game-theoretic model is presented in [16] for analyzing nodes' behaviors and the incentive mechanism's influence by using a mental cost in order to demonstrate the level of the peer's altruism. In addition, we came up with a game-theoretic framework in [28] for designing attack-resistant and distributed cheat-proof cooperative stimulation strategies for P2P live streaming social networks.

Every peer is treated as an independent individual by most of the existing schemes; however, every peer is capable of having a large quantity of geographically neighboring peers with large intragroup upload and download bandwidths in reality (e.g., peers within the same campus, lab, or building). In this chapter, we label those geographically neighboring peers with large intragroup upload and download bandwidths as *group peers*, and the possible cooperation among *group peers* will be explored regardless of each peer's independent strategy for declining unnecessary traversal links and improving the efficiency of the network. Moreover, peers would act as free riders if doing so is capable of improving their utility since they are naturally selfish, in which case full cooperation cannot be ensured. Instead, through learning from their own payoff histories, rational peers would adapt their degree of cooperation to achieve better payoffs. Hence, an important question is: How should a group of selfish peers cooperate with each other to achieve better streaming performance?

6.2   The System Model and Utility Functions

6.2.1   System Model

Within Figure 6.1, there is a set of *group peers*[1] (three in this example) that are willing to view a real-time video streaming simultaneously. Each peer is capable of choosing either to be a normal peer or an *agent* peer within a group. If they serve as an agent, they would need to act as a client to download video data from the

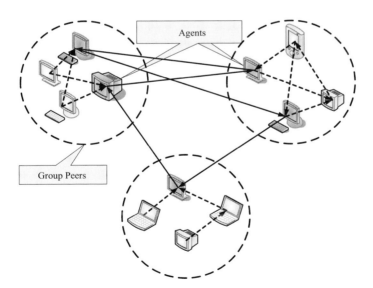

Figure 6.1 A cooperative streaming example.

---

[1] How to group the peers itself is an interesting problem. In this chapter, however, we assume that the peers have already been grouped and focus mainly on how the *group peers* cooperate with each other to achieve better streaming performance.

agents in other groups and as a server to upload video streams for the agents both in the same group and in other groups. If they decide not to be an agent, they will only need to download/upload data from/to the peers within the same group. Peers tend to be normal with the assumption that compared with those cross-groups, the download and upload bandwidth within the group is larger on the basis of their selfish nature. Because there might not be sufficient agents to download data from other groups, normal peers suffer the risk of receiving degraded streaming performance. The following question needs to be addressed for achieving good streaming performance through cooperation: Given a group of peers, which peers ought to serve as agents?

6.2.2   Utility Functions

Within a P2P network, a peer can not only benefit from downloading data from the other peers as a client, but also incurs a cost due to uploading data for the other peers acting as servers, in which case the cost could be the resources spent on uploading data, such as buffer size and bandwidth.

Given the *group peers* $u_1, u_2, \ldots, u_N$, it can be presumed that k peers are willing to serve as agents for downloading multimedia data from the peers outside the group. Let the download rate be the transmission speed between a corresponding peer outside the group and an agent. If the k agents' download rates are $r_1, r_2, \ldots, r_k$, then the total download rate of the *group peers* can be computed by

$$y_k = \sum_{i=1}^{k} r_i. \tag{6.1}$$

The download rates r_i are random variables since the agents choose peers outside the group independently and aimlessly for downloading data. The cumulative distribution function (CDF) of a peer's download bandwidth could be modeled as a linear function according to [29], and this means that the probability density function of a peer's download bandwidth is capable of being modeled as a uniform distribution (i.e., the r_i rates are distributed without exception).

We first consider a simple scenario without buffering to provide more insight into the cooperative streaming problem. Later we extend our discussion to the case where there is a buffering effect. For the scenario without buffering, the group peers could achieve real-time streaming and all of the group peers are capable of obtaining a certain gain G if, compared with the source rate r, the total download rate y_k is not smaller; otherwise some delay would arise. Within this circumstance, the gain is assumed to be zero. Hence, given the source rate r and the total download rate y_k, if peer u_i decides to be an agent, then the utility function of u_i can be calculated by

$$U_{A,i}(k) = Pr(y_k \geq r)G - C_i, \forall k \in [1, N], \tag{6.2}$$

where the cost of u_i is represented by C_i when they serve as an agent and the probability of achieving real-time streaming is represented by $Pr(y_k \geq r)$, which is capable of being calculated on the basis of Theorem 6.1.

The cost of uploading data to the other peers within the group can be negligible because the download and upload bandwidths within the group are large. Within this kind of circumstance, if peer u_i decides not to be an agent, then there is no cost for u_i and the utility function becomes

$$U_{N,i}(k) = \begin{cases} Pr(y_k \geq r)G, & \text{if } k \in [1, N-1]; \\ 0, & \text{if } k = 0. \end{cases} \tag{6.3}$$

THEOREM 6.1 *If $r_1, r_2, \ldots, r_k$ are independent and identically uniformly distributed within $[r^L, r^U]$, then $Pr(y_k \geq r)$ is computed by*

$$Pr(y_k \geq r) = \frac{1}{2k!} \sum_{l=0}^{k} (-1)^l \binom{k}{l} [(k-l)^k - sgn(\hat{r} - l)(\hat{r} - l)^k], \tag{6.4}$$

and when k is sufficiently large, $Pr(y_k \geq r)$ is capable of being approximated as

$$Pr(y_k \geq r) \approx Q\left(\frac{\hat{r} - \frac{k}{2}}{\sqrt{\frac{k}{12}}}\right), \tag{6.5}$$

where $\hat{r} = \frac{r - kr^L}{r^U - r^L}$ and $Q(x)$ represents the Gaussian tail function $\int_x^{\infty} \frac{1}{\sqrt{2\pi}} \exp^{-\frac{x^2}{2}} dx$.

Proof Let $\hat{r}_l = \frac{r_l - r^L}{r^U - r^L}, \forall l$, then $\hat{r}_1, \hat{r}_2, \ldots, \hat{r}_k$ are independent and identically uniformly distributed with $[0, 1]$. The characteristic function of $\hat{r}_l$ is calculated by

$$\phi(t) = \frac{i(1 - e^{it})}{t}. \tag{6.6}$$

Let $\hat{y}_k = \sum_{l=1}^{k} \hat{r}_l$, then the characteristic function of $\hat{y}_k$ is computed by

$$\phi_{\hat{y}_k}(t) = \left(\frac{i(1 - e^{it})}{t}\right)^k. \tag{6.7}$$

Therefore, the density function of $\hat{y}_k$ is

$$f_{\hat{y}_k}(y) = \mathcal{F}_t^{-1}\left[\left(\frac{i(1 - e^{it})}{t}\right)^k\right](y)$$

$$= \frac{1}{2(k-1)!} \sum_{l=0}^{k} (-1)^l \binom{k}{l} sgn(y - l)(y - l)^{k-1}. \tag{6.8}$$

Because $Pr(y_k \geq r) = Pr(\hat{y}_k \geq \hat{r})$, on the basis of (6.8), we have

$$Pr(y_k \geq r) = Pr(\hat{y}_k \geq \hat{r}) = \int_{\hat{r}}^{\infty} f_{\hat{y}_k}(y) dy$$

$$= \frac{1}{2k!} \sum_{l=0}^{k} (-1)^l \binom{k}{l} [(k-l)^k - sgn(\hat{r} - l)(\hat{r} - l)^k]. \tag{6.9}$$

When k is sufficiently large, based on the central limit theory, the distribution of $\hat{y}_k$ could be approximated as the Gaussian distribution $N(\frac{k}{2}, \frac{k}{12})$. Hence, we have

$$Pr(y_k \geq r) = Pr(\hat{y}_k \geq \hat{r}) \approx Q \left(\frac{\hat{r} - \frac{k}{2}}{\sqrt{\frac{k}{12}}} \right). \qquad (6.10)$$

6.3   Agent Selection within a Homogeneous Group

In the previous section, the system model and the peer utility function that represents that proper peers ought to serve as agents to download data from the peers outside the group in order to optimize the streaming performance were discussed. In this section, we will discuss the way of selecting agents within a homogeneous group in which the cost for all peers serving as agents is presumed to be the same.

6.3.1   Centralized Agent Selection

If there is a central controller that is capable of deciding which peers ought to act as agents, then a straightforward criterion for selecting proper agents is to maximize the social welfare and the sum of all peers' utilities.

Let $C_i = C$ be the cost of a peer serving as an agent within a homogeneous group. Thus the social welfare of an $N - peer$ group with k agents could be computed by

$$SW(k) = Pr(y_k \geq r)GN - kC. \qquad (6.11)$$

On the basis of (6.11), the agent selection problem for maximizing social welfare could be signified as

$$\max_k SW(k) = \max_k \left[Pr(y_k \geq r)GN - kC \right], \qquad (6.12)$$

where $k \in \{1, 2, \ldots, N\}$.

Through solving (6.12) the optimal $k^\star$ with the maximized social welfare could be found. Then the central controller could choose $k^\star$ peers from the group as agents for downloading data from the peers outside the group on the basis of some mechanism (e.g., the peers take turns serving as agents). But peers might take part in or leave the P2P network at any time since their behaviors are highly dynamic, and so the centralized approach might not be practical in such a case.

6.3.2   Distributed Agent Selection

A distributed approach in which every peer acts as an agent with probability x could be considered in order to overcome the drawbacks of the centralized approach. Then, due to (6.2) and (6.3), the group's social welfare could be calculated by

$$U_{total}(x) = \sum_{i=1}^{N} \binom{N}{i} x^i (1-x)^{N-i} [Pr(y_i \geq r)GN - iC]. \qquad (6.13)$$

The problem of finding an optimal x for maximizing social welfare could be signified as

$$\max_{x} \sum_{i=1}^{N} \binom{N}{i} x^i (1-x)^{N-i} [Pr(y_i \geq r)GN - iC]$$

$$s.t. \quad 0 \leq x \leq 1. \qquad (6.14)$$

However, peers are not as cooperative as a system controller/designer desires since they are selfish by nature. Though we are capable of finding the optimal $x^\star$ that maximizes social welfare by solving (6.14), this cannot maximize each peer's own utility. Hence, when peers are selfish, the optimal $x^\star$ is not attainable. Furthermore, the optimization problem's solution represented within (6.14) is not stable because any perturbation would lead to a new solution.

6.3.3   Evolutionary Cooperative Streaming Game

The concept of an ESS [30,31] is adopted to provide a robust equilibrium strategy for selfish peers, which can be defined as follows.

DEFINITION 6.2   A strategy $a^\star$ stands for an ESS if and only if, $\forall a \neq a^\star$, $a^\star$ satisfies

* Equilibrium condition: $U_i(a, a^\star) \leq U_i(a^\star, a^\star)$, and
* Stability condition: if $U_i(a, a^\star) = U_i(a^\star, a^\star)$, $U_i(a, a) < U_i(a^\star, a)$,

where the utility of player i is represented by $U_i(a_1, a_2)$ when they adopt strategy a_1 and another player adopts strategy a_2.

All peers would cheat if cheating could improve their payoffs owing to their selfish natures, and this means that all peers are uncertain of the utilities and actions of the other peers. Within this circumstance, different strategies would be tried by peers in each iteration of the game. The peers would learn from their strategic interactions using the methodology of understanding by building in order to improve their utility. During the process, the proportion of peers using a certain pure strategy might alter. Such a population evolution could be modeled by replicator dynamics; specifically, let x_a stands for the probability of a peer using pure strategy $a \in \mathcal{A}$, where $\mathcal{A} = \{A, N\}$ represents the set of pure strategies including being an agent (A) and never being an agent (N). Through replicator dynamics, the evolution dynamics of x_a are computed using the following differential equation:

$$\dot{x}_a = \eta [\bar{U}(a, x_{-a}) - \bar{U}(x_a)] x_a, \qquad (6.15)$$

where a positive scale factor is represented by η, the average payoff of the peers using pure strategy a is represented by $\bar{U}(a, x_{-a})$, the set of peers that adopt pure strategies other than a is represented by x_{-a}, and the average payoff of all peers is represented by $\bar{U}(x_a)$.

Within (6.15), compared with the average level, if pure strategy a could lead to a higher payoff, the probability of a peer adopting it would grow at the rate $\dot{x}_a / x_a$, which is proportional to the difference between the average payoff of all peers (i.e., $\bar{U}(x_a)$) and the average payoff of using strategy a (i.e., $\bar{U}(a, x_{-a})$).

6.3.4 Analysis of the Cooperative Streaming Game

According to (6.2) and (6.3), if a peer chooses to be an agent, their average payoff could be calculated by

$$\bar{U}_A(x) = \sum_{i=0}^{N-1} \binom{N-1}{i} x^i (1-x)^{N-1-i} [Pr(y_{i+1} \geq r)G - C], \tag{6.16}$$

where x stands for the probability of a peer being an agent and $\binom{N-1}{i} x^i (1-x)^{N-1-i}$ represents the probability that there are i agents out of $N-1$ other peers.

Similarly, the average payoff of a peer if they choose not to be an agent is signified by

$$\bar{U}_N(x) = \sum_{i=1}^{N-1} \binom{N-1}{i} x^i (1-x)^{N-1-i} Pr(y_i \geq r)G. \tag{6.17}$$

On the basis of (6.16) and (6.17), the average payoff of a peer is

$$\bar{U}(x) = x\bar{U}_A(x) + (1-x)\bar{U}_N(x). \tag{6.18}$$

Substituting (6.18) back into (6.15), we have

$$\dot{x} = \eta x(1-x)[\bar{U}_A(x) - \bar{U}_N(x)]. \tag{6.19}$$

No player would deviate from the optimal strategy at equilibrium $x^\star$, and this means $\dot{x}^\star = 0$. We could obtain $x^\star = 0$, 1, or the solutions to $\bar{U}_A(x) = \bar{U}_N(x)$. Because $\dot{x}^\star = 0$ is the only necessary condition in order for $x^\star$ to be an ESS, the sufficient condition for every ESS candidate is examined, and we draw the following conclusions with the proofs within Theorems 6.4, 6.5, and 6.6.

- $x^\star = 0$ represents an ESS only when $Pr(y_1 \geq r)G - C \leq 0$.
- $x^\star = 1$ represents an ESS only when $Pr(y_N \geq r)G - Pr(y_{N-1} \geq r)G \geq C$.
- Let $x^\star$ be the solution to $\bar{U}_A(x) = \bar{U}_N(x)$ and $x^\star \in (0, 1)$. Then, $x^\star$ represents an ESS.

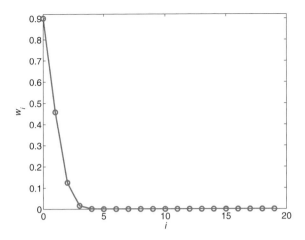

Figure 6.2 The deceasing property of w_i.

LEMMA 6.3   *Let* $f(x) = \bar{U}_A(x) - \bar{U}_N(x)$, *then* $f'(x) < 0$, $\forall x \in [0,1]$.

Proof   On the basis of (6.16) and (6.17), we have

$$f(x) = \sum_{i=0}^{N-1} \binom{N-1}{i} x^i (1-x)^{N-1-i} w_i - C, \tag{6.20}$$

where $w_i = [Pr(y_{i+1} \geq r) - Pr(y_i \geq r)]G$.

- $\forall x \in (0,1)$, through taking the derivative of $f(x)$ over x, we have

$$f'(x) = \sum_{i=0}^{N-1} \binom{N-1}{i} x^{i-1}(1-x)^{N-2-i}[i-(N-1)x]w_i,$$

$$= \sum_{i=0}^{i_1} \binom{N-1}{i} x^{i-1}(1-x)^{N-2-i}[i-(N-1)x]w_i$$

$$+ \sum_{i=i_1+1}^{N-1} \binom{N-1}{i} x^{i-1}(1-x)^{N-2-i}[i-(N-1)x]w_i, \tag{6.21}$$

where i_1 is the integer such that $i_1 \leq (N-1)x$ and $i_1 + 1 > (N-1)x$.

Because w_i represents the additional gain through introducing one more agent into the i-agent system, as is shown in Figure 6.2, it is a decreasing function due to i, and this means that $w_i \geq w_{i_1}, \forall i \leq i_1$ and $w_i \leq w_{i_1}, \forall i > i_1$. Therefore, according to (6.21), we have

$$f'(x) < \sum_{i=0}^{i_1} \binom{N-1}{i} x^{i-1}(1-x)^{N-2-i}[i-(N-1)x]w_{i_1}$$

$$+ \sum_{i=i_1+1}^{N-1} \binom{N-1}{i} x^{i-1}(1-x)^{N-2-i}[i-(N-1)x]w_{i_1},$$

$$= w_{i_1} \sum_{i=0}^{N-1} \binom{N-1}{i} x^{i-1}(1-x)^{N-2-i}[i-(N-1)x],$$

$$= w_{i_1} \frac{d\left[\sum_{i=0}^{N-1} \binom{N-1}{i} x^i(1-x)^{N-1-i}\right]}{dx},$$

$$= 0. \tag{6.22}$$

Hence, $f'(x) < 0, \forall x \in (0,1)$.

- The derivative of $f(x)$ over x at $x = 0$ could be calculated by

$$f'(0) = \lim_{\varepsilon \to 0} \frac{f(\varepsilon) - f(0)}{\varepsilon}$$

$$= \lim_{\varepsilon \to 0} \frac{\sum_{i=0}^{N-1} \binom{N-1}{i} \varepsilon^i(1-\varepsilon)^{N-1-i}w_i - w_0}{\varepsilon}$$

$$= \lim_{\varepsilon \to 0} \frac{(1-\varepsilon)^{N-1}w_0 - w_0}{\varepsilon} + \lim_{\varepsilon \to 0} \frac{(N-1)\varepsilon(1-\varepsilon)^{N-2}w_1}{\varepsilon}$$

$$= (N-1)(w_1 - w_0)$$

$$< 0. \tag{6.23}$$

where the last inequality comes from the fact that w_i represents a decreasing function in terms of i.

- Similarly, the derivative of $f(x)$ over x at $x = 1$ can be computed by

$$f'(1) = \lim_{\varepsilon \to 0} \frac{f(1) - f(1-\varepsilon)}{\varepsilon}$$

$$= \lim_{\varepsilon \to 0} \frac{w_{N-1} - \sum_{i=0}^{N-1} \binom{N-1}{i}(1-\varepsilon)^i \varepsilon^{N-1-i}w_i}{\varepsilon}$$

$$= \lim_{\varepsilon \to 0} \frac{w_{N-1} - (1-\varepsilon)^{N-1}w_{N-1}}{\varepsilon} + \lim_{\varepsilon \to 0} \frac{-(N-1)(1-\varepsilon)^{N-2}\varepsilon w_{N-2}}{\varepsilon}$$

$$= (N-1)(w_{N-1} - w_{N-2})$$

$$< 0. \tag{6.24}$$

where the last inequality comes from the fact that w_i is a decreasing function due to i.

In all, $f'(x) < 0, \forall x \in [0,1]$.

THEOREM 6.4   *The condition for $x^\star = 0$ to be an ESS is $Pr(y_1 \geq r)G - C \leq 0$.*

Proof   On the basis of (6.16)–(6.18), the utility of a peer adopting mixed strategy x and of the other peers adopting mixed strategy $x^\star = 0$ could be signified as

$$\bar{U}(x,0) = \bar{U}_N(0) + (\bar{U}_A(0) - \bar{U}_N(0))x,$$

where $\bar{U}_A(0) = Pr(y_1 \geq r)G - C$ and $\bar{U}_N(0) = 0$.

- If $Pr(y_1 \geq r)G - C > 0$ (i.e., $\bar{U}_A(0) > \bar{U}_N(0)$), every peer would deviate to $x = 1$ for obtaining $\bar{U}_A(0)$ rather than $\bar{U}_N(0)$.
- If $Pr(y_1 \geq r)G - C < 0$ (i.e., $\bar{U}_A(0) < \bar{U}_N(0)$), every peer would stay at $x = 0$ to obtain $\bar{U}_N(0)$ rather than $\bar{U}_A(0)$.
- If $Pr(y_1 \geq r)G - C = 0$ (i.e., $\bar{U}_A(0) = \bar{U}_N(0)$), then $\bar{U}(x,0) = 0 \; \forall x$ and $f(0) = \bar{U}_A(0) - \bar{U}_N(0) = 0$. On the basis of Lemma 6.3, it can be seen that $f'(x) < 0 \; \forall x \in [0,1]$, so $f(x) = \bar{U}_A(x) - \bar{U}_N(x) < 0$. Within this circumstance, $\bar{U}(0,x) = \bar{U}_N(x) > \bar{U}(x,x) = \bar{U}_N(x) + (\bar{U}_A(x) - \bar{U}_N(x))x$, which means $x^\star = 0$ represents an ESS based on Definition 6.2.

Hence, $x^\star = 0$ represents an ESS only when $Pr(y_1 \geq r)G - C \leq 0$.

THEOREM 6.5   *The condition for $x^\star = 1$ to be an ESS is $Pr(y_N \geq r)G - Pr(y_{N-1} \geq r)G \geq C$.*

Proof   On the basis of (6.16)–(6.18), the utility of a peer adopting mixed strategy x and of the other peers adopting mixed strategy $x^\star = 1$ could be signified as

$$\bar{U}(x,1) = \bar{U}_N(1) + (\bar{U}_A(1) - \bar{U}_N(1))x,$$

where $\bar{U}_A(1) = Pr(y_N \geq r)G - C$ and $\bar{U}_N(1) = Pr(y_{N-1} \geq r)G$.

- If $Pr(y_N \geq r)G - Pr(y_{N-1} \geq r)G < C$ (i.e., $\bar{U}_N(1) > \bar{U}_A(1)$), every peer would deviate to $x = 0$ for obtaining $\bar{U}_N(1)$ rather than $\bar{U}_A(1)$.
- If $Pr(y_N \geq r)G - Pr(y_{N-1} \geq r)G > C$ (i.e., $\bar{U}_N(1) < \bar{U}_A(1)$), every peer would stay at $x = 1$ for obtaining $\bar{U}_A(1)$ rather than $\bar{U}_N(1)$.
- If $Pr(y_N \geq r)G - Pr(y_{N-1} \geq r)G = C$ (i.e., $\bar{U}_N(1) = \bar{U}_A(1)$), then $\bar{U}(x,1) = \bar{U}_N(1) \; \forall x$ and $f(1) = \bar{U}_A(1) - \bar{U}_N(1) = 0$. On the basis of Lemma 6.3, it can be seen that $f'(x) < 0 \; \forall x \in [0,1]$, so $f(x) = \bar{U}_A(x) - \bar{U}_N(x) > 0$. In such a case, $\bar{U}(1,x) = \bar{U}_N(x) + (\bar{U}_A(x) - \bar{U}_N(x))1 > \bar{U}(x,x) = \bar{U}_N(x) + (\bar{U}_A(x) - \bar{U}_N(x))x$, which means $x^\star = 1$ is an ESS based on Definition 6.2.

Hence, $x^\star = 1$ represents an ESS only when $Pr(y_N \geq r)G - Pr(y_{N-1} \geq r)G \geq C$.

THEOREM 6.6   *If $x^\star \in (0,1)$ represents a solution to $\bar{U}_A(x) = \bar{U}_N(x)$, then $x^\star$ represents an ESS.*

Proof   Let $\bar{U}_i(x,x^\star)$ be the utility of player i when player i adopts mixed strategy x and other users adopt mixed strategy $x^\star$. Then we have

$$\bar{U}_i(x,x^\star) = x\bar{U}_A(x^\star) + (1-x)\bar{U}_N(x^\star). \tag{6.25}$$

Since $x^\star$ is a solution to $\bar{U}_A(x) = \bar{U}_N(x)$, we have $\bar{U}_A(x^\star) = \bar{U}_N(x^\star)$. Hence, (6.25) turns into

$$\bar{U}_i(x, x^\star) = \bar{U}_A(x^\star) = \bar{U}_i(x^\star, x^\star), \tag{6.26}$$

which means $x^\star$ satisfies the equilibrium condition represented in Definition 6.2.

Furthermore, on the basis of (6.18), we have

$$\bar{U}_i(x, x) = \bar{U}_N(x) + (\bar{U}_A(x) - \bar{U}_N(x))x, \tag{6.27}$$

and

$$\bar{U}_i(x^\star, x) = \bar{U}_N(x) + (\bar{U}_A(x) - \bar{U}_N(x))x^\star. \tag{6.28}$$

Hence we have

$$\bar{U}_i(x^\star, x) - \bar{U}_i(x, x) = (\bar{U}_A(x) - \bar{U}_N(x))(x^\star - x). \tag{6.29}$$

From Lemma 6.3 it can be seen that $f(x) = \bar{U}_A(x) - \bar{U}_N(x)$ is a monotonically decreasing function. Because $\bar{U}_A(x^\star) = \bar{U}_N(x^\star)$, $\bar{U}_A(x) - \bar{U}_N(x) > 0$ if $x < x^\star$ and $\bar{U}_A(x) - \bar{U}_N(x) < 0$ if $x > x^\star$. Hence, $(\bar{U}_A(x) - \bar{U}_N(x))(x^\star - x) > 0, \forall x \neq x^\star$, i.e.,

$$\bar{U}_i(x^\star, x) > \bar{U}_i(x, x), \forall x \neq x^\star, \tag{6.30}$$

which means $x^\star$ satisfies the stability condition represented in Definition 6.2.

On the basis of (6.26) and (6.30), it can be seen that $x^\star$ represents an ESS.

6.4   Agent Selection within a Heterogeneous Group

In this section, the methods of selecting agents within a heterogeneous group in which the costs of the peers acting as agents are different will be discussed.

Let x_{i,a_i} stand for the probability of peer u_i adopting the pure strategy $a_i \in \mathcal{A}$. Through replicator dynamics, the evolution dynamics of x_{i,a_i} are signified by the following differential equation:

$$\dot{x}_{i,a_i} = \eta[\bar{U}_i(a_i, x_{-i}) - \bar{U}_i(x_i)]x_{i,a_i}, \tag{6.31}$$

where a positive scale factor is represented by η, the average payoff of peer u_i using pure strategy a_i is represented by $\bar{U}_i(a_i, x_{-i})$, and the average payoff of peer u_i using mixed strategy x_i is represented by $\bar{U}_i(x_i)$.

We analyze a two-player game first because it is not easy to signify $\bar{U}_i(a_i, x_{-i})$ and $\bar{U}_i(x_i)$ within a compact form generally. The observations in the two-player game are then generalized to the multiplayer game.

6.4.1   Two-Player Game

Let x_2 and x_1 be the probability of u_2 and u_1 being agents, respectively, and let $B_1 = Pr(y_1 \geq r)G$ and $B_2 = Pr(y_2 \geq r)G$. Then the payoff matrix of u_1 and u_2 could be signified as in Table 6.1. Hence the average payoff $\bar{U}_1(A, x_2)$ could be calculated by

Table 6.1. Utility table of a two-player game.

	"A"	"N"
"A"	$(B_2 - C_1, B_2 - C_2)$	$(B_1 - C_1, B_1)$
"N"	$(B_1, B_1 - C_2)$	$(0,0)$

$$\bar{U}_1(A, x_2) = (B_2 - C_1)x_2 + (B_1 - C_1)(1 - x_2), \tag{6.32}$$

and the average payoff $\bar{U}_1(x_1)$ turns into

$$\bar{U}_1(x_1) = (B_2 - C_1)x_1x_2 + (B_1 - C_1)x_1(1 - x_2) + B_1(1 - x_1)x_2. \tag{6.33}$$

On the basis of (6.31), the replicator dynamics equation of u_1 is signified by

$$\dot{x}_1 = \eta x_1(1 - x_1)[B_1 - C_1 - (2B_1 - B_2)x_2]. \tag{6.34}$$

Similarly, the replicator dynamics equation of u_2 could be calculated by

$$\dot{x}_2 = \eta x_2(1 - x_2)[B_1 - C_2 - (2B_1 - B_2)x_1]. \tag{6.35}$$

At equilibrium, it can be seen that $\dot{x}_1 = 0$ and $\dot{x}_2 = 0$. On the basis of (6.34) and (6.35), we can obtain five equilibria: $(0,0)$, $(0,1)$, $(1,0)$, $(1,1)$, and the mixed strategy equilibrium $\left(\frac{B_1 - C_2}{2B_1 - B_2}, \frac{B_1 - C_1}{2B_1 - B_2}\right)$.

According to [32], the equilibrium of the replicator dynamics equations is an ESS if it is a locally and asymptotically stable point within a dynamic system. Therefore, we can examine whether the five equilibria are ESSs by regarding (6.34) and (6.35) as a nonlinear dynamic system and analyzing the corresponding Jacobian matrix. Through taking partial derivatives of (6.34) and (6.35), the Jacobian matrix could be signified as

$$J = \begin{bmatrix} \frac{\partial \dot{x}_1}{\partial x_1} & \frac{\partial \dot{x}_1}{\partial x_2} \\ \frac{\partial \dot{x}_2}{\partial x_1} & \frac{\partial \dot{x}_2}{\partial x_2} \end{bmatrix} = \eta \begin{bmatrix} J_{11} & J_{12} \\ J_{21} & J_{22} \end{bmatrix}, \tag{6.36}$$

where $J_{11} = (1 - 2x_1)(B_1 - C_1 - (2B_1 - B_2)x_2)$, $J_{12} = -x_1(1 - x_1)(2B_1 - B_2)$, $J_{21} = -x_2(1 - x_2)(2B_1 - B_2)$, and $J_{22} = (1 - 2x_2)(B_1 - C_2 - (2B_1 - B_2)x_1)$.

Asymptotic stability demands that $det(J) > 0$ and $tr(J) < 0$ [32]. By substituting the five equilibria (i.e., $(0,0)$, $(0,1)$, $(1,0)$, $(1,1)$, and $\left(\frac{B_1 - C_2}{2B_1 - B_2}, \frac{B_1 - C_1}{2B_1 - B_2}\right)$), into (6.36), it can be concluded that

- If $B_2 - B_1 - C_1 > 0$ and $B_2 - B_1 - C_2 > 0$, there is a unique ESS $(1,1)$ where both u_1 and u_2 converge to be agents.
- Else if $B_2 - B_1 - C_1 > 0$ and $B_2 - B_1 - C_2 < 0$, there is a unique ESS $(1,0)$ where u_1 converges to be an agent and u_2 converges to be a free rider.
- Else if $B_2 - B_1 - C_1 < 0$ and $B_2 - B_1 - C_2 > 0$, there is a unique ESS $(0,1)$ where u_2 converges to be an agent and u_1 converges to be a free rider.
- Else there are two ESSs $(1,0)$ and $(0,1)$ where the converged strategy profiles rely on the initial strategy profiles.

From the analysis above, the peer tends to be an agent when the gain of being an agent $(B_2 - B_1)$ is greater than the cost $(C_1$ or $C_2)$, and the peer with a higher cost tends to be a free rider and depends on the peer with a lower cost.

6.4.2   Multiplayer Game

From the analysis of the two-player game, it could be inferred that the peer with a higher cost (C_i) tends to obtain benefits from the peer with a lower cost, and this observation could be extended to the multiplayer game. If there are more than two peers within the game, the strategy of the peers with higher $C_i's$ would converge to "N" with a greater probability, and the peers with lower $C_i's$ tend to be agents because they would endure relatively heavier losses if there is no one to serve as an agent.

6.5   A Distributed Learning Algorithm for an ESS

Within Sections 6.3 and 6.4, the ESS could be found through solving the replicator dynamics equations ((6.19) or (6.31)), yet this demands the exchange of private information and strategies that are adopted by other peers. In this section, we will discuss a distributed learning algorithm that could converge to an ESS gradually without information exchange.

First, we discretize the replicator dynamics equation represented in (6.31) as

$$x_i(t + 1) = x_i(t) + \eta \left[\bar{U}_i(A, x_{-i}(t)) - \bar{U}_i(x_i(t)) \right] x_i(t), \qquad (6.37)$$

where t represents the slot index and $x_i(t)$ represents the probability of u_i being an agent during slot t. Here we presume that every slot could be further divided into M subslots and every peer is capable of choosing to be an agent or not at the beginning of every subslot.

Within (6.37), first we ought to calculate $\bar{U}_i(A, x_{-i}(t))$ and $\bar{U}_i(x_i(t))$ for updating $x_i(t + 1)$. Let us signify an indicator function $\mathbf{1}_i(t, k)$ as

$$\mathbf{1}_i(t, q) = \begin{cases} 1, & \text{if } u_i \text{ is an agent at subslot } q \text{ in slot } t, \\ 0, & \text{else,} \end{cases} \qquad (6.38)$$

where the subslot index is represented by q.

The immediate utility of u_i at subslot q within slot t could be calculated by

$$U_i(t, q) = \begin{cases} G - C_i, & \text{if } u_i \text{ is an agent and } r^t \geq r, \\ -C_i, & \text{if } u_i \text{ is an agent and } r^t < r, \\ G, & \text{if } u_i \text{ is not an agent and } r^t \geq r, \\ 0, & \text{if } u_i \text{ is not an agent and } r^t < r, \end{cases} \qquad (6.39)$$

where r^t stands for the total download rate of the agents and r stands for the source rate.

Algorithm 6: A distributed learning algorithm for an ESS.

(1) Given the step size η and the slot index $t = 0$, every peer u_i initializes x_i with $x_i(0)$.

(2) During slot t, for $q = 1 : M$,

- u_i tosses a coin with probability $x_i(t)$ being heads. If the outcome is heads, u_i serves as an agent and downloads data from the peers outside the group with download rate $r_i(t, q)$. In addition, if the outcome is tails, u_i acts as a free rider and downloads the data from the agents.
- u_i computes their utility by adopting (6.39).
- u_i computes the indicator function by adopting (6.38).

(3) Then u_i approximates $\bar{U}_i(A, x_{-i}(t))$ and $\bar{U}_i(x_i(t))$ by adopting (6.40) and (6.41).

(4) Finally, u_i updates the probability of being an agent $x_i(t)$ by adopting (6.37).

Then, $\bar{U}_i(A, x_{-i}(t))$ could be approximated by adopting

$$\bar{U}_i(A, x_{-i}(t)) = \frac{\sum_{q=1}^{M} U_i(t, q) \mathbf{1}_i(t, q)}{\sum_{q=1}^{M} \mathbf{1}_i(t, q)}. \tag{6.40}$$

Similarly $\bar{U}_i(x_i(t))$ can be approximated as

$$\bar{U}_i(x_i(t)) = \frac{1}{M} \sum_{q=1}^{M} U_i(t, q). \tag{6.41}$$

In view of (6.37)–(6.41), u_i could learn the ESS gradually. Within Algorithm 6, the detailed procedures of the proposed distributed learning algorithm are summarized.

6.6 Simulation Results

Within all of the following simulations, we set the parameters G, r^L, and r^U to be 1, 50, and 800, respectively. In the rest of this chapter, we signify the centralized approach maximizing the social welfare represented within (6.12) as **MSW-C**, the distributed approach maximizing the social welfare represented within (6.14) as **MSW-D**, and the ESS-based approach as **ESS-D** for convenience. The methods proposed are compared with the traditional P2P noncooperation method, signified as **Non-Coop**. Within **Non-Coop**, every peer acts as an individual and aimlessly selects some peers for downloading video streams. This kind of protocol has been universally adopted within the existing P2P systems such as PPLive [9] and Coolstreaming [7].

We illustrate the social welfare (the sum of all peers' utilities) comparison between different approaches in the first simulation where it is assumed that there are 20 homogeneous peers and the cost C is 0.1. **MSW-C** achieves the best social welfare performance, as is shown in Figure 6.3, because its objective function is maximizing

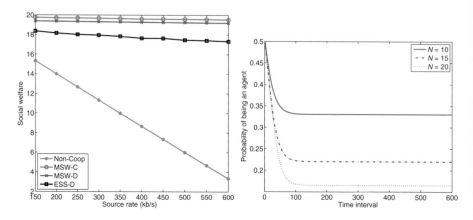

Figure 6.3 The social welfare comparison among **Non-Coop**, **MSW-C**, **MSW-D**, and **ESS-D**.

Figure 6.4 Behavior dynamics of a homogeneous group of peers.

social welfare with a pure strategy. **MSW-D** achieves the second best social welfare performance by adopting the mixed strategy for maximizing social welfare. However, the solution to **MSW-D** is not stable, as discussed previously. Yet a stable NE solution could be obtained through **ESS-D**, at the cost of a slight loss of social welfare. Nevertheless, all three algorithms perform much better compared with the **Non-Coop** method. In **Non-Coop**, social welfare performance decreases linearly with regard to the source rate. All three discussed algorithms could maintain high social welfare performance even with large source rates through cooperation and selecting the proper number of agents adaptively.

In the second simulation, the convergence property of **ESS-D** is evaluated. Figure 6.4 shows the replicator dynamics of the cooperation streaming game with homogeneous peers where $C = 0.1$ and $r = 500$ and in which, starting from a high initial value, all peers constantly reduce their probabilities of being an agent because each peer is more often able to achieve a higher payoff through being a free rider. However, the probability of being an agent would finally converge to a certain value that is determined by the number of peers since an extremely low probability of being an agent increases the possibility of no peer being an agent.

Th replicator dynamics of the cooperation streaming game with 20 heterogeneous peers are represented in Figure 6.5, where $r = 500$ and the cost C_i is selected from $[0.1, 0.3]$ aimlessly. Then we further presume that C_i increases monotonically within i, in which the lowest cost is experienced by u_1 and the highest cost is experienced by u_{20}. In Figure 6.5, the peers with lower costs (u_1, u_2, and u_3 in this simulation) converge to be agents, while the peers with higher costs ($u_4 - u_{20}$ in this simulation) converge to be free riders, which coincides with the conclusion "*the peers with lower costs tend to be agents since they suffer relatively higher losses if no one serves as an agent.*" We only represent the behavior dynamics of $u_1 - u_4$. All other peers $u_5 - u_{20}$ show similar behavior dynamics to u_4, and they all converge to be free riders.

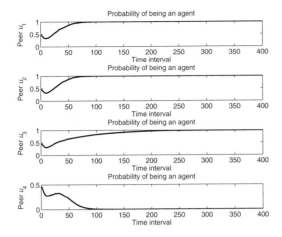

Figure 6.5 Behavior dynamics of a heterogeneous group of peers.

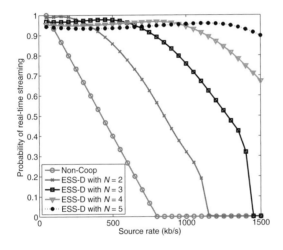

Figure 6.6 Comparison of the probability of real-time streaming between **Non-Coop** and **ESS-D**.

In the third simulation, the performance of **ESS-D** and **Non-Coop** in terms of the probability of real-time streaming is compared, which is signified by the probability of the total download rate being greater than the source rate. The simulation results are represented in Figure 6.6, which shows that the probability of achieving real-time streaming could be significantly improved with cooperation, especially in the high source rate region. We also show that the probability of achieving of real-time streaming rises when N rises in the high source rate region.

The visual quality comparison between **ESS-D** and **Non-Coop** is represented in Figure 6.7. In this simulation, the probability of achieving real-time streaming is fixed at 0.85. Based on Figure 6.6, the corresponding source rates for "**Non-Coop**," "**ESS-D** with $N = 2$," "**ESS-D** with $N = 3$," and "**ESS-D** with $N = 4$" are around 100 kb/s,

Figure 6.7 Visual quality comparison: (a) **Non-Coop**; (b) **ESS-D** with $N = 2$; (c) **ESS-D** with $N = 3$; (d) **ESS-D** with $N = 4$.

300 kb/s, 520 kb/s, and 720 kb/s, respectively. Through setting the above source rates as the target bit rates, we encode the Foreman sequence in the Common Intermediate Format (CIF) by adopting the H.264 encoder. From Figure 6.7, the video visual quality with the proposed **ESS-D** is much better than that with **Non-Coop**.

We then represent the simulation results of the source rate versus utility. As is shown in Figure 6.8, without cooperation, the source rate cannot be larger than 130 kb/s if the peer requires a utility of around 0.8. However, with cooperation, the source rate is capable of being more than 400 kb/s, even when there are only two peers. Hence cooperation enables peers to achieve much higher-quality video with the same utility.

In the fourth simulation, the case in which the peers in the same group are viewing multiple channels is considered, with L being the number of the channels. It is assumed that for all channels the source rate is the same, there are 20 homogenous peers with cost $C = 0.1$, and the downloading and uploading are decoupled within the proposed **ESS-D** algorithm, which is similar to the view-upload decoupling scheme [33]. Cooperation among all peers is allowed, by which the agent could download source data that they are not viewing. The source rate could not be larger than 130 kb/s in the **Non-Coop** method without cooperation if the peer requires a utility of around 0.8, as is shown in Figure 6.9. But with the **ESS-D** algorithm, the

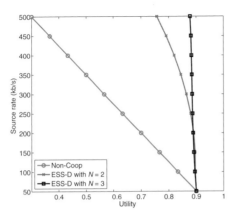

Figure 6.8 Single-source rate comparison between **Non-Coop** and **ESS-D**.

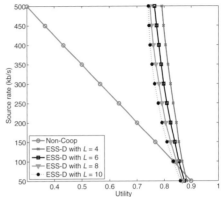

Figure 6.9 Multisource rate comparison between **Non-Coop** and **ESS-D**.

source rate is capable of being around 240 kb/s, even when eight different channels are viewed by the peers. This phenomenon fully illustrates the efficiency of the discussed method.

In the last simulation, buffering effects are taken into consideration, in which the gain in utility would not drop to zero but rather retain a positive value when compared with the source rate, and the total download rate is smaller due to the existence of the buffering effects. One possible utility function that considers the buffering effect is represented by

$$U_{A,i}(k) = \frac{1}{\ln(r)} E\left[\ln(y_k)\right] G - C_i, \forall k \in [1, N],$$

$$U_{N,i}(k) = \begin{cases} \frac{1}{\ln(r)} E\left[\ln(y_k)\right] G, & \text{if } k \in [1, N-1]; \\ 0, & \text{if } k = 0. \end{cases} \quad (6.42)$$

From the utility function (6.42), the gain rises as the total download rate y_k rises for any given source rate r. Moreover, an increase within the high-y_k region ought to lead to a less significant gain than that in the low-y_k region [34] since the increased data in the buffer leads to a smaller probability of playback delay. Here we adopt the ln(.) function for characterizing such properties. However, other functions that have similar properties could also be adopted.

The social welfare comparison between **Non-Coop** and **ESS-D** using the utility function from (6.42) is represented in Figure 6.10. From Figure 6.10, the social welfare performance of **Non-Coop** no longer declines linearly with the source rate when the utility function in (6.42) is adopted because the gain would not drop to zero when compared with the source rate with the existence of buffers, for which the total download rate is smaller. Nevertheless, **ESS-D** could still lead to a much higher social welfare performance for all source rates compared with **Non-Coop**. Moreover, notice that all of the analyses within Section 6.3 are still applicable to the utility function in (6.42).

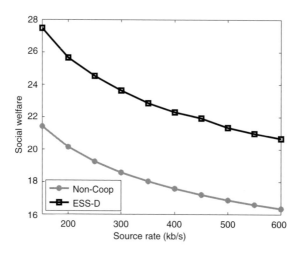

Figure 6.10 The social welfare comparison between **Non-Coop** and **ESS-D** when the utility function is defined as (6.42).

6.7   Conclusion

In this chapter, we discuss a cooperative streaming scheme for addressing the network inefficiency of traditional noncooperative P2P schemes. We answer the question of how a group of selfish peers with large intragroup upload and download bandwidths cooperate with each other to achieve better streaming performance through formulating the problem as an evolutionary game and introducing the ESS for each peer. Then we further discuss a distributed learning algorithm for each peer to converge to the ESS through learning from their own past payoff history. From the simulation results, and compared with the traditional noncooperative P2P schemes, much better social welfare is achieved using the discussed algorithm, the probability of achieving real-time streaming is higher, and video quality (higher source rate) is better. Moreover, the discussed cooperative streaming scheme permits peers that are viewing different videos to cooperate with each other, mutually improving the streaming performance by incorporating the recently presented view-upload decoupling scheme.

References

[1] "AccuStream media research." www.accustreamresearch.com.

[2] "YouTube." www.youtube.com.

[3] S. Deering and D. Cheriton, "Multicast routing in datagram inter-networks and extended lans," *ACM Transactions on Computer Systems*, vol. 8, pp. 85–111, 1990.

[4] L. Kontothanassis, R. Sitaraman, J. Wein, D. Hong, R. Kleinberg, B. Mancuso, D. Shaw, and D. Stodolsky, "A transport layer for live streaming in a content delivery network," *Proceedings of the IEEE*, vol. 92, pp. 1408–1419, 2004.

[5] Y. Liu, Y. Guo, and C. Liang, "A survey on peer-to-peer video streaming systems," *Journal of Peer-to-Peer Networking and Applications*, vol. 1, pp. 18–28, 2008.

[6] Y. Chu, S. G. Rao, and H. Zhang, "A case for end system multicast," in *ACM SIGMETRICS*, 2000.

[7] X. Zhang, J. Liu, B. Li, and T.-S. P. Yum, "Coolstreaming: A data-driven overlay network for peer-to-peer live media streaming," in *IEEE Conference on Computer Communications (INFOCOM)*, 2005.

[8] "Sopcast." www.sopcast.com.

[9] "PPLive." www.pplive.com.

[10] "PPStream." www.ppstream.com.

[11] "UUSee." www.uusee.com.

[12] X. Hei, C. Liang, J. Liang, Y. Liu, and K. W. Ross, "A measurement study of a large-scale P2P IPTV system," *IEEE Transactions on Multimedia*, vol. 9, pp. 1672–1687, 2007.

[13] H. Xie, Y. R. Yang, A. Krishnamurthy, Y. Liu, and A. Siberschatz, "P4P: provider portal for applications," in *ACM SIGCOMM*, 2008.

[14] T. Karagiannis, P. Rodriguez, and K. Papagiannaki, "Should Internet service providers fear peer-assisted content distribution?" in *Proc. Internet Measurement Conference*, 2005.

[15] S. Seetharaman and M. Ammar, "Characterizing and mitigating inter-domain policy violations in overlay routes," in *Proc. IEEE International Conference on Network Protocols*, 2006.

[16] M. Xiao and D. Xiao, "Understanding peer behavior and designing incentive mechanism in peer-to-peer networks: An analytical model based on game theory," in *Proc. International Conference on Algorithms and Architectures for Parallel Processing (ICA3PP)*, 2007.

[17] A. Habib and J. Chuang, "Service differentiated peer selection: An incentive mechanism for peer-to-peer media streaming," *IEEE Transactions on Multimedia*, vol. 8, pp. 610–621, 2006.

[18] H. V. Madhyastha, T. Isdal, M. Piatek, C. Dixon, T. Anderson, A. Krishnamurthy, and A. Venkataramani, "iPlane: An information plane for distributed services," in *7th Symposium on Operating Systems Design and Implementation (OSDI)*, 2006.

[19] D. Purandare and R. Guha, "An alliance based peering scheme for P2P live media streaming," *IEEE Transactions on Multimedia*, vol. 9, pp. 1633–1644, 2007.

[20] S. Marti and H. Garcia-Molina, "Limited reputation sharing in P2P systems," in *Proc. 5th ACM Conference on Electronic Commerce*, 2004.

[21] M. Gupta, P. Judge, and M. Ammar, "A reputation system for peer-to-peer networks," in *Proc. ACM 13th International Workshop on Network and Operating Systems Support for Digital Audio and Video*, 2003.

[22] V. Vishumurthy, S. Chandrakumar, and E. Sirer, "Karma: A secure economic framework for peer-to-peer resource sharing," in *Proc. 2003 Workshop on Economics of Peer-to-Peer Systems*, 2003.

[23] P. Golle, K. Leyton-Brown, and I. Mironov, "Incentive for sharing in peer-to-peer networks," in *Proc. ACM Conference on Electronic Commerce*, 2001.

[24] H. V. Zhao, W. S. Lin, and K. J. R. Liu, "Behavior modeling and forensics for multimedia social networks," *IEEE Signal Processing Magazine*, vol. 26, pp. 118–139, 2009.

[25] B. Wang, Y. Wu, and K. J. R. Liu, "Game theory for cognitive radio networks: An overview," *Computer Networks*, vol. 54, pp. 2537–2561, 2010.

[26] Y. Chen, B. Wang, and K. J. R. Liu, "A game-theoretic framework for multi-user multimedia rate allocation," in *2009 IEEE International Conference on Acoustics, Speech and Signal Processing*, 2009.

[27] J. Luo and I. Ahmad, "Using game theory for perceptual tuned rate control algorithm in video coding," in *Image and Video Communications and Processing 2005* (A. Said and J. G. Apostolopoulos, eds.), vol. 5685, pp. 297–308, International Society for Optics and Photonics, SPIE, 2005.

[28] W. S. Lin, H. V. Zhao, and K. J. R. Liu, "Incentive cooperation strategies for peer-to-peer live multimedia streaming social networks," *IEEE Transactions on Multimedia, Special Issues on Community and Media Computing*, vol. 11, pp. 396–412, 2009.

[29] C. Huang, J. Li, and K. W. Ross, "Can Internet video-on-demand be profitable?" in *ACM SIGCOMM*, 2007.

[30] J. M. Smith, *Evolution and the Theory of Games*. Cambridge University Press, 1982.

[31] B. Wang, K. J. R. Liu, and T. Clancy, "Evolutionary cooperative spectrum sensing game: how to collaborate?" *IEEE Transactions on Communications*, vol. 58, pp. 890–900, 2010.

[32] R. Cressman, *Evolutionary Dynamics and Extensive Form Games*. MIT Press, 2003.

[33] D. Wu, C. Liang, Y. Liu, and K. W. Ross, "View-upload decoupling: A redesign of multi-channel P2P video systems," in *IEEE Conference on Computer Communications (IEEE INFOCOM '09), Mini-Conference*, 2009.

[34] Y. Chen, Y. Wu, B. Wang, and K. J. R. Liu, "Spectrum auction games for multimedia streaming over cognitive radio networks," *IEEE Transactions on Communications*, vol. 58, pp. 2381–2390, 2010.

7 Evolutionary Game for Spectrum Sensing and Access in Cognitive Networks

In order to give the secondary users (SUs) more opportunities to draw on the primary users' (PUs') spectrum resources, several spectrum sensing methods and dynamic access algorithms have been proposed. However, few of them have thought about the integration of spectrum sensing design and access algorithms by considering their mutual influences. This chapter sets out to analyze the spectrum sensing and access problem based on studies of two scenarios: a synchronous scenario and a nonslotted asynchronous scenario. The primary network of the former is slotted. As SUs are selfish, they tend to access the channel without contributing to the spectrum sensing. Furthermore, being uncertain about others' strategies, they are likely to adopt out-of-equilibrium schemes. For simulation of the interplay among SUs, the problem of joint spectrum sensing and access is shaped into an evolutionary game, and studies are conducted on the evolutionarily stable strategy (ESS) from which no users will deviate. Moreover, a distributed learning algorithm applicable to SUs' convergence to the ESS is introduced. The algorithm enables SUs to sense and access the primary channel with the probabilities based purely on their own utility history, so that the desired ESS will be achieved in the end. The simulation results reveal the system's rapid convergence to an ESS that shows robustness in the case of selfish SUs' sudden undesirable deviations.

7.1 Introduction

Regarding the mitigation of the crowded radio spectrum, the cognitive radio network is a communication paradigm that has shown considerable effectiveness. Great improvements can be seen in the utilization efficiency of existing spectrum resources via dynamic spectrum access (DSA) [1,2]. In DSA, when the impact on the PUs in the licensed spectrum is kept to a minimum, it will be possible for cognitive devices, called SUs, to seize the opportunity to access the licensed spectrum in a dynamic way [3].

The detection of the available spectrum requires the monitoring of the PUs' activities through spectrum sensing by the SUs. The literature offers plenty of spectrum sensing algorithms. The authors of [4] and [5] introduced spectrum sensing methods based on energy detection and waveform sensing, respectively. To improve sensing performance, Ghasemi et al. used cooperative spectrum sensing to tackle shadowing/fading effects [6], while Visotsky et al. carried out research on ways to combine the outcomes of spectrum sensing with cooperative schemes for spectrum sensing [7]. The closed-form expressions for detection and the false-alarm probabilities of cooperative spectrum sensing are available in [8]. In [9], an investigation was launched into two media access control-layer sensing modes, including slotted-time sensing and continuous-time sensing. In [10], research was carried out on distributed compressive spectrum sensing in cooperative multi-hop cognitive networks.

Upon detecting the available spectrum, SUs are required to figure out a way of accessing the spectrum. A number of spectrum access methods developed on the basis of various mathematical models have been introduced: Markov decision process (MDP)-based approaches [11], queuing theoretic approaches [12], and game-theoretic approaches [13]. In [11], Zhao et al. proposed a decentralized spectrum access protocol on the basis of a partially observable MDP (POMDP). Afterwards, the authors of [14] acquired the unknown statistics of the primary signals so as to extend the POMDP framework. In [12,15,16], models of the SUs were shaped into detached queuing systems, and a multiple-access strategy with cooperative relays was proposed. Wu et al. in [17] introduced a spectrum auction game with multiple winners to guard against the SUs' collision behaviors in the course of spectrum access, while Li et al. [18] proposed a coalitional game-theoretic approach to the spectrum access of the SUs.

The analysis of spectrum sensing and access is separated in most existing works. For instance, spectrum sensing performance is optimized irrespective of the spectrum sharing effect. Another example is the design of the multiuser access algorithm without regard to spectrum sensing. In this chapter, a joint spectrum sensing and access game is taken into account so as to achieve integration of the SUs' spectrum sensing and access. When the contribution to spectrum sensing is only available from a small number of SUs, the relatively high false-alarm probability tends to yield low throughput during channel access. In addition, when accessing the primary channel is attempted by a large number of SUs, the channel is apt to be too crowded for an individual SU to gain sufficient throughput. Consequently, each SU is supposed to be aware of its strategic interactions with other SUs so as to dynamically adjust its strategy accordingly. In [19], studies were carried out on a joint design of spectrum sensing and access from the perspective of a queuing theoretic approach that takes into account the effects of inaccuracies in spectrum sensing in terms of the SUs' performance at multichannel access. In [20], to tackle the problem of joint spectrum sensing and access, a coalition game-theoretic approach that focused on SUs forming coalitions that constituted a Nash-stable network partition was proposed.

Being naturally selfish, the SUs tend to access channels without contributing to spectrum sensing. Furthermore, being uncertain about others' strategies, they are likely to adopt out-of-equilibrium strategies. As a result, it is desirable for each SU to have a robust Nash equilibrium (NE). To simulate the intricate interplay among the SUs and to figure out a stable NE for them, the problem of joint spectrum sensing and access is shaped into an evolutionary game, and the ESS is thus obtained. Evolutionary games have been applied to the simulation of behaviors performed by users in a variety of fields, such as image processing [21], communication and networking [22,23], congestion control [24], cooperative sensing [25], and cooperative peer-to-peer (P2P) streaming [26]. According to these papers, evolutionary games represent a feasible approach for the simulation of the dynamic social interactions among network users.

The PU's communication mechanism makes two scenarios possible for the joint spectrum sensing and access evolutionary game. In the first scenario, the primary network is slotted and there is synchronization between the SUs and the PU, whereas in the second scenario, the primary network is kept intact without SU–PU synchronization. In this chapter, the ESSs of these two scenarios are obtained and approaches to achieving a favorable ESS in a distributive manner are discussed. In a distributed network, SUs are faced with the common difficulty of knowing the strategies of others as well as the relevant usages of the spectrum. Furthermore, the SUs behave dynamically; for instance, they can join or depart from the secondary network whenever they like. In view of the aforementioned problems, a distributed learning algorithm is proposed so that the SUs can achieve an ESS based exclusively on their own utility histories.

7.2 System Model

7.2.1 Network Entity

It is demonstrated in Figure 7.1 that, in this chapter, we discuss a cognitive radio network featuring a single licensed primary channel and M SUs. The PU is prioritized to access the channel whenever it likes, whereas the SUs are prevented from occupying the channel unless preceded by the guarantee of the PU's communication quality of service (QoS). It is feasible for all SUs to conduct spectrum sensing independently through energy detection and to share their results with others afterwards. A narrowband signaling channel available in the secondary network enables the SUs to exchange their sensing results [27]. Nevertheless, to achieve greater bandwidth for high-data-rate transmissions such as multimedia transmissions, it is necessary for the

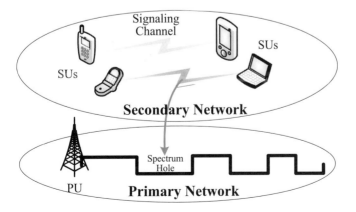

Figure 7.1 The network entity.

SUs to opportunistically access the primary channel. In view of the SUs' small size and power limits in mobile terminals, they are all assumed to be half-duplex. This means that on the one hand the SUs are unable to send and accept data concurrently, and on the other hand they are in no position to conduct spectrum sensing while maintaining data communication [28].

7.2.2   Spectrum Sensing Model

Cooperative spectrum sensing technology is in a position to play an effective role in tackling the problems of the channel fading and shadowing in spectrum sensing [6]. In the distributed cooperative sensing architecture adopted, each SU independently determines the presence or absence of the PU via the combination of its own sensing results and those of other SUs. To improve sensing performance, it is assumed that SUs share all of their sensing information with others, which is called *soft* combination rules [29].

Let $\mathcal{H}_0$ and $\mathcal{H}_1$ denote the PU being absent and present, respectively. The signals received by the SUs under $\mathcal{H}_0$ and $\mathcal{H}_1$ can be written by

$$
\begin{aligned}
\mathcal{H}_0: \quad & y_m[n] = u_m[n], & \text{the PU is absent,} \\
\mathcal{H}_1: \quad & y_m[n] = s_m[n] + u_m[n], & \text{the PU is present,}
\end{aligned}
\tag{7.1}
$$

where $y_m[n]$ denotes the nth sample of the mth SU's sensing signal, u_m denotes the noise, which is assumed to be circular symmetric complex Gaussian (CSCG) with zero mean and variance σ^2 [8], and s_m is the PU's signal, which is regarded as an independent and identically distributed random process with zero mean and variance σ_p^2. In this case, for the mth SU, the average energy of sensed signal Y_m is calculated by

$$
Y_m = \frac{1}{\lambda T_s} \sum_{n=1}^{\lambda T_s} \left| y_m^{(i)}[n] \right|^2,
\tag{7.2}
$$

where T_s stands for the sensing time and λ refers to the sampling rate. Then, each SU transmits its sensing data Y_m to the entire network. Therefore, the overall average energy Y can be written as

$$
Y = \frac{1}{M} \sum_{m=1}^{M} Y_m = \frac{1}{\lambda M T_s} \sum_{m=1}^{M} \sum_{n=1}^{\lambda T_s} \left| y_m[n] \right|^2.
\tag{7.3}
$$

Finally, the SUs make a comparison of Y and the threshold Y_{th} determined beforehand so as to determine the absence or presence of the PU as follows:

$$
\begin{aligned}
\mathcal{D}_0: \quad & Y < Y_{th}, & \text{the SUs decide on the absence of the PU,} \\
\mathcal{D}_1: \quad & Y \geq Y_{th}, & \text{the SUs decide on the presence of the PU.}
\end{aligned}
$$

Two terms are commonly used to measure the performance of spectrum sensing: detection probability P_d and false-alarm probability P_f. P_d is defined as the probability that the SUs can detect the presence of the PU, while P_f represents the probability

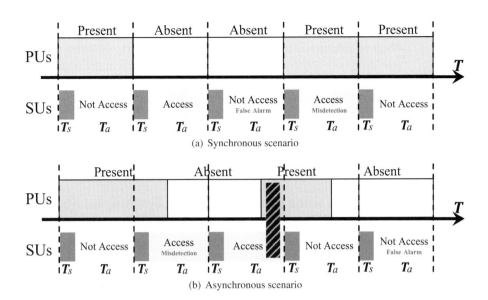

Figure 7.2 Illustration of the two scenarios.

that the SUs make an untruthful report of the presence of the PU during its actual absence. Due to the fact that P_d is usually preceded by the PU, the corresponding P_f can be calculated by [25]

$$P_f = \frac{1}{2}\mathrm{erfc}\left(\sqrt{2\gamma+1}\cdot\mathrm{erfc}^{-1}(2P_d) + \gamma\sqrt{\frac{M\lambda T_s}{2}}\right),$$

$$= \frac{1}{2}\mathrm{erfc}\left(\Omega + \gamma\sqrt{\frac{M\lambda T_s}{2}}\right), \qquad (7.4)$$

where $\gamma = \sigma_p/\sigma$ represents the SUs' received signal-to-noise ratio (SNR) of the PU's signal under $\mathcal{H}_1$ and erfc$(\cdot)$ stands for the complementary error function erfc$(x) = \frac{2}{\sqrt{\pi}}\int_x^{+\infty} e^{-t^2} dt$.

7.2.3 Synchronous and Asynchronous Scenarios

Studies were conducted on the joint spectrum sensing and access problem under two scenarios: a synchronous scenario and an asynchronous scenario. As is shown in Figure 7.2(a), in the synchronous scenario, the primary channel is assumed to be slotted and the SUs show synchrony with the PU's time slots. In the asynchronous scenario, the privacy of primary communication and the SUs' unawareness of the definite form of the PU's exchange are assumed. In this case, as is presented in Figure 7.2(b), asynchrony is found between the system clock of the secondary network and that of the primary network [30]. For the two scenarios, at the start of each slot, the SUs sense the primary channel at time T_s and tend to access the channel at time T_a when the PU's absence is observable.

In the secondary network, to obtain maximum data throughput with minimal contribution to spectrum sensing, each SU tends to maximize its access time. It is unavoidable that such selfish behavior of the SUs will result in the worst-case scenario in which no one is able to detect the primary channel, culminating in an exceedingly high false-alarm probability P_f, and thus there is nearly zero throughput. Furthermore, despite all SUs' contributions to spectrum sensing, the access of the primary channel by a large number of SUs tends to trigger congestion in the channel, again resulting in low throughput.

7.3   Evolutionary Game Formulation for the Synchronous Scenario

7.3.1   Evolutionary Game

In the evolutionary game, all players dynamically adjust their strategies based on their observance of the utilities under different strategies. Following a period of strategic interaction, it is effective for players who belong to the same group to converge to a stable equilibrium: namely, the ESS. In accordance with evolutionary game theory [22], for a game with M players, a strategy profile $\mathbf{a}^* = (a_1^*, \ldots, a_M^*)$ is an ESS if and only if, $\forall \mathbf{a} \neq \mathbf{a}^*$, $\mathbf{a}^*$ satisfies the following:

(1) $U_i(a_i, \mathbf{a}_{-i}^*) \leq U_i(a_i^*, \mathbf{a}_{-i}^*),$ (7.5)

(2) If $U_i(a_i, \mathbf{a}_{-i}^*) = U_i(a_i^*, \mathbf{a}_{-i}^*),$ $U_i(a_i, \mathbf{a}_{-i}) < U_i(a_i^*, \mathbf{a}_{-i}),$ (7.6)

where U_i stands for the utility of player i and $\mathbf{a}_{-i}$ denotes the strategies of all players other than player i. It is clear that the first condition refers to the NE condition and the second condition ensures strategic stability. Furthermore, it can be seen that every strict NE is an ESS.

In a distributed scheme, no player is able to be fully aware of the actions taken by other players and their corresponding utilities. To improve their own utility, all players tend to try various strategies in different rounds of play and so acquire knowledge of their interplay by drawing on the understanding-by-building methodology. In the course of this process, the number of players adopting a certain pure strategy tends to change with the passage of time. In the evolutionary game, replicator dynamics are applied to the simulation of this population evolution. In the system, two strategy sets for the SUs are available: one is spectrum sensing strategy set $\Lambda_1 = (s, \bar{s})$, where strategy s denotes sensing and strategy $\bar{s}$ denotes not sensing, and the other is spectrum access strategy set $\Lambda_2 = (a, \bar{a})$, where strategy a denotes access and strategy $\bar{a}$ denotes not access. Let p_s denote the portion of SUs who sense the primary channel and let p_a denote the portion of SUs who access the channel if the absence of the PU is observable after cooperative spectrum sensing (i.e., $p(a)|_{\mathcal{D}_0} = p_a$ and $p(a)|_{\mathcal{D}_1} = 0$). Then the evolution dynamics of p_s and p_a are given by

$$\dot{p}_s = \eta p_s (\mathbb{U}_s - \mathbb{U}), \tag{7.7}$$

$$\dot{p}_a = \eta p_a (\mathbb{U}_a|_{\mathcal{D}_0} - \mathbb{U}|_{\mathcal{D}_0}), \tag{7.8}$$

where $\mathbb{U}_s$ stands for the average utility of the SUs who are engaged in the cooperative spectrum sensing, $\mathbb{U}$ is the average utility of all SUs, $\mathbb{U}_a|_{\mathcal{D}_0}$ denotes the average utility of the SUs who access the primary channel conditioning on $\mathcal{D}_0$, $\mathbb{U}|_{\mathcal{D}_0}$ refers to the mean utility of all SUs when $\mathcal{D}_0$ is available, and η is a positive scale factor. From (7.7), it can be shown that if spectrum sensing can result in a higher utility than the average level, then the portion p_s will increase and the increasing rate $\dot{p}_s/p_s$ is proportional to the difference between $\mathbb{U}_s$ and $\mathbb{U}$. A similar phenomenon can be found for the evolution of p_a.

For the joint spectrum sensing and access game, both p_s and p_a can serve as determinants of the utility functions. Given the absence of the PU (i.e., given $\mathcal{H}_0$), the utility functions of the SUs that take four divergent actions $\{sa, \bar{s}a, s\bar{a}, \overline{sa}\}$ can be put as follows:

$$U_{sa}|_{\mathcal{H}_0} = \mathbb{F}(Mp_a) - \Theta_a - \Theta_s, \tag{7.9}$$

$$U_{\bar{s}a}|_{\mathcal{H}_0} = \mathbb{F}(Mp_a) - \Theta_a, \tag{7.10}$$

$$U_{s\bar{a}}|_{\mathcal{H}_0} = -\Theta_s + R, \tag{7.11}$$

$$U_{\overline{sa}}|_{\mathcal{H}_0} = 0, \tag{7.12}$$

where $\mathbb{F}(\cdot)$ symbolizes the reward an SU obtains from channel access, $\Theta_a = T_a E_2$ stands for the energy consumed in the course of data transmission, $\Theta_s = T_s E_3$ denotes the energy consumed by spectrum sensing, and the constant R represents the energy reward for the SU who contributes to channel sensing without accessing the channel and $R > \Theta_s$. When the cognitive radio network is put into practice, the energy reward R is can be regarded as credit for the SUs, or as a period of cost-free network access time. Here $\mathbb{F}(Mp_a)$ stands for the throughput of an SU calculated by

$$\mathbb{F}(Mp_a) = B \log \left(1 + \frac{\text{SNR}}{(Mp_a - 1) \cdot \text{INR} + 1} \right) \cdot T_a E_1, \tag{7.13}$$

where Mp_a is the number of SUs that tend to access the channel on the condition of $\mathcal{D}_0$, B denotes the bandwidth of the primary channel, INR denotes the interference-to-noise ratio from each of the rest of SUs where it is assumed that the SUs cause identical and mutual impacts, and E_1 represents the parameter that converts an SU's throughput reward into its energy reward.

Similarly to the case for $\mathcal{H}_0$, the SUs' utility functions under $\mathcal{H}_1$ can be summarized as follows:

$$U_{sa}|_{\mathcal{H}_1} = -\Theta_a - \Theta_s, \tag{7.14}$$

$$U_{\bar{s}a}|_{\mathcal{H}_1} = -\Theta_a, \tag{7.15}$$

$$U_{s\bar{a}}|_{\mathcal{H}_1} = -\Theta_s + R, \tag{7.16}$$

$$U_{\overline{sa}}|_{\mathcal{H}_1} = 0, \tag{7.17}$$

where it is assumed that there is no reward for the SU by accessing the channel under the condition of $\mathcal{H}_1$ when the PU is present.

7.3.2   Replicator Dynamics of Spectrum Sensing

The replicator dynamics of spectrum sensing can be found in (7.7), where it is crucial to be aware of the average utility of the SUs that conduct channel sensing $\mathbb{U}_s$ and the average utility of all SUs $\mathbb{U}$. In accordance with utility functions (7.9)–(7.17), we can calculate the average utility of performing sensing and not performing sensing given $\mathcal{H}_0$ or $\mathcal{H}_1$ as follows:

$$\mathbb{U}_s|_{\mathcal{H}_0} = p(a)|_{\mathcal{H}_0} \cdot U_{sa}|_{\mathcal{H}_0} + p(\bar{a})|_{\mathcal{H}_0} \cdot U_{s\bar{a}}|_{\mathcal{H}_0}, \tag{7.18}$$

$$\mathbb{U}_s|_{\mathcal{H}_1} = p(a)|_{\mathcal{H}_1} \cdot U_{sa}|_{\mathcal{H}_1} + p(\bar{a})|_{\mathcal{H}_1} \cdot U_{s\bar{a}}|_{\mathcal{H}_1}, \tag{7.19}$$

$$\mathbb{U}_{\bar{s}}|_{\mathcal{H}_0} = p(a)|_{\mathcal{H}_0} \cdot U_{\bar{s}a}|_{\mathcal{H}_0} + p(\bar{a})|_{\mathcal{H}_0} \cdot U_{\bar{s}\bar{a}}|_{\mathcal{H}_0}, \tag{7.20}$$

$$\mathbb{U}_{\bar{s}}|_{\mathcal{H}_1} = p(a)|_{\mathcal{H}_1} \cdot U_{\bar{s}a}|_{\mathcal{H}_1} + p(\bar{a})|_{\mathcal{H}_1} \cdot U_{\bar{s}\bar{a}}|_{\mathcal{H}_1}, \tag{7.21}$$

where $p(a)|_{\mathcal{H}_0}$ and $p(a)|_{\mathcal{H}_1}$ denote the portion of SUs that access the primary channel given the channel conditions in $\mathcal{H}_0$ and $\mathcal{H}_1$, respectively, which are written as

$$p(a)|_{\mathcal{H}_0} = p(a, \mathcal{D}_0)|_{\mathcal{H}_0} = p(a)|_{(\mathcal{D}_0, \mathcal{H}_0)} \cdot p(\mathcal{D}_0)|_{\mathcal{H}_0} = p_a(1 - P_f(Mp_s)), \tag{7.22}$$

$$p(a)|_{\mathcal{H}_1} = p(a, \mathcal{D}_0)|_{\mathcal{H}_1} = p(a)|_{(\mathcal{D}_0, \mathcal{H}_1)} \cdot p(\mathcal{D}_0)|_{\mathcal{H}_1} = p_a(1 - P_d), \tag{7.23}$$

where $P_f(Mp_s)$ represents the false-alarm probability when Mp_s SUs cooperatively sense the primary channel.

Accordingly, the average utility of SUs who sense the primary channel, $\mathbb{U}_s$, the average utility of SUs who do not sense, $\mathbb{U}_{\bar{s}}$, and the average utility of all SUs, $\mathbb{U}$, can be derived as follows:

$$\mathbb{U}_s = p_0 \cdot \mathbb{U}_s|_{\mathcal{H}_0} + p_1 \cdot \mathbb{U}_s|_{\mathcal{H}_1}, \tag{7.24}$$

$$\mathbb{U}_{\bar{s}} = p_0 \cdot \mathbb{U}_{\bar{s}}|_{\mathcal{H}_0} + p_1 \cdot \mathbb{U}_{\bar{s}}|_{\mathcal{H}_1}, \tag{7.25}$$

$$\mathbb{U} = p_s \cdot \mathbb{U}_s + (1 - p_s) \cdot \mathbb{U}_{\bar{s}}. \tag{7.26}$$

The probability of the PU's absence is given by p_0 (i.e., the probability of $\mathcal{H}_0$), and $p_1 = 1 - p_0$ represents the probability of the PU's presence (i.e., the probability of $\mathcal{H}_1$). Combining (7.7) and (7.9)–(7.26), the replicator dynamics of spectrum sensing by (7.27) can be rewritten as follows:

$$\dot{p}_s = \eta p_s (1 - p_s)(\mathbb{U}_s - \mathbb{U}_{\bar{s}})$$
$$= \eta p_s (1 - p_s)\big(-\Theta_s + (1 - p_a + p_a(p_0 P_f(Mp_s) + p_1 P_d))R\big). \tag{7.27}$$

7.3.3   Replicator Dynamics of Spectrum Access

The analysis of the replicator dynamics of spectrum sensing starts with a particular initial calculation, and likewise the average utility of SUs accessing the primary channel, $\mathbb{U}_a|_{\mathcal{D}_0}$, and the average utility of all SUs given $\mathcal{D}_0$, $\mathbb{U}|_{\mathcal{D}_0}$, should be calculated first.

The utilities of the SUs that adopt the four pure strategies $\{sa, \bar{s}a, s\bar{a}, \bar{s}\bar{a}\}$ given $\mathcal{D}_0$ can be calculated using (7.28)–(7.31) as follows:

$$U_{sa|\mathcal{D}_0} = p(\mathcal{H}_0)|_{(a,\mathcal{D}_0)} \cdot U_{sa}|_{(\mathcal{D}_0,\mathcal{H}_0)} + (1 - p(\mathcal{H}_0)|_{(a,\mathcal{D}_0)}) \cdot U_{sa}|_{(\mathcal{D}_0,\mathcal{H}_1)}, \quad (7.28)$$

$$U_{\bar{s}a|\mathcal{D}_0} = p(\mathcal{H}_0)|_{(a,\mathcal{D}_0)} \cdot U_{\bar{s}a}|_{(\mathcal{D}_0,\mathcal{H}_0)} + (1 - p(\mathcal{H}_0)|_{(a,\mathcal{D}_0)}) \cdot U_{\bar{s}a}|_{(\mathcal{D}_0,\mathcal{H}_1)}, \quad (7.29)$$

$$U_{s\bar{a}|\mathcal{D}_0} = p(\mathcal{H}_0)|_{(\bar{a},\mathcal{D}_0)} \cdot U_{s\bar{a}}|_{(\mathcal{D}_0,\mathcal{H}_0)} + (1 - p(\mathcal{H}_0)|_{(\bar{a},\mathcal{D}_0)}) \cdot U_{s\bar{a}}|_{(\mathcal{D}_0,\mathcal{H}_1)}, \quad (7.30)$$

$$U_{\bar{s}\bar{a}|\mathcal{D}_0} = p(\mathcal{H}_0)|_{(\bar{a},\mathcal{D}_0)} \cdot U_{\bar{s}\bar{a}}|_{(\mathcal{D}_0,\mathcal{H}_0)} + (1 - p(\mathcal{H}_0)|_{(\bar{a},\mathcal{D}_0)}) \cdot U_{\bar{s}\bar{a}}|_{(\mathcal{D}_0,\mathcal{H}_1)}, \quad (7.31)$$

where $p(\mathcal{H}_0)|_{(a,\mathcal{D}_0)}$ refers to the probability of the absence of the PU when the SUs choose to access, while $p(\mathcal{H}_0)|_{(\bar{a},\mathcal{D}_0)}$ stands for the case in which the SUs decide not to access. $U_{..}|_{(\mathcal{D}_0,\mathcal{H}_0)}$ and $U_{..}|_{(\mathcal{D}_0,\mathcal{H}_1)}$ are the SUs' utility functions when given $\{\mathcal{D}_0,\mathcal{H}_0\}$ and $\{\mathcal{D}_0,\mathcal{H}_1\}$, respectively. Due to the given $\mathcal{D}_0$, the accessing behavior is independent of the status of the PU, $p(\mathcal{H}_0)|_{(a,\mathcal{D}_0)} = p(\mathcal{H}_0)|_{(\bar{a},\mathcal{D}_0)} = p(\mathcal{H}_0)|_{\mathcal{D}_0}$, where $p(\mathcal{H}_0)|_{\mathcal{D}_0}$ is subject to the Bayes' rule calculation as

$$\begin{aligned} p(\mathcal{H}_0)|_{\mathcal{D}_0} &= \frac{p_0 \cdot p(\mathcal{D}_0)|_{\mathcal{H}_0}}{p_0 \cdot p(\mathcal{D}_0)|_{\mathcal{H}_0} + p_1 \cdot p(\mathcal{D}_0)|_{\mathcal{H}_1}}, \\ &= \frac{p_0(1 - P_f(Mp_s))}{1 - p_0 P_f(Mp_s) - p_1 P_d}. \end{aligned} \quad (7.32)$$

Given the actions, the SUs' utilities are not determined by $\mathcal{D}_0$ (i.e., $U_{..}|_{(\mathcal{D}_0,\mathcal{H}_0)} = U_{..}|_{\mathcal{H}_0}$ and $U_{..}|_{(\mathcal{D}_0,\mathcal{H}_1)} = U_{..}|_{\mathcal{H}_1}$). In this case, the average utilities of the SUs who access and those who refrain from accessing the primary channel, $U_a|_{\mathcal{D}_0}$ and $U_{\bar{a}}|_{\mathcal{D}_0}$, and the average utility of all SUs, $\mathbb{U}|_{\mathcal{D}_0}$, are written as follows:

$$\mathbb{U}_a|_{\mathcal{D}_0} = p_s \cdot U_{sa}|_{\mathcal{D}_0} + (1 - p_s) \cdot U_{\bar{s}a}|_{\mathcal{D}_0}, \quad (7.33)$$

$$\mathbb{U}_{\bar{a}}|_{\mathcal{D}_0} = p_s \cdot U_{s\bar{a}}|_{\mathcal{D}_0} + (1 - p_s) \cdot U_{\bar{s}\bar{a}}|_{\mathcal{D}_0}, \quad (7.34)$$

$$\mathbb{U}|_{\mathcal{D}_0} = p_a \cdot \mathbb{U}_a|_{\mathcal{D}_0} + (1 - p_a) \cdot \mathbb{U}_{\bar{a}}|_{\mathcal{D}_0}. \quad (7.35)$$

Combining (7.8) and (7.28)–(7.35), the replicator dynamics of spectrum access can be rewritten as follows:

$$\begin{aligned} \dot{p}_a &= \eta p_a(1 - p_a)(\mathbb{U}_a|_{\mathcal{D}_0} - \mathbb{U}_{\bar{a}}|_{\mathcal{D}_0}) \\ &= \eta p_a(1 - p_a)\left(\frac{p_0(1 - P_f(Mp_s))}{1 - p_0 P_f(Mp_s) - p_1 P_d}\mathbb{F}(Mp_a) - \Theta_a - p_s R\right). \end{aligned} \quad (7.36)$$

7.3.4 Analysis of the ESS

At equilibrium, $\dot{p}_s = 0$ and $\dot{p}_a = 0$ are available. In accordance with (7.27) and (7.36), there are seven possible equilibria: $(0,0)$, $(0,1)$, $(1,0)$, $(1,1)$, $(p_{s_1}, 1)$, $(1, p_{a_1})$, and

(p_{s_2}, p_{a_2}), where p_{s_1} satisfies $P_f(Mp_{s_1}) = \left(\frac{\Theta_s}{R} - p_1 P_d\right)/p_0$, p_{a_1} satisfies $\mathbb{F}(Mp_{a_1}) = \frac{(\Theta_a + R)\left(1 - p_0 P_f(M) - p_1 P_d\right)}{p_0\left(1 - P_f(M)\right)}$, and (p_{s_2}, p_{a_2}) is the solution to the following equations:

$$
\begin{cases}
-\Theta_s + \left(1 - p_a + p_a(p_0 P_f(Mp_s) + p_1 P_d)\right) R = 0, \\[2mm]
\dfrac{p_0\left(1 - P_f(Mp_s)\right)}{1 - p_0 P_f(Mp_s) - p_1 P_d} \mathbb{F}(Mp_a) - \Theta_a - p_s R = 0.
\end{cases}
\tag{7.37}
$$

In accordance with evolutionary game theory [22], an equilibrium of the replicator dynamics equation is an ESS if and if only it is a locally asymptotically stable point in a dynamic system. In Lemma 7.1 and Theorem 7.2, we will determine which of the equilibria are ESSs.

LEMMA 7.1   *The false-alarm probability P_f is a decreasing function in the light of p_s and the reward from channel access $\mathbb{F}$ is a decreasing function based on p_a (i.e., $\frac{dP_f(Mp_s)}{dp_s} < 0$ and $\frac{d\mathbb{F}(Mp_a)}{dp_a} < 0$).*

Proof   According to (7.4), we have

$$
\frac{dP_f(Mp_s)}{dp_s} = -\frac{\gamma}{2\sqrt{\pi}}\sqrt{\frac{\lambda T_s M}{2p_s}}\, e^{-\left(\Omega + \sqrt{\frac{\lambda T_s Mp_s}{2}}\gamma\right)^2} < 0.
\tag{7.38}
$$

According to (7.13) and (7.38), we have

$$
\frac{d\mathbb{F}(Mp_a)}{dp_a} = -\frac{B \cdot T_a \cdot E_1}{(Mp_a - 1)\text{INR} + 1 + \text{SNR}} \cdot \frac{M \cdot \text{SNR} \cdot \text{INR}}{(Mp_a - 1)\text{INR} + 1} < 0.
\tag{7.39}
$$

Equation (7.38) means that the larger p_s is, the greater the potential contribution of SUs to the cooperative spectrum sensing and the lower the P_f that can be achieved, while (7.39) refers to the fact that when the number of SUs accessing the primary channel increases, the reward obtained through channel access by each SU is going to decrease.

THEOREM 7.2   *In terms of the joint spectrum sensing and access evolutionary game under the synchronous scenario, three ESSs are available: $(p_s^*, p_a^*) = (1, 0)$, $(1, p_{a_1})$, and (p_{s_2}, p_{a_2}) under different conditions of the rewards R, as in (7.40).*

$$
(p_s^*, p_a^*) =
\begin{cases}
(1, 0), & R > \dfrac{p_0(1 - P_f(M))}{1 - p_0 P_f(M) - p_1 P_d}\mathbb{F}(1) - \Theta_a, \\[4mm]
(1, p_{a_1}), & R > \dfrac{\Theta_s}{1 - p_{a_1}(1 - p_0 P_f(M) - p_1 P_d)}, \\[4mm]
(p_{s_2}, p_{a_2}), & R < \dfrac{p_0^2 p_{s_2}(1 - P_f(Mp_{s_2}))\frac{d\mathbb{F}(Mp_{a_2})}{dp_{a_2}} - \frac{p_0 p_1(1 - P_d)\mathbb{F}(Mp_{a_2})}{1 - p_0 P_f(Mp_{s_2}) - p_1 P_d}}{(1 - p_0 P_f(Mp_{s_2}) - p_1 P_d)^2}\dfrac{dP_f(Mp_{s_2})}{dp_{s_2}}.
\end{cases}
\tag{7.40}
$$

Proof   Considering (7.27) and (7.36) as a nonlinear dynamic system, we are in a position to discern the possible ESSs from the seven equilibria through the analysis of the Jacobian matrix of the replicator dynamics equations as follows:

$$J = \begin{pmatrix} \frac{\partial \dot{p}_s}{\partial p_s} & \frac{\partial \dot{p}_s}{\partial p_a} \\ \frac{\partial \dot{p}_a}{\partial p_s} & \frac{\partial \dot{p}_a}{\partial p_a} \end{pmatrix} = \eta \begin{pmatrix} J_{11} & J_{12}, \\ J_{21} & J_{22} \end{pmatrix}, \tag{7.41}$$

where J_{11}, J_{12}, J_{21}, and J_{22} are listed in (7.42)–(7.45).

$$J_{11} = (1 - 2p_s)(-\Theta_s + (1 - p_a + p_a(p_0 P_f(Mp_s) + p_1 P_d))R)$$
$$+ p_0 p_s (1 - p_s) p_a \frac{d P_f(Mp_s)}{dp_s} R, \tag{7.42}$$

$$J_{12} = -p_s(1 - p_s)(1 - p_0 P_f(Mp_s) - p_1 P_d)R, \tag{7.43}$$

$$J_{21} = p_a(1 - p_a)\left(-\frac{p_0 p_1 (1 - P_d)\mathbb{F}(Mp_a)}{(1 - p_0 P_f(Mp_s) - p_1 P_d)^2} \frac{d P_f(Mp_s)}{dp_s} - R\right), \tag{7.44}$$

$$J_{22} = (1 - 2p_a)\left(\frac{p_0(1 - P_f(Mp_s))\mathbb{F}(Mp_a)}{1 - p_0 P_f(Mp_s) - p_1 P_d} - \Theta_a - p_s R\right)$$
$$+ p_0 \frac{p_a(1 - p_a)(1 - P_f(Mp_s))}{1 - p_0 P_f(Mp_s) - p_1 P_d} \frac{d\mathbb{F}(Mp_a)}{dp_a}. \tag{7.45}$$

The asymptotic stability is preconditioned by $det(J) > 0$ and $tr(J) < 0$ [22]. Substituting the seven equilibria into (7.41) separately, we are in a postion to determine whether they are ESSs or not. For the equilibrium $(0,0)$ (i.e., no SU senses and accesses the primary channel), we have $\lim_{p_s \to 0} J_{12} \cdot J_{21} = 0$ because

$$\lim_{p_s \to 0} p_s \frac{d P_f(Mp_s)}{dp_s} = \lim_{p_s \to 0} -\frac{\gamma}{2\sqrt{\pi}} \sqrt{\frac{\lambda T_s M p_s}{2}} e^{-\left(\Omega + \sqrt{\frac{\lambda T_s M p_s}{2}}\gamma\right)^2} = 0. \tag{7.46}$$

In such a case, $(0,0)$ is an ESS if and only if $\lim_{p_s \to 0} J_{11} < 0$ and $\lim_{p_s \to 0} J_{22} < 0$. However, $\lim_{p_s \to 0} J_{11} = -\Theta_s + R > 0$. Therefore, $(0,0)$ is not an ESS. Similarly, the equilibrium $(0,1)$ (i.e., no SU senses but all SUs access the primary channel) is not an ESS due to the fact that when $p_a = 1$, the channel will be subject to congestion and $\mathbb{F}(M) \to 0$, leading to $J_{22} \to \Theta_a > 0$. In addition, the equilibrium $(1,1)$ (i.e., all SUs sense and access the channel) and the equilibrium $(p_{s_1}, 1)$ (i.e., a portion of SUs sense but all SUs access the channel) are both not considered to be ESSs due to the fact that $J_{22} \to \Theta_a + R > 0$ and $J_{12} \cdot J_{21} = 0$.

In terms of the equilibrium $(1,0)$, which means all SUs sense but no SUs access the channel, we have

$$\lim_{p_a \to 0} J_{11} = \Theta_s - R < 0, \tag{7.47}$$

$$\lim_{p_a \to 0} J_{22} = \frac{p_0(1 - P_f(M))}{1 - p_0 P_f(M) - p_1 P_d}\mathbb{F}(1) - \Theta_a - R, \tag{7.48}$$

$$\lim_{p_a \to 0} J_{12} \cdot J_{21} = 0. \tag{7.49}$$

Therefore, $(1,0)$ is an ESS when the reward R satisfies

$$R > \frac{p_0(1 - P_f(M))}{1 - p_0 P_f(M) - p_1 P_d} \mathbb{F}(1) - \Theta_a. \tag{7.50}$$

From (7.50), it is clear that if the reward for an SU who senses but does not access, R, outstrips the reward that the SU is able to acquire when it occupies the channel exlusively, $p(\mathcal{H}_0)|_{\mathcal{D}_0} \cdot \mathbb{F}(1) - \Theta_a$ according to (7.32), then all SUs will tend to decide to sense but not to access the channel. This kind of ESS would reduce the utilization of the spectrum. As a consequence, to prevent such a system from converging to this type of undesired ESS, R should be set properly.

For the equilibrium $(1, p_{a_1})$ (i.e., all SUs sense but only a portion of SUs choose to access the primary channel), we have $J_{12} \cdot J_{21} = 0$ and, according to Lemma 7.1,

$$J_{11} = \Theta_s - \left(1 - p_{a_1}(1 - p_0 P_f(M) - p_1 P_d)\right) R, \tag{7.51}$$

$$J_{22} = \frac{p_0 p_{a_1}(1 - p_{a_1})(1 - P_f(M))}{1 - p_0 P_f(M) - p_1 P_d} \frac{d\mathbb{F}(M p_{a_2})}{dp_{a_2}} < 0. \tag{7.52}$$

In this case, $(1, p_{a_1})$ becomes an ESS if reward R is in line with

$$R > \frac{\Theta_s}{1 - p_{a_1}(1 - p_0 P_f(M) - p_1 P_d)}. \tag{7.53}$$

For the solution (p_{s_2}, p_{a_2}) (i.e., a portion of SUs sense and access the primary channel), we have

$$J_{11} = p_0 p_{s_2}(1 - p_{s_2}) p_{a_2} \frac{dP_f(M p_{s_2})}{dp_{s_2}} R < 0, \tag{7.54}$$

$$J_{12} = -p_{s_2}(1 - p_{s_2})(1 - p_0 P_f(M p_{s_2}) - p_1 P_d) R, \tag{7.55}$$

$$J_{21} = p_{a_2}(1 - p_{a_2}) \left(-\frac{p_0 p_1(1 - P_d)\mathbb{F}(M p_{a_2})}{(1 - p_0 P_f(M p_{a_2}) - p_1 P_d)^2} \frac{dP_f(M p_{s_2})}{dp_{s_2}} - R\right), \tag{7.56}$$

$$J_{22} = p_0 \frac{p_{a_2}(1 - p_{a_2})(1 - P_f(M p_{s_2}))}{1 - p_0 P_f(M p_{a_2}) - p_1 P_d} \frac{d\mathbb{F}(M p_{a_2})}{dp_{a_2}} < 0. \tag{7.57}$$

With (7.54)–(7.57), we calculate $det(J)$ in (7.58) as

$$det(J) = \frac{p_{s_1}(1 - p_{s_1}) p_{a_1}(1 - p_{a_1}) R}{1 - p_0 P_f(M p_{s_2}) - p_1 P_d} \left(p_0^2 p_{a_2}(1 - P_f(M p_{s_2}))\right) \frac{d\mathbb{F}(M p_{a_2})}{dp_{a_2}} \frac{dP_f(M p_{s_2})}{dp_{s_2}}$$
$$- \frac{p_0 p_1(1 - P_d)\mathbb{F}(M p_{s_2})}{1 - p_0 P_f(M p_{s_2}) - p_1 P_d} \frac{dP_f(M p_{s_2})}{dp_{s_2}} - \left(1 - p_0 P_f(M p_{s_2}) - p_1 P_d\right)^2 R\right). \tag{7.58}$$

Thus, (p_{s_2}, p_{a_2}) is an ESS when the reward R satisfies

$$R < \frac{p_0^2 p_{s_2}(1 - P_f(Mp_{s_2}))\frac{d\mathbb{F}(Mp_{a_2})}{dp_{a_2}} - \frac{p_0 p_1(1-P_d)\mathbb{F}(Mp_{a_2})}{1-p_0 P_f(Mp_{s_2})-p_1 P_d}}{(1 - p_0 P_f(Mp_{s_2}) - p_1 P_d)^2} \cdot \frac{d P_f(Mp_{s_2})}{dp_{s_2}}. \quad (7.59)$$

It can be concluded that (7.50), (7.53), and (7.59) are the respective conditions for the three ESSs $(p_s^*, p_a^*) = (1, 0)$, $(1, p_{a_1})$, and (p_{s_2}, p_{a_2}). This demonstrates the proof of the theorem.

7.4 Evolutionary Game Formulation for the Asynchronous Scenario

This section considers the scenario featuring desynchrony between the SUs and the PU. The SUs act in a similar way to that in the synchronous scenario: if the PU's absence is observable, they are going to access the primary channel on the condition of time T_a; if not, they are going to await the next slot and sense the channel again. The synchronous scenario is different from the asynchronous scenario in that the impact on the PU originates exclusively from the SUs' imperfect spectrum sensing in the former, whereas in the latter, as is represented by the diagonally striped area in Figure 7.2(b), extra interference may arise due to the SUs' possible failure to discover the PU's recurrence during its packet transmission in the primary channel. Essentially, this is grounded in the half-duplex SUs' inability to perform sensing during data transmission [31]. Therefore, to gain control over the interference and to ensure the PU's QoS in the asynchronous scenario, the SUs' access time T_a should be appropriately chosen. In this section, the model of the primary channel as an ON–OFF process together with the proper T_a is introduced, followed by the definition of the SUs' utility functions under the asynchronous scenario. Finally, we discuss the ESS of spectrum sensing and access.

7.4.1 ON–OFF Primary Channel Model

Due to the fact that SUs are not sure of the definite communication mechanism of the primary network and the subsequent asynchrony with the PU, the notion of a time slot in the primary channel from the perspective of SUs [32] can be used in the asynchronous scenario. Rather, as is shown in Figure 7.3, the primary channel simply alternately shifts between the ON state and OFF state. The ON state represents the occupation of the channel by the PU, while the OFF state denotes the "spectrum hole"

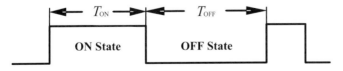

Figure 7.3 Illustration of the ON–OFF primary channel state.

that can be freely accessed by the SUs. Two random variables T_{ON} and T_{OFF} stand for the lengths of the ON state and OFF state, respectively. According to different types of primary services (e.g., digital TV broadcasting or cellular communication), T_{ON} and T_{OFF} statistically obey different distributions. Here we assume that T_{ON} and T_{OFF} are independent and satisfy exponential distributions with parameters λ_1 and λ_0, respectively, denoted by $f_{ON}(t)$ and $f_{OFF}(t)$ as follows:

$$\begin{cases} T_{ON} \sim f_{ON}(t) = \frac{1}{\lambda_1} e^{-t/\lambda_1}, \\ T_{OFF} \sim f_{OFF}(t) = \frac{1}{\lambda_0} e^{-t/\lambda_0}. \end{cases} \tag{7.60}$$

In this case, correspondingly, the anticipated lengths of the ON state and OFF state are λ_1 and λ_0. Effective estimation of the two parameters λ_1 and λ_0 can be achieved through a maximum likelihood estimator [33]. Such an ON–OFF behavior of the PU is the result of the combination of two Poisson processes and is a renewal process [34]. The renewal interval is $T_p = T_{ON} + T_{OFF}$ and the distribution of T_p, denoted by $f_p(t)$, is

$$f_p(t) = f_{ON}(t) * f_{OFF}(t), \tag{7.61}$$

where the symbol "$*$" is the convolution operation. As a result, $\mu_1 = \lambda_1/(\lambda_0 + \lambda_1)$ represents the occurrence probability of the ON state: namely, the channel utilization ratio. Similarly, $\mu_0 = \lambda_0/(\lambda_0 + \lambda_1)$ denotes the occurrence probability of the OFF state.

7.4.2   Analysis of SUs' Access Time T_a

In order to obtain higher throughput, the SUs are always inclined to access the primary channel for a longer time. However, the larger T_a is, the greater interference to the PU will be. To calculate an appropriate T_a for both SUs and the PU, a variable Q_I is introduced for the quantification of the interference from the SUs. The Q_I is defined as the portion of the periods that cause interference to the PU during the PU's total communication time (i.e., the length of all the ON states). Based on the fact that interference may arise only in the period of the SUs' access time, two cases become possible:

(1)   The PU is absent (i.e., the channel is in the OFF state), the SUs manage to detect it and then choose to access the channel, but the PU comes back to this channel during the SUs' access time, according to Figure 7.2(b).

(2)   The PU is present (i.e., the channel is in the ON state) and the SUs fail to discover this and access the channel.

In this case, Q_I is given by

$$\begin{aligned} Q_I &= \lim_{N \to \infty} \frac{N\mu_0(1 - P_f)I_1(T_a) + N\mu_1(1 - P_d)I_2(T_a)}{NT_a \cdot \mu_1}, \\ &= \frac{\mu_0(1 - P_f)I_1(T_a) + \mu_1(1 - P_d)I_2(T_a)}{\mu_1 T_a}, \\ &\leq \frac{\mu_0 I_1(T_a) + \mu_1(1 - P_d)I_2(T_a)}{\mu_1 T_a}, \end{aligned} \tag{7.62}$$

where the denominator stands for the expected length of all ON states during a long interval NT_a and the numerator refers to the interference originating from the SUs during NT_a. $I_1(T_a)$ is the expected length of all ON states within time T_a, given T_a starts from the OFF state, while $I_2(T_a)$ is that given T_a starts from the ON state. According to the definition of Q_1, it stands for the probability of the occurrence of interference to the PU. In this case, the PU's average data rate $R_{av} = (1 - Q_1)R_p$, where R_p is the PU's data rate when SUs generate no interference. To guarantee the PU's reliable communication, the data rate should not be smaller than the average date rate $R_{av}^{\downarrow}$ (i.e., $R_{av} \geq R_{av}^{\downarrow}$), which means that $Q_1 \leq 1 - \frac{R_{av}^{\downarrow}}{R_p}$ is kept to a minimum. Drawing on the combination of this PU's QoS constraint and (7.62), we have

$$\frac{\mu_0 I_1(T_a) + \mu_1(1 - P_d)I_2(T_a)}{\mu_1 T_a} = 1 - \frac{R_{av}^{\downarrow}}{R_p}. \tag{7.63}$$

In [31], the closed-form expression for $I_1(T_a)$ using the renewal theory is given as

$$I_1(T_a) = \frac{\lambda_1}{\lambda_0 + \lambda_1} T_a - \frac{\lambda_0 \lambda_1^2}{(\lambda_0 + \lambda_1)^2}\left(1 - e^{-\frac{\lambda_0 + \lambda_1}{\lambda_0 \lambda_1} T_a}\right). \tag{7.64}$$

Similarly, based on the renewal theory, the closed-form expression for $I_2(T_a)$ can also be obtained.

LEMMA 7.3 $I_2(t)$ satisfies the renewal equation given by

$$I_2(t) = \lambda_1 F_{ON}(t) + \int_0^t I_2(t - w) f_p(w)dw, \tag{7.65}$$

where $F_{ON}(t) = \int_0^t f_{ON}(t)dt = 1 - e^{-\frac{t}{\lambda_1}}$ is the cumulative distribution function of the ON state and $f_p(t)$ is the probability density function of the PU's renewal interval given in (7.61).

Proof In accordance with Figure 7.4, the recursive expression of the function $I_2(t)$ can be rewritten as follows:

$$I_2(t) = \begin{cases} t & t \leq X, \\ X & X \leq t \leq X + Y, \\ X + I_2(t - X - Y) & X + Y \leq t, \end{cases} \tag{7.66}$$

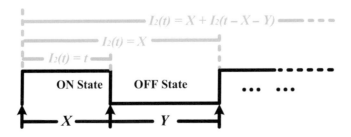

Figure 7.4 Illustration of the function $I_2(t)$.

where X denotes the length of the first ON state and Y represents the length of the first OFF state. Furthermore, $X \sim f_{\text{ON}}(x) = \frac{1}{\lambda_1} e^{-x/\lambda_1}$ and $Y \sim f_{\text{OFF}}(y) = \frac{1}{\lambda_0} e^{-y/\lambda_0}$. Due to the independence of X and Y, their joint distribution is $f_{XY}(x, y) = f_{\text{ON}}(x) f_{\text{OFF}}(y)$. In this case, we can rewrite $I_2(t)$ as

$$I_2(t) = \int_{x \geq t} t f_{\text{ON}}(x) dx + \iint_{x \leq t \leq x+y} x f_{XY}(x, y) dx dy$$

$$+ \iint_{x+y \leq t} [x + I_2(t - x - y)] f_{XY}(x, y) dx dy,$$

$$= t - \int_0^t (t - x) f_{\text{ON}}(x) dx + \iint_{x+y \leq t} I_2(t - x - y) f_{\text{ON}}(x) f_{\text{OFF}}(y) dx dy,$$

$$= t - t * f_{\text{ON}}(t) + I_2(t) * f_p(t). \tag{7.67}$$

By taking Laplace transforms of the two sides of (7.67), we have

$$\mathbb{I}_2(s) = \frac{1}{s^2} - \frac{1}{s^2} \mathbb{F}_{\text{ON}}(s) + \mathbb{I}_2(s) \mathbb{F}_p(s),$$

$$= \lambda_1 \frac{\mathbb{F}_{\text{ON}}(s)}{s} + \mathbb{I}_2(s) \mathbb{F}_p(s), \tag{7.68}$$

where $\mathbb{I}_2(s)$ stands for the Laplace transform of $I_2(t)$, $\mathbb{F}_{\text{ON}}(s) = \frac{1}{\lambda_1 s + 1}$ is the Laplace transform of $f_{\text{ON}}(t)$, and $\mathbb{F}_p(s) = \frac{1}{(\lambda_1 s + 1)(\lambda_0 s + 1)}$ is the Laplace transform of $f_p(t)$. Then by taking the inverse Laplace transform on both sides of (7.68), we have

$$I_2(t) = \lambda_1 \int_0^t f_{\text{ON}}(w) dw + \int_0^t I_2(t - w) f_p(w) dw,$$

$$= \lambda_1 F_{\text{ON}}(t) + \int_0^t I_2(t - w) f_p(w) dw. \tag{7.69}$$

This completes the proof of the lemma.

Thus, by solving (7.68) in Lemma 7.3, the closed-form expression for $I_2(T_a)$ is given as

$$I_2(T_a) = \frac{\lambda_1}{\lambda_0 + \lambda_1} T_a + \frac{\lambda_0^2 \lambda_1}{(\lambda_0 + \lambda_1)^2} \left(1 - e^{-\frac{\lambda_0 + \lambda_1}{\lambda_0 \lambda_1} T_a} \right). \tag{7.70}$$

Substituting (7.64) and (7.70) into (7.63), the proper T_a that satisfies the PU's QoS constraint is obtained.

7.4.3   Analysis of the ESS

The difference between the asynchronous scenario and the synchronous scenario is shown in terms of the utility functions. The PU's recurrences may trigger interference to the SUs when they choose to access the primary channel during the PU's absence. In addition, given the PU's presence and the SUs' failure to discover this and access the primary channel, a certain throughput is still attainable due to the possible case in which the channel switches to the OFF state during the SUs' access time. Considering both of the cases, we may put the utility functions in the asynchronous scenario as follows:

$$
\begin{cases}
U_{sa}|_{\mathcal{H}_0} = \mathbb{W}_1(Mp_a) - \Theta_a - \Theta_s, \\
U_{\bar{s}a}|_{\mathcal{H}_0} = -\Theta_s + R, \\
U_{\bar{s}a}|_{\mathcal{H}_0} = \mathbb{W}_1(Mp_a) - \Theta_a, \\
U_{\overline{sa}}|_{\mathcal{H}_0} = 0,
\end{cases}
\tag{7.71}
$$

$$
\begin{cases}
U_{sa}|_{\mathcal{H}_1} = \mathbb{W}_2(Mp_a) - \Theta_a - \Theta_s, \\
U_{\bar{s}a}|_{\mathcal{H}_1} = -\Theta_s + R, \\
U_{\bar{s}a}|_{\mathcal{H}_1} = \mathbb{W}_2(Mp_a) - \Theta_a, \\
U_{\overline{sa}}|_{\mathcal{H}_1} = 0,
\end{cases}
\tag{7.72}
$$

$$
\text{and} \quad
\begin{cases}
\mathbb{W}_1(Mp_a) = \phi(Mp_a)(T_a - I_1(T_a))E_1, \\
\mathbb{W}_2(Mp_a) = \phi(Mp_a)(T_a - I_2(T_a))E_1,
\end{cases}
\tag{7.73}
$$

where $\phi(Mp_a) = B \log \left(1 + \dfrac{\text{SNR}}{(Mp_a-1)\text{INR}+1}\right)$. Similar to the synchronous scenario, we can write the replicator dynamics equations of the asynchronous scenario as

$$
\dot{p}_s = \eta p_s (1 - p_s)\big(-\Theta_s + (1 - p_a + p_a(p_0 P_f + p_1 P_d))R \big),
\tag{7.74}
$$

$$
\dot{p}_a = \eta p_a (1 - p_a) \left(\frac{p_0(1 - P_f(Mp_s))\mathbb{W}_1(Mp_a)}{1 - p_0 P_f(Mp_s) - p_1 P_d} \right.
$$

$$
\left. + \frac{p_1(1 - P_d)\mathbb{W}_2(Mp_a)}{1 - p_0 P_f(Mp_s) - p_1 P_d} - \Theta_a - p_s R \right),
$$

$$
= \eta p_a (1 - p_a) \left(\left((\xi_1 - \xi_2)\frac{p_0(1 - P_f(Mp_s))}{1 - p_0 P_f(Mp_s) - p_1 P_d} + \xi_2 \right) \right.
$$

$$
\left. \times \mathbb{F}(Mp_a) - \Theta_a - p_s R \right).
\tag{7.75}
$$

where $\xi_1 = \frac{T_a - I_1(T_a)}{T_a}$ and $\xi_2 = \frac{T_a - I_2(T_a)}{T_a}$. When $T_a \ll \lambda_1$ and λ_0, it can be seen that $I_1(T_a)$ goes to 0 and $I_2(T_a)$ goes to T_a according to (7.64) and (7.70). In this case, $\xi_1 \to 1$ and $\xi_2 \to 0$, which represents the fact that the asynchronous scenario is reduced to the synchronous scenario when $T_a \ll \lambda_1$ and λ_0. Based on the analysis of the replicator dynamics equations (7.74) and (7.75), which resembles the ESS analysis in the synchronous scenario, Theorem 7.4 can be obtained.

THEOREM 7.4   *Three ESSs are available for the joint spectrum sensing and access evolutionary game under the asynchronous scenario:* $(p_s^*, p_a^*) = (1,0)$, $(1, p_{a_1})$, *and* (p_{s_2}, p_{a_2}), *under different conditions of the rewards R as follows:*

$$(p_s^*, p_a^*) = \begin{cases} (1,0), & R > \left((\xi_1 - \xi_2)\frac{p_0(1-P_f(M))}{1-p_0 P_f(M)-p_1 P_d} + \xi_2 \right) \mathbb{F}(1) - \Theta_a, \\[2ex] (1, p_{a_1}), & R > \frac{\Theta_s}{1-p_{a_1}(1-p_0 P_f(M)-p_1 P_d)}, \\[2ex] (p_{s_2}, p_{a_2}), & R < \frac{p_0^2 p_{s_2}(1-P_f(Mp_{s_2}))\frac{d\mathbb{F}(Mp_{a_2})}{dp_{a_2}} - \frac{p_0 p_1(1-P_d)\mathbb{F}(Mp_{a_2})}{1-p_0 P_f(Mp_{s_2})-p_1 P_d}}{(1-p_0 P_f(Mp_{s_2})-p_1 P_d)^2/(\xi_1-\xi_2)} \frac{dP_f(Mp_{s_2})}{dp_{s_2}}. \end{cases}$$

$$(7.76)$$

7.5   A Distributed Learning Algorithm for the ESSs

Based on the aforementioned joint spectrum sensing and access evolutionary games, the ESSs for the SUs have been obtained. Therefore, through the replicator dynamics equations (7.27) and (7.36) in the synchronous scenario and (7.74) and (7.75) in the asynchronous scenario, a group of SUs is in a position to achieve the ESSs. It can be inferred that solving these equations entails the exchange of utilities among all SUs in order to work out the average utilities, such as $\mathbb{U}_s$ and $\mathbb{U}_a|_{\mathcal{D}_0}$. In a distributed network, however, the disclosure of such private information by each SU is a commonly encountered difficulty. This section introduces a distributed learning algorithm that may gradually converge to an ESS with no exchange of private utility information.

In evolutionary biology, research on population reproduction dynamics under natural selection is characterized by the prevalent application of the Wright–Fisher model [35]. In this model, it is assumed that the probability of an individual's adoption of a certain strategy is in proportion to the expected utility of the population using that strategy. Let $\tilde{p}_s$ and $\tilde{p}_a$ be the probabilities of an SU sensing and accessing the primary channel, respectively. In line with the Wright–Fisher model, $\tilde{p}_s$ is in proportion to the total utility of the SUs sensing the channel. In this case, the SUs' strategy of spectrum sensing at time slot $t + 1$, $\tilde{p}_s(t + 1)$, can be calculated by

$$\tilde{p}_s(t+1) = \frac{p_s(t)\tilde{\mathbb{U}}_s(t)}{p_s(t)\tilde{\mathbb{U}}_s(t) + \left(1 - p_s(t)\right)\tilde{\mathbb{U}}_{\bar{s}}(t)} = \frac{p_s(t)\tilde{\mathbb{U}}_s(t)}{\tilde{\mathbb{U}}(t)}, \qquad (7.77)$$

where $\tilde{\mathbb{U}}_s(t)$ and $\tilde{\mathbb{U}}_{\bar{s}}(t)$ are the average utilities of the SUs who have sensed and not sensed the channel at the tth time slot, respectively, and the denominator $\tilde{\mathbb{U}}(t)$ is the average utility of all SUs, which is the normalization term that ensures $\tilde{p}_s + \tilde{p}_{\bar{s}} = 1$. After cooperative spectrum sensing at the beginning of the time slot, when the presence of the PU is observable, under no circumstances will the SUs access the primary channel within this slot. Rather, each SU will access the channel with probability $\tilde{p}_a$. According to the Wright–Fisher model, $\tilde{p}_a$ is in proportion to the total utility of the SUs who decide to access the channel. In this case, one strategy for the SUs to access the channel $\tilde{p}_a$ can be calculated by

$$\tilde{p}_a(t'+1) = \frac{p_a(t')\widetilde{U}_a(t')}{p_a(t')\widetilde{U}_a(t') + (1 - p_a(t'))\widetilde{U}_{\bar{a}}(t')} = \frac{p_a(t')\widetilde{U}_a(t')}{\widetilde{U}(t')}, \qquad (7.78)$$

where t' and $t'+1$ stand for the time slots when the absence of the PU is observable to the SUs, $\widetilde{U}_a(t')$ and $\widetilde{U}_{\bar{a}}(t')$ refer to the average utilities of the SUs who have accessed and not accessed the channel at the t'th time slot, respectively, and $\widetilde{U}(t')$ represents the average utility of all SUs when the absence of the PU is observable.

When the number of SUs M is assumed to be sufficiently large, the portion of the SUs who sense the primary channel equals the probability that one individual SU decides on sensing the channel (i.e., $p_s = \tilde{p}_s$). Similarly, $p_a = \tilde{p}_a$ if the absence of the PU is observable by SUs. In this case, we have

$$\tilde{p}_s(t+1) = \frac{\tilde{p}_s(t)\widetilde{U}_s(t)}{\tilde{p}_s(t)\widetilde{U}_s(t) + (1 - \tilde{p}_s(t))\widetilde{U}_{\bar{s}}(t)},$$

$$= \frac{\tilde{p}_s(t)\widetilde{U}_s(t)}{\widetilde{U}(t)}, \qquad (7.79)$$

$$\tilde{p}_a(t'+1) = \frac{\tilde{p}_a(t')\widetilde{U}_a(t')}{\tilde{p}_a(t')\widetilde{U}_a(t') + (1 - \tilde{p}_a(t'))\widetilde{U}_{\bar{a}}(t')},$$

$$= \frac{\tilde{p}_a(t')\widetilde{U}_a(t')}{\widetilde{U}(t')}. \qquad (7.80)$$

According to (7.79), it can be known that when $\widetilde{U}_s = \widetilde{U}_{\bar{s}}$ or $\tilde{p}_s = 0$ or 1, $\dot{\tilde{p}}_s = 0$ (i.e., it is possible to achieve the equilibrium). In accordance with the replicator dynamics equation of spectrum sensing in (7.27), $\widetilde{U}_s = \widetilde{U}_{\bar{s}}$ and $\tilde{p}_s = 0$ or 1 are the solutions for the replicator dynamics. The same argument is true of p_a. Consequently, when M is large enough, the Wright–Fisher model will equalize the replicator dynamics equations.

According to (7.79), it can be known that all SUs have to be aware of the average utilities $\widetilde{U}_s(t)$ and $\widetilde{U}_{\bar{s}}(t)$ so as to update $\tilde{p}_s(t+1)$. There are assumptions that it is possible to further divide each slot into L subslots and that each SU adopts an identical strategy of channel sensing and access constantly during all L subslots. An effective method for utility learning is proposed in [36]. Drawing on the method in the chapter, we have

$$\widetilde{U}_s(t,n+1) = \begin{cases} (1 - \tau(n))\widetilde{U}_s(t,n) + \tau(n)U_{sa}(t,n), & \text{sensing and accessing,} \\ (1 - \tau(n))\widetilde{U}_s(t,n) + \tau(n)U_{s\bar{a}}(t,n), & \text{sensing but not accessing,} \\ \widetilde{U}_s(t,n), & \text{not sensing,} \end{cases} \qquad (7.81)$$

$$\widetilde{U}_{\bar{s}}(t,n+1) = \begin{cases} (1 - \tau(n))\widetilde{U}_{\bar{s}}(t,n) + \tau(n)U_{\bar{s}a}(t,n), & \text{not sensing but accessing,} \\ (1 - \tau(n))\widetilde{U}_{\bar{s}}(t,n) + \tau(n)U_{\bar{s}\bar{a}}(t,n), & \text{not sensing and accessing,} \\ \widetilde{U}_{\bar{s}}(t,n), & \text{sensing,} \end{cases} \qquad (7.82)$$

where $1 \leq n \leq L - 1$, $\tau(n) \in (0,1)$ is a sequence of averaging factors $\sum_n \tau(n) = \infty$ and $\sum_n \tau^2(n) < \infty$ [36]. $\tau(n)$ is set as $\tau(n) = \frac{1}{n}$. The SUs also need to acquire

---

Algorithm 7: A distributed learning algorithm for the ESSs.

---

(1) When the time slot index $t = 0$ is available, the SU initializes its strategy $\tilde{p}_s$ and $\tilde{p}_a$ with $\tilde{p}_s(0)$ and $\tilde{p}_a(0)$.

(2) **for** each time slot t **do**

(3) 　**for** $n = 1 : L$ **do**

(4) 　　• Sense the primary channel with probability $\tilde{p}_s(t)$.

(5) 　　• Share its sensing data with others on the signaling channel.

(6) 　　**if** the SU observes that the PU is absent **then**

(7) 　　　• Access the primary channel with probability $\tilde{p}_a(t)$.

(8) 　　　• Estimate the average utilities of sensing and not sensing using (7.81) and (7.82).

(9) 　　　• Estimate the average utilities of accessing and not accessing using (7.83) and (7.84).

(10) 　　**else**

(11) 　　　• Do not access the primary channel.

(12) 　　　• Estimate the average utilities of sensing and not sensing using (7.81) and (7.82).

(13) 　　**end if**

(14) 　**end for**

(15) 　• Update the probability of sensing and accessing, $\tilde{p}_s(t + 1)$ and $\tilde{p}_a(t + 1)$, using (7.79) and (7.80).

(16) **end for**

---

knowledge of the average utilities $\widetilde{\mathbb{U}}_a(t)$ and $\widetilde{\mathbb{U}}_{\bar{a}}(t)$ to update $\tilde{p}_a(t + 1)$ in (7.80). Similarly to $\tilde{p}_s(t + 1)$, we have

$$\widetilde{\mathbb{U}}_a(t', n + 1) = \begin{cases} (1 - \tau(n))\widetilde{\mathbb{U}}_a(t', n) + \tau(n)U_{sa}(t', n), & \text{sensing and accessing,} \\ (1 - \tau(n))\widetilde{\mathbb{U}}_a(t', n) + \tau(n)U_{\bar{s}a}(t', n), & \text{not sensing but accessing,} \\ \widetilde{\mathbb{U}}_a(t', n), & \text{not accessing,} \end{cases}$$

(7.83)

$$\widetilde{\mathbb{U}}_{\bar{a}}(t', n + 1) = \begin{cases} (1 - \tau(n))\widetilde{\mathbb{U}}_{\bar{a}}(t', n) + \tau(n)U_{s\bar{a}}(t', n), & \text{sensing but not accessing,} \\ (1 - \tau(n))\widetilde{\mathbb{U}}_{\bar{a}}(t', n) + \tau(n)U_{\bar{s}\bar{a}}(t', n), & \text{not sensing and accessing,} \\ \widetilde{\mathbb{U}}_{\bar{a}}(t', n), & \text{accessing.} \end{cases}$$

(7.84)

Each SU is able to gradually come to know the ESS on the basis of (7.79)–(7.84). In Algorithm 7, a detailed summary is given for the procedures of the distributed learning algorithm.

Table 7.1. Parameters used in the simulation.

Parameter	Value	Description
M	20	The number of SUs
γ	-15 dB	The SUs' received SNR of the PU's signal under $\mathcal{H}_1$
P_d	0.9	Detection probability given by the PU
T_s	10 ms	Sensing time of each SU
T_a	100 ms	Accessing time of each SU
λ	1 MHz	Sampling rate of the energy detection
B	8 MHz	Bandwidth of the primary channel
SNR	-10 dB	Each SU's signal-to-noise ratio
INR	-20 dB	The interference-to-noise ratio from each transmitting SU
E_1	0.03 mw/bit	Factor that translates one SU's throughput reward into its energy reward
E_2	0.5 mw/s	Energy consumed per second by data transmission
E_3	2 mw/s	Energy consumed per second by spectrum sensing
p_0	0.9	Probability that the PU is absent
λ_0	2000 ms	Average length of the OFF state
λ_1	222 ms	Average length of the ON state
$R_{av}^{\downarrow}$	10 Mbps	PU's minimum average data rate
R_p	15 Mbps	PU's data rate when there is no interference from the SUs

7.6 Simulation Results

To verify the effectiveness of the theoretical analysis, simulations are conducted in this section. Table 7.1 shows all of the relevant parameters.

7.6.1 ESSs of the Synchronous and Asynchronous Scenarios

The process begins with the illustration of the ESS of the synchronous scenario where all SUs update their strategies through the proposed learning alogrithm shown in Algorithm 7. The convergence of the population states p_s and p_a is shown in Figure 7.5, where the reward to the SUs that merely contribute to sensing but do not access the channel, R, is set as 40, 100, or 400. In the simulation, the initial population states are set as $p_s = 0.1$ and $p_a = 0.9$, which indicates that a large portion of the SUs access the primary channel without contributing to channel sensing. Figure 7.5 shows that, with this scheme, the SUs tend to leave such an undesired strategy immediately, and the system culminates in the convergence to different ESSs under various settings of the reward R.

It can be seen from Figure 7.5(a) that when the reward $R = 40$, the ESS is $(p_s^*, p_a^*) = (0.6, 0.4)$, which is in line with the case that a portion of the SUs sense

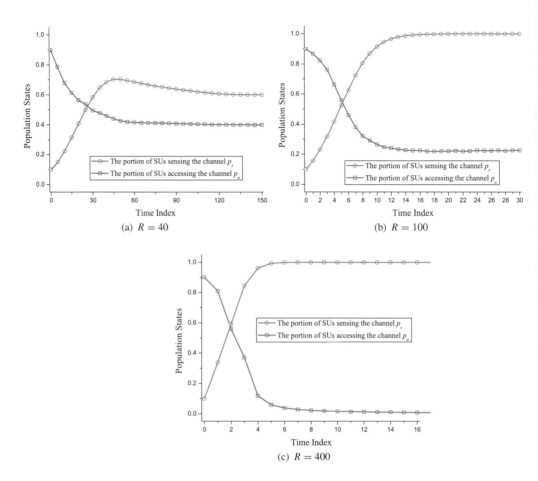

Figure 7.5 Population states of the synchronous scenario.

and access the primary channel. In this case, the convergence of p_s to 0.6 is based on the fact that 60% of SUs cooperatively sensing the channel can already achieve a relatively low false-alarm probability, and the convergence of p_a to 0.4 is grounded in the fact that over 40% of the SUs simultaneously accessing the channel will cause serious damage to mutual throughput.

According to Figure 7.5(b), when the reward $R = 100$, the ESS is $(p_s^*, p_a^*) = (1, 0.25)$, which is in line with the case that all SUs sense but a portion of them access the primary channel. When $p_s = 0.6$, despite the sufficiently low false-alarm probability, the increase in the reward R improves the utility of sensing but not accessing, which indicates an increase in the number of SUs who sense but a decrease in the number of SUs who access the primary channel.

According to Figure 7.5(c), when the reward $R = 400$, the ESS is $(p_s^*, p_a^*) = (1, 0)$, which is in line with the case that all SUs sense but none access the primary channel. In this case, the reward R is high enough for each SU to derive relatively high utility from mere sensing without accessing the channel. Consequently, to ensure the network's convergence to a desired ESS, R should be set appropriately.

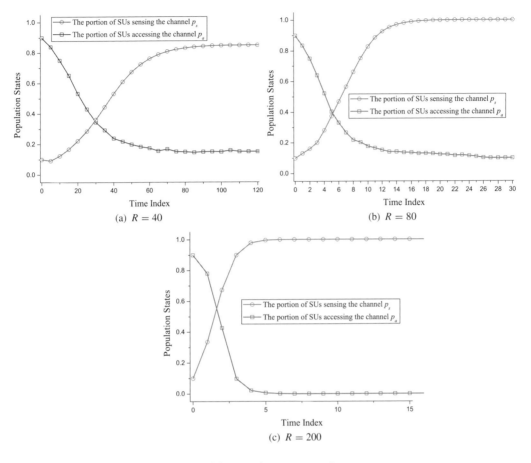

Figure 7.6 Population states of the asynchronous scenario.

We then analyze the ESS of the asynchronous scenario. In light of the parameters in Table 7.1, the SUs' access time is calculated as $T_a = 150$ ms from (7.63), (7.64), and (7.70). The convergence of the population states p_s and p_a with various settings of the reward R under the asynchronous scenario is shown in Figure 7.6. Here the initial population states are also set as $p_s = 0.1$ and $p_a = 0.9$. It is shown in Figure 7.6(a) that when the reward $R = 40$, the ESS is $(p_s^*, p_a^*) = (0.85, 0.15)$. According to Figure 7.6(b), when the reward $R = 80$, the ESS is $(p_s^*, p_a^*) = (1, 0.1)$. It is shown in in Figure 7.6(c) that when the reward $R = 200$, the ESS is $(p_s^*, p_a^*) = (1, 0)$. The simulation results of these two scenarios are in line with the ESS analysis in Sections 7.3 and 7.4.

7.6.2 Stability of the ESSs

When the system is at ESS, verification of the stability of the ESS requires the SUs to deviate from the equilibrium. According to Figure 7.7(a), in the synchronous scenario, the SUs deviate from cooperative sensing by setting $p_s = 0.1$ at $t = 200$ when the system has already converged to the ESS. It is clear that both p_s and p_a return to

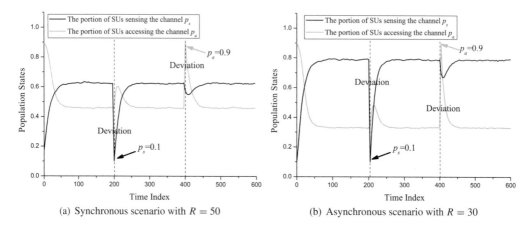

(a) Synchronous scenario with $R = 50$ (b) Asynchronous scenario with $R = 30$

Figure 7.7 Stability of the ESSs.

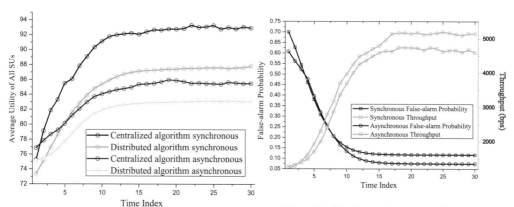

Figure 7.8 Utility comparison of the synchronous scenario with $R = 50$ and the asynchronous scenario with $R = 30$.

Figure 7.9 Sensing and access performances under the synchronous scenario with $R = 100$ and the asynchronous scenario with $R = 80$.

the ESS quickly after the perturbation. When p_s falls to 0.1, a minor increase can be found in p_a. This is based on the fact that a remarkable reduction in p_s will result in the decrease of both $\mathbb{U}_a$ and $\mathbb{U}_{\bar{a}}$. If the reduction $\Delta\mathbb{U}_a < \Delta\mathbb{U}_{\bar{a}}$, $\dot{p}_a$ is larger than 0 based on (7.8), this leads to the increase of p_a. When $t = 400$, the SUs deviate from the equilibrium again when $p_a = 0.9$. In this case, the utility from channel access is extremely low and the SUs will not sense and access the channel. This explains the decrease of p_s when p_a is set at 0.9. As is shown in Figure 7.7(b), similar phenomena can be found in the asynchronous scenario.

7.6.3   Performance Evaluation

First, the performance of the distributed learning algorithm is compared with that of the centralized algorithm. In the centralized model, a data center is responsible for the collection of information about the utility of each SU in each slot and about the global adjustment to the SUs' strategies p_s and p_a in the next time slot. Figure 7.8 shows the results of the comparison in terms of the average utility of all SUs, from which the gap between the distributed algorithm and the centralized one is revealed to be around 6%. Nevertheless, the centralized algorithm provides a truthful report of the private utility information of all of the SUs, whereas the distributed learning algorithm does not.

Furthermore, a simulation is conducted for the evaluation of the performance of the joint channel sensing and access algorithm. The performances of the SUs' false-alarm probability and throughput during the ESS convergence process within the synchronous and asynchronous scenarios can be found in Figure 7.9. Along with the system's convergence to the ESS for the two scenarios, the false-alarm probability gradually approaches a minimum, while the throughput gradually reaches a peak. Additionally, as is shown in Figures 7.5(b), 7.6(b), and 7.9, it is clear that the false-alarm probability is a decreasing function according to p_s and the SUs' throughput is a decreasing function according to p_a, which is in line with the results proved in Lemma 7.1.

7.7   Conclusion

In this chapter, by utilizing evolutionary game theory, we determine how to make the SUs choose cooperation in the joint spectrum sensing and access problem. We discuss the behavior dynamics of the SUs within two scenarios: synchronous and asynchronous. Different ESSs under various conditions are obtained from the solution of the joint replicator dynamics equations of channel sensing and accessing. In accordance with natural selection theory, a distributed learning algorithm that enables the SUs to achieve the ESSs on the basis of their own utility histories is introduced. Simulation results show that convergence of the population states of the network to the desired ESS is achieved via adjustment of the reward to the contributors.

In this chapter, the single-channel case is discussed as one of the system models. Further studies will be done on the multichannel case in which Markov processes are applicable to the simulation of the transition process of the channel state, where the system state space refers to the set of all possible combinations of all channel states (if the channels are independent). In this case, the utility functions rely on the system state, while the analysis of replicator dynamics and ESS derivations resembles that of the single-channel case. Based on the fact that the system state space increases in an exponential manner according to the number of channels, it is necessary to design a fast, suboptimal learning algorithm for the SUs to converge to the ESS.

References

[1] S. Haykin, "Cognitive radio: brain-empowered wireless communications," *IEEE Journal of Selected Areas in Communications*, vol. 23, pp. 201–220, 2005.

[2] B. Wang and K. J. R. Liu, "Advances in cognitive radios: A survey," *IEEE Journal of Selected Topics in Signal Processing*, vol. 5, pp. 5–23, 2011.

[3] K. J. R. Liu and B. Wang, *Cognitive Radio Networking and Security: A Game-theoretic View*. Cambridge University Press, 2010.

[4] S. Shankar, C. Cordeiro, and K. Challapali, "Spectrum agile radios: utilization and sensing architectures," in *Proc. IEEE DySPAN*, 2005.

[5] H. Tang, "Some physical layer issues of wide-band cognitive radio systems," in *Proc. IEEE DySPAN*, 2005.

[6] A. Ghasemi and E. S. Sousa, "Collaborative spectrum sensing for opportunistic access in fading environments," in *Proc. IEEE DySPAN*, 2005.

[7] E. Visotsky, S. Kuffner, and R. Peterson, "On collaborative detection of TV transmissions in support of dynamic spectrum sharing," in *Proc. IEEE DySPAN*, 2005.

[8] Y. C. Liang, Y. Zeng, E. C. Y. Peh, and A. T. Hoang, "Sensing–throughput tradeoff for cognitive radio networks," *IEEE Transactions on Wireless Communications*, vol. 7, pp. 1326–1337, 2008.

[9] R. Fan and H. Jiang, "Optimal multi-channel cooperative sensing in cognitive radio networks," *IEEE Transactions on Wireless Communications*, vol. 9, pp. 1128–1138, 2010.

[10] F. Zeng, C. Li, and Z. Tian, "Distributed compressive spectrum sensing in cooperative multihop cognitive networks," *IEEE Journal of Selected Topics in Signal Processing*, vol. 5, pp. 37–48, 2011.

[11] Q. Zhao, L. Tong, A. Swami, and Y. Chen, "Decentralized cognitive MAC for opportunistic spectrum access in ad hoc networks: A POMDP framework," *IEEE Journal of Selected Areas in Communications*, vol. 25, pp. 589–600, 2007.

[12] A. K. Sadek, K. J. R. Liu, and A. Ephremides, "Cognitive multiple access via cooperation: protocol design and performance analysis," *IEEE Transactions on Information Theory*, vol. 53, pp. 3677–3695, 2007.

[13] Z. Ji and K. J. R. Liu, "Dynamic spectrum sharing: A game theoretical overview," *IEEE Communications Magazine*, vol. 45, pp. 88–94, 2007.

[14] J. Unnikrishnan and V. V. Veeravalli, "Algorithms for dynamic spectrum access with learning for cognitive radio," *IEEE Transactions on Signal Processing*, vol. 58, pp. 750–760, 2010.

[15] A. A. El-Sherif, A. Kwasinski, A. Sadek, and K. J. R. Liu, "Content-aware cognitive multiple access protocol for cooperative packet speech communications," *IEEE Transactions on Wireless Communications*, vol. 8, pp. 995–1005, 2009.

[16] A. A. El-Sherif, A. K. Sadek, and K. J. R. Liu, "Opportunistic multiple access for cognitive radio networks," *IEEE Journal of Selected Areas Communications*, vol. 29, pp. 704–715, 2011.

[17] Y. Wu, B. Wang, K. J. R. Liu, and T. Clancy, "A scalable collusion-resistant multi-winner cognitive spectrum auction game," *IEEE Transactions on Communications*, vol. 57, pp. 3805–3816, 2009.

[18] D. Li, Y. Xu, X. Wang, and M. Guizani, "Coalitional game theoretic approach for secondary spectrum access in cooperative cognitive radio networks," *IEEE Transactions on Wireless Communications*, vol. 10, pp. 844–856, 2011.

[19] A. A. El-Sherif and K. J. R. Liu, "Joint design of spectrum sensing and channel access in cognitive radio networks," *IEEE Transactions on Wireless Communications*, vol. 10, pp. 1743–1753, 2011.

[20] W. Saad, Z. Han, R. Zheng, A. Hjorungnes, T. Basar, and H. V. Poor, "Coalitional games in partition form for joint spectrum sensing and access in cognitive radio networks," *IEEE Journal of Selected Topics in Signal Processing*, vol. 6, pp. 195–209, 2012.

[21] Y. Chen, Y. Gao, and K. J. R. Liu, "An evolutionary game-theoretic approach for image interpolation," in *Proc. IEEE International Conference on Acoustics, Speech, and Signal Processing (ICASSP)*, 2011.

[22] R. Cressman, *Evolutionary Dynamics and Extensive Form Games*. MIT Press, 2003.

[23] B. Wang, Y. Wu, and K. J. R. Liu, "Game theory for cognitive radio networks: An overview," *Computer Networks*, vol. 54, pp. 2537–2561, 2010.

[24] E. H. Watanabe, D. Menasché, E. Silva, and R. M. Leão, "Modeling resource sharing dynamics of VoIP users over a WLAN using a game-theoretic approach," in *Proc. IEEE INFOCOM*, 2008.

[25] B. Wang, K. J. R. Liu, and T. Clancy, "Evolutionary cooperative spectrum sensing game: How to collaborate?" *IEEE Transactions on Communications*, vol. 58, pp. 890–900, 2010.

[26] Y. Chen, B. Wang, W. S. Lin, Y. Wu, and K. J. R. Liu, "Cooperative peer-to-peer streaming: An evolutionary game-theoretic approach," *IEEE Transactions on Circuits and Systems for Video Technology*, vol. 20, pp. 1346–1357, 2010.

[27] P. Baronti, P. Pillai, V. Chook, S. Chessa, A. Gotta, and Y. Hu, "Wireless sensor networks: A survey on the state of the art and the 802.15.4 and ZigBee standards," *Computer Communications*, vol. 30, pp. 1655–1695, 2007.

[28] C. Buratti, A. Conti, D. Dardari, and R. Verdone, "An overview on wireless sensor networks technology and evolution," *Sensors*, vol. 9, pp. 6869–6896, 2009.

[29] I. F. Akyildiz, B. F. Lo, and R. Balakrishnan, "Cooperative spectrum sensing in cognitive radio networks: A survey," *Physical Communication*, vol. 4, pp. 40–62, 2011.

[30] C. Jiang, Y. Chen, K. J. R. Liu, and Y. Ren, "Renewal-theoretical dynamic spectrum access in cognitive radio networks with unknown primary behavior," *IEEE Journal of Selected Areas in Communications*, vol. 31, pp. 1–11, 2013.

[31] C. Jiang, Y. Chen, and K. J. R. Liu, "A renewal-theoretical framework for dynamic spectrum access with unknown primary behavior," in *Proc. IEEE Globecom*, 2012.

[32] C. Jiang, Y. Chen, K. J. R. Liu, and Y. Ren, "Analysis of interference in cognitive radio networks with unknown primary behavior," in *Proc. IEEE ICC*, 2012.

[33] H. Kim and K. G. Shin, "Efficient discovery of spectrum opportunities with MAC-layer sensing in cognitive radio networks," *IEEE Transactions on Mobile Computing*, vol. 7, pp. 533–545, 2008.

[34] D. R. Cox, *Renewal Theory*. Butler and Tanner, 1967.

[35] R. Fisher, *The Genetical Theory of Natural Selection*. Clarendon Press, 1930.

[36] R. Cominetti, E. Melo, and S. Sorin, "A payoff-based learning procedure and its application to traffic games," *Games and Economic Behavior*, vol. 70, pp. 71–83, 2010.

8 Graphical Evolutionary Game for Distributed Adaptive Networks

Distributed adaptive filtering is now regarded as an efficient method to process and estimate data over distributed networks. Nevertheless, the majority of existent distributed adaptive filtering algorithms neglect the distributed network's natural evolutionary attributes, and they focus on devising different information propagation rules. In this chapter, the adaptive network is studied from the perspective of game theory, and the graphical evolutionary game is utilized to formulate the distributed adaptive filtering problem. In this case, we consider the nodes as players and regard the nearby combiner of estimation data from diverse neighbors as a form of diverse strategy determination. It is shown that this general graphical evolutionary game framework is able to unify the existing adaptive network algorithms. As examples, we will discuss two error-aware adaptive filtering algorithms based on this framework. Furthermore, graphical evolutionary game theory (EGT) is used to determine the process of information diffusion over adaptive networks and the system's evolutionarily stable strategy (ESS). Finally, simulation results are presented verifying that the method discussed in this chapter is effective.

8.1 Introduction

Recently, the notion of adaptive filter networks has developed from conventional adaptive filtering. In this concept, a group of nodes cooperate with each other and estimate a number of parameters of interest from noisy measurements [1]. This kind of distributed estimation architecture is feasible in cases such as distributed cooperative sensing in cognitive radio networks, wireless ad hoc networks for military event localization, wireless sensor networks for environmental monitoring, etc. [2,3]. The distributed architecture, compared with the classic centralized one, is more robust in case the central node operates improperly, and it is also more adaptable if the nodes are mobile. As a result, the adaptive filter network is regarded as an effective method for achieving data diffusion, data fusion, and data processing on distributed networks [4].

In a distributed adaptive filter network, node i receives a set of data $\{d_i(t), \boldsymbol{u}_{i,t}\}$ at every time index t, and the data meet a linear regression model as follows:

$$d_i(t) = \boldsymbol{u}_{i,t}\boldsymbol{w}^0 + v_i(t). \tag{8.1}$$

Here w^0 denotes a deterministic but unknown $M \times 1$ vector, $d_i(t)$ denotes a scalar measurement of some random process d_i, $u_{i,t}$ represents the regression vector with dimensions $1 \times M$ at time t with zero mean and covariance matrix $R_{u_i} = \mathbb{E}(u_{i,t}^* u_{i,t}) > 0$, and $v_i(t)$ is the signal of random noise with zero mean and variance σ_i^2 at time t. It is worth noting that the measurement process d_i and the regression data $u_{i,t}$ are spatially independent and temporally white. Each node's target is to estimate parameter w^0 by using the data set $\{d_i(t), u_{i,t}\}$.

In existing works, a number of distributed adaptive filtering algorithms for estimating parameter w^0 have been proposed. For instance, the incremental least mean square (LMS) algorithm was introduced in [5], which is one kind of incremental algorithm. In these algorithms, node i updates w (i.e., the estimation of w^0) by merging the observed data sets of node $i - 1$ and itself. The diffusion algorithms (e.g., diffusion recursive least square [6] and diffusion LMS [7,8]) are quite different, enabling node i to combine all of its neighbors' data sets. In addition, [9] introduced projection-based adaptive filtering algorithms (e.g., the combine–project–adapt algorithm [10] and the projected subgradient algorithm [11]). The authors of [12] gave consideration to the mobility of the node and analyzed mobile adaptive networks as well.

Although these conventional distributed adaptive filtering algorithms show promising performance, they are generally centered on the design of various information diffusion rules or combination rules within their neighborhoods. This can be done by using nodes' statistics and/or the information on the network's topology. For instance, the degree of information of each node is considered in the relative degree rule [6], and the variance in information of each node is further incorporated in the relative degree–variance rule [7]. Nevertheless, the majority of the existing algorithms are intuitively created to achieve particular goals, which are bottom-up methods. There is no existing work that offers a design philosophy to explain why combination and/or diffusion rules are developed and how they are related in a unified view. Is there a common system that can uncover the ties among the existing rules and guide us toward the better design of distributed adaptive filtering algorithms? It has been found that the parameter updating process in distributed adaptive networks resembles the process of evolution in natural ecological systems. Thus, we introduce a general framework in this chapter on the basis of the graphical evolutionary game. This framework provides a consolidated overview of existing distributed adaptive algorithms and offers ideas clues for future new designs, and it also provides a top-down design philosophy to explain the basic relationships between distributed adaptive networks, making it different from the conventional bottom-up approaches focusing on particular rules.

8.2   Related Works

Let us think about an adaptive filter network composed of N nodes. In the case in which a fusion center that gathers information from every node exists, then we can use global (centralized) optimization methods to acquire the optimal updating rule for w, in which w is a deterministic but unknown $M \times 1$ vector for estimation, as presented

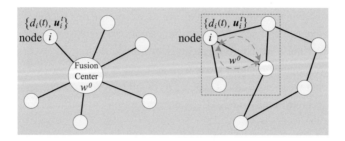

Figure 8.1 Left: centralized model. Right: distributed model.

in the left part of Figure 8.1. In the global LMS algorithm, for example, we are able to write the parameter updating rule as [7]

$$w_{t+1} = w_t + \mu \sum_{i=1}^{N} u_{i,t}^{*}(d_i(t) - u_{i,t}w_t), \tag{8.2}$$

where μ represents the step size and $\{\cdot\}^*$ is a complex conjugation operation. It can be seen that with (8.2) the centralized LMS algorithm demands the information of $\{d_i(t), u_{i,t}\}$ beyond the whole network, which is usually unrealistic. This kind of centralized architecture has a high dependence on the fusion center, and it would break if some data links are not connected or the fusion center becomes dysfunctional.

If a fusion center does not exist in the network, then as is shown in the right part of Figure 8.1, every node should exchange information with its neighbors to update the parameter. In the literature, some distributed adaptive filtering algorithms have been proposed, such as distributed LMS [7,8], projection-based algorithms [10,11], and distributed incremental algorithms [5]. These distributed algorithms are based on classic adaptive filtering algorithms in which nodes can estimate the parameter w^0 by utilizing information from their neighbors. We take Adapt-then-Combine Diffusion LMS (ATC) [7], one of the distributed LMS algorithms, as an example, for which the parameter updating rule of node i is

$$\begin{cases} \chi_{i,t+1} = w_{i,t} + \mu_i \sum_{j \in \mathcal{N}_i} o_{ij} u_{j,t}^{*}(d_j(t) - u_{j,t}w_{j,t}), \\ \\ w_{i,t+1} = \sum_{j \in \mathcal{N}_i} a_{ij}\chi_{j,t+1}, \end{cases} \tag{8.3}$$

where $\mathcal{N}_i$ stands for node i's neighboring node set (including node i itself) and o_{ij} and a_{ij} are linear weights that satisfy the following conditions:

$$\begin{cases} o_{ij} = a_{ij} = 0, \quad \text{if } j \notin \mathcal{N}_i, \\ \\ \sum_{j=1}^{N} o_{ij} = 1, \quad \sum_{j=1}^{N} a_{ij} = 1. \end{cases} \tag{8.4}$$

Because the interchange of full raw data $\{d_i(t), u_{i,t}\}$ with neighbors exacts a high price in practical situations, we usually set the weight o_{ij} as $o_{ij} = 0$, if $j \neq i$, as is

Table 8.1. Different combination rules.

Name	Rule: $A_i(j) =$
Uniform [10,13]	$\frac{1}{n_i}$, for all $j \in \mathcal{N}_i$
Maximum degree [6,14]	$\begin{cases} \frac{1}{N}, & \text{for } j \neq i, \\ 1 - \frac{n_i - 1}{N}, & \text{for } j = i \end{cases}$
Laplacian [15,16]	$\begin{cases} \frac{1}{n_{\max}}, & \text{for } j \neq i \\ 1 - \frac{n_i - 1}{n_{\max}}, & \text{for } j = i \end{cases}$
Relative degree [6]	$\frac{n_j}{\sum_{k \in \mathcal{N}_i} n_k}$, for all $j \in \mathcal{N}_i$
Relative degree–variance [7]	$\frac{n_j \sigma_j^{-2}}{\sum_{k \in \mathcal{N}_i} n_k \sigma_k^{-2}}$, for all $j \in \mathcal{N}_i$
Metropolis [16,17]	$\begin{cases} \frac{1}{\max\{\lvert\mathcal{N}_i\rvert, \lvert\mathcal{N}_j\rvert\}}, & \text{for } j \neq i, \\ 1 - \sum_{k \neq i} A_i(k), & \text{for } j = i \end{cases}$
Hastings [17]	$\begin{cases} \frac{\sigma_j^2}{\max\{\lvert\mathcal{N}_i\rvert\sigma_i^2, \lvert\mathcal{N}_j\rvert\sigma_j^2\}}, & \text{for } j \neq i, \\ 1 - \sum_{k \neq i} A_i(k), & \text{for } j = i \end{cases}$

shown in [7]. In this case, when node i has neighbour set $\{i_1, i_2, \ldots, i_{n_i}\}$ and owns degree n_i (including node i itself; i.e., the cardinality of set $\mathcal{N}_i$), the general parameter updating rule can be written as

$$w_{i,t+1} = A_{i,t+1}(F(w_{i_1,t}), F(w_{i_2,t}), \ldots, F(w_{i_{n_i},t})),$$

$$= \sum_{j \in \mathcal{N}_i} A_{i,t+1}(j) F(w_{j,t}), \tag{8.5}$$

where $F(\cdot)$ could be any adaptive filtering algorithm (e.g. $F(w_{i,t}) = w_{i,t} + \mu u_{i,t}^*(d_i(t) - u_{i,t}w_{i,t})$ for the LMS algorithm). $A_{i,t+1}(\cdot)$ denotes a few particular linear combination rules. Equation (8.5) provides a general expression for existing distributed adaptive filtering algorithms. Under this circumstance, performance is mainly determined by the combination rule $A_{i,t+1}(\cdot)$. Table 8.1 sums up the existing combination rules in which $A_{i,t+1}(j) = 0$, if $j \notin \mathcal{N}_i$ is satisfied.

It can be seen from Table 8.1 that the network topology alone determines the weights of the first four combination rules. However, sensitivity to the spatial difference of noise and signal statistics among the network is the shortcoming of such topology-based rules. The relative degree–variance rule has a better mean-square performance than others, but this requires knowledge of the noise variances of all neighbors. All of these distributed algorithms focus on the creation of combination rules only. However, the nodes in a distributed network are just like individuals in a system, and the network can be seen as a natural ecological system that may follow some nature evolutionary rules spontaneously, rather than some particular artificially predefined rules. In addition, there is still no general method that can uncover the unifying fundamentals of distributed adaptive filtering problems, despite the fact that scholars have developed various kinds of combination rules. In the next section, graphical EGT theory will be used to set up a general framework for unifying existing algorithms, and we will provide an overview of the distributed adaptive filtering problem.

8.3   Graphical Evolutionary Game Formulation

8.3.1   Introduction to the Graphical Evolutionary Game

EGT starts from ecological biology [18]. Instead of paying attention only to the characteristics of the equilibrium, EGT focuses more on the stability and dynamics of the whole population's strategies [19], which is a different approach from that of classical game theory. It has broad applications for modeling users' behaviors in networking and communication areas [20,21], such as cooperative sensing [22], congestion control [23], dynamic spectrum access [24], and cooperative peer-to-peer (P2P) streaming [25]. It is also applied in the field of image processing [26]. Evolutionary games have been shown to be efficient ways of modeling the dynamic social interactions between users of a network.

In studying the ways in which players converge on a stable equilibrium after a period of strategic interactions, EGT is quite effective. An ESS is the definition of such an equilibrium strategy. In an evolutionary game with N players, a strategy profile $\mathbf{a}^* = (a_1^*, \ldots, a_N^*)$, where $\mathcal{X}$ is the action space and $a_i^* \in \mathcal{X}$, is an ESS if and only if, $\forall \mathbf{a} \neq \mathbf{a}^*$, $\mathbf{a}^*$ satisfies [19]:

$$(1) \ U_i(a_i, \mathbf{a}_{-i}^*) \leq U_i(a_i^*, \mathbf{a}_{-i}^*), \tag{8.6}$$

$$(2) \text{ if } U_i(a_i, \mathbf{a}_{-i}^*) = U_i(a_i^*, \mathbf{a}_{-i}^*), \qquad U_i(a_i, \mathbf{a}_{-i}) < U_i(a_i^*, \mathbf{a}_{-i}), \tag{8.7}$$

where U_i is player i's utility and $\mathbf{a}_{-i}$ represents the strategies of all players other than player i. It can be seen that the first case is the Nash equilibrium (NE) condition and the second case ensures the strategy's stability. Furthermore, it can also be seen that a strict NE is an ESS consistently. Under the effects of natural selection, no mutant strategy is able to infect the population when all players adopt the ESS. An ESS can still be a locally stable state even though there may be some irrational players who may use out-of-equilibrium strategies.

Let us think about an evolutionary game in which there are m strategies $\mathcal{X} = \{1, 2, \ldots, m\}$. U, the utility matrix, is an $m \times m$ matrix whose element u_{ij} is the utility for strategy i versus strategy j. We use p_i to represent the population fraction of strategy i, where $\sum_{i=1}^{m} p_i = 1$, and we use $f_i = \sum_{j=1}^{m} p_j u_{ij}$ to represent the fitness of strategy i. We have $\phi = \sum_{i=1}^{m} p_i f_i$ as the the whole population's average fitness. To prompt players to converge to the ESS, the Wright–Fisher model has been extensively utilized [27], where each player's strategy updating equation can be denoted as

$$p_i(t+1) = \frac{p_i(t) f_i(t)}{\phi(t)}. \tag{8.8}$$

In the Wright–Fisher model, one assumption is that the probability of an individual player using strategy i can represent the fraction of players using strategy i when the total population is large enough. It can be seen from (8.8) that there is similarity between the parameter updating process in the adaptive filter problem and the strategy updating process in the evolutionary game. Intuitively, the evolutionary game can be used to formulate the distributed adaptive filter problem.

In traditional EGT, a population with M individuals in a complete graph is considered. However, in many scenarios, players' spatial locations may lead to an incomplete graph structure. Thus, in such a finite structured population, graphical EGT is adopted to study strategy evolution [28], where every edge stands for the reproductive relationship between valid neighbors and every vertex stands for a player. In other words, θ_{ij} is the possibility of node i's strategy replacing node j's, as is shown in Figure 8.2. Graphical EGT is devoted to analyzing the capacity of a mutant gene to

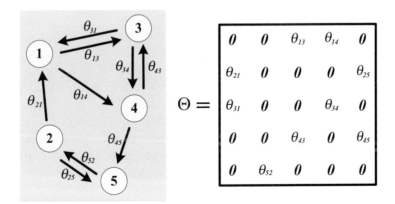

Figure 8.2 Graphical evolutionary game model.

Table 8.2. Correspondence between graphical EGT and a distributed adaptive network.

Graphical EGT	Distributed adaptive network
N players	N nodes in the network
Pure strategy of player i with n_i neighbors $\{i_1, i_2, \ldots, i_{n_i}\}$	Node i combines information from one of its neighbors $\{i_1, i_2, \ldots, i_{n_i}\}$
Mixed strategy of player i with n_i neighbors $\{p_1, p_2, \ldots, p_{n_i}\}$	Node i's combiner (weight) $\{A_i(1), A_i(2), \ldots, A_i(n_i)\}$
Mixed strategy update of player i	Combiner update of node i
Equilibrium	Convergence network state

surpass a group of finite structured residents. Finding a method to calculate the fixation probability (i.e., the probability of the mutant finally surpassing the whole structured population) is one of the most significant research issues in graphical EGT [29]. Next, graphical EGT will be used to model the dynamic parameter updating process in a distributed adaptive filter network.

8.3.2   Graphical Evolutionary Game Formulation

After interacting with neighbors, players in graphical EGT update their strategies based on their fitness in each round. In the same way, nodes in distributed adaptive filtering update their own parameters w by absorbing information from their neighbors. The nodes in a distributed filter network under this situation can be treated as players in a graphical evolutionary game. The node i who has n_i neighbors has n_i pure strategies $\{i_1, i_2, \ldots, i_{n_i}\}$, in which strategy j indicates updating $w_{i,t+1}$ with the updated information from its neighbor j, $A_{i,t+1}(j)$. It can be seen that (8.5) means that the mixed strategy is adopted. In this case, we can regard the parameter updating process in a distributed adaptive filter network as the strategy updating process in graphical EGT. The connection between the terminologies in a distributed adaptive network and those in graphical EGT is summarized in Table 8.2.

We first talk about the updating process of players' strategies in graphical EGT. We then apply it to parameter updating in distributed adaptive filtering. A player's fitness in graphical EGT is decided by mutual interactions with all neighbor players locally. We define this as [30]

$$f = (1 - \alpha) \cdot B + \alpha \cdot U, \tag{8.9}$$

in which B is the baseline fitness representing the inherent property of the player. For instance, a node's baseline fitness in a distributed adaptive network could be given as the quality of its noise variance. U denotes the utility of a player that is affected by the predefined utility matrix. α, the parameter of selection intensity, means the

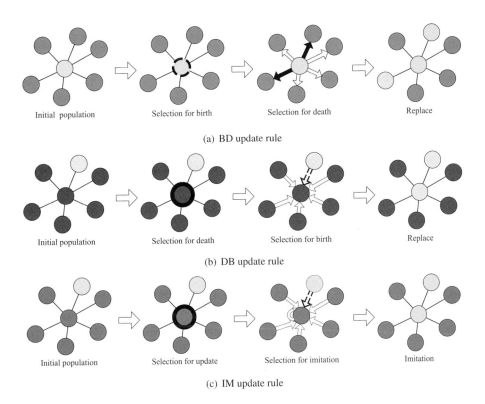

(a) BD update rule

(b) DB update rule

(c) IM update rule

Figure 8.3 Three different update rules, where death selections are shown in black and birth selections are shown with dash lines.

relative contribution of the game to fitness. When $\alpha \rightarrow 0$, this signifies that the case is weak selection [31], while $\alpha = 1$ signifies strong selection, in which utility and fitness are identical. In terms of evolution dynamics, birth-death (BD), death-birth (DB), and imitation (IM) [32] are three general strategy updating rules.

- BD update rule: choose a player for reproduction with the probability being proportional to fitness (birth process). Then the chosen player's strategy takes the place of a neighbor's strategy uniformly (death process), as is shown in Figure 8.3(a).
- DB update rule: choose a random player to abandon their current strategy (death process). Then the chosen player adopts a neighbor's strategy with the probability being proportional to their fitness (birth process), as is shown in Figure 8.3(b).
- IM update rule: each player either adopts the strategy of a neighbor or remains with their current strategy, with the probability being proportional to fitness, as is shown in Figure 8.3(c).

We can match the three strategy updating rules to three different parameter updating algorithms in distributed adaptive filtering. We assume that in a structured network there are N nodes and the degree of each node i is denoted as n_i. The set of all nodes is denoted as $\mathcal{N}$ and the neighborhood set of node i, which includes node i itself, is denoted as $\mathcal{N}_i$.

For the BD update rule, we include the possibility that node i adopts strategy j (i.e., utilizing updated information from its adjacent node j) as

$$P_j = \frac{f_j}{\sum_{k \in \mathcal{N}} f_k} \frac{1}{n_j}. \tag{8.10}$$

Here the first term $\frac{f_j}{\sum_{k \in \mathcal{N}} f_k}$ represents the possibility that the neighbor node j is selected for reproduction, which is proportional to its fitness f_j. The second term $\frac{1}{n_j}$ represents the possibility of selected node i adopting strategy j. Notice that we need to calculate the network topology information (n_j) (8.10). Under this circumstance, we can write the equivalent parameter updating rule for node i as

$$\boldsymbol{w}_{i,t+1} = \sum_{j \in \mathcal{N}_i \backslash \{i\}} \left(\frac{f_j}{\sum_{k \in \mathcal{N}} f_k} \frac{1}{n_j} \right) F(\boldsymbol{w}_{j,t}) + \left(1 - \sum_{j \in \mathcal{N}_i \backslash \{i\}} \left(\frac{f_j}{\sum_{k \in \mathcal{N}} f_k} \frac{1}{n_j} \right) \right) F(\boldsymbol{w}_{i,t}).$$

$$\tag{8.11}$$

Similarly, we are able to represent the corresponding parameter updating rule of node i for the DB updating rule as

$$\boldsymbol{w}_{i,t+1} = \frac{1}{n_i} \sum_{j \in \mathcal{N}_i \backslash \{i\}} \left(\frac{f_j}{\sum_{k \in \mathcal{N}_i} f_k} \right) F(\boldsymbol{w}_{j,t}) + \left(1 - \frac{1}{n_i} \sum_{j \in \mathcal{N}_i \backslash \{i\}} \left(\frac{f_j}{\sum_{k \in \mathcal{N}_i} f_k} \right) \right) F(\boldsymbol{w}_{i,t}).$$

$$\tag{8.12}$$

For the IM updating rule, we have

$$\boldsymbol{w}_{i,t+1} = \sum_{j \in \mathcal{N}_i} \left(\frac{f_j}{\sum_{k \in \mathcal{N}_i} f_k} \right) F(\boldsymbol{w}_{j,t}). \tag{8.13}$$

Note that (8.11), (8.12), and (8.13) are the expected outcomes of BD, DB, and IM update rules, respectively.

We usually use two measures to evaluate the performance of adaptive filtering algorithms: mean-square deviation (MSD) and excess-mean-square error (EMSE). They are defined as

$$\text{MSD} = \mathrm{E}\|\boldsymbol{w}_t - \boldsymbol{w}^0\|^2, \tag{8.14}$$

$$\text{EMSE} = \mathrm{E}\left|\boldsymbol{u}_t(\boldsymbol{w}_{t-1} - \boldsymbol{w}^0)\right|^2. \tag{8.15}$$

According to [7], we are able to compute the network MSD and EMSE of these three update rules through (8.11), (8.12), and (8.13).

8.3.3   Relationship to Existing Distributed Adaptive Filtering Algorithms

In (8.5) and Table 8.1, the existing distributed adaptive filtering algorithms have been summarized. In this section, it will be shown that every algorithm is a special case of the IM update rule in the graphical EGT framework. By comparing (8.5) and (8.13), it can be seen that various fitness definitions correspond to various distributed adaptive filtering algorithms in Table 8.1. We define the fitness uniformly as $f_i = 1$ for the uniform rule, and with the IM update rule we have

$$w_{i,t+1} = \sum_{j \in \mathcal{N}_i} \frac{1}{n_i} F(w_{j,t}), \qquad (8.16)$$

which corresponds to the uniform rule in Table 8.1. The definition of $f_i = 1$ here refers to the setting of weak selection ($\alpha \ll 1$) and fixed fitness. For the Laplacian rule, if node i's parameter is updated, the fitness of nodes in $\mathcal{N}_i$ is defined as

$$f_j = \begin{cases} 1, & \text{for } j \neq i, \\ n_{\max} - n_i + 1, & \text{for } j = i. \end{cases} \qquad (8.17)$$

From (8.17), it can be seen that by enhancing fitness, each node gives more weight to its own information. In the same way, for the relative degree–variance rule, we define fitness as

$$f_j = n_j \sigma_j^{-2}, \quad \text{for all } j \in \mathcal{N}_i. \qquad (8.18)$$

For the Hastings rule and metropolis rule, the corresponding fitness is defined on the basis of the strong selection model ($\alpha \to 1$). In this model, utility plays a dominant role in (8.9). For the metropolis rule, we define the nodes' utility matrix as

$$\begin{array}{cc} \text{Node } i & \text{Node } j \neq i \end{array}$$
$$\begin{array}{c} \text{Node } i \\ \text{Node } j \neq i \end{array} \begin{pmatrix} 1 - \sum_{k \neq i} A_i(k) & \frac{1}{\max\{|\mathcal{N}_i|, |\mathcal{N}_j|\}} \\ \frac{1}{\max\{|\mathcal{N}_i|, |\mathcal{N}_j|\}} & 1 - \sum_{k \neq j} A_j(k) \end{pmatrix} \qquad (8.19)$$

For the Hastings rule, we define the utility matrix as

$$\begin{array}{cc} \text{Node } i & \text{Node } j \neq i \end{array}$$
$$\begin{array}{c} \text{Node } i \\ \text{Node } j \neq i \end{array} \begin{pmatrix} 1 - \sum_{k \neq i} A_i(k) & \frac{\sigma_{(i,j)}^2}{\max\{|\mathcal{N}_i|\sigma_i^2, |\mathcal{N}_j|\sigma_j^2\}} \\ \frac{\sigma_{(j,i)}^2}{\max\{|\mathcal{N}_i|\sigma_i^2, |\mathcal{N}_j|\sigma_j^2\}} & 1 - \sum_{k \neq j} A_j(k) \end{pmatrix} \qquad (8.20)$$

The different corresponding definitions of fitness for the different combination rules in Table 8.1 are summarized in Table 8.3. Thus, with corresponding fitness definitions, the EGT framework can summarize the existing algorithms.

8.3.4   Error-Aware Distributed Adaptive Filtering Algorithm

In this section, by choosing different fitness functions, two distributed adaptive algorithms are further designed as examples to demonstrate the graphical EGT framework. Now all existing distributed adaptive filtering algorithms are dependent on either the requirement of additional network statistics or prior knowledge of network topology, so for a dynamic network where the location of the node as well as its noise variance may change with time, they are not robust. Due to these issues, error-aware algorithms

Table 8.3. Different fitness definitions.

Name	Fitness: $f_j =$
Uniform [10,13]	1, for all $j \in \mathcal{N}_i$
Maximum degree [6,14]	$\begin{cases} 1, & \text{for } j \neq i, \\ N - n_i + 1, & \text{for } j = i \end{cases}$
Laplacian [15,16]	$\begin{cases} 1, & \text{for } j \neq i \\ n_{\max} - n_i + 1, & \text{for } j = i \end{cases}$
Relative degree [6]	n_j, for all $j \in \mathcal{N}_i$
Relative degree–variance [7]	$n_j \sigma_j^{-2}$, for all $j \in \mathcal{N}_i$
Metropolis [16,17]	$\begin{pmatrix} 1 - \sum_{k \neq i} A_i(k) & \frac{1}{\max\{|\mathcal{N}_i|,|\mathcal{N}_j|\}} \\ \frac{1}{\max\{|\mathcal{N}_i|,|\mathcal{N}_j|\}} & 1 - \sum_{k \neq j} A_j(k) \end{pmatrix}$
Hastings [17]	$\begin{pmatrix} 1 - \sum_{k \neq i} A_i(k) & \frac{\sigma_{(i,j)}^2}{\max\{|\mathcal{N}_i|\sigma_i^2,|\mathcal{N}_j|\sigma_j^2\}} \\ \frac{\sigma_{(j,i)}^2}{\max\{|\mathcal{N}_i|\sigma_i^2,|\mathcal{N}_j|\sigma_j^2\}} & 1 - \sum_{k \neq j} A_j(k) \end{pmatrix}$

are discussed on account of the intuition that neighbor nodes who have a high mean-square error (MSE) deserve less weight while neighbor nodes who have a low MSE deserve more weight. We can calculate node i's instantaneous error, ϱ_i, by

$$\varrho_{i,t} = \left| d_i(t) - \boldsymbol{u}_{i,t} \boldsymbol{w}_{i,t-1} \right|^2, \tag{8.21}$$

Here we only use local data $\{d_i(t), \boldsymbol{u}_{i,t}\}$. Then node i's approximated MSE in each time slot can be estimated by the following update rule:

$$\beta_{i,t} = (1 - v_{i,t})\beta_{i,t-1} + v_{i,t}\varrho_{i,t}, \tag{8.22}$$

in which $v_{i,t}$ is a positive parameter. Suppose that nodes could share instantaneous MSE information with their neighbors. According to the estimated MSE, two forms of fitness – power form and exponential form – are designed as follows:

$$\text{Power: } f_i = \beta_i^{-\lambda}, \tag{8.23}$$

$$\text{Exponential: } f_i = e^{-\lambda \beta_i}, \tag{8.24}$$

in which λ is a positive coefficient. These two kinds of fitness are only two cases of the framework, and we can consider many other forms of fitness (e.g., $f_i = \log(\lambda \beta_i^{-1})$). With the IM update rule, we have

$$\boldsymbol{w}_{i,t+1} = \sum_{j \in \mathcal{N}_i} \frac{\beta_{j,t}^{-\lambda}}{\sum_{k \in \mathcal{N}_i} \beta_{k,t}^{-\lambda}} F(\boldsymbol{w}_{j,t}), \tag{8.25}$$

$$w_{i,t+1} = \sum_{j \in \mathcal{N}_i} \frac{e^{-\lambda \beta_{j,t}}}{\sum_{k \in \mathcal{N}_i} e^{-\lambda \beta_{k,t}}} F(w_{j,t}). \tag{8.26}$$

It can be seen from (8.25) and (8.26) that network topology information is not a direct influence factor for the algorithms. Since the weights could be accordingly adjusted instantly, the algorithms can also become accustomed to a dynamic environment in which the nodes' noise variance may suddenly change or be unknown. In [33], a similar algorithm on the basis of the instantaneous MSE information was also illustrated, which can be regarded as a particular case of an error-aware algorithm with the power form of $\lambda = 2$. Notice that when implementing (8.25) and (8.26), deterministic coefficients instead of randomly combining coefficients with some possibility are used. Nevertheless, we can also implement the algorithm by adopting a random selection with probabilities. The same expected outcome determines that there is no performance loss, but the efficiency (convergence speed) would be lower.

8.4 Diffusion Analysis

Within the distributed adaptive filter network, both nodes with good signals (i.e., lower noise variance) and nodes with poor signals exist. The primary purpose of distributed adaptive filtering algorithms is improving network performance by stimulating the good signals' diffusion to the whole network. In this section, the EGT is used to investigate such a dynamic diffusion process and to acquire the closed-form expression of the diffusion probability. In the subsequent analysis, we assume that the regressor statistics $\mathbf{R_u}$ are the same for all nodes, but that they have different noise statistics.

The structured population consists of either mutants or residents in a graphical evolutionary game. In the game, fixation probability is a crucial concept, representing the probability that the whole population will eventually be overtaken by the mutants [34]. As is shown in Figure 8.4, we consider a local adaptive filter network in which the gray points represent good nodes whose noise variance σ_m^2 is lower and the white points represent common nodes whose noise variance σ_r^2 is common. The connection

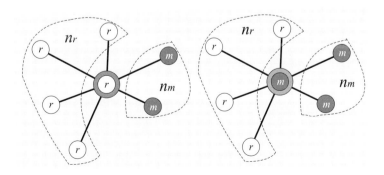

Figure 8.4 Graphical evolutionary game model.

between σ_m^2 and σ_r^2 is $\sigma_r^2 \gg \sigma_m^2$. To better display good signals' diffusion processes, here the binary signal model is adopted. If the good nodes are regarded as mutants and the common nodes are regarded as residents, we can apply the concept of fixation probability in EGT to the analysis of the good signals' diffusion. Based on the definition of fixation probability, the diffusion probability for the distributed filter network is defined as the probability that all nodes will update the parameters in the network with a good signal.

8.4.1   Strategies and Utility Matrix

The neighbors of the center node cover both good and common nodes, as is shown in Figure 8.4. When the node at the center updates its parameter w_i, there are only two possible strategies available to it:

$$\begin{cases} S_r, & \text{using information from common nodes,} \\ S_m, & \text{using information from good nodes.} \end{cases} \tag{8.27}$$

The utility matrix in this case can be defined as follows:

$$\begin{array}{cc} & \begin{array}{cc} S_r & \quad\quad S_m \end{array} \\ \begin{array}{c} S_r \\ S_m \end{array} & \left(\begin{array}{cc} \pi^{-1}(\sigma_r, \sigma_r) & \pi^{-1}(\sigma_m, \sigma_r) \\ \pi^{-1}(\sigma_r, \sigma_m) & \pi^{-1}(\sigma_m, \sigma_m) \end{array} \right) \end{array} = \left(\begin{array}{cc} u_1 & u_2 \\ u_3 & u_4 \end{array} \right), \tag{8.28}$$

in which $\pi(x, y)$ denotes the steady EMSE of the node with noise variance x^2 when it uses information from the node with noise variance y^2. For instance, $\pi(\sigma_r, \sigma_m)$ represents the steady EMSE of the node with noise variance σ_r^2 adopting strategy S_m (i.e., updating its w utilizing information from the node with noise variance σ_m^2, which in turn adopts strategy S_r). In the diffusion analysis, we suppose that at one time instant there are only two players interacting mutually. In other words, at one time instant only two nodes are exchanging and combining information with each other. Under this circumstance, the payoff matrix is a two-user case. It should be noted that the selection process of the specific neighbor by the node occurs with some probability, which can be regarded as the weight that the node gives to that neighbor.

Because the information combining rule determines the steady EMSE $\pi(x, y)$ in the utility matrix, $\pi(x, y)$ has no general expression. But intuitively we know that since $\sigma_r^2 \gg \sigma_m^2$, the steady EMSE of the node with variance σ_r^2 ought to be larger than that of the node with variance σ_m^2, and strategy S_m is a more beneficial strategy than S_r because the node could obtain better information from the other nodes (i.e., $\pi(\sigma_r, \sigma_r) > \pi(\sigma_r, \sigma_m) > \pi(\sigma_m, \sigma_r) > \pi(\sigma_m, \sigma_m)$). As a result, it is assumed that the utility matrix defined in (8.28) has the following quality:

$$u_1 < u_3 < u_2 < u_4. \tag{8.29}$$

Here an example in [17] is used to obtain $\pi(x, y)$ with a closed-form expression so as to interpret and confirm this intuition. Based on [17], with an adequately small step size μ, we can calculate the optimal $\pi(x, y)$ by

$$\pi(x, y) = c_1\sigma_1^2 + c_2\frac{x^4}{\sigma_2^2}, \tag{8.30}$$

$$\begin{cases} c_1 = \frac{\mu\text{Tr}(\mathbf{R}_u)}{4}, & c_2 = \frac{\mu^2\|\zeta\|^2}{2}, \\ \sigma_1^2 = \frac{2x^2y^2}{x^2+y^2}, & \sigma_2^2 = \frac{x^2y^2}{2}, \end{cases} \tag{8.31}$$

where $\zeta = \text{col}\{\zeta_1, \ldots, \zeta_N\}$ is composed of the eigenvalues of $\mathbf{R}_u$ ($\mathbf{R}_u$ is the covariance matrix of the observed regression data $\mathbf{u}_t$). Based on (8.30) and (8.31), we get

$$\pi(\sigma_r, \sigma_r) = c_1\sigma_r^2 + 2c_2, \tag{8.32}$$

$$\pi(\sigma_r, \sigma_m) = c_1\frac{2\sigma_m^2\sigma_r^2}{\sigma_m^2 + \sigma_r^2} + 2c_2\frac{\sigma_r^2}{\sigma_m^2}, \tag{8.33}$$

$$\pi(\sigma_m, \sigma_r) = c_1\frac{2\sigma_m^2\sigma_r^2}{\sigma_m^2 + \sigma_r^2} + 2c_2\frac{\sigma_m^2}{\sigma_r^2}, \tag{8.34}$$

$$\pi(\sigma_m, \sigma_m) = c_1\sigma_m^2 + 2c_2. \tag{8.35}$$

Suppose $\sigma_m^2 = \tau\sigma_r^2$; through comparing (8.32)–(8.35), the condition for $\pi(\sigma_r, \sigma_r) > \pi(\sigma_r, \sigma_m) > \pi(\sigma_m, \sigma_r) > \pi(\sigma_m, \sigma_m)$ is as follows:

$$\mu < \frac{\tau\text{Tr}(\mathbf{R}_u)\sigma_r^2}{4(1 + \tau)\|\zeta\|^2}. \tag{8.36}$$

According to [17], the premise of the optimal $\pi(x, y)$'s derivation in (8.30) and (8.31) is the assumption that μ is small enough. Hence, the condition of μ in (8.36) holds. Thus, it can be concluded that $\pi(\sigma_r, \sigma_r) > \pi(\sigma_r, \sigma_m) > \pi(\sigma_m, \sigma_r) > \pi(\sigma_m, \sigma_m)$, which implies that $u_1 < u_3 < u_2 < u_4$.

In the following, the diffusion process of strategy S_m (i.e., good signals' capability to diffuse through the whole network) will be analyzed. We will consider an adaptive filter network regarded as a homogeneous graph whose degree is n generally, and we will use the IM update rule for the parameter update [35]. We use p_r and p_m to stand for the proportions of nodes adopting strategies S_r and S_m in the population, respectively. p_{rr}, p_{rm}, p_{mr}, and p_{mm} stand for the percentages of edges, in which p_{rm} is the proportion of edges at which both nodes use strategy S_r and S_m. We use $q_{m|r}$ to represent the conditional probability of a node adopting strategy S_m when the neighbor node is adopting strategy S_r, and similarly for $q_{r|r}$, $q_{r|m}$ and $q_{m|m}$. Thus, we can get

$$p_r + p_m = 1, \quad q_{r|X} + q_{m|X} = 1, \tag{8.37}$$

$$p_{XY} = p_Y \cdot q_{X|Y}, \quad p_{rm} = p_{mr}, \tag{8.38}$$

in which X and Y are either m or r. Equations (8.37) and (8.38) indicate that only two variables, p_m and $q_{m|m}$, can describe the state of the whole network. The dynamics of p_m and $q_{m|m}$ will be calculated under the IM update rule in the following.

8.4.2   Dynamics of p_m and $q_{m|m}$

To derive the diffusion probability, the diffusion process of the system should be analyzed first. As discussed above, parameters p_m and $q_{m|m}$ can represent the dynamics of the system under the IM update rule. In this section, the dynamics of p_m and $q_{m|m}$ will be analyzed first so that we can determine the dynamic diffusion process for the adaptive network. Based on the IM update rule, the probability of a node with strategy S_r being chosen for imitation is p_r. We can see from the left part of Figure 8.4 that there are n_m neighbor nodes adopting strategy S_m and n_r neighbor nodes adopting strategy S_r among all n neighbors (not including the node itself), in which $n_r + n_m = n$. The percentage of such a configuration is $\binom{n}{n_m} q_{m|r}^{n_m} q_{r|r}^{n_r}$. The fitness of this node under such a situation is

$$f_0 = (1 - \alpha) + \alpha(n_r u_1 + n_m u_2), \tag{8.39}$$

in which the baseline fitness is normalized as 1. It can be seen that in addition to the normalized baseline fitness, (8.39) also includes the fitness from utility, which is the standard definition of fitness used in the EGT field as in (8.9). The fitness of those neighbor nodes with strategy S_m is

$$f_m = (1 - \alpha) + \alpha([(n - 1)q_{r|m} + 1]u_3 + (n - 1)q_{m|m}u_4), \tag{8.40}$$

and the fitness of those neighbor nodes with strategy S_r is

$$f_r = (1 - \alpha) + \alpha([(n - 1)q_{r|r} + 1]u_1 + (n - 1)q_{m|r}u_2). \tag{8.41}$$

Under these circumstances, the node with strategy S_r is substituted by S_m with probability

$$P_{r \to m} = \frac{n_m f_m}{n_m f_m + n_r f_r + f_0}. \tag{8.42}$$

Thus, the probability of the proportion of nodes with strategy S_m, p_m, increasing by $1/N$ is

$$\text{Prob}\left(\Delta p_m = \frac{1}{N}\right) = p_r \sum_{n_r + n_m = n} \binom{n}{n_m} q_{m|r}^{n_m} q_{r|r}^{n_r} \cdot \frac{n_m f_m}{n_m f_m + n_r f_r + f_0}. \tag{8.43}$$

At the same time, the edges on which both nodes adopt strategy S_m would increase by n_m. Therefore, we can get

$$\text{Prob}\left(\Delta p_{mm} = \frac{2n_m}{nN}\right) = p_r \binom{n}{n_m} q_{m|r}^{n_m} q_{r|r}^{n_r} \cdot \frac{n_m f_m}{n_m f_m + n_r f_r + f_0}. \tag{8.44}$$

We can apply a similar analysis to the node with strategy S_m. Based on the IM update rule, the probability of a node with strategy S_m being chosen for imitation is p_m. As is shown on the right side of Figure 8.4, it is assumed that among all n neighbors, there are n_m nodes adopting strategy S_m and n_r nodes adopting strategy S_r. Such a phenomenon appears with percentage $\binom{n}{n_m} q_{m|m}^{n_m} q_{r|m}^{n_r}$. Therefore, the fitness of this node could be written as

$$g_0 = (1 - \alpha) + \alpha(n_r u_2 + n_m u_3). \tag{8.45}$$

In those n neighbors, the fitness of the node with strategy S_m is

$$g_m = (1 - \alpha) + \alpha\big((n - 1)q_{r|m}u_3 + [(n - 1)q_{m|m} + 1]u_4\big), \tag{8.46}$$

and the fitness of the node with strategy S_r is

$$g_r = (1 - \alpha) + \alpha\big((n - 1)q_{r|r}u_1 + [(n - 1)q_{m|r} + 1]u_2\big). \tag{8.47}$$

Under this circumstance, the node with strategy S_m is substituted by S_r with probability

$$P_{m \to r} = \frac{n_r g_r}{n_m g_m + n_r g_r + g_0}. \tag{8.48}$$

Thus, the probability of p_m, the percentage of nodes with strategy S_m, decreasing by $1/N$ is

$$\mathrm{Prob}\left(\Delta p_m = -\frac{1}{N}\right) = p_m \sum_{n_r + n_m = n} \binom{n}{n_m} q_{m|m}^{n_m} q_{r|m}^{n_r} \cdot \frac{n_r g_r}{n_m g_m + n_r g_r + g_0}. \tag{8.49}$$

In this case, the edges on which both nodes adopt strategy S_m would decrease by n_m. Therefore, we get

$$\mathrm{Prob}\left(\Delta p_{mm} = -\frac{2n_m}{nN}\right) = p_m \binom{n}{n_m} q_{m|m}^{n_m} q_{r|m}^{n_r} \cdot \frac{n_r g_r}{n_m g_m + n_r g_r + g_0}. \tag{8.50}$$

After combining (8.43) and (8.49), we will have the dynamic of p_m as

$$\dot{p}_m = \frac{1}{N}\mathrm{Prob}\left(\Delta p_m = \frac{1}{N}\right) - \frac{1}{N}\mathrm{Prob}\left(\Delta p_m = -\frac{1}{N}\right)$$

$$= \frac{\alpha n(n - 1)p_{rm}}{N(n + 1)^2}(\gamma_1 u_1 + \gamma_2 u_2 + \gamma_3 u_3 + \gamma_4 u_4) + O(\alpha^2), \tag{8.51}$$

in which the second equality is based on the weak selection assumption with α close to zero and Taylor's theorem [36], and we define the parameters γ_1, γ_2, γ_3, and γ_4 as follows:

$$\gamma_1 = -q_{r|r}[(n - 1)(q_{r|r} + q_{m|m}) + 3], \tag{8.52}$$

$$\gamma_2 = -q_{m|m} - q_{m|r}[(n - 1)(q_{r|r} + q_{m|m}) + 2] - \frac{2}{n - 1}, \tag{8.53}$$

$$\gamma_3 = q_{r|r} + q_{r|m}[(n - 1)(q_{r|r} + q_{m|m}) + 2] + \frac{2}{n - 1}, \tag{8.54}$$

$$\gamma_4 = q_{m|m}[(n - 1)(q_{r|r} + q_{m|m}) + 3]. \tag{8.55}$$

The dot notation $\dot{p}_m$ in (8.51) denotes the dynamics of p_m (i.e., the change of p_m in a very small period of time). Therefore, each player's utility received from the interactions can be regarded as a finite contribution to the whole fitness. On the one hand, in the case of a larger selection strength, the results of weak selection are usually still valid approximations [31]. On the other hand, in theoretical biology, the weak selection limit has been traditionally used for a long time [37]. What is more, the assumption of weak selection not only lets us obtain a closed-form analysis of the diffusion process, but also better determines the process of strategy diffusion among the whole network. In the same way, after combining (8.44) and (8.50), the dynamics of p_{mm} can be obtained as

$$
\dot{p}_{mm} = \sum_{n_m=0}^{n} \frac{2n_m}{nN} \text{Prob}\left(\Delta p_{mm} = \frac{2n_m}{nN}\right) - \sum_{n_m=0}^{n} \frac{2n_m}{nN} \text{Prob}\left(\Delta p_{mm} = -\frac{2n_m}{nN}\right)
$$

$$
= \frac{2p_{rm}}{(n+1)N}(1 + (n-1)(q_{m|r} - q_{m|m})) + O(\alpha), \tag{8.56}
$$

and the dynamics of $q_{m|m}$ can also be obtained as

$$
\dot{q}_{m|m} = \frac{d}{dt}\left(\frac{p_{mm}}{p_m}\right) = \frac{2}{(n+1)N}\frac{p_{rm}}{p_m}(1 + (n-1)(q_{m|r} - q_{m|m})) + O(\alpha). \tag{8.57}
$$

8.4.3   Diffusion Probability Analysis

The dynamics of p_m denoted in (8.51) demonstrate the dynamic processes of nodes who update w utilizing good nodes' information, meaning the diffusion status of good signals in the network. When $\dot{p}_m$ is positive, this indicates that good signals are spreading over the network, while $\dot{p}_m$ being negative refers to good signals not being well used. The good nodes' noise variance σ_m largely determines the diffusion probability of good signals. Our intuition tells us that a lower σ_m leads to a higher diffusion probability of good signals over the whole network. So in this section, the closed-form expression for the diffusion probability will be analyzed.

As was stated above, only p_m and $q_{m|m}$ can describe the state of the whole network. Under these circumstances, we can rewrite (8.51) and (8.57) as functions of p_m and $q_{m|m}$ as

$$
\dot{p}_m = \alpha \cdot G_1(p_m, q_{m|m}) + O(\alpha^2), \tag{8.58}
$$

$$
\dot{q}_{m|m} = G_2(p_m, q_{m|m}) + O(\alpha). \tag{8.59}
$$

From (8.58) and (8.59), it can be seen that under the weak selection assumption, p_m approaches the equilibrium much more slowly than $q_{m|m}$. When $q_{m|m}$ is at a steady state (i.e., $\dot{q}_{m|m} = 0$), we can get

$$
q_{m|m} - q_{m|r} = \frac{1}{n-1}. \tag{8.60}
$$

In such a situation, the dynamic network will quickly converge to the slow manifold given by $G_2(p_m, q_{m|m}) = 0$. Thus, it can be assumed that (8.60) is satisfied over the whole convergence process of p_m. Based on (8.37), (8.38), and (8.60), we have

$$
q_{m|m} = p_m + \frac{1}{n-1}(1 - p_m), \tag{8.61}
$$

$$
q_{m|r} = \frac{n-2}{n-1}p_m, \tag{8.62}
$$

$$q_{r|m} = \frac{n-2}{n-1}(1 - p_m), \tag{8.63}$$

$$q_{r|r} = 1 - \frac{n-2}{n-1}p_m. \tag{8.64}$$

Thus, only p_m can characterize the diffusion process, and in order to get the diffusion probability we need only pay attention to the dynamics of p_m. Then Theorem 8.1 gives the expression of the diffusion probability.

THEOREM 8.1 *In a distributed adaptive filter network that can be characterized by an N-node regular graph with degree n, suppose that there are common nodes with noise variance σ_r and good nodes with noise variance σ_m, and each common node has a connection edge with only one good node. If each node updates its parameter w using the IM update rule, the diffusion probability of the good signal can be approximated by*

$$P_{diff} = \frac{1}{n+1} + \frac{\alpha n N}{6(n+1)^3}(\xi_1 u_1 + \xi_2 u_2 + \xi_3 u_3 + \xi_4 u_4), \tag{8.65}$$

where the parameters ξ_1, ξ_2, ξ_3, and ξ_4 are as follows:

$$\xi_1 = -2n^2 - 5n + 3, \quad \xi_2 = -n^2 - n - 3, \tag{8.66}$$

$$\xi_3 = 2n^2 + 2n - 3, \quad \xi_4 = n^2 + 4n + 3. \tag{8.67}$$

Proof First, we define $m(p_m)$ as the mean of the increment of p_m per unit time given as follows:

$$m(p_m) = \frac{\dot{p}_m}{1/N} \simeq \frac{\alpha n(n-2)}{(n-1)(n+1)^2}p_m(1-p_m)(ap_m + b), \tag{8.68}$$

in which the approximation step is obtained by replacing (8.51) with (8.60)–(8.64) and the parameters a and b are defined as

$$a = (n-2)(n+3)(u_1 - u_2 - u_3 + u_4), \tag{8.69}$$

$$b = -(n-1)(n+3)u_1 - 3u_2 + (n^2 + n - 3)u_3 + (n+3)u_4. \tag{8.70}$$

Then we define $v(p_m)$ as the variance of the increment of p_m per unit time and compute it by

$$v(p_m) = \frac{\dot{p}_m^2 - (\dot{p}_m)^2}{1/N}, \tag{8.71}$$

where $\dot{p}_m^2$ can be calculated by

$$\dot{p}_m^2 = \frac{1}{N^2}\left(\text{Prob}\left(\Delta p_m = \frac{1}{N}\right) + \text{Prob}\left(\Delta p_m = -\frac{1}{N}\right)\right)$$

$$= \frac{2}{N^2}\frac{n(n-2)}{(n-1)(n+1)}p_m(1-p_m) + O(\alpha). \tag{8.72}$$

In such a case, $v(p_m)$ can be approximated by

$$v(p_m) \simeq \frac{2}{N} \frac{n(n-2)}{(n-1)(n+1)} p_m(1-p_m). \tag{8.73}$$

We set p_{m0} as the initial proportion of good nodes in the network. Let us define $H(p_{m0})$ as the possibility of good signals being adopted in the overall network (i.e., information from good nodes is used by all nodes to update their own w). Based on the backward Kolmogorov equation [38], $H(p_{m0})$ satisfies the following differential equation:

$$0 = m(p_{m0}) \frac{dH(p_{m0})}{dp_{m0}} + \frac{v(p_{m0})}{2} \frac{d^2 H(p_{m0})}{dp_{m0}^2}. \tag{8.74}$$

With the assumption of weak selection, the approximate solution of $H(p_{m0})$ can be obtained as

$$H(p_{m0}) = p_{m0} + \frac{\alpha N}{6(n+1)} p_{m0}(1-p_{m0})((a+3b)+ap_{m0}). \tag{8.75}$$

When the worst initial system state is considered, in which every common node links to only one good node (i.e., $p_{m0} = \frac{1}{n+1}$), we have

$$H\left(\frac{1}{n+1}\right) \simeq \frac{1}{n+1} + \frac{\alpha n N}{6(n+1)^3}(a+3b). \tag{8.76}$$

Finally, we can get (8.65), the closed-form expression of the diffusion probability, by substituting (8.69) and (8.70) into (8.76). This completes the proof of the theorem.

Through Theorem 8.1, the diffusion probability of the good signals in the network can be calculated. This can also be used in the evaluation of an adaptive filter network's performance. In a similar way, by using the same analysis we can derive the probabilities and diffusion dynamics under the BD and DB update rules. Theorem 8.2 reveals an interesting consequence of this, which derives from a vital theorem in [29] stating that in undirected regular graphs there is no difference between the evolutionary dynamics under BD, DB, and IM.

THEOREM 8.2   *In a distributed adaptive filter network that can be characterized by an N-node regular graph with degree n, suppose that there are common nodes with noise variance σ_r and good nodes with noise variance σ_m, and each common node has a connection edge with only one good node. If each node updates its parameter w using the IM update rule, the diffusion probabilities of good signals under the BD and DB update rules are the same as that under the IM update rule.*

8.5   Evolutionarily Stable Strategy

In the previous section, the information diffusion process under the IM update rule in an adaptive network has been analyzed and the diffusion probability for strategy S_m that makes use of good nodes' information has been presented. If we suppose that

S_m, as the favorable strategy, has already been selected for adoption by the whole network, is the current state a stable network state despite the adoption of the other strategy S_r by a small portion of nodes? These questions will be answered subsequently with the concept of the ESS in EGT. The ESS guarantees that one strategy is able to resist another strategy's invasion [39]. In the system model discussed in this chapter, utilizing good nodes' information (i.e., S_m) is obviously favored, and this strategy is the desired ESS in the network. So in this section we will verify whether the strategy S_m is the ESS.

8.5.1   ESS in Complete Graphs

First, we will discuss whether the strategy S_m is an ESS in complete graphs. The result is given in Theorem 8.3.

THEOREM 8.3   *In a distributed adaptive filter network that can be characterized by complete graphs, strategy S_m is always an ESS strategy.*

Proof   Every node has the same probability of meeting other nodes in a complete graph, and from the utility matrix in (8.28), we have the average utilities of adopting strategies S_r and S_m

$$U_r = p_r u_1 + p_m u_2, \tag{8.77}$$

$$U_m = p_r u_3 + p_m u_4, \tag{8.78}$$

where p_m and p_r denote the proportions of the population adopting strategies S_m and S_r, respectively. If a small portion of the population uses S_r, which could be regarded as invasion, while the main portion of the population uses strategy S_m, $p_r = \epsilon$. Under this circumstance, strategy S_m is evolutionarily stable if $U_m > U_r$ for $(p_r, p_m) = (\epsilon, 1 - \epsilon)$, i.e.,

$$\epsilon(u_3 - u_1) + (1 - \epsilon)(u_4 - u_2) > 0. \tag{8.79}$$

For $\epsilon \to 0$, the left-hand side of (8.79) is positive if and only if

$$\text{``}u_4 > u_2\text{''} \quad \text{or} \quad \text{``}u_4 = u_2 \text{ and } u_3 > u_1.\text{''} \tag{8.80}$$

Equation (8.80) provides the sufficient evolutionarily stable condition for strategy S_m. In the model, we have $u_4 > u_2 > u_3 > u_1$, which indicates (8.80) always holds. So if the adaptive filter network is a complete graph, strategy S_m is always an ESS.

8.5.2   ESS in Incomplete Graphs

We consider an adaptive filter network that is an incomplete regular graph with degree n. Theorem 8.4 indicates that in such an incomplete graph strategy S_m is an ESS all of the time.

THEOREM 8.4   *In a distributed adaptive filter network that can be characterized by a regular graph with degree n, strategy S_m is always an ESS strategy.*

Proof Based on the pair approximation method [32], we can represent the approximation of the replicator dynamics for strategies S_r and S_m on a common graph with degree n simply as

$$\dot{p}_r = p_r(p_r u'_1 + p_m u'_2 - \phi), \tag{8.81}$$

$$\dot{p}_m = p_m(p_r u'_3 + p_m u'_4 - \phi), \tag{8.82}$$

where $\phi = p_r p_r u'_1 + p_r p_m(u'_2 + u'_3) + p_m p_m u'_4$ represents the average utility and u'_1, u'_2, u'_3, and u'_4 are

$$\begin{cases} u'_1 = u_1, \\ u'_2 = u_2 + u', \\ u'_3 = u_3 - u', \\ u'_4 = u_4. \end{cases} \tag{8.83}$$

The parameter u' is given by the form of the update rule employed (IM, BD, or DB), and it can be written as [32]

$$\text{IM: } u' = \frac{(n+3)u_1 + u_2 - u_3 - (n+3)u_4}{(n+3)(n-2)}, \tag{8.84}$$

$$\text{BD: } u' = \frac{(n+1)u_1 + u_2 - u_3 - (n+1)u_4}{(n+1)(n-2)}, \tag{8.85}$$

$$\text{DB: } u' = \frac{u_1 + u_2 - u_3 - u_4}{n-2}. \tag{8.86}$$

The equivalent utility matrix in such a case is

$$\begin{array}{c} \begin{array}{cc} S_r & S_m \end{array} \\ \begin{array}{c} S_r \\ S_m \end{array} \left(\begin{array}{cc} u_1 & u_2 + u' \\ u_3 - u' & u_4 \end{array} \right). \end{array} \tag{8.87}$$

Based on (8.80), the evolutionarily stable condition for strategy S_m is

$$u_4 > u_2 + u'. \tag{8.88}$$

Since $u_1 < u_3 < u_2 < u_4$, we have $u' < 0$ for all three update rules. In this case, (8.88) is always true, indicating that strategy S_m is an ESS all of the time. This completes the proof of the theorem.

8.6   Simulation Results

In this section, simulations comparing various adaptive filtering algorithms' performances are conducted. We also validate the results regarding the information diffusion probability as well as the ESS.

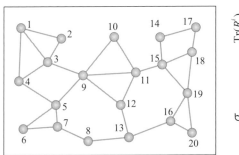 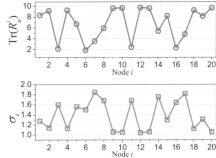

Figure 8.5 Network information for simulation, including the network topology for 20 nodes (left), the trace of regressor covariance $\text{Tr}(\boldsymbol{R}_u)$ (top right) and the noise variance σ_i (bottom right).

8.6.1 Mean-Square Performance

The left-hand side of Figure 8.5 shows the network topology used for the simulations, in which the locations of 20 nodes are random. Each node's information regarding the signal and noise power is also displayed on the right-hand side of Figure 8.5. We assume that the regressors with size $M = 5$ are zero-mean Gaussian and are independent in space and time. We set the unknown vector as $w^0 = \mathbb{1}_5/\sqrt{2}$ and the step size of the LMS algorithm for each node i as $\mu_i = 0.01$. Five hundred independent runs are done for all simulation results, from which the average is taken. In the simulations, six different distributed adaptive filtering algorithms are compared:

- Relative degree algorithm [6];
- Hastings algorithm [17];
- Adaptive combiner algorithm [8];
- Relative degree–variance algorithm [7];
- Error-aware algorithm with power form;
- Error-aware algorithm with exponential form.

Among them, the error-aware algorithm and the adaptive combiner algorithm [8] depend on dynamic combiners (weights) that are updated at every time instant. What is different between them is the update rule: the error-aware algorithms utilize the approximated EMSE information, while the adaptive combiner algorithm in [8] utilizes the projection method and optimization.

In the first comparison, we assume that the Hastings and relative degree–variance algorithms know each node's noise variance. In Figure 8.6, the results of the transient network performance comparison of the six different algorithms with respect to MSD and EMSE are shown. With a similar rate of convergence, it can be seen that the relative degree–variance algorithm shows the optimum performance. The error-aware algorithm with exponential form has a better performance than the relative degree algorithm. With power form fitness, the performance of the error-aware algorithm is similar if not better than that of the adaptive combiner algorithm,

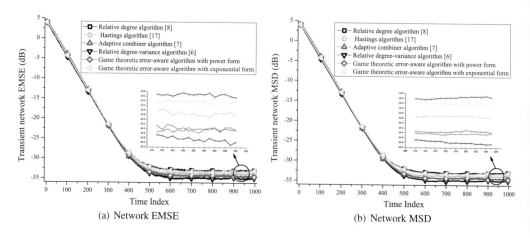

Figure 8.6 Transient performance comparison with known noise variances.

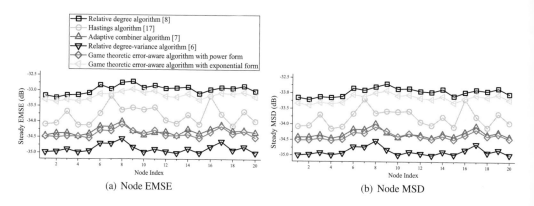

Figure 8.7 Steady-state performance comparison with known noise variances.

and these two algorithms have a better performance than all other algorithms apart from the relative degree–variance algorithm. Nevertheless, the error-aware algorithm does not need each node's information regarding noise variance, while the relative degree–variance algorithm does. In Figure 8.7, each node's corresponding steady-state performance for six distributed adaptive filtering algorithms in terms of EMSE and MSD are exhibited. Since the steady-state result is for each node, in addition to averaging over 500 independent runs, we average at each node over 100 time slots after convergence. It can be seen that the results of the transient performances and the steady-state performances are similar.

In the second comparison, we make the assumption that each node's information regarding the noise variance is unknown, but that we can use the approach developed in [17] to estimate it. With similar convergence rates, Figures 8.8 and 8.9 display the results regarding the transient and steady-state performances in terms of EMSE and MSD for the six algorithms. Because additional complexity is required in the noise variance estimation, the Hastings and relative degree–variance algorithms without variance estimation are also simulated to make the comparison fairer, and the

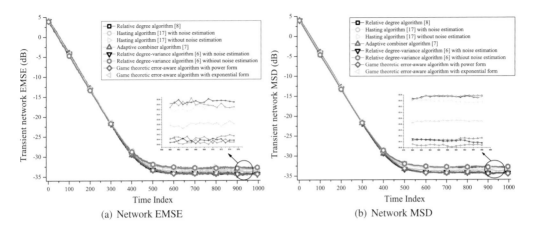

Figure 8.8 Transient performance comparison with unknown noise variances.

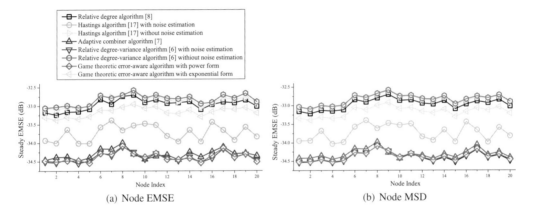

Figure 8.9 Steady-state performances comparison with unknown noise variances.

noise variance is set as the network's average variance, which is considered to be prior information. Compared with Figure 8.7, it can be seen that even though there is noise variance estimation, once we cannot know the information regarding noise variance, the performance of the relative degree–variance algorithm degrades significantly by nearly 0.5 dB (12% more error). However, as the Hastings algorithm depends less on information regarding noise variance, the degradation of its performance is not as severe. In Figure 8.8(b), it can be seen that if we do not adopt the variance estimation method, the error-aware algorithm with power form performs optimally. If we adopt the variance estimation method, the relative degree–variance algorithm, the adaptive combiner algorithm, and the error-aware algorithm with power form have similar performances, and they show better performance than the other algorithms. However, the adaptive combiner algorithm and the relative degree–variance algorithm with variance estimation are more complex than the error-aware algorithm with power form. Such results clearly demonstrate the advantages of the general framework. It should be noted that by selecting more appropriate fitness functions we can design more algorithms that perform better under particular criteria based on the framework.

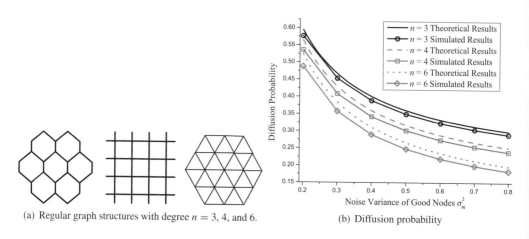

(a) Regular graph structures with degree $n = 3, 4$, and 6.   (b) Diffusion probability

Figure 8.10 Diffusion probabilities under three types of regular graphs

8.6.2   Diffusion Probability

In order to validate the analysis of the diffusion probability, we conduct another simulation here. As is shown in Figure 8.10(a), we generate three kinds of regular graphs with different degrees: $n = 3, 4$, and 6. In these three graphs, it is assumed that there are $N = 100$ nodes. We set the trace of regressor covariance for each node as $\text{Tr}(\boldsymbol{R}_u) = 10$, the noise variance of common nodes as $\sigma_r^2 = 1.5$, and the noise variance of good nodes as $\sigma_m^2 \in [0.2, 0.8]$. The initial state of the network in the simulation is that all common nodes choose to adopt strategy S_r. Then, at each time slot, based on the IM rules, we update the strategy of a randomly chosen node under weak selection ($w = 0.01$). We repeat the update steps until either the number of steps has reached the limit or strategy S_m has reached fixation. The fraction of runs where strategy S_m reached fixation out of 10^6 runs is computed as the diffusion probability. The simulation results are presented in Figure 8.10(b), in which all of the emulated results tally with the corresponding theoretical analysis and the gaps between them are because we make approximations in the derivations. It can also be seen that when the good signals' noise variance increases, their diffusion probability declines (i.e., a better signal has a better diffusion capability).

8.6.3   Evolutionarily Stable Strategy

As is shown in Figure 8.11, the IM update rule is further simulated over a 10×10 grid network with $N = 100$ nodes and degree $n = 4$ so as to prove that strategy S_m is an ESS in the adaptive network. Here we view the solid points as good nodes and the hollow points as common nodes. All of the settings, except the initial network settings, are the same as those in the simulation of the diffusion probability. The network state begins with only a few nodes adopting strategy S_r, denoted in gray, while the main portion of nodes adopts strategy S_m, denoted in black (including both solid and hollow nodes) in Figure 8.11. It can be seen from Figure 8.11, which illustrates the whole

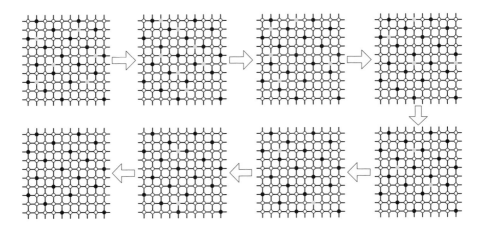

Figure 8.11 Strategy updating process in a 10×10 grid network with degree $n = 4$ and number of nodes $N = 100$.

network's strategy updating process, that the unfavorable strategy S_r is eventually abandoned by the network, verifying the stability of strategy S_m.

8.7   Conclusion

In this chapter, we introduce an evolutionary game-theoretic framework offering a very general view of the distributed adaptive filtering problems and unifying existing algorithms. As illustrations, we present two error-aware adaptive filtering algorithms based on this framework. With graphical EGT, the information diffusion process under the IM update rule in the network is analyzed, and it is verified that the strategy of utilizing good nodes' information is always an ESS. Differently from the traditional bottom-up approaches, the graphical evolutionary game-theoretic framework offers a top-down design philosophy for understanding the basics of distributed adaptive algorithms. As it provides us with a unified view and could stimulate us to design new distributed adaptive algorithms in the future, such a top-down design philosophy is of vital importance to the area of distributed adaptive signal processes.

References

[1] V. D. Blondel, J. M. Hendrickx, A. Olshevsky, and J. N. Tsitsiklis, "Distributed processing over adaptive networks," in *Proc. Adaptive Sensor Array Processing Workshop*, 2006.

[2] D. Li, K. D. Wong, Y. H. Hu, and A. M. Sayed, "Detection, classification, and tracking of targets," *IEEE Signal Processing Magazine*, vol. 19, pp. 17–29, 2002.

[3] F. C. Ribeiro Jr., M. L. R. de Campos, and S. Werner, "Distributed cooperative spectrum sensing with selective updating," in *Proc. European Signal Processing Conference (EUSIPCO)*, 2012.

[4] S. Haykin and K. J. R. Liu, *Handbook on Array Processing and Sensor Networks*. IEEE-Wiley, 2009.

[5] C. G. Lopes and A. H. Sayed, "Incremental adaptive strategies over distributed networks," *IEEE Transactions on Signal Processing*, vol. 55, pp. 4064–4077, 2007.

[6] F. S. Cattivelli, C. G. Lopes, and A. H. Sayed, "Diffusion recursive least-squares for distributed etimation over adaptive networks," *IEEE Transactions on Signal Processing*, vol. 56, pp. 1865–1877, 2008.

[7] F. S. Cattivelli and A. H. Sayed, "Diffusion LMS strategies for distributed estimation," *IEEE Transactions on Signal Processing*, vol. 58, pp. 1035–1048, 2010.

[8] N. Takahashi, I. Yamada, and A. H. Sayed, "Diffusion least-mean squares with adaptive combiners: formulation and performance analysis," *IEEE Transactions on Signal Processing*, vol. 58, pp. 4795–4810, 2010.

[9] S. Theodoridis, K. Slavakis, and I. Yamada, "Adaptive learning in a world of projections," *IEEE Signal Processing Magazine*, vol. 28, pp. 97–123, 2011.

[10] S. Chouvardas, K. Slavakis, and S. Theodoridis, "Adaptive robust distributed learning in diffusion sensor networks," *IEEE Transactions on Signal Processing*, vol. 59, pp. 4692–4707, 2011.

[11] R. L. G. Cavalcante, I. Yamada, and B. Mulgrew, "An adaptive projected subgradient approach to learning in diffusion networks," *IEEE Transactions on Signal Processing*, vol. 57, pp. 2762–2774, 2009.

[12] S.-Y. Tu and A. H. Sayed, "Mobile adaptive networks," *IEEE Journal of Selected Topics in Signal Processing*, vol. 5, pp. 649–664, 2011.

[13] V. D. Blondel, J. M. Hendrickx, A. Olshevsky, and J. N. Tsitsiklis, "Convergence in multiagent coordination, consensus, and flocking," in *Proc. Joint 44th IEEE Conference on Decision and Control and European Control Conference (CDC-ECC)*, 2005.

[14] L. Xiao, S. Boyd, and S. Lall, "A scheme for robust distributed sensor fusion based on average consensus," in *Proc. Information Processing Sensor Networks (IPSN)*, 2005.

[15] D. S. Scherber and H. C. Papadopoulos, "Locally constructed algorithms for distributed computations in ad hoc networks," in *Proc. Information Processing Sensor Networks (IPSN)*, 2004.

[16] L. Xiao and S. Boyd, "Fast linear iterations for distributed averaging," *Systems & Control Letters*, vol. 53, pp. 65–78, 2004.

[17] X. Zhao and A. H. Sayed, "Performance limits for distributed estimation over LMS adaptive networks," *IEEE Transactions on Signal Processing*, vol. 60, pp. 5107–5124, 2012.

[18] J. Smith, *Evolution and the Theory of Games*. Cambridge University Press, 1982.

[19] R. Cressman, *Evolutionary Dynamics and Extensive Form Games*. MIT Press, 2003.

[20] K. J. R. Liu and B. Wang, *Cognitive Radio Networking and Security: A Game-Theoretic View*. Cambridge University Press, 2010.

[21] B. Wang, Y. Wu, and K. J. R. Liu, "Game theory for cognitive radio networks: An overview," *Computer Networks*, vol. 54, pp. 2537–2561, 2010.

[22] B. Wang, K. J. R. Liu, and T. Clancy, "Evolutionary cooperative spectrum sensing game: How to collaborate?," *IEEE Transactions on Communications*, vol. 58, pp. 890–900, 2010.

[23] E. H. Watanabe, D. Menasché, E. Silva, and R. M. Leão, "Modeling resource sharing dynamics of VoIP users over a WLAN using a game-theoretic approach," in *Proc. IEEE INFOCOM*, 2008.

[24] C. Jiang, Y. Chen, Y. Gao, and K. J. R. Liu, "Joint spectrum sensing and access evolutionary game in cognitive radio networks," *IEEE Transactions on Wireless Communications*, vol. 12, pp. 2470–2483, 2013.

[25] Y. Chen, B. Wang, W. S. Lin, Y. Wu, and K. J. R. Liu, "Cooperative peer-to-peer streaming: An evolutionary game-theoretic approach," *IEEE Transactions on Circuits and Systems for Video Technology*, vol. 20, pp. 1346–1357, Oct. 2010.

[26] Y. Chen, Y. Gao, and K. J. R. Liu, "An evolutionary game-theoretic approach for image interpolation," in *Proc. IEEE International Conference on Acoustics, Speech and Signal Processing (ICASSP)*, 2011.

[27] R. Fisher, *The Genetical Theory of Natural Selection*. Clarendon Press, 1930.

[28] E. Lieberman, C. Hauert, and M. A. Nowak, "Evolutionary dynamics on graphs," *Nature*, vol. 433, pp. 312–316, 2005.

[29] P. Shakarian, P. Roos, and A. Johnson, "A review of evolutionary graph theory with applications to game theory," *Biosystems*, vol. 107, pp. 66–80, 2012.

[30] M. A. Nowak and K. Sigmund, "Evolutionary dynamics of biological games," *Science*, vol. 303, pp. 793–799, 2004.

[31] H. Ohtsuki, M. A. Nowak, and J. M. Pacheco, "Breaking the symmetry between interaction and replacement in evolutionary dynamics on graphs," *Physical Review Letters*, vol. 98, p. 108–106, 2007.

[32] H. Ohtsuki and M. A. Nowak, "The replicator equation on graphs," *Journal of Theoretical Biology*, vol. 243, pp. 86–97, 2006.

[33] X. Zhao and A. H. Sayed, "Clustering via diffusion adaptation over networks," in *Proc. International Workshop on Cognitive Information Processing*, (Spain), 2012.

[34] M. Slatkin, "Fixation probabilities and fixation times in a subdivided population," *Journal of Theoretical Biology*, vol. 35, pp. 477–488, 1981.

[35] H. Ohtsuki, C. Hauert, E. Lieberman, and M. A. Nowak, "A simple rule for the evolution of cooperation on graphs and social networks," *Nature*, vol. 441, pp. 502–505, 2006.

[36] F. Fu, L. Wang, M. A. Nowak, and C. Hauert, "Evolutionary dynamics on graphs: efficient method for weak selection," *Physical Review E*, vol. 79, p. 046707, 2009.

[37] G. Wild and A. Traulsen, "The different limits of weak selection and the evolutionary dynamics of finite populations," *Journal of Theoretical Biology*, vol. 247, pp. 382–390, 2007.

[38] W. J. Ewense, *Mathematical Population Genetics: Theoretical Introduction*. Spinger, 2004.

[39] H. Ohtsukia and M. A. Nowak, "Evolutionary stability on graphs," *Journal of Theoretical Biology*, vol. 251, pp. 698–707, 2008.

9 Graphical Evolutionary Game for Information Diffusion in Social Networks

Current social networks operate at an extremely large scale, which generates a huge number of information flows at any moment. Both industry and academics have paid attention to the ways in which information diffuses over social networks. Machine learning methods, which focus on empirical data mining and social network structure analysis, form the basis for analyzing information diffusion in most existing works. However, most existing works ignore the actions, decisions, and socioeconomic interactions of network users. In this chapter, in order to model the process of dynamic information spread in social networks, an evolutionary game-theoretic framework will be introduced. The information diffusion dynamics in complete networks, uniform-degree networks, and nonuniform-degree networks, particularly for two special networks – the Barabási–Albert scale-free network and the Erdős–Rényi random network – are derived. It is found that when the network scale is large enough, the information diffusion dynamics for these three types of networks are identical and thus scale-free. In order to substantiate the theoretical analysis, we simulate the process of information propagation in both synthetic networks and real-world Facebook networks. An experiment on a Twitter hashtag data set is also conducted, indicating that this game-theoretic model accords well with the situation in real social networks and can also forecast information diffusion processes.

9.1 Introduction

Currently, "social networks" are highly prevalent in our daily lives. Studying social networking from different perspectives is a hot topic for researchers from different disciplines due to the diverse implications of social networks [1]. A social network refers to a social structure that consists of social actors such as websites, individuals, organizations, or even equipment, and a set of interactions and relationships among those actors [2]. It is an important medium for the propagation of ideas, influences, and information between users. Today, mobile technologies and the Internet are developing rapidly, leading to social networks being achieving a very large scale. For example, there were around 1,000,000,000 active users of Facebook as of September 2012 [3]. At the same time, the amount of information on social networks is increasingly at a tremendous rate (e.g., every day throughout 2012, users sent 175 million tweets on Twitter [4]).

A variety of new information is generated on social networks every day, such as announcing a new cell phone model, the release of trade advertisements, a party's political statements are declared, or rumors circulating around singers and actors are reported. This sort of information may stir up heated discussions or vanish quickly. In order to know or even foretell the diffusion consequences of a new message on an underlying social network, it is essential to learn about information diffusion dynamics. As social network is influenced by a lot of factors (e.g., "word-of-mouth" effects, users' social interactions with and influence over each other, and users' interest in the information). Industry and academia currently pay much attention to the ways in which information diffuses over social networks. Politicians/enterprises can achieve effective and efficient advocation/advertisements by studying information diffusion. In addition, from the perspective of security, studying information propagation contributes to preventing the spread of harmful information, such as fake news, rumors, and computer viruses.

A typical example is the mention times of Twitter hashtags illustrated in [5], which presents the 1,000 highest total volume hashtags among 6 million hashtags from June to December 2009. The keyword "DavidArchuleta," which is a singer's name, is at the peak. He won the Rising Male Star award at the ALMA Awards in September 2009 and he also won second place in *American Idol*. His agency can use his information dynamics to learn his approval degree and thus improve future marketing planning. Another example is the Twitter political index [6]. During the 2012 US president election, this index provided the approval ratings of Obama and Romney by utilizing Twitter users' comment behaviors and online information diffusion, particularly after the candidates gave speeches. With such information, candidates are able to adjust their attitudes in future speeches so as to gain more approval. It can be seen from these examples that researching information diffusion is of significant importance in advocation and advertisements.

There are a large number of works on the information diffusion over social networks, and those that are most relevant and representative to our study are summarized. We can place the existing works into two categories: diffusion dynamics analysis and diffusion stability analysis. By utilizing different mathematical models, the former approach focuses on studying the process of dynamic information propagation over various types of networks [7–12]. One of the earliest works studying information propagation dynamics using the blogspace from both microscopic and macroscopic perspectives can be found in [7]. Subsequently, in [13], the ways in which social network influencing behaviors spread is studied and the network structure's influence on the behavior diffusion of users is investigated. The authors of [9] adopted an experimental approach to research the role of social networks in general information diffusion instead of focusing on behavior diffusion. Recently, with the increasing popularity of online social networks (e.g., Facebook and Twitter), researchers have conducted empirical analyses using large-scale data sets, including modeling the global influence of a node on the rate of diffusion on Memetracker [11], illustrating the statistical mechanics of rumor spreading on Facebook [12], and predicting the speed and range of information diffusion on Twitter [14]. In contrast to analyzing the process of dynamic information diffusion with some existing networks, some works focus on the reverse procedure (i.e., learning about and draw inferences from the hidden networks by mining the information diffusion data set [15–18]). The second category of information diffusion analysis attaches importance to the consequences and stability of information diffusion [19–23]. In [19], the ways of extracting the most influential nodes over a large-scale social network were analyzed by the author. Then, in order to find the top-k influential nodes in mobile social networks, the author proposed a community-based greedy algorithm in [21]. Further authors studied how to confine the contaminated or private information propagation in [20] and [22] by identifying crucial information links and hubs, respectively. On the other hand, information spread maximization was analyzed in [23] by designing effective neighbor selection strategies. The analysis of this chapter belongs to the first category; that is, modeling the dynamic process of information diffusion.

Machine learning methods using empirical data mining are adopted in the majority of existing works on information diffusion analysis. They all assume that the training set is consistent with the testing set statistically. But there is an obvious disadvantage: the results learned from a specified data set depend on the corresponding social network structure, and they might fail to analyze or predict future networks as social networks are quite different in a highly dynamic environment. In addition, this machine learning-based method disregards the decision-making and actions of users, while the influence of users' actions, decisions, and socioeconomic connections in terms of forwarding the information is vital in the process of information diffusion. Suppose that an individual or some people release some new information – whether other users forward the information largely determines the quick diffusion or sudden disappearance of the information. For users, decisions on forwarding or not forwarding rely on a number of factors, such as whether their friends are interested in the information, whether it is exciting, etc. We can often model interactions of this type through utilizing game theory [24]. Hence, in this chapter, a game-theoretic framework will be discussed regarding the dynamics of information diffusion over social networks. What is more, the game-theoretic method, compared with the machine learning-based one, focuses on the behavior of users from a microcosmic perspective, and the results do not depend on the assumptions of a steady network structure and could be utilized to analyze and predict a future network generally.

In the process of dynamic information diffusion, on the one hand, the users' neighbors can exert influence over whether they forward certain information or not; on the other hand, the neighbors' forwarding actions can also be impacted by the users. Actually, this kind of dynamic mutual influence process resembles the evolutionary processes in natural ecological systems [25], in which users with new messages could be seen as mutants and information propagation could be regarded as the mutants spreading. So the evolutionary game is considered for analyzing the process of dynamic information diffusion. The information diffusion dynamics of users in the model are revealed by analyzing their interactions, learning, and decision-making. On the basis of the evolutionary game-theoretic formulation, information diffusion dynamics over complete networks, uniform-degree networks, and nonuniform-degree networks are analyzed, and two special networks – the Barabási–Albert scale-free network and the Erdős–Rényi random network – are particularly researched. It has been found that when the scale of the network is large enough, the information diffusion dynamics for these three networks are identical and scale-free. We conduct our experiments using synthetic networks, the real-world Facebook network, and the Twitter hashtag data set to substantiate the theoretical analysis.

9.2 Diffusion Dynamics over Complete Networks

9.2.1 Basic Concepts of Evolutionary Game Theory

A fixed set of players is considered in classical game theory, and analyzing the static Nash equilibrium is its focus. Derived from ecological biology [25], evolutionary game theory (EGT) introduces the concept of "population" to enlarge the game formulation and focuses more on the dynamics of strategy updating in the whole population [26]. It is an efficient modeling tool in the field of signal processing, including wireless multicast [27], peer-to-peer streaming [28], adaptive filtering networks [29,30] and image interpolation [31], as well as networking and communications areas including wireless communications [32,33] and cognitive radio networks [34,35].

In EGT, "replicator dynamics" is one of the most significant concepts. It illustrates the strategies' dynamic processes in the whole population and offers information regarding the system state at any given moment. The player, who can reproduce their strategy according to some particular rules of mutation and selection, is represented as the replicator. To tally with the theory of natural selection, it is defined in EGT that the replicator with a higher payoff can reproduce at a higher rate. Under this situation, the replicators' dynamics could be demonstrated as a set of differential equations. Let us consider an evolutionary game with M pure strategies $\mathcal{X} = \{1, 2, \dots, M\}$ and a population of N players. Use n_i to represent the number of players who adopt strategy i and $x_i = \frac{n_i}{N}$ to stand for the percentage of players who adopt strategy i among the whole population. Under this circumstance, a vector $\mathbf{x} = [x_1, x_2, \dots, x_M]$ can illustrate the population state. In EGT, a player's utility is referred as "fitness" [36], which is denoted as

$$\Psi = (1 - \alpha) \cdot B + \alpha \cdot U. \tag{9.1}$$

Here B is the baseline fitness, which stands for the inherent property of the players. For instance, in a social network, a user's interests in the posted message can represent their baseline fitness. U is the payoff of the player, which is decided by the players' mutual interactions and the predefined payoff matrix. The parameter α denotes the selection intensity, representing the relative contribution of the game to fitness. The case $\alpha \to 1$ represents strong selection in which fitness and payoff are identical, while $\alpha \to 0$ stands for the limit of weak selection [37]. Notice that the selection intensity can be time variant (e.g., $\alpha(t) = \beta e^{-\epsilon t}$), indicating that as time proceeds, the contribution of game interactions drops.

Based on EGT, a set of discrete differential equations could represent the replicator dynamics, which are as follows:

$$
\begin{cases}
\dot{x}_1(t) = x_1(t)\left[\overline{\Psi}_1(t) - \overline{\Psi}(t)\right], \\
\quad \vdots \\
\dot{x}_i(t) = x_i(t)\left[\overline{\Psi}_i(t) - \overline{\Psi}(t)\right], \\
\quad \vdots \\
\dot{x}_M(t) = x_M(t)\left[\overline{\Psi}_M(t) - \overline{\Psi}(t)\right],
\end{cases}
\tag{9.2}
$$

where $\dot{x}_i(t)$ denotes the variation of x_i at time t (i.e., $x_i(t+1) = x_i(t) + \dot{x}_i(t)$), $\overline{\Psi}_i(t)$ stands for players' average fitness when they adopt strategy i at time t, and $\overline{\Psi}(t)$ symbolizes the whole population's average fitness at time t. It can be seen that if a higher fitness than the average degree could be achieved by adopting strategy i, the percentage x_i is going to rise and the rate of increase $\dot{x}_i/x_i$ is proportional to the difference between $\overline{\Psi}_i$ and $\overline{\Psi}$. It should be noted that if the overall population is homogeneous and large enough, the probability of an individual using strategy i can represent the proportion of players who use strategy i. In other words, $\mathbf{x}$ could be described as the mixed strategy of each player, and the replicator dynamics could be described as the mixed strategy updating of each player.

9.2.2   Evolutionary Game Formulation

When one user or a small group of users release a series of new information in the social network, the process of dynamic information diffusion relies on whether other users forward the information or not. Some factors can impact whether or not a user forwards such information, including their neighbor's actions and the user's own interest in the information. For example, the user is more likely to forward the information if all of their neighbors forward the information. This users' dynamic information forwarding process greatly resembles the process of players' strategy updating in the aforementioned EGT. As a result, the information diffusion dynamics over a complete network can be modeled by making use of the following evolutionary game:

- *Population and players*: A population means all of the users in a specific social network (e.g., Facebook or Twitter). "Players" refers to the users of the social network. Moreover, a population can also mean a large group of users in a social network (e.g., a circle in Google+).
- *Strategy*: Each user has two possible actions during the information diffusion process: to forward the received information or not. The two actions correspond to the following two strategies:

$$
\begin{cases}
S_f, & \text{forward the information,} \\
S_n, & \text{not forward the information.}
\end{cases}
\tag{9.3}
$$

- *Payoff*: Many factors can influence users' payoffs in social networks. They include the cost for forwarding the information and the reward received by forwarding or not (e.g., the hit rate of a website or the popularity of a user in a social network). In this chapter, the payoff matrix of users is modeled as

$$
\begin{array}{cc}
 & \begin{array}{cc} S_f & S_n \end{array} \\
\begin{array}{c} S_f \\ S_n \end{array} & \left(\begin{array}{cc} u_{ff} & u_{fn} \\ u_{fn} & u_{nn} \end{array} \right)
\end{array}
\tag{9.4}
$$

from which we can see that the payoff structure is symmetric (i.e., if a user with strategy S_f meets a user with strategy S_n, both of them receive the same payoff u_{fn}). Due to the heterogeneity of users, their mutual influences may not be symmetric. Thus, instead of focusing on the influence between users, we set our sights on the interactions among the strategies of users (i.e., to forward or not). Under this circumstance, we regard the nodes' interactions as undirected. This assumption is acceptable because users generally cannot obtain their neighbors' extra information in the information diffusion process (e.g., the interests or types of neighbors). So the influence of neighbors is unknown for users. All that they can do is to observe the strategies of neighbors (i.e., forwarding information or not). It should be noted that the asymmetric payoff matrix scenario can be easily obtained through extending all of the theoretical analysis for information diffusion in this chapter, as the payoff matrix is not considered in the analytical method. It is assumed that the payoff has been normalized within interval $(0, 1)$ (i.e., $0 < u_{ff}, u_{fn}, u_{nn} < 1$). Notice that the payoff matrix's value can vary under different application circumstances. For instance, the payoff matrix would satisfy $u_{ff} \geq u_{fn} \geq u_{nn}$ when the massage has something to do with the latest hot topics and forwarding is the best choice as it attracts more attention from other websites or users. By contrast, the payoff matrix would exhibit $u_{nn} \geq u_{fn} \geq u_{ff}$ when the information is related to unnecessary ads.

It can be seen from this formulation that there are strong similarities between strategy updating in the evolutionary game and information diffusion dynamics in social networks. In the following section, replicator dynamics will be used to model the process of dynamic information diffusion.

9.2.3   Information Diffusion Dynamics over a Complete Network

Each user is likely to interact with all other users in a complete network. In this way, the information published by a user is supposed to be received by all other users. Nevertheless, the decision on forwarding the information is determined by different users' strategies. In such a case, the network is considered to be a crowd of users who release new information constantly. For example, such a group of users, in practical social networks, may be a group in Facebook or a circle in Google+. As users in the group also link with other users outside the group, the information will spread more widely if there are more users in the group forwarding the information. Thus, we are able to deduce the process of information propagating to other users outside the group by analyzing the dynamics of users' strategies on information forwarding. Let us define x_f as the percentage of users who use strategy S_f and $x_n = 1 - x_f$ as the percentage of users who use strategy S_n. Under this situation, $\mathbf{x} = [x_f, x_n]$ can describe the network state.

By discretizing the process of dynamic information diffusion into time slots, we can consider the dynamic changing of $\mathbf{x}$ over time. In each time slot, the users in the complete network are supposed to have the ability to observe other users' strategies and fitness (the users are in the population). On the basis of the observed information, every user's decision (whether to forward or not) in the next time slot is decided by which strategy gives them higher fitness. Therefore, the network state $\mathbf{x}$ keeps changing slot by slot as the users' strategies update. Let us define the network state's changing rate as the *population dynamics* of information diffusion, $[\dot{x}_f, \dot{x}_n]$. Based on the replicator dynamics in (9.2), the population dynamics can be modeled as follows:

$$\dot{x}_f(t) = x_f(t)(\overline{\Psi}_f - \overline{\Psi}), \tag{9.5}$$

$$\dot{x}_n(t) = x_n(t)(\overline{\Psi}_n - \overline{\Psi}), \tag{9.6}$$

where $\overline{\Psi}_f$ represents the average fitness for using strategy S_f, which means forwarding the information, $\overline{\Psi}_n$ denotes the average fitness of using strategy S_n, which means not forwarding the information, and $\overline{\Psi}$ denotes the whole population's average fitness. To make the formulation more simple, we omit the time notation (t) in the subsequent analysis. Only one replicator dynamics equation (either (9.5) or (9.6)) can describe the network state because $x_f + x_n = 1$. It can be seen from the replicator dynamics of $\dot{x}_f$ and $\dot{x}_n$ that, if the average fitness of forwarding surpasses the average overall fitness, the number of users forwarding the information goes up. By contrast, if the average fitness of not forwarding exceeds the average overall fitness, the number of users not forwarding the information will increase.

Suppose that $[x_f, 1 - x_f]$ represents the current network state. The probability of two users with strategy S_f meeting is x_f and the probability of a user with strategy S_f meeting a user with strategy S_n is $1 - x_f$. Hence, based on the payoff matrix defined in (9.4), the average fitness for using strategy S_f is calculated as

$$\overline{\Psi}_f = 1 - \alpha + \alpha[x_f u_{ff} + (1 - x_f)u_{fn}], \tag{9.7}$$

which is based on the assumption of a large number of users N. It should be noted that throughout this chapter the baseline fitness is normalized as 1. Similarly, the average fitness for using strategy S_n can be calculated as

$$\overline{\Psi}_n = 1 - \alpha + \alpha[x_f u_{fn} + (1 - x_f)u_{nn}]. \tag{9.8}$$

Then we can get the average fitness for the whole population as

$$\overline{\Psi} = x_f \overline{\Psi}_f + (1 - x_f)\overline{\Psi}_n$$

$$= 1 - \alpha + \alpha[x_f^2 u_{ff} + x_f(1 - x_f)u_{fn} + (1 - x_f)^2 u_{nn}]. \tag{9.9}$$

By substituting (9.7)–(9.9) into (9.5), we have

$$\dot{x}_f = x_f(1 - x_f)(\overline{\Psi}_f - \overline{\Psi}_n)$$

$$= \alpha x_f(1 - x_f)[(u_{ff} - 2u_{fn} + u_{nn})x_f + u_{fn} - u_{nn}], \tag{9.10}$$

where we can see that the speed of users' observations and strategy adjustments is controlled by the selection intensity parameter α. Therefore, the following proposition can be given.

PROPOSITION 9.1   The population dynamics of information diffusion over complete networks given by replicator dynamics (9.5) and (9.6) can be described as the following:

$$\dot{x}_f = \alpha x_f(1 - x_f)\left(a_1 x_f + b_1\right), \tag{9.11}$$

$$\text{where} \quad \begin{cases} a_1 = u_{ff} - 2u_{fn} + u_{nn}, \\ b_1 = u_{fn} - u_{nn}. \end{cases} \tag{9.12}$$

Remarks: It can be seen that the information on network scale (i.e., the number of users in the network) was not used in the derivation of Proposition 9.1. Notice that the conclusion is based on the assumption that the number of users N is large enough. Only the values of the payoff matrix and initial state $x_f(0)$ determine the information diffusion dynamics in (9.11), which also exhibits the property of being scale-free.

9.3   Diffusion Dynamics over Uniform-Degree Networks

9.3.1   Basic Concepts of Graphical EGT

A fully connected population is considered in traditional EGT (i.e., a complete graph is considered for the population). Nevertheless, in many cases, the spatial locations of players can result in an incomplete graph structure. Then we introduce graphical EGT to work on the evolution of strategies in such a structured population [38]. In graphical EGT, besides the payoff matrix, strategies, and identities of the players, a graph structure is also linked to each game model. In the graph, the vertices represent players and the edges decide the interactions among players. As the mutual connections are limited among players, the fitness of each player is locally decided by interactions with all neighbor players. In nature, when the graph structure of graphical EGT is complete, the traditional evolutionary game could be seen as its special case. Previously, the stable state of information diffusion in social networks [39] and adaptive networks [30] has been modeled using graphical EGT. In this chapter, we focus on information diffusion dynamics by using replicator dynamics, while [39] is different because it laid emphasis on the information diffusion's final stable state by analyzing the evolutionarily stable state (ESS), which is also a significant concept in EGT.

In graphical EGT, replicator dynamics is an important concept, just like the ESS in traditional EGT. The difference is that replicator dynamics are generally analyzed

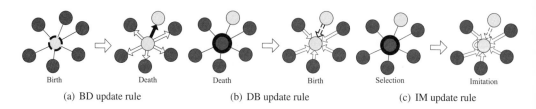

Birth   Death   Death   Birth   Selection   Imitation
(a) BD update rule   (b) DB update rule   (c) IM update rule

Figure 9.1 Three different strategy updating rules.

under some predefined rules for strategy updating, such as birth-death (BD), death-birth (DB), and imitation (IM) [40]. These strategy updating rules come from the field of evolutionary biology, and they are utilized to model the mutant/resident evolution process as follows. In the BD strategy updating rule, a player is selected for reproduction with the probability being proportional to fitness (birth process). Then the strategy of the chosen player takes the place of the strategy of a neighbor with uniform probability (death process). This process is shown in Figure 9.1(a). In the DB strategy updating rule, a player is randomly selected to give up their present strategy (death process). Then the selected player uses the strategy of one of their neighbors with the probability being proportional to their fitness (birth process). This process is shown in Figure 9.1(b). In the IM strategy updating rule, every player can choose to use a neighbor's strategy or continue adopting their present strategy, with the probability being proportional to fitness. This process is shown in Figure 9.1(c). Next, under the BD strategy updating rule, we will first analyze the dynamics of information diffusion, and then we will analyze the dynamics under the DB and IM strategy updating rules. It can be seen that if the network degree is sufficiently large, the results of these three rules are identical.

9.3.2   Graphical Evolutionary Game Formulation

In graphical EGT, a graph can represent a social network. In the graph, users are denoted as nodes and relationships between users are denoted as edges. Websites on the Internet or humans in a social network can represent users, and corresponding hyperlinks between web pages or friendships between users can represent relationships. When a series of new information is released by a user, the information may spread over the graph or disappear, and this is decided by the information forwarding actions of a user's neighbors, as well as the information forwarding actions of neighbors' neighbors. Similarly, through utilizing graphical EGT, the information diffusion dynamics over the graph-based networks can be modeled as follows:

- *Graph structure*: The graph structure of the game corresponds to the social network topology.
- *Players and population, payoff, and strategy*: The formulations resemble those in Section 9.2.

9.3.3   Diffusion Dynamics over Uniform-Degree Networks

In this section, on the basis of the previous graphical evolutionary game formulation, the information diffusion dynamics in uniform-degree networks will be analyzed. Here we consider an N-user homogeneous social network with general degree k. Just like the complete network scenario, $\mathbf{x} = [x_f, 1 - x_f]$ can also describe the network state of information diffusion. x_f represents the percentage of users forwarding the information in the whole population. The goal of this uniform-degree network scenario is to obtain the dynamics of x_f, which represents the information's diffusion scale. In addition, differently from the scenario of a complete network, in which the global network state x_f is simply the probability of a player meeting a player who adopts strategy S_f, x_f is not always equivalent to that probability in a social network based on an incomplete graph, as every user only has possible connections with neighbors. Under this situation, because of the limited dispersal, clusters are likely to form among users with the same strategy (either forwarding the information or not). To take the correlation of two neighboring players' strategies into account, the local network states are defined as $x_{f|f}$ and $x_{f|n}$, which denote the percentages of a user's neighbors using strategy S_f when this user adopts strategy S_f and S_n, respectively. To put it another way, $x_{f|f}$ or $x_{f|n}$ is the local network state around a user who adopts strategy S_f or S_n. It should be noted that the relationship between the global network state and local network state is

$$x_{f|f} = x_{ff}/x_f, \quad (1 - x_{f|f})x_f = x_{f|n}x_n, \qquad (9.13)$$

where x_{ff} denotes the global edge state (i.e., the percentage of edges at which both users adopt strategy S_f). In the same way, we have x_{fn} and x_{nn}, where $x_{ff} + x_{fn} + x_{nn} = 1$. Therefore, based on the definitions of local and global network states and the global edge states, three dynamics of information diffusion over graph-based networks are defined as follows:

- *Population dynamics*: $\dot{x}_f$, which resembles that in the complete networks.
- *Relationship dynamics*: $\dot{x}_{ff}$ and $\dot{x}_{nn}$, which are the dynamics of global edge states and demonstrate the dynamics of users' relationship. Note that $\dot{x}_{fn} = -\dot{x}_{ff} - \dot{x}_{nn}$.
- *Influence dynamics*: $\dot{x}_{f|f}$ and $\dot{x}_{f|n}$, which are the dynamics of local network state and demonstrate the users' influence over their neighbors (e.g., $\dot{x}_{f|f} = 1$ refers to the user's forwarding strategy being adopted by all their neighbors; i.e., the neighbors of this user tend to be affected by them or the user is more influential). By contrast, $\dot{x}_{f|n} = 1$ denotes the opposite situation.

In what follows, these information diffusion dynamics over uniform-degree networks will be analyzed to derive the population dynamics with closed-form expression.

Just like the scenario of a complete network, the dynamic information diffusion process will also be discretized into time slots, and the global and local dynamics will be analyzed under the BD strategy updating rule. Based on the BD updating rule, a user is chosen from the whole population with a probability proportional to their fitness at each time slot. Then the strategy of the chosen user (i.e., forwarding the information or not) randomly takes the place of one of their neighbors' strategies. That is, the user affects one of their neighbors and then their strategy is replicated by the neighbor. As the strategy of the user selected for reproduction is likely to have higher fitness than average, this dynamic strategy updating rule's physical meaning equals that of the replicator dynamics. Thus, a set of differential equations can be used to represent the dynamics of the network states under the BD updating rule, as in (9.2). In the subsequent deduction, only the weak selection scenario is taken into account (i.e., the selection intensity parameter satisfies $\alpha \to 0$). With the assumption of $\alpha \to 0$, the contribution of the payoff acquired from interactions is limited to every player's overall fitness, as is shown in (9.1). It should be noted that the results derived from weak selection often remain as valid approximations for larger selection strength [37]. Furthermore, a closed form in the dynamic information diffusion derivation is easier to achieve with the weak selection assumption, and the results also more clearly reveal the process of strategy diffusion over the network.

Influence Dynamics and Relationship Dynamics

Let us consider an N-user social network with uniform degree k. If a user releases some new messages, the BD strategy updating rule is regarded as the guidance for other users' forwarding the information or not. First, it is possible that when there are neighbors adopting strategy S_f, the user with strategy S_n may be affected by them and then change their current strategy. This phenomenon in the social network corresponds with the circumstance that when a user sees their friends forward some information, then the user would follow their friends. Under the BD strategy updating rule, this case only occurs when a user with strategy S_f is chosen for reproduction and then their strategy takes the place of the strategy of a neighbor who adopts S_n. Under this situation, the (S_f, S_f) pair will replace the original (S_f, S_n) pair. At the same time, another $(k-1)x_{f|n}$ (S_f, S_f) pairs are generated by the replaced neighbor on average. Therefore, if this case occurs, the (S_f, S_f) pairs add $1 + (k-1)x_{f|n}$ in total. It should be noted that this instance occurs with probability $x_f(1 - x_{f|f})$, in which x_f represents the probability of local selection and $1 - x_{f|f}$ represents the probability of local replacement. In summary, it can be seen that when the network degree is large enough, the (S_f, S_f) pairs in a unit update period increase on average by

$$P_i = x_f(1 - x_{f|f})[1 + (k-1)x_{f|n}]. \tag{9.14}$$

Second, another possible case is that of a user who uses strategy S_f under the influence of their neighbors using strategy S_n and then abandoning their current strategy. In a social network, this corresponds to the scenario in which a user finds that the forwarded information has drawn little attention from their friends, so that then the user would decide not to forward such kinds of information in the future. Based on the BD strategy updating rule, this occurs if a user with strategy S_n is chosen for reproduction and then their strategy takes the place of the strategy of a neighbor who use S_f, resulting in the (S_f, S_f) pairs reducing $(k-1)x_{f|f}$. Under this situation, when the network degree is large enough, the (S_f, S_f) pairs in a unit update period decrease on average by

$$P_d = (1 - x_f)x_{f|n}(k - 1)x_{f|f}. \qquad (9.15)$$

Because in each time slot N users are going to update their strategies and only one user can update at one time, it is assumed that there are N unit periods in every time slot (i.e., there are N subslots). By combining (9.14) and (9.15), we can write the relationship dynamics $\dot{x}_{ff}$ (i.e., the expected changes of the global edge state x_{ff} at one time slot) as

$$\dot{x}_{ff} = \frac{Nx_f(1 - x_{f|f})[1 + (k - 1)x_{f|n}] - N(1 - x_f)x_{f|n}(k - 1)x_{f|f}}{Nk/2}, \qquad (9.16)$$

where the denominator $Nk/2$ is the total number of edges in the network and it is assumed that the number of users N is large. In the same way, the other relationship dynamics $\dot{x}_{nn}$ can be written as

$$\dot{x}_{nn} = \frac{N(1 - x_f)[1 + (k - 1)x_{n|f}] - Nx_f(1 - x_{f|f})(k - 1)x_{n|n}}{Nk/2}. \qquad (9.17)$$

Ohtsukia and Nowak in [40] discovered that the global network state x_f changes at a rate of order α, while the changing rate orders of local network states $x_{f|f}$ and $x_{f|n}$ are 1, so the global network state x_f dominates the speed of dynamics. Under this situation, the global network state will converge to equilibria at a much slower rate than the local network states on account of the weak selection. Thus, two timescales can be separated. In this way, when influence dynamics $\dot{x}_{f|f}$ and $\dot{x}_{f|n}$ are converging, the global network state x_f can be viewed as a constant. The reason for this is that the local network dynamics are only in terms of a local area that includes k users at most. So at such a small scale the local dynamics vary and converge at rather high speed. Nevertheless, the dynamics of a global network state would be much slower due to the state's association of all users (i.e., the whole network). With weak selection and the relationship dynamics in (9.16) and (9.17), we can derive the influence dynamics $\dot{x}_{f|f}$ and $\dot{x}_{f|n}$ as follows:

$$
\begin{aligned}
\dot{x}_{f|f} = \frac{\dot{x}_{ff}}{x_f} &= \frac{x_f(1 - x_{f|f})[1 + (k - 1)x_{f|n}] - (1 - x_f)x_{f|n}(k - 1)x_{f|f}}{kx_f/2} \\
&= \frac{(1 - x_{f|f})[1 + (k - 1)x_{f|n}] - (1 - x_{f|f})(k - 1)x_{f|f}}{k/2} \\
&= \frac{2}{k}\{1 + (k - 1)[x_{f|f}x_{f|f} + x_{f|n}(1 - x_{f|f})] - kx_{f|f}\},
\end{aligned} \qquad (9.18)
$$

and

$$\dot{x}_{f|n} = 1 - \frac{\dot{x}_{nn}}{1 - x_f} = \frac{2}{k}\{(k - 1)[x_{f|f}x_{f|n} + x_{f|n}(1 - x_{f|n})] - kx_{f|n}\}. \qquad (9.19)$$

By setting $\dot{x}_{f|n} = \dot{x}_{f|f} = 0$ and utilizing the relationships described in (9.13), the stable points (equilibria) of the influence dynamics can be obtained as

$$x_{f|n}^{*} = \frac{(k-2)x_f}{k-1}, \quad x_{f|f}^{*} = \frac{(k-2)x_f + 1}{k-1}. \tag{9.20}$$

Population Dynamics

Using the dynamics of local network states (i.e., the influence dynamics) we could analyze the global strategy updating of users to obtain the population dynamics. Two cases that result in the dynamics of global network state x_f are as follows:

- *Case 1:* The global network state x_f will increase by a unit when the strategy of a user is changed from S_n to S_f.
- *Case 2:* The global network state x_f will decrease by a unit when the strategy of a user is changed from S_f to S_n.

Based on the BD strategy updating rule, when a user is chosen for reproduction because of higher fitness, the strategy replacement (replication) of a neighbor will occur, and thus there is a change in the user's strategy. Under this circumstance, *Case 1* applies for a user with strategy S_n whose neighbor, adopting strategy S_f, is selected for reproduction, and then this user is chosen to replicate strategy S_f. That is to say, this user is affected by their neighbor via interaction and observation and replaces strategy S_n with S_f. *Case 2* applies for a user with strategy S_f whose neighbor, adopting strategy S_n, is selected for reproduction, and then this user is chosen to replicate strategy S_n. That is to say, this user is affected by their neighbor and replaces strategy S_f with S_n. After the analysis of *Case 1*'s and *Case 2*'s occurrence probabilities, in each time slot, the expected change in the global state x_f can be calculated, which is just the population dynamics, as is shown in the following proposition.

PROPOSITION 9.2   Under the weak selection scenario and BD strategy updating rule, the population dynamics of information diffusion over uniform-degree networks can be denoted as follows:

$$\dot{x}_f = \frac{\alpha(k-2)}{(k-1)}x_f(1-x_f)\left(a_2 x_f + b_2\right) + o(\alpha^2), \tag{9.21}$$

$$\text{where} \begin{cases} a_2 = (k-2)(u_{ff} - 2u_{fn} + u_{nn}), \\ b_2 = u_{ff} + (k-2)u_{fn} - (k-1)u_{nn}. \end{cases} \tag{9.22}$$

Proof Two probable cases of the global network state x_f changing are summarized in *Case 1* and *Case 2* given in Section 9.3.3. *Case 1* corresponds with the situation in which a user who adopts strategy S_f is chosen for reproduction and takes the place of the strategy of a neighbor who adopt strategy S_n. Assume that there are k_f neighbors using strategy S_f and $k - k_f$ neighbors using strategy S_n. According to the BD strategy updating rule, the overall probability for being selected is proportional to the fitness. Under this situation, the user adopting strategy S_f is chosen with probability

$x_f \Psi_f / \overline{\Psi}$ and the replacement probability is $(k - k_f)/k$. Here Ψ_f stands for the fitness of the user who adopts strategy S_f and $\overline{\Psi}$ represents the whole population's average fitness. Under this circumstance, the expected occurrence probability of *Case 1* is

$$P_1^{BD} = \sum_{k_f=0}^{k} \frac{k!}{k_f!(k-k_f)!} x_{f|f}^{k_f} (1 - x_{f|f})^{k-k_f} \frac{x_f \Psi_f}{\overline{\Psi}} \frac{k-k_f}{k}, \qquad (9.23)$$

which is also the expected probability for the global network state x_f increasing by $1/N$. In the same way, *Case 2* corresponds with the situation in which a user who adopts strategy S_n is chosen for reproduction and takes the place of the strategy of a neighbor who adopts strategy S_f. The expected occurrence probability of *Case 2* can be calculated as a dual expression of (9.23) as follows:

$$P_2^{BD} = \sum_{k_f=0}^{k} \frac{k!}{k_f!(k-k_f)!} x_{f|n}^{k_f} (1 - x_{f|n})^{k-k_f} \frac{(1 - x_f)\Psi_n}{\overline{\Psi}} \frac{k_f}{k}, \qquad (9.24)$$

which is also the expected probability of the global network state x_f decreasing by $1/N$. Ψ_n represents the fitness of the user who adopts strategy S_n.

It is assumed that in each time slot there are N unit periods (i.e., only one update appears in one subslot, although there are N subslots). Combining (9.23) and (9.24), in one time slot the expected change of the global network state x_f is

$$\dot{x}_f = \sum_{k_f=0}^{k} \frac{k!}{k_f!(k-k_f)!} \left\{ x_{f|f}^{k_f} (1 - x_{f|f})^{k-k_f} \frac{x_f \Psi_f}{\overline{\Psi}} \frac{k-k_f}{k} \right.$$
$$\left. - x_{f|n}^{k_f} (1 - x_{f|n})^{k-k_f} \frac{(1 - x_f)\Psi_n}{\overline{\Psi}} \frac{k_f}{k} \right\}, \qquad (9.25)$$

$$\text{where} \quad \begin{cases} \Psi_f = 1 - \alpha + \alpha[k_f u_{ff} + (k - k_f)u_{fn}], \\ \Psi_n = 1 - \alpha + \alpha[k_f u_{fn} + (k - k_f)u_{nn}]. \end{cases} \qquad (9.26)$$

By substituting (9.26) into (9.25), the dynamics of the global network state can be simplified as

$$\dot{x}_f = \frac{\alpha x_f(1 - x_{f|f})(k - 1)}{\overline{\Psi}} \cdot [(u_{ff} - u_{fn})x_{f|f} - (u_{nn} - u_{fn})(1 - x_{f|n})], \quad (9.27)$$

from which we can see that the numerator is dominant by α, which is sufficiently small compared with 1 in the weak selection scenario, while the denominator $\overline{\Psi} = 1 - \alpha + \alpha \overline{U}$ is dominant by 1. Under this circumstance, (9.27) can be approximated by replacing (9.27) with the local equilibria (9.20) as follows:

$$\dot{x}_f \doteq \alpha x_f(1 - x_{f|f})(k - 1) \cdot [(u_{ff} - u_{fn})x_{f|f} - (u_{nn} - u_{fn})(1 - x_{f|n})]$$

$$= \frac{\alpha(k - 2)}{(k - 1)} x_f(1 - x_f)[(k - 2)(u_{ff} - 2u_{fn} + u_{nn})x_f$$

$$+ u_{ff} + (k - 2)u_{fn} - (k - 1)u_{nn}]. \qquad (9.28)$$

Remarks: From Proposition 9.2 it can be seen that the forms of the population dynamics of information diffusion over uniform-degree networks and that over the complete network in (9.11) are rather similar. The dynamics in (9.21) only depend on the values of the payoff matrix, the degree of the network, and the initial state $x_f(0)$, regardless of the network scale information. Thus, the scale-free property is also shown in the population dynamics of information diffusion over uniform-degree networks. In real social networks, each user's degree generally satisfies $k \gg 2$. Under this circumstance, we can further approximate (9.21) as

$$\dot{x}_f = \frac{\alpha(k-2)^2}{(k-1)} x_f(1-x_f) \left[(u_{ff} - 2u_{fn} + u_{nn})x_f + \frac{u_{ff} - u_{nn}}{k-2} + u_{fn} - u_{nn} \right]$$

$$= \alpha' x_f(1-x_f)[(u_{ff} - 2u_{fn} + u_{nn})x_f + u_{fn} - u_{nn}], \tag{9.29}$$

where $\alpha' = \frac{\alpha(k-2)^2}{(k-1)}$. It can be seen that the population dynamics of information diffusion over uniform-degree networks are indeed identical to those over a complete network as shown in (9.11). The reason for this is that with sufficiently large degree in a uniform-degree network (i.e., every user has the same sufficiently large number of neighbors) a user's information forwarding strategy is affected by many other users, which is similar to that in complete networks. In nature, when $k \to N$, the complete network can be seen as a special case of the uniform-degree networks. Furthermore, this phenomenon also verifies that under the BD strategy updating rule the dynamics are equivalent to the replicator dynamics in complete networks. So far, Proposition 9.2 demonstrates the dynamics of information diffusion under BD strategy updating rule. The relationship between the dynamics of information diffusion under the BD, DB, and IM strategy updating rules will be revealed by the following proposition.

PROPOSITION 9.3   Under the weak selection scenario and the assumption of the network degree being sufficiently large, the population dynamics of information diffusion over uniform-degree networks under BD, DB, and IM strategy updating rules are equivalent.

Proof   In this proof, first, the analysis of information diffusion dynamics under the BD rule will be extended to the scenario under the DB and IM strategy updating rules, respectively. Second, assuming that network degree is large enough, equivalence will be demonstrated by comparing the derived approximation of the diffusion dynamics under the three different rules.

Diffusion Dynamics under the DB Rule

Just like the analysis under the BD rule, for the diffusion dynamics under the DB strategy updating rule, the influence dynamics' stable point (i.e., the local equilibria of the information diffusion) should be calculated first, and then the population dynamics will be calculated through the analysis of the two cases in Section 9.3.3. It should be noted that we omit the complicated process of derivation here because the influence dynamics' stable point under the BD rule as shown in (9.20) can be directly applied to that under the DB strategy updating rule. What is more, the analyses of population dynamics under the BD and DB rules are similar to each other as well, since the DB rule is dual with the BD rule. Recall that *Case 1* in Section 9.3.3 corresponds with the situation in which a user who adopts strategy S_f is chosen for reproduction and takes the place of the strategy of a neighbor who adopts strategy S_n. Under the DB strategy updating rule, we calculate *Case 1*'s expected occurrence probability as

$$P_1^{DB} = \sum_{k_f=0}^{k} \frac{k!}{k_f!(k-k_f)!} x_{f|n}^{k_f} (1-x_{f|n})^{k-k_f} \frac{(1-x_f)\Psi_f}{\overline{\Psi}_1} \frac{k_f}{k}. \tag{9.30}$$

In the same way, *Case 2* in Section 9.3.3 corresponds with the situation in which a user who adopts strategy S_n is chosen for reproduction and takes the place of the strategy of a neighbor who adopts strategy S_f, and the corresponding expected occurrence probability is

$$P_2^{DB} = \sum_{k_f=0}^{k} \frac{k!}{k_f!(k-k_f)!} x_{f|f}^{k_f} (1-x_{f|f})^{k-k_f} \frac{x_f \Psi_n}{\overline{\Psi}_2} \frac{k-k_f}{k}. \tag{9.31}$$

Combining (9.30) and (9.31), in one time slot the expected change of the global network state x_f is

$$\dot{x}_f = \sum_{k_f=0}^{k} \frac{k!}{k_f!(k-k_f)!} \left\{ x_{f|n}^{k_f} (1-x_{f|n})^{k-k_f} \frac{(1-x_f)\Psi_f}{\overline{\Psi}} \frac{k_f}{k} \right.$$
$$\left. - x_{f|f}^{k_f} (1-x_{f|f})^{k-k_f} \frac{x_f \Psi_n}{\overline{\Psi}} \frac{k-k_f}{k} \right\}, \tag{9.32}$$

where

$$\begin{cases} \Psi_f = 1 - \alpha + \alpha[(k-1)(x_{f|f}u_{ff} + (1-x_{f|f})u_{fn}) + u_{fn}], \\ \Psi_n = 1 - \alpha + \alpha[(k-1)(x_{f|n}u_{fn} + (1-x_{f|n})u_{nn}) + u_{fn}]. \end{cases} \tag{9.33}$$

Through substituting (9.33) and the local equilibria (9.20) into (9.32), (9.32) can be simplified as

$$\dot{x}_f^{DB} = \frac{\alpha(k-2)(k+1)}{k(k-1)} x_f(1-x_f)[(k-2)(u_{ff} - 2u_{fn}$$
$$+ u_{nn})x_f + u_{ff} + (k-2)u_{fn} - (k-1)u_{nn}], \tag{9.34}$$

which represents the diffusion dynamics under the DB strategy updating rule.

Diffusion Dynamics under the IM Rule

Similarly, we can derive the diffusion dynamics under the IM strategy updating rule. First, the influence dynamics' stable point under the IM rule is identical to that under the BD and DB strategy updating rules as shown in (9.20). Second, under the IM strategy updating rule, the analysis of population dynamics is similar to that under the DB rule, as the user being able to mimic their own strategy in the IM rule is the only difference between these two strategy updating rules, as is shown in

Figure 9.1(b) and (c). Therefore, under the IM strategy updating rule we can derive the diffusion dynamics through considering the possibility of one user keeping their strategy unchanged, which is

$$\dot{x}_f^{IM} = \frac{\alpha k(k-2)(k+3)}{(k-1)(k+1)^2} x_f (1-x_f)[(k-2)(u_{ff}-2u_{fn}$$

$$+ u_{nn})x_f + u_{ff} + (k-2)u_{fn} - (k-1)u_{nn}]. \tag{9.35}$$

Equivalence

Comparing (9.28), (9.34), and (9.35) (i.e., the diffusion dynamics under three different strategy updating rules), it can be seen that apart from the coefficient (i.e., the BD rule with coefficient $\frac{\alpha(k-2)}{(k-1)}$, the DB rule with coefficient $\frac{\alpha(k-2)(k+1)}{k(k-1)}$, and the IM rule with coefficient $\frac{\alpha k(k-2)(k+3)}{(k-1)(k+1)^2}$), the expressions of the diffusion dynamics are exactly the same. Under this situation, all three coefficients would tend to be α under the assumption of network degree k being large enough, indicating that under these three different strategy updating rules the diffusion dynamics over uniform-degree networks are equivalent to each other.

9.4   Diffusion Dynamics over Nonuniform-Degree Networks

In this section, the analysis in the previous section is extended to the scenario of nonuniform-degree networks. For the nonuniform-degree network, an N-user social network in which the degree obeys distribution $\lambda(k)$ is considered. This distribution indicates that when selecting a random user from the network, the possibility that the selected user has k neighbors is $\lambda(k)$. Under this situation, the network's average degree is

$$\bar{k} = \sum_{k=0}^{+\infty} \lambda(k)k. \tag{9.36}$$

It should be noted that degree correlation is not taken into account (i.e., all users' degrees are independent of each other). Graphical EGT can also model the dynamics of information diffusion over nonuniform-degree networks, and apart from the structure of the graph, the formulation is the same as that in the previous section. In what follows, under the BD strategy updating rule, the general case for the dynamics of information diffusion over nonuniform-degree networks will be analyzed first. Then two special instances (i.e., two types of typical networks, Erdős–Rényi random network and Barabási–Albert scale-free networks), will be highlighted.

9.4.1   General Case

For the nonuniform scenario, the analytical method is no different from that in the previous section: first acquire the influence dynamics and relationship and find the corresponding equilibrium, then obtain the population dynamics. Thus, the same derivations in the previous section can be used to derive the population dynamics of information diffusion over nonuniform-degree networks. The only distinction is that we should take into account the distribution of the users' degrees. There are two kinds of users according to the BD strategy updating rule: the selected user and the replaced neighbor. Conspicuously, the degree of the selected user complies with distribution $\lambda(k)$. Nevertheless, the replaced neighbor does not, because if a random pair is chosen, $\frac{k\lambda(k)}{\sum_{k=0}^{+\infty} k\lambda(k)}$ rather than $\lambda(k)$ represents the distribution degree of the user in the specific pair [41]. The population dynamics of information diffusion over nonuniform-degree networks could be derived as in Proposition 9.4 by having different expectations with respect to the various kinds of users' degrees.

PROPOSITION 9.4 Under the weak selection scenario and the BD strategy updating rule, the population dynamics of information diffusion over nonuniform-degree networks can be described as follows:

$$\dot{x}_f = \frac{\alpha(\overline{k}-1)(\overline{k^2}-2\overline{k})}{(\overline{k^2}-\overline{k})^2} x_f(1-x_f)\left(a_3 x_f + b_3\right) + o(\alpha^2), \tag{9.37}$$

$$\text{where} \begin{cases} a_3 = (\overline{k^2}-2\overline{k})(u_{ff}-2u_{fn}+u_{nn}), \\ b_3 = \overline{k}u_{ff} + (\overline{k^2}-2\overline{k})u_{fn} - (\overline{k^2}-\overline{k})u_{nn}. \end{cases} \tag{9.38}$$

Proof In the expression of local dynamics of uniform-degree networks, the "k" in (9.14) and (9.15) denotes the replaced neighbor's degree. In the nonuniform scenario, the replaced neighbor's degree follows a specific distribution rather than the constant k. It should be noted that if a random pair is chosen, $\frac{k\lambda(k)}{\sum_{k=0}^{+\infty} k\lambda(k)}$ instead of $\lambda(k)$ represents the distribution degree of the user in the specific pair. Under this circumstance, the replaced neighbor's average degree is

$$\sum_{k=0}^{+\infty} k \frac{k\lambda(k)}{\sum_{k=0}^{+\infty} k\lambda(k)} = \frac{\overline{k^2}}{\overline{k}}, \tag{9.39}$$

where $\overline{k^2} = \sum_{k=0}^{+\infty} k^2\lambda(k)$ is the expectation of k^2. In the nonuniform scenario, when we calculate the average decrease and increase of the (S_f, S_f) pairs in a unit update period, we need to take expectations into account with respect to the "k" in (9.14) and (9.15). What is more, the denominator in (9.16) denoting the total number of network edges should be $N\overline{k}/2$. Hence, we denote the local dynamics of the nonuniform-degree networks as

$$\dot{x}_{f|n} = \frac{2}{\overline{k}}\left\{\left(\frac{\overline{k^2}}{\overline{k}}-1\right)[x_{f|f}x_{f|n} + x_{f|n}(1-x_{f|n})] - \frac{\overline{k^2}}{\overline{k}}x_{f|n}\right\}, \tag{9.40}$$

$$\dot{x}_{f|f} = \frac{2}{\overline{k}}\left\{1+\left(\frac{\overline{k^2}}{\overline{k}}-1\right)[x_{f|f}x_{f|f} + x_{f|n}(1-x_{f|f})] - \frac{\overline{k^2}}{\overline{k}}x_{f|f}\right\}. \tag{9.41}$$

Then the local equilibrium of the information diffusion dynamics over nonuniform-degree networks is

$$x_{f|n}^* = \frac{(\overline{k^2} - 2\overline{k})x_f}{\overline{k^2} - \overline{k}}, \quad x_{f|f}^* = \frac{(\overline{k^2} - 2\overline{k})x_f + \overline{k}}{\overline{k^2} - \overline{k}}. \tag{9.42}$$

For the global dynamics, the distribution degree of users should also be considered. Since the degree of the selected user is represented by the "k" in (9.27), we could base our expectation on this and obtain the global dynamics of the nonuniform-degree networks as

$$\dot{x}_f = \frac{\alpha x_f(1 - x_{f|f})(\overline{k} - 1)}{\overline{\Psi}} \cdot [(u_{ff} - u_{fn})x_{f|f} - (u_{nn} - u_{fn})(1 - x_{f|n})]. \tag{9.43}$$

In the same way, through substituting (9.42) into (9.43) and approximating $\overline{\Psi}$, we have

$$\dot{x}_f = \frac{\alpha(\overline{k} - 1)(\overline{k^2} - 2\overline{k})}{(\overline{k^2} - \overline{k})^2}x_f(1 - x_f)[(\overline{k^2} - 2\overline{k})(u_{ff} - 2u_{fn} + u_{nn})x_f$$

$$+ \overline{k}u_{ff} + (\overline{k^2} - 2\overline{k})u_{fn} - (\overline{k^2} - \overline{k})u_{nn}]. \tag{9.44}$$

Remarks: It can be seen from Proposition 9.4 that the form of information diffusion dynamics over nonuniform-degree networks is similar to that in Propositions 9.1 and 9.2. Nevertheless, the scale-free property may not hold because of the term $\overline{k^2} = \sum_{k=0}^{+\infty} k^2 \lambda(k)$, which is the expectation of k^2 and probably includes information on the network scale. We can find from Proposition 9.4 that there are three stable states 0, 1, and $\frac{b_3}{a_3}$ in (9.37), and this tallies with the results in [39].

9.4.2   Two Special Cases

In this section, two special instances of the nonuniform-degree networks will be discussed, which are Erdős–Rényi random (ER) networks [42] and Barabási–Albert scale-free (BA) networks [43]. The degree of ER networks obeys a Poisson distribution, i.e.,

$$\lambda_{\mathrm{ER}}(k) = \frac{e^{-\overline{k}}\overline{k}^k}{k!} \quad \text{and} \quad \overline{k^2} = \overline{k}(\overline{k} + 1). \tag{9.45}$$

Under this situation, based on Proposition 9.4, we can obtain the population dynamics of information diffusion over ER networks as

$$\dot{x}_f^{\mathrm{ER}} = \alpha\left(\frac{\overline{k} - 1}{\overline{k}}\right)^2 x_f^{\mathrm{ER}}(1 - x_f^{\mathrm{ER}})[(\overline{k} - 1)(u_{ff} - 2u_{fn} + u_{nn})x_f^{\mathrm{ER}}$$

$$+ u_{ff} + (\overline{k} - 1)u_{fn} - \overline{k}u_{nn}]. \tag{9.46}$$

With the assumption of the network's average degree $\overline{k} \gg 1$, we can approximate $\dot{x}_f^{\mathrm{ER}}$ in (9.46) as

$$\dot{x}_f^{\text{ER}} = \alpha_{\text{ER}} x_f^{\text{ER}} (1 - x_f^{\text{ER}})[(u_{ff} - 2u_{fn} + u_{nn})x_f + u_{fn} - u_{nn}], \tag{9.47}$$

where $\alpha_{\text{ER}} = \alpha \frac{(\overline{k}-1)^3}{\overline{k}^2} \approx \alpha \overline{k}$. It can be seen that the forms of the population dynamics in ER networks, complete networks and uniform-degree networks are the same (when the uniform degree $k \gg 2$). What is more, since α is adjustable, it can be seen that $\dot{x}_f^{\text{ER}}$ would also become scale-free by taking $\alpha = \frac{\alpha'}{\overline{k}}$.

As for the BA network, the degree obeys a power law distribution, i.e.,

$$\lambda_{\text{BA}}(k) \propto k^{-\xi} \quad \text{and} \quad \overline{k^2} \doteq \overline{k}^2 \log N/4 \text{ (when } \xi = 3). \tag{9.48}$$

Under this circumstance, based on Proposition 9.4, we can derive the information diffusion dynamics of BA networks as

$$\dot{x}_f^{\text{BA}} = \frac{\alpha(\overline{k} - 1)(\overline{k} \log N/4 - 2)}{(\overline{k} \log N/4 - 1)^2} x_f^{\text{BA}}(1 - x_f^{\text{BA}})$$
$$\times [(\overline{k} \log N/4 - 2)(u_{ff} - 2u_{fn} + u_{nn})x_f^{\text{BA}}$$
$$+ u_{ff} + (\overline{k} \log N/4 - 2)u_{fn} - (\overline{k} \log N/4 - 1)u_{nn}]. \tag{9.49}$$

If the network scale N is large enough, $\dot{x}_f^{\text{BA}}$ in (9.49) can be approximated by

$$\dot{x}_f^{\text{BA}} = \alpha_{\text{BA}} x_f^{\text{BA}}(1 - x_f^{\text{BA}})[(u_{ff} - 2u_{fn} + u_{nn})x_f^{\text{BA}} + u_{fn} - u_{nn}], \tag{9.50}$$

where $\alpha_{\text{BA}} = \frac{\alpha(\overline{k}-1)(\overline{k} \log N/4-2)^2}{(\overline{k} \log N/4-1)^2} \approx \alpha(\overline{k} - 1)$. Therefore, the form of population dynamics in BA networks is also the same as that in complete networks, and the scale-free property would also be satisfied in $\dot{x}_f^{\text{BA}}$ by taking $\alpha = \frac{\alpha'}{\overline{k}-1}$.

9.5 Experiments

In this section, experiments are performed to substantiate our analysis of information diffusion dynamics. First, the information diffusion process in synthetic networks and a real-world network (i.e., the Facebook social network) is simulated to validate the theoretical results through setting various payoff matrices. Then, by fitting the curve of the real-world information diffusion process, we estimate each hashtag's corresponding payoff matrix by using of the Twitter hashtag data set.

9.5.1 Synthetic Networks and a Real-World Network

For the experiment on synthetic networks, four types of networks are generated to simulate the process of information diffusion:

- The complete network;
- The uniform-degree network;
- The ER random network;
- The BA network.

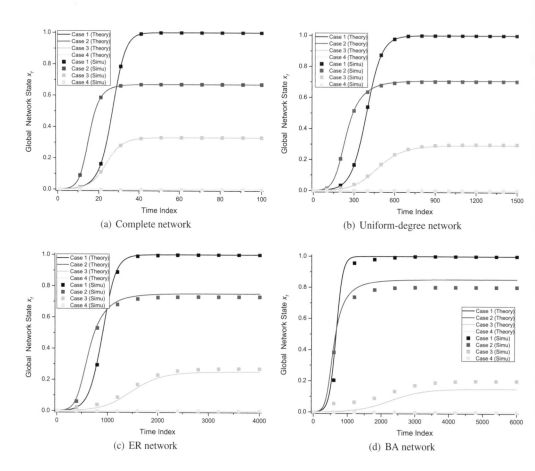

Figure 9.2 Simulation results for synthetic networks.

In total, 1,000 users are generated for each network, and initially only one user uses strategy S_f while all other users use S_n. Selection intensity α is set to be 0.1, which means weak selection, and we consider four kinds of payoff matrix:

- Case 1: $u_{ff} = 0.8 > u_{fn} = 0.6 > u_{nn} = 0.4$;
- Case 2: $u_{fn} = 0.8 > u_{ff} = 0.6 > u_{nn} = 0.4$;
- Case 3: $u_{fn} = 0.8 > u_{nn} = 0.6 > u_{ff} = 0.4$;
- Case 4: $u_{nn} = 0.8 > u_{fn} = 0.6 > u_{ff} = 0.4$.

For the scenario of complete and uniform-degree networks, the experiment results with various payoff matrices are shown in Figure 9.2(a) and (b), respectively. The theoretical results are directly calculated from Propositions 9.1 and 9.2 and the simulation results are acquired by the simulation of the BD strategy updating rule over the generated network. In each run of the simulation, the step of strategy updating is repeated until the global network state x_f converges. Furthermore, in order to avoid any spurious results based on one specific realization of a particular network type, we regenerate the network structure every 500 runs. It can be seen from Figure 9.2(a) and (b) that all of the simulation results tally with the theoretical analysis, substantiating the validity of the conclusions in Propositions 9.1 and 9.2. Diverse settings of the payoff matrix can result in various dynamics of information diffusion. In *Case 1* where $u_{ff} > u_{fn} > u_{nn}$, the global network state has the trend of being 1, indicating that all users are willing to forward the information due to its higher utility than that of not forwarding. In contrast, every user would not forward the information in *Case 4* where $u_{nn} > u_{fn} > u_{ff}$. For *Case 2* and *Case 3*, it can be seen from the results that some users would forward the information, and this is decided by the connection between u_{nn} and u_{ff} (i.e., less than half of the population would forward the information when $u_{ff} < u_{nn}$ and more than half of the population would forward the information when $u_{ff} > u_{nn}$).

The experimental results for the nonuniform-degree networks with various payoff matrices are exhibited in Figure 9.2(c) and (d), including the ER network and the BA network. The theoretical results are directly calculated from (9.46) and (9.49) and the simulation results are acquired by the simulation of the BD strategy updating rule over the two generated networks. It can be seen that all of the simulation results also tally with the theoretical analysis very well. In Figure 9.2(d), the reason for the gap in the BA network is that the network degree and the global network state have weak correlation, and this correlation in the diffusion analysis was neglected. In the same way, diverse settings of payoff matrices (i.e., the relationships between u_{ff}, u_{fn}, and u_{nn}) can result in various information diffusion dynamics.

For the experiment on a real-world network, the Facebook social network is used to evaluate the information diffusion process [44]. There are 4,039 users and 88,234 edges in total in the Facebook data set, with the average degree being around 40 [5]. The experimental results under various payoff matrix settings are shown in Figure 9.3.

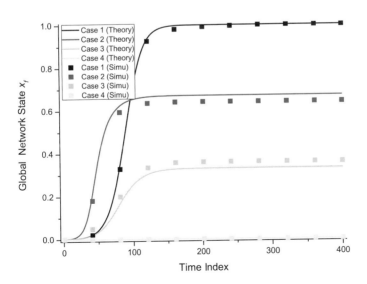

Figure 9.3 Simulation results for the real-world Facebook network.

We obtain the theoretical results by calculation from Proposition 9.2, while we obtain the simulation results through the simulation of the BD strategy updating rule over the Facebook graph. It is obvious that the simulation results tally with the theoretical analysis very well, although there are some small gaps mainly caused by the ignored correlation between the network degree and the global network state. Thus, the theoretical analysis is validated on the real-world network by the experimental results.

9.5.2   Twitter Hashtag Data Set Evaluation

In Section 9.5.1, we first set the payoff matrix of users and then conducted experiments to verify the information diffusion dynamics over different kinds of networks. In this section, a reversal procedure is carried out in which the Twitter hashtag data set is utilized to estimate the payoff matrices corresponding to different hashtags through fitting the hashtags' mention times in an hour. The Twitter hashtag data set contains the number of mention times per hour of 1,000 Twitter hashtags with corresponding time series, which are the 1,000 hashtags with the highest total mention times among 6 million hashtags from June to December 2009 [5].

First, we acquire the closed-form expression of the global network state $x_f(t)$. It can be seen from Propositions 9.1, 9.2, and 9.4 that the information diffusion dynamics over the three types of networks have the same form as follows:

$$\frac{dx_f}{dt} = \beta e^{-\epsilon t} x_f (1 - x_f)(x_f + \gamma), \tag{9.51}$$

where $\alpha = e^{-\epsilon t}$ is regarded as the time variance and the coefficients β and γ differ in the various types of networks. The implicit closed-form expression of x_f can be derived by the separation of variables method as follows:

$$\frac{(\gamma + 1)\ln x_f - \gamma \ln(1 - x_f) + \ln(-x_f - \gamma)}{\gamma(\gamma + 1)} = -\frac{\beta}{\epsilon} e^{-\epsilon t} + c, \tag{9.52}$$

in which c is a constant and could be computed from the initial condition $x_f(t = 0)$. Under this situation, the parameters $\epsilon, \beta,$ and γ can be estimated from (9.52) by fitting the Twitter hashtag data set. Figure 9.4 exhibits four hashtags' curve fitting results through making use of the least squares method, where the vertical axis is the global network state $x_f(t)$. In order to obtain the proportion of users that have mentioned the hashtag, the mention times need to be divided by the number of users. Due to the fact that in the data set there is no information regarding user numbers, it is assumed that the maximum mention times in the data set represent the users' total number, and all of the mention times are divided by the maximum (i.e., all of the mention times are normalized to the interval [0,1]). Then we assemble the normalized mention times over time to obtain the cumulative mention times as shown by the solid black squares in Figure 9.4. It can be seen from Figure 9.4 that the proposed model is able to perfectly fit the data from real-world information diffusion, indicating that the global network state of information diffusion can be predicted by the evolutionary game-theoretic model accurately.

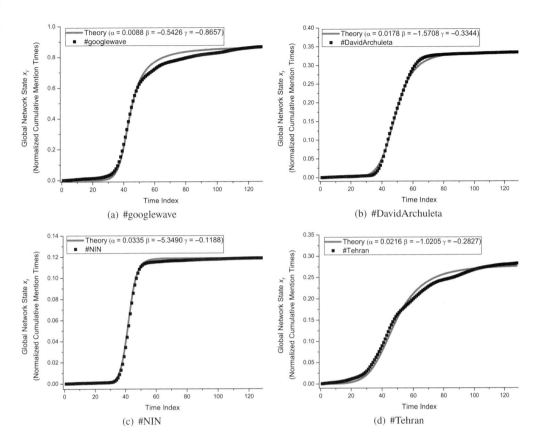

Figure 9.4 The curve fitting of different hashtag diffusion dynamics.

In view of a sufficiently large network scale and the scale-free property of the Twitter social network, according to (9.50), the relationship of the payoff matrix can be acquired by setting $\alpha_{BA} = \frac{e^{-\bar{\epsilon}t}}{k-1}$ as follows:

$$u_{ff} - 2u_{fn} + u_{nn} = \beta, \tag{9.53}$$

$$u_{fn} - u_{nn} = \beta\gamma. \tag{9.54}$$

u_{ff} and u_{nn} can be calculated by solving (9.53) and (9.54) if u_{fn} is normalized as 1. The difference between u_{ff} and u_{nn} could indicate a hashtag's popularity (i.e., $u_{ff} - u_{nn} < 0$ refers to low popularity and $u_{ff} - u_{nn} > 0$ stands for high popularity as higher utility will be obtained by forwarding the information than not forwarding). The distribution of $u_{ff} - u_{nn}$ among all 1,000 hashtags in the Twitter data set is shown in Figure 9.5. It can be seen that the majority of hashtags are of high popularity, since these 1,000 hashtags have the highest total mention times among 6 million hashtags from June to December 2009. Hence, based on popularity, we can categorize the information over the social network into different levels with such an analytical method. This can also be extended to categorize users in the social network.

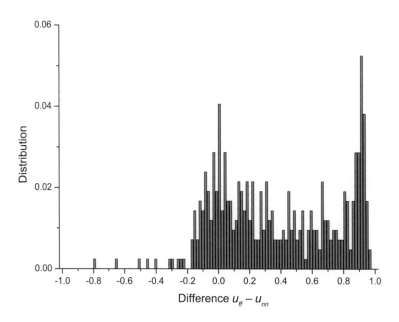

Figure 9.5 Distribution of $u_{ff} - u_{nn}$ among all 1,000 hashtags.

For example, if a group of users always show high interest in sport-related information (i.e., it is of high popularity among these users), then those users are likely to love things about sports. This indicates that sport-related advertisements may be more effective among those users.

On the basis of the estimated payoff matrix, the dynamics $\dot{x}_f(t)$ can be further simulated by the game-theoretic model discussed in this chapter. In this experiment, the results are compared with one of the most relevant existing works [45] that uses the data mining method. In this model, the information diffusion dynamics are predicted by

$$\frac{dx_f}{dt} = q_1 t^{q_2} e^{-q_3 t}, \tag{9.55}$$

in which we can similarly estimate the parameters q_1, q_2, and q_3 by least-squares curve fitting. The comparison results are shown in Figure 9.6, where the vertical axis represents the dynamics $\dot{x}_f(t)$. We also normalize different hastags' mention times per hour within interval $[0, 1]$ and denote them by solid black squares. It can be seen from Figure 9.6 that the game-theoretic model matches the dynamics of information diffusion in the real world better than the data mining method in [45], as the decision-making behaviors and interactions of users are considered.

Finally, we carry out an experiment to verify whether the game-theoretic model is able to predict the information diffusion dynamics. In this experiment, only a portion of the data are used to estimate the payoff matrix, and then with the estimated payoff matrix the game-theoretic model is examined in terms of whether it is able to predict

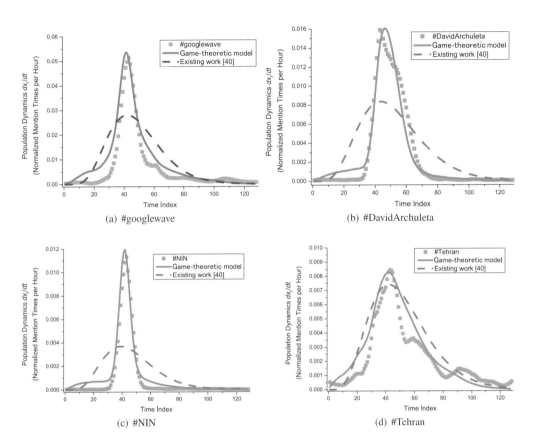

(a) #googlewave

(b) #DavidArchuleta

(c) #NIN

(d) #Tehran

Figure 9.6 Comparison with the existing work.

the remaining diffusion dynamics. In Figure 9.7(a), only 25% of the data for the hashtag #googlewave (i.e., the data represented by solid squares) are utilized for estimating the payoff matrix, and then we plot the prediction results with estimated parameters. It can be seen that when we only use 25% of the data, the prediction is effective until time index 40 (i.e., the near future). Then when 30% of the data are utilized in Figure 9.7(b), the game-theoretic model can predict the peak time accurately, and the prediction is effective until time index 45. The predictions become more and more precise in Figure 9.7(c) and (d) in which 40% and 60% of the data are utilized, respectively. The reason for this is that as long as the time index of dynamics and the peak value are included when estimating the payoff, the precision for prediction will go up to a large extent, as the time index and peak value represent the most significant information for dynamics. What is more, the performance of prediction is also evaluated among the whole data set. In Figure 9.8, we show the relationship between the percentage of correct predicted data and the percentage of data used in curve fitting, and the error bars represent the variance. In the experiment, the predicted data are considered as "correct predicted" when they fall into $[-10\%, +10\%]$ of the

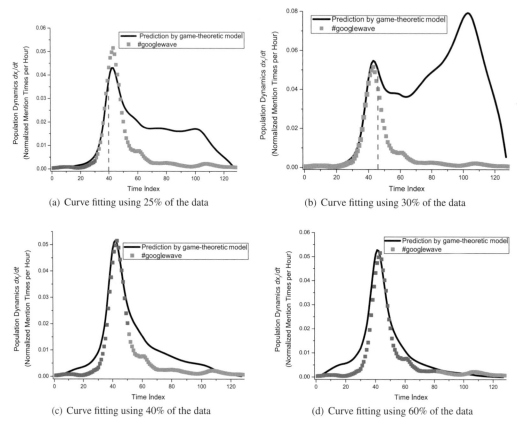

(a) Curve fitting using 25% of the data

(b) Curve fitting using 30% of the data

(c) Curve fitting using 40% of the data

(d) Curve fitting using 60% of the data

Figure 9.7 Prediction simulation results. The vertical dashed lines represent the time indices up to which the predictions are effective.

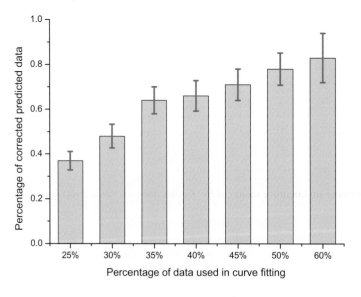

Figure 9.8 Prediction evaluation among all 1,000 hashtags.

corresponding real data. It can be seen that all of the hashtags' variance is small, indicating that the results are consistent for all hashtags. The probability of a correct prediction can reach 80% if more than 50% of the data are utilized for prediction.

9.6   Conclusion

In this chapter, the information diffusion dynamics over social networks are formulated using EGT. In this problem, the players, payoff matrices, and strategies are defined and the correspondence between the information diffusion and EGT is highlighted. With the derived dynamics of information diffusion, we analyze three types of networks: complete, uniform-degree and nonuniform-degree social networks. What is more, two representative networks are also analyzed: the ER network and the BA network. In order to validate the theoretical analysis, experiments are carried out on synthetic networks, a real-world Facebook network, and a Twitter hashtags data set. All of the theoretical results and experimental results are consistent, which verifies the hypothesis that when modeling the dynamics of the information diffusion problem, the EGT model is feasible and effective.

References

[1] H. V. Zhao, W. S. Lin, and K. J. R. Liu, *Behavior Dynamics in Media-Sharing Social Networks*. Cambridge University Press, 2011.

[2] Wikipedia, "Social network." http://en.wikipedia.org/wiki/Social_network.

[3] Wikipedia, "Facebook." http://en.wikipedia.org/wiki/Facebook.

[4] A. Stadd, "20 Twitter stats from 2012." www.mediabistro.com/alltwitter/twitter-stats_b32050.

[5] J. Leskovec, "Stanford large network dataset collection." http://snap.stanford.edu/data.

[6] Twitter, "Twitter political index." https://election.twitter.com.

[7] D. Gruhl, R. Guha, D. Liben-Nowell, and A. Tomkins, "Information diffusion through blogspace," in *Proc. 13th International Conference on the World Wide Web (WWW)*, 2004.

[8] F. Zeng, C. Li, and Z. Tian, "Distributed compressive spectrum sensing in cooperative multihop cognitive networks," *IEEE Journal of Selected Topics on Signal Processing*, vol. 5, pp. 37–48, 2011.

[9] E. Bakshy, I. Rosenn, C. Marlow, and L. Adamic, "The role of social networks in information diffusion," in *Proc. 21st International Conference on the World Wide Web (WWW)*, 2012.

[10] J. Unnikrishnan and V. V. Veeravalli, "Algorithms for dynamic spectrum access with learning for cognitive radio," *IEEE Transactions on Signal Processing*, vol. 58, pp. 750–760, 2010.

[11] J. Yang and J. Leskovec, "Modeling information diffusion in implicit networks," in *IEEE International Conference on Data Mining (ICDM)*, 2010.

[12] M. Ostilli, E. Yoneki, I. X. Leung, J. F. Mendes, P. Lio, and J. Crowcroft, "Statistical mechanics of rumor spreading in network communities," in *Prof. International Conference on Computational Science*, 2010.

[13] D. Centola, "The spread of behavior in an online social network experiment," *Science*, vol. 329, pp. 1194–1197, 2010.

[14] J. Yang and S. Counts, "Predicting the speed, scale, and range of information diffusion in twitter," in *Proc. Fourth International AAAI Conference on Weblogs and Social Media*, 2010.

[15] M. G. Rodriguez, J. Leskovec, and A. Krause, "Inferring networks of diffusion and influence," in *Proc. ACM SIGKDD International Conference on Knowledge Discovery and Data Mining (KDD)*, 2010.

[16] M. G. Rodriguez, J. Leskovec, and A. Krause, "Uncovering the temporal dynamics of diffusion networks," in *Proc. International Conference on Machine Learning (ICML)*, 2011.

[17] F. Biebmann, J.-M. Papaioannou, M. Braun, and A. Harth, "Canonical trends: detecting trend setters in web data," in *Proc. International Conference on Machine Learning (ICML)*, 2012.

[18] N. Du, L. Song, A. Smola, and M. Yuan, "Learning networks of heterogeneous influence," in *Proc. Neural Information Processing Systems Conference (NIPS)*, 2012.

[19] M. Kimura, K. Saito, and R. Nakano, "Extracting influential nodes for information diffusion on a social network," in *Prof. AAAI Conference on Artificial Intelligence*, 2007.

[20] M. Kimura, K. Saito, and H. Motoda, "Blocking links to minimize contamination spread in a social network," *ACM Transactions on Knowledge Discovery from Data*, vol. 3, pp. 9:1–9:23, 2009.

[21] Y. Wang, G. Cong, G. Song, and K. Xie, "Community-based greedy algorithm for mining top-k influential nodes in mobile social networks," in *Proc. 16th ACM SIGKDD International Conference on Knowledge Discovery and Data Mining*, 2010.

[22] M. U. Ilyas, M. Z. Shafiq, A. X. Liu, and H. Radha, "A distributed and privacy preserving algorithm for identifying information hubs in social networks," in *Prof. IEEE INFOCOM*, 2011.

[23] H. Kim and E. Yoneki, "Influential neighbours selection for information diffusion in online social networks," in *Prof. IEEE ICCCN*, 2012.

[24] Y. Chen and K. J. R. Liu, "Understanding microeconomic behaviors in social networking: An engineering view," *IEEE Signal Processing Magazine*, vol. 29, pp. 53–64, 2012.

[25] J. Smith, *Evolution and the Theory of Games*. Cambridge University Press, 1982.

[26] R. Cressman, *Evolutionary Dynamics and Extensive Form Games*. MIT Press, 2003.

[27] B. Hu, H. V. Zhao, and H. Jiang, "Incentive mechanism in wireless multicast," in *Proc. IEEE ICASSP*, 2011.

[28] Y. Chen, B. Wang, W. S. Lin, Y. Wu, and K. J. R. Liu, "Cooperative peer-to-peer streaming: An evolutionary game-theoretic approach," *IEEE Transactions on Circuits and Systems for Video Technology*, vol. 20, pp. 1346–1357, 2010.

[29] C. Jiang, Y. Chen, and K. J. R. Liu, "Graphical evolutionary game theoretical framework for distributed adaptive filtering networks," in *Proc. IEEE GlobalSIP*, 2013.

[30] C. Jiang, Y. Chen, and K. J. R. Liu, "Distributed adaptive networks: A graphical evolutionary game-theoretic view," *IEEE Transactions on Signal Processing*, vol. 61, pp. 5675–5688, 2013.

[31] Y. Chen, Y. Gao, and K. J. R. Liu, "An evolutionary game-theoretic approach for image interpolation," in *Proc. IEEE International Conference on Acoustics, Speech and Signal Processing (ICASSP)*, 2011.

[32] H. Tembine, E. Altman, R. Azouzi, and Y. Hayel, "Evolutionary games in wireless networks," *IEEE Transactions on Systems, Man, and Cybernetics B*, vol. 40, pp. 634–646, 2010.

[33] P. Wiecek, E. Altman, and Y. Hayel, "Stochastic state dependent population games in wireless communication," *IEEE Transactions on Automatic Control*, vol. 56, pp. 492–505, 2011.

[34] B. Wang, K. J. R. Liu, and T. Clancy, "Evolutionary cooperative spectrum sensing game: How to collaborate?" *IEEE Transactions on Communications*, vol. 58, pp. 890–900, 2010.

[35] C. Jiang, Y. Chen, Y. Gao, and K. J. R. Liu, "Joint spectrum sensing and access evolutionary game in cognitive radio networks," *IEEE Transactions Wireless Communications*, vol. 12, pp. 2470–2483, 2013.

[36] M. A. Nowak and K. Sigmund, "Evolutionary dynamics of biological games," *Science*, vol. 303, pp. 793–799, 2004.

[37] H. Ohtsuki, M. A. Nowak, and J. M. Pacheco, "Breaking the symmetry between interaction and replacement in evolutionary dynamics on graphs," *Physical Review Letters*, vol. 98, p. 108106 2007.

[38] P. Shakarian, P. Roos, and A. Johnson, "A review of evolutionary graph theory with applications to game theory," *Biosystems*, vol. 107, pp. 66–80, 2012.

[39] C. Jiang, Y. Chen, and K. J. R. Liu, "Graphical evolutionary game for information diffusion over social networks," *IEEE Journal of Selected Topics in Signal Processing*, vol. 8, pp. 524–536, 2014.

[40] H. Ohtsuki and M. A. Nowak, "The replicator equation on graphs," *Journal of Theoretical Biology*, vol. 243, pp. 86–97, 2006.

[41] M. Newman, "Ego-centered networks and the ripple effect," *Social Networks*, vol. 25, pp. 83–95, 2003.

[42] P. Erdős and A. Rényi, "On random graphs I," *Publicationes Mathematicae Debrecen*, pp. 290–297, 1959.

[43] A. Barabási and R. Albert, "Emergence of scaling in random networks," *Science*, vol. 286, pp. 509–512, 1999.

[44] J. McAuley and J. Leskovec, "Learning to discover social circles in ego networks," in *Proc. Neural Information Processing Systems Conference (NIPS)*, 2012.

[45] J. Leskovec, L. Backstrom, and J. Kleinberg, "Meme-tracking and the dynamics of the news cycle," in *ACM SIGKDD International Conference on Knowledge Discovery and Data Mining (KDD)*, 2009.

10 Graphical Evolutionary Game for Information Diffusion in Heterogeneous Social Networks

Every day, millions of people with various characteristics create and forward a huge amount of information, which spreads over online social networks. For different applications, including website management and online advertisements, it is critical to understand the mechanisms of information diffusion over social networks. Unlike most existing work in this area, here we study information diffusion from the perspective of evolutionary game theory, and we attempt to uncover the underlying principles that dominate the complicated process of information diffusion over heterogeneous social networks. The heterogeneous users' mutual interactions are first modeled as a graphical evolutionary game, and then we obtain the evolutionary dynamics and evolutionarily stable states (ESSs) of the diffusion. The heterogeneous users' various payoffs result in various diffusion dynamics and ESSs, which is consistent with the heterogeneity detected in real-world data sets. Simulations confirm the theoretical analysis. The theory is also tested with the Twitter hashtag data set. It is found that the evolutionary dynamics match rather well with the data and are able to predict the data of future diffusion.

10.1 Introduction

In our daily lives, online social networks (e.g., Facebook, Twitter, and YouTube), are everywhere. On these social networks, billions of people with diverse characteristics interact with each other, and they both receive and create a huge amount of information. For instance, there are nearly 300,000 status updates per minute on Facebook [1], and around 500 million tweets are sent on Twitter each day [2]. Every piece of information will either become rather well known or will vanish instantly with little influence. When user-generated information (e.g., Twitter hashtags [3] and memes [4]), spreads over the social networks, information diffusion dynamics of all kinds can be detected [5]. Numerous users' complex decision-making and interactions involving the heterogeneous influences and interests of users determine the diffusion dynamics or the information's popularity. For example, a football fan is more likely to retweet a tweet related to football, and a user is inclined to forward a piece of news when it has been posted by many of their friends. In practice, a number of applications are associated with information diffusion analysis over social networks (e.g., political statements, online advertisements, rumor detection and control). Better insight into the information diffusion processes over social networks containing all types of users is needed for all of these applications. Thus, great effort has been spent on studying the processes of information diffusion in recent decades.

There are two categories of existing works on information diffusion: (1), making predictions and inferences using data mining or machine learning (ML) approaches and (2), explaining information diffusion in terms of the interactions of individual users by analysing the underlying microscopic mechanisms. Among the first category, future diffusion was predicted by Pinto et al. with the help of early diffusion data [6], while other authors further utilized the community structure to enhance the prediction performance of viral memes in [7]. A clustering algorithm was put forward by Yang and Leskovec to determine the patterns of the diffusion dynamics of online content [5]. With the data relating to information diffusion, some authors have developed efficient algorithms to derive the underlying information diffusion network [8–10]. Moreover, individuals' global influence on the process of information diffusion was estimated in [11]. In [12] the interactions between several pieces of informations' diffusion were studied, while in [13] the influence of exterior sources on information diffusion was investigated. The authors in [14] attempted to predict the cascades of information diffusion. The cluster structure's influence on the diffusion of behaviors in social networks was investigated based on the data from a real-world experiment in [15]. In the same way, using an experimental approach, the role of social ties in information diffusion was investigated by Bakshy et al. [16]. These data mining- or ML-based methods have a common limitation, which is the lack of analysis of the underlying microscopic mechanisms of the decision-making of individuals that govern the information diffusion process, and these are the targets of works in the second category. In such works, competitive contagions in networks (e.g., the competition among firms for users' purchase) have been analyzed using game-theoretic mechanisms in [17,18]. Granovetter worked on collective behavior diffusion, defined as the adoption of one of two alternative behaviors, based on a threshold model [19]. In [20], the conditions for global contagion of behaviors were studied with the assumption that every user played the best response to the strategies of the population. In [21], the network structure's influence on viral propagation was studied. Furthermore, to maximize future contagions over these networks, algorithms to find initial targets were demonstrated in [22]. By using a model-based approach, the community structure's influence on information diffusion was investigated in [23].

An evolutionary game-theoretic framework was recently put forward by the authors of [24,25] to model the interactions of the users during the information diffusion process. Originating from evolutionary biology [26], evolutionary game theory, as a promising modeling tool, has been utilized in diverse areas of signal processing (e.g., image processing and communication networking) [27–31]. It could be found in

[24,25] that the dynamics obtained by using the evolutionary game framework match well with the information diffusion dynamics in the real world, and they are even able to predict future diffusion dynamics, indicating that this is a tractable and suitable paradigm for information diffusion analysis.

The majority of the existing works do not consider users' heterogeneity, regarding network users as homogeneous individuals. But significant heterogeneity can often be found in real-world social networks. For instance, Twitter network's heterogeneity can be demonstrated in numerous ways: (1) the tweet count distribution is of high heterogeneity, as the top 15% of users send 85% of all tweets, indicating the heterogeneity of the user's activity strength [32]; (2) all kinds of topics coexist due to users' heterogeneous interests; and (3) different users have highly varying follower counts, which indicates diverse effects [33]. Information diffusion can be affected greatly by the heterogeneity of users' activities, influences, and interests. For instance, when a user receives a piece of information associated with football, whether they are a football fan or not can greatly affect the user's decision-making (forwarding that information or not).

Based on a graphical evolutionary game method, information diffusion in heterogeneous social networks will be studied in this chapter. We conduct the analysis on the dynamics of information diffusion by regarding the decision-making of users as an evolutionary game. Based on the work in this chapter, we provide a microeconomic framework through utilizing some utility parameters to model the mechanisms of the users' decision-making in the process of information diffusion over real-world heterogeneous social networks.

10.2   Heterogeneous System Model

In this section, first, a concise introduction to evolutionary game theory's preliminary concepts is given. Then the evolutionary game-theoretic formulations for information diffusion are presented regarding heterogeneous social networks.

10.2.1   Basics of Evolutionary Game Theory

In traditional game theory, the focus is on a game with static players and with a static Nash equilibrium (NE) as its solution concept. By contrast, evolutionary game theory [26] centers on the investigation of the stable states and dynamics of a large population of evolving agents with mutual interactions. Just as its name implies, evolutionary game theory originates from the field of biology concerning the evolution of species, in which plants or animals are modeled as players with mutual interactions. Recent works [24,25] show that evolutionary game theory is a useful model for analyzing the social interactions among social network users as well.

The ESS is a vital solution concept in evolutionary game theory. In an evolutionary game, the ESS predicts the eventual equilibrium of the evolutionary dynamics. Let us consider a large population of players in an evolutionary game. Assume there are m strategies $\{1, \ldots, m\}$ and an $m \times m$ payoff matrix U in which the (i, j)-th entry u_{ij} represents the payoff for strategy i versus strategy j (i.e., the payoff for the user with strategy i interacting with a player with strategy j is u_{ij}). We use p_i to denote the percentage of players using strategy i, and $p = [p_1, p_2, \ldots, p_m]^T$ is the system state in this evolutionary game. Therefore, when interacting the whole population with state p, the payoff for any subpopulation with state q is $q^T U p$. The state p^* is called an ESS if for any $q \neq p^*$ when the following, two conditions are satisfied [26]:

(1) $q^T U p^* \leq p^{*^T} U p^*$.
(2) If $q^T U p^* = p^{*^T} U p^*$, then $p^{*^T} U q > q^T U q$.

The first condition is an NE condition, which indicates that no better payoff can be achieved by any mutant that deviates from the ESS p^* of any subpopulation. The second condition ensures that when a payoff is unchanged in the deviation, then the ESS is rigidly better than the deviated state q among the mutated subpopulation (i.e., interacting with the subpopulation state q). This further guarantees the stability of the state p^*. Computing the ESSs is an important step in evolutionary game theory. There is a general method for this, which is to determine the evolutionary dynamics' locally stable state as a dynamical system $\dot{p} = f(p)$, in which f is some function.

In classical evolutionary game theory, it is assumed that any two players can have mutual interactions, clearly leading to the hypothesis that the underlying interaction network is a complete graph. The graphical evolutionary game is a useful generalization of the classical evolutionary game. However, for the graphical evolutionary game, the interaction network may be incomplete. In graphical evolutionary game theory [34,35], users' *fitness* is directly determined by the player strategy updating rule, and this can be defined by combining the payoff U and the baseline fitness B convexly, i.e.,

$$\pi = (1 - \alpha)B + \alpha U, \tag{10.1}$$

in which π denotes the fitness and, α denotes the selection strength that controls the influence of the payoff on the fitness and satisfies $0 < \alpha < 1$. In the works related to graphical evolutionary game theory [24,25,36,37], a general assumption is that α is very small, and this assumption is also made in the rest of the chapter. The reason for this assumption is that adaptations are expected to happen gently and slowly. For example, species evolve quite slowly in the field of biology; in adaptive signal processing such as that in the least mean square algorithm, a small step size is usually adopted to constrain instability or abrupt intense changes. The influence of payoff differences on fitness degree is limited by small α, so the gaps between different players' fitnesses are reduced, slowing down the evolution. It will be seen later that the evolution dynamics are always proportional to α. For the definition of fitness, three general strategy updating rules in the literature of graphical evolutionary game theory can be introduced. The three rules are birth-death (BD), death-birth (DB), and imitation (IM).

- BD updating rule: one player is selected for reproduction with probability proportional to fitness. Then the strategy of the selected player takes the place of one of their neighbor's strategies with uniform probability.
- DB updating rule: one player is selected to give up their current strategy with uniform probability. They will use one of their neighbors' strategies with probability proportional to their fitness.
- IM updating rule: one player is selected to update their strategy with uniform probability. They may keep their current strategies or use one of their neighbors' strategies, with probability proportional to their fitness.

The DB updating rule is adopted in this chapter. Similar analyses can be made for other updating rules. In the following, utilizing evolutionary game theory to model information diffusion over heterogeneous social networks will be explained.

Generally, a graph can be used to model a social network, with users denoted as nodes and relationships denoted as edges. It is assumed that the network has N nodes (users), and each of them has a number of neighbors to interact with. $\lambda(k)$ (the fraction of the number of neighbors k) is the distribution of neighbors' number k in real social networks. For instance, the power law distribution is exhibited in Barabási–Albert scale-free networks [38] and the Poisson distribution is exhibited in Erdős–Rényi networks [39]. What is more, users in real-world social networks generally belong to different groups since they have diverse activities, influences, and interests. In order to describe this heterogeneity, users are categorized into M types, and $q(i), i = 1, 2, \ldots, M$ represents the proportion of type-i users among the whole. In the formulation based on evolutionary game theory, all users are viewed as players. When meeting a new piece of information (e.g., a meme, a status, or a hashtag), every user can choose one of two possible strategies: forwarding it ($\mathcal{S}_f$) or not ($\mathcal{S}_n$). We denote $p_f(i)$ as the proportion of users who use $\mathcal{S}_f$ among all the type-i users and p_f as the proportion of users who use $\mathcal{S}_f$ among the whole population. In the rest of this chapter, $p_f(i)$ and p_f are called *popularity dynamics* or *population dynamics*.

10.2.2   Unknown User-Type Model

In social networks in our real lives, users usually have no idea of their friends'/neighbors' types (e.g., a user is probably unaware of whether their friend is a particular singer's fan or not). A model is presented in this section in which the information about user type is unknown to others (i.e., it is private information). Let us consider a social interaction where a type-i user A is having an interaction with one neighbor who is a type-j user B. Since the type of B is unknown to A, the type of B should not determine the payoff of A in this social interaction. Therefore, the type-i node A's payoff matrix can be denoted by

$$
\begin{array}{cc}
 & \begin{array}{cc} \mathcal{S}_f & \quad \mathcal{S}_n \end{array} \\
\begin{array}{c} \mathcal{S}_f \\ \mathcal{S}_n \end{array} & \begin{pmatrix} u_{ff}(i) & u_{fn}(i) \\ u_{fn}(i) & u_{nn}(i) \end{pmatrix}
\end{array} .
$$

$u_{ff}(i)$ is the payoff of A in the case of A and B both adopting $\mathcal{S}_f$, which ignores the type of B. We can define $u_{fn}(i)$ and $u_{nn}(i)$ in the same way. As in [24,25], the structure of the payoff matrix is considered as symmetric (i.e., the payoff of a type-i user with strategy $\mathcal{S}_f$ ($\mathcal{S}_n$) is $u_{fn}(i)$ when meeting a user with strategy $\mathcal{S}_n$ ($\mathcal{S}_f$)). This assumption of a symmetric payoff structure is reasonable because disagreement (one adopts strategy $\mathcal{S}_f$ and the other adopts strategy $\mathcal{S}_n$) usually results in the same payoff to both sides. For example, if a user does not talk about a hashtag while another user is interested in it, they cannot discuss this topic when interacting and both would get the same payoff. The payoff's physical meaning relies on the applications: if nodes are social network users, then the payoffs correspond to their popularity; if nodes are websites, then the payoffs correspond to their hit rates. Users' types and the content of the information jointly determine the values of the payoff matrix. For instance, when forwarding information relating to the latest hot topic (e.g., the soccer World Cup in the summer of 2014) enhances the popularity of users, then $u_{nn}(i)$ is small and $u_{ff}(i)$ is large, and when some users are very interested in that hot topic (e.g., soccer fans), then compared with other users, their $u_{nn}(i)$ is probably smaller and $u_{ff}(i)$ is even larger. The fitness can be written as $\pi = 1 - \alpha + \alpha U$ (U is the payoff and π is the fitness) by taking the baseline fitness to be 1 in (10.1). Conventionally, the selection strength α is assumed to be rather small and satisfies $0 < \alpha < 1$. It should be noted that unlike payoff, fitness stands for a user's fitness level in the social network. This fitness level consists of not only the payoff acquired from extrinsic interactions, but also a baseline fitness that includes users' intrinsic attributes (e.g., satisfaction with the social network/website). If we assume that there are k_f neighbors using $\mathcal{S}_f$ for user A, then A's fitness is

$$\pi_f(i, k_f) = 1 - \alpha + \alpha[k_f u_{ff}(i) + (k - k_f)u_{fn}(i)]. \qquad (10.2)$$

When A uses $\mathcal{S}_n$, A's fitness $\pi_n(i, k_f)$ can be similarly obtained as follows:

$$\pi_n(i, k_f) = 1 - \alpha + \alpha[k_f u_{fn}(i) + (k - k_f)u_{nn}(i)]. \qquad (10.3)$$

Moreover, since A has no idea of its neighbors' types and only knows its neighbors' strategies, it considers all neighbors' types as type-i, the same as itself. That is to say, A regards the fitness as $\pi_f(i, k_f)$ when interacting with a neighbor with strategy $\mathcal{S}_f$, or A regards the fitness as $\pi_n(i, k_f)$.

10.2.3 Known User-Type Model

Users may sometimes get to know their neighbors' types by interacting with them repeatedly. For example, when a user notices that one of their friends releases news related to soccer matches frequently, they would probably regard this friend as a soccer fan. A model is presented in this section in which the types of users are revealed. Let us consider a social interaction where a type-i user A is having interactions with a type-j neighbor B. The type of B is known to A here, which is different from the unknown user-type model. Therefore, in this social interaction, the type of B determines the payoff of A. To be specific, A will get a payoff $u_{ff}(i,j)$ when both A and B use $\mathcal{S}_f$, and the payoff of A will be $u_{fn}(i,j)$ when A and B use strategies $\mathcal{S}_f$ and $\mathcal{S}_n$, respectively. In the same way, $u_{nf}(i,j)$ and $u_{nn}(i,j)$ can be defined.

Take the baseline fitness to be 1 in (10.1). Thus we can obtain the fitnesses of users with strategies $\mathcal{S}_f$ or $\mathcal{S}_n$, respectively, as

$$\pi_f(i) = 1 - \alpha + \alpha \sum_{j=1}^{M} [k_f(j)u_{ff}(i,j) + k_n(j)u_{fn}(i,j)], \qquad (10.4)$$

$$\pi_n(i) = 1 - \alpha + \alpha \sum_{j=1}^{M} [k_f(j)u_{nf}(i,j) + k_n(j)u_{nn}(i,j)], \qquad (10.5)$$

where $k_f(j)$ $(k_n(j))$ represents the numer of type-j neighbors who adopt strategy $\mathcal{S}_f$ $(\mathcal{S}_n)$. As discussed previously for the unknown-type model, DB is still the updating rule. The difference between these two models is that now the player knows their neighbors' types and consequently can only learn strategies from those neighbors with the same type.

10.3　Theoretical Analysis for the Unknown User-Type Model

In this section, under the unknown user-type model, we obtain $p_f(i), p_f$, which are the evolutionary dynamics of the network states as well as the corresponding ESSs. With the payoff matrices of heterogeneous users, the information diffusion process and the final steady states are clearly connected by the derived dynamics and ESSs. From the perspective of the payoff matrix, simple explanations for the ESSs in the information diffusion can be given.

Consider a type-i user who adopts strategy $\mathcal{S}_f$ (this user will be called the center user in the following). It is assumed that the center node has k_f users using strategy $\mathcal{S}_f$ and $(k - k_f)$ users using strategy $\mathcal{S}_n$ among its total k neighbors. (10.2) shows the fitness $\pi_f(i,k_f)$ of the center user. The center's fitness $\pi_n(i,k_f)$ becomes (10.3) if they change strategy to $\mathcal{S}_n$. In the eyes of the center user, the fitness for the neighbor with strategy $\mathcal{S}_f$ (or $\mathcal{S}_n$) is $\pi_f(i,k_f)$ (or $\pi_n(i,k_f)$, respectively). The center user will, based on the DB updating rule, choose to use the strategy of one neighbor with the probability proportional to the neighbor's fitness. Therefore, we have the probability of the center node changing to strategy $\mathcal{S}_n$ from $\mathcal{S}_f$ as

$$\mathbb{P}_{f \to n}(i,k_f) = \frac{(k - k_f)\pi_n(i,k_f)}{k_f \pi_f(i,k_f) + (k - k_f)\pi_n(i,k_f)}. \qquad (10.6)$$

Substituting the expressions of $\pi_f(i,k_f)$ and $\pi_n(i,k_f)$ in (10.2) and (10.3) into (10.6) yields (10.7)

$$\mathbb{P}_{f \to n}(i, k_f)$$

$$= \frac{k - k_f}{k} \frac{1 + \alpha[k_f u_{fn}(i) + (k - k_f)u_{nn}(i) - 1]}{1 + \alpha\left[\frac{k_f}{k}(k_f u_{ff}(i) + (k - k_f)u_{fn}(i) - 1) + \left(1 - \frac{k_f}{k}\right)(k_f u_{ff}(i) + (k - k_f)u_{fn}(i) - 1)\right]}$$

$$= \frac{k - k_f}{k} + \alpha(k - k_f)\left[\frac{k_f^2}{k^2}\Delta(i) + \frac{k_f}{k}\Delta_n(i)\right] + O(\alpha^2), \tag{10.7}$$

where $\Delta(i) := 2u_{fn}(i) - u_{ff}(i) - u_{nn}(i)$ and, $\Delta_n(i) := u_{nn}(i) - u_{fn}(i)$. The fact that $\frac{1+ax}{1+bx} = 1 + (a - b)x + O(x^2)$ for small x is invoked in the last equation. The $O(\alpha^2)$ term will be omitted in the following due to the fact that α is a small quantity. Every neighbor has probability p_f for using strategy $\mathcal{S}_f$ because the proportion of users adopting strategy $\mathcal{S}_f$ is p_f over the whole network. Therefore, k_f can be regarded as a random variable that obeys a binomial distribution, and its probability mass function is

$$\theta(k, k_f) = \binom{k}{k_f} p_f^{k_f}(1 - p_f)^{k - k_f}. \tag{10.8}$$

Thus, taking the expectation of (10.7) (notice that k is a random variable as well and it should also be taken as an expectation) gives

$$\mathbb{E}[\mathbb{P}_{f \to n}(i, k_f)] = 1 - p_f + \alpha\Delta(i)[(-\bar{k} + 3 - 2\overline{k^{-1}})p_f^3 + (\bar{k} - 4 + 3\overline{k^{-1}})p_f^2$$

$$+ (1 - \overline{k^{-1}})p_f] + \alpha\Delta_n(i)[-(\bar{k} - 1)p_f^2 + (\bar{k} - 1)p_f], \tag{10.9}$$

where $\overline{k^{-1}}$ and $\bar{k}$, respectively, stand for the expectation of k^{-1} and k. During the derivation process of (10.9), the moments of binomial distribution are utilized: $\mathbb{E}[k_f|k] = kp_f$, $\mathbb{E}[k_f^2|k] = k^2 p_f^2 - kp_f^2 + kp_f$, $\mathbb{E}[k_f^3|k] = k(k - 1)(k - 2)p_f^3 + 2(k - 1)kp_f^2 + kp_f$. According to the DB strategy updating rule, one of the N users will be randomly chosen to update the current strategy in each round. $p_f(i)q(i)$ is the proportion of type-i users with strategy $\mathcal{S}_f$ among all of the users. Based on the DB rule, the case of $p_f(i)$ decreasing by $\frac{1}{Nq(i)}$ (i.e., one type-i user deviates its strategy from $\mathcal{S}_f$ to $\mathcal{S}_n$), happens only if the selected user is a type-i user adopting strategy $\mathcal{S}_f$, and its probability of occurrence is $q(i)p_f(i)$. Then the user should change its strategy from $\mathcal{S}_f$ to $\mathcal{S}_n$, which happens with probability $\mathbb{E}[\mathbb{P}_{f \to n}(i, k_f)]$, where we take the expectation on node degree k. Thus we have

$$\mathbb{P}\left(\delta p_f(i) = -\frac{1}{Nq(i)}\right) = p_f(i)q(i)\mathbb{E}[\mathbb{P}_{f \to n}(i, k_f)], \tag{10.10}$$

where δ represents the increment. Similarly to the previous statements, the probability of one type-i user changing its strategy from $\mathcal{S}_n$ to $\mathcal{S}_f$ can be calculated as

$$\mathbb{P}\left(\delta p_f(i) = \frac{1}{Nq(i)}\right) = p_n(i)q(i)(1 - \mathbb{E}[\mathbb{P}_{f \to n}(i, k_f)]). \tag{10.11}$$

By combining (10.9), (10.10), and (10.11), the expected change of $p_f(i)$ (i.e., the dynamic of $p_f(i)$) can be deduced as

$$\dot{p}_f(i) = -\frac{1}{Nq(i)}\mathbb{P}\left(\delta p_f(i) = -\frac{1}{Nq(i)}\right) + \frac{1}{Nq(i)}\mathbb{P}\left(\delta p_f(i) = \frac{1}{Nq(i)}\right)$$

$$= \frac{1}{N}p_f - \frac{1}{N}p_f(i) + \frac{\alpha}{N}p_f(p_f - 1) \tag{10.12}$$

$$\times\, [\Delta(i)((\overline{k} - 3 + 2\overline{k^{-1}})p_f + 1 - \overline{k^{-1}}) + \Delta_n(i)(\overline{k} - 1)].$$

Based on (10.12), we can denote the dynamic of p_f as

$$\dot{p}_f = \sum_{i=1}^{M} q(i)\dot{p}_f(i)$$

$$= \frac{\alpha}{N}p_f(p_f - 1)[\overline{\Delta}((\overline{k} - 3 + 2\overline{k^{-1}})p_f + 1 - \overline{k^{-1}}) + \overline{\Delta}_n(\overline{k} - 1)], \tag{10.13}$$

where $\overline{\Delta} := \sum_{i=1}^{M} q(i)\Delta(i)$ and $\overline{\Delta}_n := \sum_{i=1}^{M} q(i)\Delta_n(i)$. The results of the theoretical evolutionary dynamics are summarized in Theorem 10.1.

THEOREM 10.1   (Evolutionary dynamics) *In the unknown user-type model, the evolutionary dynamics for the network states $p_f(i)$ and p_f are given in (10.12) and (10.13), respectively.*

It can be observed from Theorem 10.1 that both the type-specific utility-related parameters $\Delta(i)$ and $\Delta_n(i)$ and the global population dynamics p_f determine the population dynamics $p_f(i)$ in (10.12). Hence, a relation between the heterogeneous information diffusion dynamics at each time and the heterogeneous type-specific payoff matrix is clearly built. Moreover, by comparing (10.13) with [24,25], where the evolutionary population dynamics of a homogeneous social network are given, it should be noted that the global population dynamics p_f evolve as if the network is homogeneous, with the corresponding payoff matrix being the weighted average (with weights $q(i)$) of those among all of the types.

Based on Theorem 10.1, in which the dynamical system is described, we would like to obtain its ESSs, which are realized by Theorem 10.2.

THEOREM 10.2   (ESSs) *The ESSs of the network in the unknown user-type model are as follows:*

$$p_f^* = \begin{cases} 0, & \textit{if } \overline{u}_{nn} > \overline{u}_{fn}, \\ 1, & \textit{if } \overline{u}_{ff} > \overline{u}_{fn}, \\ \dfrac{\overline{\Delta}_n(1 - \overline{k}) + \overline{\Delta}(\overline{k^{-1}} - 1)}{\overline{\Delta}(\overline{k} - 3 + 2\overline{k^{-1}})}, & \textit{if } \max\{\overline{u}_{ff}, \overline{u}_{nn}\} < \overline{u}_{fn}, \end{cases} \tag{10.14}$$

$$p_f^*(i) = p_f^* + \alpha p_f^*(p_f^* - 1)[\Delta(i)((\overline{k} - 3 + 2\overline{k^{-1}})p_f^* + 1 - \overline{k^{-1}}) + \Delta_n(i)(\overline{k} - 1)],$$
$$(10.15)$$

where $\overline{u}_{ff} = \sum_{i=1}^{M} q(i)u_{ff}(i)$ *and* $\overline{u}_{fn}$ *and* $\overline{u}_{nn}$ *are similarly defined. Recall that* $\Delta(i) = 2u_{fn}(i) - u_{ff}(i) - u_{nn}(i), \Delta_n(i) = u_{nn}(i) - u_{fn}(i),$ *and* $\overline{\Delta} = \sum_{i=1}^{M} q(i)\Delta(i),$ $\overline{\Delta}_n = \sum_{i=1}^{M} q(i)\Delta_n(i).$ *It should be noted that there is more than one ESS in the system.*

Proof Setting the right-hand side of (10.12) as zero, the three equilibrium points for the dynamic of p_f are obtained as

$$p_f^* = 0, \ 1, \ \frac{\overline{\Delta}_n(1 - \overline{k}) + \overline{\Delta}(\overline{k^{-1}} - 1)}{\overline{\Delta}(\overline{k} - 3 + 2\overline{k^{-1}})}. \qquad (10.16)$$

With p_f^*, we can derive the equilibrium state of $p_f(i)$ from (10.12) as shown in (10.15).

For the underlying dynamical system, the condition of an equilibrium point being an ESS is that the equilibrium point should satisfy locally asymptotic stability. Notice that for each i, $p_f(i)$ and p_f can be considered as dynamical systems that are made up of two states as indicated by (10.12) and (10.13). The Jacobian matrix of the system is given by

$$\mathbf{J} = \begin{bmatrix} \dfrac{\partial \dot{p}_f(i)}{\partial p_f(i)} & \dfrac{\partial \dot{p}_f(i)}{\partial p_f} \\[3ex] \dfrac{\partial \dot{p}_f}{\partial p_f(i)} & \dfrac{\partial \dot{p}_f}{\partial p_f} \end{bmatrix}, \qquad (10.17)$$

where

$$\frac{\partial \dot{p}_f(i)}{\partial p_f(i)} = -\frac{1}{N},$$

$$\frac{\partial \dot{p}_f(i)}{\partial p_f} = \frac{1}{N} + \frac{\alpha}{N}(2p_f - 1)[\Delta(i)(\overline{k} - 3 + 2\overline{k^{-1}})p_f + \Delta(i)(1 - \overline{k^{-1}})$$
$$+ \Delta_n(i)(\overline{k} - 1)] + \frac{\alpha \Delta(i)}{N}(p_f^2 - p_f)(\overline{k} - 3 + 2\overline{k^{-1}}),$$
$$(10.18)$$

$$\frac{\partial \dot{p}_f}{\partial p_f(i)} = 0,$$

$$\frac{\partial \dot{p}_f}{\partial p_f} = \frac{\alpha}{N}(2p_f - 1)[\overline{\Delta}(\overline{k} - 3 + 2\overline{k^{-1}})p_f + \overline{\Delta}(1 - \overline{k^{-1}}) + \overline{\Delta}_n(\overline{k} - 1)]$$
$$+ \frac{\alpha \overline{\Delta}}{N}(p_f^2 - p_f)(\overline{k} - 3 + 2\overline{k^{-1}}).$$

The condition for stability is simply $\frac{\partial \dot{p}_f}{\partial p_f} < 0$, as $\mathbf{J}$ is an upper triangular matrix and $\frac{\partial \dot{p}_f(i)}{\partial p_f(i)}$ is always negative. Substituting the three equilibrium points in (10.16) into (10.17) generates the three possible ESS conditions given in (10.14), in which the fact that in practice the node degree k is usually much larger than 1 is utilized.

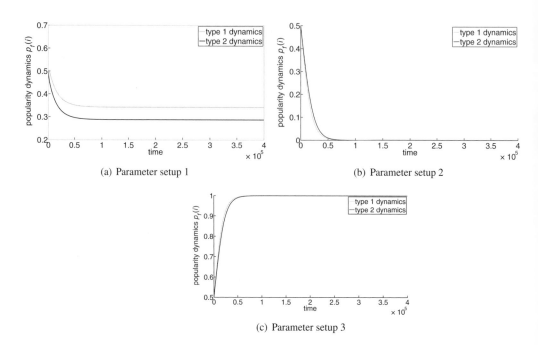

(a) Parameter setup 1   (b) Parameter setup 2

(c) Parameter setup 3

Figure 10.1 Evolutionary dynamics under diverse parameter setups. parameter setup 1: $u_{ff}(1) = 0.4, u_{ff}(2) = 0.2, u_{fn} = 0.6, u_{fn}(2) = 0.4, u_{nn}(1) = 0.3, u_{nn}(2) = 0.5$; Parameter setup 2: $u_{ff}(1) = 0.4$, parameter setup 3: $u_{ff}(2) = 0.2, u_{fn} = 0.3, u_{fn}(2) = 0.5$, $u_{nn}(1) = 0.6, u_{nn}(2) = 0.4$; $u_{ff}(1) = 0.6, u_{ff}(2) = 0.4, u_{fn} = 0.3, u_{fn}(2) = 0.5$, $u_{nn}(1) = 0.4, u_{nn}(2) = 0.2$. We have $q(1) = q(2) = 0.5, N = 1000, k = 20$ in every setup. The ESSs match the assertions in Theorem 10.2: some dynamics go down to 0 (b) or go up to 1 (c), while some will stay at some stable state between 0 and 1 (a).

The ESS results (10.14) in Theorem 10.2 can be clarified easily as the following: when $\bar{u}_{ff}$ is sufficiently large (larger than $\bar{u}_{fn}$); i.e., the players tend to forward the information on average) then the network's ESS is $p_f^* = 1$. The ESS $p_f^* = 0$ can be interpreted in a similar way. By contrast, if neither $\bar{u}_{ff}$ nor $\bar{u}_{nn}$ is sufficiently large (both are smaller than $\bar{u}_{fn}$), then there will be an ESS between 0 and 1. It can be seen in Figure 10.1 that we have different evolutionary dynamics for various parameter setups. Some dynamics go down to 0 (Figure 10.1b) or go up to 1 (Figure 10.1c), and some would be in some stable state within the interval of 0 and 1 (Figure 10.1). Theorem 10.2 directly predicts the corresponding ESSs. It is found that initially the population dynamics $p_f(i)$ always change quickly, and then gradually slow down until finally reaching a stable state. (10.13) can give an explanation for this. With p_f being closer and closer to the ESS (be it 1, 0, or some number between 0 and 1), the absolute value of the right-hand side of (10.13) gets smaller, and the changing speed of p_f thus slows down until it eventually reaches the ESS. In addition, according to (10.12), when p_f is stable, the entire type-specific population dynamics $p_f(i)$ will converge to their respective ESSs as well.

10.4   Theoretical Analysis for the Known User-Type Model

The evolutionary dynamics for the known user-type model are obtained in this section. It is found that the influence states (which will be defined later) always keep track of the corresponding population states, which could be utilized for the further simplification of the dynamics.

A user's neighbors' strategies may also be influenced by the user due to the fact that the user's strategy and type exert influence on neighbors' payoffs. Therefore, to thoroughly characterize the network state, the edge information is also required. Specifically, network edge states are defined as $p_{ff}(i,j), p_{fn}(i,j)$, and $p_{nn}(i,j)$, where $p_{ff}(i,j)$ ($p_{nn}(i,j)$) stands for the percentage of edges on which a type-i user adopting strategy $\mathcal{S}_f$ ($\mathcal{S}_n$) and a type-j user adopting strategy $\mathcal{S}_f$ ($\mathcal{S}_n$) are connected, and $p_{fn}(i,j)$ represents the percentage of edges on which a type-i user adopting strategy $\mathcal{S}_f$ and a type-j user adopting strategy $\mathcal{S}_n$ are connected. What is more, $p_{f|f}(i,j)$ is defined as the proportion of type-i neighbors with strategy $\mathcal{S}_f$ when the center type-j user is adopting strategy $\mathcal{S}_f$. $p_{f|n}(i,j), p_{n|f}(i,j)$, and $p_{n|n}(i,j)$ can be defined in a similar way. To sum up, network states include *population states* (e.g., $p_f(i)$), *influence states* (e.g., $p_{f|f}(i,j)$), and *relationship states* (e.g., $p_{ff}(i,j)$). For characterizing the whole network state, we only need a subset of these states, as the states are associated with each other. For instance, all of the other states can be calculated by $p_f(i), 1 \le i \le M$ and $p_{ff}(i,j), 1 \le i \le j \le M$.

Suppose a type-i user uses strategy $\mathcal{S}_f$. Strictly speaking, $k_f(j)$ and $k_n(j)$ are random variables with expectations $kq(j)p_{f|f}(j,i)$ and $kq(j)p_{n|f}(j,i)$, respectively. In social networks in real life, a small number of types M are able to characterize the behaviors of users and the number of neighbors k is comparably large (more than 100 for typical online social networks such as Facebook), so in the following, $k_f(j)$ and $k_n(j)$ are approximated with their expectations to facilitate analysis. We can justify this approximating operation as follows: recall the Chernoff bound and suppose that $X_1, X_2, \ldots, X_n$ are independent random variables whose values are in $[0,1]$, $X = \sum_{i=1}^{n} X_i$, and $\mu = \mathbb{E}(X)$. Then for any $0 < \delta < 1$, we have: (1) $\mathbb{P}(X \ge (1+\delta)\mu) \le \exp\left(-\frac{\delta^2 \mu}{3}\right)$ and (2) $\mathbb{P}(X \le (1-\delta)\mu) \le \exp\left(-\frac{\delta^2 \mu}{2}\right)$. For the case in this section, when there are k neighbors for a type-i user adopting strategy $\mathcal{S}_f$, the probability of every one of their neighbors being a type-j user with strategy $\mathcal{S}_f$ is $q(j)p_{f|f}(j,i)$. We assume that if a user's l-th neighbor is a type-j user adopting strategy $\mathcal{S}_f$, then the random variable X_l ($l = 1, \ldots, k$) is 1. Otherwise, it will be 0. Therefore, X_l values are independent and identically distributed random variables. We use $X = \sum_{l=1}^{k} X_i$ to denote the total number of type-j neighbors adopting strategy $\mathcal{S}_f$, equivalent to $k_f(j)$ in the formulation in this chapter. Every $q(j), j = 1, 2, \ldots, M$ (altogether summing to 1), is usually not too small due to the fact that M is small. Moreover, k is quite large and $p_{f|f}(j,i)$ is usually not too small. Thus, $\mu = \mathbb{E}(X) = kq(j)p_{f|f}(j,i)$ is large. Using the Chernoff bound's multiplicative form, it can be claimed that X has a high probability of being close to its expectation.

Therefore, replacing $k_f(j)$ with its expectation is reasonable. Similar arguments hold for $k_n(j)$. With this approximation, (10.4) becomes

$$\pi_f(i) = 1 - \alpha + \alpha k \sum_{j=1}^{M} q(j)[p_{f|f}(j,i)u_{ff}(i,j) + p_{n|f}(j,i)u_{fn}(i,j)]. \quad (10.19)$$

In the same way, the fitness (10.5) for a type-i user adopting strategy $\mathcal{S}_n$ can be approximated as

$$\pi_n(i) = 1 - \alpha + \alpha k \sum_{j=1}^{M} q(j)[p_{f|n}(j,i)u_{nf}(i,j) + p_{n|n}(j,i)u_{nn}(i,j)]. \quad (10.20)$$

Now suppose a type-i center user with strategy $\mathcal{S}_f$ is chosen to update the current strategy. On average, the number of type-i neighbors who adopt strategy $\mathcal{S}_f$ is $kp_{f|f}(i,i)$ and the number of type-i neighbors who adopts strategy $\mathcal{S}_n$ is $kp_{n|f}(i,i)$. So based on the DB updating rule, the center user would update their strategy to $\mathcal{S}_n$ with probability

$$\mathbb{P}_{f \to n}(i) = \frac{\pi_n(i)p_{n|f}(i,i)}{\pi_f(i)p_{f|f}(i,i) + \pi_n(i)p_{n|f}(i,i)}. \quad (10.21)$$

Meanwhile, a type-i user adopting strategy $\mathcal{S}_f$ may be selected to update the current strategy, and the probability of this is $q(i)p_f(i)$. Thus we have

$$\mathbb{P}\left(\delta p_f(i) = -\frac{1}{Nq(i)}\right) = q(i)p_f(i)\mathbb{E}[\mathbb{P}_{f \to n}(i)]. \quad (10.22)$$

In the same way, the case of a type-i user adopting strategy $\mathcal{S}_n$ being chosen to update their strategy can be analyzed. Thus we have

$$\mathbb{P}_{n \to f}(i) = \frac{\pi_f(i)p_{f|n}(i,i)}{p_{f|n}(i,i)\pi_f(i) + p_{n|n}(i,i)\pi_n(i)}. \quad (10.23)$$

$$\mathbb{P}\left(\delta p_f(i) = \frac{1}{Nq(i)}\right) = q(i)p_n(i)\mathbb{E}[\mathbb{P}_{n \to f}(i)]. \quad (10.24)$$

We know that

$$\dot{p}_f(i) = -\frac{1}{Nq(i)}\mathbb{P}\left(\delta p_f(i) = -\frac{1}{Nq(i)}\right) + \frac{1}{Nq(i)}\mathbb{P}\left(\delta p_f(i) = \frac{1}{Nq(i)}\right). \quad (10.25)$$

In order to facilitate notation, we temporarily denote that $a = k\sum_{j=1}^{M} q(j)[p_{f|n}(j,i) u_{nf}(i,j) + p_{n|n}(j,i)u_{nn}(i,j)]$ and $b = k\sum_{j=1}^{M} q(j)[p_{f|f}(j,i)u_{ff}(i,j) + p_{n|f}(j,i) u_{fn}(i,j)]$. Therefore, we can rewrite the first term in (10.25) as

$$-\frac{1}{Nq(i)}\mathbb{P}\left(\delta p_f(i) = -\frac{1}{Nq(i)}\right) \tag{10.26}$$

$$= -\frac{p_f(i)p_{n|f}(i,i)}{N} \times \mathbb{E}\left\{\frac{1 + \alpha(a-1)}{1 + \alpha[(b-1)p_{f|f}(i,i) + (a-1)p_{n|f}(i,i)]}\right\} \tag{10.27}$$

$$= -\frac{p_f(i)p_{n|f}(i,i)}{N}\mathbb{E}[1 + p_{f|f}(i,i)(a-b)\alpha] + O(\alpha^2), \tag{10.28}$$

in which the fact that $p_{f|f}(i,i) + p_{n|f}(i,i) = 1$ is used is easy to deduce from the definition. The expectation is taken over k. In the same way, the second term in (10.25) can be derived as

$$\frac{1}{Nq(i)}\mathbb{P}\left(\delta p_f(i) = \frac{1}{Nq(i)}\right) = \frac{p_n(i)p_{f|n}(i,i)}{N}\mathbb{E}[1 + \alpha p_{n|n}(i,i)(b-a)] + O(\alpha^2). \tag{10.29}$$

Noting that $p_f(i)p_{n|f}(i,i) = p_n(i)p_{f|n}(i,i)$, we have

$$\dot{p}_f(i) \approx \frac{\alpha\overline{k}}{N}p_f(i)p_{n|f}(i,i)(p_{n|n}(i,i) + p_{f|f}(i,i))$$

$$\times \sum_{j=1}^{M} q(j)[p_{f|f}(j,i)u_{ff}(i,j) + p_{n|f}(j,i)u_{fn}(i,j) \tag{10.30}$$

$$- p_{f|n}(j,i)u_{nf}(i,j) - p_{n|n}(j,i)u_{nn}(i,j)],$$

in which $\overline{k}$ represents the network's average degree and the $O(\alpha^2)$ terms are omitted. Then the dynamics of $p_{ff}(i,l)$ (or $p_{f|f}(i,l)$ equivalently) are computed. If the value of $p_{ff}(i,l)$ changes, either a type-l user or a type-i user changes their strategy. There are four situations in total if $i \neq l$. The situations are: (1) a type-i user deviates from strategy $\mathcal{S}_n$ to $\mathcal{S}_f$; (2) a type-i user deviates from strategy $\mathcal{S}_f$ to $\mathcal{S}_n$; (3) a type-l user deviates from strategy $\mathcal{S}_n$ to $\mathcal{S}_f$; and (4) a type-l user deviates from strategy $\mathcal{S}_f$ to $\mathcal{S}_n$. They correspond to the following four equations in the following:

$$\mathbb{P}\left(\delta p_{ff}(i,l) = -\frac{2}{N}q(i)p_{f|f}(i,l)\right) = q(l)p_f(l)\mathbb{P}_{f\to n}(l) \approx q(l)p_f(l)p_{n|f}(l,l),$$

$$\mathbb{P}\left(\delta p_{ff}(i,l) = -\frac{2}{N}q(l)p_{f|f}(l,i)\right) = q(i)p_f(i)\mathbb{P}_{f\to n}(i) \approx q(i)p_f(i)p_{n|f}(i,i),$$

$$\mathbb{P}\left(\delta p_{ff}(i,l) = \frac{2}{N}q(i)p_{f|n}(i,l)\right) = q(l)p_n(l)\mathbb{P}_{n\to f}(l) \approx q(l)p_n(l)p_{f|n}(l,l),$$

$$\mathbb{P}\left(\delta p_{ff}(i,l) = \frac{2}{N}q(l)p_{f|n}(l,i)\right) = q(i)p_n(i)\mathbb{P}_{n\to f}(i) \approx q(i)p_n(i)p_{f|n}(i,i),$$

$$\tag{10.31}$$

where $O(\alpha)$ terms are omitted in the last step (i.e., regarding α as 0). Since there are nonzero $O(1)$ terms here, $O(\alpha)$ terms are omitted while $O(\alpha^2)$ terms are not, as before. For $i \neq l$, this can be obtained by combining the four equations in (10.31) such that

$$
\begin{aligned}
\dot{p}_{ff}(i,l) = & -\frac{2}{N}q(l)p_{f|f}(l,i)\mathbb{P}\left(\delta p_{ff}(i,l) = -\frac{2}{N}q(l)p_{f|f}(l,i)\right) \\
& -\frac{2}{N}q(i)p_{f|f}(i,l)\mathbb{P}\left(\delta p_{ff}(i,l) = -\frac{2}{N}q(i)p_{f|f}(i,l)\right) \\
& +\frac{2}{N}q(l)p_{f|n}(l,i)\mathbb{P}\left(\delta p_{ff}(i,l) = \frac{2}{N}q(l)p_{f|n}(l,i)\right) \\
& +\frac{2}{N}q(i)p_{f|n}(i,l)\mathbb{P}\left(\delta p_{ff}(i,l) = \frac{2}{N}q(i)p_{f|n}(i,l)\right) \\
= & \frac{2}{N}q(i)q(l)p_f(i)p_{n|f}(i,i)(p_{f|n}(l,i) - p_{f|f}(l,i)) \\
& +\frac{2}{N}q(i)q(l)p_f(l)p_{n|f}(l,l)(p_{f|n}(i,l) - p_{f|f}(i,l)) \\
= & \frac{2}{N}q(i)q(l)p_f(i)(1 - p_{f|f}(i,i)) \times \left[\frac{p_f(l)}{p_n(i)}(1 - p_{f|f}(i,l)) - p_{f|f}(l,i)\right] \\
& +\frac{2}{N}q(i)q(l)p_f(l)(1 - p_{f|f}(l,l)) \times \left[\frac{p_f(i)}{p_n(l)}(1 - p_{f|f}(l,i)) - p_{f|f}(i,l)\right],
\end{aligned}
$$

(10.32)

where in the last step the equalities $p_{n|f}(i,i) = 1 - p_{f|f}(i,i)$ and $p_{f|n}(l,i) = \frac{p_f(l)}{p_n(i)}(1 - p_{f|f}(i,l))$ are used to replace all of the influence states by $p_{f|f}(\cdot,\cdot)$. In a similar way, the dynamics of $p_{ff}(i,i)$ can be derived as follows:

$$
\dot{p}_{ff}(i,i) = \frac{2}{Np_n(i)}q^2(i)p_f(i)(1 - p_{f|f}(i,i))(p_f(i) - p_{f|f}(i,i)).
$$

(10.33)

Recall (10.30), in which it is noted that the evolving speed of population dynamics $p_f(\cdot)$ is $O(\alpha)$. It can be seen from (10.32) and (10.33) that the evolving speed of relationship dynamics $p_{ff}(\cdot,\cdot)$ (hence the influence dynamics $p_{f|f}(\cdot,\cdot)$) is $O(1)$. With the assumption of α being sufficiently small, the population dynamics evolve at a much slower speed than do the influence dynamics and relationship dynamics. This indicates that if a time window with a proper length is selected, the population dynamics $p_f(\cdot)$ remain largely unchanged, while the influence dynamics $p_{f|f}(\cdot,\cdot)$ and relationship dynamics $p_{ff}(\cdot,\cdot)$ change significantly. Such a time period is our focus in the following. In this kind of period, the population dynamics $p_f(\cdot)$ remain constant, while only the influence dynamics and relationship dynamics change along with time. Taking the derivative with respect to time on both sides of the equation $p_{ff}(i,l) = 2q(i)q(l)p_f(i)p_{f|f}(l,i), i \neq l$, we obtain

$$
\dot{p}_{ff}(i,l) = 2q(i)q(l)p_f(i)\dot{p}_{f|f}(l,i).
$$

(10.34)

Combining (10.32) and (10.34) generates the dynamics of $p_{f|f}(l,i), l \neq i$, as follows:

$$\dot{p}_{f|f}(l,i) = \frac{1}{N}(1 - p_{f|f}(i,i))\left[\frac{p_f(l)}{p_n(i)}(1 - p_{f|f}(i,l)) - p_{f|f}(l,i)\right]$$

$$+ \frac{1}{N}(1 - p_{f|f}(l,l)) \times \left[\frac{p_f(l)}{p_n(l)}(1 - p_{f|f}(l,i)) - \frac{p_f(l)}{p_f(i)}p_{f|f}(i,l)\right].$$

(10.35)

Furthermore, we could simplify (10.35) by leveraging the equation $p_f(i)p_{f|f}(l,i) = p_f(l)p_{f|f}(i,l)$ as

$$\dot{p}_{f|f}(l,i) = \frac{1}{N}(p_f(l) - p_{f|f}(l,i)) \times \left[\frac{1 - p_{f|f}(i,i)}{p_n(i)} + \frac{1 - p_{f|f}(l,l)}{p_n(l)}\right], \forall l \neq i.$$

(10.36)

On the other hand, if $l = i$, then $\dot{p}_{ff}(i,i) = q^2(i)p_f(i)\dot{p}_{f|f}(i,i)$. Therefore, based on (10.33), we have

$$\dot{p}_{f|f}(i,i) = \frac{2}{Np_n(i)}(1 - p_{f|f}(i,i))(p_f(i) - p_{f|f}(i,i)), \forall i.$$

(10.37)

It is known that any i,l is satisfied in (10.36) (not necessarily unequal), as (10.37) is equivalent to setting $i = l$ in (10.36). Recall that in (10.36) the population dynamics $p_f(i)$ and $p_n(i)$ are regarded as constants. That is to say, a small time period is considered. In this period, the influence dynamics $p_{f|f}(\cdot,\cdot)$ change in accordance with the deduced dynamics (10.36), while the population dynamics do not change along with time. It is then shown that the influence dynamics $p_{f|f}(\cdot,\cdot)$ will converge to the corresponding population dynamics $p_f(\cdot)$ in this small period of time.

First, the ordinary differential equation (10.37) is solved with the single variable $p_{f|f}(i,i)$. Generally, it is assumed that the initial value of $p_f(i)$ is larger than $p_{f|f}(i,i)$. Therefore, through solving (10.37), we have

$$p_{f|f}(i,i) = p_f(i) - \frac{p_n(i)}{e^{\frac{4t}{N}+C_i} - 1},$$

(10.38)

where $C_i := \ln\left(1 - p_{f|f}(i,i)\big|_{t=0}\right) - \ln\left(p_f(i) - p_{f|f}(i,i)\big|_{t=0}\right)$ is a constant. It can be seen from (10.38) that $\lim_{t \to +\infty} p_{f|f}(i,i) = p_f(i)$. By substituting (10.38) into (10.36), we have

$$\dot{p}_{f|f}(l,i) = \frac{1}{N}(p_f(l) - p_{f|f}(l,i))\left[\frac{e^{\frac{4t}{N}+C_i}}{e^{\frac{4t}{N}+C_i} - 1} + \frac{e^{\frac{4t}{N}+C_l}}{e^{\frac{4t}{N}+C_l} - 1}\right].$$

(10.39)

Thus, through solving for $p_{f|f}(l,i)$, it can be obtained that

$$
\ln\left|p_f(l) - p_{f|f}(l,i)\right| - \ln\left|p_f(l) - p_{f|f}(l,i)\right|_{t=0} + \frac{2t}{N}
$$

$$
= -\frac{1}{N}\int_0^t\left(\frac{1}{e^{\frac{4\sigma}{N}+C_i}-1} + \frac{1}{e^{\frac{4\sigma}{N}+C_l}-1}\right)d\sigma. \tag{10.40}
$$

With t going to infinity, the right-hand side of (10.40) is clearly a bounded quantity. Thus it can be observed from the left-hand side of (10.40) that $\ln\left|p_f(l) - p_{f|f}(l,i)\right| \to -\infty$ as $t \to +\infty$. That is to say, $\lim_{t\to+\infty}p_{f|f}(l,i) = p_f(l), \forall l \neq i$. Thus for the known user-type model, the results of the evolutionary dynamics are summarized in Theorem 10.3.

THEOREM 10.3   *In the known user-type model, the population dynamics $p_f(i)$ are given in (10.30), while the relationship dynamics $p_{ff}(i,l)$ are given in (10.32) (for $i \neq l$) and (10.33) (for $i = l$).*

The evolving speed of the population dynamics is much slower than that of the relationship dynamics and the influence dynamics. In a small time period in which the population states $p_f(\cdot)$ stay unchanged, the influence dynamics $p_{f|f}(l,i)$ are given by (10.36) (for any l,i). Each influence state $p_{f|f}(l,i)$ will converge to the corresponding fixed population state $p_f(l)$ in such a small period of time.

According to Theorem 10.3, the approximation that $p_{f|f}(l,i) = p_f(l), \forall l,i$, can be made as the influence state would keep track of the corresponding population state. Therefore, we can further simplify the population dynamics into the following form: under the known user-type model, we have the population dynamics $p_f(i)$ for every type $i = 1, 2, \ldots, M$ (approximately) as

$$
\dot{p}_f(i) = \frac{\alpha\bar{k}}{N}p_f(i)p_n(i)\sum_{j=1}^{M}q(j)[p_f(j)(u_{ff}(i,j) - u_{nf}(i,j))
$$

$$
+ p_n(j)(u_{fn}(i,j) - u_{nn}(i,j))]. \tag{10.41}
$$

10.5   Experiments

In this section, experiments on synthetic data and real data are implemented to substantiate the theoretical analysis of information diffusion dynamics as well as ESSs. First, it is shown that by using synthetic data, the simulations match well with the theoretical findings. It is then found that by using real data, the theoretical dynamics match well with the dynamics of real-world information diffusion as well, and they are even able to predict future diffusion dynamics.

10.5.1   Synthetic Data Experiments

Simulations are conducted in this section to verify the theoretical evolutionary dynamics and ESSs. Suppose $M = 2$ (i.e., there are two types of users in the network).

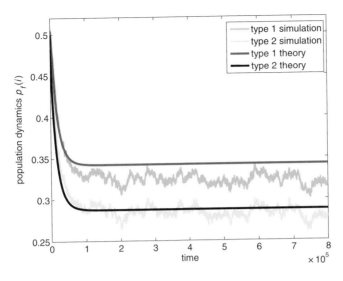

Figure 10.2 Simulation results of the evolution dynamics for the unknown user-type model. The theoretical dynamics fit the simulation dynamics well, and the ESSs are precisely predicted. The heterogeneous model has an average relative ESS error of 3.54%, and this becomes 6.83% if the entire network is modeled as a homogeneous one, which shows the heterogeneous model's advantages in this chapter.

A constant-degree network in which every node has the same degree (k is a certain constant) is synthesized. First, the unknown user-type model is considered. We set two types of players' payoff parameters as follows: $u_{ff}(1) = 0.4, u_{ff}(2) = 0.2$, $u_{fn}(1) = 0.6, u_{fn}(2) = 0.4, u_{nn}(1) = 0.3$, and $u_{nn}(2) = 0.5$. We set the other parameters as $N = 1000, k = 20, q(1) = q(2) = 0.5$, and $\alpha = 0.05$. Figure 10.2 shows the results. The theoretical dynamics fit the simulation dynamics well and the average relative ESS error[1] between the theoretical ESSs and corresponding simulated ESSs is 3.54%. If a homogeneous network such as those in [24,25] is used to model the heterogeneous network (i.e., all of the payoffs are set as the average over all types), the average relative ESS error is 6.83%. This demonstrates the heterogeneous model's advantages. What is more, with another utility parameter setup, the evolutionary dynamics are simulated in Figure 10.3, and it is observed that the simulation still matches the theoretical analysis well. Moreover, in order to demonstrate the extreme ESSs of 0 and 1 stressed in Theorem 10.2, the parameters of utility are changed in the simulation. Figure 10.4 shows the results, in which the population dynamics with ESSs of 0 and 1 are displayed. It is observed that the simulated dynamics still fit the

---

[1] The average relative ESS error is calculated as follows: we denote these two simulated ESSs (for two different types, respectively) as x_1 and x_2. The two theoretical ESSs are denoted as y_1 and y_2. Then the average relative ESS error is $\frac{1}{2}(|y_1 - x_1|/x_1 + |y_2 - x_2|/x_2)$. We only have one global theoretical ESS z if a homogeneous network is utilized for modeling. Under this situation, the average relative ESS error is computed as $\frac{1}{2}(|z - x_1|/x_1 + |z - x_2|/x_2)$.

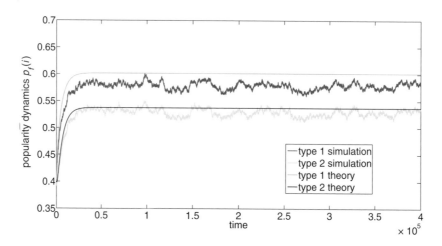

Figure 10.3 Simulation results of the evolution dynamics for the unknown user-type model with another utility parameter setup: $u_{ff}(1) = 0.5$, $u_{ff}(2) = 0.1$, $u_{fn}(1) = 0.8$, $u_{fn}(2) = 0.5$, $u_{nn}(1) = 0.1$, and $u_{nn}(2) = 0.3$. We observe that the simulated dynamics still fit the theoretical ones well.

theoretical ones well. Figure 10.5(a) and 10.5(b), respectively, show the simulation results for an Erdős–Rényi network [39] and a Barabási–Albert network [38] under the same setting parameter settings. The results of the population dynamics strongly resemble those of the constant-degree network, and the simulated dynamics again match well with the theoretical ones. When there are three types of users, the information diffusion over the heterogeneous network is simulated in Figure 10.6. It is observed that the theoretical dynamics still fit the simulated ones well. The accuracy and effectiveness of the heterogeneous network theory are validated by all of the results above.

Then, for the known user-type model, simulations are implemented with randomly selected payoff parameters as follows:

$$u_{ff} = \begin{bmatrix} 0.5882 & 0.0116 \\ 0.8688 & 0.1590 \end{bmatrix}, u_{fn} = \begin{bmatrix} 0.9619 & 0.7370 \\ 0.5595 & 0.7180 \end{bmatrix},$$

$$u_{nf} = \begin{bmatrix} 0.9339 & 0.9864 \\ 0.3288 & 0.4593 \end{bmatrix}, u_{nn} = \begin{bmatrix} 0.2479 & 0.3385 \\ 0.6570 & 0.2437 \end{bmatrix}. \tag{10.42}$$

The other parameters are $\alpha = 0.05, k = 20, N = 1000, q(1) = 0.5518$, and $q(2) = 0.4482$. Figure 10.7 shows the theoretical and simulated population dynamics. Here, the theoretical dynamics for the known user-type model match well with the simulated ones. The evolutionary dynamics for the unknown user-type model are also plotted in Figure 10.7. These do not fit the simulated evolutionary dynamics, implying that the theory of the known user-type model is necessary. Figure 10.8 shows the simulations with two different parameter settings. Figure 10.8 shows that

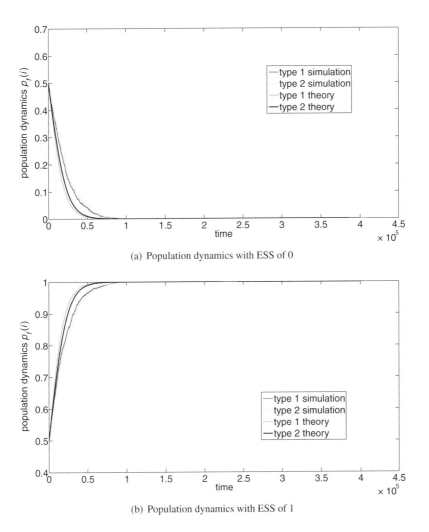

(a) Population dynamics with ESS of 0

(b) Population dynamics with ESS of 1

Figure 10.4 Simulations for the unknown user-type model: population dynamics with ESSs of 0 and 1. The utility parameters in (a) are: $u_{ff}(1) = 0.4$, $u_{ff}(2) = 0.2$, $u_{fn}(1) = 0.3$, $u_{fn}(2) = 0.5$, $u_{nn}(1) = 0.6$, and $u_{nn}(2) = 0.4$. In (b), the utility parameters are: $u_{ff}(1) = 0.6$, $u_{ff}(2) = 0.4$, $u_{fn}(1) = 0.3$, $u_{fn}(2) = 0.5$, $u_{nn}(1) = 0.4$, and $u_{nn}(2) = 0.2$.

the simulated dynamics match the theoretical dynamics. In Figure 10.8(a), we set the utility parameters as follows:

$$u_{ff} = \begin{bmatrix} 0.4228 & 0.1052 \\ 0.9184 & 0.5182 \end{bmatrix}, u_{fn} = \begin{bmatrix} 0.9641 & 0.9865 \\ 0.3008 & 0.7058 \end{bmatrix},$$

$$u_{nf} = \begin{bmatrix} 0.7453 & 0.7104 \\ 0.8943 & 0.9505 \end{bmatrix}, u_{nn} = \begin{bmatrix} 0.3199 & 0.6119 \\ 0.3162 & 0.4556 \end{bmatrix}.$$

(10.43)

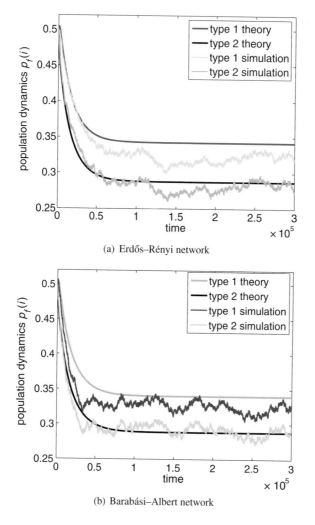

(a) Erdős–Rényi network

(b) Barabási–Albert network

Figure 10.5 More simulations of the evolutionary dynamics for the unknown user-type model with diverse networks.

In Figure 10.8(b), the utility parameters are set as follows:

$$u_{ff} = \begin{bmatrix} 0.6673 & 0.1855 \\ 0.0703 & 0.2549 \end{bmatrix}, u_{fn} = \begin{bmatrix} 0.7964 & 0.1144 \\ 0.9288 & 0.9262 \end{bmatrix},$$

$$u_{nf} = \begin{bmatrix} 0.7979 & 0.1071 \\ 0.8047 & 0.4854 \end{bmatrix}, u_{nn} = \begin{bmatrix} 0.2721 & 0.7794 \\ 0.7564 & 0.0574 \end{bmatrix}. \tag{10.44}$$

Some fluctuations of the simulated dynamics are observed in Figure 10.8(b). A possible reason for this is that for the known user-type model, the number of parameters is quite large and the strategy updating rule is more complex than for the unknown user-type model, likely resulting in the users having unstable behaviors.

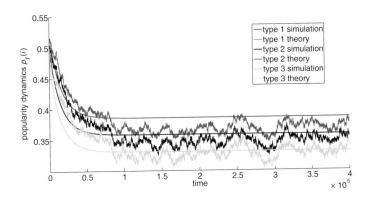

Figure 10.6 Simulation results for the unknown user-type model with three types of users. It is observed that the theoretical dynamics still match the simulated ones well.

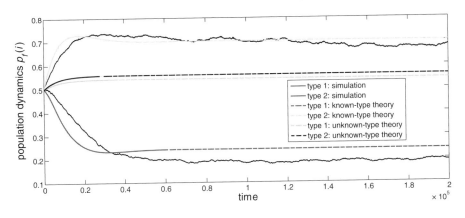

Figure 10.7 Simulation of evolutionary dynamics: the known user-type model.

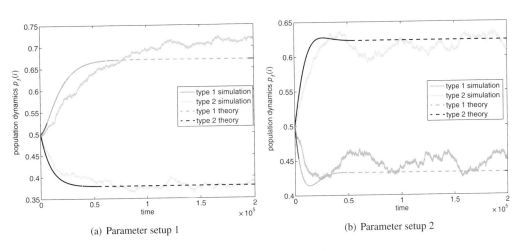

(a) Parameter setup 1   (b) Parameter setup 2

Figure 10.8 Known user-type model: more simulations of the evolutionary dynamics with diverse parameter setups.

10.5.2   Real Data Experiments

In this section, the theoretical analysis is validated by the Twitter hashtag data set in [7], which is based on sampled public tweets from March 24, 2012 to April 25, 2012 and consists of sequences of timestamps and adopters of the observed hashtags. The users are divided into two types to describe their heterogeneity, and the classification is based on the activity of users. Specifically, each user's mention number of hashtags is computed. We then classify the top 10% of users whose hashtag mention number is the highest as type-1 users and we classify the rest as type-2 users. There are 62,757 type-1 users and 533, 262 type-2 users after categorization. k is set to be 100, and in social networks, this is a common number of friends/neighbors. Since there is no network structure of the users in the data set, the network is postulated to be a constant-degree network in which users have a uniform degree $k = 100$. In the curve prediction/fitting process, the selection strength α is of no significance because it can be absorbed into the payoff parameters as it often multiplies with all of the payoff parameters. The time indices' physical units are not specified in the data set. An appropriate time slot length is selected in the following experiments so that (1) the data dynamics are smooth (indicating the length of the time slot cannot be too small) and (2) the data dynamics constantly change and can reveal the variation in the diffusion dynamics of real data correctly (indicating the length of the time slot cannot be too large).

First, under the unknown user-type model, the theoretic dynamics in (10.12) and (10.13) are fitted with the real data. The parameters (i.e., $\Delta(i)$ and $\Delta_n(i)$) in (10.12) and (10.13) can be estimated by real data, and then on the basis of the estimated parameters, the theoretical dynamics are calculated. In order to finish the curve fitting (i.e., to estimate the payoff parameters), the MATLAB function `lsqcurvefit` is invoked. This MATLAB function contains the theory of parameter estimation. When the function to be fit and the data are given, the optimal parameters are selected by `lsqcurvefit` to minimize the squared fitting error. Figure 10.9 shows the fitting results of four popular hashtags. As the population state $p_f(1)$ is usually bigger than $p_f(2)$, type-1 users are more active than type-2 users. It is observed that the theoretical dynamics match well with the dynamics of real-world information diffusion, which implies that considering the heterogeneous users' decision-making and interactions is effective. During the curve fitting of the dynamics of the hashtag #Thoughts-DuringSchool, the utility parameters are estimated as: $u_{ff}(1) - u_{fn}(1) = -3.32$, $u_{nn}(1) - u_{fn}(1) = -0.578$, $u_{ff}(2) - u_{fn}(2) = -0.64$, and $u_{nn}(2) - u_{fn}(2) = -0.004$. It can be seen from these relationships that the estimated utility parameters of real-world information diffusion data generally meet the condition $\bar{u}_{fn} > \max\{\bar{u}_{ff}, \bar{u}_{nn}\}$. We can observe from Theorem 10.2 that an ESS between 0 and 1 is the result of this condition, which is the case in the majority of real-world applications. In the simulations from the previous section, we also selected the utility parameters that complied with this condition (e.g., Figures 10.3 and 10.4), and we found them to be justified by the real data. Moreover, it can be seen that $u_{nn}(1)$ is much smaller than $u_{fn}(1)$, but $u_{nn}(2)$ is approximately the same as $u_{fn}(2)$. This, to some extent, can explain why type-1 users are more active than type-2 users. Furthermore, two less popular hashtags #ididnttextback and #imhappywhen (with peak mention counts

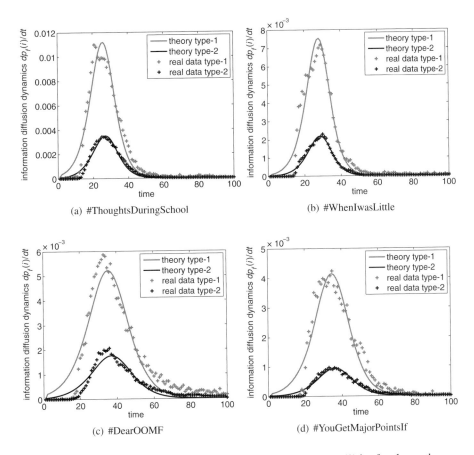

Figure 10.9 Fitting results for the unknown user-type model. Since $p_f(1)$ is often larger than $p_f(2)$, type-1 users are often more active than type-2 users. The theoretical dynamics match the information diffusion dynamics of the real-world heterogeneous social networks well, which substantiates the effectiveness of considering the individuals' interactions. It is indicated from the theory that the heterogeneous behavior dynamics of online users are the consequences of their heterogeneous payoff structures.

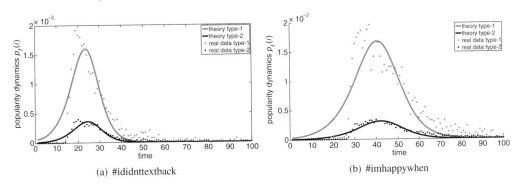

Figure 10.10 Fitting results for the unknown user-type model. Two less popular hashtags, #ididnttextback and #imhappywhen, are fitted. The fitting is still accurate, though the data become more noisy as these two hashtags are less popular.

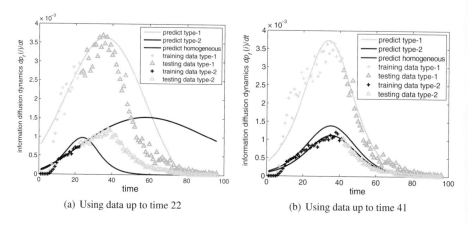

Figure 10.11 Predictions. Future diffusion dynamics can be predicted by the heterogeneous game-theoretic model, and the predictions performs better than those of the homogeneous model.

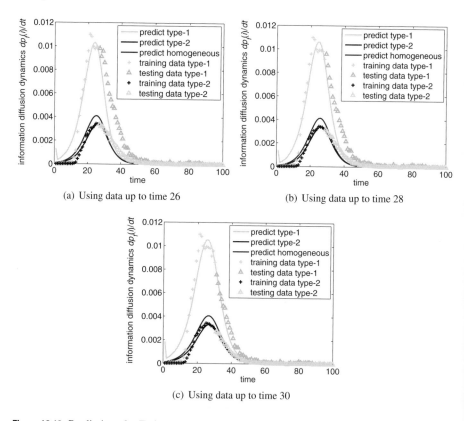

Figure 10.12 Predictions for Twitter hashtag #ThoughtsDuringSchool.

being about a sixth of that of the hashtag #ThougtsDuringSchool) are fitted. It can be seen from the results in Figure 10.10 that the fitting is still accurate, although the data are more noisy for these two less popular hashtags, which implies that the method is robust.

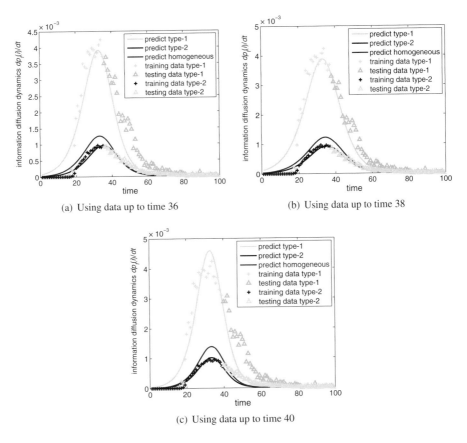

(a) Using data up to time 36   (b) Using data up to time 38

(c) Using data up to time 40

Figure 10.13 Predictions for the Twitter hashtag #YouGetMajorPointsIf.

Experiments to predict future diffusion dynamics were also conducted. In particular, only a portion of the data are used to train the payoff parameters in (10.12) and (10.13), and the trained parameters are utilized for the prediction of future diffusion dynamics. The heterogeneous network is modeled as a homogeneous one, and the homogeneous network theory in [25] is utilized to make predictions, both of which act as benchmarks for comparison with the homogeneous model in [24] and [25]. Figure 10.11 shows the prediction results for one, popular hashtag, #WhenIwasLittle. Two kinds of training data lengths are studied. The future diffusion dynamics can be well predicted by the heterogeneous game-theoretic model. By contrast, through modeling the network as a homogeneous model, the predicted results do not fit the real data well, particularly for type-1 users. This is because we can regard the prediction under the homogeneous model as a prediction of the overall diffusion dynamics averaged over the two types of users. However, type-1 users are the minority who are active among the whole (10% of all users). Thus their diffusion dynamics not only are poorly predicted, but also are far from the average. Figures 10.12 and 10.13, respectively, show the prediction results for two other Twitter hashtags, #ThoughtsDuringSchool and #YouGetMajorPointsIf.

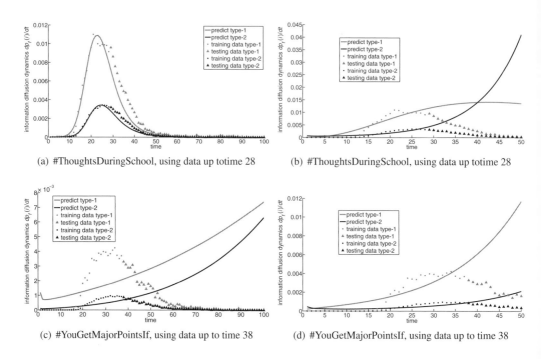

(a) #ThoughtsDuringSchool, using data up totime 28

(b) #ThoughtsDuringSchool, using data up totime 28

(c) #YouGetMajorPointsIf, using data up to time 38

(d) #YouGetMajorPointsIf, using data up to time 38

Figure 10.14 Prediction results.

The heterogeneous model's performance on prediction is good for both hashtags. What is more, after the diffusion dynamics' peak is seen for the 8 most popular hashtags in the data set, predictions for 10 future time slots are performed. The heterogeneous game model's average relative error is 23% and the homogeneous game model's in [25] is 47%. Moreover, Figure 10.14 shows the prediction results of the existing approaches in [4,40]. The game-theoretic approach's advantage is shown through the comparison with the corresponding prediction results of the approaches in Figures 10.12(b) and 10.13(b).

Finally, using the real data of the four popular Twitter hashtags, the theoretical dynamics under the known user-type model are fitted. It can be seen from Figure 10.15 that the real data and the theoretical dynamics are well fitted. But in Figure 10.16 we can see that the prediction performance of the known user-type model is not steady. A likely explanation for this is that more parameters are involved in the known user-type model and the quality of observed data is not sufficiently high to precisely estimate them.

10.6   Discussion and Conclusion

It can be seen from the experiments on real data that the known user-type model is sometimes not able to function well in predicting the future dynamics of information

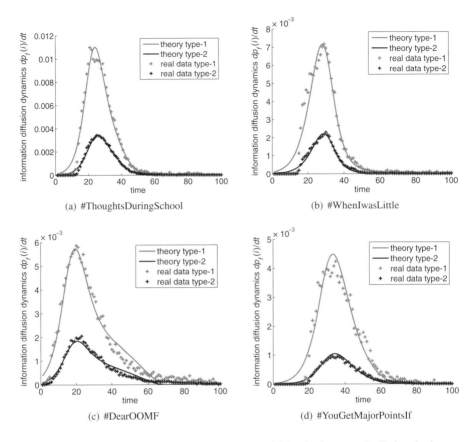

(a) #ThoughtsDuringSchool

(b) #WhenIwasLittle

(c) #DearOOMF

(d) #YouGetMajorPointsIf

Figure 10.15 Fitting results of the known user-type model for the four popular Twitter hashtags.

diffusion. We think the first reason for this is the data's quality: the data's time resolution is not good enough or equivalently the data are not adequately smooth when we narrow the time window, because more parameters are involved in the known user-type model than in the unknown user-type model and better data for the accurate estimation of all of the parameters are also required for the known user-type model. The second reason is as follows: differently from Facebook, in the Twitter network (from which the data are collected) users generally are more interested in famous people rather than the people around them, indicating that Twitter users probably are not familiar with the types of their friends. Thus it is likely that the known user-type model does not fit the Twitter network well. However, in the corresponding simulations, the theoretical dynamics still match well with the simulated dynamics, as the setup is simply the known user-type model. This indicates that the theory itself is accurate.

In summary, an evolutionary game-theoretic framework is presented in this chapter to analyze information diffusion over heterogeneous social networks. Theoretical results' fitting and prediction for the information diffusion data from real-world social networks are good, which proves that the heterogeneous game-theoretic modeling

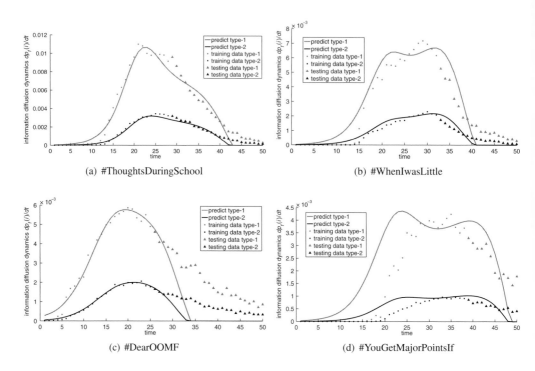

(a) #ThoughtsDuringSchool

(b) #WhenIwasLittle

(c) #DearOOMF

(d) #YouGetMajorPointsIf

Figure 10.16 Known user-type model: prediction results for various Twitter hashtags. The prediction performance of the known user-type model is not steady. Sometimes it is accurate ((a) and (b)), but sometimes it is not ((c) and (d)).

method is effective. The acquired evolutionary dynamics in this chapter could be incorporated to enhance the state-of-the-art approaches based on ML in the literature on information diffusion. What is more, with only a small number of parameters, the model offers a game-theoretic interpretation to the mechanism of individuals' decision-making in the information diffusion process over heterogeneous social networks.

References

[1] D. Noyes, "The top 20 valuable Facebook statistics – updated October 2014." https://zephoria.com/social-media/top-15-valuable-facebook-statistics/

[2] C. Smith, "By the numbers: 250 amazing Twitter statistics." http://expandedramblings.com/index.php/march-2013-by-the-numbers-a-few-amazing-twitter-stats/

[3] M. D. Domenico, A. Lima, P. Mougel, and M. Musolesi, "The anatomy of a scientific rumor," *Scientific Reports*, vol. 3, p. 2980, 2013.

[4] J. Leskovec, L. Backstrom, and J. Kleinberg, "Meme-tracking and the dynamics of the news cycle," in *ACM SIGKDD International Conference on Knowledge Discovery and Data Mining (KDD)*, 2009.

[5] J. Yang and J. Leskovec, "Patterns of temporal variation in online media," in *ACM International Conference on Web Search and Data Mining (WSDM '11)*, 2011.

[6] H. Pinto, J. Almeida, and M. Goncalves, "Using early view patterns to predict the popularity of youtube videos," in *Proc. ACM International Conference on Web Search and Data Mining (WSDM)*, 2013.

[7] L. Weng, F. Menczer, and Y.-Y. Ahn, "Predicting successful memes using network and community structure," in *8th AAAI International Conference on Weblogs and Social Media (ICWSM)*, 2014.

[8] M. Rodriguez, J. Leskovec, D. Balduzzi, and B. Scholkopf, "Uncovering the structure and temporal dynamics of information propagation," in *Network Science*, vol. 2, pp. 26–65, 2014.

[9] M. Rodriguez, J. Leskovec, D. Balduzzi, and B. Scholkopf, "Modeling information propagation with survival theory," in *International Conference on Machine Learning (ICML)*, 2013.

[10] M. Rodriguez, J. Leskovec, D. Balduzzi, and B. Scholkopf, "Structure and dynamics of information pathways in online media," in *ACM International Conference on Web Search and Data Mining (WSDM)*, 2013.

[11] J. Yang and J. Leskovec, "Modeling information diffusion in implicit networks," in *IEEE International Conference on Data Mining (ICDM)*, 2010.

[12] S. Myers and J. Leskovec, "Clash of the contagions: cooperation and competition in information diffusion," in *IEEE International Conference on Data Mining (ICDM)*, 2012.

[13] S. Myers, C. Zhu, and J. Leskovec, "Information diffusion and external influence in networks," in *ACM SIGKDD International Conference on Knowledge Discovery and Data Mining (KDD)*, 2012.

[14] J. Cheng, L. Adamic, P. Dow, J. Kleinberg, and J. Leskovec, "Can cascades be predicted?" in *ACM International Conference on World Wide Web (WWW)*, 2014.

[15] D. Centola, "The spread of behavior in an online social network experiment," *Science*, vol. 329, pp. 1194–1197, 2010.

[16] E. Bakshy, I. Rosenn, C. Marlow, and L. Adamic, "The role of social networks in information diffusion," in *Proc. 21st International Conference on the World Wide Web (WWW)*, 2012.

[17] S. Goyal and M. Kearns, "Competitive contagion in networks," in *45th ACM Symposium on the Theory of Computing (STOC)*, 2012.

[18] V. Tzoumas, C. Amanatidis, and E. Markakis, "A game-theoretic analysis of a competitive diffusion process over social networks," in *8th Conference on Web and Internet Economics*, 2012.

[19] M. Granovetter, "Threshold models of collective behavior," *American Journal of Sociology*, vol. 83, pp. 1420–1443, 1978.

[20] S. Morris, "Contagion," *Review of Economic Studies*, vol. 67, pp. 57–78, 2000.

[21] P. Mieghem, J. Omic, and R. Kooij, "Virus spread in networks," *IEEE/ACM Transactions on Networking*, vol. 17, pp. 1–14, 2009.

[22] D. Kempe, J. Kleinberg, and E. Tardos, "Maximizing the spread of influence through a social network," in *ACM SIGKDD*, 2003.

[23] A. Nematzadeh, E. Ferrara, A. Flammini, and Y.-Y. Ahn, "Optimal network modulariy for information diffusion," *Physical Review Letters*, vol. 113, p. 088701, 2014.

[24] C. Jiang, Y. Chen, and K. J. R. Liu, "Graphical evolutionary game for information diffusion over social networks," *IEEE Journal of Selected Topics in Signal Processing*, vol. 8, pp. 524–536, 2014.

[25] C. Jiang, Y. Chen, and K. J. R. Liu, "Evolutionary dynamics of information diffusion over social networks," *IEEE Transactions on Signal Processing*, vol. 62, pp. 4573–4586, 2014.

[26] J. Smith, *Evolution and the Theory of Games*. Cambridge University Press, 1982.

[27] Y. Chen, B. Wang, W. S. Lin, Y. Wu, and K. J. R. Liu, "Cooperative peer-to-peer streaming: An evolutionary game-theoretic approach," *IEEE Transactions on Circuits and Systems for Video Technology*, vol. 20, pp. 1346–1357, 2010.

[28] Y. Chen, Y. Gao, and K. J. R. Liu, "An evolutionary game-theoretic approach for image interpolation," in *Proc. IEEE International Conference on Acoustics, Speech and Signal Processing (ICASSP)*, 2011.

[29] C. Jiang, Y. Chen, and K. J. R. Liu, "Distributed adaptive networks: A graphical evolutionary game-theoretic view," *IEEE Transactions on Signal Processing*, vol. 61, pp. 5675–5688, 2013.

[30] B. Wang, K. J. R. Liu, and T. Clancy, "Evolutionary cooperative spectrum sensing game: How to collaborate?" *IEEE Transactions on Communications*, vol. 58, pp. 890–900, 2010.

[31] H. Tembine, E. Altman, R. Azouzi, and Y. Hayel, "Evolutionary games in wireless networks," *IEEE Transactions on Systems, Man, and Cybernetics, Part B (Cybernetics)*, vol. 40, pp. 634–646, 2010.

[32] F. Richter, "Top 15% of Twitter users account for 85% of all tweets." www.statista.com/chart/1098/distribution-of-of-tweets-among-twitter-users/

[33] Beevolve, "An exhaustive study of Twitter users across the world." www.beevolve.com/twitter-statistics/

[34] P. Shakarian, P. Roos, and A. Johnson, "A review of evolutionary graph theory with applications to game theory," *Biosystems*, vol. 107, pp. 66–80, 2012.

[35] M. A. Nowak and K. Sigmund, "Evolutionary dynamics of biological games," *Science*, vol. 303, pp. 793–799, 2004.

[36] H. Ohtsuki, M. A. Nowak, and J. M. Pacheco, "Breaking the symmetry between interaction and replacement in evolutionary dynamics on graphs," *Physical Review Letters*, vol. 98, p. 108106, 2007.

[37] H. Ohtsuki and M. A. Nowak, "The replicator equation on graphs," *Journal of Theoretical Biology*, vol. 243, pp. 86–97, 2006.

[38] A. Barabási and R. Albert, "Emergence of scaling in random networks," *Science*, vol. 286, pp. 509–512, 1999.

[39] P. Erdős and A. Rényi, "On random graphs I," *Publicationes Mathematicae Debrecen*, vol. 6, pp. 290–297, 1959.

[40] D. Wang, C. Song, and A. Barabasi, "Quantifying long-term scientific impact," *Science*, vol. 342, pp. 127–132, 2013.

Part III

Sequential Decision-Making

11 Introduction to Sequential Decision-Making

In Part III of this book, the third branch of modern game theory, sequential decision-making, is presented. The important components in sequential decision-making, such as network externality, information asymmetry, and user rationality, are presented and defined. The limitations of the existing approaches, such as social learning and multiarmed bandit problems, are also presented.

11.1 Decision-Making in Networks

People form networks through relationships. The relationships can be friendships, kinships, colleagues, location proximity, preferences, etc. The relationships suggest that one's actions will influence others' in the same network, and vice versa. Typically, these relations in networks have significant impacts on the decisions of rational agents.

Let us consider the food corner problem as an example. You enter a new food corner containing restaurants you have never been to before. You need to choose one for lunch, but you have no idea which one is best. How do you choose? A common strategy in this problem is to observe the waiting lines in front of each restaurant. A longer line suggests that the restaurant is a preferred choice by the general public. This strategy relies on the fact that some people in the network make decisions before you and their decisions contain some information that you could learn from. We call this *learning* in the network.

Nevertheless, you may find that even if you already know the best restaurant in the food corner, you may choose another restaurant for lunch due to the long waiting line in front of that restaurant. This decision comes from the fact that others' decisions will have impacts on the utility you may derive from certain choices. We call this *externality* in the network.

Through the above simple example, we observe several important characteristics of decision-making in networks:

(1)   Decisions are usually made sequentially. Some people make decisions before you and some after you. You may be able to observe some of these decisions when you are making your own decision.

(2)   Decisions may contain useful information. Some agents may know more than others when there is unknown or uncertain information in the network. Nevertheless, their decisions may leak information, and agents making decisions later may be able to learn this information.

(3)   The utility of an agent is influenced by the decisions of all agents, which we call externality. The externality could be positive or negative, and the influence could depend on the number of agents, the system state, or the agent's own preferences.

Concluding from the above, rational sequential decision-making in networks should be conducted as follows:

- Collect information (learn) about uncertain states.
    - Signals and, rumors collected by the agents.
    - Information shared by other agents.
    - Actions revealed by other agents.
- Estimate (predict) the corresponding utility.
    - Conditioning on the available information.
    - Predicting the decisions of subsequent agents.
- Make the optimal decision by maximizing the expected utility.

We find that in order to completely analyze the above rational decision-making process in a network, it is necessary to understand both the learning and prediction processes in rational settings. In the literature, rational learning and prediction processes are studied in different areas. In the following, we list several research areas that are closely related to sequential decision-making.

11.2   Social Learning

The study of social learning aims to understand how agents learn about information and actions through observing or imitating others. In this area, learning behavior is considered to be a cognitive process regarding social contents and interactions. Let us consider a social network in an uncertain system state. The state has an impact on the agents' rewards. When the impact is differential (i.e., one action results in a higher reward than other actions in one state but not in all states), the state information becomes critical for agents to make correct decisions.

In most of the social learning literature, the state information is unknown to agents. Nevertheless, agents may learn the state through signals or actions revealed by other agents through social interactions. Initially agents may have prior knowledge of the unknown state due to observed signals. Then the agents make their decisions sequentially, while their actions/signals may be fully or partially observed by other agents. Most of the existing works in this area study how the beliefs of agents are formed through learning in the sequential decision-making process and how accurate the beliefs will be when more information is revealed.

Although the social learning problem is very similar to the sequential decision-making problem, one popular assumption in the traditional social learning literature is that there is no network externality (i.e., the actions of subsequent agents do not influence the rewards of the preceding agents). In such a case, agents will make their decisions purely based on their own beliefs without considering the actions of subsequent agents. In other words, predictions of the decisions of later agents are ignored in this area.

11.3 Multiarmed Bandit

The multiarmed bandit problem is studied in order to understand the optimal allocation of resources to certain choices so as to maximize the (expected) reward. The rewards of these choices are unknown at first, and they could be stochastic. The multiarmed bandit problem can be illustrated as follows: a gambler stands at a row of slot machines. Each returns a random reward if the gambler plays. Nevertheless, the gambler has limited coins to play with. In this problem, the gambler aims to find the optimal strategy by selecting the machine (bandit) to maximize their long-term reward.

In such a setting, the agent is facing a trade-off: exploring new options to learn their unknown rewards, with the risk to lowering the total received reward, and exploiting the existing best option to utilize the learned knowledge so far, with the risk of falling into the local optimal choices. The studies of the multiarmed bandit problem focus on the optimal policy that minimizes *regret*: that is, the maximum potential loss if a certain action is selected.

One may find that this is similar to the action selection problem in sequential decision-making given an unknown state and limited knowledge derived from learning. Nevertheless, the multiarmed bandit problem is a single-agent learning problem: that is, only one agent is considered in the system. The derived solutions would be impractical in sequential decision-making problems since they ignore the externality and rationality of other agents, which are critical aspects in sequential decision-making.

11.4 Reinforcement Learning

Reinforcement learning is studied in machine learning in order to understand how agents may interact with the environment to maximize their received reward. It has received a lot of attention in various areas due to its generality, simplicity, and effectiveness. The general idea of reinforcement learning is to reinforce the actions that have better rewards in a gradual way in order to balance the trade-off between exploration and exploitation in unknown problems.

The reinforcement learning problem is usually formulated as a Markov decision process, but there are some pieces of information or structures that are unknown to the problem solver, such as the state transition probability or immediate rewards. Reinforcement learning algorithms are designed to explore the rewards from these actions and state transitions. The derived knowledge is stored in memory. Through reinforcing better actions that are learned from past explorations, reinforcement learning will converge to the optimal policy in a fairly general set of problems.

Nevertheless, the proper scenarios to apply reinforcement learning are: (1) when the problem itself is not well defined and may lack some important system structures or parameters, such as the state transition probability or distributions and (2) when the problem is too complicated to solve in a theoretical way. In addition, reinforcement learning can only derive solutions without providing proper insights and reasoning behind the policy. In this book, we tend to study the sequential decision-making problem given a well-defined system in a theoretical way so that we can fully understand how rational agents make decisions in a network. The reinforcement learning approach is not suitable for this purpose.

12 Chinese Restaurant Game

Sequential Decision-Making in Static Systems

Agents in a social network are smart and are able to decide on things based on trying to maximize their utility. They are able to either make good decisions through learning from the experiences of other agents or make timely decisions to avoid large-scale competition. The two effects of negative network externality and social learning are significant in the process of an agent's decision-making. Although there exist some works on negative network externality and social learning, general research on these two effects is still limited. It is found that a popular random process named the Chinese restaurant process offers a well-defined structure for modeling an agent's decision-making process under these two effects.

In this chapter, the "Chinese restaurant game" is introduced to formulate the social learning problem with negative network externality through incorporating the non-strategic Chinese restaurant process with strategic behavior. Through an analysis of the Chinese restaurant game, each agent's optimal strategy is derived, and a recursive method is provided to reach the optimal strategy. Through simulations, the ways in which negative network externality and social learning affect each other in diverse settings are investigated. In addition, as one of the applications of the Chinese restaurant game, the spectrum access problem is illustrated in cognitive radio networks. It is found that the Chinese restaurant game-theoretic method can help users to better decide and enhance the overall performance of the system.

12.1 Introduction

In many research fields (e.g., cognitive adaptation in cognitive radio networks, machine learning with communications among devices, and social learning in social networks), the ways in which agents learn and decide in a network is an issue of vital significance. The objective of agents in a network making decisions is to realize some purpose. Nevertheless, due to an agent's external uncertainty regarding the system or limited observational ability, what they know about the system may be limited, which weakens their utility as they need sufficient knowledge to decide correctly. Learning can enrich an agent's limited knowledge, and the information sources may consist of their previous shopping experience, a brands' advertisements, or other agents' decisions. Generally, the accuracy of agents' decisions could be increased through learning from the collected information.

In the literature, learning behavior in a social network is a hot topic. Consider a social network in an uncertain system state that affects the rewards of agents. If the influence is differential (i.e., in one state but not in all states a higher reward is caused by one action rather than other actions), the state information is important in order for an agent to decide correctly. Agents do not know the state information in the majority of the social learning literature. However, some signals associated with the system state are known to the agents. The agents make decisions accordingly, and other agents may fully or partially notice these actions/signals. The majority of existing works [1–3] study the ways in which agents' beliefs are formed by learning in a sequential decision-making process and the degree of the beliefs' precision as more information is released. In the traditional social learning literature, there is a common assumption that network externality does not exist (i.e., the subsequent agents' actions do not affect the former agents' rewards. Under this circumstance, agents will make decisions simply on the basis of their own beliefs, and they will not take the subsequent agents' actions into account. These existing works' potential applications are significantly limited by this assumption.

In economics, network externality (i.e., the effect of other agents' behaviors on the reward of one agent), is a classical topic. In coordination game theory, researchers investigated the ways in which agents' relations affect the behavior of an agent [4]. The coordination game can be used to model this problem if the network externality is positive. A number of works on coupling social learning and positive network externality can be found in the literature (e.g., voting games [5–7] and investment games [8–11]). In the voting game, there is an election with several candidates and voters have their own preferences on the candidates. A voter's preference on the candidates is determined by how they can benefit from a supposed election winner. When a candidate gets more votes, it becomes more likely that they will win the election and hence the voters can benefit. In the investment game, there are investors and multiple projects, and each project has diverse payoffs. If the same project is invested in by more investors, the project's possibility of winning goes up, which brings benefits to all investors who have invested in this project. It should be noted that the decision of the agent in both the voting and investment games affects decisions positively. When a decision is made by one agent, this decision will often be followed by the subsequent agents due to two aspects: the probability of getting a positive outcome from this action goes up because of the decision of this agent, and this action's potential reward is likely to be large based on this agent's belief.

This will become an anticoordination game when the externality is negative. In such a game, agents would prefer to shun the same decisions as others [12–14]. However, it is hard analyze the combination of network externality with social learning. If the network externality is negative, the game becomes an anticoordination game, and consequently one agent tries to make different decisions to maximize their own reward. However, under this situation, the decision of the agent also includes some information related to their belief regarding the system state, which can be learned through social learning algorithms by subsequent agents. Therefore, subsequent agents are likely to be aware that the first agent's decision is better than the others, and then follow that agent's decision. The information revealed by the decision of the agent maybe decrease the reward that the agent can get as the network externality is negative. Thus, in order to maximize their own rewards, rational agents ought to consider the possible reactions of subsequent players.

In a number of applications and diverse research fields, the role of negative network externality is rather significant. In cognitive radio networks, one important application is spectrum access. In the problem of spectrum access, secondary users who access the same spectrum should share with each other. If there are more secondary users accessing the same channel, then the interference for each of them will be higher or available access time will be less. Under this circumstance, the utility of the agents who made the same decision is decreased by the negative network externality. As is explained in [15], the interference from other secondary users would degrade the transmission quality of a secondary user, and this could be regarded as the negative network externality effect. Thus, during the decision-making process, the agents ought to consider the possibility of degraded utility. In other applications, similar features can also be found (e.g., deal selection in the Groupon website and service selection in cloud computing).

The most strategic methods are the social learning approaches mentioned before. In these approaches, agents can be viewed as players with bounded or unbounded rationality in maximizing their rewards. Another type of approach for the problem of learning is machine learning, which centers on designing algorithms that utilize previous experience to enhance performance on future similar tasks [16]. In general, there are some training data, and a learning method designed by the system designer is followed by devices to study and enhance performance on some particular tasks. The majority of learning methods researched in machine learning are nonstrategic without rationality for considering their own benefit. Under the situation where devices are sufficiently intelligent and rational to select actions that maximize their own benefits instead of following the rule designed by the system designer, it is likely that such nonstrategic learning methods would become unfeasible.

In machine learning [17], the Chinese restaurant process is a nonparametric learning approach that offers an interesting nonstrategic learning approach for unbounded numbers of objects. In this process, there are infinite numbers of tables in a Chinese restaurant, with each table having infinite numbers of seats. Infinite numbers of customers will come into the restaurant. When one customer enters the restaurant, the probabilities of them sitting at a new table or sharing a table with other customers are predefined by the process. In general, if more customers occupy a table, then it is more likely that a new customer will join the table, and a parameter can control the possibility of a new table being sat at by a customer [18]. A systematic method is offered by this process to construct the parameters for modeling unknown distributions. However, in the Chinese restaurant game, customers' behavior is nonstrategic, indicating that they obey predefined rules without considering their own utility rationally. It is observed that if strategic behaviors are introduced to the Chinese restaurant process, the model can be regarded as a general framework for analyzing social learning with negative network externality.

In this chapter, a new game – the Chinese restaurant game – is introduced to formulate the social learning problem with negative network externality by adding strategic behavior to the nonstrategic Chinese restaurant process. Suppose there are J tables in a Chinese restaurant. In order to have meals, N customers sequentially request for seats from these J tables. One customer is likely to request one of the tables, and then will be seated at the required table. It is assumed that all of the customers are rational (i.e., they like having more space so as to have an enjoyable eating experience). Therefore, one probably feels happy when getting a bigger table. Nevertheless, the table may be shared with others if this is wanted by multiple customers due to the fact that all tables are available to all customers. Under this situation, the customer's eating space is reduced and consequently their eating experience is negatively impacted. Thus, the ways by which customers choose the tables to improve their own eating experience is the critical problem in the Chinese restaurant game. Due to the fact that the eating experience of customers is worsened if they and others use the same table, this model incorporates negative network externality. What is more, when the customers do not know the table size and each customer gets some signals associated with the table size, this game contains the process of learning if previous signals or actions can be observed by customers.

12.2   System Model

Suppose there are N customers labeled with $1, 2, \ldots, N$ and J tables numbered $1, 2, \ldots, J$ in a Chinese restaurant. To have a meal, every customer asks for a table. There are infinite seats at each table, which may be of various sizes. A restaurant's table sizes are modeled with two components: the restaurant state θ and the table size functions $\{R_1(\theta), R_2(\theta), \ldots, R_J(\theta)\}$. The state θ denotes an objective parameter that maybe change if the restaurant is remodeled. The table size function $R_j(\theta)$ is fixed (i.e., each time the restaurant is remodeled, the functions $\{R_1(\theta), R_2(\theta), \ldots, R_J(\theta)\}$ would not change). The order of existing tables is an example of θ. Assume that there are two tables in the restaurant and the sizes of them are L and S. The owner of the restaurant may number them as table 1 for the large one and table 2 for the small one. We can model the process of numbering the tables as $\theta \in \{1, 2\}$, while the table size functions $R_1(\theta)$ and $R_2(\theta)$ are given as $R_1(1) = L$, $R_1(2) = S$ and $R_2(1) = S$, $R_2(2) = L$. Denote Θ as the set of all possible states of the restaurant. In this case, $\Theta = \{1, 2\}$.

The problem of table selection is formulated as a game, which is called the *Chinese restaurant game*. First, $\mathcal{X} = \{1, \ldots, J\}$ is denoted as the action set (tables) form which the customer can choose, where $x_i \in \mathcal{X}$ refers to the notion that table x_i is chosen by customer i who requires a seat. Then, customer i's utility function is $U(R_{x_i}, n_{x_i})$, in which n_{x_i} is the number of customers who select table x_i. Based on discussion above, the utility function needs to be an increasing function with respect to R_{x_i} and a decreasing function with respect to n_{x_i}. It should be noted that the negative network externality effect can explain the decreasing characteristic of $U(R_{x_i}, n_{x_i})$ over n_{x_i}, because it is the joining of other customers that leads to the utility's degradation.

Finally, let $\mathbf{n} = (n_1, n_2, \ldots, n_J)$ be the numbers of customers on the J tables (i.e., the *grouping* of customers in the restaurant).

The restaurant, as mentioned earlier, is in a state $\theta \in \Theta$. But the exact state θ may be unknown to customers (i.e., they probably have no idea of each table's exact size before requiring a seat). They may instead collect some impressions or see some advertisements for the restaurant. This information could be considered as signals associated with the restaurant's true state. Under this circumstance, they are able to estimate θ by referring to the accessible information (i.e., the information they collect and/or learn in the game process). Consequently, it is assumed that every customer knows the prior distribution of the state information θ represented by $\mathbf{g_0} = \{g_{0,l} | g_{0,l} = Pr(\theta = l), \forall l \in \Theta\}$. The signal that every customer gets $s_i \in \mathcal{S}$ is derived from a predefined distribution $f(s|\theta)$. Note that the signal quality is likely to change due to it, relying on the accuracy of the signal reflecting the state. As a simple example, consider the system state space $\Theta = \{1,2\}$ and a signal space $\mathcal{S} = \{1,2\}$. The signal distribution is defined as the follows:

$$Pr(s = \theta|\theta) = p, \; Pr(s \neq \theta|\theta) = 1 - p, \; 0.5 \leq p \leq 1. \tag{12.1}$$

Here the parameter p represents this signal distribution's signal quality. The signal is more likely to reflect the real system state when p is higher.

Belief [2] describes how customers estimate the system state θ. Due to the fact that customers make decisions sequentially, customers making decisions later may learn from the signals of those making decisions earlier. We use $\mathbf{h_i} = \{s\}$ to stand for the signals that customer i learn, excluding their own signal s_i. With their own signal s_i, signals $\mathbf{h_i}$, the prior distribution $\mathbf{g_0}$, and the conditional distribution $f(s|\theta)$, the current system state can be estimated by each customer i in probability terms with the belief being defined as

$$\mathbf{g_i} = \{g_{i,l} | g_{i,l} = Pr(\theta = l | \mathbf{h_i}, s_i, \mathbf{g_0}), \forall l \in \Theta\} \; \forall i \in N. \tag{12.2}$$

Based on the previous definition, $g_{i,l}$ denotes the probability that system state θ is the same as l conditional on the received signal s_i, the gathered signals $\mathbf{h_i}$, the prior probability $\mathbf{g_0}$, and the conditional distribution $f(s|\theta)$. It should be noted that in the literature of social learning, belief is able to be acquired through either fully rational Bayesian rules [2] or non-Bayesian updating rules [1,19]. In the fully rational Bayesian rules, customers are completely rational, with the possibility of taking optimal actions and no limit on the fixed belief updating rule. As we consider the customers here as completely rational, they will update their beliefs following the Bayesian rule as follows:

$$g_{i,l} = \frac{g_{0,l} \, Pr(\mathbf{h_i}, s_i | \theta = l)}{\sum_{l' \in \Theta} g_{0,l'} \, Pr(\mathbf{h_i}, s_i | \theta = l')}. \tag{12.3}$$

Note that a certain expression of belief relies on how the signals are learned and generated, which is usually influenced by the game structure and the conditional distribution $f(s|\theta)$. The non-Bayesian updating rule is implicitly on the basis of the assumption that customers are limitedly rational, and so in order to calculate their beliefs they follow some predefined rules. All learned information, the game structure, and the non-Bayesian updating rules constrain customers' ability to maximize their utility.

12.3   Equilibrium Grouping and Advantage in Decision Order

First, the perfect signal case is studied. In this case, all customers know the system state θ. Suppose there are N customers and J tables in a Chinese restaurant game. Customers know the sizes of tables $R_1(\theta), R_2(\theta), \ldots, R_J(\theta)$ exactly because they know θ.

Customers in the Chinese restaurant game make decisions sequentially in a predefined order that all customers know (e.g., queuing up outside the restaurant). Without loss of generality, in the remaining part of this chapter, it is assumed that the number of customers is their order. It is also assumed that the decisions of the previous customers are all known to each customer (i.e., customer i knows the customers' decisions $\{1, \ldots, i - 1\}$). Denote $\mathbf{n_i} = (n_{i,1}, n_{i,2}, \ldots, n_{i,J})$ as the current grouping (i.e., the number of customers selecting table $\{1, 2, \ldots, J\}$ before customer i). $\mathbf{n_i}$ practically stands for the degree of crowdedness at every table when customer i gets into the restaurant. Note that $\mathbf{n_i}$ would not be the same as $\mathbf{n}$, which is the final grouping determining the utilities of customers.

Given any possible situation in the game, how a player will play is described by a strategy. In the Chinese restaurant game, the strategy of a customer should be a mapping from other customers' table choices to their own choice. Recall that n_j represents the number of customers who choose table j. We define $\mathbf{n_{-i}} = (n_{-i,1}, n_{-i,2}, \ldots, n_{-i,J})$, in which $n_{-i,j}$ is the number of customers apart from customer i selecting table j. So with $\mathbf{n_{-i}}$, a rational customer i's best response should be

$$BE_i(\mathbf{n_{-i}}, \theta) = \arg\max_{x \in \mathcal{X}} U(R_x(\theta), n_{-i,x} + 1). \tag{12.4}$$

Note that given $\mathbf{n_{-i}}$, $n_j = n_{-i,j} + 1$ if $x = j$. Nevertheless, customer i cannot fully observe $\mathbf{n_{-i}}$, because customers $i + 1 \sim N$ make decisions after customer i. Thus customer i ought to make predictions regarding the subsequent customers' decisions when state θ and current observation $\mathbf{n_i}$ are given, which is shown in the next section.

12.3.1   Equilibrium Grouping

First, the probable equilibria of the Chinese restaurant game are investigated. When it comes to the prediction of the outcome of a game with rational customers, the Nash equilibrium is a popular concept. Informally speaking, a Nash equilibrium is an action profile in which the reaction of each customer is the best response to the actions of other customers in the profile. Due to the fact that best responses are used by all customers, no one intends to deviate from the current action. It is observed that a Nash equilibrium could be translated into an equilibrium grouping in the Chinese restaurant game. An equilibrium grouping is defined as follows.

DEFINITION 12.1   Given the customer set $\{1, \ldots, N\}$, the table set $\mathcal{X} = \{1, \ldots, J\}$, and the current system state θ, an *equilibrium grouping* $\mathbf{n}^*$ satisfies the following conditions:

$$U(R_x(\theta), n_x^*) \geq U(R_y(\theta), n_y^* + 1), \text{ if } n_x^* > 0, \forall x, y \in \mathcal{X}. \tag{12.5}$$

Conspicuously, there will be more than one Nash equilibrium, because any two customers' actions in one Nash equilibrium can always be exchanged to establish a new Nash equilibrium without violating the necessary and sufficient condition shown in (12.5). However, even though there are multiple Nash equilibria, the equilibrium grouping $\mathbf{n}^*$ may be unique. In order to ensure the equilibrium grouping's uniqueness, we will state the sufficient condition in Theorem 12.2.

THEOREM 12.2   *If the inequality in* (12.5) *strictly holds for all* $x, y \in \mathcal{X}$, *then the equilibrium grouping* $\mathbf{n}^* = (n_1^*, \ldots, n_J^*)$ *is unique.*

Proof   Contradiction is used to finish proof here. Assume that there is another Nash equilibrium with equilibrium grouping $\mathbf{n}' = (n_1', \ldots, n_J')$, where $n_j' \neq n_j^*$ for some $j \in \mathcal{X}$. We have $\sum_{j=1}^{J} n_j' = \sum_{j=1}^{J} n_j^* = N$, as both $\mathbf{n}'$ and $\mathbf{n}^*$ are equilibrium groupings. Under this circumstance, there are two tables x and y with $n_x' > n_x^*$ and $n_y' < n_y^*$. Then because $\mathbf{n}^*$ is an equilibrium grouping, we obtain

$$U(R_y(\theta), n_y^*) > U(R_x(\theta), n_x^* + 1). \tag{12.6}$$

As $n_x' > n_x^*, n_y' < n_y^*$, and $U(\cdot)$ is a decreasing function with respect to n, we have

$$U(R_x(\theta), n_x^*) > U(R_x(\theta), n_x^* + 1) \geq U(R_x(\theta), n_x'), \tag{12.7}$$

$$U(R_y(\theta), n_y') > U(R_y(\theta), n_y' + 1) \geq U(R_y(\theta), n_y^*). \tag{12.8}$$

As $\mathbf{n}'$ is also an equilibrium grouping, we have

$$U(R_x(\theta), n_x') \geq U(R_y(\theta), n_y' + 1). \tag{12.9}$$

According to (12.7), (12.8), and (12.9) we have

$$U(R_x(\theta), n_x^* + 1) \geq U(R_x(\theta), n_x') \geq U(R_y(\theta), n_y' + 1) \geq U(R_y(\theta), n_y^*), \tag{12.10}$$

which contradicts (12.6). Thus, if the inequality in (12.5) is strictly satisfied, the equilibrium grouping $\mathbf{n}^*$ is unique.

The following is a specific instance in which the equilibrium grouping is and is not unique. Let us consider that there are two tables with sizes R_1 and R_2 and three customers in a Chinese restaurant. If $R_1 = R_2$, there are two equilibrium groupings: $\mathbf{n}^1 = (1, 2)$ and $\mathbf{n}^2 = (2, 1)$. In this case, the equilibrium grouping is not unique since the inequality of (12.5) does not strictly hold, indicating that the same utility may be received for the customer they choose another table based on others' decisions. By contrast, if $R_1 > R_2$ and $U(R_1, 3) < U(R_2, 1)$, there is a unique equilibrium grouping $\mathbf{n}^3 = (2, 1)$, because as proved in Theorem 12.2, it is impossible for all other groupings to be the equilibrium output.

By a simple greedy algorithm, we can find the equilibrium grouping. In this algorithm, customers act in the myopic way (i.e., they select the tables that are able to maximize their current utilities only on the basis of their observed information). Denote $\mathbf{n_i} = (n_{i,1}, n_{i,2}, \ldots, n_{i,J})$ with $\sum_{j=1}^{J} n_{i,j} = i - 1$ as the grouping observed by customer i. Then customer i will choose the myopic action given by

$$BE_i^{myopic}(\mathbf{n_i}, \theta) = \arg\max_{x \in \mathcal{X}} U(R_x(\theta), n_{i,x} + 1). \tag{12.11}$$

Whether the greedy algorithm actually outputs an equilibrium grouping is checked. Denote $\mathbf{n}^* = (n_1^*, n_2^*, \ldots, n_J^*)$ as the corresponding grouping. Consider a table j with $n_j^* > 0$, and we assume that customer k is the last customer who chooses table j. According to (12.11) we have

$$U(R_j(\theta), n_{k,j} + 1) \geq U(R_{j'}(\theta), n_{k,j'} + 1) \geq U(R_{j'}(\theta), n_{j'}^* + 1), \forall j' \in \mathcal{X}. \tag{12.12}$$

It should be noted that (12.12) is satisfied for all $j, j' \in \mathcal{X}$ with $n_j^* > 0$ (i.e., $U(R_j(\theta), n_j^*) \geq U(R_{j'}(\theta), n_{j'}^* + 1), \forall j, j' \in \mathcal{X}$ with $n_j^* > 0$). The output grouping $\mathbf{n}^*$ deduced by the greedy algorithm is an equilibrium grouping according to Definition 12.1.

12.3.2   Subgame-Perfect Nash Equilibrium

The subgame-perfect Nash equilibrium will be studied in a sequential game. Within the sequential game, the subgame-perfect Nash equilibrium is a popular improvement to the Nash equilibrium. It ensures that in every possible subgame all players choose strategies rationally. A subgame is a part of the original game. In the Chinese restaurant game, when all possible actions before player i are given, any game process starting from player i can be a subgame.

DEFINITION 12.3   In the Chinese restaurant game, a subgame consists of two elements: (1) it starts from customer i and (2) the current grouping before customer i is $\mathbf{n_i} = (n_{i,1}, \ldots, n_{i,J})$ with $\sum_{j=1}^{J} n_{i,j} = i - 1$.

DEFINITION 12.4   A Nash equilibrium is a subgame-perfect Nash equilibrium if and only if it is a Nash equilibrium for any subgame.

In the Chinese restaurant game, the existence of a subgame-perfect Nash equilibrium is shown through building one. Generally, the customer i who is rational ought to predict the final equilibrium grouping on the basis of their present knowledge about the system state θ and the choices of previous customers $\mathbf{n_i}$. Then, based on the prediction, they would probably choose the table with the highest expected utility. On the basis of this idea, customers' best responses in a subgame are derived.

The prediction part is implemented through the following two functions. First, denote $EG(\mathcal{X}^s, N^s)$ as the function that produces the number of customers N^s and the equilibrium grouping for a table set $\mathcal{X}^s$. We generate the equilibrium grouping through the greedy algorithm from the previous section with N being substituted by

N^s and $\mathcal{X}$ being substituted by $\mathcal{X}^s$. Note that N^s is less than or the same as N, and $\mathcal{X}^s$ can be any subset of the total table set $\mathcal{X} = \{1, \ldots, J\}$.

Next, denote $PC(\mathcal{X}^s, \mathbf{n}^s, N^s)$, in which $\mathbf{n}^s$ represents the current grouping seen by the customer, as the algorithm that produces the set of available tables given $\mathbf{n}^s$ in the subgame. The algorithm removes the tables that are occupied by customers yet whose number is more than expected in the equilibrium grouping. This helps the customer to remove irrational selection and predict the final equilibrium grouping in every subgame correctly. This algorithm's fundamental procedure is as follows: (1) compute the equilibrium grouping $\mathbf{n}^e$ with the number of customers N^s and the table set $\mathcal{X}^s$; (2) check whether there is any table that is occupied in excess by comparing $\mathbf{n}^s$ with $\mathbf{n}^e$; if so (3) remove these tables from $\mathcal{X}^s$ and also the customers who occupy these tables from N^s, and then go back to (1). Otherwise, the algorithm terminates. How to implement $PC(\mathcal{X}^s, \mathbf{n}^s, N^s)$ is described as follows:

(1) Initialize: $\mathcal{X}^o = \mathcal{X}^s$, $N^t = N^s$.
(2) $\mathcal{X}^t = \mathcal{X}^o$, $\mathbf{n}^e = EG(\mathcal{X}^t, N^t)$, $\mathcal{X}^o = \{x | x \in \mathcal{X}^t, n_j^e \geq n_j^s\}$,
$N^t = N^s - \sum_{x \in \mathcal{X}^s \setminus \mathcal{X}^o} n_x^s$.
(3) If $\mathcal{X}^o \neq \mathcal{X}^t$, go back to Step (2).
(4) Output $\mathcal{X}^o$.

A method will now be introduced to build a subgame-perfect Nash equilibrium. This equilibrium satisfies (12.5) too. In a subgame, the strategy of each customer i is

$$BE_i^{se}(\mathbf{n_i}, \theta) = \arg \max_{x \in \mathcal{X}^{i,cand}, n_{i,x} < n_x^{i,cand}} U(R_x(\theta), n_x^{i,cand}), \qquad (12.13)$$

where $\mathcal{X}^{i,cand} = PC(\mathcal{X}, \mathbf{n_i}, N)$, $N^{i,cand} = N - \sum_{x \in \mathcal{X} \setminus \mathcal{X}^{i,cand}} n_{i,x}$, and $\mathbf{n}^{i,cand} = EG(\mathcal{X}^{i,cand}, N^{i,cand})$. The optimal response $BE_i^{se*}(\mathbf{n_i}, \theta)$ is to choose the table with the highest utility based on the candidate table set $\mathcal{X}^{i,cand}$ and the predicted equilibrium grouping $\mathbf{n}^{i,cand}$. We obtain the equilibrium grouping $\mathbf{n}^{i,cand}$ by $EG(\mathcal{X}^{i,cand}, N^{i,cand})$, where the candidate table set $\mathcal{X}^{i,cand}$ is derived by $PC(\mathcal{X}, \mathbf{n_i}, N)$. In Lemma 12.5, the previous strategy's results in the equilibrium grouping in any subgame are shown.

LEMMA 12.5 *Given the available table set* $\mathcal{X}^s = PC(\mathcal{X}, \mathbf{n}^s, N)$, $N^s = N - \sum_{x \in \mathcal{X} \setminus \mathcal{X}^s} n_x^s$, *the strategy shown in* (12.13) *leads to an equilibrium grouping* $\mathbf{n}^* = EG(\mathcal{X}^s, N^s)$ *over* $\mathcal{X}^s$.

Proof This is substantiated by contradiction. Denote $\mathbf{n} = (n_j | j \in \mathcal{X}^s)$ as the final grouping after all customers select their tables on the basis of (12.13). Assume that $\mathbf{n} \neq \mathbf{n}^* = EG(\mathcal{X}^s, N^s)$, then there are some tables j for which $n_j > n_j^*$. Let table j be the first table exceeding n_j^s in this sequential subgame. Due to the fact that $n_j > n_j^*$, there are at least $n_j^* + 1$ customers who choose table j. Assume that customer i is the $n_j^* + 1$-th customer who chooses table j. Denote $\mathbf{n_i} = (n_{i,1}, n_{i,2}, \ldots, n_{i,J})$ as the current grouping seen by customer i before they make their choice. Since customer i is the $n_j^* + 1$-th customer who chooses table j, we have $n_{i,j} = n_j^*$. Since table j is the first table that exceeds $\mathbf{n}^*$ after customer i's choice, we obtain $n_{i,x} \leq n_x^* \ \forall x \in \mathcal{X}^s$.

No table is going to be removed from candidates based on the definition of $PC(\cdot)$. Therefore, $\mathcal{X}^{i,cand} = \mathcal{X}^s$ and $N^{i,cand} = N^s$. We have

$$\mathbf{n}^{i,\,cand} = EG(\mathcal{X}^{i,cand}, N^{i,cand}) = EG(\mathcal{X}^s, N^s) = \mathbf{n}^*. \qquad (12.14)$$

But according to (12.13), due to the fact that $n_{i,j} = n_j^* = n_j^{i,cand}$, customer i should not choose table j. This conflicts with our assumption that customer i is the $n_j^* + 1$-th customer who chooses table j. Therefore, strategy (12.13) ought to bring about the equilibrium grouping $\mathbf{n}^* = EG(\mathcal{X}^s, N^s)$.

It should be noticed that it is also shown from Lemma 12.5 that if all customers follow the strategy introduced in (12.13), the final grouping of the sequential game should be $\mathbf{n}^* = EG(\mathcal{X}, N)$. It is shown in Lemma 12.6 that $PC(\mathcal{X}^s, \mathbf{n}^s, N^s)$ removes the tables dominated by other tables if all customers follow (12.13).

LEMMA 12.6   *Given a subgame with current grouping $\mathbf{n}^s$, if table $j \notin \mathcal{X}^s = PC(\mathcal{X}, \mathbf{n}^s, N)$, then table j can never be the optimal response of the customer if all other customers follow (12.13).*

Proof   Let $\mathbf{n}' = EG(\mathcal{X}, N)$ and the final grouping be $\mathbf{n}^*$. First, it is shown that for every table under the final grouping $\mathbf{n}^*$, there is always a table offering a lesser or equal utility under the grouping $\mathbf{n}'$. Based on Lemma 12.5, if all customers follow (12.13), then the final grouping $\mathbf{n}^*$ is an equilibrium grouping over $\mathcal{X}^s$. What is more, as no customers will choose table j, $n_j^* = n_j^s$. Suppose that there is a table $k \in \mathcal{X}^s$ with $n_k' < n_k^*$. Because $n_j^* = n_j^s > n_j'$, we obtain $\sum_{x \in \mathcal{X} \setminus \{j\}} n_x^* < \sum_{x \in \mathcal{X} \setminus \{j\}} n_x'$. Thus, $\exists k' \in \mathcal{X}^s$ that $n_{k'}' > n_{k'}^*$. Since $\mathbf{n}'$ and $\mathbf{n}^*$ are equilibrium groupings over $\mathcal{X}^s$, similar to (12.10), we have

$$U(R_k(\theta), n_k' + 1) \geq U(R_k(\theta), n_k^*) \geq U(R_{k'}(\theta), n_{k'}^* + 1)$$
$$\geq U(R_{k'}(\theta), n_{k'}') \geq U(R_k(\theta), n_k' + 1). \qquad (12.15)$$

The first and third inequalities are because of $n_k' < n_k^*$ and $n_{k'}' > n_{k'}^*$. The second and fourth inequalities are derived from the equilibrium grouping condition in (12.5). Only when all equalities hold is the equation valid. Therefore, if $n_k' < n_k^*$, $\exists k' \in \mathcal{X}^s$ that $U(R_k(\theta), n_k^*) = U(R_{k'}(\theta), n_{k'}')$, indicating that a table k' that provides the same utility as $U(R_k(\theta), n_k^*)$ under grouping $\mathbf{n}'$ can always be found. When $n_k' \geq n_k^*$, $U(R_k(\theta), n_k^*) \geq U(R_k(\theta), n_k')$. Thus, $\forall k \in \mathcal{X}^s$, $\exists k' \in \mathcal{X}^s$ that $U(R_k(\theta), n_k^*) \geq U(R_{k'}(\theta), n_{k'}')$.

Next, it will be shown that all other tables under $\mathbf{n}^*$ dominate table j. Since table j is removed by $PC(\mathcal{X}, \mathbf{n}^s, N)$, we have $n_j^s > n_j'$. Thus, on the basis of the discussion above and the truth that $\mathbf{n}'$ is an equilibrium grouping, we have $\forall k \in \mathcal{X}^s$

$$U(R_k(\theta), n_k^*) \geq \min_{k' \in \mathcal{X}^s} U(R_{k'}(\theta), n_{k'}') \geq U(R_j(\theta), n_j' + 1) > U(R_j(\theta), n_j^s + 1).$$

$$(12.16)$$

Since table j can offer the highest utility $U(R_j(\theta), n_j^s + 1)$, the utility is dominated by all other tables in $\mathcal{X}^s$ under the final grouping $\mathbf{n}^*$. Thus a customer's optimal response is never table j.

THEOREM 12.7 *There is always a subgame-perfect Nash equilibrium with the corresponding equilibrium grouping $\mathbf{n}^*$ satisfying (12.5) in a sequential Chinese restaurant game.*

Proof It could be shown that a Nash equilibrium is formed by the proposed strategy in (12.13). Assume that table j is chosen by customer i in their round based on (12.13). Then the utility of customer i is $u_i = U(R_j(\theta), n_j^*)$ because, according to Lemma 12.5, the equilibrium grouping $\mathbf{n}^*$ will finally be realized.

Now it is shown that customer i's best response is actually table j. Assuming that the last customer is customer i (i.e., $i = N$) and another table $j' \neq j$ is chosen by customer i in their round, then the utility is $U(R_{j'}(\theta), n_{j'}^* + 1)$. But in accordance with (12.5), we have

$$u_j^* = U(R_j(\theta), n_j^*) \geq U(R_{j'}(\theta), n_{j'}^* + 1). \tag{12.17}$$

Therefore, for customer N, selecting table j is always better than selecting table j'.

For the situation where the last customer is not customer i, it is assumed that in their round, they select table j' rather than table j. As all customers before customer i follow (12.13), we have $n_{i,j} \leq n_j^* \; \forall j \in \mathcal{X}$. Otherwise, $\mathbf{n}^*$ cannot be realized, which conflicts with Lemma 12.5.

When $n_{i,j'} < n_{j'}^*$, we have $n_{i+1,j'} \leq n_{j'}^*$. What is more, $n_{i+1,j} = n_{i,j} \leq n_j^* \; \forall j \in \mathcal{X} \setminus \{j'\}$ because customer i does not choose other tables. Therefore, $\mathcal{X}^{i+1,cand} = PC(\mathcal{X}, \mathbf{n}_{i+1}, N)$ and $N^{i,cand} = N$. The final grouping, according to Lemma 12.5, ought to be $\mathbf{n}^* = EG(\mathcal{X}, N)$. Therefore, customer i's new utility is $u_i' = U(R_{j'}(\theta), n_{j'}^*)$. Nevertheless, according to (12.13), we have

$$u_i = U(R_j(\theta), n_j^*) = \arg \max_{x \in \mathcal{X}, n_{i,x} < n_x^*} U(R_x(\theta), n_x^*)$$

$$\geq U(R_{j'}(\theta), n_{j'}^*) = u_i'. \tag{12.18}$$

Therefore, selecting table j' does not lead to a higher utility for customer i.

When $n_{i,j'} = n_{j'}^*$, the final grouping is $\mathbf{n}' = (n_1', n_2', \ldots, n_J')$. Because table j' is chosen by customer i when $n_{i,j'} = n_{j'}^*$, we have $n_{j'}' \geq n_{i+1,j'} = n_{i,j'} + 1 = n_{j'}^* + 1$. So we obtain

$$u_i = U(R_j(\theta), n_j^*) \geq U(R_{j'}(\theta), n_{j'}^* + 1)$$

$$\geq U(R_{j'}(\theta), n_{j'}') = u_i', \; \forall j' \in X, \tag{12.19}$$

in which the first inequality is derived from the equilibrium grouping condition in (12.5) and the second inequality is derived from the fact that $U(R, n)$ decreases over n and $n_{j'}' \geq n_{j'}^* + 1$. Therefore, in the two situations, selecting table j' is always worse than selecting table j. It is concluded that $\{BE_i^{se}(\cdot)\}$ in (12.13) reaches a Nash equilibrium in which the grouping is the equilibrium grouping $\mathbf{n}^*$.

Finally, it is shown that in every subgame the strategy forms a Nash equilibrium. In Lemma 12.6, it is shown that if table j is removed by $PC(\mathcal{X}, \mathbf{n}^s, N)$, it is impossibly all of the remaining customers' optimal response. Therefore, only the remaining table candidates $\mathcal{X}^s = PC(\mathcal{X}, \mathbf{n}^s, N)$ in the subgame need to be considered. Then, with Lemma 12.5, it is shown that for every possible subgame with corresponding $\mathcal{X}^s$, the equilibrium grouping $\mathbf{n}^* = EG(\mathcal{X}^s, N^s)$ would be implemented at the end of the subgame. What is more, the proof above indicates that $BE_i^{se}(\cdot)$ is the best response function if at the end of the subgame the equilibrium grouping $\mathbf{n}^s$ would be realized. Thus, in every subgame, the strategy forms a Nash equilibrium (i.e., there is a subgame-perfect Nash equilibrium).

It is observed in the proof of Theorem 12.7 that the sequential game structure is advantageous for those customers who make early decisions. In accordance with (12.13), customers who make decisions early are able to select the table that offers the highest utility in the equilibrium. If the number of customers who select that table reaches the equilibrium number, customers will select the second-best table until it is full again. There is no choice for the last customer and they can only select the worst table.

12.4   Signals: Learning Unknown States

It is shown in Section 12.3 that customers who choose first have the possibility of obtaining better tables and thus larger utilities in the Chinese restaurant game with perfect signaling. Nevertheless, if the signals are not perfect, such a conclusion may not be correct. In the case of uncertainties existing regarding table sizes, customers who arrive first probably cannot select the best tables, which may result in lower utility. By contrast, perhaps customers arriving later would have a better chance of eventually getting better tables because they are able to gather more information in order to decide correctly. That is to say, if signals are not perfect, there will be learning that probably leads to larger utilities for customers who choose tables later. Thus, there is a trade-off between more precise signals when playing later and more choices when playing first. In this section, this trade-off is investigated through a discussion of the imperfect signal model.

In the imperfect signal model, it is assumed that all N customers have no idea of the system state $\theta \in \Theta = \{1, 2, \ldots, L\}$. The functions of θ can express the sizes of J tables, which are represented as $R_1(\theta), R_2(\theta), \ldots, R_J(\theta)$. We suppose that all customers know the prior probability of θ, $\mathbf{g_0} = \{g_{0,1}, g_{0,2}, \ldots, g_{0,J}\}$ with $g_{0,l} = Pr(\theta = l)$. What is more, every customer gets a private signal $s_i \in \mathcal{S}$, which follows a probability density function $f(s|\theta)$. It is assumed that here $f(s|\theta)$ is public information available to all customers. While conditioning on the system state θ, the customers' received signals are uncorrelated.

With the imperfect signal model, the customers follow the order according to their number, thereby making decisions sequentially in the Chinese restaurant game. After a decision is made by a customer i, they cannot change it at any subsequent time, and all other customers can know their signal and decision. As signals are shown sequentially, more information could be gathered by the customers making decisions later, enabling them to estimate the system state better. It is assumed that customers are fully rational, indicating that in their decision-making process they should use the Bayesian learning rule [2]. Thus, when a new signal is released, all customers obey the Bayesian rule for updating their beliefs on the basis of their present beliefs. From (12.3), the belief updating function is deduced as follows:

$$g_{i,l} = \frac{g_{i-1,l} f(s_i|\theta = l)}{\sum_{w \in \Theta} g_{i-1,w} f(s_i|\theta = w)}. \tag{12.20}$$

12.4.1 Best Response of Customers

As the customers are rational, they will choose the action to maximize their own expected utility conditional on the information that they collect. Denote $\mathbf{n_i} = (n_{i,1}, n_{i,2}, \ldots, n_{i,J})$ as the present grouping seen by customer i before choosing a table, in which $n_{i,j}$ is the number of customers who choose table j before customer i. Then, denote $\mathbf{h_i} = \{s_1, s_2, \ldots, s_{i-1}\}$ as the history of revealed signals before customer i. Under this situation, we can write customer i's best response as

$$BE_i(\mathbf{n_i}, \mathbf{h_i}, s_i) = \arg\max_j \mathbb{E}[U(R_j(\theta), n_j)|\mathbf{n_i}, \mathbf{h_i}, s_i]. \tag{12.21}$$

It can be seen from (12.21) that while making an estimation of the expected utility in the optimal response function, two critical terms should be estimated by the customer: the final grouping $\mathbf{n} = (n_1, n_2, \ldots, n_J)$ and the system state θ. We can estimate the system state θ by utilizing the concept of belief represented as $\mathbf{g_i} = \{g_{i,1}, g_{i,2}, \ldots, g_{i,L}\}$ with $g_{i,l} = Pr(\theta = l|\mathbf{h_i}, s_i)$. Because $\mathbf{h_i}$ fully shows the information about the system state θ in $\mathbf{n_i}$, with $\mathbf{h_i}$, $\mathbf{g_i}$ is independent with $\mathbf{n_i}$. Thus, when the belief of customer $\mathbf{g_i}$ is given, the expected utility of customer i choosing table j is

$$\mathbb{E}[U(R_j(\theta), n_j)|\mathbf{n_i}, \mathbf{h_i}, s_i, x_i = j] = \sum_{w \in \Theta} g_{i,w} \mathbb{E}[U(R_j(w), n_j)|\mathbf{n_i}, \mathbf{h_i}, s_i, x_i = j, \theta = w]. \tag{12.22}$$

It should be noted that while customer i is making their decision, they do not know the decisions of customers $i+1, \ldots, N$. Thus it is generally unfeasible and impossible to achieve a closed-form solution to (12.22). In this chapter, a recursive method is proposed to calculate the expected utility.

12.4.2 Recursive Form of the Best Response

Denote $BE_{i+1}(\mathbf{n_{i+1}}, h_{i+1}, s_{i+1})$ as the optimal response function for customer $i+1$. Then, based on $BE_{i+1}(\mathbf{n_{i+1}}, \mathbf{h_{i+1}}, s_{i+1})$, we can partition the signal space $\mathcal{S}$ into $\mathcal{S}_{i+1,1}, \ldots, \mathcal{S}_{i+1,J}$ subspaces with

$$\mathcal{S}_{i+1,j}(\mathbf{n_{i+1}}, \mathbf{h_{i+1}}) = \{s|s \in \mathcal{S}, BE_{i+1}(\mathbf{n_{i+1}}, \mathbf{h_{i+1}}, s) = j\}, \forall j \in \{1, \ldots, J\}. \tag{12.23}$$

It can be seen on the basis of (12.23) that, given $\mathbf{n_{i+1}}$ and $\mathbf{h_{i+1}}$, $BE_{i+1}(\mathbf{n_{i+1}}, \mathbf{h_{i+1}}, s_{i+1}) = j$ if and only if $s_{i+1} \in \mathcal{S}_{i+1,j}$. Thus, customer $i + 1$'s decision is able to be predicted based on the signal distribution $f(s|\theta)$ given by

$$Pr(x_{i+1} = j|\mathbf{n_{i+1}}, \mathbf{h_{i+1}}) = \int_{s \in \mathcal{S}_{i+1,j}(\mathbf{n_{i+1}}, \mathbf{h_{i+1}})} f(s)ds. \qquad (12.24)$$

We define $m_{i,j}$ as the number of customers who choose table j after customer i (including customer i themself). Then, $n_j = n_{i,j} + m_{i,j}$, in which n_j represents the final number of customers who choose table j at the end of the game. In accordance with the definition of $m_{i,j}$, we obtain

$$m_{i,j} = \begin{cases} 1 + m_{i+1,j}, & x_i = j; \\ m_{i+1,j}, & \text{else.} \end{cases} \qquad (12.25)$$

In the following, the recursive relation of $m_{i,j}$ in (12.25) will be utilized to obtain the best response function's recursive form. First, the recursive form of the distribution of $m_{i,j}$ is derived; in other words, $Pr(m_{i,j} = X|\mathbf{n_i}, \mathbf{h_i}, s_i, x_i, \theta)$ could be represented as a function of $Pr(m_{i+1,j} = X|\mathbf{n_{i+1}}, \mathbf{h_{i+1}}, s_{i+1}, x_{i+1} = j, \theta = l)$, $\forall l \in \Theta$, $0 \le j \le J$, as in (12.26)

$$Pr(m_{i,j} = X|\mathbf{n_i}, \mathbf{h_i}, s_i, x_i, \theta = l)$$

$$= \begin{cases} Pr(m_{i+1,j} = X - 1|\mathbf{n_i}, \mathbf{h_i}, s_i, x_i, \theta = l), & x_i = j, \\ Pr(m_{i+1,j} = X|\mathbf{n_i}, \mathbf{h_i}, s_i, x_i, \theta = l), & x_i \ne j, \end{cases}$$

$$= \begin{cases} \sum_{u \in \{1,\dots,J\}} \int_{s \in \mathcal{S}_{i+1,u}(\mathbf{n_{i+1}}, \mathbf{h_{i+1}})} Pr(m_{i+1,j} = X - 1|\mathbf{n_{i+1}}, \mathbf{h_{i+1}}, s_{i+1} = s, x_{i+1} = u, \theta = l) \\ \qquad\qquad\qquad\qquad\qquad f(s|\theta = l)ds, \quad x_i = j, \\ \sum_{u \in \{1,\dots,J\}} \int_{s \in \mathcal{S}_{i+1,u}(\mathbf{n_{i+1}}, \mathbf{h_{i+1}})} Pr(m_{i+1,j} = X|\mathbf{n_{i+1}}, \mathbf{h_{i+1}}, s_{i+1} = s, x_{i+1} = u, \theta = l) \\ \qquad\qquad\qquad\qquad\qquad f(s|\theta = l)ds, \quad x_i \ne j, \end{cases}$$

$$\qquad (12.26)$$

where $\mathbf{h_{i+1}}$ and $\mathbf{n_{i+1}}$ can be acquired by using

$$\mathbf{h_{i+1}} = \{h_i, s_i\} \text{ and } \mathbf{n_{i+1}} = (n_{i+1,1}, \dots, n_{i+1,J}), \qquad (12.27)$$

with

$$n_{i+1,k} = \begin{cases} n_{i,k} + 1, & \text{if } x_i = k, \\ n_{i,k}, & \text{otherwise.} \end{cases} \qquad (12.28)$$

$Pr(m_{i,j} = X|\mathbf{n_i}, \mathbf{h_i}, s_i, x_i, \theta = l)$ can be computed recursively on the basis of (12.26). So the expected utility $\mathbb{E}[U(R_j(\theta), n_j)|\mathbf{n_i}, \mathbf{h_i}, s_i]$ could be calculated by (12.29)

$$\mathbb{E}[U(R_j(\theta), n_j)|\mathbf{n_i}, \mathbf{h_i}, s_i]$$

$$= \sum_{l \in \Theta} \sum_{x=0}^{N-i+1} g_{i,l} Pr(m_{i,j} = x|\mathbf{n_i}, \mathbf{h_i}, s_i, x_i = j, \theta = l) U(R_j(l), n_{i,j} + x). \qquad (12.29)$$

Finally, we can derive customer i's optimal response function by (12.30)

$$BE_i(\mathbf{n_i}, \mathbf{h_i}, s_i)$$

$$= \arg\max_j \sum_{l \in \Theta} \sum_{x=0}^{N-i+1} g_{i,l} Pr(m_{i,j} = x | \mathbf{n_i}, \mathbf{h_i}, s_i, x_i = j, \theta = l) U(R_j(l), n_{i,j} + x).$$

$$(12.30)$$

Given the recursive form, we can obtain all customers' optimal response functions by utilizing backward induction. The last customer N's optimal response function can be found as

$$BE_N(\mathbf{n_N}, h_N, s_N) = \arg\max_j \sum_{l \in \Theta} g_{N,l} u_N(R_j(l), n_{N,j} + 1). \qquad (12.31)$$

It should be noted that $Pr(m_{N,j} = X | \mathbf{n_N}, \mathbf{h_N}, s_N, x_N, \theta)$ can be derived with ease as follows:

$$Pr(m_{N,j} = 1 | \mathbf{n_N}, \mathbf{h_N}, s_N, x_N, \theta) = \begin{cases} 1, & \text{if } x_N = j, \\ 0, & \text{otherwise.} \end{cases} \qquad (12.32)$$

As the convergence of the recursive best response is based on the traditional backward induction technique, it converges due to there being finite players in this game. Given a Chinese restaurant game with N players, only N recursive calls are needed to obtain all of the best responses.

12.5 Simulation Results and Analysis

The recursive best response and corresponding equilibrium are verified in this section. A Chinese restaurant with two tables $\{1, 2\}$ and two possible states $\theta \in \{1, 2\}$ are simulated here. If $\theta = 1$, table 1's size is $R_1(1) = 100$ and table 2's size is $R_2(1) = 100r$, in which r is the ratio of table sizes. If $\theta = 2$, $R_1(2) = 100r$ and $R_2(2) = 100$. The state is chosen randomly with $Pr(\theta = 1) = Pr(\theta = 2) = 0.5$. There is a fixed number of customers. At the beginning of the simulation, every customer gets a randomly generated signal s_i. The signal distribution $f(s|\theta)$ is given by $Pr(s = 1|\theta = 1) = Pr(s = 2|\theta = 2) = p$, $Pr(s = 2|\theta = 1) = Pr(s = 1|\theta = 2) = 1 - p$, in which $p \geq 0.5$ could be considered as the signal quality. The signal is more likely to reflect the true state θ when the quality of this signal p is closer to 1. Customers make decisions sequentially with the signals. After the i-th customer makes their choice, the other customers know their signal and decision. After the last customer makes their decision, the game comes to an end. Then the utility of customer i who chooses table j is given by $U(R_j(\theta), n_j) = \frac{R_j}{n_j}$, where n_j is the number of customers who choose table j.

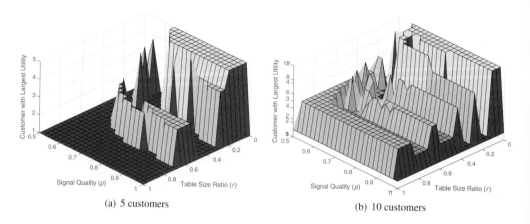

(a) 5 customers   (b) 10 customers

Figure 12.1 The effect of different table size ratios and signal qualities.

12.5.1   Advantage of Playing Positions vs. Signal Quality

First, how the signal quality and decision order influence customers' utility is studied. One table's size is fixed to be 100. Another table's size is $r \times 100$, in which r is the ratio of the table sizes. We assume the ratio $r \in [0, 1]$ in the simulations. If the ratio $r = 1$, two tables are the same as each other, but each table probably has different utilities, because we may have an odd number of customers. If $r = 0$, this means that there is a size of 0 for one table, indicating that a positive utility can be obtained only when the customer selects the table correctly.

In general, the effect of table size ratio and signal quality is nonlinear in the Chinese restaurant game because of the complicated game structure. As is shown in Figure 12.1(a), if the number of customers is 5, then customer 5 has the biggest utility when the table size ratio is low and the signal quality is high, and customer 1 has the biggest utility when the table size ratio is high and the signal quality is low. The explanation for these circumstances is as follows: when the table size ratio is lower, the larger table is desired by all of the customers, because even if all of them select the larger one, every one of them still has a larger utility than when selecting the smaller one. Under this situation, customers making later choices tend to have superiority for they have gathered more signals and are more likely to identify the large table. However, if the signal quality is low, the learned state cannot be strongly believed even by the last customer. Under this situation, each table's expected size becomes less important, and the decisions of customers depend more on the negative network externality effect (i.e., the degree of crowededness for each table). Under this circumstance, the first customer has the possibility of selecting the table with fewer expected customers.

However, it is observed that in some situations customer 3 is the one with the highest utility. The explanation for this is as follows: in these situations, customers' expected number at the larger table is 3, and at equilibrium, a larger utility is offered for customers by this table. Thus customers tend to identify this table and choose it on the basis of their own beliefs. Customer 3 identifies the correct table with higher probability as they gather more signals than customers 1 and 2. What is more, this table is always available to them as they are the third customer. Thus, in these cases, customer 3 has the biggest expected utility.

It should be noted that both the table size ratio and the signal quality determine the expected table size. In general, if the signal quality is low, the probability of a customer believing the true state strongly (i.e., both tables' expected table sizes are similar) is low. This indicates that a lower signal quality exerts similar influence on the expected table size as a higher table size ratio. The concentric-like structure exhibited in Figure 12.1(a) can support our arguments. For the 10-customer scheme that is shown in Figure 12.1(b), the same arguments hold. A similar concentric-like structure can be observed. What is more, it is observed that if the table size ratio goes up, the order of the customer who has the highest utility in the peaks goes down to 5 from 10. This conforms to the arguments because customers' equilibrium number at the large table goes down to 5 from 10 if the table size ratio goes up. This can also be considered the reason for why customer 1 does not have the highest utility when the table size ratio is high. Under this circumstance, customers' equilibrium number at the large table is 5, and at equilibrium, higher utilities are available to customers at the large table. Customer 5 knows the table size better than customers 1–4 because customer 5 is able to gather more signals than the previous customers. Furthermore, as customer 5 is the fifth one to choose a table, they always have the chance to choose the large table. Under this situation, when the table size ratio is high, customer 5 has the highest expected utility.

12.5.2 Price of Anarchy

The efficiency of the equilibrium grouping is now studied in a Chinese restaurant game by utilizing price of anarchy, which is a popular measurement in game theory of the degradation of system efficiency due to players' rational behaviors. Basically, in a game-theoretic system, the ratio of the social welfare under the worst equilibrium in the system to the one under the centralized-optimal solution is used to defined the price of anarchy. As a result, universal rational behaviors will not lead to efficiency loss in the system when the price of anarchy is close or the same as 1.

First, the social welfare function $W(\mathbf{B})$ in the Chinese restaurant game is defined as the sum of customers, expected utilities; that is, $W(\mathbf{B}) = \mathbb{E}[\sum_{i=1}^{N} U(R_{x_i}(\theta), n_{x_i})|\mathbf{B}]$, in which $\mathbf{B}$ represents customers' strategies applied in the Chinese restaurant game. Denote $\mathcal{B}^{\mathcal{E}}$ as the set of all equilibria in the Chinese restaurant game and $\mathcal{B}^{\mathcal{U}}$ as the general set of all possible strategies. We define the price of anarchy as

$$PoA = \frac{\max_{\mathbf{B} \in \mathcal{B}^{\mathcal{U}}} W(\mathbf{B})}{\min_{\mathbf{B}' \in \mathcal{B}^{\mathcal{E}}} W(\mathbf{B}')}. \tag{12.33}$$

A restaurant with five customers, two tables, and two states is simulated. Except for the utility function, all of the other settings are the same as those in Section 12.5.1.

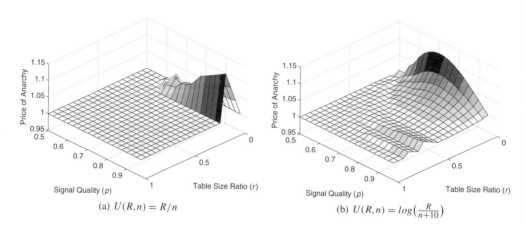

(a) $U(R,n) = R/n$ (b) $U(R,n) = log\left(\frac{R}{n+10}\right)$

Figure 12.2 Price of anarchy with different utility functions.

Two utility functions are applied in this simulation: $U(R,n) = R/N$ and $U(R,n) = log\left(\frac{R}{n+10}\right)$. The former stands for the situation in which the resource is equally shared, while the latter roughly stands for the signal-to-interference-plus-noise ratio throughput in wireless networks. Based on exhaustive search, the centralized-optimal solution is found. Figure 12.2 shows the prices of anarchy under all combinations of table size ratio and signal quality.

It can be seen from Figure 12.2(a) that if the utility function is R/n, the price of anarchy is equal to 1 under most combinations apart from that when the table size ratio is close to 0. Since the smaller table is so small that there are bigger utilities for all customers even if they share the larger table, the price of anarchy is larger than 1 at these points. Under this situation, customers will not choose the small table, and the resources offered by this table are lost because of the customers' rational behaviors. In the situation of the utility function being $U(R,n) = log\left(\frac{R}{n+10}\right)$, the price of anarchy never exceeds 1.06 (Figure 12.2(b)). The reason for this is that under this situation social welfare will be broadly increased by a proper balance in loadings on tables, and it is automatically implemented through customers' rational choices owing to their concerns regarding negative network externality. Thus, in general, in the Chinese restaurant game, rational behaviors do not impair the system efficiency much, and the equilibrium discovered by us is effective even in comparison with the centralized-optimal solution.

12.5.3   Case Study: Resource Pool and Availability Scenarios

Finally, two particular cases are discussed here: the resource pool case with $r = 0.4$ and available/unavailable cases with $r = 0$. In the resource pool case, the second table's size is 40. In order to realize the maximization of utilities, users act rationally and sequentially to select the two tables. In the available/unavailable case, the size of the second table is 0, indicating that only when a customer chooses the right table can they have positive utility. For both cases, the schemes are examined with $N = 3$ and $N = 5$.

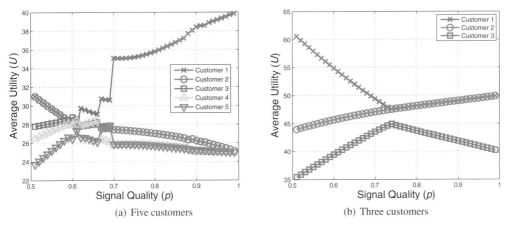

(a) Five customers

(b) Three customers

Signals	Best Response	
s_1, s_2, s_3	$p = 0.9$	$p = 0.6$
2,2,2	2,2,1	1,2,2
1,2,2	1,2,2	2,1,2
2,1,2	2,1,2	1,2,2
1,1,2	1,1,2	2,1,1
2,2,1	2,2,1	1,2,2
1,2,1	1,2,1	2,1,1
2,1,1	2,1,1	1,2,1
1,1,1	1,1,2	2,1,1

(c) Best response when $N = 3$

Figure 12.3 Average utility of customers in the resource pool scenario when $r = 0.4$.

It can be seen from Figure 12.3 that in the resource pool case with $r = 0.4$, customer 1 has significantly higher utility on average, which conforms to the results in Figure 12.1(a). Taking the scheme with five customers shown in Figure 12.3(a) as an example, the benefits of playing first are large if the signal quality is high ($p > 0.7$) or if it becomes too low ($p < 0.6$). It is also found that for most signal qualities p, customer 5 has the lowest average utility. A more distinct view on this can be seen in the scheme with three customers. In Figure 12.3(c), customers' best responses with the received signals are listed. It is observed that if signal quality p is large, both customers 1 and 2 choose tables on the basis of the signals they received. Nevertheless, when the same table is selected by the first two customers, customer 3 does not follows their signal, and will instead choose an empty table. Here customer 3 is likely to be aware of which table is larger, but they do not select the larger one if it has already been occupied by the first two customers. In this case, the learning advantage is dominated by the network externality effect.

However, customer 1's optimal response is the opposite if p is low (i.e., they would, according to the received signal, choose a smaller table). Although customer 1's optimal response seems to be irrational, such a strategy is actually the best response of customer 1 in view of the expected equilibrium in this case. Based on Theorem 12.7, when given perfect signals ($p = 1$), customers 1 and 2 ought to choose the large table as, at equilibrium, the large table's utility of $100/2 = 50$ is larger than the

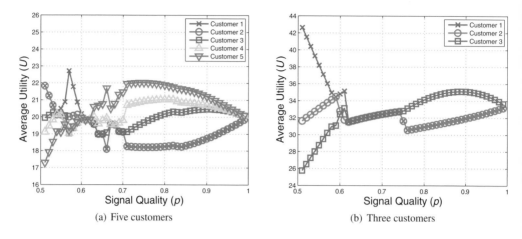

(a) Five customers   (b) Three customers

Signals	Best Response		
s_1, s_2, s_3	$p = 0.9$	$p = 0.7$	$p = 0.55$
2,2,2	2,2,2	2,2,2	1,2,2
1,2,2	1,2,2	1,2,2	2,1,2
2,1,2	2,1,2	2,1,2	1,2,2
1,1,2	1,1,1	1,1,2	2,1,1
2,2,1	2,2,2	2,2,1	1,2,2
1,2,1	1,2,1	1,2,1	2,1,1
2,1,1	2,1,1	2,1,1	1,2,1
1,1,1	1,1,1	1,1,1	2,1,1

(c) Best response when $N = 3$

Figure 12.4 Average utility of customers in the available/unavailable scenario when $r = 0$.

small table's utility of $40/1 = 40$. Nevertheless, customers choose the tables on the basis of the expected table sizes if imperfect signals are released. If signal quality is low, the table sizes' uncertainty is large, resulting in similar expected table sizes for both tables. Under this situation, compared with the choice of sharing with another customer at the larger table, the smaller table is preferred by customer 1 as it offers a higher expected utility.

As is indicated in Figure 12.4, in the available/unavailable case, the benefit of customer 1 playing first is less important. Taking the scheme with five customers shown in Figure 12.4(a) as an example, customer 1 has the smallest average utility and customer 5 has the largest one if signal quality p is larger than 0.6. The reason for this is that when $r = 0$ customers ought to spare every effort to identify the available table. In this case, the later customers acquire a significant advantage by learning from previous signals.

However, it is observed that selecting the table that is available with higher probability is not necessarily always the best response of later customers. Take the scheme with three customers as an illustrative example. In Figure 12.4(c), with the received signals, all customers' best responses are listed. If the signal quality is quire low ($p = 0.55$), the best response will be the same as that in the resource pool case, where the network externality effect is still important. Taking $(s_1, s_2, s_3) = (2, 2, 1)$ as an example, even though customer 3 notices that table 2 is available with higher probability, choosing table 1 is still their best response, because both customers 1 and 2 have chosen table 2, and the expected utility of choosing table 2 with two other customers is lower than that of choosing table 2 with only customer 3 themself. With signal quality p being high (e.g., $p = 0.9$), customer 3 would select the table on the basis of all signals s_1, s_2, s_3 that they have gathered, because now the belief derived from the signals is sufficiently strong to overcome the loss in the network externality effect.

12.6 Application: Cooperative Spectrum Access in Cognitive Radio Networks

In this section, a crucial application of the Chinese restaurant game is illustrated: cooperative spectrum access in cognitive radio networks. Identifying the available spectrum by spectrum sensing is at the core of traditional dynamic spectrum access methods. As a potential scheme, cooperative spectrum sensing can improve the efficiency and accuracy for detecting the available spectrum [20–22]. All members within the same or neighboring networks are able to know the sensing consequences from the secondary users in cooperative spectrum sensing. These secondary users then make spectrum access decisions individually or collaboratively by assessing the gathered results. If users' sensing results are independent, the cooperative spectrum sensing is able to improve the accuracy of detecting the activity of the primary user. Secondary users could improve insights into the primary user's activity by learning from others' sensing results. After the available spectrum is detected, secondary users should share the spectrum according to some predetermined access policy. Generally, if there are more secondary users accessing the same channel, the available access time is less for each of them (i.e., there is a negative network externality in this problem). Thus, before deciding on spectrum access, both the probable number of secondary users who access the same spectrum and the activity of a primary user should be estimated by a secondary user.

12.6.1 System Model

Suppose there are J channels, one primary user, and N secondary transmitter–receiver pairs in a cognitive radio system. It is assumed that an access point organizes the secondary users' spectrum access behavior through a control channel. The secondary users are able to synchronize their channel sensing and selection times through this organization. Assume that the primary user is often active and transmits a certain amount of data through one of the channels. What is more, we slot the access time of primary use. At each time slot, the probability of being chosen by the primary user for transmission is $1/J$, and the same is ture for each channel. Figure 12.5 shows the secondary users' activities. At the beginning of each time slot, secondary users, or transmitters, start to sense on all channels $1 \sim J$ individually. Next, they decide on which channel to access in this time slot sequentially according to a predefined order. Without loss of generality, it is assumed that the order for them is the same

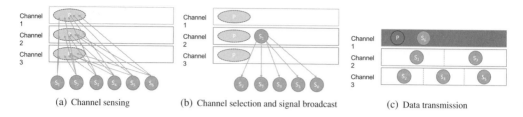

(a) Channel sensing   (b) Channel selection and signal broadcast   (c) Data transmission

Figure 12.5 Sequential cooperative spectrum sensing and accessing.

as their indices. Through a preallocated control channel, a secondary user i reports their sensing result and decision to the access point. Meanwhile, this report is received by all secondary users too through overhearing. After all secondary users have finished making decisions, the access policy of each channel is declared by the access point through the control channel; secondary users who choose the same channel share the slot time equally. However, for the case in which the primary users occupy the channel, secondary users' transmission would break down because of interference from the transmission of the primary user.

We can model this kind of cognitive radio system as a Chinese restaurant game. Denote H_j as the hypothesis that primary users occupy the channel j. Then denote the sensing results of secondary user $i \in \{1, 2, \ldots, N\}$ on channel $j \in \{1, 2, \ldots, J\}$ as $s_{i,j}$. A simple binary model is used on the sensing result in this example, in which $s_{i,j} = 1$ when some activities on channel j have been detected by the secondary user and $s_{i,j} = 0$ when no activity on channel j is detected. For secondary user i, we denote their own sensing results as $\mathbf{s_i} = (s_{i,1}, s_{i,2}, \ldots, s_{i,J})$. What is more, the results that they gathered from previous users' reports are represented as $\mathbf{h_i} = \{\mathbf{s_1}, \mathbf{s_2}, \ldots \mathbf{s_{i-1}}\}$.

A secondary user i's belief on the occupation of channels is defined as $\mathbf{g_i} = \{g_{i,1}, g_{i,2}, \ldots, g_{i,J}\}$, where $g_{i,j} = Pr(H_j | \mathbf{h_i}, \mathbf{s_i})$. Denote the probability of false alarm and miss detection of the sensing technique on a single channel as p_f and p_m, respectively. The probability of $\mathbf{s_i}$ conditioning on H_j is

$$Pr(\mathbf{s_i} | H_j) = p_m^{1-s_{i,j}} (1 - p_m)^{s_{i,j}} \prod_{k \in \{1, \ldots, J\} \setminus \{j\}} p_f^{s_{i,k}} (1 - p_f)^{1-s_{i,k}}. \qquad (12.34)$$

Therefore, the following belief updating rule is obtained:

$$g_{i,j} = \frac{g_{i-1,j} Pr(\mathbf{s_i} | H_j)}{\sum_{k=1}^{J} g_{i-1,k} Pr(\mathbf{s_i} | H_k)}. \qquad (12.35)$$

When the access point receives a new sensing result, secondary user i's belief is updated with this rule. Channel j's available access time within a slot is its slot time, which is represented as T. However, when the channel is occupied by the primary user, its access time turns to 0. Channel j's access time is consequently defined as

$$R_j(H_k) = \begin{cases} 0, & j = k. \\ T, & \text{otherwise.} \end{cases} \qquad (12.36)$$

Next, let x_i be the choice of secondary user i on the channels and n_j be the number of secondary users who choose channel j. We define secondary user i's utility as

$$u_i = U(x_i) = \frac{Q_{x_i} R_{x_i}(\theta)}{n_{x_i}}, \qquad (12.37)$$

where $\theta \in \{H_j\}$ is the hypothesis of this being true and Q_{x_i} is channel x_i's channel quality. It is assumed here that the secondary users are near to each other and similar channel conditions are shared by them, which are principally determined by the background noise and the external interference. The differences in channel gains are affected by time-dependent external interference or frequency. In the case of the channel having higher quality, higher data rates and higher utilities are received by the secondary users who choose the channel consequently. Then secondary user i's best response is as follows:

$$BE_i(\mathbf{n_i}, \mathbf{h_i}, \mathbf{s_i}) = \arg\max_x \sum_{k \in \{1,2,\dots,J\} \setminus \{x\}} g_{i,k} E\left[\frac{Q_x T}{n_x} | \mathbf{n_i}, \mathbf{h_i}, \mathbf{s_i}, H_k\right]. \qquad (12.38)$$

With the recursive equations in (12.26) and (12.30), we can solve this best response function recursively.

12.6.2 Simulation Results

A simulation of a cognitive radio network with one primary user, seven secondary transmitter–receiver pairs, and three channels is conducted. In one time slot, the secondary users' available access time is 100 ms if the primary user does not occupy the channel. At the beginning of the time slot, secondary users (i.e., transmitters), sense the activity of the primary user in all three channels. It is assumed that the probabilities of the primary user occupying one of three channels are the same. Conditional on the primary user's occupation of the channel, the probabilities of false alarm and miss detection when sensing one channel are 0.1. Channel 1's channel quality factor is $Q_1 = 1$, while channel 2's and Channel 3's are $1 - d$ and $1 - 2d$, respectively. The degraded factor is denoted as d, which is within $[5\%, 50\%]$ in the simulations.

The best response strategy in (12.30) is compared with the following four strategies: random, signal, learning, and myopic strategies. In the random strategy, strategies are chosen by customers randomly and uniformly (i.e., under the random strategy, the probability of being chosen is the same as $\frac{1}{J}$ for all J tables). In the signal strategy, customers makes decisions purely on the basis of their own signal. Other customers' information (including their choices on tables and the revealed signals) is neglected. The goal of the signal strategy is choosing the biggest expected table size conditional on their signal given by

$$x_i^{signal} = \arg\max_x \sum_{l \in \Theta} Pr(\theta = l | \mathbf{s_i}) Q_x R_x(l). \qquad (12.39)$$

As an extension of the signal strategy, we have the learning strategy. In this strategy, not only the customer's own signal but also the signals uncovered by the previous customers are utilized by the customer to learn about the system state. Thus the learning strategy can be denoted as

$$x_i^{learn} = \arg\max_x \sum_{l\in\Theta} g_{i,l} Q_x R_x(l), \tag{12.40}$$

where $g_{i,l} = Pr(\theta = l | \mathbf{h_i}, \mathbf{s_i}, \mathbf{g_0})$ is the belief of the customer regarding the state.

Finally, a myopic player's behavior is simulated by the myopic strategy. Under the myopic strategy, a customer's goal is to maximize their present utility; in other words, the customer decides based on their own signal, all uncovered signals, and the current grouping $\mathbf{n_i}$ as the follows:

$$x_i^{myopic} = \arg\max_x \sum_{l\in\Theta} g_{i,l} \frac{Q_x R_x(l)}{n_{i,x} + 1}. \tag{12.41}$$

It can be seen from (12.41) that the myopic strategy resembles the best response strategy apart from the Bayesian prediction of the decisions of subsequent customers. In the following applications, all four of these strategies' performances will be evaluated in all simulations. They could be viewed as the baseline of the system performance without customers showing fully rational behaviors.

Figure 12.6 shows the simulation results. From Figure 12.6(a), (b), and (d), it can be seen that under different orders and schemes secondary users have different utilities. For both the best response and the myopic schemes, when the degraded factor is low, the utility of secondary user 3 is larger than that of secondary user 1. The reason for this is that in terms of identifying the occupied channel, secondary user 3 is better than secondary user 1 at gathering more signals. What is more, the loadings of the other two channels are far from their expected equilibrium loadings at this point, because only two secondary users have made choices. Thus, secondary user 3 has a larger utility than secondary user 1. However, it can be seen that when there is a high degraded factor, secondary user 1 has a larger utility than secondary user 3. The reason for this is that if the degraded factor goes up, the quality difference among channels goes up as well. Under this situation, although the occupied channel is successfully identified by secondary user 3, the expected number of secondary users who access this channel is two or even one, and secondary user 3 cannot select those channels with freedom. For secondary user 7, as six secondary users have made decisions beforehand, they usually have no choice, so their utility is the smallest.

In general, for secondary users who make decisions early (e.g., secondary user 1), the myopic scheme offers the same or lower utility than the best response scheme, because secondary users in the myopic scheme do not predict subsequent users' decisions. Nevertheless, some benefits from the early mistakes of secondary users will be obtained by later secondary users eventually. From Figure 12.6(b) and (c), it can be seen that for some cases, because of customer 1's and/or customer 2's mistakes, there will be a higher utility for customers 3 and 4 under the myopic scheme than under the best response scheme. From Figure 12.6(e), it can also be seen that both the myopic scheme and the best response scheme offer the same average utility for all secondary users. Under this circumstance, some secondary users' loss of utility under

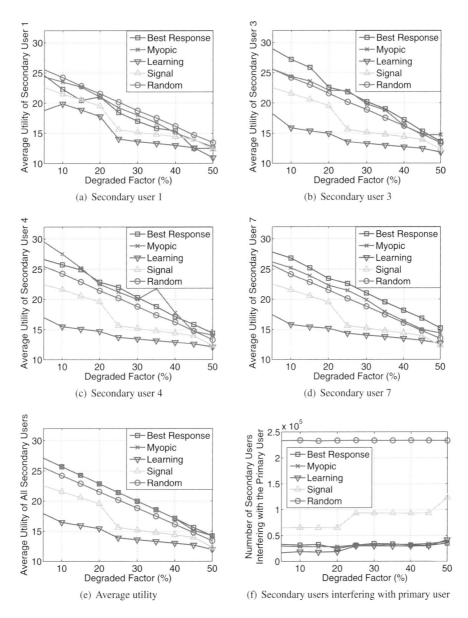

Figure 12.6 Spectrum accessing in a cognitive radio network under different schemes.

the myopic scheme would result in increasing some other secondary users' utilities. In the random and signal schemes, differences do not exist among the average utilities of secondary users 1, 3, and 7, because under these two schemes secondary users do not learn from other agents' signals and actions. In the learning scheme, it can be seen that the utility of secondary user 1 is much larger than those of secondary users 3 and 7. The reason for this is that when deciding on the channel selection, the negative network externality is not taken into account by secondary users in the learning scheme. As secondary users making later decisions identify the activity of the primary user with higher probability, it is more possible for them to select the same channels, and their utilities are degraded because of the negative network externality.

Let us take a deeper look at all secondary users' average utilities shown in Figure 12.6(e). It can be seen that all secondary users have the highest average utility in both the myopic and best response schemes. Strategic secondary users are forced by the network externality effects in spectrum access to access different channels rather than accessing the same high-quality channels. In addition, learning and signal schemes result in low average utilities because the network externality is not considered in these two schemes in the process of decision-making. All secondary users are inclined to access the same available high-quality channel, and thus the spectrum resources in other available channels are wasted. This is also the reason for why the learning scheme resulted in worse performance than the signal scheme. In the learning scheme, it is more possible for secondary users to reach a consensus on the activity of the primary user and choose channels in the same way, which impairs the overall system performance.

Finally, in Figure 12.6(f), the number of secondary users who cause interference to the primary user is shown. It can be seen that the interference to the primary user of those schemes involving learning, which are the best response, learning, and myopic schemes, is low. The channel occupied by the primary user is efficiently avoided through secondary users learning from the signals of others.

12.7   Conclusion

In this chapter, a new game–the Chinese restaurant game–is introduced by coupling the nonstrategic machine learning technique with strategic game-theoretic analysis. A new general framework can be offered by the Chinese restaurant game for the analysis of strategic learning and for predicting the behaviors of rational agents in a social network with negative network externality. Through analyzing the game, each agent's best strategy is derived and a recursive method to realize the equilibrium is offered. The trade-off between two contradictory advantages is discussed using simulations: making decisions earlier to choose better tables and making decisions later to obtain more accurate beliefs. It is discovered that the expected utilities of customers with different decision orders are determined by both the table size ratio and the signal quality of the unknown system state. In general, the benefit from learning is dominated by the advantage of playing first if the table size ratio is high and the signal quality is low. By contrast, the advantage of playing later in order to better learn the true state improves the later agents' expected utilities if the table size ratio is low and the signal quality is high. It can also be seen from the simulations that in the Chinese restaurant game, the price of anarchy is close to 1, indicating that the efficiency loss because of customers' rational behaviors is close to 0. The small price of anarchy is realized by the loading balance among tables, which is automatically achieved in the Chinese restaurant game. Finally, the cooperative spectrum access problem in cognitive radio networks, which is a specific application of the Chinese restaurant game, is illustrated in wireless networking. It is shown that global channel utilization can be enhanced through considering the negative network externality in the decision processes of secondary users. In addition, secondary users' interference with the primary user can be decreased by learning from others' sensing results.

References

[1] V. Bala and S. Goyal, "Learning from neighbours," *Review of Economic Studies*, vol. 65, p. 595, 1998.

[2] D. Acemoglu, M. Dahleh, I. Lobel, and A. Ozdaglar, "Bayesian learning in social networks." *Review of Economic Studies*, January 2011.

[3] D. Acemoglu and A. Ozdaglar, "Opinion dynamics and learning in social networks." *Dynamic Games and Applications*, vol. 1, pp. 3–49, 2011.

[4] R. Cooper, *Coordination Games: Complementarities and Macroeconomics*. Cambridge University Press, 1999.

[5] J. Wit, "Social learning in a common interest voting game," *Games and Economic Behavior*, vol. 26, pp. 131–156, 1999.

[6] M. Battaglini, "Sequential voting with abstention." *Games and Economic Behavior*, vol. 51, pp. 445–463, 2005.

[7] S. N. Ali and N. Kartik, "Observational learning with collective preferences." Manuscript, Columbia University, 2010.

[8] D. Gale, "Dynamic coordination games," *Economic Theory*, vol. 5, pp. 1–18, 1995.

[9] A. Dasgupta, "Social learning with payoff complementarities." Econometric Society World Congress 2000 Contributed Paper 0322, Econometric Society.

[10] A. Dasgupta, "Coordination and delay in global games," *Journal of Economic Theory*, vol. 134, pp. 195–225, 2007.

[11] S. Choi, D. Gale, S. Kariv, and T. Palfrey, "Network architecture, salience and coordination", *Games and Economic Behavior*, vol. 73, pp. 76–90, 2011.

[12] M. Katz and C. Shapiro, "Technology adoption in the presence of network externalities," *Journal of Political Economy*, vol. 94, pp. 822–841, 1986.

[13] W. Sandholm, "Negative externalities and evolutionary implementation," *Review of Economic Studies*, vol. 72, pp. 885–915, 2005.

[14] G. Fagiolo, "Endogenous neighborhood formation in a local coordination model with negative network externalities," *Journal of Economic Dynamics and Control*, vol. 29, pp. 297–319, 2005.

[15] S.-J. Kim and G. Giannakis, "Optimal resource allocation for MIMO ad hoc cognitive radio networks," *IEEE Transactions on Information Theory*, vol. 57, pp. 3117–3131, 2011.

[16] T. Mitchell. *Machine learning*. McGraw-Hill, 1997.

[17] D. Aldous, I. Ibragimov, J. Jacod, and D. Aldous, "Exchangeability and related topics," in *Lecture Notes in Mathematics*, vol. 1117, pp. 1–198. Springer Berlin/Heidelberg, 1985.

[18] J. Pitman, "Exchangeable and partially exchangeable random partitions," *Probability Theory and Related Fields*, vol. 102, pp. 145–158, 1995.

[19] B. Golub and M. O. Jackson, "Naive learning in social networks: convergence, influence, and the wisdom of crowds," https://web.stanford.edu/~jacksonm/naivelearning.pdf

[20] S. Mishra, A. Sahai, and R. Brodersen. "Cooperative sensing among cognitive radios," in *IEEE International Conference on Communications*, 2006.

[21] B. Wang, K. J. R. Liu, and T. C. Clancy, "Evolutionary cooperative spectrum sensing game: How to collaborate?" *IEEE Transactions on Communications*, vol. 58, pp. 890–900, 2010.

[22] K. J. R. Liu and B. Wang. *Cognitive Radio Networking and Security: A Game-Theoretic View*. Cambridge University Press, 2010.

13 Dynamic Chinese Restaurant Game

Sequential Decision-Making in Dynamic Systems

In a social network, users always perform decision-making in an uncertain network state. There are plenty of works in the field of social learning that discuss how to construct beliefs in an uncertain network state, but there are few studies on combining learning with decision-making in the case of users being uncertain about the network state where their decisions are subject to a certain interplay. What is more, in a social network, the population often turns out to be dynamic, for users may enter and depart from the network at any time, bringing more variability to the problem. In this chapter, a dynamic Chinese restaurant game is introduced to investigate how a user in a dynamic social network learns about the uncertain network state and makes optimal decisions through considering the immediate utility on the one hand and subsequent users' negative influences on the other hand. A Bayesian learning- based method is introduced so that users are able to acquire knowledge regarding the network state, and a multidimensional Markov decision process (MDP)-based method for users to make the best decisions is discussed. Finally, the dynamic Chinese restaurant game is applied to cognitive radio networks, and simulations show that the scheme is both effective and efficient.

13.1 Introduction

When making decisions [1], users in a social network [2] usually have no precise information about the network state. For instance, users are inclined to be uncertain about the exact reliability and effectiveness of each service provider when they choose a cloud storage service. In addition, users must take into account the decisions made by subsequent customers, because users overwhelmingly using the same storage service inevitably increase waiting times and blocking rates. This kind of phenomenon is usually referred to as negative network externality [3] (i.e., the negative effects of other users' behaviors on a user's reward). Because of this, users are inclined to shun identical decisions to those of others for the sake of their own interests. For example, in the selection of a deal on the Groupon website or the choice of a Wi-Fi access point in a conference hall similar problems will arise. Thus, the ways in which users in a social network acquire knowledge of the network state and make the best decisions through the prediction of the effects of others' possible decisions represent research topic of vital significance in social networking.

Despite the fact that in a social network users are not fully aware of the network state, they are in a position to glean some information from certain external information sources (e.g., the experiences of other users) to form a belief that is mostly probabilistic regarding the uncertain network state. In to the social learning literature [4–9], how a user forms accurate beliefs by using various learning rules has been investigated. However, the concept of network externality has not been taken into account in these traditional social learning works (i.e., there is a prevalent assumption that a user's reward is independent of subsequent users' actions). Under this situation, a user's decision-making is exclusively on the basis of their beliefs without considering the decisions made by other users. As mentioned previously, in social networking, the negative network externality is a common phenomenon that can greatly affect users' rewards and decisions. When integrating the negative network externality into social learning, it is inevitable that the decision-making of users should have something to do with game-theoretic analysis, which explains the interplay among the decisions made by different users [10].

In Chapter 12, a new game – the Chinese restaurant game – was introduced to determine a possible way to integrate strategic decision-making with social learning in terms of social networking problems with negative network externality. This game concept is derived from the Chinese restaurant process [11], which is applied to non-parameter learning approaches in machine learning to give shape to the parameters for the simulation of unknown distributions. There are finite tables of diverse size in the Chinese restaurant game and a limited number of customers are choosing tables for a meal in a sequential manner. On the grounds that customers have no idea of the exact size of each table, it is necessary for them to learn these sizes on the basis of some external information. When requesting a table, each customer should consider the subsequent customers' decisions because of the limited dining space at each table (i.e., the negative network externality). Based on the investigation of such a Chinese restaurant game model, a new general framework was provided to analyze the strategic learning and to predict the behaviors of rational users in a social network. In addition discussions were carried out on the applications of the Chinese restaurant game in different research avenues.

In the Chinese restaurant game, one assumption is the fixed population setting (i.e., there are finite customers who choose the tables sequentially) [12,13]. However, in many practical scenarios, the setting often has a dynamic population, since customers may come and leave at any time. Under this situation, customers' utilities will vary from time to time because of the dynamic number of customers at each table. In the light of such problems, in this chapter, the Chinese restaurant game is extended to the dynamic population setting, in which the scenario of customers arriving at and departing from the restaurant is considered as a random process. Under this situation, it is possible for each new customer to acquire knowledge of the system state on the basis of the information received and uncovered by previous customers and to make predictions about the decisions of subsequent customers during their stay to maximize their utility. The Chinese restaurant game framework becomes more universal and feasible with this dynamic model.

The dynamic Chinese restaurant game is applicable to a wide range of fields (e.g., storage service selection in cloud computing, deal selection on the Groupon website in online social networking, and Wi-Fi access point selection in wireless networking) in line with the initial discussion. Its application to cognitive radio networks [14] is the focus of this chapter. Recently, it has been shown that dynamic spectrum access in cognitive radio networks may contribute to greater efficiency of spectrum utilization, where cognitive devices, namely secondary users (SUs), are able to access the licensed spectrum in a dynamic manner, provided there is minimal interference to the primary user (PU) [15]. For dynamic spectrum access, SUs are required to perform spectrum sensing to acquire knowledge of the state of the primary channel and share the available primary channel with other SUs. The throughput acquired by each individual SU decrease with increasing numbers of SUs accessing the identical channel (i.e., negative network externality is revealed in this case). Thus, for the dynamic spectrum access problems, the dynamic Chinese restaurant game is an effective tool to investigate how SUs acquire knowledge of the state of primary channels and of the ways in which they access the primary channels based on the prediction of the effects of subsequent SUs' decisions.

13.2 System Model

The dynamic Chinese restaurant game will be introduced in this section. Specifically, how customers learn the restaurant state is first discussed using the Bayesian learning rule, and then how customers choose a table on the basis of the learning result is investigated so as to maximize their own expected utility during their stay in the restaurant.

Consider a Chinese restaurant with N independent tables numbered $1, 2, \ldots, N$, and each table has a limited number of L seats to serve finite customers. In the model, all of the tables have the same size, which means that these tables have the same number of seats. It is assumed that the customers arrive and leave in a Bernoulli process [16], where a customer arrives with probability λ or a customer leaves with probability μ in each time slot. It can be seen from Figure 13.1 that when arriving at the restaurant each customer chooses one table for their meal. As long as a customer

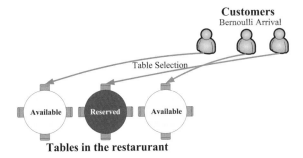

Figure 13.1 System model of the dynamic Chinese restaurant game.

selects a certain table, they will stay there until they finish their meal. What is more, the tables may be reserved beforehand so that they cannot be chosen by new customers until the reservation becomes invalid. In this case, the restaurant state is denoted as $\theta = (\theta_1, \theta_2, \ldots, \theta_N)$ (all of the subscripts refer to table number index in this chapter), where $\theta_i \in \{\mathcal{H}_0, \mathcal{H}_1\}$ represents the state of table i and, $\mathcal{H}_0$ indicates that the table is available while $\mathcal{H}_1$ means that the table is already reserved. It should be noticed that the state of each table θ_i varies along with time, because the table can be reserved at any time and the reservation can also be canceled at all hours.

The dynamic Chinese restaurant game aims to formulate the problem of how a new customer chooses a table. Each customer's action set is $\mathcal{A} = \{1, 2, \ldots, N\}$ (i.e., choosing one table from all N tables). It should be noted that in this chapter only pure strategies are considered. Let us define the grouping state when the jth customer arrives, $G^j = (g_1^j, g_2^j, \ldots, g_N^j)$ (all of the superscripts refer to the customer index in this chapter), where $g_i^j \in \{0, 1, \ldots, L\}$ represents the number of customers at table i. Suppose that the jth customer chooses table i. Their utility function can be given by $U(\theta_i^j, g_i^j)$, where θ_i^j stands for the state of table i and g_i^j represents the number of customers who choose table i during the jth customer's mealtime at table i. It should be noted that the utility function is a decreasing function in terms of g_i^j, which is reflective of negative network externality, because the utility of the jth customer is going to decrease with increasing numbers of subsequent customers joining table i.

As mentioned above, the restaurant state θ varies with time. The jth customer may be unaware of the real reservation information of each table θ_i^j. However, some external information (e.g., advertisements and reviews), can help customers estimate the reservation information. Thus, it is assumed that the customers may have an initial prior distribution of the state θ_i for each table, which is represented as $b^0 = \{b_i^0 | b_i^0 = \Pr(\theta_i = \mathcal{H}_0), \forall i \in 1, 2, \ldots, N\}$. What is more, every customer can receive a signal $s^j = \{s_i^j, \forall i \in 1, 2, \ldots, N\}$ derived from a predefined distribution $f(s_i | \theta_i)$. Such signals can be considered as the observation (estimation) of the restaurant state by customers. Table 13.1 shows all of the notations.

13.2.1   Bayesian Learning for the Restaurant State

In this section, we discuss the ways in which customers estimate the restaurant state based on some external information. On the grounds that the restaurant state θ varies with time, customers must learn each θ_i before choosing tables in order to shun the reserved ones. As mentioned above, every customer receives a signal related to the state of the restaurant. Customers also receive former customers' remarks on the restaurant (i.e., the beliefs of previous customers). With the collected information, a Bayesian learning model can be adopted to update the beliefs on the restaurant's current state.

First, the concept of belief is introduced to denote customers' uncertainty about the state of the tables. The belief b_i^j represents the jth customer's belief on the state of table i. It is supposed that every customer reveals their beliefs after choosing tables. The restaurant state θ is different from the previous static Chinese restaurant game

Table 13.1. Notations.

Notation	Meanings
N	Number of tables
L	Number of seats at each table
M	Number of quantized belief levels
λ	Customers' arrival rate
μ	Customers' leaving rate
θ_i	State of availability at table i
g_i	Number of customers at table i
b_i	Customers' continuous belief on the state of table i
B_i	Customers' quantized belief on the state of table i
$\hat{b}_i$	Customers' mapping belief on the state of table i
s_i	Signal received by customers at table i
V_i	The ith customer's expected utility
π	Customers' strategy profile
r_0	Average length of channel's OFF state
r_1	Average length of channel's ON state

model where signals instead of beliefs are revealed because the restaurant state θ varies with time in this dynamic model. Under this situation, for customer j, signals $s^{j-2}, s^{j-3}, \ldots$ become increasingly useless for them to form their belief. Furthermore, belief b^{j-1} comprises more information than signal s^{j-1}, which may facilitate the calculation of the subsequent customers' beliefs. Thus every customer's belief about table i is the result of the study of previous customer's belief b_i^{j-1}, their own signal s_i^j, and the conditional distribution $f(s_i|\theta_i)$, which can be defined as

$$b^j = \{ b_i^j | b_i^j = \Pr(\theta_i^j = \mathcal{H}_0 | b_i^{j-1}, s_i^j, f), \forall i \in 1, 2, \ldots, N \}. \tag{13.1}$$

It can be seen from the above definition that the belief $b_i^j \in [0, 1]$ is a continuous parameter. In a practical system, a customer can never reveal their continuous belief using infinite data bits. Thus the continuous belief is quantized into M belief levels $\{\mathbb{B}_1, \mathbb{B}_2, \ldots, \mathbb{B}_M\}$, which indicates that if we have $b_i^j \in \left[\frac{k-1}{M}, \frac{k}{M}\right]$, then $B_i^j = \mathbb{B}_k$. On the grounds that each customer can only reveal and receive quantized belief, the previous customer's quantized belief B^{j-1} is first shaped into a belief $\hat{b}^{j-1}$ in accordance with the rule that if $B_i^{j-1} = \mathbb{B}_k$ then $\hat{b}_i^{j-1} = \frac{1}{2}\left(\frac{k-1}{M} + \frac{k}{M}\right)$. It should be noted that here the mapping belief $\hat{b}_i^{j-1}$ is not the previous customer's true continuous belief b_i^{j-1}. Next, $\hat{b}^{j-1}$ is coupled with the signal s^j to calculate the continuous belief b^j. Finally, b^j is quantized into the belief B^j. Therefore, the learning process for the jth customer can be concluded as $B^{j-1} \xrightarrow{\text{Mapping}} \hat{b}^{j-1} \xrightarrow{s^j} b^j \xrightarrow{\text{Quantize}} B^j$.

The most important step in the learning process is how to calculate current belief b^j based on current signal s^j and the previous customer's belief $\hat{b}^{j-1}$, which is a classical social learning problem. Social learning, on the basis of the approaches to belief formation, can be categorized as Bayesian learning [5] and non-Bayesian

learning [7]. Bayesian learning indicates that rational individuals adopt Bayes' rule
to best estimate the unknown parameters (e.g., the restaurant state in the model),
whereas non-Bayesian learning asks individuals to obey a number of predefined rules
for updating their beliefs, which unavoidably imposes a restriction on the optimal
decision-making of rational customers. Due to the fact that customers in the dynamic
Chinese restaurant game are supposed to be fully rational, they will update their
beliefs on the restaurant state $b^j = \{b_i^j\}$ using the Bayesian learning rule as

$$b_i^j = \frac{\Pr(\theta_i^j = \mathcal{H}_0|\hat{b}_i^{j-1})f(s_i^j|\theta_i^j = \mathcal{H}_0)}{\sum_{l=0}^{1}\Pr(\theta_i^j = \mathcal{H}_l|\hat{b}_i^{j-1})f(s_i^j|\theta_i^j = \mathcal{H}_l)}, \tag{13.2}$$

where $\Pr(..|\hat{b}_i^{j-1})$ represents the probability given the belief of the $(j-1)$th customer.
For instance, $\Pr(\theta_i^j = \mathcal{H}_0|\hat{b}_i^{j-1})$ represents, given the $(j-1)$th customer's belief (i.e.,
$\Pr(\theta_i^{j-1} = \mathcal{H}_0) = \hat{b}_i^{j-1}$), what the probability $\Pr(\theta_i^j = \mathcal{H}_0)$ is. It should be noted that
(13.2) is based on the fact that the exact state θ_i^j is available and, the signal observed
by current customer s_i^j is independent of the previous customer's belief $\hat{b}_i^{j-i}$.

According to the discussion of the system model, each table's state varies with
time. In this case, the state transition probability is defined as $\Pr(\theta_i^j = \mathcal{H}_0|\theta_i^{j-1} = \mathcal{H}_0)$, which stands for the probability that table i is available at present when the
jth customer arrives provided that table i was available when the $(j-1)$th customer
arrived. In a similar way, we have $\Pr(\theta_i^j = \mathcal{H}_1|\theta_i^{j-1} = \mathcal{H}_0)$, $\Pr(\theta_i^j = \mathcal{H}_0|\theta_i^{j-1} = \mathcal{H}_1)$, and $\Pr(\theta_i^j = \mathcal{H}_1|\theta_i^{j-1} = \mathcal{H}_1)$. Under this situation, a customer can calculate the
items $\Pr(\theta_i^j = \mathcal{H}_0|\hat{b}_i^{j-1})$ and $\Pr(\theta_i^j = \mathcal{H}_1|\hat{b}_i^{j-1})$ in (13.2) using (13.3) and (13.4)

$$\Pr(\theta_i^j = \mathcal{H}_0|\hat{b}_i^{j-1}) = \Pr(\theta_i^j = \mathcal{H}_0|\theta_i^{j-1} = \mathcal{H}_0)\hat{b}_i^{j-1}$$
$$+ \Pr(\theta_i^j = \mathcal{H}_0|\theta_i^{j-1} = \mathcal{H}_1)(1 - \hat{b}_i^{j-1}), \tag{13.3}$$

$$\Pr(\theta_i^j = \mathcal{H}_1|\hat{b}_i^{j-1}) = \Pr(\theta_i^j = \mathcal{H}_1|\theta_i^{j-1} = \mathcal{H}_0)\hat{b}_i^{j-1}$$
$$+ \Pr(\theta_i^j = \mathcal{H}_1|\theta_i^{j-1} = \mathcal{H}_1)(1 - \hat{b}_i^{j-1}). \tag{13.4}$$

where the four state transition probabilities are considered as prior information for
customers.

To sum up, for the jth customer, the belief updating process for table i is
$B_i^{j-1} \xrightarrow{\text{Mapping}} \hat{b}_i^{j-1} \xrightarrow{\text{Bayesian}+s_i^j} b_i^j \xrightarrow{\text{Quantize}} B_i^j$, where the Bayesian learning from
$\hat{b}_i^{j-1}$ and s_i^j to b_i^j is (13.5)

$$b_i^j = \frac{\left(\Pr(\theta_i^j = \mathcal{H}_0|\theta_i^{j-1} = \mathcal{H}_0)\hat{b}_i^{j-1} + \Pr(\theta_i^j = \mathcal{H}_0|\theta_i^{j-1} = \mathcal{H}_1)(1 - \hat{b}_i^{j-1})\right)f(s_i^j|\theta_i^j = \mathcal{H}_0)}{\sum_{l=0}^{1}\left(\Pr(\theta_i^j = \mathcal{H}_l|\theta_i^{j-1} = \mathcal{H}_0)\hat{b}_i^{j-1} + \Pr(\theta_i^j = \mathcal{H}_l|\theta_i^{j-1} = \mathcal{H}_1)(1 - \hat{b}_i^{j-1})\right)f(s_i^j|\theta_i^j = \mathcal{H}_l)}. \tag{13.5}$$

13.3   Multidimensional MDP-based Table Selection

In this section, the table selection game is studied by modeling it as a MDP problem [17]. In this game, each customer chooses a table when they are aware of the restaurant's state, with the purpose of maximizing their own expected utility during the mealtime. In order to realize this purpose, rational customers should not only take the immediate utility into account, but also predict the choices of the subsequent customers. In the model, customers arrive by a Bernoulli process and choose their table in a sequential manner. During the decision-making process, one customer only gets to know the current grouping information G^j and belief information B^j. To consider customers' expected utility in the future, the Bellman equation is adopted to formulate a customer's utility and an MDP model is used to formulate this table selection problem. In the traditional MDP problem, if the system state varies, a player is able to adjust their decision. However, in this system, a customer cannot change their mind they have has made their decision, even if the system state has already changed. Thus the traditional MDP is not straightforwardly applicable to this case. Under such circumstances, a multidimensional MDP (M-MDP) model and a modified value iteration method are discussed to derive the best response (strategy) for every customer.

System State

First, the system state is defined and the Markov property of the state transition is substantiated to construct the MDP model. Let the quantized belief $B = (B_1, B_2, \ldots, B_N) \in \{1, 2, \ldots, M\}^N$ be the belief state. Therefore, the system state S can be defined as the belief state B with the grouping state $G = (g_1, g_2, \ldots, g_N) \in \{0, 1, \ldots, L\}^N$ (i.e., $S = (B, G)$, where the finite state space is $\mathcal{X} = (\{1, 2, \ldots, M\}^N \times \{0, 1, \ldots, L\}^N)$). It should be noted that the system state is defined at each time slot. The system that the jth customer encounters is $S^j = (B^j, G^j)$ when they reach the restaurant. Under this situation, with multiple customers arriving in a sequential manner, the system states at various arrival times $\{S^1, S^2, \ldots, S^j, \ldots\}$ form a stochastic process. According to the learning rule, only the $(j-1)$th customer's belief is adopted to update the jth customer's belief. Thus, B^j only relies on B^{j-1}. What is more, the grouping state G^j is also memoryless for customers arrive by a Bernoulli process. In such a case, it can be substantiated that $\{S^1, S^2, \ldots, S^j, \ldots\}$ is a Markov process.

Belief State Transitions

It should be noted that a customer's belief state transition has nothing to do with their action, and it is only associated with the state of the tables and the Bayesian learning rule. Here the belief state transition probability is defined as $P(B^j | B^{j-1})$. On the grounds that all tables are independent of each other, we have

$$P(B^j | B^{j-1}) = \prod_{i=1}^{N} P(B_i^j | B_i^{j-1}), \tag{13.6}$$

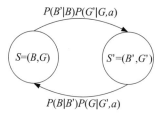

Figure 13.2 Illustration of state transition.

where $P(B_i^j|B_i^{j-1})$ is the belief state transition probability for table i. Under this situation, there exists an $M \times M$ belief state transition matrix for each table, which can be derived on the basis of the Bayesian learning rule. To find $P(B_i^j = \mathbb{B}_q|B_i^{j-1} = \mathbb{B}_p)$, with the quantized belief $B_i^{j-1} = \mathbb{B}_p$, the corresponding mapping belief $\hat{b}_i^{j-1} = \frac{1}{2}\left(\frac{p-1}{M} + \frac{p}{M}\right)$ can be calculated. Then, with $B_i^j = \mathbb{B}_q$, the value interval of $b_i^j = \left[\frac{q-1}{M}, \frac{q}{M}\right]$ can be obtained. Therefore, the belief state transition probability can be calculated as

$$P(B_i^j = \mathbb{B}_q|B_i^{j-1} = \mathbb{B}_p) = \int_{\frac{q-1}{M}}^{\frac{q}{M}} P(b_i^j|\hat{b}_i^{j-1})db_i^j, \tag{13.7}$$

where $P(b_i^j|\hat{b}_i^{j-1})$ can be computed by (13.5).

Actions and System State Transitions

The finite action set for customers is the N table set (i.e., $\mathcal{A} = \{1, 2, \ldots, N\}$). Let $a \in \mathcal{A}$ represent a new customer's action under the system state $S = (\boldsymbol{B}, \boldsymbol{G})$. Let $P(S' = (\boldsymbol{B}', \boldsymbol{G}')|S = (\boldsymbol{B}, \boldsymbol{G}), a)$ stand for the probability that action a in state S will result in state S'. It can be seen from Figure 13.2 that due to the fact that a customer's belief transition is independent on of their action, we have

$$P(S' = (\boldsymbol{B}', \boldsymbol{G}')|S = (\boldsymbol{B}, \boldsymbol{G}), a) = P(\boldsymbol{B}'|\boldsymbol{B})P(\boldsymbol{G}'|\boldsymbol{G}, a), \tag{13.8}$$

where $P(\boldsymbol{G}'|\boldsymbol{G}, a)$ is the system grouping state transition probability. Suppose that the current grouping state is $\boldsymbol{G} = (g_1, g_2, \ldots, g_N)$. On the grounds that a new customer arrives with probability λ, provided that the action of the arriving customer is table i (i.e., $a = i$), we have the arriving transition probabilities in (13.9) and (13.10).

$$P(\boldsymbol{G}' = (g_1, g_2, \ldots, g_i + 1, \ldots, g_N)|\boldsymbol{G} = (g_1, g_2, \ldots, g_i, \ldots, g_N), a = i) = \lambda, \tag{13.9}$$

$$P(\boldsymbol{G}' = (g_1, g_2, \ldots, g_j + 1, \ldots, g_N)|\boldsymbol{G} = (g_1, g_2, \ldots, g_i, \ldots, g_N), a = i) = 0,$$
$$(\forall j \neq i). \tag{13.10}$$

When no customer arrives and some customers leave the restaurant at state G, we have the leaving transition probability in (13.11)

$$P(G' = (g_1, g_2, \ldots, g_i - 1, \ldots, g_N) | G = (g_1, g_2, \ldots, g_i, \ldots, g_N)) = g_i \mu,$$

$$(\forall i \in \{1, 2, \ldots, N\}),$$ (13.11)

where μ is the probability of customers leaving, λ and μ are normalized such that $\lambda + NL\mu \le 1$ since $g_i \le L$ and $\lambda + \sum_{i=1}^{N} g_i \mu \le \lambda + NL\mu \le 1$ according to (13.12).

$$P(G' = G | G = (g_1, g_2, \ldots, g_i, \ldots, g_N)) = 1 - \lambda - \sum_{i=1}^{N} g_i \mu.$$ (13.12)

Under this situation, the system state transition probabilities $P(S'|S)$ form an $(M(L+1))^N \times (M(L+1))^N$ state transition matrix when given action a. It should be noted that (13.9)–(13.12) are based on of the assumption that the system time is discretized into small time slots and customers arrive and leave by a Bernoulli process. A single user arrives with probability λ or a single user leaves with probability μ during each time slot. There are no multiple customers who leave the same or different tables. This model is also known as a "sampled-time approximation to a Markov process" as in [16]. The state transition from one time slot to the next can only be increasing by one customer, decreasing by one customer, or remaining constant under this model.

Expected Utility

A customer's immediate utility at table i in system state S is

$$U_i(S) = \hat{b}_i \cdot R_i(g_i),$$ (13.13)

where $\hat{b}_i$ is the mapping belief of B_i and R_i is a decreasing function with respect to the number of customers at table i, g_i. Generally, customers will stay at their chosen tables for some time, and during this period the system state it likely to vary. Thus a customer should consider both the immediate and the future utilities when choosing a table. In the MDP model [17], the Bellman equation is defined as a user's long-term expected payoff with the form

$$V(S_0, a_0) = \max_{\{a_t\}_{t=0}^{\infty}} U(S_0, a_0) + \sum_{t=1}^{\infty} \beta^t U(S_t, a_t),$$ (13.14)

where the first term is the immediate utility of current state S_0, the second term is the expected utilities of the future states starting from the initial state S_0, and β^t is a discount factor series that guarantees that the summation is bounded. The Bellman equation is often written in a recursive form as the follows:

$$V(S) = \max_{a_S} U(S, a_S) + \beta \sum_{S' \in \mathcal{X}} P(S'|S, a_S) V(S'),$$ (13.15)

where S' stands for all possible next states of S and $P(S'|S)$ is the probability of transition. It can be seen from the definition of the Bellman equation that it takes both the immediate and the future utilities into account, which strongly tallies with the customers' expected utility in the Chinese restaurant game. Thus, based on the Bellman equation, a customer's expected utility at table i, $V_i(S)$, can be defined by

$$V_i(S) = U_i(S) + (1 - \mu) \sum_{S' \in \mathcal{X}} P_i(S'|S)V_i(S'), \qquad (13.16)$$

where $(1 - \mu)$ is the discount factor that can be considered as the probability that the customer only stays at the chosen table since μ is the probability of leaving. $P_i(S'|S)$ is the state transition probability defined as

$$P_i(S' = (B', G')|S = (B, G)) = P(B'|B)P_i(G'|G), \qquad (13.17)$$

where $P(B'|B)$ is the belief state transition probability and $P_i(G'|G)$ is the grouping state transition probability conditional on customers at table i conditional at table i in the next state S', which is different from $P(G'|G)$ in (13.9)–(13.12). It should be noted that $P_i(G'|G)$ is strongly associated with the action of the next arriving customer. Suppose that the new customer's action is $a_S = k$ (i.e., choosing table k at state S). We therefore have the arriving transition probability in (13.18)

$$P_i(G' = (g_1, g_2, \ldots, g_k + 1, \ldots, g_N)|G = (g_1, g_2, \ldots, g_k, \ldots, g_N)) = \lambda. \quad (13.18)$$

For the leaving transition probability, we have taken into account the discount factor $(1 - \mu)$ in the future utility (i.e., the customer will not leave the restaurant), so we have (13.19) and (13.20)

$$P_i(G' = (g_1, g_2, \ldots, g_i - 1, \ldots, g_N)|G = (g_1, g_2, \ldots, g_i, \ldots, g_N)) = (g_i - 1)\mu,$$

$$\qquad (13.19)$$

$$P_i(G' = (g_1, g_2, \ldots, g_{i' \neq i} - 1, \ldots, g_N)|G = (g_1, g_2, \ldots, g_{i' \neq i}, \ldots, g_N)) = g_{i'}\mu,$$
$$(\forall i' \in \{1, 2, \ldots, N\}), \qquad (13.20)$$

$$P_i(G' = G|G = (g_1, g_2, \ldots, g_N)) = 1 - \lambda - g\left(\sum_{i=1}^{N} g_i - 1g\right)\mu, \qquad (13.21)$$

where the item $(g_i - 1)$ is because the grouping at table i, g_i, already includes the customer who will not leave the table at state S'. Equation (13.21) is the probability of staying. Under this situation, a multidimensional expected utility function set as (13.22) can be obtained

$$
\begin{bmatrix} V_1(S) \\ V_2(S) \\ \vdots \\ V_N(S) \end{bmatrix} = \begin{bmatrix} U_1(S) \\ U_2(S) \\ \vdots \\ U_N(S) \end{bmatrix} + (1 - \mu) \begin{bmatrix} \mathbf{P}_1(S'|S) & 0 & \cdots & 0 \\ 0 & \mathbf{P}_2(S'|S) & \cdots & 0 \\ \vdots & \vdots & \ddots & \vdots \\ 0 & 0 & \cdots & \mathbf{P}_N(S'|S) \end{bmatrix} \begin{bmatrix} \mathbf{V}_1(S') \\ \mathbf{V}_2(S') \\ \vdots \\ \mathbf{V}_N(S') \end{bmatrix},
$$

$$(13.22)$$

where $\mathbf{P}_i(S'|S) = [P_i(S'|S)|\forall S' \in \mathcal{X}]$ and $\mathbf{V}_i(S'|S) = [V_i(S'|S)|\forall S' \in \mathcal{X}]^T$.

Best Strategy

The strategy profile $\pi = \{a_S|\forall S \in \mathcal{X}\}$ is a mapping from the state space to the action space (i.e., $\pi : \mathcal{X} \to \mathcal{A}$). Customers will select the best strategy to maximize their own expected utilities because of their selfish nature. Here, first, the definition of a Nash equilibrium in the dynamic Chinese restaurant game is given.

DEFINITION 13.1   A strategy profile $\pi^\star$ is a Nash equilibrium of the dynamic Chinese restaurant game if and only if, when all customers adopt $\pi^\star$, for an arriving coming customer, their utility of using any other strategy profile $\pi \neq \pi^\star$ is often no more than that of using $\pi^\star$.

It can be seen from Definition 13.1 that each customer's utility can be impaired if they unilaterally deviate from the Nash equilibrium. Suppose that one customer gets to the restaurant with system state $S = (\mathbf{B}, \mathbf{G} = (g_1, g_2, \ldots, g_i, \ldots, g_N))$. Their best strategy can be defined as

$$a_S = \underset{i \in \{1, 2, \ldots, N\}}{\operatorname{argmax}} \{V_i(\mathbf{B}, \mathbf{G} = (g_1, \ldots, g_i + 1, \ldots, g_N))\}. \qquad (13.23)$$

Since the strategy profile satisfying (13.22) and (13.23), represented by $\pi^\star$, maximizes every arriving customers' utility, $\pi^\star$ is a Nash equilibrium of the game.

Modified Value Iteration Algorithm

As was discussed at the beginning of Section 13.3, although the table selection problem of the dynamic Chinese restaurant game can be modeled as an MDP problem, there are differences between it and the traditional MDP problem, in which the customer can never adjust the action even if there is a change in the system state. In the traditional MDP problem, there is only one Bellman equation related to each system state, and the best strategy is directly acquired by the optimization of the Bellman equation. In the M-MDP problem, there is a set of Bellman equations exhibited in (13.22), and the best strategy profile should satisfy (13.22) and (13.23) simultaneously. Thus the traditional dynamic programming approach in [18] cannot be directly applied. A modified value iteration algorithm is designed to solve this problem.

When an initial strategy profile π is available, the conditional state transition probability $\mathbf{P}_i(S'|S)$ can be calculated using (13.17)–(13.21), and therefore the conditional expected utility $\mathbf{V}_i(S)$ can be found using (13.22). Then, with $\mathbf{V}_i(S)$, the strategy

---

Algorithm 8: Modified value iteration algorithm for the M-MDP Problem.

(1) • Given tolerance η_1 and η_2, set ϵ_1 and ϵ_2.
(2) • Initialize $\{V_i^{(0)}(S) = 0, \forall S \in \mathcal{X}\}$ and randomize.
(3) $\pi = \{a_S, \forall S \in \mathcal{X}\}$.
(4) **while** $\epsilon_1 > \eta_1$ or $\epsilon_2 > \eta_2$ **do**
(5)   **for** all $S \in \mathcal{X}$ **do**
(6)   • Calculate $\mathbf{P}_i(S'|S), \forall i \in \{1, 2, \ldots, N\}$ using π and (13.17)–(13.21).
(7)   • Update $\mathbf{V}_i^{(n+1)}(S), \forall i \in \{1, 2, \ldots, N\}$ using (13.22).
(8)   **end for**
(9)   **for** all $S \in \mathcal{X}$ **do**
(10)   • Update $\pi^\star = \{a_S\}$ using (13.23).
(11)   **end for**
(12)   • Update the parameter ϵ_1 by $\epsilon_1 = \|\pi - \pi^\star\|_2$.
(13)   • Update the parameter ϵ_2 by $\epsilon_2 = \|\mathbf{V}_i^{(n+1)}(S) - \mathbf{V}_i^{(n)}(S)\|_2$.
(14)   • Update the strategy file $\pi = \pi^\star$.
(15) **end while**
(16) • The best strategy profile is $\pi^\star$.

---

profile π can be updated again by using (13.23). The best strategy $\pi^\star$ can finally be found in such an iterative way. The modified value iteration algorithm for the M-MDP problem is summarized in Algorithm 8.

13.4   Application to Cognitive Radio Networks

The application of the dynamic Chinese restaurant game in cognitive radio networks is investigated in this section. In a cognitive radio network, SUs are able to utilize the PU's licensed spectrum bands in an opportunistic manner while causing no negative impact on the PU. The SUs who are inclined to access the primary channel should perform spectrum sensing first to determine the absence of the PU, which is called "Listen-before-Talk" [19]. Recently, cooperative spectrum sensing technology was proposed to deal with the channel fading and shadowing problems. Furthermore, in cooperative spectrum sensing technology, SUs report their spectrum sensing results to each other [14]. Every SU selects one primary channel to access for data transmission after spectrum sensing. Nevertheless, traditional cooperative sensing schemes simply integrate all SUs' sensing results and ignore the structure of sequential decision-making [20], especially in a dynamic situation where SUs arrive and leave stochastically. What is more, in the previous channel access methods [21], the negative network externality has not been taken into account.

It is feasible to model spectrum sensing and access in cognitive radio networks as a dynamic Chinese restaurant game. In this game, the tables are the primary channels that are likely to be reserved by the PU, and customers are the SUs looking for an available channel. Based on the dynamic Chinese restaurant game, how a SU learns about the primary channel state by using other SUs' sensing results can be considered as the way in which a customer acquires knowledge of the table state, and how an SU selects a channel to access based on the prediction about subsequent SUs' decisions can be viewed as the way in which a customer chooses a table. Despite the fact that

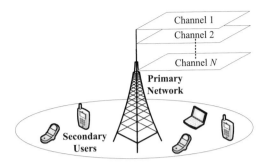

Figure 13.3 System model of the cognitive radio network.

the spectrum sensing and access problem has also been modeled by using game theory as in [22–24], there is insufficient research on the SUs' sequential decision-making structure. Approaches to applying the dynamic Chinese restaurant game to cognitive radio networks will be discussed in detail in the following sections.

13.4.1   System Model

Network Entity

It can be seen from Figure 13.3 that a primary network is considered with N independent primary channels. The PU is prioritized to occupy the channels whenever it wants to. However, SUs' channel accessing has to be preceded by the guarantee of the PU's communication quality of service. In the model, mixed underlay and overlay spectrum sharing are adopted, indicating that it is necessary for SUs to detect the PU's existence, and the interference to the PU is supposed to be kept at a minimum [25]. The primary channel state is represented as $\boldsymbol{\theta} = \{\theta_1, \theta_2, \ldots, \theta_N\}$ and $\theta_i \in \{\mathcal{H}_0, \mathcal{H}_1\}$, where $\mathcal{H}_0$ is the hypothesis of the absence of a PU and $\mathcal{H}_1$ indicates the presence of a PU.

In terms of the secondary network, SUs come and leave by a Bernoulli process with probabilities λ and μ, respectively. Spectrum sensing can be performed by all SUs using the energy detection approach. Here, a simple binary model is utilized on the spectrum sensing results, where $s_i^j = 1$ if the jth SU detects some activity on channel i and $s_i^j = 0$ if no activity is detected on channel i. Under this situation, the detection and false-alarm probabilities of channel i can be expressed as $P_i^d = \Pr(s_i = 1 | \theta_i = \mathcal{H}_1)$ and $P_i^f = \Pr(s_i = 1 | \theta_i = \mathcal{H}_0)$, which are viewed as common priors for all SUs. What is more, it is assumed that there exists a log file in the server of the secondary network that records each SU's channel belief and channel selection result. By querying this log file, the newly arriving SU is able to receive current grouping state information (i.e., the number of SUs in each primary channel and the previous SU's belief on the channel state).

ON–OFF Primary Channel Model

The PU's behavior in the primary channel is modeled as a general alternating ON–OFF renewal process. As is shown in Figure 13.4, the ON state refers to the occupation of

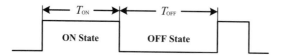

Figure 13.4 ON–OFF primary channel.

the channel by the PU, while the OFF state refers to the "spectrum hole" that can be freely accessed by SUs. This general ON–OFF switch model is applicable to the situation where SUs have no idea of the PU's exact communication mechanism [26]. Let T_{ON} and T_{OFF} represent the lengths of the ON state and OFF state, respectively. Based on a variety of primary services (e.g., digital TV broadcasting or cellular communication), T_{ON} and T_{OFF} statistically satisfy different types of distributions. In this case, it is assumed that T_{ON} and T_{OFF} are independent and satisfy exponential distributions with parameters r_1 and r_0, respectively [27], denoted by $f_{ON}(t)$ and $f_{OFF}(t)$ as follows:

$$\begin{cases} T_{ON} \sim f_{ON}(t) = \frac{1}{r_1} e^{-t/r_1}, \\ T_{OFF} \sim f_{OFF}(t) = \frac{1}{r_0} e^{-t/r_0}. \end{cases} \tag{13.24}$$

In this case, the expected lengths of the ON state and OFF state are r_1 and r_0 accordingly. These two parameters r_1 and r_0 can be effectively estimated by a maximum likelihood estimator [28]. Such an ON–OFF behavior of the PU is an integration of two Poisson processes, which is a renewal process [29]. The renewal interval is $T_p = T_{ON} + T_{OFF}$ and the distribution of T_p, denoted by $f_p(t)$, is

$$f_p(t) = f_{ON}(t) * f_{OFF}(t), \tag{13.25}$$

where the symbol "$*$" stands for the convolution operation.

13.4.2   Bayesian Channel Sensing

How SUs estimate the primary channel state by a Bayesian learning rule is discussed in this section. Define the continuous belief of the jth SU on the state of channel i as $b_i^j = \Pr(\theta_i^j = \mathcal{H}_0)$ and the quantized belief as $B_i^j \in \{\mathbb{B}_1, \mathbb{B}_2, \dots, \mathbb{B}_M\}$, where $B_i^j = \mathbb{B}_k$ if $b_i^j \in \left[\frac{k-1}{M}, \frac{k}{M}\right]$. The learning processes of all primary channels are also independent since these channels are supposed to be independent. Under this situation, for channel i, the jth SU can obtain the belief of previous SU selecting channel i, B_i^{j-1}, and their own sensing result, s_i^j. It can be seen from the discussion in

Section 13.2.1 that the learning process is $B_i^{j-1} \xrightarrow{\text{Mapping}} \hat{b}_i^{j-1} \xrightarrow{\text{Bayesian}+s_i^j} b_i^j \xrightarrow{\text{Quantize}} B_i^j$, where $\hat{b}_i^{j-1} = \left(\frac{1}{k-1} + \frac{1}{k}\right)/2$ when $B_i^{j-1} = \mathbb{B}_k$, and b_i^j can be derived according to (13.5) by a Bayesian learning rule as (13.26)

$$b_i^j = \frac{\left(P_{00}(t^j)\hat{b}_i^{j-1} + P_{10}(t^j)(1 - \hat{b}_i^{j-1})\right)\Pr(s_i^j | \theta_i^j = \mathcal{H}_0)}{\sum_{l=0}^{1} \left(P_{0l}(t^j)\hat{b}_i^{j-1} + P_{1l}(t^j)(1 - \hat{b}_i^{j-1})\right)\Pr(s_i^j | \theta_i^j = \mathcal{H}_l)}, \tag{13.26}$$

where $P_{00}(t^j)$, $P_{01}(t^j)$, $P_{10}(t^j)$, and $P_{11}(t^j)$ denote $\Pr(\theta_i^j = \mathcal{H}_0|\theta_i^{j-1} = \mathcal{H}_0)$, $\Pr(\theta_i^j = \mathcal{H}_1|\theta_i^{j-1} = \mathcal{H}_0)$, $\Pr(\theta_i^j = \mathcal{H}_0|\theta_i^{j-1} = \mathcal{H}_1)$, and $\Pr(\theta_i^j = \mathcal{H}_1|\theta_i^{j-1} = \mathcal{H}_1)$, respectively. Note that $P_{01}(t^j) = 1 - P_{00}(t^j)$ and $P_{11}(t^j) = 1 - P_{10}(t^j)$.

First, the primary channel state transition probabilities in (13.26) need to be derived to compute belief b_i^j. The channel state transition probability relies on the time interval between the $(j-1)$th and jth SUs' arrival time t^j, because the primary channel is modeled as an ON–OFF process. It should be noted that t^j can be directly acquired from the log file in the server.

The closed-form expression for $P_{01}(t^j)$ can be derived by the renewal theory as follows [30]:

$$P_{01}(t^j) = \frac{r_1}{r_0 + r_1}\left(1 - e^{-\frac{r_0+r_1}{r_0 r_1}t^j}\right). \tag{13.27}$$

Therefore, we can have $P_{00}(t^j)$ as

$$P_{00}(t^j) = 1 - P_{01}(t^j) = \frac{r_1}{r_0 + r_1}\left(\frac{r_0}{r_1} + e^{-\frac{r_0+r_1}{r_0 r_1}t^j}\right). \tag{13.28}$$

The closed-form expression for $P_{11}(t^j)$ can also be acquired in a similar way by the renewal theory as shown in Lemma 13.2.

LEMMA 13.2 $P_{11}(t)$ *satisfies the renewal equation given by*

$$P_{11}(t) = r_1 f_{ON}(t) + \int_0^t P_{11}(t-w)f_P(w)dw, \tag{13.29}$$

where $f_{ON}(t)$ is the probability density function of the ON state's length given in (13.24) and $f_P(t)$ is the probability density function of the PU's renewal interval given in (13.25).

Proof   According to Figure 13.5, the recursive expression of $P_{11}(t)$ can be written by

$$P_{11}(t) = \begin{cases} 1 & t \leq X, \\ 0 & X \leq t \leq X+Y, \\ P_{11}(t-X-Y) & X+Y \leq t, \end{cases} \tag{13.30}$$

where X represents the length of the first ON state and Y represents the length of the first OFF state. Furthermore, we have $X \sim f_{ON}(x) = \frac{1}{r_1}e^{-x/r_1}$ and $Y \sim f_{OFF}(y) = \frac{1}{r_0}e^{-y/r_0}$. On the grounds that X and Y are independent, their joint distribution $f_{XY}(x,y) = f_{ON}(x)f_{OFF}(y)$. In this case, $P_{11}(t)$ can be rewritten as the following:

$$P_{11}(t) = \int_{x \geq t} f_{ON}(x)dx + \iint_{x+y \leq t} f_{11}(t-x-y)f_{XY}(x,y)dxdy,$$

$$= 1 - F_{ON}(t) + P_{11}(t) * f_P(t), \tag{13.31}$$

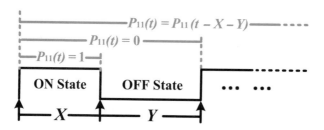

Figure 13.5 Illustration of function $P_{11}(t)$.

where $F_{\text{ON}}(t) = \int_0^t f_{\text{ON}}(x)dx = 1 - e^{-t/r_1}$ is the cumulative distribution function of the ON state's length. By taking Laplace transforms of both sides of (13.31), we have

$$\mathbb{P}_{11}(s) = \frac{1}{s} - \frac{1}{s}\mathbb{F}_{\text{ON}}(s) + \mathbb{P}_{11}(s)\mathbb{F}_p(s),$$

$$= r_1 \mathbb{F}_{\text{ON}}(s) + \mathbb{P}_{11}(s)\mathbb{F}_p(s), \tag{13.32}$$

where $\mathbb{P}_{11}(s)$ is the Laplace transform of $P_{11}(t)$, $\mathbb{F}_{\text{ON}}(s) = \frac{1}{\lambda_1 s + 1}$ is the Laplace transform of $f_{\text{ON}}(t)$, and $\mathbb{F}_p(s) = \frac{1}{(\lambda_1 s + 1)(\lambda_0 s + 1)}$ is the Laplace transform of $f_p(t)$. Then, by taking the inverse Laplace transform of (13.32), we have

$$P_{11}(t) = r_1 f_{\text{ON}}(t) + \int_0^t P_{11}(t - w) f_p(w)dw. \tag{13.33}$$

Through solving (13.29) in Lemma 13.2, we can get the closed-form expression for $P_{11}(t^j)$ given by

$$P_{11}(t^j) = \frac{r_0}{r_0 + r_1}\left(\frac{r_1}{r_0} + e^{-\frac{r_0 + r_1}{r_0 r_1}t^j}\right). \tag{13.34}$$

Then we can have $P_{10}(t_i)$ as

$$P_{10}(t^j) = 1 - P_{11}(t^j) = \frac{r_0}{r_0 + r_1}\left(1 - e^{-\frac{r_0 + r_1}{r_0 r_1}t^j}\right). \tag{13.35}$$

By substituting (13.27) and (13.28) and (13.34) and (13.35) into (13.26), we can calculate the jth SU's belief b_i^j with the corresponding sensing results $s_i^j = 1$ and $s_i^j = 0$ by (13.36) and (13.37), respectively.

$$b_i^j\big|_{s_i^j = 1} = \frac{\left(r_0 e^{\frac{r_0 + r_1}{r_0 r_1}t^j} - r_0 + (r_1 + r_0)\hat{b}_i^{j-1}\right)P_i^f}{\left(r_0 e^{\frac{r_0 + r_1}{r_0 r_1}t^j} - r_0 + (r_1 + r_0)\hat{b}_i^{j-1}\right)P_i^f + \left(r_1 e^{\frac{r_0 + r_1}{r_0 r_1}t^j} + r_0 - (r_1 + r_0)\hat{b}_i^{j-1}\right)P_i^d}, \tag{13.36}$$

$$b_i^j\big|_{s_i^j = 0} = \frac{\left(r_0 e^{\frac{r_0 + r_1}{r_0 r_1}t^j} - r_0 + (r_1 + r_0)\hat{b}_i^{j-1}\right)(1 - P_i^f)}{\left(r_0 e^{\frac{r_0 + r_1}{r_0 r_1}t^j} - r_0 + (r_1 + r_0)\hat{b}_i^{j-1}\right)(1 - P_i^f) + \left(r_1 e^{\frac{r_0 + r_1}{r_0 r_1}t^j} + r_0 - (r_1 + r_0)\hat{b}_i^{j-1}\right)(1 - P_i^d)}. \tag{13.37}$$

In the following, (13.36) is represented as $b_i^j|_{s_i^j=1} = \phi(\hat{b}_i^{j-1}, t_i, s_i^j = 1)$ and (13.37) is represented as $b_i^j|_{s_i^j=0} = \phi(\hat{b}_i^{j-1}, t_i, s_i^j = 0)$ for simplicity.

13.4.3 Belief State Transition Probability

In this section we will discuss, how to calculate the belief state transition probability matrix of each channel (i.e., $\Pr(B_i^j = \mathbb{B}_q|B_i^{j-1} = \mathbb{B}_p)$). The belief state transition probability can be acquired according to the learning rules $B_i^{j-1} \xrightarrow{\text{Mapping}}$ $\hat{b}_i^{j-1} \xrightarrow{\text{Bayesian}+s_i^j} b_i^j \xrightarrow{\text{Quantize}} B_i^j$. Note that $\hat{b}_i^{j-1} = \frac{1}{2}\left(\frac{p-1}{M} + \frac{p}{M}\right)$ if $B_i^{j-1} = \mathbb{B}_p$ and $b_i^j \in \left[\frac{q-1}{M}, \frac{q}{M}\right]$ if $B_i^j = \mathbb{B}_q$. Under this circumstance, the belief state transition probability can be calculated by

$$\Pr(B_i^j = \mathbb{B}_q|B_i^{j-1} = \mathbb{B}_p) = \int_{\frac{q-1}{M}}^{\frac{q}{M}} \Pr g\left(b_i^j \middle| \hat{b}_i^{j-1} = \frac{1}{2}\left(\frac{p-1}{M} + \frac{p}{M}\right) g\right) db_i^j. \quad (13.38)$$

According to (13.36) and (13.37), we have $b_i^j = \phi\left(\hat{b}_i^{j-1} = \frac{1}{2}\left(\frac{p-1}{M} + \frac{p}{M}\right), t^j, s_i^j\right)$. Thus the belief state transition probability can be rewritten as (13.39)

$$\Pr(B_i^j = \mathbb{B}_q|B_i^{j-1} = \mathbb{B}_p)$$

$$= \iint_{\frac{q-1}{M} \leq \phi\left(\hat{b}_i^{j-1} = \frac{1}{2}\left(\frac{p-1}{M} + \frac{p}{M}\right), t^j, s_i^j\right) \leq \frac{q}{M}} \Pr(t^j, s_i^j|\hat{b}_i^{j-1}) dt^j ds^j,$$

$$= \int_{\frac{q-1}{M} \leq \phi\left(\hat{b}_i^{j-1} = \frac{1}{2}\left(\frac{p-1}{M} + \frac{p}{M}\right), t^j, s_i^j=0\right) \leq \frac{q}{M}} \lambda e^{-\lambda t^j} \Pr(s_i^j = 0|\hat{b}_i^{j-1}) dt^j$$

$$+ \int_{\frac{q-1}{M} \leq \phi\left(\hat{b}_i^{j-1} = \frac{1}{2}\left(\frac{p-1}{M} + \frac{p}{M}\right), t^j, s_i^j=1\right) \leq \frac{q}{M}} \lambda e^{-\lambda t^j} \Pr(s_i^j = 1|\hat{b}_i^{j-1}) dt^j, \quad (13.39)$$

where the assumption "the arrival interval of two SUs t^j is in line with the exponential distribution with parameter λ and is independent of the belief" is followed by the second equality. In order to calculate (13.39), we should derive $\Pr(s_i^j|\hat{b}_i^{j-1})$, which denotes the distribution of the jth SU's received signal when given the $(j-1)$th SU's belief. It should be noted that given the current channel state θ_i^j, signal s_i^j is independent of belief $\hat{b}_i^{j-1}$. Therefore, $\Pr(s_i^j|\hat{b}_i^{j-1})$ can be calculated as follows:

$$\Pr(s_i^j|\hat{b}_i^{j-1}) = f(s_i^j|\theta_i^j = \mathcal{H}_0)\Pr(\theta_i^j = \mathcal{H}_0|\hat{b}_i^{j-1})$$

$$+ f(s_i^j|\theta_i^j = \mathcal{H}_1)\Pr(\theta_i^j = \mathcal{H}_1|\hat{b}_i^{j-1}). \quad (13.40)$$

What is more, given the previous channel state θ_i^{j-1}, the current state θ_i^j is also independent of the former SU's belief $\hat{b}_i^{j-1}$. Under this situation, $\Pr(\theta_i^j = \mathcal{H}_0|\hat{b}_i^{j-1})$ in (13.40) can be acquired as follows:

$$\Pr(\theta_i^j = \mathcal{H}_0|\hat{b}_i^{j-1}) = \Pr(\theta_i^j = \mathcal{H}_0|\theta_i^{j-1} = \mathcal{H}_0)\hat{b}_i^{j-1}$$
$$+ \Pr(\theta_i^j = \mathcal{H}_0|\theta_i^{j-1} = \mathcal{H}_1)(1 - \hat{b}_i^{j-1}),$$
$$= P_{00}(t^j)\hat{b}_i^{j-1} + P_{10}(t^j)(1 - \hat{b}_i^{j-1}). \tag{13.41}$$

Similarly, for $\Pr(\theta_i^j = \mathcal{H}_1|\hat{b}_i^{j-1})$, we have

$$\Pr(\theta_i^j = \mathcal{H}_1|\hat{b}_i^{j-1}) = P_{01}(t^j)\hat{b}_i^{j-1} + P_{11}(t^j)(1 - \hat{b}_i^{j-1}). \tag{13.42}$$

The conditional distribution of the signal can be acquired by substituting (13.41) and (13.42) into (13.40) as (13.43) and (13.44).

$$\Pr(s_i^j = 0|\hat{b}_i^{j-1}) = (1 - P_i^f)\left(P_{00}(t^j)\hat{b}_i^{j-1} + P_{10}(t^j)(1 - \hat{b}_i^{j-1})\right)$$
$$+ (1 - P_i^d)\left(P_{01}(t^j)\hat{b}_i^{j-1} + P_{11}(t^j)(1 - \hat{b}_i^{j-1})\right), \tag{13.43}$$
$$\Pr(s_i^j = 1|\hat{b}_i^{j-1}) = P_i^f\left(P_{00}(t^j)\hat{b}_i^{j-1} + P_{10}(t^j)(1 - \hat{b}_i^{j-1})\right)$$
$$+ P_i^d\left(P_{01}(t^j)\hat{b}_i^{j-1} P_{11}(t^j)(1 - \hat{b}_i^{j-1})\right). \tag{13.44}$$

Finally, with (13.43) and (13.44), the belief transition probability matrix can be calculated by using (13.39).

13.4.4 Channel Access: Two Primary Channels Case

The case where there are two primary channels is discussed in this section. Under this circumstance, the system state $S = (B_1, B_2, g_1, g_2)$, where B_1 and B_2 are the beliefs of two channels and g_1 and g_2 are the numbers of SUs in two channels. The immediate utility of the SUs in channel i, $U(B_i, g_i)$, is defined as

$$U(B_i, g_i) = \hat{b}_i R(g_i) = \hat{b}_i \log\left(1 + \frac{\text{SNR}}{(g_i - 1)\text{INR} + 1}g\right), \tag{13.45}$$

where $\hat{b}_i$ is the mapping of quantized belief B_i, SNR is the average signal-to-noise-ratio of the SUs, and INR is the average interference-to-noise ratio.

The expected utility functions of two channels, according to (13.22), can be written as

$$V_1(S) = U(B_1, g_1) + (1 - \mu)\sum_{S' \in \mathcal{X}} P_1(S'|S)V_1(S'), \tag{13.46}$$

$$V_2(S) = U(B_2, g_2) + (1 - \mu)\sum_{S' \in \mathcal{X}} P_2(S'|S)V_2(S'), \tag{13.47}$$

where P_1 and P_2 are the state transition probabilities conditional on the event that SUs stay in their chosen channels. Based on (13.17)–(13.21), P_1 and P_2 can be summarized as (13.48) and (13.49)

$$P_1(S'|S) = P\big((B_1', B_2')|(B_1, B_2)\big)$$

$$\times \begin{cases} \mathbf{1}(a_S)\lambda & \text{if } S' = (B_1', B_2', g_1 + 1, g_2), \\ (1 - \mathbf{1}(a_S))\lambda & \text{if } S' = (B_1', B_2', g_1, g_2 + 1), \\ (g_1 - 1)\mu & \text{if } S' = (B_1', B_2', g_1 - 1, g_2), \\ g_2\mu & \text{if } S' = (B_1', B_2', g_1, g_2 - 1), \\ 1 - \lambda - (g_1 + g_2 - 1)\mu & \text{if } S' = (B_1', B_2', g_1, g_2), \end{cases} \quad (13.48)$$

$$P_2(S'|S) = P\big((B_1', B_2')|(B_1, B_2)\big)$$

$$\times \begin{cases} \mathbf{1}(a_S)\lambda & \text{if } S' = (B_1', B_2', g_1 + 1, g_2), \\ (1 - \mathbf{1}(a_S))\lambda & \text{if } S' = (B_1', B_2', g_1, g_2 + 1), \\ g_1\mu & \text{if } S' = (B_1', B_2', g_1 - 1, g_2), \\ (g_2 - 1)\mu & \text{if } S' = (B_1', B_2', g_1, g_2 - 1), \\ 1 - \lambda - (g_1 + g_2 - 1)\mu & \text{if } S' = (B_1', B_2', g_1, g_2), \end{cases} \quad (13.49)$$

where $\mathbf{1}(a_S)$ is an indicator function that is defined by

$$\mathbf{1}(a_S) = \begin{cases} 1 & \text{if } a_S = 1 \text{ (i.e., selecting channnel 1)}, \\ 0 & \text{if } a_S = 2 \text{ (i.e., selecting channnel 2)}. \end{cases} \quad (13.50)$$

According to (13.23), the optimal strategy a_S for SUs arriving with system state $S = (B_1, B_2, g_1, g_2)$ can be obtained as follows:

$$a_S = \begin{cases} 1, & V_1(B_1, B_2, g_1 + 1, g_2) \geq V_2(B_1, B_2, g_1, g_2 + 1), \\ 2, & V_1(B_1, B_2, g_1 + 1, g_2) < V_2(B_1, B_2, g_1, g_2 + 1). \end{cases} \quad (13.51)$$

Therefore, with (13.45)–(13.51), the optimal strategy profile $\pi^\star = \{a_S, \forall S \in \mathcal{X}\}$ can be found by using the modified value iteration approach in Algorithm 8. It will be shown in Lemma 13.3 and Theorem 13.4 that when the beliefs regarding two channel are available, there exists a threshold structure in the optimal strategy profile $\pi^\star$.

LEMMA 13.3   *The value functions V_1 and V_2 updated by Algorithm 8 satisfy that for any $g_1 \geq 0$ and $g_2 \geq 1$*

$$V_1(B_1, B_2, g_1, g_2) \geq V_1(B_1, B_2, g_1 + 1, g_2 - 1), \quad (13.52)$$

$$V_2(B_1, B_2, g_1, g_2) \leq V_2(B_1, B_2, g_1 + 1, g_2 - 1). \quad (13.53)$$

Proof   The induction method is utilized to verify that (13.52) and (13.53) hold for all $n \geq 0$. First, since $V_1^{(0)}(B_1, B_2, g_1, g_2)$ and $V_2^{(0)}(B_1, B_2, g_1, g_2)$ are initialized by zeros in Algorithm 8, (13.52) and (13.53) hold for $n = 0$. Second, we assume that (13.52) and (13.53) hold for some $n > 0$, and we check whether (13.52) and (13.53) hold for

$(n + 1)$. We use $S_1 = (B_1, B_2, g_1, g_2)$ and $S_2 = (B_1, B_2, g_1 + 1, g_2 - 1)$ for simplicity of notation. There are three cases for action $a_{S_1}^{(n)}$ and action $a_{S_2}^{(n)}$:

- Case 1: $V_2^{(n)}(S_1) \leq V_2^{(n)}(S_2) \leq V_1^{(n)}(S_2) \leq V_1^{(n)}(S_1)$, we have $a_{S_1}^{(n)} = a_{S_2}^{(n)} = 1$;
- Case 2: $V_1^{(n)}(S_2) \leq V_1^{(n)}(S_1) \leq V_2^{(n)}(S_1) \leq V_2^{(n)}(S_2)$, we have $a_{S_1}^{(n)} = a_{S_2}^{(n)} = 2$;
- Case 3: $V_1^{(n)}(S_1) \geq V_2^{(n)}(S_1)$ and $V_1^{(n)}(S_2) \leq V_2^{(n)}(S_2)$, we have $a_{S_1}^{(n)} = 1$ and $a_{S_2}^{(n)} = 2$.

For Case 1, we have the difference of V_1 and V_2 in (13.54).

$$
V_1^{(n+1)}(S_1) - V_1^{(n+1)}(S_2) = B_1\big(R(g_1) - R(g_1 + 1)\big)
$$

$$
+ (1 - \mu)\Bigg[\lambda \sum_{B_1'} \sum_{B_2'} P\big((B_1', B_2')|(B_1, B_2)\big)
$$

$$
\times \big(V_1^{(n)}(B_1', B_2', g_1 + 1, g_2) - V_1^{(n)}(B_1', B_2', g_1 + 2, g_2 - 1)\big)
$$

$$
+ \mu(g_2 - 1) \sum_{B_1'} \sum_{B_2'} P\big((B_1', B_2')|(B_1, B_2)\big)
$$

$$
\times \big(V_1^{(n)}(B_1', B_2', g_1, g_2 - 1) - V_1^{(n)}(B_1', B_2', g_1 + 1, g_2 - 2)\big)
$$

$$
+ \mu(g_1 - 1) \sum_{B_1'} \sum_{B_2'} P\big((B_1', B_2')|(B_1, B_2)\big)
$$

$$
\times \big(V_1^{(n)}(B_1', B_2', g_1 - 1, g_2) - V_1^{(n)}(B_1', B_2', g_1, g_2 - 1)\big)
$$

$$
+ \big(1 - \lambda - \mu(g_1 + g_2 - 1)\big)
$$

$$
\times \sum_{B_1'} \sum_{B_2'} P\big((B_1', B_2')|(B_1, B_2)\big)
$$

$$
\times \big(V_1^{(n)}(B_1', B_2', g_1, g_2) - V_1^{(n)}(B_1', B_2', g_1 + 1, g_2 - 1)\big)\Bigg].
$$

$$(13.54)$$

It can be seen with this hypothesis that $V_1^{(n)}(S_1) - V_1^{(n)}(S_2) \geq 0$ that $V_1^{(n+1)}(S_1) - V_1^{(n+1)}(S_2) \geq 0$ holds according to (13.54). For Cases 2 and 3, the same conclusions can be acquired through the analysis of the difference between $V_1^{(n+1)}(S_1)$ and $V_1^{(n+1)}(S_2)$. Therefore, it is concluded that $V_1(S_1) \geq V_1(S_2)$. In a similar way, $V_2(S_1) \leq V_2(S_2)$ can be verified by induction.

It can be seen from Lemma 13.3 that when the beliefs of two channels are available, V_1 is nondecreasing and V_2 is nonincreasing along the line of $g_1 + g_2 = m, \forall m \in \{0, 1, \ldots, 2L\}$. According to Lemma 13.3, the threshold structure in the optimal strategy profile $\pi^\star$ will be as is shown by Theorem 13.4.

THEOREM 13.4 *In the two-channel case, when the belief state is available, the best strategy profile* $\pi^\star = \{a_S\}$ *derived from the modified value iteration algorithm has the following threshold structure:*

$$\text{If } a_{S=(B_1,B_2,g_1,g_2)} = 1, \text{then } a_{S=(B_1,B_2,g_1-g',g_2+g')} = 1. \tag{13.55}$$

$$\text{If } a_{S=(B_1,B_2,g_1,g_2)} = 2, \text{then } a_{S=(B_1,B_2,g_1+g',g_2-g')} = 2. \tag{13.56}$$

Proof According to Lemma 13.3, we can have

$$V_1(B_1,B_2,g_1+1,g_2) - V_2(B_1,B_2,g_1,g_2+1)$$

$$\geq V_1(B_1,B_2,g_1+2,g_2-1) - V_2(B_1,B_2,g_1+1,g_2), \tag{13.57}$$

which indicates that the difference between V_1 and V_2 is nondecreasing along $g_1 + g_2 = m, \forall m \in \{0,1,\ldots,2L\}$. In this case, on the one hand, if $V_1(B_1,B_2,g_1+1,g_2) \leq V_2(B_1,B_2,g_1,g_2+1)$ (i.e., $a_{S=(B_1,B_2,g_1,g_2)} = 2$), then for any $g' > 0$, $V_1(B_1,B_2,g_1+g'+1,g_2-g') \leq V_2(B_1,B_2,g_1+g',g_2-g'+1)$ (i.e., $a_{S=(B_1,B_2,g_1+g',g_2-g')} = 2$). On the other hand, if $V_1(B_1,B_2,g_1+1,g_2) \geq V_2(B_1,B_2,g_1,g_2+1)$ (i.e., $a_{S=(B_1,B_2,g_1,g_2)} = 1$), then for any $g' > 0$, $V_1(B_1,B_2,g_1-g'+1,g_2+g') \geq V_2(B_1,B_2,g_1-g',g_2+g'+1)$, which means $a_{S=(B_1,B_2,g_1-g',g_2+g')} = 1$. Therefore, we can conclude that if $a_{S=(B_1,B_2,g_1,g_2)} = 1$, then the upper left of line $g_1 + g_2 = m$ will be all 1, and if $a_{S=(B_1,B_2,g_1,g_2)} = 2$, then the lower right of line $g_1 + g_2 = m$ will be all 2. Thus, there exists a threshold on the line of $g_1 + g_2 = m$.

It should be noted that the best strategy profile $\pi^\star$ can be acquired off-line, and this profile can be stored in a table beforehand. It can be seen that for some fixed belief state, there are $(L+1)^2$ system states, indicating $(L+1)^2$ strategies of the corresponding strategy profile. With the proved threshold structure on each line $g_1 + g_2 = m, \forall m \in \{0,1,\ldots,2L\}$, we should simply store the threshold point on each line. Under this circumstance, the storage of the strategy profile can be decreased from $\mathcal{O}(L^2)$ to $\mathcal{O}(2L)$.

13.4.5 Channel Access: Multiple Primary Channels Case

The case where there are multiple primary channels is discussed in this section. Despite the fact that the best strategy profile of the multichannel case can also be acquired by using Algorithm 8, the computation complexity grows exponentially with the number of primary channels N. When the number of system states exponentially increases with N, there is also a challenge in terms of the storage and retrieval of the strategy profile. Therefore, developing a fast algorithm for the multichannel case becomes important.

Suppose the channel number N is even. These N primary channels can be randomly divided into $N/2$ pairs. For each pair, SUs can select one channel using the threshold strategy in Theorem 13.4. Afterwards, the chosen $N/2$ channels can be further divided into $N/4$ pairs and so on by the SUs. Under this situation, SUs can finally choose one channel to access. If the channel number N is odd, the channel can be chosen

---

Algorithm 9: Fast algorithm for the multichannel case.

---
(1) **if** N is even **then**
(2) 　**while** $N > 1$ **do**
(3) 　　• Randomly divide the N primary channels into $N/2$ pairs.
(4) 　　**for** all $N/2$ pairs **do**
(5) 　　　• Choose one channel from each pair according to Algorithm 8.
(6) 　　**end for**
(7) 　　• $N = N/2$.
(8) 　**end while**
(9) **end if**
(10) **if** N is odd **then**
(11) 　**while** $N > 1$ **do**
(12) 　　• Randomly divide the N primary channels into
(13) 　　　$(N-1)/2$ pairs and one channel.
(14) 　　**for** all $(N-1)/2$ pairs **do**
(15) 　　　• Choose one channel from each pair according to Algorithm 8.
(16) 　　**end for**
(17) 　　• $N = (N-1)/2 + 1$.
(18) 　**end while**
(19) **end if**

---

similarly. Based on such an iterative dichotomy method, an SU is able to find one suboptimal primary channel only by $\log N$ steps, and the complexity of each step is equivalent to that of the two-channel case. Algorithm 9 summarizes this fast algorithm. In Section 13.5, the performance of this fast algorithm will be compared with that of the optimal algorithm using modified value iteration.

13.4.6　Analysis of Interference to the PU

Mixed underlay and overlay spectrum sharing are utilized in this chapter; therefore, it is of vital importance to quantify the interference to the PU and evaluate the impact on the PU's data transmission. In the system, the primary channel based on the ON–OFF model, and no synchrony can be revealed between the SUs and the PU. Under this situation, the SUs may fail to discover the PU's recurrence when transmitting packets in the primary channel, which is likely to result in interference to the PU [31].

Interference to the PU is likely to occur on the condition that there are SUs in the primary channel. Thus the interference probability of channel i, P_{Ii}, is defined as the probability that the number of SUs in this channel is nonzero. Given a strategy profile $\pi = \{a_S\}$, the system state transition probability matrix $\boldsymbol{P}_s = \{P(S'|S), \forall S' \in \mathcal{X}, \forall S \in \mathcal{X}\}$ can be acquired according to (13.8)–(13.12). With $\boldsymbol{P}_s$ we derive the stationary distribution of the Markov chain, $\sigma = \{\sigma(\boldsymbol{B},\boldsymbol{G})\}$, through solving $\sigma\boldsymbol{P}_s = \sigma$. The interference probability P_{Ii} under this situation can be calculated by

$$P_{Ii} = 1 - \sum_{\boldsymbol{B}}\sum_{\boldsymbol{G}\backslash g_i} \sigma\big(\boldsymbol{B},\boldsymbol{G} = (g_1, g_2, \ldots, g_i = 0, \ldots, g_N)\big). \tag{13.58}$$

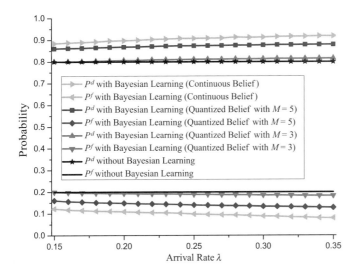

Figure 13.6 Detection and false-alarm probabilities.

If there is no interference from the SUs, the PU's instantaneous rate is $\log(1 + \mathrm{SNR}_p)$, where SNR_p is the signal-to-noise ratio of the primary signal at the PU's receiver. On the other hand, if there is interference, the PU's instantaneous rate is $\log\left(1 + \dfrac{\mathrm{SNR}_p}{\mathrm{INR}_p + 1}\right)$, where INR_p is the interference-to-noise ratio of the secondary signal received by the PU. Thus, the PU's average data rate R_i in channel i can be calculated by

$$R_{pi} = (1 - P_{Ii})\log(1 + \mathrm{SNR}_p) + P_{Ii}\log\left(1 + \frac{\mathrm{SNR}_p}{\mathrm{INR}_p + 1}g\right). \tag{13.59}$$

13.5 Simulation Results

In this section, simulations are carried out to evaluate the performance of the previously presented schemes in cognitive radio networks. Specifically, the performance of channel sensing and access and the interference to the PU are evaluated.

13.5.1 Bayesian Channel Sensing

The performance of channel sensing with Bayesian learning is evaluated in this simulation. First, one primary channel based on the ON–OFF model is generated, and the channel parameters are set to be $r_0 = 55\,\mathrm{s}$ and $r_1 = 50\,\mathrm{s}$. Then a number of SUs with some arrival rate λ sense the primary channel in sequence and form their own beliefs through the combination of the sensing result with the previous SU's belief. In Figure 13.6 a, comparison is conducted among the detection and

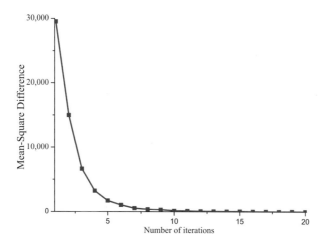

Figure 13.7 Convergence performance of the modified value iteration algorithm when $N = 3$, $M = 5$, and $L = 5$.

false-alarm probabilities between channel sensing with Bayesian learning based on continuous belief, sensing with Bayesian learning based on quantized belief (belief level $M = 5$ and 3), and sensing without Bayesian learning under a different arrival rate λ. The detection probability increases and the false-alarm probability drops when Bayesian learning is used. It can be seen that with the quantization operation of the beliefs there is some performance loss, and setting more belief levels can result in less loss. Additionally, it can be seen that with Bayesian learning the larger the arrival rate λ, the higher the detection probability and the lower the false-alarm probability. The reason for this is that a larger λ means a shorter arrival interval between two SUs, and so the previous SU's belief information contributes more to the current SU's belief construction.

13.5.2   Channel Access in the Two Primary Channels Case

In this section, the performance of the M-MDP model and the modified value iteration algorithm are evaluated for the two-channel case. The parameters of the two primary channels are set as follows: for channel 1, $r_0 = 55$ s and $r_1 = 25$ s; for channel 2, $r_0 = 25$ s and $r_1 = 55$ s, which indicates that channel 1 is statistically better than channel 2. The convergence performance of the algorithm is shown in Figure 13.7, where the x-axis is the number of iterations and the y-axis is the mean-square differences of two adjacent iterations (i.e., $E(||\pi(t+1) - \pi(t)||_2)$). It can be seen that the average number of iterations less than 20.

The strategy is compared with a centralized strategy, a myopic strategy, and a random strategy in terms of social welfare in the following simulations. First, the social welfare, W, when given a strategy profile $\pi = \{a_S, \forall S \in \mathcal{X}\}$ is defined as

$$W = \sum_{S \in \mathcal{X}} \sigma^\pi(S)(g_1 U(B_1, g_1) + g_2 U(B_2, g_2)), \qquad (13.60)$$

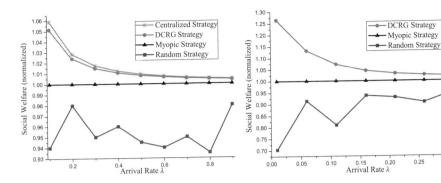

Figure 13.8 Social welfare comparison under two channels with $M = 2$ and $L = 2$.

Figure 13.9 Social welfare comparison under two channels with $M = 5$ and $L = 5$.

where $S = (B_1, B_2, g_1, g_2)$ in the two-channel case and $\sigma^{\pi}(S)$ is the stationary probability of state S. The four strategies tested are defined as follows:

- The *dynamic Chinese restaurant game (DCRG) strategy* is acquired through the value iteration algorithm in Algorithm 8.
- The *centralized strategy* is acquired by exhaustively looking for all possible $2^{|\mathcal{X}|}$ strategy profiles to maximize the social welfare (i.e., $\pi^c = \arg\max_{\pi} W^{\pi}$, where the superscript c indicates the centralized strategy). It can be seen that the complexity of finding the centralized strategy is nondeterministic polynomial (NP)-hard.
- The *myopic strategy* aims to maximize the immediate utility (i.e., to select the channel with the largest immediate reward by $\pi^m = \left\{a_S = \underset{i \in \{1,2\}}{\arg\max}\, U(B_i, g_i),\right.$ $\forall S \in \mathcal{X}\Big\}$, where the superscript m indicates the myopic strategy).
- The *random strategy* involves randomly selecting one channel with equal probability 0.5 (i.e., $\pi^r = \{a_S = \text{rand}(1,2), \forall S \in \mathcal{X}\}$, where the superscript r indicates the random strategy).

In the simulation, the myopic strategy is utilized as the comparison baseline, and the results are shown through normalizing the performance of each strategy against that of the myopic strategy.

The social welfare performance of the different methods is evaluated in Figure 13.8. Since the centralized strategy has extremely high complexity, the case with two belief levels and a maximum of two SUs is taken into account in each channel (i.e., $M = 2$ and $L = 2$). It should be noted that if $M = 2$ and $L = 3$, there are a total of $2^{2^2 \cdot (3+1)^2} = 2^{64}$ possible strategy profiles to substantiate, which is computationally intractable. Thus, as is shown in Figure 13.8, although slightly outperforming the DCRG strategy, the centralized method is not feasible for the time-varying primary channels. Furthermore, the DCRG strategy is also compared with the myopic and random strategies with $M = 5$ and $L = 5$ in Figure 13.9. It can be seen that among all of the strategies, the DCRG strategy has the best performance.

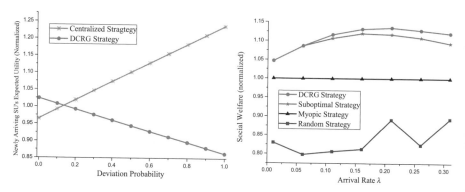

Figure 13.10 Nash equilibrium verification under two channels with $M = 2$ and $L = 2$.

Figure 13.11 Social welfare comparison under three channels.

It is shown that the DCRG strategy is a Nash equilibrium by simulating a newly arriving SU's expected utility in Figure 13.10. The deviation probability on the x-axis represents the probability that a newly arriving SU deviates from the DCRG strategy or centralized strategy. It can be seen that the DCRG strategy has a better performance than the centralized strategy when there is no deviation. The reason for this is that the centralized strategy aims to maximize social welfare and therefore sacrifices the expected utility of the newly arriving SU. Additionally, it can be seen that the expected utility of a newly arriving SU drops as the deviation probability goes up, which substantiates the notion that the DCRG strategy is a Nash equilibrium. On the other hand, higher utility can be acquired by a newly arriving SU through deviating from the centralized strategy, indicating that the centralized strategy is not a Nash equilibrium and there exists an incentive for SUs to deviate.

13.5.3   Fast Algorithm for Multichannel Access

In this simulation, the performance of the fast algorithm in the multichannel case is evaluated, and this is represented as a suboptimal strategy hereafter. In Figure 13.11, the suboptimal strategy is compared with the DCRG strategy, the myopic strategy, and the random strategy in terms of social welfare in the three-channel case, where the channel parameters are set as follows: for channel 1, $r_0 = 55$ s and $r_1 = 25$ s; for channel 2, $r_0 = 45$ s and $r_1 = 40$ s; and for channel 3, $r_0 = 25$ s and $r_1 = 55$ s. It can be seen that the suboptimal strategy achieves a social welfare performance that is very close to that of the best one (i.e., the DCRG strategy using modified value iteration, and is better than the myopic and random strategies). Thus, it is more feasible to adopt the suboptimal strategy for the multichannel case due to the low complexity of the suboptimal strategy.

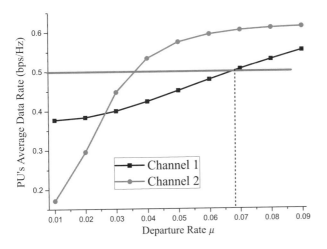

Figure 13.12 PU's average data rate when $M = 5$ and $L = 5$.

13.5.4 Interference Performance

Figure 13.12 shows the simulation results of the PU's average data rate in each channel R_{pi} versus the SUs' departure rate μ in the two-channel case, where we set $\text{SNR}_p = 5$ db and $\text{INR}_p = 3$ db. It can be seen that in terms of μ, R_{pi} is an increasing function. The reason for this is that the increase in the departure rate μ indicates that there are fewer SUs in the primary channels, which results in less interference to the PU. Suppose that the PU's data rate in each channel is at least 0.5 bps/Hz. In such a case, μ should be no smaller than the value indicated by the vertical dashed line in Figure 13.12 (i.e., μ should be larger than approximately 0.07). Thus the secondary network should properly control the SUs' departure rate μ (i.e., the average transmission time), to control the interference and guarantee the PU's average data rate.

13.6 Conclusion

In this chapter, the previous Chinese restaurant game work [12] is extended into the dynamic Chinese restaurant game where customers come and go by a Bernoulli process. On the basis of the Bayesian learning rule, a table state learning method is introduced by which customers estimate the table state. In the learning method, it is assumed that all of the customers reveal their true beliefs. Truthful reporting can be obtained through efficient mechanism design. In addition, an alternative situation can be taken into account in which each customer does not reveal their belief information and only action information can be observed. The table selection problem is modeled as an MDP problem, and an M-MDP model and a modified value iteration algorithm are discussed for reaching the optimal strategy. Furthermore, the application of the dynamic Chinese restaurant game to cognitive radio networks is discussed. It can be seen from the simulation results that compared with the centralized method maximizing social welfare with computationally intractable complexity, the DCRG scheme achieves comparable social welfare performance with much lower complexity, while compared with the random strategy and the myopic strategy, the DCRG scheme achieves much better social welfare performance. What is more, the DCRG scheme maximizes a newly arriving user's expected utility and thus achieves a Nash equilibrium where there is no incentive for the user to deviate. A universal framework for analyzing learning and strategic decision-making in a dynamic social network with negative network externality is offered by such a dynamic Chinese restaurant game.

References

[1] Y. Chen and K. J. R. Liu, "Understanding microeconomic behaviors in social networking: An engineering view," *IEEE Signal Processing Magazine*, vol. 29, pp. 53–64, 2012.

[2] H. V. Zhao, W. S. Lin, and K. J. R. Liu, *Behavior Dynamics in Media-Sharing Social Networks*. Cambridge University Press, 2011.

[3] M. Katz and C. Shapiro, "Technology adoption in the presence of network externalities," *Journal of Political Economy*, vol. 94, pp. 822–841, 1986.

[4] V. Bala and S. Goyal, "Learning from neighbours," *Review of Economic Studies*, vol. 65, pp. 595–621, 1998.

[5] D. Gale and S. Kariv, "Bayesian learning in social networks," *Games and Economic Behavior*, vol. 45, pp. 329–346, 2003.

[6] D. Acemoglu and A. Ozdaglar, "Opinion dynamics and learning in social networks," *Dynamic Games and Applications*, vol. 1, pp. 3–49, 2011.

[7] L. G. Epstein, J. Noor, and A. Sandroni, "Non-Bayesian learning," *B.E. Journal of Theoretical Economics*, vol. 10, pp. 1–16, 2010.

[8] B. Golub and M. O. Jackson, "Naive learning in social networks and the wisdom of crowds," *American Economic Journal: Microeconomics*, vol. 2, pp. 112–149, 2010.

[9] A. Jadbabaie, P. Molavi, A. Sandroni, and A. Tahbaz-Salehi, "Non-Bayesian social learning," *Games and Economic Behavior*, vol. 76, pp. 210–225, 2012.

[10] D. Fudenberg and J. Tirole, *Game Theory*. MIT Press, 1991.

[11] D. Aldous, I. Ibragimov, J. Jacod, and D. Aldous, "Exchangeability and related topics," in *Lecture Notes in Mathematics*, vol. 1117, pp. 1–198, Springer, 1985.

[12] C.-Y. Wang, Y. Chen, and K. J. R. Liu, "Chinese restaurant game," *IEEE Signal Processing Letters*, vol. 19, pp. 898–901, 2012.

[13] C. Y. Wang, Y. Chen, and K. J. R. Liu, "Sequential Chinese restaurant game," *IEEE Transactions on Signal Processing*, vol. 61, pp. 571–584, 2013.

[14] K. J. R. Liu and B. Wang, *Cognitive Radio Networking and Security: A Game-Theoretic View*. Cambridge University Press, 2010.

[15] B. Wang and K. J. R. Liu, "Advances in cognitive radios: A survey," *IEEE Journal of Selected Topics in Signal Processing*, vol. 5, pp. 5–23, 2011.

[16] R. Gallager, *Discrete Stochastic Processes*. MIT Press, 2011.

[17] M. L. Puterman, *Markov Decision Processes: Discrete Stochastic Dynamic Programming*. John Wiley & Sons, 1994.

[18] D. Bertsekas, *Dynamic Programming and Optimal Control*, 3rd ed. Athena Scientific, 2007.

[19] B. Wang, Y. Wu, and K. J. R. Liu, "Game theory for cognitive radio networks: An overview," *Computer Networks*, vol. 54, pp. 2537–2561, 2010.

[20] I. F. Akyildiz, B. F. Lo, and R. Balakrishnan, "Cooperative spectrum sensing in cognitive radio networks: A survey," *Physical Communication*, vol. 4, pp. 40–62, 2011.

[21] I. F. Akyildiz, W.-Y. Lee, M. C. Vuran, and S. Mohanty, "Next generation/dynamic spectrum access/cognitive radio wireless networks: A survey," *Computer Networks*, vol. 50, pp. 2127–2159, 2006.

[22] Z. Guan, T. Melodia, and G. Scutari, "Distributed queuing games in interference-limited wireless networks," in *Proc. IEEE ICC*, 2013.

[23] Z. Guan, T. Melodia, D. Yuan, and D. A. Pados, "Distributed spectrum management and relay selection in interference-limited cooperative wireless networks," in *Proc. ACM MobiCom*, 2011.

[24] G. S. Kasbekar and S. Sarkar, "Spectrum pricing games with bandwidth uncertainty and spatial reuse in cognitive radio networks," in *Proc. ACM MobiHoc*, 2010.

[25] M. G. Khoshkholgh, K. Navaie, and H. Yanikomeroglu, "Access strategies for spectrum sharing in fading environment: overlay, underlay, and mixed," *IEEE Transactions on Mobile Computing*, vol. 9, pp. 1780–1793, 2010.

[26] C. Jiang, Y. Chen, K. J. R. Liu, and Y. Ren, "Analysis of interference in cognitive radio networks with unknown primary behavior," in *Proc. IEEE ICC*, 2012.

[27] T. Dang, B. Sonkoly, and S. Molnar, "Fractal analysis and modeling of VoIP traffic," in *Proc. International Telecommunications Network Strategy and Planning Symposium*, 2004.

[28] H. Kim and K. G. Shin, "Efficient discovery of spectrum opportunities with MAC-layer sensing in cognitive radio networks," *IEEE Transactions on Mobile Computing*, vol. 7, pp. 533–545, 2008.

[29] D. R. Cox, *Renewal Theory*. Butler and Tanner, 1967.

[30] C. Jiang, Y. Chen, and K. J. R. Liu, "A renewal-theoretical framework for dynamic spectrum access with unknown primary behavior," in *Proc. IEEE Globecom*, 2012.

[31] C. Jiang, Y. Chen, K. J. R. Liu, and Y. Ren, "Renewal-theoretical dynamic spectrum access in cognitive radio networks with unknown primary behavior," *IEEE Journal of Selected Areas in Communications*, vol. 31, pp. 1–11, 2013.

14 Indian Buffet Game for Multiple Choices

In a dynamic system, it is crucial for users to know how to learn and make decisions. Some works are available in the social learning-related literature concerning the construction of beliefs regarding an uncertain system state; nevertheless, the incorporation of social learning into decision-making has never been a popular topic of study. Furthermore, it is possible for users to take multiple concurrent decisions in terms of various objects/resources, and usually their decisions tend to exert a negative impact on their mutual utility, which leads to an even more challenging problem. In this chapter, in order to conduct research on how users in a dynamic system acquire knowledge regarding the uncertain system state and make multiple concurrent decisions, an Indian buffet game is introduced with due consideration of both the current myopic utility and the impact exerted by the decisions of subsequent users. Analysis of the Indian buffet game is conducted under two different scenarios: first, when customers request multiple dishes without budget constraints; and second, when there are a budget constraints. To determine the subgame-perfect Nash equilibrium for customers and capture the special properties of the Nash equilibrium profile in a homogeneous setting, recursive best response algorithms are designed for both cases. Additionally, a non-Bayesian social learning algorithm is proposed, so that customers can learn the system state and theoretically prove its convergence. Finally, in order to verify the effectiveness and efficiency of the Indian buffet game, simulations are carried out.

14.1 Introduction

In a dynamic system, uncertainty regarding the system state is quite common for users during their decision-making. For instance, in the field of wireless communications, when making a choice of which channels to access, users are likely to be unaware of the exact capacity and quality of the channel. Moreover, the sharing of the same channel by plenty of users will incur an inevitable decrease in the average data rate and an increase in the end-to-end delay; therefore, users have to take others' decisions into account. This phenomenon is referred to as negative network externality [1] (i.e., the negative impact that is exerted by other users' behavior on a user's reward), and this is the reason why users are apt to refrain from making identical decisions to others so as to maximize their own utility. Our daily lives abound with similar phenomena, such as the selection of online cloud storage services and the choice of Wi-Fi access points [2].

Consequently, in a variety of fields, significant research focuses on the ways in which users in a dynamic system acquire knowledge regarding the system state and make optimal decisions with consideration of the impacts of others' decisions [3–6].

Users in a dynamic system, despite their limited awareness of the uncertain system state, are still able to generate a probabilistic belief concerning the system state on the basis of social learning. The social learning literature [7–12] offers studies on a variety of learning rules that have the aim of eventually learning the true system state. In the majority of these existing works, the learning problem is typically shaped as a dynamic game with incomplete information, and the principal focus is on determining whether users are capable of learning the true system state at the equilibria. However, all of these previous works were based on the assumption that users' utility functions were mutually independent; in other words, they excluded the concept of network externality, which is a frequently seen phenomenon in dynamic systems and can have a remarkable impact on users' utilities and decisions.

In Chapter 12, a general framework known as the Chinese restaurant game was introduced for studying the social learning problem with negative network externality. The origin of this concept can be found in the Chinese restaurant process [13], which is applied to the simulation of unknown distributions in nonparametric learning methods in the field of machine learning. In the Chinese restaurant game, there is a finite number of tables of various sizes, and a limited number of customers request tables to be seated at in sequence. Due to customers' unawareness of the exact size of each table, which influences the mutual utility, they are supposed to learn the table sizes by drawing on external information. Furthermore, each customer needs to consider subsequent customers' decisions when requesting a table, since each table has limited dining space (i.e., negative network externality). Next, in Chapter 13, an extension of the Chinese restaurant game was designed as a dynamic population setting in which customers' arrival at and departure from the restaurant followed a Poisson process. The theoretical framework of the general Chinese restaurant game makes possible the analysis of the social learning and strategic decision-making of rational users in a network [14].

It is assumed that each customer is allowed to choose only one table in the Chinese restaurant game. However, in a variety of real applications, users are entitled to multiple concurrent selections (e.g., mobile terminals are able to access multiple channels immediately and users may enjoy multiple cloud storage services). To cope with a challenge such as this, in this chapter, in analogy to the Chinese restaurant game that introduced strategic behaviors into the nonstrategic Chinese restaurant process, we introduce a new game known as the *Indian buffet game*, which introduces strategic behaviors into the nonstrategic Indian buffet process [15]. In the Indian buffet process, there is an infinite number of dishes and each customer is allowed to order several dishes according to a Poisson process. Such a stochastic process defines a probability distribution for use as a prior in probabilistic models. Through the incorporation of customers' rational behaviors, the extension of the Indian buffet process is shaped into the Indian buffet game, and studies are conducted on customers' optimal decisions in their sequential choice of dishes. The Indian buffet game is a useful framework for carrying out research on the problem of multiple dish selection through the integration of social learning and strategic decision-making with negative network externality. While much work has been done on simultaneous decision-making problems [6,16,17], the sequential decision-making problem is less frequently investigated in the literature, in which a user has to take into account previous users' decisions and predict subsequent users' decisions. Moreover, sequential decision-making scenarios are even more practically relevant, particularly in the field of wireless communications, which have to contend with the difficulty of synchronization among all users. As a consequence, in this chapter, focus is given to sequential decision-making analysis, and some insights and results regarding this problem will be offered. The discussion will be carried out using two cases: Indian buffet games with and without budget constraints, where "with budget constraints" indicates that each customer is allowed only a limited number of dishes, and "without budget constraints" represents no limitation.

14.2   System Model

14.2.1   Indian Buffet Game Formulation

We may think of an Indian buffet restaurant that provides M dishes denoted by $r_1, r_2, \ldots, r_M$. There are N customers marked as $1, 2, \ldots, N$ requesting dishes for a meal in sequence. Each dish is to be shared among a number of customers and each customer is entitled to the selection of several dishes. It is assumed that all N customers are rational in the sense that they will select dishes that enable them to achieve the greatest utility. In this case, the selection problem featuring several dishes can be shaped as a noncooperative game, known as the *Indian buffet game*, as follows:

- *Players*: N rational customers in the restaurant.
- *Strategies*: Since each customer is entitled to the selection of multiple dishes, the strategy set can be defined as

$$\mathcal{X} = \{\emptyset, \{r_1\}, \ldots, \{r_1, r_2\}, \ldots, \{r_1, r_2, \ldots, r_M\}\}, \tag{14.1}$$

where each strategy is a combination of dishes and $\emptyset$ means no dish is requested. Obviously, the customers' strategy set is finite with 2^M elements. We denote the strategy of customer i as $\mathbf{d}_i = (d_{i,1}, d_{i,2}, \ldots, d_{i,M})'$, where $d_{i,j} = 1$ represents customer i requesting dish r_j and otherwise we have $d_{i,j} = 0$. The strategy profile of all customers can be denoted by a $M \times N$ matrix as follows[1]:

$$\mathbf{D} = (\mathbf{d}_1, \mathbf{d}_2, \ldots, \mathbf{d}_N) = \begin{bmatrix} d_{1,1} & d_{2,1} & \cdots & d_{N,1} \\ d_{1,2} & d_{2,2} & \cdots & d_{N,2} \\ \vdots & \vdots & \ddots & \vdots \\ d_{1,M} & d_{2,M} & \cdots & d_{N,M} \end{bmatrix}. \tag{14.2}$$

---

[1] In this chapter, bold symbols represent vectors, bold capital symbols represent matrices, subscript i denotes the customer index, subscript j denotes the dish index, and superscript (t) denotes the time slot index.

- *Utility function*: The utility of each customer hinges on two factors: first, the quality of the dish; and second, the number of customers who share the same dish because of negative network externality. The deliciousness or the size of a dish symbolizes its quality. Let $q_j \in Q$ denote the quality of dish r_j, where Q refers to the quality space and N_j represents the total number of customers requesting dish r_j. We can then define the utility function of customer i requesting dish r_j as

$$u_{i,j}(q_j, N_j) = g_{i,j}(q_j, N_j) - c_{i,j}(q_j, N_j), \tag{14.3}$$

where $g_{i,j}(\cdot)$ is the gain function and $c_{i,j}(\cdot)$ is the cost function. Note that the utility function is an increasing function in terms of q_j and a decreasing function in terms of N_j, which can be considered as characteristic of negative network externality since the utility obtained by customer i decreases along with the increase in the number of customers requesting dish r_j. Note that if no dish is requested, the utility is zero for a customer.

We hereby define the dish state $\boldsymbol{\theta} = \{\theta_1, \theta_2, \ldots \theta_M\}$, where $\theta_j \in \Theta$ denotes the state of dish r_j. The dish state can be perceived as the quality of the ingredients or cooking. Θ represents the set of all possible states, which is assumed to be finite. The dish state remains constant over time until the remodeling of the complete Indian buffet restaurant. The quality of the dish, q_j, is assumed to be a random variable following the distribution $f_j(\cdot|\theta_j)$, which indicates that the distribution of dish quality q_j is determined by the state of the dish θ_j. Note that the dish quality is identical for every user in a certain time slot, which follows distribution $f_j(\cdot|\theta_j)$, and a realization of this exists in each time slot. No customer is informed of the dish state $\boldsymbol{\theta} \in \Theta^M$ (i.e., customers are unaware of the exact taste of the dish before requesting and tasting it). However, they may have watched some advertisements or collected certain reviews about the restaurant. Such information can be considered as types of signals regarding the true state of the restaurant. In this case, customers can evaluate $\boldsymbol{\theta}$ based on such available information (i.e., the information they collected in advance and/or gleaned from other customers).

In the Indian buffet game model, the system time is divided into time slots and the assumption is made that the dish quality q_j with $j = 1, 2, \ldots, M$ varies independently from one time slot to another according to the corresponding conditional distributions $f_j(\cdot|\theta_j)$. In each time slot, customers sequentially decide on which dishes to request. Two major issues are to be addressed in the Indian buffet game. First, owing to the unknown states, it is of great importance to design an effective social learning rule for customers to learn from others as well as from their own previous results. Second, given customers' knowledge about the state, we should characterize the equilibrium that rational customers will adopt in each time slot. In order to ensure fairness among customers, it is assumed in this chapter that customers have divergent orders for selecting dishes at various time slots. The customer index $1, 2, \ldots, N$ represents the dish request order (i.e., customer i stands for the i-th customer). In this case, it is adequate for customers to merely take into account the expected utilities at the current time slot. Furthermore, despite the fact that each customer is allowed to request more

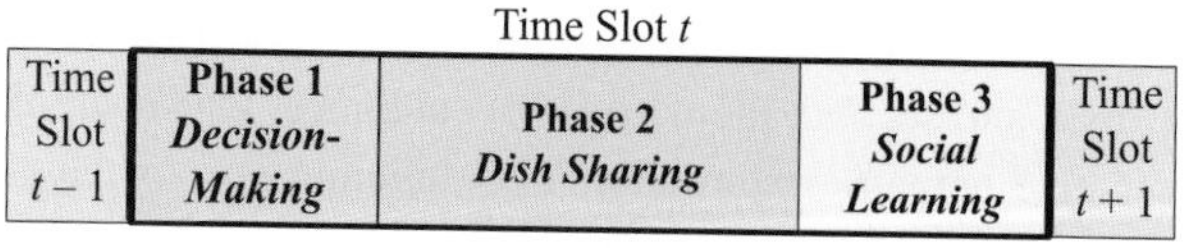

Time Slot t

Time Slot $t-1$	Phase 1 Decision-Making	Phase 2 Dish Sharing	Phase 3 Social Learning	Time Slot $t+1$

Figure 14.1 Time slot structure of the Indian buffet game.

than one dish, the total number of requests has a ceiling that is given by the budget constraint as follows:

$$\sum_{j=1}^{M} d_{i,j} \leq L, \quad \forall\, i = 1, 2, \ldots, N. \tag{14.4}$$

A special case of (14.4) states that $L \geq M$, which is identical to the case without budget constraints, where customers can request an infinite number of dishes. In the next two sections, we will discuss the Indian buffet game under two scenarios: without budget constraints ($L \geq M$) and with budget constraints ($L < M$), respectively.

14.2.2   Time Slot Structure of the Indian Buffet Game

Since customers are unaware of the dish state $\theta \in \Theta^M$, we introduce the concept of belief to describe their uncertainty regarding this state [18]. Let us represent the belief as $\mathbf{P}^{(t)} = \{\mathbf{p}_j^{(t)}, j = 1, 2, .., M\}$, where $\mathbf{p}_j^{(t)} = \{p_j^{(t)}(\theta), \theta \in \Theta\}$ stands for customers' estimation of the probability distribution related to the state of dish r_j at time slot t. Since customers are able to acquire knowledge about the dish state in advance, it is assumed that all customers begin with a prior belief $p_{i,j}^{(0)}(\theta)$ for each state $\theta \in \Theta$. Note that the prior beliefs of all customers can be divergent; however due to the fact that all customers share their beliefs with others, they will have identical beliefs after the first belief updating stage. In this section, we will discuss the social learning algorithm (i.e., the way in which customers update their belief $\mathbf{P}^{(t)}$ at each time slot).

Figure 14.1 presents an illustration of the time slot structure of the Indian buffet game. At each time slot $t \in \{1, 2, \ldots\}$, there exist three phases: the decision-making phase, the dish sharing phase, and the social learning phase.

Phase 1: Decision-Making

In this phase, customers sequentially decide on which dishes to request and share their decisions with others; in other words, everyone is informed of what others are going to get. Customer i decides to obtain the greatest expected utility in the current time slot on the basis of the belief at the current time slot $\mathbf{P}^{(t)}$, the decisions of the previous $(i - 1)$ customers $\{\mathbf{d}_1, \mathbf{d}_2, \ldots, \mathbf{d}_{i-1}\}$, and their own predictions of the subsequent $(N - i)$ customers' decisions.

Phase 2: Dish Sharing

In the second phase, each customer requests their expected dishes and receives a utility $u_{i,j}(q_j, N_j)$ in line with the dish quality q_j and the number of customers N_j

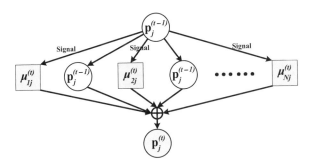

Figure 14.2 Non-Bayesian learning rule for each dish.

sharing the same dish as defined in (14.3). Note that since all customers are aware of N_j following the decision-making phase, the customers who requested dish r_j at time slot t can make a prediction regarding the dish quality q_j from the utility received. We may represent such predictions as $s_{i,j}^{(t)} \in Q, s_{i,j} \sim f_j(\cdot|\theta_j)$, which serves as the signal in the learning procedure. In addition, the customers who have not requested r_j at time slot t are unable to make any predictions regarding the dish quality q_j and thus have no inferred signal by themselves. Due to this asymmetric structure (i.e., not every customer infers signals), the learning problem is different from that in traditional social learning settings and thus makes learning the true state more challenging.

Phase 3: Social Learning

The observed/inferred signals in the second phase enable customers to update their beliefs according to a non-Bayesian social learning rule. Two major steps in the social learning rule are illustrated in Figure 14.2. In the first step, each customer updates their local intermediate belief on θ_j, $\mu_{i,j}^{(t)}$, and shares this intermediate belief with others afterwards. Since belief sharing helps each customer to collect more information and consequently improve their learning performance, it is assumed that the customers are motivated to do so. In the second step, each customer linearly combines their intermediate belief with those of other customers.[2] In accordance with Bayes' theorem [19], customer i's intermediate belief on the state of dish r_j, $\mu_{i,j}^{(t)} = \{\mu_{i,j}^{(t)}(\theta), \theta \in \Theta\}$, can be calculated by

$$\mu_{i,j}^{(t)}(\theta) = \frac{f_j(s_{i,j}^{(t)}|\theta)p_j^{(t-1)}(\theta)}{\sum_\Theta f_j(s_{i,j}^{(t)}|\theta)p_j^{(t-1)}(\theta)}, \quad \forall \theta \in \Theta. \tag{14.5}$$

It is shown in (14.5) that when customer i has requested r_j at time slot t, they will incorporate the corresponding signal into their intermediate belief $\mu_{i,j}^{(t)}$. Otherwise they

---

[2] Note that the state learning processes (i.e., belief updating) of all dishes are independent.

will adopt the previous belief $\mathbf{p}_j^{(t-1)}$. Afterwards, each customer linearly combines their intermediate belief with those of other customers as follows:

$$p_j^{(t)}(\theta) = \frac{1}{N} \sum_{i=1}^{N} [d_{i,j}^{(t)} \mu_{i,j}^{(t)}(\theta) + \left(1 - d_{i,j}^{(t)}\right) p_j^{(t-1)}(\theta)], \tag{14.6}$$

$$\forall \, \theta \in \Theta, \text{ and } j = 1, 2, \ldots, M,$$

where $d_{i,j}^{(t)}$ is the strategy of customer i at time slot t.

It is apparent that, unlike the Chinese restaurant game in which each customer is allowed to choose only one table [20], customers in the Indian buffet game are able to request multiple dishes concurrently. In addition, there are two more major differences between those two games. One difference is that each customer in the Chinese restaurant game is entitled to only one decision, whereas customers in the Indian buffet game are allowed to make decisions repeatedly (i.e., one-shot game vs. repeated game), and this is why customers in the Indian buffet game are in a position to learn from their previous experiences and an effective learning rule is required so that convergence can be ensured. The other difference consists of the learning rule. In the Chinese restaurant game, customers make sequential decisions and then disclose their signals to subsequent customers, where a Bayesian social learning rule is applied and thus the customers can combine the signals from previous customers. However, in the Indian buffet game, customers only disclose their intermediate beliefs rather than signals, and a non-Bayesian social learning rule is applied for the generation of their final beliefs.

14.3   Indian Buffet Game without Budget Constraints

In this section, studies are conducted on the Indian buffet game without budget constraints, which is in line with the case where $L \geq M$ in (14.4). Without budget constraints, it is advisable for customers to request all dishes that can offer them positive expected utility so as to maximize their total expected utility. Initially, it is known that without budget constraints, the decision of whether to request one dish or not is independent of other dishes (i.e., the Indian buffet game that concurrently selects multiple dishes is decomposed into a range of elementary Indian buffet games for selecting a single dish). In analogy to the Chinese restaurant game model [21], in the elementary Indian buffet game, each customer is allowed to choose only one dish; however, these games are different since all customers cooperatively estimate the dish state in the Indian buffet game model, whereas sequential learning is adopted in the Chinese restaurant game model. We propose a recursive algorithm that characterizes the subgame-perfect equilibrium of the Indian buffet game without budge constraints. Ultimately, we discuss the homogeneous case in which customers have identical utility functions.

To demonstrate the independence among different dishes, we first define the best response of a customer given other customers' actions. Let us define $\mathbf{n}_{-i} = \{n_{-i,1}, n_{-i,2}, \ldots, n_{-i,M}\}$, while

$$n_{-i,j} = \sum_{k \neq i} d_{k,j} \qquad (14.7)$$

stands for the number of customers apart from customer i choosing r_j. Let $\mathbf{P} = \{\mathbf{p}_1, \mathbf{p}_2, \ldots, \mathbf{p}_M\}$, where $\mathbf{p}_j = \{p_j(\theta), \theta \in \Theta\}$ is the customer's belief in terms of the state of dish r_j at the current time slot.[3] On the condition of $\mathbf{P}$ and $\mathbf{n}_{-i}$, the best response of customer i, $\mathbf{d}_i^* = (d_{i,1}^*, d_{i,2}^*, \ldots, d_{i,M}^*)'$, can be calculated by

$$\mathbf{d}_i^* = \mathrm{BR}_i(\mathbf{P}, \mathbf{n}_{-i}) = \underset{\mathbf{d}_i \in \{0,1\}^M}{\arg\max} \sum_{j=1}^{M} d_{i,j} \cdot U_{i,j}, \qquad (14.8)$$

where $U_{i,j}$ is customer i's expected utility for requesting dish r_j given belief $\mathbf{P}$, which can be given by

$$U_{i,j} = \sum_{\Theta} \sum_{Q} u_{i,j}(q_j, n_{-i,j} + d_{i,j}) f_j(q_j|\theta_j) p_j(\theta_j), \qquad (14.9)$$

where Q is the quality/signal set and $q_j \in Q$.

Due to the fact that the optimization problem is subject to no constraints in (14.8) and $U_{i,j}$ is only related to $d_{i,j}$, (14.8) may be put as

$$\mathbf{d}_i^* = \mathrm{BR}_i(\mathbf{P}, \mathbf{n}_{-i}) = \sum_{j=1}^{M} \underset{\mathbf{d}_i \in \{0,1\}^M}{\arg\max} \, d_{i,j} \cdot U_{i,j}, \qquad (14.10)$$

It is known from (14.10) that the optimal decision regarding one dish bears no relation to the decisions regarding other dishes, which results in independence between the different dishes. In this case, we have

$$d_{i,j}^* = \underset{d_{i,j} \in \{0,1\}}{\arg\max} \, d_{i,j} \cdot U_{i,j}. \qquad (14.11)$$

Thanks to the independence property, the analysis can be simplified through the decomposition of the original Indian buffet game into M elementary Indian buffet games. The elementary Indian buffet game refers to the case where there is only one dish for the customers, and therefore each customer has a binary decision (i.e., to request or not to request). For the rest of this section, focus will be given to the analysis of the elementary Indian buffet game, and the dish index j will be discarded for notational simplification. Consequently, we can rewrite the best response of customer i according to the latest belief information $p(\theta)$ as follows:

$$d_i^* = \mathrm{BR}_i(\mathbf{p}, n_{-i}) = \underset{d_i \in \{0,1\}}{\arg\max} \, d_i \cdot U_i \qquad (14.12)$$

$$= \begin{cases} 1, & \text{if } U_i = \sum_{\Theta} \sum_{Q} u_i(q, n_{-i} + 1) f(q|\theta) p(\theta) > 0; \\ 0, & \text{otherwise.} \end{cases}$$

---

[3] Since we are discussing the Indian buffet game in one time slot, the superscript (t) is omitted in Sections 14.3 and 14.4.

14.3.1   Recursive Best Response Algorithm

In this section, studies are conducted on the solution to the best response defined in (14.12) for each customer. According to (14.12), in order to decide whether to request the dish or not, customer i needs to know n_{-i} to calculate the expected utility U_i. However, due to the fact that the customers make sequential decisions, it is impossible for customer i to acquire any knowledge of the decisions of those who will come after them and consequently they need to make predictions regarding the subsequent customers' decisions on the basis of their beliefs and acquired information.

Let m_i represent the number of customers who will request the dish after customer i, then the recursive form of m_i can be put as

$$m_i = m_{i+1} + d_{i+1}. \tag{14.13}$$

Let $m_i|_{d_i=0}$ and $m_i|_{d_i=1}$ stand for m_i under the condition of $d_i = 0$ and $d_i = 1$, respectively. Denoted by $n_i = \sum_{k=1}^{i-1} d_k$ is the number of customers choosing the dish before customer i. The estimated number of customers who select the dish apart from customer i can then be written as follows:

$$\hat{n}_{-i}|_{d_i=0} = n_i + m_i|_{d_i=0}, \tag{14.14}$$

$$\hat{n}_{-i}|_{d_i=1} = n_i + m_i|_{d_i=1}. \tag{14.15}$$

Note that $\hat{n}_{-i}|_{d_i=0}$ and $\hat{n}_{-i}|_{d_i=1}$ are different from n_{-i} since the values of $d_{i+1}, d_{i+2}, \ldots, d_N$ are estimated rather than true observations.

In accordance with (14.15), we can quantify the expected utility of customer i when $d_i = 1$ as

$$U_i|_{d_i=1} = \sum_{\Theta} \sum_{Q} u_i(q, n_i + m_i|_{d_i=1} + 1) f(q|\theta) p(\theta). \tag{14.16}$$

Since the utility of customer i is zero when $d_i = 0$, the best response of customer i can be obtained through

$$d_i^* = \begin{cases} 1, & \text{if } U_i|_{d_i=1} > 0; \\ 0, & \text{otherwise.} \end{cases} \tag{14.17}$$

According to (14.17), we can determine the best response of customer i given belief $\mathbf{p}$, current observation n_i, and predicted number of subsequent customers who select the dish $m_i|_{d_i=1}$. To predict $m_i|_{d_i=1}$, customer i has to make predictions regarding the decisions of all customers from $i + 1$ to N. For customer N, since they are aware of the exact decisions made by all previous customers, they are able to determine the best response free from making predictions (i.e., $m_N = 0$). Along these lines, it is intuitive to design a recursive algorithm to predict $m_i|_{d_i=1}$ by taking into account all possible decisions of customers from $i + 1$ to N and sequentially updating $m_i = m_{i+1} + d_{i+1}$. In Algorithm 10, we present the recursive algorithm BR_EIBG($\mathbf{p}, n_i, i$), which describes the way to make a prediction regarding $m_i|_{d_i=1}$ and to determine the best response d_i for customer i on the condition of current belief $\mathbf{p}$ and observation n_i. Furthermore, in order to appropriately predict m_i in the recursion

---

Algorithm 10: BR_EIBG($\mathbf{p}, n_i, i$).

---

(1) **if** Customer $i == N$ **then**

(2)   //********For customer** N******//

(3)   **if** $U_N = \sum_\Theta \sum_Q u_N(q, n_N + 1) f(q|\theta) p(\theta) > 0$ **then**

(4) $d_N \leftarrow 1$

(5)   **else**

(6) $d_N \leftarrow 0$

(7)   **end if**

(8) $m_N \leftarrow 0$

(9) **else**

(10)   //********For customer** $1, 2, \ldots, N - 1$******//

(11)   //***Predicting***//

(12) $(d_{i+1}, m_{i+1}) \leftarrow$ BR_EIBG($\mathbf{p}, n_i + 1, i + 1$)

(13) $m_i \leftarrow m_{i+1} + d_{i+1}$

(14)   //***Making decision***//

(15)   **if** $U_i = \sum_\Theta \sum_Q u_i(q, n_i + m_i + 1) f(q|\theta) p(\theta) > 0$ **then**

(16) $d_i \leftarrow 1$

(17)   **else**

(18) $(d_{i+1}, m_{i+1}) \leftarrow$ BR_EIBG($\mathbf{p}, n_i, i + 1$)

(19) $m_i \leftarrow m_{i+1} + d_{i+1}$

(20) $d_i \leftarrow 0$

(21)   **end if**

(22) **end if**

(23) **return** (d_i, m_i)

---

procedure, we compute and return $m_i|_{d_i=0}$ when the best response of customer i is 0. Algorithm 10 lists all possible combinations of the choices made by customers in a dynamic programming manner. Unlike the exhaustive search with the complexity order of $O(2^N)$, Algorithm 10 has the order $O(N^2)$, in which N represents the total number of customers. Hereinafter, it will be proved that the action profile specified in BR_EIBG($\mathbf{p}, n_i, i$) serves as a subgame-perfect Nash equilibrium for the elementary Indian buffet game.

14.3.2   Subgame-Perfect Nash Equilibrium

In this section, it will be demonstrated that Algorithm 10 results in a subgame-perfect Nash equilibrium for the elementary Indian buffet game. Hereinafter, formal definitions will be rendered for Nash equilibrium, subgame, and subgame-perfect Nash equilibrium.

DEFINITION 14.1   Given the belief $\mathbf{p} = \{p(\theta), \theta \in \Theta\}$, the action profile $\mathbf{d}^* = \{d_1^*, d_2^*, \ldots, d_N^*\}$ is a Nash equilibrium of the N-customer elementary Indian buffet game if and only if $\forall\, i \in \{1, 2, \ldots, N\}, d_i^* = \mathrm{BR}_i g(\mathbf{p}, \sum_{k \neq i} d_k^* g)$ as given in (14.12).

DEFINITION 14.2   A subgame of the N-customer elementary Indian buffet game comprises three elements as follows: (1) it begins with customer i with $i = 1$, $2, \ldots, N$; (2) it has the belief $\mathbf{p}$ at the present time slot; and (3) it has the current observation n_i, which symbolizes the decisions made by the previous customers.

DEFINITION 14.3   A Nash equilibrium is a subgame-perfect Nash equilibrium if and only if it is a Nash equilibrium for every subgame.

Based on Definitions 14.1–14.3, it is shown in Theorem 14.4 that the action profile derived from Algorithm 10 is a subgame-perfect Nash equilibrium for the elementary Indian buffet game.

THEOREM 14.4   *Given the belief* $\mathbf{p} = \{p(\theta), \theta \in \Theta\}$, *the action profile* $\mathbf{d}^* = \{d_1^*, d_2^*, \ldots, d_N^*\}$, *with* d_i^* *being determined by BR_EIBG($\mathbf{p}, n_i, i$) and* $n_i = \sum_{k=1}^{i-1} d_k^*$, *is a subgame-perfect Nash equilibrium for the elementary Indian buffet game.*

Proof   Initially it is known that d_k^* is the best response of customer k in the subgame beginning with customer $i, \forall\, 1 \leq i \leq k \leq N$.

If $k = N$, it can be seen that BR_EIBG($\mathbf{p}, n_N, N$) assigns the value of d_N^* directly as

$$
d_N^* = \begin{cases} 1, & \text{if } U_N = \sum_\Theta \sum_Q u_N(q, n_N + 1) f(q|\theta) p(\theta) > 0; \\ 0, & \text{otherwise.} \end{cases}
\tag{14.18}
$$

Since $n_N = n_{-N}$, we have $d_k^* = BR_k(\mathbf{p}, n_{-k})$ when $k = N$ following (14.12) (i.e., d_k^* is the best response of customer k).

If $k < N$, suppose d_k^* is the best response of customer k derived by BR_EIBG($\mathbf{p}, n_k, k$). If $d_k^* = 0$, denoting $d_k' = 1$ as the contradiction, according to BR_EIBG($\mathbf{p}, n_k, k$)

$$
U_k|_{d_k'=1} = \sum_\Theta \sum_Q u_k(q, n_k + m_k + 1) f(q|\theta) p(\theta) < 0 = U_k|_{d_k^*=0},
\tag{14.19}
$$

which indicates that customer k is not motivated to deviate from $d_k^* = 1$ provided that the decisions of the other customers have been predicted. If $d_k^* = 1$, when $d_k' = 0$ is presented as the contradiction, it is known from BR_EIBG($\mathbf{p}, n_k, k$) that

$$
U_k|_{d_k'=0} = 0 < U_k|_{d_k^*=1} = \sum_\Theta \sum_Q u_k(q, n_k + m_k + 1) f(q|\theta) p(\theta),
\tag{14.20}
$$

which indicates that customer k is not motivated to deviate from $d_k^* = 0$ provided that the decisions of the other customers have been predicted. Therefore, $d_k^* =$ BR_EIBG($\mathbf{p}, n_k, k$) is the best response of customer k in the subgame of the elementary Indian buffet game starting with customer i. Moreover, since the statement is true for $\forall\, k$ satisfying $i \leq k \leq N$, we know that $\{d_i^*, d_{i+1}^*, \ldots, d_N^*\}$ is the Nash equilibrium for the subgame starting from customer i. Therefore, according to the definition of a subgame-perfect Nash equilibrium, we can conclude that Theorem 14.4 is true.

14.3.3   Homogeneous Case

Section 14.3.2 showed that a recursive procedure is required for the determination of the best responses in the elementary Indian buffet game. This is because a customer has to make predictions regarding the decisions made by all subsequent customers so as to decide on their best response. In this section, to obtain the best response more concisely, the game is simplified to a homogeneous setting.

In the homogeneous case, it is assumed that all customers share identical utility functions (i.e., $u_i(q,n) = u(q,n)$ for all i,q,n). In this setting, the equilibrium can be characterized in a much simpler manner, as is shown in Lemma 14.5.

LEMMA 14.5   *In the N-customer elementary Indian buffet game in a homogeneous setting, if $\mathbf{d}^* = \{d_1^*, d_2^*, \ldots, d_N^*\}$ is the Nash equilibrium action profile specified by BR_EIBG(), then we have $d_i^* = 1$ if and only if $0 \le i \le n^*$, where $n^* = \sum_{k=1}^{N} d_k^*$.*

Proof   Suppose the best response of customer i is $d_i^* = 0$. Then, according to Algorithm 10, we have

$$U_i = \sum_{\Theta} \sum_{Q} u(q, n_i + m_i|_{d_i=1} + 1) f(q|\theta) p(\theta) \le 0. \tag{14.21}$$

The prediction of m_i on the condition of $d_i = 1$ is determined by the recursive estimations of the decisions made by all subsequent customers. Specifically, we have $m_i|_{d_i=1} = d_{i+1}|_{d_i=1} + m_{i+1}|_{d_i=1}$, where the value of $d_{i+1}|_{d_i=1}$ can be calculated as follows:

$$d_{i+1}|_{d_i=1} = \begin{cases} 1, & \text{if } U_{i+1}|_{d_i=1} > 0; \\ 0, & \text{otherwise,} \end{cases} \tag{14.22}$$

with

$$U_{i+1}|_{d_i=1} = \sum_{\Theta} \sum_{Q} u(q, n_i + 1 + m_{i+1}|_{d_i=1} + 1) f(q|\theta) p(\theta). \tag{14.23}$$

Since $n_i + 1 + m_{i+1}|_{d_i=1} + 1 \ge n_i + m_i|_{d_i=1} + 1$ and $u(q,n)$ is a decreasing function in terms of n, we have $d_{i+1}|_{d_i=1} = 0$ according to (14.21) and (14.23). Following the same argument, we can show that $d_k|_{d_i=1} = 0$ for all $k = i + 1, i + 2, \ldots, N$. Therefore, we have

$$m_i|_{d_i=1} = \sum_{k=i+1}^{N} d_k|_{d_i=1} = 0. \tag{14.24}$$

Let us now consider the best response of customer $i + 1$, which can be calculated by

$$d_{i+1}^* = \begin{cases} 1, & \text{if } U_{i+1} > 0; \\ 0, & \text{otherwise,} \end{cases} \tag{14.25}$$

where

$$U_{i+1} = \sum_{\Theta} \sum_{Q} u(q, n_{i+1} + m_{i+1}|_{d_{i+1}=1} + 1) f(q|\theta) p(\theta). \tag{14.26}$$

Since $n_{i+1} = n_i + d_i$, $m_i|_{d_i=1} = 0$, and $m_{i+1}|_{d_{i+1}=1} \ge 0$, we have $n_{i+1} + m_{i+1}|_{d_{i+1}=1} + 1 \ge n_i + m_i|_{d_i=1} + 1$. According to (14.21), (14.26), and the decreasing property of the utility function in terms of the number of customers sharing the same dish, we have $d_{i+1}^* = 0$.

Following the same argument, we can show that if $d_i^* = 0$, then $d_k^* = 0$ for all $k \in \{i+1, i+2, \ldots, N\}$. Since all decisions can take values of either 0 or 1, we have $d_i^* = 1$ if and only if $0 \le i \le \sum_{k=1}^{N} d_k^*$. This completes the proof.

It is known from Lemma 14.5 that a threshold structure can be found in the Nash equilibrium of the elementary Indian buffet game in the homogeneous setting. The threshold structure is symbolized by the fact that if $d_i^* = 0$, then $d_k^* = 0, \forall k \in \{i+1, i+2, \ldots, N\}$, and if $d_i^* = 1$, then $d_k^* = 1, \forall k \in \{1, 2, \ldots i-1\}$. The result is subject to the easy extension to the Indian buffet game without budget constraints in the homogeneous setting, as is shown in Theorem 14.6.

THEOREM 14.6   *In the M-dish and N-customer Indian buffet game without budget constraints, if all of the customers have the same utility functions, there is a threshold structure in the Nash equilibrium matrix* $\mathbf{D}^*$ *presented as (14.2); in other words, for any row* $j \in \{1, 2, \ldots, M\}$ *of* $\mathbf{D}^*$, *there is a* $T_j \in \{1, 2, \ldots, N\}$ *satisfying*

$$d_{i,j}^* = \begin{cases} 1, & \forall i < T_j; \\ 0, & \forall i \ge T_j. \end{cases} \tag{14.27}$$

Proof   This theorem follows straightforwardly through the application of Lemma 14.5 to the M independent dishes case.

14.4   Indian Buffet Game with Budget Constraints

In this section, studies are conducted on the Indian buffet game with budget constraints, which is in line with the case with $L < M$ in (14.4). Differently from the previous case, in which each customer was subject to budget constraints, the selection among different dishes is no longer independent but coupled. Hereinafter, we will first discuss a recursive algorithm that is able to capture the feature of the subgame-perfect Nash equilibrium of the Indian buffet game with budget constraints. Next, to obtain more insights, we will discuss a simplified case in a homogeneous setting.

14.4.1   Recursive Best Response Algorithm

In the budget constraint cases, it is assumed that each customer is entitled to request a maximum of L dishes at each time slot with $L < M$. In this case, the best response of customer i can be determined through the following optimization problem:

$$\mathbf{d}_i^* = \mathrm{BR}_i(\mathbf{P}, \mathbf{n}_{-i}) = \underset{\mathbf{d}_i \in \{0,1\}^M}{\arg\max} \sum_{j=1}^{M} d_{i,j} \cdot U_{i,j}, \tag{14.28}$$

$$\text{s.t. } \sum_{j=1}^{M} d_{i,j} \le L < M,$$

where

$$U_{i,j} = \sum_{\Theta} \sum_{Q} u_{i,j}(q_j, n_{-i,j} + d_{i,j}) f_j(q_j|\theta_j) p_j(\theta_j). \qquad (14.29)$$

From (14.28), it is clear that customer i's decision regarding dish r_j is related to all other dishes, and consequently (14.28) is unable to be decomposed into M sub-problems. Nevertheless, we are still able to determine the best response of each customer through the comparison among all possible combinations of L dishes. Let $\Phi = \{\phi_1, \phi_2, \ldots, \phi_H\}$ denote the set of all combinations of l ($1 \le l \le L$) dishes out of M dishes, where $H = \sum_{l=1}^{L} C_M^l = \sum_{l=1}^{L} \frac{M!}{l!(M-l)!}$ and $\phi_h = (\phi_{h,1}, \phi_{h,2}, \ldots, \phi_{h,M})'$ is one possible combination, with $\phi_{h,j}$ representing whether dish r_j is requested. For example

$$\phi_h = (\underbrace{1, 1, \ldots, 1}_{l}, \underbrace{0, 0, \ldots, 0}_{M-l})' \qquad (14.30)$$

means that the customer requests dishes $r_1, r_2, \ldots, r_l$ ($1 \le l \le L$). In other words, Φ is the candidate strategy set of each customer with constraints L.

Let us define customer i's observation of previous customers' decisions as

$$\mathbf{n}_i = \{n_{i,1}, n_{i,2}, \ldots, n_{i,M}\}, \qquad (14.31)$$

where $n_{i,j} = \sum_{k=1}^{i-1} d_{k,j}$ is the number of customers choosing dish r_j before customer i. Let $\mathbf{m}_i$ denote the subsequent customers' decisions after customer i. We have its recursive form as

$$\mathbf{m}_i = \mathbf{m}_{i+1} + \mathbf{d}_{i+1}. \qquad (14.32)$$

Then let

$$\mathbf{m}_i|_{\mathbf{d}_i=\phi_h} = \{m_{i,1}|_{\mathbf{d}_i=\phi_h}, m_{i,2}|_{\mathbf{d}_i=\phi_h}, \ldots, m_{i,M}|_{\mathbf{d}_i=\phi_h}\}, \qquad (14.33)$$

with $m_{i,j}|_{\mathbf{d}_i=\phi_h}$ being the predicted number of subsequent customers who will request dish r_j under the condition that $\mathbf{d}_i = \phi_h$, where $\mathbf{d}_i = (d_{i,1}, d_{i,1}, \ldots, d_{i,M})'$ and $\phi_h \in \Phi$. In such a case, the predicted number of customers choosing different dishes excluding customer i is

$$\hat{\mathbf{n}}_{-i}|_{\mathbf{d}_i=\phi_h} = \mathbf{n}_i + \mathbf{m}_i|_{\mathbf{d}_i=\phi_h}. \qquad (14.34)$$

According to the definitions above, we can get customer i's expected utility when obtaining dish r_j when $\mathbf{d}_i = \phi_h$ as

$$U_{i,j}|_{\mathbf{d}_i=\phi_h} = \phi_{h,j} \sum_{\Theta} \sum_{Q} u_{i,j}(q_j, n_{i,j} + m_{i,j}|_{\mathbf{d}_i=\phi_h} + \phi_{h,j}) f_j(q_j|\theta_j) p_j(\theta_j).$$

$$(14.35)$$

Algorithm 11: BR_IBG($\mathbf{P}, \mathbf{n}_i, i$).

---

if Customer $i == N$ **then**

    //********For customer** N******//

    for $j = 1$ to M **do**

        $U_{i,j} = \sum_{\Theta} \sum_{Q} u_{N,j}(q_j, n_{N,j} + 1) f_j(q_j | \theta_j) p_j(\theta_j)$

    end for

    $\mathbf{j} = \{j_1, j_2, \ldots, j_L\} \leftarrow \underset{j \in \{1,2,\ldots,M\}}{\arg\max^L} \{U_{i,j}\}$

    for $j = 1$ to M **do**

        if $(U_{i,j} > 0)\&\&(j \in \mathbf{j})$ **then**

            $d_{N,j} \leftarrow 1$

        else

            $d_{N,j} \leftarrow 0$

        end if

    end for

    $\mathbf{m}_N = \mathbf{0}$

else

    //********For customer** $1, 2, \ldots, N - 1$******//

    //***_Predicting_***//

    for $\phi_h = \phi_1$ to ϕ_H **do**

        $(\mathbf{d}_{i+1}, \mathbf{m}_{i+1}) \leftarrow$ BR_IBG$(\mathbf{P}, \mathbf{n}_i + \phi_h, i + 1)$

        $\mathbf{m}_i \leftarrow \mathbf{m}_{i+1} + \mathbf{d}_{i+1}$

        $U_i(\phi_h) = \sum_M \phi_{h,j} \sum_\Theta \sum_Q u_{i,j}(q_j, n_{i,j} + m_{i,j} + \phi_{h,j})$

            $\cdot f_j(q_j | \theta_j) p_j(\theta_j)$

    end for

    //***_Making decision_***//

    $\phi_h^* \leftarrow \underset{\phi_h \in \Phi}{\arg\max} \{U_i(\phi_h)\}$

    $(\mathbf{d}_{i+1}, \mathbf{m}_{i+1}) \leftarrow$ BR_IBG$(\mathbf{P}, \mathbf{n}_i + \phi_h^*, i + 1)$

    $\mathbf{d}_i \leftarrow \phi_h^*$

    $\mathbf{m}_i \leftarrow \mathbf{m}_{i+1} + \mathbf{d}_{i+1}$

end if

return $(\mathbf{d}_i, \mathbf{m}_i)$

Then the total expected utility customer i can obtain with $\mathbf{d}_i = \phi_h$ is the sum of $U_{i,j}|_{\mathbf{d}_i=\phi_h}$ over all M dishes, i.e.,

$$U_i|_{\mathbf{d}_i=\phi_h} = \sum_{j=1}^{M} U_{i,j}|_{\mathbf{d}_i=\phi_h}. \tag{14.36}$$

In this case, we can find the optimal ϕ_h^* that maximizes customer i's expected utility $U_i|_{\mathbf{d}_i=\phi_h}$ as follows:

$$\phi_h^* = \underset{\phi_h \in \Phi}{\arg\max} \{U_i|_{\mathbf{d}_i=\phi_h}\}, \tag{14.37}$$

which is the best response of customer i.

To acquire the best response in (14.37), it is necessary for each customer to calculate the expected utilities defined in (14.35), which in turn requires them to predict $m_{i,j}|_{\mathbf{d}_i=\phi_h}$ (i.e., the number of customers who choose dish r_j after customer i). For customer N who already knows all of the previous customers' decisions, no prediction is required. Consequently, like Algorithm 10, given belief $\mathbf{P} = \{\mathbf{p}_1, \mathbf{p}_2, \ldots, \mathbf{p}_M\}$ at the current time slot and the current observation $\mathbf{n}_i = \{n_{i,1}, n_{i,2}, \ldots, n_{i,M}\}$, another recursive best response algorithm BR_IBG$(\mathbf{p}, \mathbf{n}_i, i)$ can be designed as a solution to the Indian buffet game with budget constraints, as is shown in Algorithm 11. It can be seen that customer N only needs to compare the expected utilities of requesting all M dishes and choose L or less than L dishes with the highest positive expected utilities. Note that $\max^L$ refers to determining the highest L values. For other customers, each of them needs to first make recursive predictions about subsequent customers' decisions and then makes their own decision on the basis of these predictions and the current observations.

14.4.2   Subgame-Perfect Nash Equilibrium

Similarly to the elementary Indian buffet game, we first give the formal definitions of a Nash equilibrium and a subgame of the Indian buffet game with budget constraints.

DEFINITION 14.7   Given the belief $\mathbf{P} = \{\mathbf{p}_1, \mathbf{p}_2, \ldots, \mathbf{p}_M\}$, the action profile $\mathbf{D}^* = \{\mathbf{d}_1^*, \mathbf{d}_2^*, \ldots, \mathbf{d}_N^*\}$ is a Nash equilibrium of the M-dish and N-customer Indian buffet game with budget constraints L if and only if $\mathbf{d}_i^* = \mathrm{BR}_i g\left(\mathbf{P}, \sum_{k \neq i} \mathbf{d}_k^* g\right)$ as defined in (14.28) for all i.

DEFINITION 14.8   A subgame of the M-dish and N-customer Indian buffet game with budget constraints L consists of the following three elements: (1) it starts at customer i with $i = 1, 2, \ldots, N$; (2) it has the belief $\mathbf{P}$ at the current time slot; (3) it has the current observation $\mathbf{n}_i$, which comes from the decisions of the previous customers.

Based on Definitions 14.3, 14.7, and 14.8, Theorem 14.9 shows that the action profile obtained through Algorithm 11 is a subgame-perfect Nash equilibrium of the Indian buffet game with budget constraints.

THEOREM 14.9   *Provided the belief* $\mathbf{P} = \{\mathbf{p}_1, \mathbf{p}_2, \ldots, \mathbf{p}_M\}$, *the action profile* $\mathbf{D}^* = \{\mathbf{d}_1^*, \mathbf{d}_2^*, \ldots, \mathbf{d}_N^*\}$, *where* $\mathbf{d}_i^*$ *is determined by BR_IBG*$(\mathbf{P}, \mathbf{n}_i, i)$ *and* $\mathbf{n}_i = \sum_{k=1}^{i-1} \mathbf{d}_k^*$, *is a subgame-perfect Nash equilibrium for the Indian buffet game.*

Proof   The proof of this theorem resembles that of Theorem 14.4. The proof outline is initially designed to show $\forall\, i, k$ such that $1 \leq i \leq N$ and $i \leq k \leq N$, and $\mathbf{d}_k^*$ is the best response of customer k in the subgame beginning with customer i based on the analysis of two cases: $k = N$ and $k < N$. It is therefore clear that $\{\mathbf{d}_i^*, \mathbf{d}_{i+1}^*, \ldots, \mathbf{d}_N^*\}$ is the Nash equilibrium for the subgame beginning with customer i. Finally, the definition of a subgame-perfect Nash equilibrium makes possible the verification of Theorem 14.9.

14.4.3   Homogeneous Case

For the homogeneous case, it is assumed that all customers' utility functions are identical (i.e., $u_{i,j}(q, n) = u(q, n)$) and all dishes are in an identical state (i.e., the dish state $\theta = \{\theta, \theta, \ldots, \theta\}$). Provided such conditions, we are in a position to determine certain special properties in the Nash equilibrium action profile $\mathbf{D}^*$ of the Indian buffet game with budget constraints. First, a parameter n_T is designed to satisfy

$$
\begin{cases}
\sum_{\Theta} \sum_{Q} u(q,n) f(q|\theta) p(\theta) > 0, & \text{if } n \leq n_T; \\
\sum_{\Theta} \sum_{Q} u(q,n) f(q|\theta) p(\theta) \leq 0, & \text{if } n > n_T.
\end{cases}
\tag{14.38}
$$

According to (14.38), it is clear that n_T is the critical value so that the utility of n_T customers sharing a certain dish is usually positive; however, it tends to be nonpositive with one extra customer (i.e., each dish can be requested by a maximum of n_T customers). It will be proved in Theorem 14.10 that under the homogeneous setting, all dishes will be requested by a nearly equal number of customers (i.e., equal sharing is achieved).

THEOREM 14.10   *In the M-dish and N-customer Indian buffet game with budget constraints L, if all M dishes are in identical states and all N customers share equal utility functions, the Nash equilibrium matrix $\mathbf{D}^*$ denoted by (14.2) satisfies that, for all dishes $\{r_j, j = 1, 2, \ldots, M\}$*

$$
\sum_{i=1}^{N} d_{i,j}^* =
\begin{cases}
n_T, & \text{if } n_T \leq \left\lfloor \frac{NL}{M} \right\rfloor; \\
\left\lfloor \frac{NL}{M} \right\rfloor \text{ or } \left\lceil \frac{NL}{M} \right\rceil, & \text{if } n_T \geq \left\lceil \frac{NL}{M} \right\rceil.
\end{cases}
\tag{14.39}
$$

Proof   We prove this theorem by contradiction as follows.

- Case 1: $n_T \leq \left\lfloor \frac{NL}{M} \right\rfloor$.

Suppose that there exists a Nash equilibrium $\mathbf{D}^*$ that contradicts (14.39). That is, there is a dish $r_{j'}$ such that $\sum_{i=1}^{N} d_{i,j'}^* > n_T$ or $\sum_{i=1}^{N} d_{i,j'}^* < n_T$. From (14.38) we know that each dish can be requested by a maximum of n_T customers, which means that only $\sum_{i=1}^{N} d_{i,j'}^* < n_T$ may hold. If $\sum_{i=1}^{N} d_{i,j'}^* < n_T \leq \left\lfloor \frac{NL}{M} \right\rfloor$, we have $\sum_{j=1}^{M} \sum_{i=1}^{N} d_{i,j}^* < NL$, which means that there exists at least one customer i' who requests fewer than L dishes (i.e., $\sum_{j=1}^{M} d_{i'j}^* < L$). However, according to (14.38), we have $\sum_{\Theta} \sum_{Q} u(q, \sum_{i=1}^{N} d_{i,j'}^* + 1) f(q|\theta) p(\theta) > 0$, which means that the utility of customer i' can increase if they request dish $r_{j'}$ (i.e., their utility is not maximized unless $\mathbf{D}^*$ is not a Nash equilibrium). This contradicts the assumption. Therefore, we have $\sum_{i=1}^{N} d_{i,j}^* = n_T$ for all dishes when $n_T \leq \left\lfloor \frac{NL}{M} \right\rfloor$.

- Case 2: $n_T \geq \left\lceil \frac{NL}{M} \right\rceil$.

Similarly to the arguments in Case 1, we cannot have $\sum_{j=1}^{M} \sum_{i=1}^{N} d_{i,j}^* < NL$, which means that $\sum_{j=1}^{M} \sum_{i=1}^{N} d_{i,j}^* = NL$. Let us assume that there exists a Nash equilibrium $\mathbf{D}^*$ that contradicts (14.39). Since $\sum_{j=1}^{M} \sum_{i=1}^{N} d_{i,j}^* = NL$, there is a dish r_{j_1} with $\sum_{i=1}^{N} d_{i,j_1}^* < \left\lfloor \frac{NL}{M} \right\rfloor$ and a dish r_{j_2} with $\sum_{i=1}^{N} d_{i,j_2}^* > \left\lceil \frac{NL}{M} \right\rceil$. In this case, we have $\sum_{i=1}^{N} d_{i,j_2}^* > \sum_{i=1}^{N} d_{i,j_1}^* + 1$, which leads to

$$\sum_{\Theta}\sum_{Q} u\left(q, \sum_{i=1}^{N} d_{i,j_1}^* + 1\right) f(q|\theta)p(\theta) > \sum_{\Theta}\sum_{Q} u\left(q, \sum_{i=1}^{N} d_{i,j_2}^*\right) f(q|\theta)p(\theta),$$

$$(14.40)$$

From (14.40) we can see that the customer who has requested dish r_{j_2} can obtain higher utility by unilaterally changing their decision by requesting dish r_{j_1}. Therefore, $\mathbf{D}^*$ is not a Nash equilibrium of the Indian buffet game with budget constraints L, and thus we have $\sum_{i=1}^{N} d_{i,j}^* = \lfloor \frac{NL}{M} \rfloor$ or $\lceil \frac{NL}{M} \rceil$ when $n_T \geq \lceil \frac{NL}{M} \rceil$. This completes the proof of the theorem.

14.5   Non-Bayesian Social Learning

In Sections 14.3 and 14.4, we analyzed the Indian Buffet Game and characterized the corresponding equilibrium. Based on the analysis, it can be inferred that the equilibrium is largely dependent on customers' belief $\mathbf{P} = \{\mathbf{p}_j, j = 1, 2, \ldots, M\}$ (i.e., the estimated distribution of the dish state $\theta = \{\theta_j, j = 1, 2, \ldots, M\}$). Greater accuracy of the belief will contribute to a better best response of customers and culminate in them obtaining greater utility. As a result, it is of great importance for customers to improve their beliefs through the exploitation of their inferred signals. In this section, the learning process in the Indian buffet game will be discussed. Specifically, we introduce an effective non-Bayesian social learning algorithm that ensures customers are able to learn the true system state. In social learning, the crucial difference between non-Bayesian learning and Bayesian learning consists in the users' rationality and the ways in which they process signal information, while their implementation difference is that in Bayesian learning rules, customers exchange their signal information, whereas in non-Bayesian learning rules, they exchange intermediate belief information. The incentive for designing a non-Bayesian learning rule is that customers can first distributively process their own signals and then cooperatively estimate their beliefs concerning the dish state, which can lead to a remarkable reduction in the computational cost of each customer. Note that since the learning process of one dish state θ_j is independent of all others, in the rest of this section, the dish index j will be omitted for notation simplification.

Suppose the true dish state is θ^*, given customers' beliefs at time slot t, $\mathbf{p}^{(t)} = \{p^{(t)}(\theta), \forall \theta \in \Theta\}$, their beliefs at time slot $t + 1$, $\mathbf{p}^{(t+1)} = \{p^{(t+1)}(\theta), \forall \theta \in \Theta\}$, can be updated by

$$p^{(t+1)}(\theta) = \frac{1}{N} \sum_{i=1}^{N} [d_i^{(t+1)} \mu_i^{(t+1)}(\theta) + (1 - d_i^{(t+1)})p^{(t)}(\theta)], \qquad (14.41)$$

where $d_i^{(t+1)} = 1$ or 0 is customer i's decision and $\mu_i^{(t+1)}(\theta)$ is the intermediate belief that is updated by the Bayesian learning rule for customers who have requested the dish and inferred some signal $s_i^{(t+1)} \sim f(\cdot|\theta^*)$, i.e.,

$$\mu_i^{(t+1)}(\theta) = \frac{f(s_i^{(t+1)}|\theta)p^{(t)}(\theta)}{\sum_\Theta f(s_i^{(t+1)}|\theta)p^{(t)}(\theta)}, \qquad \forall\, \theta \in \Theta. \tag{14.42}$$

DEFINITION 14.11   A learning rule has the *strong convergence* property if and only if the learning rule can learn the true state in probability such that

$$\begin{cases} p^{(t)}(\theta^*) \to 1, \\ p^{(t)}(\forall\, \theta \neq \theta^*) \to 0, \end{cases} \quad \text{as } t \to \infty. \tag{14.43}$$

By reorganizing some terms, we can rewrite the non-Bayesian learning rule in (14.41) as

$$p^{(t+1)}(\theta) = p^{(t)}(\theta) + \frac{1}{N}\sum_{i=1}^{N} d_i^{(t+1)}\left(\frac{f(s_i^{(t+1)}|\theta)}{\lambda(s_i^{(t+1)})} - 1\right)p^{(t)}(\theta), \tag{14.44}$$

with

$$\lambda(s_i^{(t+1)}) = \sum_\Theta f(s_i^{(t+1)}|\theta)p^{(t)}(\theta). \tag{14.45}$$

From (14.45), we can see that $\lambda(s_i^{(t+1)})$ is the estimation of the probability distribution of the signal $s_i^{(t+1)}$ at the next time slot. Based on $\lambda(s_i^{(t+1)})$, we can define a weak convergence, compared with the strong convergence in (14.43), as follows.

DEFINITION 14.12   A learning rule has the *weak convergence* property if and only if the learning rule can learn the true state in probability such that

$$\lambda(s) = \sum_\Theta f(s|\theta)p^{(t)}(\theta) \to f(s|\theta^*), \forall\, s \in Q, \text{ as } t \to \infty. \tag{14.46}$$

Note that the weak convergence is adequate for the Indian buffet game on the grounds that the objective of learning is to determine an accurate estimate of the expected utilities of customers and consequently acquire the best true response. From (14.9), it is known that the signal distribution $\sum_\Theta f_j(q_j|\theta_j)p_j(\theta_j)$ is a sufficient statistic of the expected utility function. As a result, if we can see that the social learning algorithm has the weak convergence property, then we are capable of obtaining the true best response for customers in the Indian buffet game. In Theorem 14.13, it will be shown and proved that the learning algorithm in (14.41) indeed has the weak convergence property. It will also be shown with simulation that the learning algorithm in (14.41) has a strong convergence property.

THEOREM 14.13   *In the Indian buffet game, suppose that the true dish state is θ^*, all customers update their belief $\mathbf{p}$ using (14.41), and their prior belief $\mathbf{p}^{(0)}$ satisfies $p^{(0)}(\theta^*) > 0$. The belief sequence $\{p^{(t)}(\theta)\}$ then ensures a weak convergence; in other words, for $\forall\, s \in Q$*

$$\lambda(s) = \sum_\Theta f(s|\theta)p^{(t)}(\theta) \to f(s|\theta^*), \quad as\ t \to \infty. \tag{14.47}$$

Intially, a probability triple is defined as $(\Omega, \mathcal{F}, \mathbb{P}^{\theta})$ in light of a few specific dish states $\theta \in \Theta$, where Ω symbolizes the space containing sequences of realizations of the signals $s_i^{(t)} \in Q$, $\mathcal{F}$ is the σ-field generated by Ω (i.e., a set of subsets of Ω), and $\mathbb{P}^{\theta}$ is the probability measure induced over sample paths in Ω (i.e., $\mathbb{P}^{\theta} = \otimes_{t=1}^{\infty} f(\cdot|\theta)$). In addition, we draw on $\mathbb{E}^{\theta}[\cdot]$ so as to denote the expectation operator associated with measure $\mathbb{P}^{\theta}$, and we define $\mathcal{F}_t$ as the smallest σ-field generated by the past history of all customers' observations within the maximum of t time slots. The proof of the weak convergence in (14.46) should be preceded by the fact that the belief sequence $\{p^{(t)}(\theta^*)\}$ converges to a positive number as $t \to \infty$ according to Lemma 14.14.

LEMMA 14.14 *Let the true dish state be θ^*, all customers update their belief **p** by following the non-Bayesian learning rule in (14.41), and their prior belief **p**$^{(0)}$ satisfies $p^{(0)}(\theta^*) > 0$. The belief sequence $\{p^{(t)}(\theta^*)\}$ then converges to a positive number as $t \to \infty$.*

Proof According to (14.41) and (14.42), it can be seen that if $p^{(t)}(\theta) > 0$, then $p^{(t+1)}(\theta) > 0$. Since the prior belief satisfies $p^{(0)}(\theta^*) > 0$, in accordance with the method of induction, we have the belief sequence $\{p^{(t)}(\theta^*)\} > 0$.

According to (14.44), for the true dish state θ^*, we have

$$p^{(t+1)}(\theta^*) = p^{(t)}(\theta^*) + \frac{1}{N} \sum_{i=1}^{N} d_i^{(t+1)} \left(\frac{f(s_i^{(t+1)}|\theta^*)}{\lambda(s_i^{(t+1)})} - 1 \right) p^{(t)}(\theta^*). \quad (14.48)$$

By taking expectation over $\mathcal{F}_t$ on both sides of (14.48), we have

$$\mathbb{E}^{\theta^*}[p^{(t+1)}(\theta^*)|\mathcal{F}_t]$$
$$= p^{(t)}(\theta^*) + \frac{1}{N} \sum_{i=1}^{N} \mathbb{E}^{\theta^*} \left[d_i^{(t+1)} \left(\frac{f(s_i^{(t+1)}|\theta^*)}{\lambda(s_i^{(t+1)})} - 1 \right) g|\mathcal{F}_t \right] p^{(t)}(\theta^*). \quad (14.49)$$

According to the time slot structure shown in Figure 14.1, each customer's decision at time slot $t + 1$ is made based on the belief updated at the end of last time slot t. In this case, when given all of the history information up to time slot t, $\mathcal{F}_t$, the decision $d_i^{(t+1)}$ is independent of the signal $s_i^{(t+1)}$ that is received at the end of time slot $t + 1$. In this case, we can separate the expectation in the second term of (14.49) as

$$\mathbb{E}^{\theta^*} \left[d_i^{(t+1)} \cdot \left(\frac{f(s_i^{(t+1)}|\theta^*)}{\lambda(s_i^{(t+1)})} - 1 \right) g|\mathcal{F}_t \right] =$$
$$\mathbb{E}^{\theta^*}[d_i^{(t+1)}|\mathcal{F}_t] \cdot \mathbb{E}^{\theta^*} \left[\left(\frac{f(s_i^{(t+1)}|\theta^*)}{\lambda(s_i^{(t+1)})} - 1 \right) g|\mathcal{F}_t \right]. \quad (14.50)$$

In (14.50), $\mathbb{E}^{\theta} \left[d_i^{(t+1)}|\mathcal{F}_t \right] \geq 0$ since $d_i^{(t+1)}$ can only be 1 or 0. Furthermore, due to the fact that $g(x) = 1/x$ is a convex function, according to Jensen's inequality, we have

$$\mathbb{E}^{\theta^*}\left[\frac{f(s_i^{(t+1)}|\theta^*)}{\lambda(s_i^{(t+1)})}g|\mathcal{F}_t\right] \geq \left(\mathbb{E}^{\theta^*}\left[\frac{\lambda(s_i^{(t+1)})}{f(s_i^{(t+1)}|\theta^*)}g|\mathcal{F}_t\right]\right)^{-1}$$

$$= \left(\sum_Q \frac{\lambda(s_i^{(t+1)})}{f(s_i^{(t+1)}|\theta^*)}f(s_i^{(t+1)}|\theta^*)\right)^{-1} = 1. \quad (14.51)$$

In this case, the equation in (14.50) becomes non-negative, which is reflective of the fact that in (14.49)

$$\mathbb{E}^{\theta^*}[p^{(t+1)}(\theta^*)|\mathcal{F}_t] \geq p^{(t)}(\theta^*). \quad (14.52)$$

Owing to the fact that customers' belief $p^{(t)}(\theta^*)$ is bounded within the interval $[0,1]$, following the martingale convergence theorem [22], it can be safely concluded that the belief sequence $\{p^{(t)}(\theta^*)\}$ converges to a positive number as $t \to \infty$.

Now we are ready to provide the proof of Theorem 14.13.

Proof Let $\mathcal{N}^{(t+1)}$ denote the set of customers who request the dish at time slot $t+1$. In such a case, we can rewrite (14.48) as

$$p^{(t+1)}(\theta^*) = \frac{1}{|\mathcal{N}^{(t+1)}|}\sum_{i\in\mathcal{N}^{(t+1)}}\frac{f(s_i^{(t+1)}|\theta^*)}{\lambda(s_i^{(t+1)})}p^{(t)}(\theta^*), \quad (14.53)$$

where $|\cdot|$ means the cardinality. By taking logarithmic operations on both sides of (14.53) and utilizing the concavity of the logarithm function, we have

$$\log p^{(t+1)}(\theta^*) \geq \log p^{(t)}(\theta^*) + \frac{1}{|\mathcal{N}^{(t+1)}|}\sum_{i\in\mathcal{N}^{(t+1)}}\log\frac{f(s_i^{(t+1)}|\theta^*)}{\lambda(s_i^{(t+1)})}. \quad (14.54)$$

Then, by taking expectation over $\mathcal{F}_t$ on both sides of (14.54), we have

$$\mathbb{E}^{\theta^*}[\log p^{(t+1)}(\theta^*)|\mathcal{F}_t] - \log p^{(t)}(\theta^*)$$

$$\geq \frac{1}{|\mathcal{N}^{(t+1)}|}\sum_{i\in\mathcal{N}^{(t+1)}}\mathbb{E}^{\theta^*}\left[\log\frac{f(s_i^{(t+1)}|\theta^*)}{\lambda(s_i^{(t+1)})}g|\mathcal{F}_t\right]. \quad (14.55)$$

In view of the left-hand side of (14.55), following Lemma 14.14, it is known that $p^{(t)}(\theta^*)$ will converge as $t \to \infty$, and thus

$$\mathbb{E}^{\theta^*}[\log p^{(t+1)}(\theta^*)|\mathcal{F}_t] - \log p^{(t)}(\theta^*) \to 0. \quad (14.56)$$

In view of the right-hand side of (14.55), it follows

$$\mathbb{E}^{\theta^*}\left[\log\frac{f(s_i^{(t+1)}|\theta^*)}{\lambda(s_i^{(t+1)})}g|\mathcal{F}_t\right] = -\mathbb{E}^{\theta^*}\left[\log\frac{\lambda(s_i^{(t+1)})}{f(s_i^{(t+1)}|\theta^*)}g|\mathcal{F}_t\right]$$

$$\geq -\log\mathbb{E}^{\theta^*}\left[\frac{\lambda(s_i^{(t+1)})}{f(s_i^{(t+1)}|\theta^*)}g|\mathcal{F}_t\right]$$

$$= 0. \quad (14.57)$$

In this case, combining (14.56) and (14.57), as $t \to \infty$, we have

$$0 \ge \frac{1}{|\mathcal{N}^{(t+1)}|} \sum_{i \in \mathcal{N}^{(t+1)}} \mathbb{E}^{\theta^*} \left[\log \frac{f(s_i^{(t+1)}|\theta^*)}{\lambda(s_i^{(t+1)})} g | \mathcal{F}_t \right] \ge 0. \qquad (14.58)$$

By squeeze theorem [23], we have for $\forall i \in \mathcal{N}^{(t+1)}$, as $t \to \infty$

$$\mathbb{E}^{\theta^*} \left[\log \frac{f(s_i^{(t+1)}|\theta^*)}{\lambda(s_i^{(t+1)})} g | \mathcal{F}_t \right] = \sum_{\Theta} f(s_i^{(t+1)}|\theta^*) \log \frac{f(s_i^{(t+1)}|\theta^*)}{\lambda(s_i^{(t+1)})} \to 0, \qquad (14.59)$$

Based on Gibbs' inequality [24], (14.59) converges to 0 if and only if as $t \to \infty$

$$\lambda(s_i^{(t+1)}) \to f(s_i^{(t+1)}|\theta^*), \quad \forall s_i^{(t+1)} \in Q. \qquad (14.60)$$

This completes the proof of the theorem.

14.6 Simulation Results

In this section, simulations are conducted to verify the performance of the non-Bayesian social learning rule and recursive best response algorithms. The simulation of an Indian buffet restaurant with five dishes $\{r_1, r_2, r_3, r_4, r_5\}$ and five possible dish states $\theta_j \in \{1, 2, 3, 4, 5\}$ is proposed. Each dish is stochastically assigned with a state. Following the request for a specific dish r_j, customer i can predict the quality of the dish and signals $s_{i,j} \in \{1, 2, 3, 4, 5\}$ in line with the conditional distribution that

$$f_j(s_{i,j}|\theta_j) = \begin{cases} w, & \text{if } s_{i,j} = \theta_j; \\ (1-w)/4, & \text{if } s_{i,j} \ne \theta_j. \end{cases} \qquad (14.61)$$

The parameter w can be perceived as the quality of the signal or customers' detection probability. When the signal quality w approaches 1, it is more probable for the customer's inferred signal to reflect the true dish state. Note that w must satisfy $w \ge 1/5$; otherwise the true state is by no means learned in a correct way. Based on the signals, customers are in a position to update their belief **P** through cooperation at a subsequent time slot and then make their sequential decisions. As soon as the i-th customer makes their dish selection, they share their decisions with the other customers. When all customers have made their decisions, they begin to reveal the corresponding dishes they have requested. Customer i's utility of requesting dish r_j is given by

$$u_{i,j} = \gamma_i \frac{s_{i,j} R}{N_j} - c_j, \qquad (14.62)$$

where γ_i denotes the utility coefficient for customer i since different customers may have different utilities in terms of the identical reward, $s_{i,j}$ is a realization of dish quality as well as the signal inferred by customer i, R represents the base award of requesting each dish such as $R = 10$, N_j stands for the overall number of customers requesting dish r_j, and c_j refers to the cost of requesting dish r_j as $\{c_j = 1, \forall j\}$. According to (14.61) and (14.62), it can be seen that by requesting a dish with higher

Table 14.1. Nash equilibrium matrix $\mathbf{D}^*$.

	1	2	3	4	5	6	7	8	9	10
r_1	1	1	0	0	0	0	0	0	0	0
r_2	1	1	1	1	0	0	0	0	0	0
r_3	1	1	1	1	1	0	0	0	0	0
r_4	1	1	1	1	1	1	0	0	0	0
r_5	1	1	1	1	1	1	1	1	0	0

state level (e.g., $\theta_j = 5$), customers can gain higher utility. However, customers are unaware of the dish state and they have to make an estimation of this based on social learning. In addition, it is also known that when the number of customers requesting the same dish increases, each customer will experience a decrease in its utility, which demonstrates the negative network externality.

14.6.1   Indian Buffet Game without Budget Constraints

In this section, the performance of the best response algorithm for the Indian buffet game without budget constraints is evaluated. First, a simulation is conducted on the homogeneous case to verify the threshold property of the Nash equilibrium matrix (i.e., Theorem 14.6), and the influence of different decision-making orders on customers' utility (i.e., making a decision earlier tends to be advantageous). We then compare the performance of the best response algorithm (i.e., Algorithm 10) with the performance of other algorithms in heterogeneous settings.

In terms of the homogeneous case, all customers' utility coefficients are set as $\gamma_i = 1$. The customers' prior belief concerning the dish state begins with a uniform distribution (i.e., $\{p_j^{(0)}(\theta) = 0.2, \forall j, \theta\}$). The dish state is set as $\Theta = [1,2,3,4,5]$ (i.e., $\theta_j = j$) in order to verify different threshold structures for divergent dish states, as is illustrated in Theorem 14.6. At each time slot, we let customers make sequential decisions in accordance with Algorithm 10 and then update their beliefs in line with the non-Bayesian learning rule. The game is played from one time slot to another until customers' belief $\mathbf{P}^{(t)}$ converges. In the first simulation, the number of customers is set as $N = 10$ for the specific verification of the threshold structure of the Nash equilibrium matrix. Table 14.1 demonstrates the Nash equilibrium matrix $\mathbf{D}^*$ obtained through Algorithm 10 after the convergence of customers' belief $\mathbf{P}^{(t)}$, where each column contains one customer's decisions $\{d_{i,j}, \forall j\}$ and each row contains all customers' decisions regarding one specific dish r_j (i.e., $\{d_{i,j}, \forall i\}$). It can be seen from Table 14.1 that once a customer does not request a specific dish, all of the subsequent customers will refrain from requesting that dish, which is consistent with the conclusion in Theorem 14.6. Furthermore, since greater utility can be obtained by requesting a dish with a higher state level (e.g., $\theta_5 = 5$), it can be inferred that most customers decide to request dish r_5. According to Table 14.1, it can be seen that customers who make decisions early are at an advantage (e.g., customer 1 can request all dishes, whereas customer 8 can only request one dish). Consequently, in

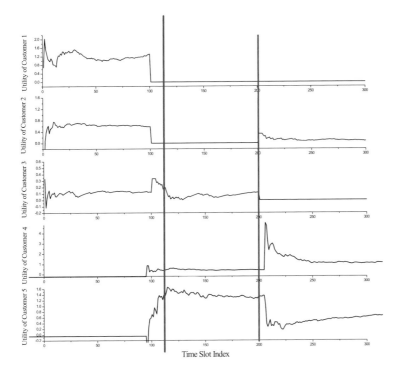

Utility of Customer 1
Utility of Customer 2
Utility of Customer 3
Utility of Customer 4
Utility of Customer 5

Time Slot Index

Figure 14.3 Each customer's utility in the homogeneous case without budget constraints.

the second simulation of the homogeneous case, to guarantee fairness, the order of decision-making is subject to dynamic adjustment. In this simulation, it is assumed that five customers share a common utility coefficient $\gamma_i = 0.4$. Figure 14.3 illustrates all customers' utilities in the simulation, where the order of decision-making varies for every 100 time slots. In the first 100 time slots, where the order of decision-making is $1 \rightarrow 2 \rightarrow 3 \rightarrow 4 \rightarrow 5$, it is clear that customer 1 obtains the highest utility and customers 4 and 5 receive 0 utility since they have not requested any dishes. In the second 100 time slots, we reverse the decision-making order to $5 \rightarrow 4 \rightarrow 3 \rightarrow 2 \rightarrow 1$, which incurs 0 utility for customers 1 and 2. Thus, based on the periodic change in the order of decision-making, it can be inferred that the expected utilities of all customers will be identical after a period of time.

For the heterogeneous case, we randomize each customer's utility coefficient γ_i between 0 and 1 and set their prior belief as $\{p_j^{(0)}(\theta) = 0.2, \forall j, \theta\}$. In this simulation, we compare the performance in terms of customers' social welfare, which is defined as the total utility sof all customers among the following different kinds of algorithms:

- *Best Response*: The recursive best response algorithm in Algorithm 10 with non-Bayesian learning.
- *Myopic*: At each time slot, customer i requests dishes according to current observation $\mathbf{n}_i = \{n_{i,j}, \forall j\}$ without social learning.
- *Learning*: At each time slot, each customer requests dishes purely based on the updated belief $\mathbf{P}^{(t)}$ using a non-Bayesian learning rule without considering negative network externality.
- *Random*: Each customer randomly requests dishes.

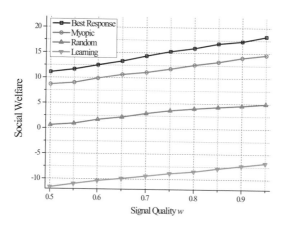

Figure 14.4 Social welfare comparison without budget constraints.

For the myopic and learning strategies, customer i's expected utility of requesting dish r_j can be calculated by

$$U_{i,j}^{\mathrm{m}} = \sum_{\Theta} \sum_{Q} u_{i,j}(q_j, n_{i,j} + d_{i,j}) f_j(q_j|\theta_j) p_j^{(0)}(\theta_j), \qquad (14.63)$$

$$U_{i,j}^{\mathrm{l}} = \sum_{\Theta} \sum_{Q} u_{i,j}(q_j, d_{i,j}) f_j(q_j|\theta_j) p_j^{(t)}(\theta_j). \qquad (14.64)$$

By drawing on these expected utilities, both myopic and learning algorithms can be derived from (14.8). It can be seen that the myopic strategy does not consider social learning, whereas the learning strategy excludes negative network externality. In the simulation, these four algorithms are averaged over hundreds of realizations. Figure 14.4 presents the results of the performance comparison, where the x-axis is the signal quality w ranging from 0.50 to 0.95 and the y-axis is the social welfare averaged over hundreds of time slots. Figure 14.4 shows that along with the increase in signal quality, social welfare grows for all algorithms. Furthermore, it can be seen that the best response algorithm performs the best while the learning algorithm performs the worst. This is due to the fact that with the learning algorithm customers can gradually learn the true dish states and then request the dish without taking other customers' decisions into account. In this case, a majority of customers may request identical dishes and each customer's utility experiences a dramatic decrease owing to the negative network externality. For the myopic algorithm, although customers are unable to learn the true dish states, by drawing on other customers' decisions, each customer can avoid requesting dishes that have been over-requested. As a result, it can be concluded that the best response algorithm achieves the best performance by taking the negative network externality into account and applying social learning to the estimation of the dish state.

Table 14.2. Nash equilibrium matrix $\mathbf{D}^*$.

	1	2	3	4	5	6	7	8	9	10
r_1	1	1	1	1	1	1	0	0	0	0
r_2	1	1	1	1	0	0	1	1	0	0
r_3	1	1	1	1	0	0	0	0	1	1
r_4	0	0	0	0	1	1	1	1	1	1
r_5	0	0	0	0	1	1	1	1	1	1

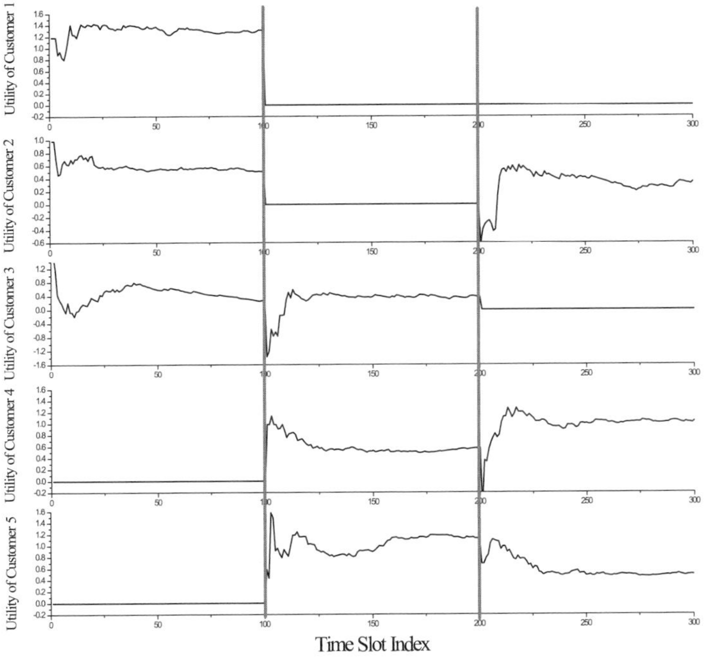

Figure 14.5 Each customer's utility in the homogeneous case with budget constraints.

14.6.2 Indian Buffet Game with Budget Constraints

In this section, the performance of the best response algorithm for the Indian buffet game with budget constraints $L = 3$ is evaluated. Analogously to Section 14.6.1, we begin with the homogeneous case, where all customers' utility coefficients are set as $\gamma_i = 1$. In the first simulation, to verify the property of the Nash equilibrium matrix illustrated in Theorem 14.10, all dish states are set as $\theta_j = 5$. Table 14.2 demonstrates the Nash equilibrium matrix $\mathbf{D}^*$ derived from Algorithm 11. It can be seen that each dish has been requested by $N \times L / M = 10 \times 3/5 = 6$ customers, which is in line with the conclusion in Theorem 14.10. In the second simulation, we dynamically change the order of customers' sequential decision-making and demonstrate each customer's utility in the simulation in Figure 14.5, in which phenomena similar to the Indian buffet game without budget constraints can be seen.

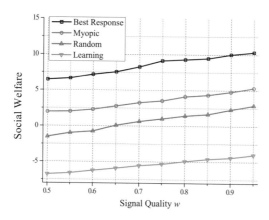

Figure 14.6 Social welfare comparison with budget constraints.

For the heterogeneous case, we randomize each customer's utility coefficient γ_i within $[0,1]$ and compare the performance of the best response algorithm (i.e., Algorithm 11) with myopic, learning, and random algorithms based on customers' social welfare. For the myopic, learning, and random algorithms, identical budget constraints are adopted (i.e., each customer is allowed to request a maximum of three dishes). Figure 14.6 displays the results of the performance comparison, from which it can be seen that the best response algorithm performs the best while the learning algorithm performs the worst.

14.6.3 Non-Bayesian Social Learning Performance

This section evaluates the performance of the non-Bayesian social learning rule. In the simulation, we start by randomizing the states of five dishes and assigning customers' prior beliefs concerning each dish state with uniform distribution (i.e., $\{p_j(\theta = 0.2), \forall j, \theta\}$). After requesting the chosen dishes, each customer can infer signals by drawing on the conditional distribution defined in (14.61) with signal quality $w = 0.6$. Figure 14.7 displays the respective learning curves of the Indian buffet game with and without budget constraints. The y-axis is the difference between customers' belief at each time slot $\mathbf{P}^{(t)}$ and the true belief $\mathbf{P}^o = \{\mathbf{p}_j = (p_j(\theta_j^*) = 1, p_j(\theta_j \neq \theta_j^*) = 0), \forall j\}$, which can be calculated by $||\mathbf{P}^{(t)} - \mathbf{P}^o||_2$. Figure 14.7 shows that customers can learn the true dish states within 15 time slots. Furthermore, the case without budget constraints enjoys a faster convergence rate than the case with budget constraints. This is due to the fact that with budget constraints, each customer requests fewer dishes at each time slot and consequently can infer fewer signals concerning the dish state, which will cause an unavoidable reduction in the customers' learning speed.

14.6.4 Application in Relay Selection of Cooperative Communication

In this section, we discuss the application of the Indian buffet game in relay selection of cooperative communications. In the application, we consider a wireless network

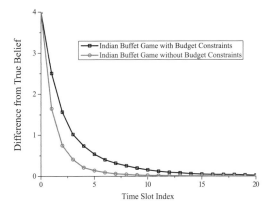

Figure 14.7 Performance of the non-Bayesian social learning rule.

with N source nodes or users that intend to send their messages to the destination nodes. There are M potential relay nodes with various relay capabilities given the different channel conditions, transmission powers, and processing speed constraints. Each source node is able to select a maximum of L relays in each time slot that assist them in relaying their messages to the destination node. All of the source nodes are assumed to be rational (i.e., each of them selects the relays that can maximize their own expected data rate). First, the more source nodes that select the same relay in a time slot, the less throughput each source node is able to obtain (i.e., negative externality). Second, since the source nodes might be unaware of the exact capacity of each relay node, they need to estimate the relay state by taking into account the history and the current signals that reflect the relay properties. Third, the source nodes are not necessarily synchronized, which means that they may make their relay selections sequentially. Taking these three properties into account, it can be seen that the Indian buffet game is a desirable tool for formulating the relay selection problem, where the source nodes are the players and the relay nodes are equivalent to the dishes in the restaurant.

In the simulation, we set five source nodes and five relay nodes with five possible relay state $\theta_j \in \{1, 2, 3, 4, 5\}$. Each source node can receive a signal regarding the capacity of the selected relay nodes after data transmission, which is consistent with the distribution $f_j(s_{i,j}|\theta_j)$ as in (14.61). Based on the assumption that the source nodes take turns in selecting the relay node, the utility of the i-th source node selecting relay node j can be defined as

$$u_{i,j} = \frac{s_{i,j}\bar{g}_{i,j}}{N_j} - c_j, \tag{14.65}$$

where $\bar{g}_{i,j}$ is the gain of the i-th source node by selecting relay j (which depends on the channel gain), N_j represents the total number of source nodes sharing relay j, and c_j refers to the cost of selecting relay j, which can be regarded as the price of the relay service. The utility definition enables us to conduct simulations to evaluate the performance of relay selection with the Indian buffet game and to compare this with those of the myopic strategy, the random strategy, and the learning strategy.

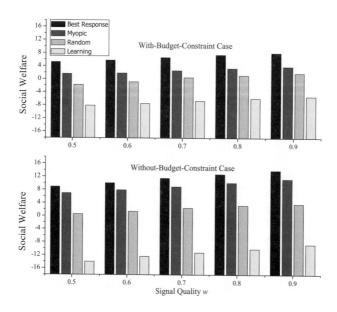

Figure 14.8 Social welfare comparison in the application of relay selection.

Figure 14.8 displays the results of the social welfare comparison for the following two cases: the with-budget-constraint case, in which each source node can select a maximum of $L = 3$ relays; and the without budget-constraint case, in which each source node can select up to $L = 5$ relays. It is shown in Figure 14.8 that, similarly to the previous comparison results, the best response algorithm performs the best in both cases. As a result, the Indian buffet game is highly applicable in the relay selection of cooperative communications.

14.7   Conclusion

In this chapter, to study how users make multiple concurrent decisions under uncertain system states, we proposed a general framework known as the Indian buffet game. Research on the Indian buffet game was carried out under two different scenarios: customers requesting multiple dishes without budget constraints and with budget constraints, respectively. Best response algorithms were designed for both cases so as to determine the subgame-perfect Nash equilibrium, and we discussed the simplified homogeneous cases in order to better understand the Indian buffet game. A non-Bayesian social learning rule was also designed for customers to learn about the dish state and theoretically prove its convergence. According to the simulation results, the best response algorithms performed much better than the myopic, learning, and random algorithms. Furthermore, the non-Bayesian learning algorithm helped customers to learn the true system state with a faster convergence speed.

This chapter focused on the analysis of the interactions and decision-making behaviors of agents in an uncertain negative-externality environment through the concept of social learning, which is considered to be a key problem in signal processing, wireless communication networks, and social networks. At the same time, this chapter is limited owing to certain assumptions of the analysis. One such assumption is that all of the customers are assumed to share their belief information with the others, given that sharing the belief information can improve learning performance on the basis of social learning. It is assumed that rational customers are motivated to do this. The other major assumption is that each customer is aware of all others' utility function forms in Algorithms 10 and 11. Note that Algorithms 10 and 11 are simply designed to determine the Nash equilibrium of the Indian buffet game. When each user is unaware of other users' utility function forms, they can form an expectation of the types of users present in accordance with some empirical user-type distribution.

The Indian buffet game is highly applicable in a variety of fields. One important application is the relay selection problem in cooperative communications, where the Indian buffet game can effectively simulate and solve the problem of such relay selection in cooperative communications. Furthermore, the Indian buffet game is also applicable to the multichannel sensing and access problem in cognitive radio networks, in which each secondary user needs to learn the primary channel state and tries to access the channel with the fewest secondary users (i.e., incorporating negative externality) [25]. For these problems, existing algorithms or models either only consider negative externality or only take social learning into account, without integrating learning and decision-making with negative externality. In this case, these algorithms perform worse than the Indian buffet game model, which can be seen from the comparison results in Figures 14.4, 14.6, and 14.8. Consequently, research on the Indian buffet game model is valuable since it provides agents with a general tool for making optimal sequential decisions in the face of an uncertain system state and negative externality characteristics.

References

[1] W. Sandholm, "Negative externalities and evolutionary implementation," *Review of Economic Studies*, vol. 72, pp. 885–915, 2005.

[2] Y.-H. Yang, Y. Chen, C. Jiang, C.-Y. Wang, and K. J. R. Liu, "Wireless access network selection game with negative network externality," *IEEE Transactions on Wireless Communications*, vol. 12, pp. 5048–5060, 2013.

[3] H. V. Zhao, W. S. Lin, and K. J. R. Liu, *Behavior Dynamics in Media-Sharing Social Networks*. Cambridge University Press, 2011.

[4] Y. Chen and K. J. R. Liu, "Understanding microeconomic behaviors in social networking: An engineering view," *IEEE Signal Processing Magazine*, vol. 29, pp. 53–64, 2012.

[5] D. Acemoglu, M. Dahleh, I. Lobel, and A. Ozdaglar, "Bayesian learning in social networks," *Review of Economic Studies*, vol. 78, pp. 1201–1236, 2011.

[6] V. Krishnamurthy and H. V. Poor, "Social learning and Bayesian games in multiagent signal processing: How do local and global decision makers interact?" *IEEE Signal Processing Magazine*, vol. 30, pp. 43–57, 2013.

[7] V. Bala and S. Goyal, "Learning from neighbours," *Review of Economic Studies*, vol. 65, pp. 595–621, 1998.

[8] D. Gale and S. Kariv, "Bayesian learning in social networks," *Games and Economic Behavior*, vol. 45, pp. 329–346, 2003.

[9] D. Acemoglu and A. Ozdaglar, "Opinion dynamics and learning in social networks," *Dynamic Games and Applications*, vol. 1, pp. 3–49, 2011.

[10] L. G. Epstein, J. Noor, and A. Sandroni, "Non-Bayesian learning," *The B.E. Journal of Theoretical Economics*, vol. 10, pp. 1–16, 2010.

[11] B. Golub and M. O. Jackson, "Naive learning in social networks and the wisdom of crowds," *American Economic Journal: Microeconomics*, vol. 2, pp. 112–149, 2010.

[12] A. Jadbabaie, P. Molavi, A. Sandroni, and A. Tahbaz-Salehi, "Non-Bayesian social learning," *Games and Economic Behavior*, vol. 76, pp. 210–225, 2012.

[13] D. Aldous, I. Ibragimov, J. Jacod, and D. Aldous, "Exchangeability and related topics," in *Lecture Notes in Mathematics*, vol. 1117, pp. 1–198, Springer 1985.

[14] C. Jiang, Y. Chen, Y.-H. Yang, C.-Y. Wang, and K. J. R. Liu, "Dynamic Chinese restaurant game: theory and application to cognitive radio networks," *IEEE Transactions on Wireless Communications*, vol. 13, pp. 1960–1973, 2014.

[15] T. L. Griffiths and Z. Ghahramani, "The Indian buffet process: An introduction and review," *Journal of Machine Learning Research*, vol. 12, pp. 1185–1224, 2011.

[16] A. Aradillas-Lopez, "Semiparametric estimation of a simultaneous game with incomplete information," *Journal of Econometrics*, vol. 157, pp. 409–431, 2010.

[17] A. Savikhin and R. M. Sheremeta, "Simultaneous decision-making in competitive and cooperative environments," *Economic Inquiry*, vol. 51, pp. 1311–1323, 2013.

[18] T. Mitchell, *Machine Learning*. McGraw Hill, 1997

[19] R. Swinburne, *Bayes's Theorem*. Oxford University Press, 2002.

[20] C. Y. Wang, Y. Chen, and K. J. R. Liu, "Sequential Chinese restaurant game," *IEEE Transactions on Signal Processing*, vol. 61, pp. 571–584, 2013.

[21] C.-Y. Wang, Y. Chen, and K. J. R. Liu, "Chinese restaurant game," *IEEE Signal Processing Letters*, vol. 19, pp. 898–901, 2012.

[22] R. Isaac, "Shorter notes: A proof of the martingale convergence theorem," *Proceedings of the American Mathematical Society*, vol. 16, pp. 842–844, 1965.

[23] J. Stewart, "Limits and continuity," in *Multivariable Calculus*, Brooks/Cole, 2011.

[24] L. M. Surhone, M. T. Tennoe, and S. F. Henssonow, *Gibbs' Inequality*. Betascript Publishing, 2010.

[25] C. Jiang, Y. Chen, and K. J. R. Liu, "Multi-channel sensing and access game: Bayesian social learning with negative network externality," *IEEE Transactions on Wireless Communications*, vol. 13, pp. 2176–2188, 2014.

15 Hidden Chinese Restaurant Game

Learning from Actions

Under many circumstances, agents in networks are required to make decisions. However, it is difficult to judge whether the decisions are effective or not on the grounds that the system state is usually concealed and the externality is often beyond agents' control. It is feasible to get rid of uncertainty by taking advantage of sources of information, such as user-generated content or revealed actions. However, user-generated content might not be truthful since other agents, induced by their selfish interests, may create misleading content in a malicious manner. Passively revealed actions tend to be more credible and easier to derive from direct observation. In this chapter, we introduce a stochastic game-theoretic framework known as the Hidden Chinese Restaurant Game (H-CRG) to take advantage of passively revealed actions in stochastic social learning processes. In order to obtain beliefs regarding the hidden information from the observed actions in a straightforward manner, grand information extraction, a novel Bayesian belief extraction process, is designed. Drawing on the relation between belief and policy, we are able to convert the original continuous belief state Markov decision process (MDP) into a discrete-state MDP. Analysis is subsequently carried out on the optimal policy with regard to both centralized and game-theoretic approaches. We then present the application of the H-CRG to the channel access problem in cognitive radio networks. Afterwards, data-driven simulations are conducted through the Community Resource for Archiving Wireless Data At Dartmouth (CRAWDAD) wireless local area network (WLAN) trace. According to the simulation results, the equilibrium strategy derived in the H-CRG provides new users with higher expected utilities and maintains reasonably high social welfare compared with other candidate strategies.

15.1 Introduction

Under many circumstances, agents in networks are required to make decisions. For instance, they may decide to buy a smartphone when their current one becomes unusable, to enjoy a meal at a restaurant when they are hungry, or to listen to music when they are suffering from loneliness. Their choices exert an impact on their utility, or the measurement of their pleasure with the outcome. Given the potential impacts of certain choices, a rational agent is supposed to seek optimal decisions so as to maximize their utility. Nevertheless, sometimes it is difficult to determine these influence of these choices due to unknown parameters, such as the quality of a meal, and external factors, such as an unfamiliar crowd within a restaurant. To make the right decisions, rational agents need to go through a learning process in which they are able to acquire knowledge regarding those uncertain parameters and external factors.

Social learning is a learning technique for acquiring knowledge by drawing on the information disclosed or publicized in a network. A paradigm refers to, for example, the selection of a smartphone in a market with a variety of available alternatives. More often than not, when deciding on which smartphone to buy, customers are usually not fully aware of the quality and usability of the smartphones. One might extract information from advertisements, one's own experience from previous purchases, reviews, or discussions shared on social networks, or some statistics on the quantity of each smartphone sold to date. All of the collected information assists the agent in the construction of their knowledge, which contributes to greater accuracy in the agent's decisions. Social relations may give rise to certain links that tend to publicize the information generated or revealed by other agents. On the grounds that each agent may have various social relations with others and make decisions at different moments, the information received by one agent tends to be different from that received by others.

The information revealed by agents and utilized through social learning could be either user-generated content or passively revealed information. User-generated content, (e.g., public reviews, comments, and ratings of restaurants) is subject to easy identification and analysis, helping agents to grasp the underlying information. The knowledge behind the generated content is implicit since such information can be treated as signals generated by the system and reported by the agent, conditional on some parameters known or unknown to the agents. A simple approach is to make the assumption that these signals are denoted by some probabilistic distribution on the condition of the values of a few unknown parameters, similarly to the assumptions in previous chapters. Agents are then able to establish their beliefs regarding the unknown parameters on the basis of their prior knowledge of the characteristics of the signals. The signaling approach is helpful for simple systematic parameters and has been put into practice through the CRG that we proposed in Chapter 12, as well as in review ratings on Yelp regarding quality of services [1] and the sensing outcomes of the primary user activities in cognitive radio networks [2,3].

However, user-generated content is likely to be untrustworthy in the case of agents having selfish interests. Rational agents are inclined to generate untruthful content for the sake of their own interests. Such content can mislead other agents to form false beliefs regarding unknown parameters and consequently make inappropriate decisions. For example, a local customer may know the best restaurants in town, but they may never disclose such as list to others lest the restaurants become so popular that this local customer needs to wait for weeks to book a table. Furthermore, this customer is apt to recommend other restaurants of lower quality. Moreover, even the providers, such as restaurant owners or movie makers, are motivated to generate untruthful content to manipulate the decisions of customers when they are competing with others. For instance, some restaurants will invite popular bloggers or critics to provide positive reviews or ratings online using discounts as a reward. Such biased content often turns out to be misleading. In cognitive radio networks, another example is that cooperative sensing utilizes the sensing results collected from several secondary users to obtain more accurate detections of the primary user's activity. A rational secondary user is likely to release an untruthful sensing outcome to mislead other users so that they alone can occupy the available channels. In these two cases, agents who hold the knowledge can decide to report content containing misleading information to mislead other agents. In addition, revealing untruthful content costs very little since such behavior requires little effor and is not detrimental to the agent's own utility. However, it requires a great deal of cost and effort, such as additional punishments or reputation systems, to ensure the credibility of content. On the condition that agents may generate untruthful content, collaboration will be impossible among agents in order to gather the truth, so they are more likely to make unwise decisions. In summary, social learning will lose its effectiveness provided that we regard user-generated content as the exclusive information source.

Passively revealed actions, such as the numbers of customers in certain restaurants or the numbers of secondary users accessing certain channels, also provide helpful information, but they entail further endeavor in order to exploit the underlying information. The connotations of such information are more explicit since they are connected with not only the systematic parameters, but also the actions of some or all agents in the system. For example, a high number of visits to a particular restaurant may suggest a high-quality service, a bad service with a short-term promotion, or the shutdown of all other restaurants. One should not only analyze the explicit information, but also take into account the reasons behind the collaborative actions.

However, in comparison with user-generated content, it is less demanding for an agent to collect passively revealed information. For example, one can easily grasp the number of customers in the restaurant, but one is unlikely to gather the opinions of these customers regarding the restaurant. In terms of a cognitive radio network, one can detect whether a channel is accessed by another agent passively, but not the sensing result that the agent holds unless an information exchange protocol and a control channel are available. Since passively revealed actions are easy to collect, this type of information is generally gathered in the real word, such as check-ins, likes in Facebook, daily visit numbers of theme parks, page views of websites, numbers of accesses to base stations/networks, etc.

Although both user-generated content and passively revealed actions are subject to potential alteration by selfish agents for the sake of their own benefits and interests, passively revealed actions are more tenable and credible if we can correctly grasp the logic behind these actions. Moreover, an agent often needs to pay a higher price if they choose to cheat through the revealed actions since they have to select a suboptimal action in order to release untruthful information, which is detrimental to their own utility. As an example, one can only mislead other agents to choose different restaurants by actually choosing a restaurant other than one's favorite. Such a decision turns out to be detrimental to one's own utility, and thus weakens one's motivation for such a cheating behavior.

In view of these advantages, a stochastic game-theoretic framework is introduced for the utilization of passively revealed actions rather than user-generated content as the main information source in social learning processes. The H-CRG makes it possible for customers to observe the actions of other customers within a limited observation space so as to determine their actions and beliefs based on hidden information in a stochastic system. Two types of information are subject to observation: history information, which is a series of actions taken by previous customers within a limited time; and grouping information, which is the number of customers at each table. The observable information may belong to either one or both types depending on the simulated network.

On the basis of the stochastic state transition structure and inspired by the Bayesian learning in the CRG, we design Grand information extraction, a novel Bayesian belief extraction process for the direct extraction of beliefs on the hidden information from the observed actions. The process is universal for any Markovian system with hidden information (state). The extracted belief is conditional on the policy applied by customers and is also likely to influence their actions. The coupling relation is applied to convert the original continuous-state formulation found in traditional partial-observed MDP (POMDP) into a discrete-state pseudo-MDP, which simplifies the problem to a great extent.

Analysis is then conducted on the optimal policy in terms of both the centralized approach and the game-theoretic approach. To determine the centralized policy in the centralized approach, a value iteration solution is introduced. Inspired by the centralized approach and the dynamic CRG (D-CRG) [3], we then propose a value iteration solution to acquire the Nash equilibrium in the H-CRG. Note that the pure-strategy Nash equilibrium is likely to be absent in the H-CRG. Specifically, the information damping phenomenon tends to emerge in a H-CRG in which customers switch from one policy to another at the same time owing to the loss of information regarding the observed action. The phenomenon resembles information cascade [4], which is a general topic of discussion in the traditional social learning literature. Fortunately, given the fact that there are a few naive customers (e.g., legacy network devices in communication networks or myopic agents in social networks), the existence of a pure-strategy Nash equilibrium is guaranteed.

We demonstrate how the H-CRG is applicable to the channel access problem in cognitive radio networks. We then embark on data-driven simulations based on the CRAWDAD WLAN trace [5,6]. According to the simulation outcomes, the equilibrium strategy obtained in H-CRG offers new customers greater expected utility, and the social welfare derived from this strategy is higher than that of other candidate strategies.

15.2   System Models

Let us think about a Chinese restaurant with M tables. It is assumed that the restaurant allows a maximum of N customers to enter, where N refers to the capacity constraint of the restaurant. We consider a time-slotted system in which customers arrive at and depart from the system according to a Bernoulli process. In other words, customers arrive at the restaurant with probability λ and leave the restaurant with probability μ. It is assumed that the time slot is so short that it only admits the arrival and departure of one customer within a slot.[1] At each arrival, the customer requests to be seated in the restaurant by choosing one table. They are probably aware or unaware of the number of customers at each table. As long as they select a table, they will remain seated at the chosen table until their departure. A customer is unlikely to choose a restaurant when (1) the restaurant is filled with customers and consequently the door is closed[2] or (2) the maximum expected utility if they enter the restaurant is negative. The latter case indicates that a customer may realize that leaving the process without entering the restaurant tends to be a more valuable option. For instance, the restaurant may provide unpalatable meals that the customer refrains from trying even though there are seats available. Let $x[t] \in \{0, 1, \ldots, M\}$ be the decision of the customer who arrives at time t, where $x[t] = 0$ denotes that the customer chooses not to enter the restaurant or there is no customer arriving at time t. Note that this is also a reflection of the fact that both of the events make no differences to agents who are merely able to observe the revealed actions.

The size of a table positively influences the dining experience of the customers, where it is assumed that a larger table is preferred by any customer provided that the number of customers choosing the table remains constant. Some tables are likely to have a smaller size or are even unavailable when they are already booked by privileged customers. The exact size of the tables is controlled by the restaurant state $\theta \in \Theta = \{1, 2, 3, \ldots\}$, where the size of each table x is given by $R_x(\theta)$. Nevertheless, the customers are unaware of the sizes of the tables before they actually enter the restaurant. That is, the restaurant state θ is given at the start of the game in advance, according to a prior distribution $Pr(\theta = k)$, but this is unknown to the customers. On the condition that θ exerts a definite influence on the dining experience of customers, it stands for the critical knowledge the customers need to acquire in the game.

15.2.1 Customers: Naive and Rational

We consider two types of customers: naive customers and rational customers. Naive customers represent the legacy agents or devices with predetermined and fixed actions without the capacity for strategic decision-making. In cognitive radio networks, for example, there may be certain legacy secondary devices with limited sensing

---

[1] Note that this assumption can be easily relaxed in the model through the expansion of the state transition probability matrix to incorporate multiple arrival and departure cases. It is believed that all methods and conclusions made in this chapter still hold with this assumption relaxed.

[2] It is also possible to provide the customers with an alternative to wait outside of the restaurant until it opens again. Specifically, we may set P as the maximum number of customers waiting outside of the restaurant when the restaurant is filled with customers, and each customer enters the restaurant in succession upon the departure of a number of customers. This can be modeled as a first in, first out queue and is subject to easy integration into the framework through appropriate adjustments to the state transition probabilities.

capability but that do not collaborate with other devices. It is easier to predict their channel access actions. These naive customers may exert either a positive or negative influence on the overall system performance and service quality experienced by other customers.

Rational customers, by contrast, select the tables in a strategic manner. They purely aim to maximize their expected utility. The utility of the customers has two determinants: the number of customers seated at the same table and the size of the table. Specifically, let $n_x[t]$ be the number of customers choosing table x at time t. The $\mathbf{n}[t] = (n_1[t], n_2[t], \ldots, n_M[t])$ represents the grouping of customers at time t (i.e., the number of customers choosing each table at time t). Then, the immediate utility of a customer choosing table x at time t is $u(R_x(\theta), n_x[t])$, where $R_x(\theta)$ means the size of table x. The influence of the number of customers (i.e., network externality), could be arbitrary and is captured by $\frac{\partial u(r,n)}{\partial n}$. The externality is positive when $\frac{\partial u(r,n)}{\partial n} > 0$, negative when $\frac{\partial u(r,n)}{\partial n} < 0$, and is zero when $\frac{\partial u(r,n)}{\partial n} = 0$ for all n. Ultimately, it is assumed that a larger table is preferred by any customer $\left(\text{i.e., } \frac{\partial u(r,n)}{\partial r} \le 0\right)$.

15.2.2   Observable Information

Knowledge regarding the unknown restaurant state can be derived from the information gathered by the customer. The basic information each customer collects serves as a private signal that they receive upon their arrival. It is assumed that the signal $s \in S$ is generated according to a probability density function $f(s|\theta)$. The signal is informative; in other words, there is a nonzero correlation between restaurant state θ and signal s. In addition, the signal is private, which means that other customers will not know the signal they received unless it is explicitly revealed. Finally, the generated signals are dependent on the true restaurant state θ.

Despite the private signaling, a customer may extract information from the other customers through observing their passively revealed actions. Such information is classified into two different types – *grouping information* and *history information* – as follows:

Grouping information: The current grouping $\mathbf{n}[t]$ of customers at time t. This represents the number of customers choosing each table at the current time. This observation sketches out the consensus among all customers in the system. However, the decision orders of these customers are not captured in grouping information. While this kind of observation is likely to be useful in some systems, one has to spend significant effort to maintain or derive it. For instance, one customer may easily determine the number of customers waiting to be served at each restaurant by simple counting, but they would remain unaware of the number of customers subscribing to each cellular service until the providers explicitly announce this information.

History information: The history of actions revealed by customers selecting tables at time $t - H, t - H + 1, \ldots, t - 1$. Here it is assumed that a customer may observe and record the actions revealed by the previous customers with a maximum of H slots before making their own decision. The history information lays emphasis on the decision orders of customers and the potential impacts of previous actions on subsequent customers. History information is easily accessible in certain networks and therefore commonly seen in the literature. Note that when H amounts to infinity, history information will become grouping information *plus* the decision order information. However, H is usually assumed to be finite so as to reflect the limited observation capability of customers.

It is assumed that the only information revealed by one customer is the table that they selected. In other words, customers will make no contribution to user-generated content such as signals, only disclosing their actions in a passive manner. This design removes the scenario in which a customer tends to unfaithfully report their private signals. Strictly speaking, the potential information space for a customer choosing a table at time t is as follows:

$$(\mathbf{n}[t], x[t - H], x[t - H + 1], \ldots, x[t - 1], s[t]) = (\mathbf{n}[t], \mathbf{h}[t], s[t]), \qquad (15.1)$$

where $\mathbf{h}[t]$ denotes the history of information (actions) revealed by customers from time $t - H$ to $t - 1$.

Rational customers aim to maximize their long-term expected utility in the system (i.e., to choose the table that maximizes their expected utility by taking into account of the unknown restaurant state and the potential network externality). Rational customers are confronted with two types of major challenge: (1) how to extract information from the observed actions for the estimation of unknown information, such as the restaurant state and (2) how to make a prediction on the impact of network externality in a stochastic system when there are naive customers.

15.3   Hidden Chinese Restaurant Game

The table selection problem is formulated as an H-CRG. The H-CRG is a stochastic game with an indeterministic number of players. The arrival and departure of the players (customers) are assumed to be in line with the Bernoulli distributions. A customer can choose the table at which to be seated or to leave right away, but they are not allowed to change their table afterwards. Their utility relies on the table they selected and the states of the system during of their stay.

Figure 15.1 presents an illustration of the H-CRG framework. In brief, the grand information extraction process is designed in the H-CRG to extract a belief regarding the hidden state from the observed information. The process entails input from the policy pursued by rational customers and the corresponding state transition probability. Rational customers then estimate the expected utilities using the belief derived from the process. The updated estimation of the expected utilities will assist them in improving their decision-making and updating their rational policy accordingly. The key in H-CRG is to determine the policy that maximizes the expected utility for each customer.

The system state sketches out the current situation of the system, including the restaurant state, grouping information, history of actions, and the generated signal.

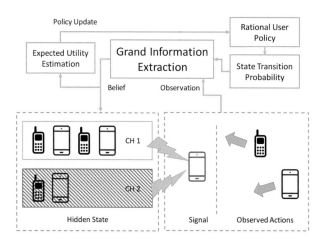

Figure 15.1 H-CRG framework.

Given the current state, one may determine the current utility of a customer completely. However, the state will transition stochastically according to a state transition probability function, which will be described subsequently. Formally speaking, the system state of H-CRG at time t is denoted as follows:

$$\mathbf{I}[t] = \{\mathbf{n}[t], \mathbf{h}[t], s[t], \theta\}. \tag{15.2}$$

The information in state $\mathbf{I}$ is classified into two types: observed state $\mathbf{I}^o$ and hidden state $\mathbf{I}^h$. The observed state refers to the information that can be readily observed by the customers upon their arrival. The hidden state represents the information that can only be extracted from belief estimations by regarding observed states as inputs. Note that both the observed state and hidden state may influence the utility of each customer.

Whether the information is observable or hidden depends on the system within which we are working. We assume that the restaurant state θ is constantly hidden based on the assumption that the value is provided beforehand but concealed from the customers. On the other hand, the signal $s[t]$ is always observable since it is assumed that each customer receives at least a private signal.

For the other two types of information–grouping information and history information–whether they are observable or hidden depends on the system settings. As an example, if we are simulating a restaurant selection problem in a food court, it is reasonable to assume that each customer is able to observe both grouping information and history information on the grounds that one can easily determine the number of customers queuing up and how these queues are formed. In this case, both grouping information and history information are observable and thus classified into the observed state. On the other hand, in the case of the simulation of a channel selection game in a cognitive radio network, it may not be feasible to assume that each secondary user is in a position to observe the grouping information as a third-party base station is required to record and broadcast such information. However, it is reasonable to assume that each secondary user can observe the choices of other users during channel access upon their arrival since this can be done through channel monitoring. In this case, the grouping information should be classified into the hidden state, whereas the history information belongs to the observed state.

A policy serves as the description of the table selection strategy a customer applies in the H-CRG given the information they observed as inputs. As we mentioned previously, a customer can only observe the information in the observed state. Consequently, a policy can be defined as follows:

$$\pi(\mathbf{I}^o) \in \mathbf{A} = \{0, 1, \ldots, M\}, \forall \mathbf{I}^o. \tag{15.3}$$

Note that $\pi(\mathbf{I}^o) = 0$ refers to the fact that the customer decides not to select any of the tables and leaves the restaurant right away when $\mathbf{I}^o$ is observable.

Recall that we have two sorts of customers: naive and rational customers. It is assumed that a ratio ρ of customers is rational, whereas the others are naive customers. Naive customers pursue a naive policy for the determination of their actions. The naive policy is fixed across the whole game. We denote the naive policy as $\pi^n(\mathbf{I}^o)$.

On the other hand, a rational customer aims to maximize their long-term expected utility. Upon the arrival of a customer at the system, they observe the system and receive the observed state. Afterwards, they choose the table with the greatest long-term expected utility by taking into account both the network externality $\mathbf{n}$ and the unknown restaurant state θ. Note that the influence of network externality tends to vary over time due to the departure and arrival of other customers. It is advisable for a rational customer to consider the currently observed state and to make a prediction regarding the decisions made by other subsequent customers (both rational and naive ones).

Recall that the immediate utility of a customer choosing table x in a given time slot t is $u(R_x(\theta), n_x[t])$. The long-term expected utility of a customer arriving at time t_a is given by

$$E[U(x)|\mathbf{I}^o[t_a]] = \sum_{t=t_a}^{\infty} (1-\mu)^{(t-t_a)} \sum_{\theta \in \Theta} Pr(\theta|\mathbf{I}^o[t_a]) E[u(R_x(\theta), n_x[t])|\mathbf{I}^o[t_a], \theta].$$
$$\tag{15.4}$$

Note that here a customer observes $\mathbf{I}^o$ without knowledge of the actual state $\mathbf{I}$. It requires further effort to estimate the corresponding hidden state, which will be introduced later.

A rational customer always tends to maximize their expected utility. Put another way, they select a table as follows:

$$\pi^r(\mathbf{I}^o) = \arg \max_{x \in \{0, 1, \ldots, M\}} E[U(x)|\mathbf{I}^o], \forall \mathbf{I}^o. \tag{15.5}$$

The key factors in the estimation of the expected utility are (1) acquiring knowledge of the hidden state based on the observed state and (2) making a prediction regarding future states based on the condition of the currently observed state.

15.3.1   System State Transition

The system state transitions over time. At each time slot, a new signal will be generated based on the condition of the restaurant state θ. Additionally, the observed actions in the history information $\mathbf{h}[t]$ will change, with the action observed at time $t - H$ forgotten and a new action observed at time t added.

The grouping information $\mathbf{n}[t]$, which is key to the estimation of the impact exerted by network externality, changes with the occurrence of any of the following events.

New Customer Arrival

When a new customer arrives, they will select a table according to either a naive policy $\pi^n(\mathbf{I}^o)$ or a rational policy $\pi^r(\mathbf{I}^o)$, depending on their type. It is also possible for the customer to choose not to enter the restaurant (i.e., $\pi^r(\mathbf{I}^o) = 0$ or $\pi^n(\mathbf{I}^o)$) with the occurrence of a certain observed state $\mathbf{I}^o$. In addition, when the restaurant accommodates as many as N customers, it may refuse any further customers irrespective of the table they select. We denotes $\mathcal{I}^{e,n}$ and $\mathcal{I}^{e,r}$ as the set of system states where naive and rational customers will not enter the restaurant, respectively. Formally speaking

$$\mathbf{I} = \{\mathbf{I}^o, \mathbf{I}^h\} \in \mathcal{I}^{e,\{n,r\}} \text{ if } \pi^{\{n,r\}}(\mathbf{I}^o) = 0 \text{ or } \sum_{j=1}^{M} n_j = N. \tag{15.6}$$

For any state $\mathbf{I} \notin \mathcal{I}^{e,\{n,r\}}$ there exists a set of states $\mathcal{I}^a_{\mathbf{I},\pi^{\{n,r\}}}$ where every state $\mathbf{I}' = \{\mathbf{n}', \mathbf{h}', s', \theta\}$ in the set satisfies

$$n'_{\pi^{\{n,r\}}(\mathbf{I}^o)} = n_{\pi^{\{n,r\}}(\mathbf{I}^o)} + 1, n'_j = n_j \forall j \neq \pi(\mathbf{I}^o),$$

$$\mathbf{h}' = \{h_2, \ldots, h_{H-1}, \pi^{\{n,r\}}(\mathbf{I}^o)\}. \tag{15.7}$$

In other words, when a new customer arrives and chooses a table according to the policy, the number of customers at the corresponding table plus 1 and the history information $\mathbf{h}$ records this choice. Note that there is likely to be more than one possible transition state in the set. For any other state $\mathbf{I} \in \mathcal{I}^{e,\{n,r\}}$ the corresponding state set $\mathcal{I}^a_{\mathbf{I},\pi^{\{n,r\}}}$ is empty.

Existing Customer Departure

When an existing customer in the restaurant leaves, the number of customers at the table decreases by one. Since no new customer enters the restaurant at this moment, the history information records zero (no observed action) for the present state. Let $\mathcal{I}^d_{\mathbf{I}}$ be the set of transition states from state $\mathbf{I}$ when one customer departs from the restaurant. For every state $\mathbf{I}' \in \mathcal{I}^d_{\mathbf{I}}$ we have

$$\exists d, n'_d = n_d - 1, n'_j = n_j \forall j \neq d, \mathbf{h}' = \{h_2, \ldots, h_{H-1}, 0\}. \tag{15.8}$$

No Change

When none of the previous events occur, the grouping information remains the same. In this case, only history information and signal change at the next time slot. We denote

$\mathcal{I}_{\mathbf{I}}^u$ as the set of transition states from state $\mathbf{I}$ when no customer arrives at or departs from the restaurant. For every state $\mathbf{I}' \in \mathcal{I}_{\mathbf{I}}^u$ we have

$$\mathbf{n}' = \mathbf{n}, \mathbf{h}' = \{h_2, \ldots, h_{H-1}, 0\}. \tag{15.9}$$

Given all of the probability distributions we defined in Section 15.2 and the previous discussion, we can derive the state transition probability from (15.10) as

$$Pr(\mathbf{I}[t+1]|\mathbf{I}[t], \pi^n, \pi^r) = \tag{15.10}$$

$$\begin{cases} \rho\lambda f(s[t+1]|\theta), & \mathbf{I}[t+1] \in \mathcal{I}_{\mathbf{I}[t], \pi^r}^a; \\ (1-\rho)\lambda f(s[t+1]|\theta), & \mathbf{I}[t+1] \in \mathcal{I}_{\mathbf{I}[t], \pi^n}^a; \\ (n_j[t])\mu f(s[t+1]|\theta), & \mathbf{I}[t+1] \in \mathcal{I}_{\mathbf{I}[t]}^d, n_j[t+1] = n_j[t]-1; \\ \left(1-\mu\sum_{j=1}^M n_j - \lambda\right) f(s[t+1]|\theta), & \mathbf{I}[t+1] \in \mathcal{I}_{\mathbf{I}[t]}^u, \mathcal{I}_{\mathbf{I}[t], \pi^r}^a \neq \emptyset, \mathcal{I}_{\mathbf{I}[t], \pi^n}^a \neq \emptyset; \\ \left(1-\mu\sum_{j=1}^M n_j - \rho\lambda\right) f(s[t+1]|\theta), & \mathbf{I}[t+1] \in \mathcal{I}_{\mathbf{I}[t]}^u, \mathcal{I}_{\mathbf{I}[t], \pi^r}^a \neq \emptyset, \mathcal{I}_{\mathbf{I}[t], \pi^n}^a = \emptyset; \\ |-|\left(1-\mu\sum_{j=1}^M n_j - (1-\rho)\lambda\right) f(s[t+1]|\theta), & \mathbf{I}[t+1] \in \mathcal{I}_{\mathbf{I}[t]}^u, \mathcal{I}_{\mathbf{I}[t], \pi^r}^a = \emptyset, \mathcal{I}_{\mathbf{I}[t], \pi^n}^a \neq \emptyset; \\ \left(1-\mu\sum_{j=1}^M n_j\right) f(s[t+1]|\theta), & \mathbf{I}[t+1] \in \mathcal{I}_{\mathbf{I}[t]}^u, \mathcal{I}_{\mathbf{I}[t], \pi^r}^a = \mathcal{I}_{\mathbf{I}[t], \pi^n}^a = \emptyset; \\ 0, & \text{else.} \end{cases}$$

15.3.2   Grand Information Extraction

The estimation of the expected utility about certain tables should be preceded by the estimation of the hidden state, which is hidden from the customer, on the condition of the observed state. Specifically, the *belief* on the hidden state (i.e., the probability distribution of the hidden state) should be acquired. This problem resembles the belief updating in POMDP apart from that the belief in POMDP is usually assumed to be an input of the policy, whereas the belief updating process is known and given. Customarily, the optimal policy is obtained through the transformation of the POMDP into a belief MDP with a continuous state space in the belief state. The optimal policy is then likely to be obtained through value iteration or policy iteration algorithms on a finite set of value functions where the expected values are formulated as a linear combination of the value function of a proper set of belief vectors. However, the major deficiency is that the exponential increase in the size of the belief vector set makes this approach computationally intractable. Approximated algorithms are more desirable for feasibility.

We propose a novel belief estimation method, grand information extraction, to extract the distribution of hidden state straightforwardly from the observed state without a belief updating process. The fundamental idea is an extension of the Bayesian belief method in the CRG from the signal domain to the system state domain. We take advantage of the stationary probability distribution of the system states, which can be derived from the state transition probability, to directly extract the belief regarding the restaurant state θ. Conditional on θ, we are then able to estimate the belief on the hidden state correspondingly. The major advantage of this process consists in the possibility of formulating the system exclusively with discrete state spaces but without a belief updating process or belief vector set. Afterwards, it is feasible to reduce the problem to the discrete-space pseudo-MDP problem.

Initially, the belief in the H-CRG is formally defined as follows:

$$g_{\mathbf{I}|\mathbf{I}^o} = Pr(\mathbf{I}|\mathbf{I}^o). \tag{15.11}$$

Provided the restaurant state $\theta = k$ and the policy applied by the customers are given, the state transition probability can be obtained directly through (15.10). Then, the stationary state distribution of the H-CRG $[Pr(\mathbf{I}|\theta = k, \pi^n, \pi^r)]$ is given as follows:

$$[Pr(\mathbf{I}|\theta = k, \pi^n, \pi^r)] = [Pr(\mathbf{I}'|\mathbf{I}, \theta = k, \pi^n, \pi^r)][Pr(\mathbf{I}|\theta = k, \pi^n, \pi^r)]. \tag{15.12}$$

The stationary state distribution of system states $\mathbf{I}$ can be obtained through finding the normalized eigenvector of the transition matrix with the eigenvalue of 1.

LEMMA 15.1   *The stationary state distribution* $[Pr(\mathbf{I}|\theta = k, \pi^n, \pi^r)]$ *is unique.*

Proof   It has been proved that the sufficient condition for a unique stationary state distribution in a Markov system is to have exactly one closed communication class in the state transition. It can be seen from (15.10) that all states have a positive probability of transitioning to the zero state with no customers in the restaurants, no actions observed in the history, and arbitrary signals when all customers depart from the restaurant. This indicates that all states will be connected with the zero state, and having two closed communication classes in the H-CRG is out of the question. As a result, the stationary state distribution, conditional on the restaurant state $\theta = k$, is unique.

The uniqueness of the stationary state distribution ensures a consensus on the beliefs among all rational customers provided they have identical observations and knowledge of the state transition.

The stationary state probability $Pr(\mathbf{I}|\theta = k, \pi^n, \pi^r)$ symbolizes the probability that a customer is subject to a certain state $\mathbf{I}$ whenever they arrive at the system, if the restaurant state θ is actually k. The Bayesian belief rule is then applicable for obtaining the probability of the restaurant state θ. Specifically, when the stationary probability distribution $Pr(\mathbf{I}|\theta, \pi^n, \pi^r)$ is derived for all $\theta \in \Theta$, we are then able to obtain the probability of the restaurant state θ as follows:

$$Pr(\theta = k|\mathbf{I}, \pi^n, \pi^r) = \frac{Pr(\mathbf{I}|\theta = k, \pi^n, \pi^r)}{\sum_{k' \in \Theta} Pr(\mathbf{I}|k', \pi^n, \pi^r)}. \tag{15.13}$$

Nevertheless, the aforementioned probability is dependent on the system state $\mathbf{I}$, whereas the customer can actually observe the observed state $\mathbf{I}^o$ only. Further effort is required to derive the actual belief of the customer regarding the hidden state. Let $\mathcal{I}_{\mathbf{I}^o}^o$ be the set that involves all of the states sharing identical observed state $\mathbf{I}^o$. The probability that one may observe a certain observed state $\mathbf{I}^o$ conditional on $\theta = k$ is the sum of the stationary state probability of all states in $\mathcal{I}_{\mathbf{I}^o}^o$, which is as follows:

$$Pr(\mathbf{I}^o|\theta = k, \pi^n, \pi^r) = \sum_{\mathbf{I} \in \mathcal{I}_{\mathbf{I}^o}^o} Pr(\mathbf{I}|\theta = k, \pi^n, \pi^r). \tag{15.14}$$

Then, once more, it is possible to evaluate the probability of the restaurant state θ conditional on the observed state $\mathbf{I}^o$ in accordance with the Bayesian rule:

$$Pr(\theta = k | \mathbf{I}^o, \pi^n, \pi^r) = \frac{Pr(\mathbf{I}^o | \theta = k, \pi^n, \pi^r) Pr(\theta = k)}{\sum_{k' \in \Theta} Pr(\mathbf{I}^o | \theta = k', \pi^n, \pi^r) Pr(\theta = k')}. \quad (15.15)$$

The above belief is adequate for the case in which only the restaurant state θ is unobservable. However, as is analyzed in Section 15.2, the grouping information or history information is also inclined to be unobservable. In this case, it is still necessary for us to estimate the hidden information in the hidden state. Recall the stationary state distribution $\left[Pr(\mathbf{I} | \theta = k, \pi^n, \pi^r) \right]$ we previously derived. Conditional on a given $\theta = k$, we can derive the probability of the actual system state $\mathbf{I}$ based on the observed state $\mathbf{I}^o$ as follows:

$$Pr(\mathbf{I} | \mathbf{I}^o, \theta = k, \pi^n, \pi^r) = \frac{Pr(\mathbf{I} | \theta = k, \pi^n, \pi^r)}{\sum_{\mathbf{I}' \in \mathcal{T}_{\mathbf{I}^o}} Pr(\mathbf{I}' | \theta = k, \pi^n, \pi^r)}. \quad (15.16)$$

Combining (15.15) with (15.16), we can derive the belief regarding the system state $\mathbf{I}$ conditional on the observed state $\mathbf{I}^o$:

$$g_{\mathbf{I} | \mathbf{I}^o, \pi^n, \pi^r} = Pr(\mathbf{I} | \mathbf{I}^o) = \sum_{k \in \Theta} Pr(\mathbf{I} | \mathbf{I}^o, \theta = k, \pi^n, \pi^r) Pr(\theta = k | \mathbf{I}^o, \pi^n, \pi^r). \quad (15.17)$$

Note that the belief from the grand information extraction process on state $\mathbf{I}$ is conditional on not only the observed state $\mathbf{I}^o$ but also the policies pursued by rational and naive customers. The accuracy of the estimated belief relies on the informativeness of the observed actions, which is determined by the policies.

15.3.3 Equilibrium Conditions

In the H-CRG, rational customers are inclined to maximize their long-term expected utility. Two determinants are involved in terms of the expected utility: the current state of the system as well as the transition of the state in the future.

The choices of customers at various states serve as determinants of the state transition. For grouping $\mathbf{n}$, as an example, two major determinants are involved: the policy pursued by the naive customers and that pursued by other subsequent rational customers. Moreover, the belief of a customer regarding the hidden state depends on the observed state containing the actions of other previous customers. Changes in the actions taken by other customers lead to alterations in the state transition as well as the expected utility experienced by the customer. To sum up, the belief regarding the hidden state and the state transition depends on the choices of all customers, whereas each customer's choice relies on their belief regarding the states. The complex interactions among customers are consequently captured by the H-CRG.

An analysis is carried out on the pure-strategy Nash equilibrium of the H-CRG. A Nash equilibrium is a popular solution concept in game theory that is applicable to the prediction of the outcome of a game. Let $E[U(x_{\mathbf{I}^o}, \mathbf{x}_{-\mathbf{I}^o})]$ be the expected utility of a customer observing $\mathbf{I}^o$, where $x_{\mathbf{I}^o}$ is their choice and $\mathbf{x}_{-\mathbf{I}^o}$ are the choices of other customers at other states. The pure-strategy Nash equilibrium of the H-CRG is defined as follows:

DEFINITION 15.2 (Nash Equilibrium)   The Nash equilibrium, or pure-strategy Nash equilibrium, in the H-CRG is a policy π^* where for all $\mathbf{I}^o$

$$E[U(x^*_{\mathbf{I}^o}, \mathbf{x}^*_{-\mathbf{I}^o})] \geq E[U(x, \mathbf{x}^*_{-\mathbf{I}^o})], \forall x \in \{0, 1, 2, \ldots, M\}, \tag{15.18}$$

where $x^*_{\mathbf{I}^o} = \pi^*(\mathbf{I}^o)$, $\mathbf{x}^*_{-\mathbf{I}^o} = \{\pi^*(\mathbf{I}'^o) | \mathbf{I}'^o \neq \mathbf{I}^o\}$.

The expected utility in (15.18) can be analyzed by modeling the H-CRG as a multidimensional MDP(M-MDP) [7]. Let the system state $\mathbf{I}$ be the state and $\pi^r(\mathbf{I}^o)$ be the policy in the M-MDP. The immediate reward is defined as follows:

$$R(\mathbf{I}, x) = R(\mathbf{n}, \mathbf{h}, s, \theta, x) = u(R_x(\theta), n_x). \tag{15.19}$$

The expected reward of a customer choosing table x at state $\mathbf{I}$ in the system can be presented as $W^I(\mathbf{I}, x)$ and derived from the Bellman equation. When the game reaches the stationary states, the expected reward for a customer staying at a table x equals the immediate reward they receive at the current state plus the expected reward they are going to receive in the days to come if they continue their stay at the restaurant. As a consequence, we have

$$W^I(\mathbf{I}, x, \pi^r) = R(\mathbf{I}, x) + (1 - \mu) \sum_{\mathbf{I}'} Pr(\mathbf{I}' | \mathbf{I}, \pi^n, \pi^r, x) W^I(\mathbf{I}', x, \pi^r), \forall \mathbf{I}, x. \tag{15.20}$$

Nevertheless, the state transition probability $Pr(\mathbf{I}' | \mathbf{I}, \pi^n, \pi^r, x)$ we denote here is different from (15.10) since it is on the grounds that this customer does not leave at the next time slot. Specifically, when $x > 0$, the number of customers who may depart from table x will be $n_x[t] - 1$ rather than $n_x[t]$. The transition probability is therefore given by (15.21).

$$Pr(\mathbf{I}[t+1] | \mathbf{I}[t], \pi^n, \pi^r, x) = \tag{15.21}$$

$$\begin{cases} \rho\lambda f(s[t+1] | \theta), & \mathbf{I}[t+1] \in \mathcal{I}^a_{\mathbf{I}[t], \pi^r}; \\ (1 - \rho)\lambda f(s[t+1] | \theta), & \mathbf{I}[t+1] \in \mathcal{I}^a_{\mathbf{I}[t], \pi^n}; \\ (n_j[t])\mu f(s[t+1] | \theta), & \mathbf{I}[t+1] \in \mathcal{I}^d_{\mathbf{I}[t]}, n_j[t+1] = n_j[t] - 1, j \neq x; \\ (n_x[t] - 1)\mu f(s[t+1] | \theta), & \mathbf{I}[t+1] \in \mathcal{I}^d_{\mathbf{I}[t]}, n_x[t+1] = n_x[t] - 1; \\ \left(1 - \mu\left(\sum_{j=1}^M n_j - 1\right) - \lambda\right) f(s[t+1] | \theta), & \mathbf{I}[t+1] \in \mathcal{I}^u_{\mathbf{I}[t]}, \mathcal{I}^a_{\mathbf{I}[t], \pi^r} \neq \emptyset, \mathcal{I}^a_{\mathbf{I}[t], \pi^n} \neq \emptyset; \\ \left(1 - \mu\left(\sum_{j=1}^M n_j - 1\right) - \rho\lambda\right) f(s[t+1] | \theta), & \mathbf{I}[t+1] \in \mathcal{I}^u_{\mathbf{I}[t]}, \mathcal{I}^a_{\mathbf{I}[t], \pi^r} \neq \emptyset, \mathcal{I}^a_{\mathbf{I}[t], \pi^n} = \emptyset; \\ \left(1 - \mu\left(\sum_{j=1}^M n_j - 1\right) - (1-\rho)\lambda\right) f(s[t+1] | \theta), & \mathbf{I}[t+1] \in \mathcal{I}^u_{\mathbf{I}[t]}, \mathcal{I}^a_{\mathbf{I}[t], \pi^r} = \emptyset, \mathcal{I}^a_{\mathbf{I}[t], \pi^n} \neq \emptyset; \\ \left(1 - \mu\left(\sum_{j=1}^M n_j - 1\right)\right) f(s[t+1] | \theta), & \mathbf{I}[t+1] \in \mathcal{I}^u_{\mathbf{I}[t]}, \mathcal{I}^a_{\mathbf{I}[t], \pi^r} = \mathcal{I}^a_{\mathbf{I}[t], \pi^n} = \emptyset; \\ 0, & \text{else.} \end{cases}$$

The Bellman equations in (15.20) describe the inherent expected rewards if one has been fully aware of the system state. However, customers know nothing about the inherent expected reward since they are only informed of observed state $\mathbf{I}^o$. One has to go to great lengths to estimate the expected utility on the condition of the observed state $\mathbf{I}^o$. The idea is to draw on the belief extracted from grand information extraction so as to estimate the expected immediate reward and corresponding state transition probability. Let $W(\mathbf{I}^o, x)$ be the expected utility of a customer at table x if they observe $\mathbf{I}^o$. Recall that $\mathcal{I}_{\mathbf{I}^o}^o$ is the set of states sharing identical observed state $\mathbf{I}^o$ and $g_{\mathbf{I}|\mathbf{I}^o}$ is the distribution of the states in the set conditional on the observed state $\mathbf{I}^o$. We have

$$W(\mathbf{I}^o, x) = \sum_{\mathbf{I} \in \mathcal{I}_{\mathbf{I}^o}^o} g_{\mathbf{I}|\mathbf{I}^o, \pi^n, \pi^r} W^I(\mathbf{I}, x), \forall \mathbf{I}^o, x \in \{1, 2, \dots, M\}. \tag{15.22}$$

Additionally, let $W(\mathbf{I}^o, 0)$ be the utility if the customer chooses to depart from the system right away. This represents the lower bound of the expected utility for a customer entering the restaurant. In this chapter, we discuss $W(\mathbf{I}^o, 0) = 0, \forall \mathbf{I}^o$ without any losses in generality.

Rational customers intend to maximize their long-term expected utility given the actions taken by other customers in previous and future states. The actions taken by other customers are captured by the rational policy π^r. Nevertheless, a customer's own action will also exert an impact on the system state transition. Let $Pr(\mathbf{I}^{'o}|\mathbf{I}^o, \pi^r, x)$ be the probability that the observed state transits from $\mathbf{I}^o$ to $\mathbf{I}^{'o}$ if the customer selects table x. From the standpoint of the customer, it is ideal to choose the table that maximizes the expected utility. Consequently, we have

$$\pi^r(\mathbf{I}^o) = \arg \max_{x \in \{0, 1, 2, \dots, M\}} \sum_{\mathbf{I}^{'o}} Pr(\mathbf{I}^{'o}|\mathbf{I}^o, \pi^r, x) W(\mathbf{I}^{'o}, x). \tag{15.23}$$

The exact transition probability from $\mathbf{I}^o$ to $\mathbf{I}^{'o}$ depends on the form of the observed state. On the grounds that merely one customer is to be seated at a table, the transition in grouping information and history information often turns out to be unique. It is apparent that when $x > 0$, we have $n_x' = n_x + 1$ and $\mathbf{h}' = \{h_2, h_3, \dots, x\}$ in the transition state $\mathbf{I}$ and the corresponding $\mathbf{I}^o$. By constrast, if the customer refrains from entering the restaurant, there will be no changes in the grouping. As a result, we have $n_x' = n_x$ and $\mathbf{h}' = \{h_2, h_3, \dots, 0\}$ when $x = 0$.

However, the newly generated signal s' depends on the restaurant state θ, which is in the hidden state $\mathbf{I}^h$. Consequently, it is necessary to estimate the new signal s' on the basis of the belief regarding the restaurant state. In conclusion, we have the transition probability of observed states in (15.24) based on the observed state $\mathbf{I}^o$ and the belief from grand information extraction $g_{\mathbf{I}|\mathbf{I}^o, \pi^n, \pi}$.

$$Pr(\mathbf{I}^{'o}|\mathbf{I}^o, \pi^r, x) = \tag{15.24}$$

$$\begin{cases} \sum_{\theta \in \Theta} Pr(\theta = k|\mathbf{I}^o, \pi^n, \pi^r) f(s'|\theta), & \mathbf{h}' = \{h_2, h_3, \dots, x\}, n_x' = n_x + 1, n_j' = n_j, \forall j, x > 0; \\ \sum_{\theta \in \Theta} Pr(\theta = k|\mathbf{I}^o, \pi^n, \pi^r) f(s'|\theta), & \mathbf{h}' = \{h_2, h_3, \dots, 0\}, \mathbf{n}' = \mathbf{n}, x = 0 \text{ or } \sum_{j=1}^M n_j = N; \\ 0, & \text{else.} \end{cases}$$

The coupling relation between the long-term expected utility $W(\mathbf{I}^o)$ and the rational policy $\pi^r(\mathbf{I}^o)$ captures the impact of any customer's action on the expected utility. Then, in accordance with the Nash equilibrium of the H-CRG we defined in Definition 15.2, we have the equilibrium conditions of the H-CRG as follows:

THEOREM 15.3   *The Nash equilibrium of the H-CRG is* $\pi^*(\mathbf{I}^o)$ *if*

$$W^{I*}(\mathbf{I}, x, \pi^*) = R(\mathbf{I}, x) + (1 - \mu) \sum_{\mathbf{I}'} Pr(\mathbf{I}'|\mathbf{I}, \pi^n, \pi^*, x) W^{I*}(\mathbf{I}', x, \pi^*), \quad (15.25)$$

$$W^*(\mathbf{I}^o, x) = \sum_{\mathbf{I} \in \mathcal{I}_{\mathbf{I}^o}^o} g_{\mathbf{I}|\mathbf{I}^o, \pi^n, \pi^*} W^I(\mathbf{I}, x), \quad (15.26)$$

$$\pi^*(\mathbf{I}^o) = \arg \max_x \sum_{\mathbf{I}'^o} Pr(\mathbf{I}'^o|\mathbf{I}^o, \pi^*, x) W^*(\mathbf{I}'^o, x), \quad (15.27)$$

for all $\mathbf{I}$, $\mathbf{I}^o$, $x \in \{1, 2, \ldots, M\}$.

Proof   Given a policy π^*, the expected utility of any rational customer applying action x at state $\mathbf{I}^o$ is given by (15.26). In addition, given (15.27), we have

$$E[U(\pi^*(\mathbf{I}^o), \pi^*_{-\mathbf{I}^o}(\mathbf{I}^o))] = W^*(\mathbf{I}^o, \pi^*(\mathbf{I}^o)) \geq W^*(\mathbf{I}^o, x) = E[U(x, \pi^*_{-\mathbf{I}^o}(\mathbf{I}^o))].$$

Therefore, the policy π^* is a Nash equilibrium according to Definition 15.2.

15.4   Solutions

15.4.1   Centralized Policy

To begin with, we analyze the socially optimal policy for the H-CRG. The socially optimal policy is the solution for the maximization of the expected social welfare of the whole system. This solution serves as the performance bound provided by centralized control solutions. The social welfare is defined as the average total utility of all customers in the restaurant

$$SW = \lim_{T \to \infty} \sum_{t=0}^{T} \frac{\sum_{j=1}^{M} n_j U(R_j(\theta), n_j)|_{\mathbf{I}[t]}}{T}. \quad (15.28)$$

The expected total utility given the observed state $\mathbf{I}^o$, which we defined as $W^s(\mathbf{I}^o)$, can be obtained through the Bellman equation

$$W^s(\mathbf{I}^o) = \mu' \sum_{\mathbf{I}'^o} Pr(\mathbf{I}'^o|\mathbf{I}^o, \pi^r) W^s(\mathbf{I}'^o) + \sum_{\mathbf{I} \in \mathcal{I}_{\mathbf{I}^o}^o} g_{\mathbf{I}|\mathbf{I}^o, \pi^n, \pi^r} \sum_{j=1}^{M} n_j U(R_j(\theta), n_j)|_{\mathbf{I}}. $$

$$(15.29)$$

Note that $Pr(\mathbf{I}'^o|\mathbf{I}^o, \pi^r)$ can be obtained through reducing (15.10) to the observed state domain.

This form is similar to an MDP apart from that the immediate reward concerns not only the current action but also the actions in other states due to the grand information extraction. In this case, determining the socially optimal solution is quite a challenge. Instead, we try to find the centralized policy for the maximization of the current expected social welfare at each instance, or the expected social welfare

---

Algorithm 12: Value iteration for centralized solutions.
___

(1) Initialize $\pi^{s,0}, W^{s,0}, l = 0$

(2) **while** 1 **do**

(3) $l \leftarrow l + 1$

(4) $Pr(\mathbf{I}'^o | \mathbf{I}^o, \pi^n, \pi^r) \leftarrow (15.24)$

(5)   **for all $\mathbf{I}^o$ do**

(6) $\pi^{s,l} \leftarrow (15.30)$

(7) $W^{s,l} \leftarrow (15.29)$

(8)   **end for**

(9) $W^{s,d} \leftarrow W^{s,l+1} - W^{s,l}$

(10)   **if** $\max W^{s,d} - \min W^{s,d} < \epsilon$ **then**

(11)   Break

(12)   **end if**

(13) **end while**

(14) Output $\pi^{r,l}$ and $W^{s,l}$
___

given the policy pursued in the present. Note that this is also a shared objective in traditional MDP problems.

The centralized policy is given by

$$\pi^s(\mathbf{I}^o) = \arg \max_{x \in \{0, 1, 2, ..., M\}} \sum_{\mathbf{I}'^o} Pr(\mathbf{I}'^o | \mathbf{I}^o, x) W^s(\mathbf{I}'^o). \qquad (15.30)$$

The value iteration algorithm is then utilized to determine the centralized policy. Differences can be found between the algorithm and the traditional value iteration algorithms in MDPs. The updating of a policy will lead to the updating of two elements: the expected social welfare as well as the immediate social welfare. The immediate social welfare is updated through the grand information extraction in order to acquire the correct belief regarding the hidden states under the new policy. The algorithm is shown in Algorithm 12.

It is possible for the centralized policy to provide superior performance from the perspective of the service operator (i.e., restaurant owner). However, it excludes the rationality of rational customers. In certain cases, the centralized policy requires some rational customers to choose the tables that can benefit the system but are suboptimal for their own utility. In this case, these customers tend to deviate from the centralized policy when no extra incentive mechanism is available [8].

15.4.2   Nash Equilibrium

In terms of the original H-CRG setup in which rational customers choose to maximize their own long-term expected utilities, to obtain the final outcome (i.e., the Nash equilibrium) often turns out to be a more daunting challenge due to the competition among customers. Taking advantage of the inspiration from the value iteration algorithm for

---

Algorithm 13: Value-iteration algorithm for the Nash equilibrium.

(1) Initialize π^r, W, W^I;

(2) **while** 1 **do**

(3) $g_{I|I^o, \pi^n, \pi^r} \leftarrow$ (15.17)

(4)   **for all I^o do**

(5) $\pi^{r'} \leftarrow$ (15.27);

(6) $W^{I'} \leftarrow$ (15.25);

(7) $W' \leftarrow$ (15.26);

(8)   **end for**

(9) $W^d \leftarrow W' - W$

(10)   **if** $\max W^d - \min W^d < \epsilon$ **then**

(11)   Break

(12)   **else**

(13) $W \leftarrow W', W^I \leftarrow W^{I'}, \pi^r \leftarrow \pi^{r'}$

(14)   **end if**

(15) **end while**

(16) Output π^r, W, and W^I

---

the centralized solution, we design a value iteration algorithm to determine the Nash equilibrium in the H-CRG. This is Algorithm 13.

LEMMA 15.4   *The output of Algorithm 13, if converged, is the Nash equilibrium of the H-CRG when $\epsilon \to 0$.*

Proof It is apparent that when Algorithm 13 converges with $\epsilon = 0$, all conditions in Theorem 15.3 (i.e., (15.25), (15.26), and (15.27)) are satisfied. Therefore, the output policy π^r is the Nash equilibrium of the H-CRG.

Unfortunately, it is found that the pure-strategy Nash equilibrium is likely to be absent when the belief regarding the hidden state is seriously affected by the choices of other customers observed in the history information. In certain cases, the rational policy pursued by rational customers may change from one to another in the stochastic system, which is referred to as *information damping*. Specifically, the optimal choice of a rational customer is determined by their belief regarding the restaurant state. This belief is conditional on both their received signal and their observed actions, whereas the information contained in the observed actions relies on whether other customers make decisions according to their signals or not. When all rational customers follow their own signals, the information contained in previous actions tends to be more effective than their own signals when the observed history is sufficiently long. When the information is effective enough to overcome the signal, the customers are inclined to choose to follow the actions rather than their own signals. This decision, on the other hand, reduces the information contained in the observed actions. In certain cases, the information in the action is reduced to such an extent that the received signal becomes more informative than the observed actions. Customers then switch back to following the observed signals rather than the observed actions. This is called information damping since customers have the alternatives of following the signals or the actions of others. This phenomenon resembles information cascade in traditional social learning problems, where the information contained in the observed actions is subject to certain constraints on account of the information diffusion structure [9,10]. Information damping is one of the key factors that results in the absence of the pure-strategy Nash equilibrium, which may affect the stability of the system.

Information damping is fundamentally caused by the loss of information in the observed actions due to customers' rational choices. However, a way to avoid this is to take into account both the rational customers and the naive customers in the system. The naive customers, who pursue a predetermined policy for choosing the table given the observed state, are generally found in most systems. In wireless networks, for instance, the naive customers could be the legacy devices following existing protocols without strategic thinking. In social networks, by contrast, the naive customers could be agents who are naive in terms of short-term memory, which are discussed in the literature [11,12]. The naive policy π^n followed by the naive customers is predictable, unaffected by rational customers, and potentially informative if the received signal influences the output of the policy π^n.

The actions of these naive customers will be regarded as an external information source for revealing the hidden state in the grand information extraction process. However, it can be intractable to differentiate the actions of naive customers from those of rational ones. In the H-CRG, according to the illustration in Section 15.2, it is assumed that these actions are indistinguishable. The naive policy π^n pursued by these naive customers, on the other hand, is known by the rational customers. As the ratio of naive customers increases, the observed actions become potentially more informative and predictable. The grand information extraction process will automatically extract the information according to the naive policy and the customer type ratio.

15.5   Application: Channel Access in Cognitive Radio Networks

In this section, we introduce an important application of the H-CRG: channel access in cognitive radio networks. Initially, the problem is described and then the illustration of its corresponding H-CRG model is given. Afterwards, we evaluate the performance of the H-CRG through data-driven simulations [5].

We consider a cognitive radio network with some primary users and secondary users sharing the channels. The primary users are prioritized to access the channels. In other words, secondary users are not allowed to access the channel if they are occupied the primary users. In certain cases, the secondary users are likely to be punished if they interfere with the primary users' transmissions by accident. Therefore, it is necessary for secondary users to detect the activity of primary users through channel sensing before their actual transmission. However, the channel sensing has certain deficiencies, particularly when the protocol of the primary users is kept secret. Both misdetections and false alarms can be detrimental to the service quality experienced by both primary and secondary users. Cooperative sensing is a prevalently applied approach for improving the detection accuracy through the aggregation of the sensing results of all nodes. The aggregated outcomes could contribute to a more desired consensus regarding the channel states and hence better decisions in terms of channel access.

In this sense, we discuss a new approach to cooperative sensing inspired by the stochastic social learning techniques in the H-CRG. In this case, the secondary users can detect two major sorts of information: the activity of primary users as well as the access attempts of other secondary users. Specifically, a secondary user will first wait for a few time slots and detect the access attempts of other secondary users in the channels. Afterwards, it will detect the activity of the primary users through traditional channel sensing. The secondary user may derive the sensing results of other secondary users from the collected channel access patterns. This approach has the advantage of requiring no control channels or signaling exchanges between secondary users, which makes it more feasible for networks with limited channel resources. However, this is a costly advantage: each secondary user has to wait for a while before accessing the channel. This triggers an extra delay and thus decreases the average throughput. When the accuracy of sensing result is high, the cost in extra delay may cancel out the benefit obtained in the learning process.

The system model can now be formulated. Let us take M channels into account, and the primary users currently occupy one of them. The secondary users sense the channels and decide on the channel that is occupied by the primary users. It is assumed that the sensing has certain deficiencies (i.e., there is a probability of $p < 1$ for the correct detection of the occupied channel). The access probability of the secondary users per slot is given by $p_a < 1$. Note that when several user access the channel concurrently, the transmissions tend to collide with each other and fail. As a consequence, given that the channel is free from occupation by the primary users and k secondary users choose the same channel, the expected access opportunity for a secondary user is

$$E[u(1,k)] = p_a(1 - p_a)^{k-1}. \qquad (15.31)$$

By contrast, if a primary user occupies the channel, the following penalty has to be paid by the secondary user who attempts to access the same channel:

$$E[u(0,k)] = C < 0. \qquad (15.32)$$

When a secondary user arrives, they choose a channel to access. It is assumed that they will wait for H slots and detect the access patterns of other customers. At the final slot, they will also sense the actions of primary users in each channel. These slots are referred to as sensing slots. Afterwards, they will choose the channel to access before their departure. The following slots are known as accessing slots. It is assumed that there are two types of secondary users: legacy and strategic users. The legacy secondary users will access the channel according to their own sensing results. This symbolizes the legacy devices without cooperative sensing capability. Strategic secondary users, on the other hand, will draw on all of the observed information so as to select the channel based on the largest expected utility.

The long-term expected utility of a secondary user is the average expected successful access attempts before their departure from the system, including both sensing slots and accessing slots. Note that all secondary users will wait in the sensing slots before accessing the channel, which indicates that each secondary user has zero access opportunities for the first H slots. The larger H is, the smaller will be the portion of accessing slots during a secondary user's stay.

We can model the channel access problem as a H-CRG if we regard M channels as tables, the sensing results as the signal s, and the utility as the access opportunity minus the penalty. Moreover, the restaurant state $\theta = \{1, 2, \ldots, M\}$ represents the channel occupied by the primary users. We may derive both the centralized policy and the Nash equilibrium policy for the strategic secondary users. Note that in this system a secondary user may observe the actions taken by previous users instead of the current grouping. Put another way, the observed state is $\mathbf{I}^o = \{\mathbf{h}, s\}$. Consequently, not only should the rational customers derive a belief regarding the primary user channel occupation, but also they have to estimate the number of secondary users choosing the same channel.

15.5.1   Simulation Results

We evaluate the performance of policies through data-driven simulations with user process and network models by drawing on time-invariant parameters extracted from a real data set. Specifically, the H-CRG framework requires a variety of components, such as a user arrival process, departure process, and utility functions. We extract the necessary parameters for each component from the data set and construct the appropriate settings for the problem. In the simulation, the parameters of user process and network models are extracted from the CRAWDAD WLAN trace [5,6]. The arrival and departure of secondary users follow the distribution extracted from the trace in the data set. In terms of the utility function, we take the slotted ALOHA access mechanism into account and make the assumption that secondary users focus on successful access attempts, with a penalty imposed by the primary users in the case of interference. The sensing accuracy, on the other hand, rests with the sensing techniques applied by the system, and here we treat it as an adjustable parameter in the simulations. It can be replaced with the corresponding accuracy given the adoption of certain sensing techniques.

The simulation is conducted on a cognitive radio network with two channels and a maximum of eight secondary users. Each slot lasts five minutes. The probability of primary users choosing either channel to occupy is equal. The arrival and departure of secondary users follow the distribution extracted from [5]; in other words, the arrival rates of naive and strategic secondary users are 0.2106 and 0.1479 per slot, respectively. The departure rate per secondary user is 0.0715 per slot [6]. For each secondary user in the network, the access probability per slot is 0.7. The penalty for interfering with primary user is -0.7 per slot.

We compare the performance of the policy derived from the H-CRG and four other policies: signal, belief, myopic, and centralized. The signal policy is identical to the policy pursued by legacy devices, where the users always comply with their own signal to access the channel. This demonstrates the performance bound in the case of the secondary users' noncooperation. The belief policy represents the strategy for following the belief regarding the primary users' channel occupation extracted from the grand information extraction through (15.15), but the estimation of the number of users is excluded. This demonstrates the performance upper bound provided that there is cooperation among secondary users in sensing, but the effect of network externality is ignored. The myopic policy represents the strategy in which both the primary users' channel occupation and number of secondary users are estimated by grand information extraction, but the payoff in the future slots is excluded. This demonstrates the performance bound if secondary users take into account both the sensing results and network externality, but the impact of other subsequent secondary users is ignored. Finally, the centralized policy is the one that we obtained through Algorithm 12. This represents the policy in which there is a centralized control node that determines the channel access policy for secondary users. It turns out to be the performance upper bound for social welfare provided that there is adoption of a centralized control mechanism.

The performance of the different policies is evaluated based on two metrics: expected long-term individual utility for new strategic users and average social welfare per slot.

Initially, we evaluate the influence of history length on the performance of all policies. We set the signal quality as $p = 0.85$ and then simulate history lengths from 1 to 5. This simulation improves our understandings of whether the increased history information can enhance the accuracy of the belief regarding the hidden state and the utilities of the secondary users. Figure 15.2 presents the simulation results. It is apparent that increasing history length improves the expected individual utility of the user. This is due to the increase in the observed state space, which contains more information to be extracted from grand information extraction. It is known that the equilibrium policy from the H-CRG offers the highest individual expected utility among all of the policies. Furthermore, the H-CRG is the only policy that ensures a positive expected utility for new users. It is interesting that the increase in H also has a positive effect on the expected utility of the signal policy. This is due to the fact that the signal policy receives a negative expected utility and the accuracy is unaffected by history length. Given the negative expected utility of accessing slots, a reduction in the portion of access slots will exert a positive impact on the expected utility under the signal policy.

Regarding social welfare, on the other hand, an inverse trend is shown for the equilibrium policy in the H-CRG. This is due to the fact that the increase in history length leads to better understanding of the hidden state, which also results in fiercer competition among the secondary users. This tends to exert a negative impact on social welfare. However, the equilibrium policy is still the closest to the centralized policy. It is also known that the H-CRG outperforms centralized policy in terms of the expected utility of new secondary users but not social welfare. This is grounded in the fact that in the centralized policy, better social welfare might be achieved at the expense of certain users. For instance, some secondary users may be rejected

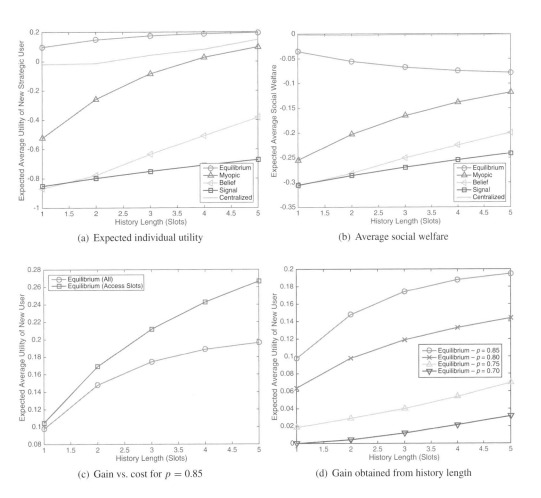

(a) Expected individual utility

(b) Average social welfare

(c) Gain vs. cost for $p = 0.85$

(d) Gain obtained from history length

Figure 15.2 Influence of history length.

by the system in the centralized policy for the purpose of protecting other existing users from higher collision rates in channel access, even if these new users would have received a positive utility if they had been allowed to enter. Such protection contributes to higher social welfare, but may be detrimental to the utility of new users. For the H-CRG, on the other hand, new secondary users will access the channel that maximizes their own utility, irrespective of whether this attempt is detrimental to social welfare. Consequently, the expected utility of new customers should be higher under this policy, in exchange for lower social welfare.

We now discuss the influence of sensing slots on average utility. Figure 15.2(c) illustrates the average utility of secondary users across the whole duration and all access slots. The difference between the two lines in Figure 15.2(c) consists of the overheads due to the extra delay in sensing slots. It is observable that the overheads brought about by the sensing slots increase remarkably with increasing history length. By contrast, the increase in the average utility of access slots diminishes

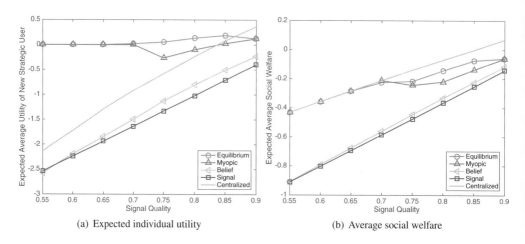

(a) Expected individual utility   (b) Average social welfare

Figure 15.3 Influence of signal quality.

with increasing history length. This indicates that a reasonable history length balances the accuracy and the extra overheads brought about by the sensing slots. The results also suggest that the resulting performance is concave with regard to history length, thus the optimal history length can be determined with ease. Figure 15.2(d) illustrates the average utility of secondary users under different signal qualities. It is shown that the increase of utility brought about by greater history lengths becomes more significant in the case of low quality of the signal. This is due to the fact that when the signal quality is low, the increase in accuracy due to the greater history length is sufficient to offset the overheads brought about by the extra delay. According to these results, the sensing slots need to be extended when the signal quality is low, and vice versa.

We now evaluate the influence of signal quality (channel sensing accuracy) on the performance of all policies. We set the history length as $H = 4$ and then simulate a range of signal qualities from 0.90 to 0.45. The results are presented in Figure 15.3. It is shown that the increase in signal quality is beneficial to the expected individual utility of the user. This is due to the increased signal quality and thus the increased information contained. However, it is clear that the equilibrium policy from the H-CRG still offers the highest individual expected utility compared with all other policies, apart from in the case of high signal quality. When the signal quality is high, the centralized policy provides a higher expected utility. However, the centralized policy is suboptimal for some users at certain states, and hence it is unsteady and impossible to implement unless additional incentive mechanisms are available.

On the other hand, it is shown that the equilibrium, myopic, and centralized policies provide identical social welfare when the signal quality is low, but in the case of high signal quality, social welfare diminishes for both the equilibrium and myopic policies. This is due to the influence of fiercer competition when the system state is identified with greater accuracy by better signals. This may exert a negative impact

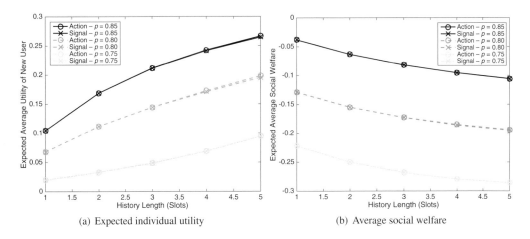

(a) Expected individual utility   (b) Average social welfare

Figure 15.4 Action vs. signal-based models.

on social welfare. Nevertheless, the performance of the equilibrium policy is still the closest to the centralized policy in the majority of cases.

Finally, we compare the performance of the framework with that of various information sources. Specifically, the actions revealed in the observed state in the H-CRG are replaced with the signals each user receives upon their arrival at the system. Put another way, users share their signals with other users when they access the channel in the revised model. The original H-CRG is defined as the action-based model; the revised one is defined as the signal-based model. The revised model refers to the social learning system treating user-generated signals as an information source. Note that all algorithms are still applicable to the revised model. Figure 15.4 presents the expected utility of new customers and social welfare in both models. It can be seen that the performance loss from signal-based to action-based models, if any, is trivial. The results show that the revealed actions already contain sufficient information for rational customers to acquire the hidden information and make appropriate decisions.

15.6   Conclusion

We proposed a stochastic game-theoretic framework called the H-CRG, to utilize passively revealed actions rather than user-generated content as the main source of information in social learning processes. On the basis of the stochastic state transition structure and inspired by the Bayesian learning in CRG, the grand information extraction can extract the belief regarding the hidden information straightforwardly from the observed actions. The belief extraction process can be applied to any Markovian system. To convert the original continuous-state formulation in traditional POMDP into a discrete-state MDP, further exploitation is conducted as to the coupling relation between the belief and the policy. Analysis of the optimal policy is then conducted in terms of both the centralized approach and the game-theoretic approach. It is notable that the pure-strategy Nash equilibrium may be absent in the H-CRG. Specifically, the information damping phenomenon may arise in a particular H-CRG in which customers synchronously switch from one policy to another owing to the information loss in the observed actions. Fortunately, the existence of naive customers contributes to the guarantee of the existence of a pure-strategy Nash equilibrium. Their actions can be regarded as signals to stabilize the beliefs of agents on the observed actions. We conducted an evaluation of the performance of the H-CRG through simulations while drawing on the framework for the channel access problem in cognitive radio networks. We conducted data-driven simulations based on the CRAWDAD WLAN trace. According to the simulation outcomes, the equilibrium strategy derived in the H-CRG provides new users with higher expected utility and maintains a reasonably high social welfare in comparison with other candidate strategies.

15.7   Literature Review

Social learning is one of the major areas of research that focus on both economy and network science. Users in a social network may not be fully aware of the current state of the network. Consequently, they may actively reveal their private information or passively observe the actions taken by others to improve their understanding of the network state. The majority of the existing literature focuses on how agents could achieve a proper consensus through social learning [4,13–15]. These studies were confined to the scenario in which network externality was excluded (i.e., the choice of one agent would not affect the payoff received by other agents). This assumption helps researchers to focus on belief formation, but is limited in terms of applications. One has to go to great lengths to extend the traditional social learning framework to include network externality [16,17]. These models are still troubled by limited applicability due to the assumptions they depend on, such as a binary state space, no decision order information, and positive network externality only. Some studies on social learning in the stochastic system can be found in [18,19]. They focus on the equilibrium learning strategy concerning the stochastic characteristics of a hidden state. However, none of these studies take into account network externality and a dynamic agent population.

The framework resembles the POMDP model, which is a generalization of MDPs with hidden states. In the POMDP model, a centralized user who determines the action cannot straightforwardly observe the true state of the system. Some observations concerning the true state can be derived by the agent as a clue to the true underlying state. The belief and the probability distribution of the true state serve as the determinants of the uncertainty and the knowledge of the true state. The agent intends to determine the optimal policy for controlling the system in order to maximize their long-term reward. It has been shown that POMDPs can be shaped into a belief MDP in which the belief is captured by additional continuous belief states. The optimal policy can then be obtained through the application of point-based methods [20,21]. Point-based methods are based on the observations that the optimal expected value function can be formulated as a combination of the value function on a proper set of belief vectors in which the optimal action in each segment can be obtained. The optimal policy can be derived afterwards. Determining the feasible belief vectors is of great significance for obtaining an exact optimal policy. Approximated algorithms for finding suboptimal but tractable belief vectors thus have been proposed [21]. Another approach is to control the POMDP system through finite-state controllers [22]. A feasible control policy can be formulated as a policy graph depicting the actions to take upon the receipt of certain observations, without the need for additional belief states [23]. The solution space is then reducible to the policy space depicted by the graph. However, the size of the policy graph is likely to be intractable if we would like to guarantee the optimality of the solution. The differences between the POMDP model and the H-CRG consist of two factors: the number of objective functions and the complexity of the belief updating process. In traditional MDP or POMDP problems, we only have one expected value function to serve as the only objective function for maximization. In the H-CRG framework, on the other hand, we are tackling multiple objective functions, or the utilities of agents entering the system at different states and choosing different tables. According to the illustrations in previous works [7,8], this major difference constitutes a daunting challenge for solving the Nash equilibrium in the game since these objective functions will influence each other in a nonlinear fashion. Additionally, the belief updating process, as is illustrated in Section 15.3.2, is no longer Markovian since the updated belief relies on not only the current state, prior belief, and current action, but also the actions of other agents in previous and future time slots. As a consequence, none of the current algorithms, including point-based methods and policy graphs, can be utilized directly to derive the Nash equilibrium. This offers the incentive for us to search for an alternative approach to this problem.

Cooperative sensing in cognitive radio networks is an important application of the H-CRG framework. In cognitive radio networks, secondary users are allowed to access the channels only when they are not occupied by primary users. However, there is no direct interaction between primary and secondary users. In an attempt to guard against interference, secondary users are supposed to detect the activities of primary users through channel sensing. We introduce cooperative sensing so as to enhance sensing accuracy by allowing secondary users to share their sensing results in order to make decisions through collaboration [24]. Various signaling exchange schemes have been put forward, including centralized or distributed modes and soft or hard collaborative decisions [25]. Overall, greater accuracy (e.g., using the soft decision mode in the centralized sharing scheme) is brought about, along with longer latency and greater overheads due to the increase in signal exchanges. Cheating behavior in cooperative sensing, or Byzantine attacks, has attracted wider attention in recent years [26]. In an attempt to gain advantages in channel access, secondary users are likely to intentionally report false sensing results to others. Various defense mechanisms have been introduced based on the statistical difference between false reports and other normal reports. Some extra penalties may be applied in utility-based approaches to discourage rational users from launching attacks. The majority of proposed designs bring about greater overheads in the cooperative sensing system in the form of either implementation costs or accuracy losses. The main overheads in cooperative sensing come from the cost of sharing sensing results among members through signal exchanges. In this chapter, we used the H-CRG to thoroughly remove the need for signal exchange processes while maintaining sensing accuracy.

References

[1] Y. Chen, C. Jiang, C. Y. Wang, Y. Gao, and K. J. R. Liu, "Decision learning: data analytic learning with strategic decision making," *IEEE Signal Processing Magazine*, vol. 33, pp. 37–56, 2016.

[2] C. Y. Wang, Y. Chen, and K. J. R. Liu, "Sequential Chinese restaurant game," *IEEE Transactions on Signal Processing*, vol. 61, pp. 571–584, 2013.

[3] C. Jiang, Y. Chen, Y.-H. Yang, C.-Y. Wang, and K. J. R. Liu, "Dynamic Chinese restaurant game: theory and application to cognitive radio networks," *IEEE Transactions on Wireless Communications*, vol. 13, pp. 1960–1973, 2014.

[4] V. Bala and S. Goyal, "Learning from neighbours," *Review of Economic Studies*, vol. 65, pp. 595–621, 1998.

[5] D. Kotz, T. Henderson, I. Abyzov, and J. Yeo, "CRAWDAD dataset Dartmouth/campus (v. 2009-09-09)." http://crawdad.org/dartmouth/campus/20090909.

[6] Y. H. Yang, Y. Chen, C. Jiang, and K. J. R. Liu, "Wireless network association game with data-driven statistical modeling," *IEEE Transactions on Wireless Communications*, vol. 15, pp. 512–524, 2016.

[7] Y.-H. Yang, Y. Chen, C. Jiang, C.-Y. Wang, and K. J. R. Liu, "Wireless access network selection game with negative network externality," *IEEE Transactions on Wireless Communications*, vol. 12, pp. 5048–5060, 2013.

[8] C. Y. Wang, Y. Chen, H. Y. Wei, and K. J. R. Liu, "Scalable video multicasting: A stochastic game approach with optimal pricing," *IEEE Transactions on Wireless Communications*, vol. 14, pp. 2353–2367, 2015.

[9] F. Chierichetti, J. Kleinberg, and A. Panconesi, "How to schedule a cascade in an arbitrary graph," in *Proc. of the 13th ACM Conference on Electronic Commerce (EC)*, 2012.

[10] M. Hajiaghayi, H. Mahini, and D. Malec, "The polarizing effect of network influences," in *Proc. 15th ACM Conference on Economics and Computation (EC)*, 2014.

[11] D. Fudenberg and A. Peysakhovich, "Recency, records and recaps: learning and non-equilibrium behavior in a simple decision problem," in *Proc. 15th ACM Conference on Economics and Computation (EC)*, 2014.

[12] S. Zhang and A. J. Yu, "Forgetful Bayes and myopic planning: human learning and decision-making in a bandit setting," in *Advances in Neural Information Processing Systems (NIPS)*, 2013.

[13] B. Golub and M. O. Jackson, "Naive learning in social networks and the wisdom of crowds," *American Economic Journal: Microeconomics*, vol. 2, pp. 112–149, 2010.

[14] D. Acemoglu, M. Dahleh, I. Lobel, and A. Ozdaglar, "Bayesian learning in social networks," *Review of Economic Studies*, vol. 78, 1201–1236, 2011.

[15] D. Acemoglu and A. Ozdaglar, "Opinion dynamics and learning in social networks," *Dynamic Games and Applications*, vol. 1, pp. 3–49, 2011.

[16] G. Angeletos, C. Hellwig, and A. Pavan, "Dynamic global games of regime change: learning, multiplicity, and the timing of attacks," *Econometrica*, vol. 75, pp. 711–756, 2007.

[17] J. Costain, "A herding perspective on global games and multiplicity," *BE Journal of Theoretical Economics*, vol. 7, p. 22, 2007.

[18] V. Krishnamurthy, "Quickest detection pomdps with social learning: interaction of local and global decision makers," *IEEE Transactions on Information Theory*, vol. 58, pp. 5563–5587, 2012.

[19] J. A. Bohren, "Stochastic games in continuous time: persistent actions in long-run relationships, second version," *SSRN Electronic Journal*, 2014.

[20] H. Zhang, "Partially observable Markov decision processes: A geometric technique and analysis," *Operations Research*, vol. 58, pp. 214–228, 2009.

[21] G. Shani, J. Pineau, and R. Kaplow, "A survey of point-based POMDP solvers," *Autonomous Agents and Multi-Agent Systems*, vol. 27, pp. 1–51, 2013.

[22] N. Meuleau, L. Peshkin, K.-E. Kim, and L. P. Kaelbling, "Learning finite-state controllers for partially observable environments," in *Proc. 15th Conference on Uncertainty in Artificial Intelligence*, 1999.

[23] N. Meuleau, K.-E. Kim, L. P. Kaelbling, and A. R. Cassandra, "Solving POMDPs by searching the space of finite policies," in *Proc. 15th Fifteenth Conference on Uncertainty in Artificial Intelligence*, 1999.

[24] T. Yucek and H. Arslan, "A survey of spectrum sensing algorithms for cognitive radio applications," *IEEE Communications Surveys & Tutorials*, vol. 11, pp. 116–130, 2009.

[25] A. Ali and W. Hamouda, "Advances on spectrum sensing for cognitive radio networks: theory and applications," *IEEE Communications Surveys & Tutorials*, vol. 19, pp. 1277–1304, 2017.

[26] L. Zhang, G. Ding, Q. Wu, Y. Zou, Z. Han, and J. Wang, "Byzantine attack and defense in cognitive radio networks: A survey," *IEEE Communications Surveys & Tutorials*, vol. 17, pp. 1342–1363, 2015.

16 Wireless Network Access with Mechanism Design

In a wireless environment, the selection of a wireless access network is required for network service acquisition. A key problem in wireless access network selection is studying rational strategies that consider negative network externality (i.e., the influence of subsequent users' decisions on an individual's throughput due to the limited available resources). Within this chapter, the wireless network selection problem as a stochastic game with negative network externality is formulated, and it shows that the process of finding the optimal decision rule could be modeled as a multidimensional Markov decision process (M-MDP). We utilize a modified value iteration algorithm for obtaining efficiently the optimal decision rule with a simple threshold structure, reducing the strategy profile's storage space. Furthermore, we investigate the mechanism design problem with incentive compatibility (IC) constraints that force the networks to reveal truthful state information. As a mixed integer program, the formulated problem generally lacks an efficient solution. We introduce a dynamic programming (DP) algorithm that is capable of solving the problem within the two-network scenario optimally by exploiting the optimality of the substructures. In a multinetwork scenario, the heuristic greedy approach can be outperformed by the DP algorithm within polynomial time complexity.

16.1 Introduction

Today, wireless network services such as femtocells [1] and Wi-Fi access points (APs) are universally deployed to provide Internet access in areas such as hotels, homes, offices, airports, etc. However, only one can be joined by the user among multiple available wireless networks. Figure 16.1 represents an example of Wi-Fi network selection in a smartphone. The network selection that used to be resolved in a centralized manner by admission control [2,3] ought to be investigated from a distributed perspective by considering users' own interests, since the networks can be owned by different operators. A myopic strategy can often be adopted through choosing that which has the strongest signal within the wireless access network selection, leading to user congestion in terms of communicating with certain network controllers such as routers, APs, or switches. Inefficient resource utilization for service providers and poor quality of service (QoS) for users occur because an unbalanced load is created by the users' concentration within the network.

Figure 16.1 Wi-Fi network selection.

While efficient resource utilization is an important issue within modern wireless access networks as the available resources, such as signal power and spatial and temporal bandwidth, are limited. On the one hand, the available resources can accommodate as many users as possible since the service provider aims to maximize resource utilization. On the one hand, a user aims at to optimize their own utility according to their selfish nature and individual rationality (IR). Therefore, the optimal strategy of a user under such a resource-sharing scenario must take *negative network externality* [4,5] into consideration (i.e., the influence of other users' strategies on the user's own utility). Negative network externality, a concept used commonly in economics and business, represents the effect that occurs when the value of a resource becomes less when there are more users; for instance, traffic congestion overloads a highway and large numbers of customers degrade the QoS within a restaurant, which hinder the utilities of users making the same decision.

Within this chapter, we first focus on the ways of a user choosing one of the available wireless access networks by taking negative network externality into consideration. We consider the problem within a different scenario in which users make decisions *sequentially* and their optimal decisions involve the prediction of subsequent users' decisions on the basis of negative network externality, yet most of the existing works study this problem under the scenario in which users make decisions simultaneously. We study sequential decisions taking negative network externality into account in the Chinese restaurant game [6–8], in which we characterize the equilibrium of the grouping of a certain number of players within the scenario. In this chapter, the wireless access network selection problem is formulated as a stochastic game with negative network externality in which users arrive at and depart from networks in a probabilistic manner. Discovering the optimal decision rule is represented as an M-MDP that has multiple potential functions, unlike a conventional MDP [9]. Hence, DP [10] cannot be adopted directly. We then introduce a modified value iteration algorithm in order to find the equilibrium of the M-MDP. The analysis shows that the strategy profile generated by the modified value iteration algorithm has a threshold structure, enabling us to preserve the storage space of the strategy profile from $\mathcal{O}(N^2)$ to $\mathcal{O}(N \log N)$, where N^2 stands for the number of system states within the two-network scenario. Simulation results prove the analysis and illustrate the effectiveness and efficiency of the M-MDP (i.e., the M-MDP shows similar performance in terms of social welfare to that of the centralized method where social welfare is maximized while achieving the optimal strategy for the individual).

Second, we focus on truthful mechanism design [11–15] for the network selection game. Mechanism design devises rules of allocation and pricing that satisfy IC [12,13]. Within the network selection game, if making a deceitful claim is profitable, the reported state might be untruthful because users make decisions depending on the system state where the system states consist of the information provided by the networks, possibly owned by different operators with different interests. We investigate the mechanism design problem with IC constraints that incline the networks to report truthfully while the utility of users is optimized. As a mixed integer programming problem, the formulated problem lacks an efficient solution in general. We introduce a DP algorithm that could solve the problem within the two-network scenario efficiently and optimally by exploiting the optimality of the substructures. This algorithm is capable of outperforming the heuristic greedy approach within polynomial time complexity for the multinetwork scenario. We present simulation results to validate the analysis and illustrate the DP algorithm's effectiveness.

16.2   System Model and Problem Formulation

Within this section, the system model and the formulation of the wireless access network selection problem are presented in detail. To better illustrate the idea, we first introduce some necessary notation, including the probabilistic model, and then characterize the (approximate) equilibrium. Note that the model is quite general and could be adapted to not only the network selection problem, but also other problems with negative network externality.

16.2.1   System Model

The system we consider comprises a capacity of N users of K wireless access networks (i.e., a network is capable of serving at most N users simultaneously). For the sake of notation simplicity, it is considered that all networks have the same capacity. The analysis could be extended without difficulty to systems with networks of different capacities. The networks are assumed to have no buffer room for users, and this means that users are not capable of making connections demands to the network when it is full. Every user within network k acquires a utility $R_k(s_k)$ per unit time, in which s_k represents the users' current number within network k. The utility function is signified as the individual throughput $\left(\text{i.e., } R_k(s_k) = \log\left(1 + \frac{P_S/N_0}{(s_k-1)P_I/N_0+1}\right), \forall k\right)$, which signifies the achievable data rate within interuser interference in which the signal-to-noise power ratio is represented by P_S/N_0 and the interference-to-noise power ratio is represented by P_I/N_0. The utility stands for the QoS ensured by the network; however, it is restricted by the available resources such as the bandwidth of the radiofrequency and the total transmission power. The data rate's reduction as the number of users within the network rises due to negative network externality is manifested by a higher interuser interference. Note that we assume that users share the same utility within the same network at each time slot owing to the fact that the network is capable of providing the same QoS to every user through resource allocation, even though the different users' instantaneous channel conditions might differ. For instance, the network can use the centralized downlink power control algorithms [16,17] to obtain a common signal-to-interference-plus-noise ratio (SINR) or to maximize the minimum SINR among the users.

The users with a Poisson distributed arrival rate $\bar{\lambda}_0$ (users per second) are capable of choosing to connect to one of the K networks. During a period of time with an exponential distribution of parameter $\bar{\mu}$ after making a decision, a user is not capable of switching to other networks and must stay, and this is presumed to be the same for all networks for simplicity. Only network k can be chosen by the users with arrival rate $\bar{\lambda}_k$, for $k = 1, \ldots, K$, and these could be envisioned as either the users with certain deterministic behaviors or the users that are capable of only accessing one specific network based on their geographic distribution. Note that incorporating this type of user only makes the system model more general since we can simply set these rates to zero if there are no such users.[1]

The system state $\mathbf{s} = (s_1, \ldots, s_K)$ holds its value from the state space $\mathcal{S} = \{(s_1, \ldots, s_K)|s_k = 0, 1, \ldots, N, k = 1, \ldots, K\}$ and stands for the state that s_k users are within network k, for $k = 1, \ldots, K$. First, a discrete time Markov system in which a time slot has duration T (seconds) is considered. Then the arrival and departure probabilities $\lambda_k = \bar{\lambda}_k T e^{-\bar{\lambda}_k T}$ and $\mu = \bar{\mu} T e^{-\bar{\mu} T}$ could be approximated as $\lambda_k \approx \bar{\lambda}_k T, k = 0, \ldots, K$ and $\mu \approx \bar{\mu} T$ when T is sufficiently small [18–20]. Let $\mathcal{F}(\mathbf{s}) = \{k|s_k = N, k = 1, \ldots, K\}$ be the index set of the full networks that are serving the maximum user number and thus cannot accept any more. The complement set of $\mathcal{F}(\mathbf{s})$ is signified by $\bar{\mathcal{F}}(\mathbf{s}) = \{k|s_k < N, k = 1, \ldots, K\}$ (i.e., the index set of the nonfull networks). The network selection's strategy space is restricted within $\bar{\mathcal{F}}(\mathbf{s})$ when $\mathbf{s}$ represents a boundary state (i.e., when $\sigma_\mathbf{s} \in \bar{\mathcal{F}}(\mathbf{s})$). We presume that the connection requests from users arriving at the full networks are denied and the traffic goes to other nonfull networks. We assume that the traffic flows to the nonfull networks immediately for modeling such a traffic transition. For the two-network case, the traffic goes to nonfull networks since for those users only one nonfull networks has room; for the

---

[1] We can consider more general types of users, such as users who can only connect to one of a subset of K networks, but we only consider two types of users for simplicity (i.e., users who can choose any one of K networks and users who can choose only one specific network).

multinetwork case, multiple nonfull networks are capable of accommodating those users. To simplify the notation and provided that there is a well-defined Markov system, we presume that the traffic goes to a specific network (i.e., $\min \bar{\mathcal{F}}(\mathbf{s})$, the network with the minimum index). Notice that no connection demand is capable of being accepted if $\bar{\mathcal{F}}(\mathbf{s}) = \phi$ (i.e., all networks are full). The network selection strategy is denoted as $\sigma_{\mathbf{s}}$ when the user observes state $\mathbf{s}$, which holds value within $\bar{\mathcal{F}}(\mathbf{s})$. We signify $\sigma_{\mathbf{s}} = j$ if network j is selected. The indicator function $I_k(\sigma_{\mathbf{s}})$ is then defined as: if $\sigma_{\mathbf{s}} = j$, $I_j(\sigma_{\mathbf{s}}) = 1$; otherwise $I_j(\sigma_{\mathbf{s}}) = 0$. The state transition probability of an arrival event can be computed as

$$P_{\text{sys}}\left(\mathbf{s} + \mathbf{e}_j | \mathbf{s}\right) = \begin{cases} \sum_{i \in \mathcal{F}(\mathbf{s})} \lambda_i + \lambda_j + I_j(\sigma_{\mathbf{s}})\lambda_0, & \text{if } j = \min \bar{\mathcal{F}}(\mathbf{s}), \\ \lambda_j + I_j(\sigma_{\mathbf{s}})\lambda_0, & \text{if } j \in \bar{\mathcal{F}}(\mathbf{s}) \setminus \left\{ \min \bar{\mathcal{F}}(\mathbf{s}) \right\}, \end{cases} \quad (16.1)$$

where $\mathbf{s} + \mathbf{e}_j$ and $\mathbf{s}$ signify the system states at the next time slot, and the current time slot respectively, and $\mathbf{e}_j$ stands for a standard basis vector whose j-th coordinate is 1 and other coordinates are 0. Within system state $\mathbf{s}$, because the number of users within network j is s_j, a departure event's transition probability is given by

$$P_{\text{sys}}(\mathbf{s} - \mathbf{e}_j | \mathbf{s}) = s_j \mu, \ j = 1, \dots, K. \quad (16.2)$$

Moreover, the probability that the system state remains the same is

$$P_{\text{sys}}(\mathbf{s}|\mathbf{s}) = \begin{cases} 1 - \sum_{j=0}^{K} \lambda_j - \sum_{j=1}^{K} s_j \mu, & \text{if } \bar{\mathcal{F}}(\mathbf{s}) \neq \phi, \\ 1 - \sum_{j=1}^{K} s_j \mu, & \text{if } \bar{\mathcal{F}}(\mathbf{s}) = \phi. \end{cases} \quad (16.3)$$

The duration of a time slot T ought to be chosen such that $\sum_{j=0}^{K} \lambda_j + K N \mu \leq 1$ (i.e., $T \leq 1/\left(\sum_{j=0}^{K} \bar{\lambda}_j + K N \bar{\mu}\right)$).

For instance, when $K = 2$, $0 \leq s_1 \leq N - 1$, and $0 \leq s_2 \leq N - 1$, the transition probability is calculated by

$$P_{\text{sys}}\left\{\mathbf{s}' | \mathbf{s} = (s_1, s_2)\right\} = \begin{cases} I_1(\sigma_{\mathbf{s}})\lambda_0 + \lambda_1, & \text{if } \mathbf{s}' = (s_1 + 1, s_2), \\ I_2(\sigma_{\mathbf{s}})\lambda_0 + \lambda_2, & \text{if } \mathbf{s}' = (s_1, s_2 + 1), \\ s_1 \mu, & \text{if } \mathbf{s}' = (s_1 - 1, s_2), \\ s_2 \mu, & \text{if } \mathbf{s}' = (s_1, s_2 - 1), \\ 1 - \lambda_0 - \lambda_1 - \lambda_2 - s_1 \mu - s_2 \mu, & \text{if } \mathbf{s}' = (s_1, s_2), \\ 0, & \text{otherwise.} \end{cases}$$

$$(16.4)$$

Similarly, the corresponding transition probabilities for $s_1 = N$, $0 \leq s_2 \leq N - 1$, or $0 \leq s_1 \leq N - 1$, $s_2 = N$ could also be signified. Figure 16.2 illustrates the state transition diagram when $K = 2$. The dynamics of the two-network system can be shown using a two-dimensional Markov chain, in which the probability $P_{\text{sys}}(\mathbf{s}|\mathbf{s})$ is not represented within Figure 16.2 for conciseness.

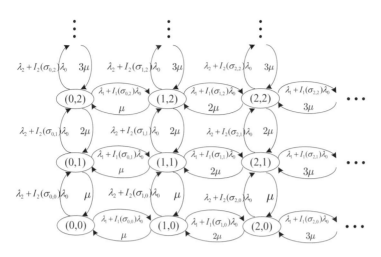

Figure 16.2 State diagram of the two-dimensional Markov chain.

16.2.2 Expected Utility

The strategy profile $\sigma = \{\sigma_{\mathbf{s}}|\forall \mathbf{s} \in \mathcal{S}\}$ is a mapping from the aggregate state space to the action space (i.e., $\sigma : \{0, 1, \ldots, N\}^K \mapsto \{1, 2, \ldots, K\}$). Given a strategy profile σ, the system transition probability within (16.1)–(16.3) can be obtained. A rational user makes the decision $\sigma_{\mathbf{s}_0} = \hat{k}$ when they arrive and observe system state $\mathbf{s}_0$, leading to the new system state $\mathbf{s}_1 = \mathbf{s}_0 + \mathbf{e}_{\hat{k}}$. After that, the rational user's expected utility is signified by

$$V_{\hat{k}}(\mathbf{s}_1) = E\left[\sum_{t=1}^{\infty}(1 - \mu)^{t-1} R_{\hat{k}}(\mathbf{s}_t)\,\middle|\, \mathbf{s}_1\right], \tag{16.5}$$

where the system state at time t is signified by $\mathbf{s}_t$. Because μ represents the probability that the service is terminated within one time slot, then $(1 - \mu)$ can be seen as the probability of the user staying in the network within one time slot. The value $(1 - \mu)$ can also be seen as the discounting factor for the future utility, which will be shown later within (16.6). The strategy $\sigma_{\mathbf{s}_0} = \hat{k}$ determines the network that would be entered by the user and the expected utility function that would be obtained by the user. Signified by $V_{\hat{k}}(\mathbf{s}_1)$, the expected utility function is the expected value of the discounted sum of the immediate utilities $R_{\hat{k}}(\mathbf{s}_t)$ accumulated from the next time slot. Notice that $\mathbf{s}_1 = \mathbf{s}_0 + \mathbf{e}_{\hat{k}}$ is uniquely determined by the user's strategy $\sigma_{\mathbf{s}_0}$, but the subsequent states $\mathbf{s}_t$, for $t \geq 2$, are stochastic and dependent on the arrival of other users, including users from the user arrival stream k, $1 \leq k \leq K$, and other rational users.

Within the Bellman equation [9], the expected utility within (16.5) can be represented as satisfying the following recursive expression:

$$V_k(\mathbf{s}) = R_k(s_k) + (1 - \mu)\sum_{\mathbf{s}'} P_k\left(\mathbf{s}'|\mathbf{s}\right) V_k(\mathbf{s}'), \tag{16.6}$$

where

$$
P_k\left(\mathbf{s}'|\mathbf{s}\right) = \begin{cases}
\sum_{i \in \mathcal{F}(\mathbf{s})} \lambda_i + \lambda_j + I_j(\sigma_{\mathbf{s}})\lambda_0, & \text{if } j = \min \bar{\mathcal{F}}(\mathbf{s}), \\
\lambda_j + I_j(\sigma_{\mathbf{s}})\lambda_0, & \text{if } j \in \bar{\mathcal{F}}(\mathbf{s}) \backslash \{\min \bar{\mathcal{F}}(\mathbf{s})\}, \\
s_i \mu, & \text{if } \mathbf{s}' = \mathbf{s} - \mathbf{e}_i, \forall i \neq k, \\
(s_k - 1)\mu, & \text{if } \mathbf{s}' = \mathbf{s} - \mathbf{e}_k, \\
1 - \sum_{j=0}^{K} \lambda_j - \sum_{j=1}^{K} s_j \mu + \mu, & \text{if } \mathbf{s}' = \mathbf{s}, \\
0, & \text{otherwise,}
\end{cases} \tag{16.7}
$$

which is the transition probability given that the user remains within network k. The probability of transitioning from $\mathbf{s}$ to $\mathbf{s} - \mathbf{e}_k$ is $(s_k - 1)\mu$, because $s_k - 1$ users might leave. In addition, the probability of transitioning from $\mathbf{s}$ to other states is similar to the definition of P_{sys} within (16.4).

16.2.3 Best Response of Rational Users

The strategy $\sigma_{\mathbf{s}}$ would be chosen by a rational user for maximizing their expected utility when observing the state $\mathbf{s}$ due to their selfish nature. Hence the rational strategy $\sigma_{\mathbf{s}}$ needs to satisfy

$$
\sigma_{\mathbf{s}} = \arg\max_k V_k(\mathbf{s} + \mathbf{e}_k). \tag{16.8}
$$

It shows that no user is capable of obtaining a higher expected utility through unilateral deviation to any other strategy with the strategy profile where the strategy of each state satisfies (16.8). Hence the strategy profile satisfying (16.6)–(16.8) is a Nash equilibrium (NE) of the stochastic game.

16.3 Modified Value Iteration Algorithm

Finding the strategy profile satisfying (16.6)–(16.8) is not a conventional MDP problem. A conventional MDP problem [9] can usually be solved through the theory of DP [10] in which the optimal strategy could be acquired directly by optimizing the potential function that is associated with each system state. But within our model, multiple potential functions are related in the following vector form:

$$
\begin{bmatrix} V_1(\mathbf{s}) \\ V_2(\mathbf{s}) \\ \vdots \\ V_K(\mathbf{s}) \end{bmatrix} = \begin{bmatrix} R_1(s_1) \\ R_2(s_2) \\ \vdots \\ R_K(s_K) \end{bmatrix} + (1 - \mu) \begin{bmatrix} \mathbf{p}_1 & \mathbf{0} & \cdots & \mathbf{0} \\ \mathbf{0} & \mathbf{p}_2 & \cdots & \mathbf{0} \\ \vdots & & \ddots & \vdots \\ \mathbf{0} & \mathbf{0} & \cdots & \mathbf{p}_K \end{bmatrix}^T \begin{bmatrix} \mathbf{v}_1 \\ \mathbf{v}_2 \\ \vdots \\ \mathbf{v}_K \end{bmatrix},
$$

$$
\tag{16.9}
$$

where an all-zero vector is signified by $\mathbf{0}$, $\mathbf{v}_k$ and $\mathbf{p}_k$ represent vectors comprising $V_k(\mathbf{s}')$ and $P_k(\mathbf{s}'|\mathbf{s})$ as elements, and $k = 1, \ldots, K$. The transpose operator is signified by $(\cdot)^T$.

The strategy $\sigma_{\mathbf{s}}$ is determined by comparing $V_k(\mathbf{s} + \mathbf{e}_k)$ for all k as in (16.8). Hence, DP could not be adopted directly within such a problem. Before making a decision, a user arrives and observes that the system state $\mathbf{s}$ is quite important. Led by their strategy, the user enters some network k and causes an expected utility $V_k(\mathbf{s} + \mathbf{e}_k)$, and they cannot change from this network is staying currently to any another network in subsequent time slots. The strategies of others affect the expected utility through the transition probabilities that are signified within (16.6).

Given the expected utilities $\{V_k\}_{k=1}^K$, the rational strategy profile σ ought to satisfy (16.8). Moreover, given a strategy profile σ, the expected utilities $\{V_k\}_{k=1}^K$ can be found by (16.6), in which the transition probability $P_k(\mathbf{s}'|\mathbf{s})$ stands for a function of the strategy $\sigma_{\mathbf{s}}$. To acquire the optimal strategy profile σ^* satisfying (16.6)–(16.8), we introduce a modified value iteration algorithm in order to solve the problem iteratively. At the n-th iteration, the rational strategy profile is calculated as

$$\sigma_{\mathbf{s}}^{(n+1)} = \arg\max_k V_k^{(n)}(\mathbf{s} + \mathbf{e}_k), \forall \mathbf{s} \in \mathcal{S}. \tag{16.10}$$

The expected utility functions could be acquired through solving

$$V_k^{(n+1)}(\mathbf{s}) = R_k(s_k) + (1 - \mu) \sum_{\mathbf{s}' \in \mathcal{S}} P_k^{(n+1)}(\mathbf{s}'|\mathbf{s}) V_k^{(n+1)}(\mathbf{s}'),$$

$$\forall \mathbf{s} \in \mathcal{S}, \forall k \in \{1, \dots, K\}, \tag{16.11}$$

in which the transition probability $P_k^{(n+1)}(\mathbf{s}'|\mathbf{s})$ is updated by adopting the corresponding updated strategies, i.e.,

$$P_k^{(n+1)}(\mathbf{s}'|\mathbf{s}) = \begin{cases} \sum_{i \in \mathcal{F}(\mathbf{s})} \lambda_i + \lambda_j + I_j(\sigma_{\mathbf{s}}^{(n+1)})\lambda_0, \text{if } \mathbf{s}' = \mathbf{s} + \mathbf{e}_j, j = \min\bar{\mathcal{F}}(\mathbf{s}) \\ \lambda_j + I_j(\sigma_{\mathbf{s}}^{(n+1)})\lambda_0, \qquad \text{if } \mathbf{s}' = \mathbf{s} + \mathbf{e}_j, j \in \bar{\mathcal{F}}(\mathbf{s}) \backslash \{\min\bar{\mathcal{F}}(\mathbf{s})\} \\ s_j \mu, \qquad\qquad\qquad\qquad\qquad \text{if } \mathbf{s}' = \mathbf{s} - \mathbf{e}_j, j \neq k \\ (s_k - 1)\mu, \qquad\qquad\qquad\qquad \text{if } \mathbf{s}' = \mathbf{s} - \mathbf{e}_k \\ 1 - \sum_{j \in \bar{\mathcal{F}}_{\mathbf{s}}} P_k(\mathbf{s} + \mathbf{e}_j|\mathbf{s}) - \sum_{j=1}^K P_k(\mathbf{s} - \mathbf{e}_j|\mathbf{s}), \qquad \mathbf{s}' = \mathbf{s}, \\ 0, \qquad\qquad\qquad\qquad\qquad\qquad\qquad\qquad\qquad \text{otherwise.} \end{cases} \tag{16.12}$$

The solution to (16.11) can be obtained through several approaches. The value iteration algorithm [9] is one such approach that initializes $V_k^{(n+1)}(\mathbf{s})$ to be an arbitrary value such as zero and updates it using (16.11) iteratively. The iteration function stands for a contraction mapping, thus it guarantees the convergence to a fixed and unique point. Another approach is considering (16.11) to be K sets of linear systems in which every set obtains N^2 unknown variables corresponding to $\{V_k^{(n+1)}(\mathbf{s}), \forall \mathbf{s}\}$ and N^2 equations, which could be solved by matrix inversion or linear programming.

In the next section, we will show theoretically that for $K = 2$, the algorithm lead to a threshold structure of the strategy profile at each iteration, which is also observed for $K > 2$ generally. But due to the hard decision rule in (16.8), the strategy profile may

Table 16.1. Modified value iteration algorithm.

---

(1) Initialize: $V_k^{(0)}(\mathbf{s}) = 0$, $\forall k \in \{1, \ldots, K\}$, $\forall \mathbf{s} \in \mathcal{S}$. $T = \phi$.
(2) **Loop**:

    (i) Update $\{\sigma_{\mathbf{s}}^{(n+1)}\}$ by (16.13).

        If $\{\sigma_{\mathbf{s}}^{(n+1)}\} = \{\sigma_{\mathbf{s}}^{(n)}\}$, then stop loop.

        else if $\{\sigma_{\mathbf{s}}^{(n+1)}\} \in T$, then

               choose a $\{\sigma_{\mathbf{s}}\} \in \bar{T}$, and let $\{\sigma_{\mathbf{s}}^{(n+1)}\} = \{\sigma_{\mathbf{s}}\}$.

        end if

        $T = T \cup \{\sigma_{\mathbf{s}}^{(n+1)}\}$.

    (ii) Update $\{P_k^{(n+1)}(\mathbf{s}'|\mathbf{s})\}$ by (16.12).

    (iii) Solve $\{V_k^{(n+1)}(\mathbf{s})\}$ in (16.11) by value iteration or linear
        programming.

    Until $\bar{T} = \phi$ or $\{\sigma_{\mathbf{s}}^{(n+1)}\} = \{\sigma_{\mathbf{s}}^{(n)}\}$.

---

not converge when the rational strategy of the state around the threshold oscillates between different choices each time when the expected utility is updated. Under this circumstance, the expected utilities corresponding to different strategies are quite close to each other. Thus the hard decision rule is relaxed through allowing a small region of tolerance to switch among the strategies [21] for solving this problem, leading to the soft decision rule that can be defined by

$$
\sigma_{\mathbf{s}}^{(n+1)} = \begin{cases} \sigma_{\mathbf{s}}^{(n)}, & \text{if } V_{\sigma_{\mathbf{s}}^{(n)}}^{(n)}(\mathbf{s} + \mathbf{e}_{\sigma_{\mathbf{s}}^{(n)}}) \geq \max_k V_k^{(n)}(\mathbf{s} + \mathbf{e}_k) - \epsilon, \\ \arg\max_k V_k^{(n)}(\mathbf{s} + \mathbf{e}_k), & \text{if } V_{\sigma_{\mathbf{s}}^{(n)}}^{(n)}(\mathbf{s} + \mathbf{e}_{\sigma_{\mathbf{s}}^{(n)}}) < \max_k V_k^{(n)}(\mathbf{s} + \mathbf{e}_k) - \epsilon, \end{cases}
$$

$$(16.13)$$

where a small constant is represented by $\epsilon > 0$. Table 16.1 summarizes the modified value iteration algorithm for the M-MDP. Notice that the algorithm stops when all of the strategy profiles are searched or an equilibrium is found. Based on this definition, the resulting strategy profile is an ϵ-approximate NE [22] when the algorithm obtains a solution where the strategy at each state has an expected utility that is at most ϵ less than that of any other strategy. It also should be noted that there might be multiple ϵ-approximate NEs, especially for a larger ϵ when a larger region of tolerance is permitted for switching among the strategies.

16.4   Threshold Structure of the Strategy Profile

Within this section, we prove that the strategy profile produced by the modified value iteration algorithm in every iteration exhibits a threshold structure for two-network systems. With the presumption that $R_k(s_k)$, $k = 1, 2$, are nonincreasing, Lemma 16.1 shows that $V_1(\mathbf{s})$ is nondecreasing and $V_2(\mathbf{s})$ is nonincreasing along the line of $s_1 + s_2 = m$, $\forall m \in \{1, 2, \ldots, 2N\}$.

LEMMA 16.1 *For $n \geq 0$,*

$$V_1^{(n)}(\mathbf{s}) \geq V_1^{(n)}(\mathbf{s} + \mathbf{e}_1 - \mathbf{e}_2), \tag{16.14}$$

$$V_2^{(n)}(\mathbf{s}) \leq V_2^{(n)}(\mathbf{s} + \mathbf{e}_1 - \mathbf{e}_2). \tag{16.15}$$

Proof Induction is adopted to show that (16.14) and (16.15) hold for all $n \geq 0$.

(1) Because $V_1^{(0)}(\mathbf{s})$ and $V_2^{(0)}(\mathbf{s})$ are initialized as zeros, (16.14) and (16.15) hold for $n = 0$.

(2) We presume that the induction hypothesis holds for some $n \geq 0$. Then we can show that (16.14) and (16.15) also hold for $(n + 1)$ through analyzing the following difference: let $\mathbf{s}' = \mathbf{s} + \mathbf{e}_1 - \mathbf{e}_2$. For $0 \leq s_1 \leq N - 2$ and $1 \leq s_2 \leq N - 1$,

$$V_1^{(n+1)}(\mathbf{s}) - V_1^{(n+1)}(\mathbf{s}') = R_1(s_1) - R_1(s_1 + 1)$$

$$+ (1 - \mu)[\lambda_1(V_1^{(n)}(\mathbf{s} + \mathbf{e}_1) - V_1^{(n)}(\mathbf{s}' + \mathbf{e}_1)).$$

$$+ \lambda_0(I_1(\sigma_\mathbf{s})V_1^{(n)}(\mathbf{s} + \mathbf{e}_1) - I_1(\sigma_{\mathbf{s}'})V_1^{(n)}(\mathbf{s}' + \mathbf{e}_1))$$

$$+ \lambda_2(V_1^{(n)}(\mathbf{s} + \mathbf{e}_2) - V_1^{(n)}(\mathbf{s}' + \mathbf{e}_2))$$

$$+ \lambda_0(I_2(\sigma_\mathbf{s})V_1^{(n)}(\mathbf{s} + \mathbf{e}_2) - I_2(\sigma_{\mathbf{s}'})V_1^{(n)}(\mathbf{s}' + \mathbf{e}_2))$$

$$+ (s_1 - 1)\mu V_1^{(n)}(\mathbf{s} - \mathbf{e}_1) - s_1\mu V_1^{(n)}(\mathbf{s}' - \mathbf{e}_1)$$

$$+ s_2\mu V_1^{(n)}(\mathbf{s} - \mathbf{e}_2) - (s_2 - 1)\mu V_1^{(n)}(\mathbf{s}' - \mathbf{e}_2)$$

$$+ (1 - \lambda_0 - \lambda_1 - \lambda_2 - s_1\mu - s_2\mu)(V_1^{(n)}(\mathbf{s}) - V_1^{(n)}(\mathbf{s}'))].$$
$$\tag{16.16}$$

It is sufficient to discuss the following cases by rearranging a few terms based on the fact that the utility function $R_1(s_1)$ is nonincreasing within s_1 and the induction hypothesis ensures the non-negativeness of many terms' differences within (16.16).

Case 1: $\sigma_\mathbf{s}^{(n)} = \sigma_{\mathbf{s}'}^{(n)} = 1$. Then, $V_1^{(n)}(\mathbf{s} + \mathbf{e}_1) - V_1^{(n)}(\mathbf{s}' + \mathbf{e}_1) \geq 0$ by the induction hypothesis.

Case 2: $\sigma_\mathbf{s}^{(n)} = \sigma_{\mathbf{s}'}^{(n)} = 2$. Then, $V_1^{(n)}(\mathbf{s} + \mathbf{e}_2) - V_1^{(n)}(\mathbf{s}' + \mathbf{e}_2) \geq 0$ by the induction hypothesis.

Case 3: $\sigma_\mathbf{s}^{(n)} = 1$ and $\sigma_{\mathbf{s}'}^{(n)} = 2$. Then, $V_1^{(n)}(\mathbf{s} + \mathbf{e}_1) - V_1^{(n)}(\mathbf{s}' + \mathbf{e}_2) = 0$.

Case 4: $\sigma_\mathbf{s}^{(n)} = 2$ and $\sigma_{\mathbf{s}'}^{(n)} = 1$. Then, $V_1^{(n)}(\mathbf{s} + \mathbf{e}_2) - V_1^{(n)}(\mathbf{s}' + \mathbf{e}_1) \geq 0$ by the induction hypothesis.

Hence, we have $V_1^{(n+1)}(\mathbf{s}) - V_1^{(n+1)}(\mathbf{s}') \geq 0$ for $0 \leq s_1 \leq N - 2$ and $1 \leq s_2 \leq N - 1$. Then we can easily check that the inequality still holds for the case of $s_1 = N - 1, 1 \leq s_2 \leq N - 1$, and the case of $0 \leq s_1 \leq N - 1, s_2 = N$. Similarly, $V_2^{(n)}(\mathbf{s}) \leq V_2^{(n)}(\mathbf{s}')$ can also be set.

Lemma 16.2 shows that the difference between $V_1(\mathbf{s} + \mathbf{e}_1)$ and $V_2(\mathbf{s} + \mathbf{e}_2)$ is nonincreasing along the line of $s_1 + s_2 = m, \forall m \in \{1, 2, \dots, 2N\}$.

LEMMA 16.2 $V_1^{(n)}(\mathbf{s} + \mathbf{e}_1) - V_2^{(n)}(\mathbf{s} + \mathbf{e}_2) \geq V_1^{(n)}(\mathbf{s}' + \mathbf{e}_1) - V_2^{(n)}(\mathbf{s}' + \mathbf{e}_2)$, *where*
$\mathbf{s}' = \mathbf{s} + \mathbf{e}_1 - \mathbf{e}_2$.

Proof   This can be easily proven by adopting Lemma 16.1.

THEOREM 16.3   *The strategy profile generated by the modified value iteration algorithm obtains a threshold structure for $K = 2$.*

Proof   The soft decision rule within (16.13) for $K = 2$ could be signified as

$$\sigma_{\mathbf{s}}^{(n+1)} = \begin{cases} \sigma_{\mathbf{s}}^{(n)}, & \text{if } |V_1^{(n)}(\mathbf{s} + \mathbf{e}_1) - V_2^{(n)}(\mathbf{s} + \mathbf{e}_2)| \leq \epsilon, \\ 1, & \text{if } V_1^{(n)}(\mathbf{s} + \mathbf{e}_1) > V_2^{(n)}(\mathbf{s} + \mathbf{e}_2) + \epsilon, \\ 2, & \text{if } V_2^{(n)}(\mathbf{s} + \mathbf{e}_2) > V_1^{(n)}(\mathbf{s} + \mathbf{e}_1) + \epsilon. \end{cases} \quad (16.17)$$

If $\sigma_{\mathbf{s}}^{(n+1)} = 1$ and $\sigma_{\mathbf{s}}^{(n)} = 2$ (i.e., the strategy of the current iteration is updated to be different from the one of the previous iteration), then it must be calculated by $V_1^{(n)}(\mathbf{s} + \mathbf{e}_1) > V_2^{(n)}(\mathbf{s} + \mathbf{e}_2) + \epsilon$. Lemma 16.2 implies that $V_1(\mathbf{s}' + \mathbf{e}_1) - V_2(\mathbf{s}' + \mathbf{e}_2)$ is nonincreasing along the line of $s_1' + s_2' = s_1 + s_2$. Thus, for $\mathbf{s}' = \mathbf{s} - k\mathbf{e}_1 + k\mathbf{e}_2, k = 1, 2, \ldots, \min\{s_1, N - s_2\}$, we have

$$V_1(\mathbf{s}' + \mathbf{e}_1) - V_2(\mathbf{s}' + \mathbf{e}_2) \geq V_1(\mathbf{s} + \mathbf{e}_1) - V_2(\mathbf{s} + \mathbf{e}_2) > \epsilon > 0.$$

Therefore, $\sigma_{\mathbf{s}'}^{(n+1)} = 1$ for $\mathbf{s}' = \mathbf{s} - k\mathbf{e}_1 + k\mathbf{e}_2, k = 1, 2, \ldots, \min\{s_1, N - s_2\}$. Similarly, if $\sigma_{\mathbf{s}}^{(n)} = 1$ and $\sigma_{\mathbf{s}}^{(n+1)} = 2$, then $\sigma_{\mathbf{s}''}^{(n+1)} = 2$ for $\mathbf{s}'' = \mathbf{s} + k\mathbf{e}_1 - k\mathbf{e}_2, k = 1, 2, \ldots, \min\{N - s_1, s_2\}$. From the discussion above, the strategies along the line of $s_1 + s_2 = m, \forall m \in \{1, 2, \ldots, 2N\}$ retain a threshold structure within every iteration. In addition, the strategy profile acquired within every iteration of the algorithm obtains a threshold structure because the strategy profile's initialization exhibits a threshold structure trivially.

In a two-network system, the number of system states is N^2, and thus N^2 strategies need to be stored without the threshold structure. The storage space of each strategy is 1 bit. Thus, with such a threshold structure on each line $s_1 + s_2 = m, m = 1, 2, \ldots, 2N$, the threshold point on each line can be easily stored. The strategy profile storage can be reduced from $\mathcal{O}(N^2)$ to $\mathcal{O}(N \log N)$ since every threshold point demands the storage space of $\log N$ bits.

Within this chapter, only an analysis of the two-network systems is provided. It is difficult to analyze systems with more than two networks due to the lack of optimality in a single potential function as in the admission control problem [23,24]. From the simulation results within Section 16.6 multinetwork systems also have, strategy profiles with threshold structures.

16.5   Truthful Mechanism Design

In the discussion above, the networks are assumed to report their states s_k truthfully, thus the user can observe the true system state $\mathbf{s}$ and make a decision to maximize their utility on the basis of this observation. However, the networks may not report their states truthfully without appropriate incentives, and they might even report some state s'_k that is different from the true state s_k if this is profitable. In this section, enforcing truth-telling as a dominant strategy for the networks is considered through incorporating pricing rules into the wireless access network selection game.

A mechanism consists of allocation rules $\{a_k(\mathbf{s})\}$ and pricing rules $\{P_k(\mathbf{s})\}$ in which $P_k(\mathbf{s})$ signifies the unit price of the expected rate $V_k(\mathbf{s})$ supported by network k at state $\mathbf{s}$ and $a_k(\mathbf{s})$ signifies the allocation probability, which is either 0 or 1 (i.e., whether the user gains access to network k or not). The utility of network k is given by

$$U_k(\mathbf{s}) = V_k(\mathbf{s} + \mathbf{e}_k)P_k(\mathbf{s}) - c_k(\mathbf{s} + \mathbf{e}_k)a_k(\mathbf{s}), \tag{16.18}$$

where $c_k(\mathbf{s} + \mathbf{e}_k)$ is the cost per user. With the states reported from the networks, these rules determine the user allocation and the price that the user should pay, both as functions of the reports from networks. For example, if network k reports its state as s'_k and others report $s_{-k} = \{s_j : j \neq k\}$, network k's utility becomes $V_k(\mathbf{s} + \mathbf{e}_k)P_k(s'_k, s_{-k}) - c_k(\mathbf{s} + \mathbf{e}_k)a_k(s'_k, s_{-k})$. Notice that $V_k(\mathbf{s} + \mathbf{e}_k)$ and $c_k(\mathbf{s} + \mathbf{e}_k)$ are functions of true states that do not depend on the reports. Thus the truth-telling or the IC constraints are, $\forall s_k, s'_k, s_{-k}$,

$$V_k(s_k + 1, s_{-k})P_k(s_k, s_{-k}) - c_k(s_k + 1, s_{-k})a_k(s_k, s_{-k})$$
$$\geq V_k(s_k + 1, s_{-k})P_k(s'_k, s_{-k}) - c_k(s_k + 1, s_{-k})a_k(s'_k, s_{-k}),$$

which means truth-telling is a dominant strategy for each network at each state. The mechanism also has to satisfy the IR constraints; in other words, $\forall s_k, s_{-k}$,

$$V_k(s_k + 1, s_{-k})P_k(s_k, s_{-k}) - c_k(s_k + 1, s_{-k})a_k(s_k, s_{-k}) \geq 0, \tag{16.19}$$

which guarantees the non-negative utility of attending to the mechanism for all networks.

Within this section, we study the interplay among the networks through the network selection game by taking the interdependence between the users within the previous sections as the focus. We assume that users' strategies are chosen on the basis of *ex ante* optimality [12,22] (i.e., the allocation rule is based on optimizing the expected objective over the state probability). The truthful mechanism design aims at constructing a set of allocation and pricing rules by which a specific objective can be optimized while satisfying IR and IC constraints. For instance, the mechanism design problem $\mathcal{P}_p$ for minimizing the expected payment could be computed as follows:

$$\mathcal{P}_p : \min_{\{P_k\}, \{a_k\}} \sum_{\mathbf{s} \in \mathcal{S}} \pi(\mathbf{s}) \sum_{k=1}^{K} P_k(\mathbf{s})V_k(\mathbf{s} + \mathbf{e}_k) \tag{16.20}$$

$$\text{s.t.} \quad \text{(IC), (IR)}, a_k(\mathbf{s}) \in \{0, 1\}, \forall \mathbf{s}, \forall k. \tag{16.21}$$

$$\sum_{k=1}^{K} a_k(\mathbf{s}) = 1, \forall \mathbf{s} \in \mathcal{S}. \tag{16.22}$$

Other mechanism design objectives such as the utility maximization $\mathcal{P}_u$ can be calculated through substituting (16.20) with users' expected utility function as follows:

$$\max_{\{P_k\},\{a_k\}} \sum_{\mathbf{s}\in\mathcal{S}} \pi(\mathbf{s}) \sum_{k=1}^{K} \left[\lambda a_k(\mathbf{s}) V_k(\mathbf{s}+\mathbf{e}_k) - P_k(\mathbf{s}) V_k(\mathbf{s}+\mathbf{e}_k) \right]$$

s.t. (16.21),(16.22).

The unit cost $c_k(\mathbf{s}+\mathbf{e}_k)/V_k(\mathbf{s}+\mathbf{e}_k)$ is signified as $w_k(\mathbf{s})$. The IC constraints become

$$P_k(s_k,s_{-k}) - w_k(s_k,s_{-k})a_k(s_k,s_{-k})$$

$$\geq P_k(s'_k,s_{-k}) - w_k(s_k,s_{-k})a_k(s'_k,s_{-k}), \forall s_k,s'_k,s_{-k}. \tag{16.23}$$

A monotonicity assumption for the unit cost is needed (i.e., $w_k(s_k,s_{-k})$ is nondecreasing within s_k; e.g., $w_k(s_k,s_{-k}) \geq w_k(s'_k,s_{-k})$ if $s_k \geq s'_k$). The assumption holds when $c_k(s_k,s_{-k})$ is nondecreasing within s_k since $V_k(s_k,s_{-k})$ is nonincreasing within s_k (e.g., the assumption holds if the per-user cost is a constant with every network; i.e., $c_k(s_k,s_{-k}) = C_k$). The monotonicity of $w_k(s_k,s_{-k})$ leads to the threshold structure of $a_k(s_k,s_{-k})$ as in Lemma 16.4.

LEMMA 16.4   *Under IC constraints, there is a threshold value of s_k on the allocation rule $a_k(s_k,s_{-k})$; in other words, given s_{-k}, there is $s_k^*(s_{-k}) \in \{-1,0,1,\ldots,N\}$ such that*

$$a_k(s_k,s_{-k}) = \begin{cases} 1, & s_k \leq s_k^*(s_{-k}) \\ 0, & s_k > s_k^*(s_{-k}). \end{cases} \tag{16.24}$$

Proof   From (16.23) we have

$$P_k(s_k,s_{-k}) - P_k(s'_k,s_{-k}) \geq w_k(s_k,s_{-k})[a_k(s_k,s_{-k}) - a_k(s'_k,s_{-k})]. \tag{16.25}$$

Interchanging s_k and s'_k, we also have

$$P_k(s'_k,s_{-k}) - P_k(s_k,s_{-k}) \geq w_k(s'_k,s_{-k})[a_k(s'_k,s_{-k}) - a_k(s_k,s_{-k})]. \tag{16.26}$$

Combining the above two inequalities leads to

$$[w_k(s_k,s_{-k}) - w_k(s'_k,s_{-k})][a_k(s_k,s_{-k}) - a_k(s'_k,s_{-k})] \leq 0. \tag{16.27}$$

Thus, since $w_k(s_k,s_{-k})$ is nondecreasing within s_k, the allocation rule $a_k(s_k,s_{-k})$ needs to be nonincreasing within s_k. Based on this monotonicity and the fact that $a_k(s_k,s_{-k})$ can only obtain a value of 0 or 1, there is a threshold of $a_k(s_k,s_{-k})$ in s_k that is demonstrated within (16.24).

COROLLARY 16.5   *If $K = 2$, then $s_1^*(s_2)$ is nondecreasing within s_2 and $s_2^*(s_1)$ is nondecreasing within s_1.*

Proof   Assume $\exists s_2$ such that $s_1^*(s_2 + 1) < s_1^*(s_2)$. From Lemma 16.4, we have $a_1(s_1,s_2+1) = 0$ for $s_1 > s_1^*(s_2+1)$, which implies $a_2(s_1,s_2 + 1) = 1$ for $s_1 > s_1^*(s_2 + 1)$ due to the constraint that $a_1(\mathbf{s})+a_2(\mathbf{s}) = 1, \forall \mathbf{s}$. Therefore, $a_2(s_1^*(s_2),s_2+1) = 1$, which implies $a_2(s_1^*(s_2), s_2) = 1$ from Lemma 16.4, but we also have $a_1(s_1^*(s_2), s_1) = 1$, leading to a contradiction.

Lemma 16.6 shows that only adjacent IC constraints are essential.

LEMMA 16.6 *Nonadjacent IC constraints are redundant.*

Proof Let us consider the following two adjacent IC constraints:

$$P_k(s_k, s_{-k}) - w_k(s_k, s_{-k})a_k(s_k, s_{-k})$$
$$\geq P_k(s_k - 1, s_{-k}) - w_k(s_k, s_{-k})a_k(s_k - 1, s_{-k}), \qquad (16.28)$$
$$P_k(s_k - 1, s_{-k}) - w_k(s_k - 1, s_{-k})a_k(s_k - 1, s_{-k})$$
$$\geq P_k(s_k - 2, s_{-k}) - w_k(s_k - 1, s_{-k}).a_k(s_k - 2, s_{-k}) \qquad (16.29)$$

Adding (16.28) and (16.29), we have

$$P_k(s_k, s_{-k}) - w_k(s_k, s_{-k})a_k(s_k, s_{-k})$$
$$\geq P_k(s_k - 2, s_{-k}) - w_k(s_k, s_{-k})a_k(s_k - 2, s_{-k})$$
$$\quad - w_k(s_k, s_{-k})[a_k(s_k - 1, s_{-k}) - a_k(s_k - 2, s_{-k})]$$
$$\quad + w_k(s_k - 1, s_{-k})[a_k(s_k - 1, s_{-k}) - a_k(s_k - 2, s_{-k})]$$
$$\geq P_k(s_k - 2, s_{-k}) - w_k(s_k, s_{-k})a_k(s_k - 2, s_{-k}). \qquad (16.30)$$

The last inequality is based on the notion that $w_k(s_k, s_{-k})$ is increasing within s_k and $a_k(s_k, s_{-k})$ is decreasing within s_k. This shows that the nonadjacent IC constraints could be inferred from the adjacent ones.

We can obtain the bounds for the payments using the adjacent IC constraints; in other words, given an allocation rule $\{a_k(\mathbf{s})\}$, the incentive-compatible payment rule $\{P_k(\mathbf{s})\}$ satisfies

$$P_k(s_k, s_{-k}) + w_k(s_k, s_{-k})[a_k(s_k - 1, s_{-k}) - a_k(s_k, s_{-k})] \geq P_k(s_k - 1, s_{-k})$$
$$\geq P_k(s_k, s_{-k}) \quad + w_k(s_k - 1, s_{-k})[a_k(s_k - 1, s_{-k}) - a_k(s_k, s_{-k})]. \qquad (16.31)$$

Within the optimization problems $\mathcal{P}_p$, we focus on minimizing a linear combination of $P_k(s_k, s_{-k})$ with non-negative coefficients. The lower bound within (16.31) ought be binding, or the objective function should always be capable of being better optimized through decreasing the nonbinding $P_k(s_k, s_{-k})$. Thus the payment rule could be signified as

$$P_k(s_k, s_{-k}) = P_k(N, s_{-k}) + \sum_{r=s_k+1}^{N} w_k(r - 1, s_{-k})\left[a_k(r - 1, s_{-k}) - a_k(r, s_{-k})\right].$$
$$(16.32)$$

To minimize $P_k(s_k, s_{-k})$ while satisfying the IR constraint in (16.19), $P_k(N, s_{-k})$ ought to be set as 0. Substituting Lemma 16.4 into (16.32), we can conclude

$$P_k(s_k, s_{-k}) = \begin{cases} w_k(s_k^*, s_{-k}), & s_k \leq s_k^*, \\ 0, & s_k > s_k^*, \end{cases} \tag{16.33}$$

where s_k^* signifies $s_k^*(s_{-k})$ for notational simplicity.

From the IC and IR constraints, the pricing rule $\{P_k\}$ could be determined given the allocation rule $\{a_k\}$, and it is specified by the thresholds $\{s_k^*\}$. Thus (16.33) means simply that the pricing rule $\{P_k\}$ is also specified by the thresholds $\{s_k^*\}$. Adopting $\{s_k^*\}$ to be optimization variables, the problem $\mathcal{P}_p$ could be signified as

$$\min_{\{s_k^*\}} \sum_{s \in \mathcal{S}} \pi(s) \sum_{k=1}^{K} P_k(s) V_k(s) \tag{16.34}$$

s.t. (16.22), (16.24), (16.33).

But the optimization problem is still difficult to solve optimally with the simplification since the optimization variables $\{s_k^*\}$ are discrete and an exhaustive search demands exponential time complexity within N. For this problem, a DP algorithm is introduced that is instigated by the optimal substructures within the two-network case. The optimal solution to the primary problem is capable of being broken down into finding the optimal solutions to its subproblems, which can be tackled using the DP technique that essentially behaves in a recursive divide-and-conquer fashion. The performance of the DP approach is satisfactory compared with the greedy method, although it is suboptimal for the multinetwork case. Other traditional optimization algorithms such as branch-and-bound could be adopted for solving the mixed integer programming problem optimally; however, their computational complexity is prohibitively high (exponential in terms of the number of states) because this kind of algorithm basically performs exhaustive tree searches using certain pruning strategies. Generally, there are no efficient solutions for a mixed integer programming problem. Within this chapter, we focus on introducing an algorithm that is capable of achieving satisfactory performance with reasonable complexity (polynomial in terms of the number of states).

16.5.1   Solution

Since the number of states is NK, the exhaustive search over all possible allocation rules requires a complexity of $\mathcal{O}(K^{N^K})$. Such exponential complexity is formidably high even for a moderate N. Within this section, we introduce a polynomial time algorithm on the basis of DP in order to search for the thresholds $\{s_k^*\}$. Let $f_k^{\text{DP}}(\{s_i : i \in \mathcal{I}\}|\{s_j : j \in \mathcal{J}\})$ signify the optimal value of a set of system states specified by $(\{s_i : i \in \mathcal{I}\}|\{s_j : j \in \mathcal{J}\})$ in which the set $\mathcal{J}$ consists of coordinates with coordinate j being fixed as s_j. The set $\mathcal{I}$ consists of the coordinates with ranges in which coordinate i ranges from 1 to s_i. The set $\mathcal{I}$ has k coordinates (i.e., the considered set of system states is k-dimensional). The optimal value function f_k^{DP} can be calculated by adopting lower-dimensional optimal value functions. The recursive calculation is demonstrated by the following equations. For $k = 2, \ldots, K$,

$$f_k^{DP}(\{s_i : i \in \mathcal{I}\}|\{s_j : j \in \mathcal{J}\})$$

$$= \min_{i \in \mathcal{I}} \left\{ f_k^{DP}(s_i - 1, s_{-i}|\{s_j : j \in \mathcal{J}\}) + f_{k-1}^{DP}(s_{-i}|\{s_j : j \in \mathcal{J} \cup \{i\}\}) \right\},$$

where $s_{-i} = \{s_l : l \neq i, l \in \mathcal{I}\}$. $\qquad (16.35)$

$$a_{i^*}(s_{i^*}, s'_{-i^*}, s_j, s_{-j}) = 0, \forall s'_{-i^*} \preceq s_{-i^*}, \qquad (16.36)$$

$$i^* = \arg\min_{i \in \mathcal{I}} \left\{ f_k^{DP}(s_i - 1, s_{-i}|\{s_j : j \in \mathcal{J}\}) + f_{k-1}^{DP}(s_{-i}|\{s_j : j \in \mathcal{J} \cup \{i\}\}) \right\},$$

$$\qquad (16.37)$$

where $s'_{-i^*} \preceq s_{-i^*}$ signifies $s'_{-i^*} \in \{s'_l : s'_l \leq s_l, l \neq i^*, l \in \mathcal{I}\}$. The boundary condition is

$$f_1^{DP}(s_i|s_{-i}) = f_1^{DP}(s_i - 1|s_{-i}) \frac{w_i(s_i, s_{-i})}{w_i(s_i - 1, s_{-i})} + \pi(s_i, s_{-i})V_i(s_i + 1, s_{-i})w_i(s_i, s_{-i}),$$

$$\qquad (16.38)$$

$$a_{-i^*}(s_{i^*}, s'_{-i^*}, s_j, s_{-j}) = 1, \forall s'_{-i^*} \leq s_{-i^*}, \qquad (16.39)$$

where i^* is the minimizer in (16.37) when $k = 2$. Notice that (16.38) is equivalent to $f_1^{DP}(s_i|s_{-i}) = \sum_{r=0}^{s_i} \pi(r, s_{-i})V_i(r + 1, s_{-i})w_i(s_i, s_{-i})$, but the recursive form within (16.38) is more efficient in terms of computation at the cost of using more storage space. The algorithm aims to evaluate $f_K^{DP}(N, \ldots, N)$ with $\mathcal{I} = \{1, \ldots, K\}$ and $\mathcal{J} = \phi$ through using (16.35)–(16.39). Theorem 16.7 demonstrates the optimality of the solution that is acquired by the algorithm when $K = 2$.

THEOREM 16.7 *For $K = 2$, the algorithm optimally solves $\mathcal{P}_p$ in $\mathcal{O}(N^2)$.*

For $K \geq 3$, the solution acquired by the algorithm might be suboptimal the because the monotonicity of allocation thresholds within Corollary 16.5 only holds when $K = 2$, which still outperforms the heuristic greedy method, as is shown in Section 16.6. For a general K, the computational complexity of the algorithm can be represented as $\mathcal{O}(N^K)$ that is polynomial within N.

Given the stationary probability $\{\pi(\mathbf{s})\}$ and the expected rate $\{V_k(\mathbf{s})\}$, the DP can discover solutions of the pricing rule $\{P_k(\mathbf{s})\}$ and the allocation rule $\{a_k(\mathbf{s})\}$ in the problem $\mathcal{P}_p$ efficiently. But $\{\pi(\mathbf{s})\}$ and $\{V_k(\mathbf{s})\}$ rely on $\{a_k(\mathbf{s})\}$ because the state transition probability relies on $\{a_k(\mathbf{s})\}$. Thus we update $\{V_k(\mathbf{s})\}$, $\{\pi(\mathbf{s})\}$, and $\{a_k(\mathbf{s})\}$ iteratively. The mechanism design algorithm for the network selection game are summarized in Table 16.2. It is observed that the iterative algorithm exhibits quite fast convergence, with a typical number of iterations to converge of between five and eight within the numerical simulation.

The algorithm can be modified without difficulty for solving $\mathcal{P}_u$ through replacing the min within (16.35) and (16.37) with the max and changing the boundary condition within (16.38) to be $f_1(s_i|s_{-i}) = \sum_{r=0}^{s_i} \pi(r, s_{-i})V_k(r, s_{-i})(\lambda - w(s_i, s_{-i}))$.

Table 16.2. DP algorithm for mechanism design.

---

(1) Initialization: obtain $\{V_k^{(0)}(\mathbf{s})\}$ and $\{\pi^{(0)}(\mathbf{s})\}$ using Table 16.1.
(2) **Loop**:
    (i) With initial $\mathcal{I} = \{1, \ldots, K\}$, $\mathcal{J} = \phi$, evaluate
        $f_K^{(n)}(N, \ldots, N)$ using (16.35)–(16.39) to obtain $\{a_k^{(n+1)}(\mathbf{s})\}$
        and $\{P_k^{(n+1)}(\mathbf{s})\}$.
    (ii) Calculate $\{V_k^{(n+1)}(\mathbf{s})\}$ and $\{\pi^{(n+1)}(\mathbf{s})\}$.
    Until $\{a_k^{(n+1)}(\mathbf{s})\}$ and $\{P_k^{(n+1)}(\mathbf{s})\}$ converge.

16.6   Numerical Simulation

In this section, we evaluate the performance of the modified value iteration algorithm as a rational strategy through numerical simulation. We compare the M-MDP method with the myopic, centralized, and random strategies as follows: first, we signify the social welfare given a strategy profile σ as $SW^{\sigma} = \sum_{\mathbf{s} \in \mathcal{S}} \pi^{\sigma}(\mathbf{s}) \sum_{k=1}^{K} s_k R_k(s_k)$, where $\pi^{\sigma}(\mathbf{s})$ represents the stationary probability at system state $\mathbf{s}$. The centralized method demands a computational complexity of $\mathcal{O}(K^{|\mathcal{S}|})$ that increases exponentially with the number of system states and is impossible to adopt in practice because it searches exhaustively through all of the possible strategy profiles and chooses the one by which the largest social welfare is achieved (i.e., $\sigma^{\mathrm{cent}} = \arg\max_{\sigma} SW^{\sigma}$). After making the decision, the myopic strategy is acquired through choosing the largest immediate utility (i.e., $\sigma_{\mathbf{s}}^{\mathrm{myop}} = \arg\max_{k \in \{1, \ldots, K\}} R_k(s_k + 1)$). In current cellular systems, cell selection is achieved by choosing the base station with the highest detected SNR. Such an approach is similar to the myopic strategy since it is only concerned with immediate utility. Finally, the random strategy randomly makes decisions with equal probability (i.e., $Pr\{\sigma_{\mathbf{s}}^{\mathrm{rand}} = k\} = \frac{1}{|\bar{\mathcal{F}}(\mathbf{s})|}, \forall k \in \bar{\mathcal{F}}(\mathbf{s})$, where the cardinality of a set is signified by $|\cdot|$). Within the following simulation, the random strategy's performance is acquired through averaging the performance of 1000 instances for every set of parameters.

The algorithm analysis within Section 16.4 shows that there is a threshold structure of the strategies along each line of $s_1 + s_2 = m$, $\forall m \in \{1, 2, \ldots, 2N\}$. With the numerical simulation in Figure 16.3, we verify this analysis. The strategy profile calculated by the algorithm within a two-network system is illustrated in Figure 16.3 where $P_s/N_0 = 50$, $P_I/N_0 = 10$, $T = 0.08$ (sec), $\bar{\lambda}_0 = 0.5$ (users/sec), $\bar{\lambda}_1 = 0.125$ (users/sec), $\bar{\lambda}_2 = 2.5$ (users/sec), $\bar{\mu} = 1.25$ (users/sec), $\epsilon = 0.05$, and $N = 8$. The x-axis (y-axis) signifies s_1 (s_2); in other words, the users' number within network 1 (network 2). The number marked at the coordinate $\mathbf{s} = (s_1, s_2)$ signifies the computed strategy $\sigma_{\mathbf{s}}$ that is either 2 or 1 within this scenario. Figure 16.3 shows that the strategy profile converges in 30 iterations. The dot-dashed line is drawn in between the different strategies to emphasize the threshold. The threshold lines of certain iterations (1, 2, and 10) are also shown in Figure 16.3 to illustrate the evolution of the strategy profile during the iterations of the modified value iteration algorithm. It is observed that at each iteration, the threshold structure of the strategies always exists along the diagonal

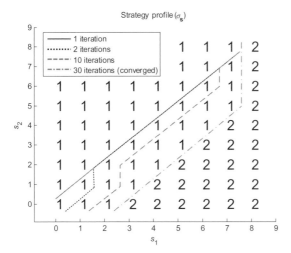

Figure 16.3 The threshold structure of the strategy profile during iterations of the algorithm.

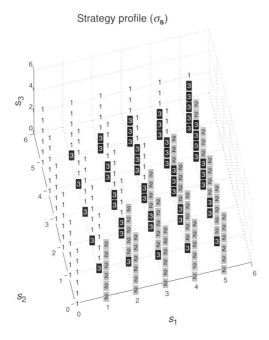

Figure 16.4 The threshold structure of the strategy profile for a three-network system.

lines, as in the analysis in Section 16.4. Within the rest of simulations, we consider the parameters as transition probabilities regardless of the time slot and arrival rate duration because the resulting performance is influenced by the relative values of these probabilities directly. Figure 16.4 shows the converged strategy profile of a three-network system in which $P_s/N_0 = 50$, $P_I/N_0 = 10$, $\lambda_0 = 0.1$, $\lambda_1 = 0.1$, $\lambda_2 = 0.2$, $\lambda_3 = 0.3$, $\mu = 0.1$, $\epsilon = 0.05$, and $N = 5$. It shows that a threshold structure within the strategy profile also exists.

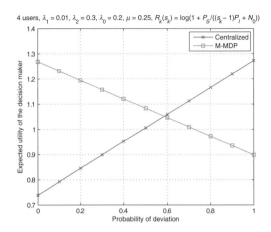

Figure 16.5 Comparison of the M-MDP method and the centralized method for the decision-maker's expected utility versus probability of deviation.

Figure 16.5 validates the IR of the M-MDP method within a two-network system in which the parameters are set as $P_s/N_0 = 50$, $P_I/N_0 = 10$, $\lambda_0 = 0.2$, $\lambda_1 = 0.01$, $\lambda_2 = 0.3$, $\mu = 0.25$, $\epsilon = 0.05$, and $N = 4$. The decision-maker's expected utility, computed by $E[V_{\sigma_s}(\mathbf{s} + \mathbf{e}_{\sigma_s})]$, is evaluated versus the probability of deviation p_d. The number of users N is set as four for computational tractability of the centralized method. Assume that the time slot duration is chosen for ensuring that $\lambda_0 + \lambda_1 + \lambda_2 + 2N\mu \leq 1$; however, these probabilities' relative values are preserved. The user at state $\mathbf{s}$ deviates from the given strategy σ_s with probability p_d. The expected utility of a decision-maker can only be impaired when they deviate from the strategy profile that is generated by the M-MDP method. But the centralized strategy does not satisfy IR because a decision-maker can obtain a higher expected utility (about 70% performance improvement within Figure 16.5) by deviating from the strategy that maximizes social welfare.

Figures 16.6(a) and 16.6(b) compare the decision-maker's expected utility with different strategy profiles within a two-network system in which $N = 4$, $P_s/N_0 = 50$, $P_I/N_0 = 10$, $\lambda_1 = 0.01$, $\mu = 0.15$, and $\epsilon = 0.5$. We adopt the myopic strategy to be the baseline through normalizing the performance of the other methods with that of the myopic strategy. Within Figure 16.6(a), $\lambda_2 = \lambda_0 = 0.2$ varies from 0.75 to 0.05. Within Figure 16.7(b), $\lambda_0 = \lambda_2 = 0.3$ varies from 0.75 to 0.05. It can be seen that the M-MDP method performs best among all schemes because the decision-maker optimizes their expected utility through choosing the network that is to their best advantage. According to the normalization, the myopic strategy always obtains performance 1 and it is better than the random strategy because it exploits the immediate utility's information. The centralized method performs the worst owing to the fact that it maximizes social welfare, sacrificing the decision-maker's expected utility.

In Figures 16.7(a) and 16.7(b), the strategy profiles' social welfare performance generated by different approaches is compared within a two-network system in which the parameters are $N = 4$, $P_s/N_0 = 50$, $P_I/N_0 = 10$, $\lambda_0 = 0.2$, $\mu = 0.25$, and

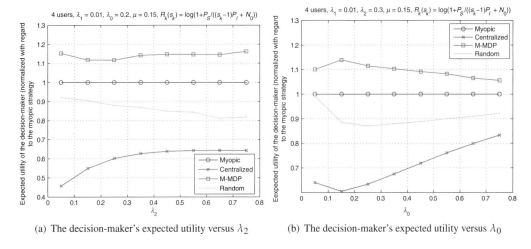

(a) The decision-maker's expected utility versus λ_2 (b) The decision-maker's expected utility versus λ_0

Figure 16.6 Comparison of the different strategies in terms of the decision-maker's expected utility.

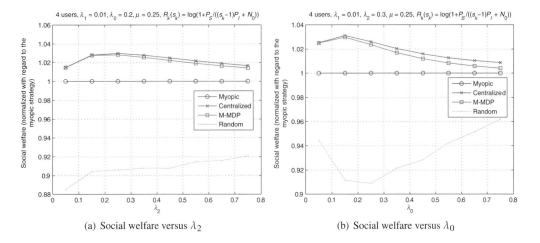

(a) Social welfare versus λ_2 (b) Social welfare versus λ_0

Figure 16.7 Comparison of the different strategies in terms of social welfare.

$\epsilon = 0.05$. Within Figure 16.7(a), $\lambda_2 = \lambda_1 = 0.01$ varies from 0.75 to 0.05. Within Figure 16.7(b), $\lambda_0 = \lambda_2 = 0.3$ varies from 0.75 to 0.05. Every method's performance is normalized against that of the myopic strategy. It can be seen that the performance of the M-MDP method is similar to that of the centralized method by which the social welfare is maximized. Figure 16.8 shows the impact of ϵ on the number of iterations taken for the strategy profile to converge when adopting the modified value iteration algorithm, and we can see that it requires a smaller number of iterations to converge because the region of tolerance for switching among the strategy profiles is larger, and possibly more ϵ-approximate NEs are available when ϵ increases.

Figures 16.9 and 16.10 provide performance comparisons for the different mechanism designs when $K = 2$ and $K = 3$, respectively. Determining the rule with the

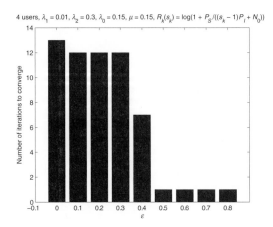

Figure 16.8 The impact of ϵ on the number of iterations taken for the strategy profile to converge.

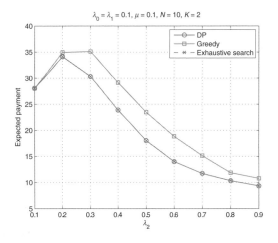

Figure 16.9 Comparison of the different mechanism designs in terms of the expected payment versus λ_2 when $K = 2$.

optimal objective value through searching over all possible allocation rules is the aim of the exhaustive search approach. The following recursive formula characterizes the greedy algorithm:

$$f_k^G(\{s_i, i \in \mathcal{I}\}|\{s_j, j \in \mathcal{J}\}) = \min_{i \in \mathcal{I}} \{f_{k-1}^G(s_{-i}|\{s_j, j \in \mathcal{J} \cup \{i\}\})\}, \tag{16.40}$$

$$a_{i^*}(s_{i^*}, s'_{-i^*}, s_j, s_{-j}) = 0, \forall s'_{-i^*} \preceq s_{-i^*},$$

$$\text{where } i^* = \arg \min_{i \in \mathcal{I}} \{f_{k-1}^G(s_{-i}|s_j, j \in \mathcal{J} \cup \{i\})\}. \tag{16.41}$$

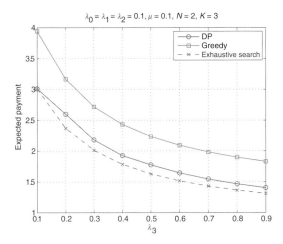

Figure 16.10 Comparison of the different mechanism designs in terms of the expected payment versus λ_3 when $K = 3$.

The boundary condition is

$$f_1^G(s_i|s_{-i}) = f_1^G(s_i - 1|s_{-i})\frac{w_i(s_i, s_{-i})}{w_i(s_i - 1, s_{-i})} + \pi(s_i, s_{-i})V_i(s_i + 1, s_{-i})w_i(s_i, s_{-i}),$$

$$(16.42)$$

$$a_{-i^*}(s_{i^*}, s'_{-i^*}, s_j, s_{-j}) = 1, \forall s'_{-i^*} \le s_{-i^*},$$

where i^* is the minimizer in (16.41) when $k = 2$.   (16.43)

The greedy algorithm evaluates $f_K^G(N, \dots, N)$ with $\mathcal{I} = \{1, \dots, K\}$ and $\mathcal{J} = \phi$ by adopting (16.40)–(16.43). With a similar analysis, its computational complexity can be shown as $\mathcal{O}(N^K)$. As a heuristic approach, a local optimal decision is made by it based on lower-dimensional results compared with the DP algorithm. This can be seen more clearly through considering the case of $K = 2$, i.e.,

$$f_2^G(s_1, s_2) = \min\left\{f_1^G(s_2|s_1), f_1^G(s_1|s_2)\right\},$$

$$(16.44)$$

$$\left(a_1(s_1, s'_2), a_2(s_1, s'_2)\right) = (0, 1), \forall s'_2 \le s_2, \text{ if } f_1^G(s_2|s_1) > f_1^G(s_1|s_2),$$

$$(16.45)$$

$$\left(a_1(s'_1, s_2), a_2(s'_1, s_2)\right) = (1, 0), \forall s'_1 \le s_1, \text{ if } f_1^G(s_2|s_1) \le f_1^G(s_1|s_2).$$

$$(16.46)$$

For example, state (N, N) will be allocated to network 1 if $f_1^G(s_2 = N|s_1 = N)$ is larger than $f_2^G(s_1 = N|s_2 = N)$ while evaluating $f_2^G(N, N)$. Based on Lemma 16.4, the states $\{(s_1, N), \forall s_1 \le N\}$ are all allocated to network 1. We can evaluate $f_2^G(N, N - 1)$ and so on since the unallocated states so far are $\{(s_1, s_2), 0 \le s_1 \le N, 0 \le s_2 \le N - 1\}$. Within Figure 16.9, the DP algorithm is able to achieve the same performance as the exhaustive search approach when $K = 2$ with the requirement of polynomial time complexity. A worse performance is shown by the greedy algorithm because a local optimal decision is made by it for determining the thresholds of the allocation rules. Within Figure 16.10, we compare the different mechanism design approaches for $K = 3$, showing that the greedy method is still outperformed by the DP algorithm. Therefore, the DP algorithm has a much lower complexity compared with the exhaustive search approach, and such an approximate approach could provide reasonably good results, although it might not achieve the global optimum for a general K as discussed within Section 16.5.

16.7   Discussion

We can see that the model demonstrated within this chapter is quite general and can be adapted to many problems, although our focus is the wireless access network selection problem. The cell selection problem within cellular networks [25–27] is a closely related scenario. When a mobile station wishes to inform the cellular system as to whether it is on the air, it registers to a base station that corresponds to a cellular cell. A local SNR-based strategy is applied to accomplish the cell selection process within most current cellular systems, which choose the cell with the largest SNR [26] after detecting the SNR of each cell, without considering others' strategies (i.e., negative network externality). However, the QoS experienced by a mobile station would be degraded if the limited resources are shared among a large quantity of users, and the utilization of system resources would also be degraded owing to the fact that the strategy causes cellular cells to have unbalanced loads.

It can be seen that the cell selection problem has the same structure as the wireless access network selection problem. Mobile stations choose one cellular cell (corresponding to a base station) sequentially for registering on the basis of the acquired information about every available cell, and during the period it stays within the cell, the utility each of them is determined by the expected throughput. A mobile station's instantaneous throughput within a certain cell is influenced by the the cell's crowdedness according to the limited bandwidth and the delay caused by the scheduling overheads. Thus a rational mobile station ought to consider other mobile stations' decisions while choosing a cellular cell in order to avoid crowdedness.

16.8   Conclusion

Within this chapter, the wireless access network selection problem was studied, which was shown to be an M-MDP as a stochastic game with negative network externality in which a user chooses a network through considering the subsequent decisions of the users. To obtain the optimal strategy profile for each selfish user, a modified value iteration algorithm was introduced, and we showed that the resulting strategy profile exhibited a threshold structure along every diagonal line. This kind of threshold structure can be adopted to save the strategy profile's storage space, going from $\mathcal{O}(N^2)$ to $\mathcal{O}(N \log N)$, within the two-network scenario. Simulation results validated the analysis and illustrated that rational users would not deviate from the strategy profile acquired by the modified value iteration algorithm. In terms of the expected utility of the decision-maker, the M-MDP method was superior to other approaches, and its social welfare performance was similar to that of the centralized strategy by which social welfare was maximized.

We further investigated truth-telling enforcement mechanism designs within the wireless access network selection problem, which captured the IR and IC constraints while the utility of users was optimized. Though the formulated problem as a mixed integer program generally has no efficient solutions, a DP algorithm was utilized for optimally solving the mixed integer programming problem within the two-network scenario through exploiting the optimal substructures. For the multinetwork scenario, the heuristic greedy approach in polynomial time complexity was outperformed by the DP algorithm. Finally, the optimality in the two-network case was substantiated by simulation results and the effectiveness of the DP algorithm in the multinetwork scenario was illustrated.

16.9 Literature Review

As an essential problem of resource utilization, wireless access network selection has attracted much attention recently [28–39]. In [35], centralized approaches are investigated for providing congestion relief through network-directed roaming and explicit channel switching. In [36], a distributed AP selection algorithm based on no-regret learning is proposed that could ensure convergence to an equilibrium. The departure and arrival of users within network selection problems are also considered in [38,39]. Another network selection approach is based on game theory. Game theory has been regarded as an ideal tool for studying interactions among users [22,40] and has been universally used within wireless networking and communications for many different problems [40–44], including power control [41], security enforcement [45], and cooperation stimulation [44]. In [29], Mittal et al. consider users changing locations as strategies for obtaining more resources, and the authors analyze the corresponding NEs. In [34], network selection is modeled as a congestion game in which decisions are made simultaneously by players for optimizing the throughput and interference, and the congestion within the game is similar to that within the channel selection game (e.g., [46–48]). In [46], an atomic congestion game is taken into consideration where resources are allowed to be readopted among noninterfering users. In [47,48], game-theoretic solutions are investigated by the authors for the distributed channel selection problem within opportunistic spectrum access systems. In [49], the existing decision-theoretic solutions are comprehensively reviewed and compared by the authors, including stochastic control, MDPs, and game theory.

References

[1] V. Chandrasekhar, J. Andrews, and A. Gatherer, "Femtocell networks: A survey," *IEEE Communications Magazine*, vol. 46, pp. 59–67, 2008.

[2] M. Ahmed, "Call admission control in wireless networks: A comprehensive survey," *IEEE Communications Surveys & Tutorials*, vol. 7, pp. 49–68, 2005.

[3] D. Gao, J. Cai, and K. N. Ngan, "Admission control in IEEE 802.11e wireless LANs," *IEEE Network*, vol. 19, pp. 6–13, 2005.

[4] W. Sandholm, "Negative externalities and evolutionary implementation," *Review of Economic Studies*, vol. 72, pp. 885–915, 2005.

[5] G. Fagiolo, "Endogenous neighborhood formation in a local coordination model with negative network externalities," *Journal of Economic Dynamics and Control*, vol. 29, pp. 297–319, 2005.

[6] C.-Y. Wang, Y. Chen, and K. J. R. Liu, "Chinese restaurant game," *IEEE Signal Processing Letters*, vol. 19, pp. 898–901, 2012.

[7] C. Y. Wang, Y. Chen, and K. J. R. Liu, "Sequential Chinese restaurant game," *IEEE Transactions on Signal Processing*, vol. 61, pp. 571–584, 2013.

[8] C. Jiang, Y. Chen, Y.-H. Yang, C.-Y. Wang, and K. J. R. Liu, "Dynamic Chinese restaurant game: theory and application to cognitive radio networks," *IEEE Transactions on Wireless Communications*, vol. 13, pp. 1960–1973, 2014.

[9] M. L. Puterman, *Markov Decision Processes: Discrete Stochastic Dynamic Programming*. John Wiley & Sons, 1994.

[10] D. Bertsekas, *Dynamic Programming and Optimal Control*, 3rd ed. Athena Scientific, 2007.

[11] R. B. Myerson, "Optimal auction design," *Mathematics of Operations Research*, vol. 6, pp. 58–73, 1981.

[12] V. Krishna, *Auction Theory*. Academic Press/Elsevier, 2009.

[13] N. Nisan, T. Roughgarden, E. Tardos, and V. Vazirani, *Algorithmic Game Theory*. Cambridge University Press, 2007.

[14] E. J. Friedman and D. C. Parkes, "Pricing WiFi at Starbucks: issues in online mechanism design," in *Proc. ACM Conference on Electronic Commerce (EC)*, 2003.

[15] R. Vohra, *Mechanism Design: A Linear Programming Approach*. Cambridge University Press, 2011.

[16] J. Zander, "Performance of optimum transmitter power control in cellular radio systems," *IEEE Transactions on Vehicular Technology*, vol. 41, pp. 57–62, 1992.

[17] T.-H. Lee, J.-C. Lin, and Y. Su, "Downlink power control algorithms for cellular radio systems," *IEEE Transactions on Vehicular Technology*, vol. 44, pp. 89–94, 1995.

[18] E. Parzen, *Stochastic Processes*, vol. 24. SIAM, 1999.

[19] M. Lopez-Benitez and F. Casadevall, "Discrete-time spectrum occupancy model based on Markov chain and duty cycle models," in *Proc. IEEE DySPAN*, 2011.

[20] J.-L. Wang, Y.-H. Xu, Z. Gao, and Q.-H. Wu, "Discrete-time queuing analysis of opportunistic spectrum access: Single user case," *Frequenz*, vol. 65, pp. 335–341, 2011.

[21] J. Razavilar, K. J. R. Liu, and S. Marcus, "Jointly optimized bit-rate/delay control policy for wireless packet networks with fading channels," *IEEE Transactions on Communications*, vol. 50, pp. 484–494, 2002.

[22] D. Fudenberg and J. Tirole, *Game Theory*. MIT Press, 1991.

[23] G. Koole, "Monotonicity in Markov reward and decision chains: theory and applications," *Foundations and Trends in Stochastic Systems*, vol. 1, pp. 1–76, 2007.

[24] E. Cil, E. Ormeci, and F. Karaesmen, "Effects of system parameters on the optimal policy structure in a class of queueing control problems," *Queueing Systems*, vol. 61, pp. 273–304, 2009.

[25] A. Sang, X. Wang, M. Madihian, and R. Gitlin, "Coordinated load balancing, handoff/cell-site selection, and scheduling in multi-cell packet data systems," *Wireless Networks*, vol. 14, pp. 103–120, 2008.

[26] D. Amzallag, R. Bar-Yehuda, D. Raz, and G. Scalosub, "Cell selection in 4G cellular networks," in *Proc. IEEE INFOCOM*, 2008.

[27] L. Gao, X. Wang, G. Sun, and Y. Xu, "A game approach for cell selection and resource allocation in heterogeneous wireless networks," in *Proc. IEEE SECON*, 2011.

[28] J. Hou and D. C. O'Brien, "Vertical handover-decision-making algorithm using fuzzy logic for the integrated Radio-and-OW system," *IEEE Transactions on Wireless Communications*, vol. 5, pp. 176–185, 2006.

[29] K. Mittal, E. M. Belding, and S. Suri, "A game-theoretic analysis of wireless access point selection by mobile users," *Computer Communications*, vol. 31, pp. 2049–2062, 2008.

[30] D. Niyato and E. Hossain, "Dynamics of network selection in heterogeneous wireless networks: An evolutionary game approach," *IEEE Transactions on Vehicular Technology*, vol. 58, pp. 2008–2017, 2009.

[31] Q. Song and A. Jamalipour, "Network selection in an integrated wireless LAN and UMTS environment using mathematical modeling and computing techniques," *IEEE Transactions on Wireless Communications*, vol. 12, pp. 42–48, 2005.

[32] A. Argento, M. Cesana, N. Gatti, and I. Malanchini, "A game theoretical study of access point association in wireless mesh networks," *Computer Communications*, vol. 35, pp. 541–553, 2012.

[33] D. Charilas, O. Markaki, D. Nikitopoulos, and M. Theologou, "Packet-switched network selection with the highest QoS in 4G networks," *Computer Networks*, vol. 52, pp. 248–258, 2008.

[34] M. Cesana, N. Gatti, and I. Malanchini, "Game theoretic analysis of wireless access network selection: models, inefficiency bounds, and algorithms," in *Proc. 3rd International Conference on Performance Evaluation Methodologies and Tools*, 2008.

[35] A. Balachandran, P. Bahl, and G. Voelker, "Hot-spot congestion relief in public-area wireless networks," in *Proc. IEEE 4th Workshop on Mobile Computing Systems and Applications*, 2002.

[36] L. Chen, "A distributed access point selection algorithm based on no-regret learning for wireless access networks," in *Proc. IEEE VTC 2010–Spring*, 2010.

[37] M. Satyanarayanan, "Pervasive computing: vision and challenges," *IEEE Personal Communications*, vol. 8, pp. 10–17, 2001.

[38] J. Konorski, "Multihomed wireless terminals: Mac configuration and network selection games," in *Proc. International Conference on Information Networking (ICOIN)*, 2011.

[39] F. Xu, C. Tan, Q. Li, G. Yan, and J. Wu, "Designing a practical access point association protocol," in *Proc. IEEE INFOCOM*, 2010.

[40] B. Wang, Y. Wu, and K. J. R. Liu, "Game theory for cognitive radio networks: An overview," *Computer Networks*, vol. 54, pp. 2537–2561, 2010.

[41] Z. Han and K. J. R. Liu, "Noncooperative power-control game and throughput game over wireless networks," *IEEE Transactions on Communications*, vol. 53, pp. 1625–1629, 2005.

[42] B. Wang, Z. Han, and K. J. R. Liu, "Distributed relay selection and power control for multiuser cooperative communication networks using Stackelberg game," *IEEE Transactions on Mobile Computing*, vol. 8, pp. 975–990, 2009.

[43] K. J. R. Liu and B. Wang, *Cognitive Radio Networking and Security: A Game-Theoretic View*. Cambridge University Press, 2010.

[44] Y. Chen and K. J. R. Liu, "Indirect reciprocity game modelling for cooperation stimulation in cognitive networks," *IEEE Transactions on Communications*, vol. 59, pp. 159–168, 2011.

[45] L. Xiao, Y. Chen, W. Lin, and K. J. R. Liu, "Indirect reciprocity security game for large-scale wireless networks," *IEEE Transactions on Information Forensics and Security*, vol. 7, pp. 1368–1380, 2012.

[46] C. Tekin, M. Liu, R. Southwell, J. Huang, and S. Ahmad, "Atomic congestion games on graphs and their applications in networking," *IEEE/ACM Transactions on Networking*, vol. 20, pp. 1541–1552, 2012.

[47] Y. Xu, J. Wang, Q. Wu, A. Anpalagan, and Y.-D. Yao, "Opportunistic spectrum access in cognitive radio networks: global optimization using local interaction games," *IEEE Journal on Selected Areas in Communications*, vol. 6, pp. 180–194, 2012.

[48] Y. Xu, J. Wang, Q. Wu, A. Anpalagan, and Y.-D. Yao, "Opportunistic spectrum access in unknown dynamic environment: A game-theoretic stochastic learning solution," *IEEE Transactions on Wireless Communications*, vol. 11, pp. 1380–1391, 2012.

[49] Y. Xu, A. Anpalagan, Q. Wu, L. Shen, Z. Gao, and J. Wang, "Decision-theoretic distributed channel selection for opportunistic spectrum access: strategies, challenges and solutions," *IEEE Communications Surveys & Tutorials*, vol. 15, pp. 1689–1713, 2013.

17 Deal Selection on Social Media with Behavior Prediction

Deal selection on Groupon represents a typical social learning and decision-making process in which customers are usually unaware of the quality of a deal. It is necessary for the customers to acquire this knowledge by taking advantage of social learning from other social media, such as, reviews on Yelp. In addition, the quality of a deal is determined by both the state of the vendor and the decisions of other customers on Groupon. The main focus of this chapter is how social learning and network externality influence the decisions of customers in deal selection on Groupon. We propose a data-driven game-theoretic framework to understand the rational deal selection behavior across social media. The sufficient condition of the Nash equilibrium is identified. A value iteration algorithm is utilized to determine the optimal deal selection strategy. A year-long experiment is conducted to trace the competition among deals on Groupon and the corresponding Yelp ratings. Analysis of the deal selection game (DSG) is conducted in realistic settings based on the data set. Ultimately, we evaluate the performance of the social learning framework using real data. The results suggest that customers do make decisions in a rational way rather than follow naive strategies, and there is still room for the optimization of their decisions based on the game-theoretic framework.

17.1 Introduction

Deal selection on Groupon represents a complex learning and decision-making process. Groupon is a demonstration of the new possibilities of the e-commerce business model [1]. It provides small businesses, particularly local restaurants, with a platform for product promotion with substantially discounted deals. The effectiveness of such deals is limited by time and even the amount of advertising. Customers who obtain deals on Groupon are also apt to promote the deals on other social networks such as Facebook or Twitter through the built-in tools provided by Groupon. The most attractive part for the customers to obtain certain deals is the possibility of purchasing premium products or services at a bargain price. However, the customers are usually unaware of the quality of a deal at first sight. The information provided on Groupon alone is limited and potentially biased. More often than not, it is necessary to make further efforts to acquire such knowledge from external sources.

Potential customers may obtain this information through other sources, such as experiences shared by their friends on Twitter [2], ratings on Groupon given by previous customers, or reviews on third-party websites such as Yelp. All of these information sources are treated as social media in which the information is generated by typical social entities and delivered via online social networks and/or the Internet. The information on different social media could be relevant. For instance, one may find the rating of a Groupon deal provider on Yelp, and one may be able to determine the popularity of a vendor on Yelp by checking the sales volume of its deal on Groupon. In the deal selection problem, potential customers may investigate the reviews and ratings of certain deals in the corresponding vendor records on Yelp and estimate the quality of the deal by themselves. Afterwards, based on their own estimation of the deal quality, price, and other factors, customers obtain the deals that optimally satisfy their demands.

It is quite notable that the quality of a deal is influenced by not only the state of the vendor, but also the decisions of potential customers on Groupon (i.e., network externality). Network externality, which describes the mutual influence among agents, plays a significant part in a great variety of network-related applications [3–5]. In the case of negative network externality (i.e., the utilities of agents will decrease along with the increasing number of agents making identical decisions), agents tend to refrain from making the same decisions as others in order to maximize their utility. In the case of positive externality, however, agents are inclined to make the same decision to increase their utility. This phenomenon has been found in a variety of applications in different research fields, such as storage service selection in cloud computing [6] and deal selection on Groupon [1]. It is known that when one product or service enjoys a successful promotion on Groupon, it may receive negative responses and an undesirable reputation due to the degraded quality of service or overexpectation regarding the products [7,8]. For instance, a local restaurant may offer a 50%-off deal for advertising purposes. However, the sales volume of this deal may amount to thousands, which indicates that the restaurant will have to serve a great number of customers in the coming months without obtaining a handsome profit. In this case, the quality of the meals and services will be degraded since the restaurant is limited by its resources and incentives, otherwise it may not be able to survive [9]. This effect is induced by the decisions of other customers. It is advisable for a rational agent to estimate the quality of the deal and predict this effect based on the knowledge acquired from social learning. This chapter focuses on the influence of the effects of network externality and social learning on the decisions of customers in deal selection on Groupon, supplemented by information from external social media such as Yelp.

If the agents want to enrich their knowledge of the network, they may regard social learning as an effective approach. As an example, we may imagine a scene in which an agent is in search of the best juice among thousands of options in a market. The agent may learn from advertisements offered by certain brands, their own experience from previous purchases, or reviews and discussions shared in social media. All of this information contributes to the agent's construction of a belief on the quality of the juice, due to which the accuracy of the agent's decision can be markedly improved. The latter information source (i.e., the experiences shared on social media) has recently attracted wide attention from researchers of online social networks, social media, and data science. The information of other agents is shared via the links constructed by the social relations in social media. Since each agent may have different social relations with others and may make decisions at different times, the information one agent received may be different from that received by others. The process in which an agent learns from such information is known as social learning [10–13].

Besides social learning, it is also necessary for agents to predict other agents' decisions since their rewards are generally determined by not only their own decisions, but also those of others. One paradigm relates to the selection of a cellular service provider. A user whose friends are using the same service provider is more likely to choose the same service provider so as to reduce the costs of in-network calls. Both behaviors of learning and predicting are simultaneously observable in a variety of social media, and they play a significant part in the deal selection problem.

The Chinese restaurant game (CRG) introduced in Chapter 12 is a general framework for modeling strategic learning and decision processes in the social learning problem with negative network externality. The original CRG focuses on snapshot-based scenarios; in other words, there is an assumption that the system state and customers are predetermined and fixed during the course of the game. The dynamic CRG (D-CRG) is proposed in Chapter 13 to study how a user in a dynamic social network learns about the uncertain state and makes optimal decisions. Not only should a user take into account the immediate utility they receive at a given time, but also they are supposed to know the influence of subsequent users' decisions and the transitions of the system state. In the D-CRG, a multidimensional Markov decision process (M-MDP) model is utilized to describe the decision process in the dynamic system. The system resembles the traditional MDP apart from the fact that it involves multiple reward functions and transition probability matrices. It is shown that the system is able to reach optimal social welfare when the service provider adopts an appropriate pricing strategy for the regulation of these rational users.

However, the D-CRG is still based on certain assumptions that are unrealistic in real-world scenarios and lead to the impracticality of the deal selection problem discussed in this case. Critically, it is assumed that the available choices of tables remain constant despite the passage of time. This tends to be impractical due to the fact that social media sites such as Groupon are highly dynamic and stochastic. The available choices for agents are subject to frequent changes in this sort of system. The deals offered on Groupon, for instance, are even subject to hourly changes. Every customer tends to observe various set of deals that are on sale and consequently encounters divergent deal selection problems. It is advisable for the method to tackle this phenomenon by modeling the dynamics of the available choices so as to reflect the dynamics in Groupon. Furthermore, the externality involved in the D-CRG is purely negative, which is not universal for all real-world cases. In Groupon, it is shown by the observations in the collected data set that the externality is more variable; that is, low-quality deals may have positive externality whereas high-quality ones often have negative externality. In summary, based on the features found in real data, an extension to the D-CRG is necessary here.

In this chapter, we propose a data-driven social learning model so as to understand the deal selection behavior in the real world based on the data from two specific social media sites: Groupon and Yelp. Specifically, a stochastic learning model on the basis of the CRG is utilized to understand how rational customers choose a deal according to the information they collected from external reviews concerning the externality caused by other customers. The structure of the model resembles that of the D-CRG with additional support from available dynamic deal sets, stochastic review generating processes, and general externalities in utility functions.

To construct the required data set targeting social media, a set of social media data collection tools are introduced. In order to trace the competition among deals on Groupon and the impacts on the corresponding ratings in Yelp records, we conduct a year-long experiment. By drawing on the data set, we are able to extract the necessary information from the stochastic learning model, such as regressions of arrival processes, departure processes, and utility functions. Analysis is carried out on the DSG on a deal website in a realistic settings on the basis of the learning model and data set. The sufficient condition for the Nash equilibrium in the DSG is identified. A value iteration algorithm is utilized to determine the optimal deal selection strategy. Furthermore, we evaluate how the social learning framework with the real data performs with regard to social welfare and customer utility. A more in-depth discussion is carried out on the rationality of customers in terms of deal selection in comparison with the simulation outcomes with real data.

17.2   Cross-Social Media Data Set

We first introduce the constructed Groupon and Yelp data set using the Python-based social network data collection and analysis toolbox. The toolbox offers a series of major functions:

(1)   Standard representational state transfer (REST) application programming interface (API) calls support
(2)   Scheduling-support crawler
(3)   Cross-social network identification and matching
(4)   Feature extraction
(5)   Distribution regression

For the collection of the data from Groupon and Yelp, the toolbox is applied to a Linux-based machine. Specifically, we target the Groupon deals provided in the

Washington, D.C. area and the corresponding Yelp records for each deal. Thrice daily, the Groupon crawler will first collect the deals offered on Groupon in the Washington, D.C. area through the Groupon API. Then, a social element matcher will identify each deal's corresponding Yelp record(s) via the Yelp API. Note that one deal may match multiple Yelp records when the deal is applicable to a number of stores. The IDs of the Yelp records will be marked as targets and stored in a database provided for the identification of valid records. Another Yelp crawler will collect the data of all marked Yelp records at fixed intervals in an independent manner. We are only allowed to access the latest three reviews of the records because the REST API provided by Yelp is somewhat limited. This deficiency can be offset by high-frequency data crawling (thrice daily)

It took 19 months (December 2012–July 2014) to execute the data collection process. We collected 6509 deals, among which 2389 had valid Yelp records. A Groupon–Yelp relational data set is developed with the following features:

- Groupon deals
  - Start/end time, expiry time, tags
  - Options: price, discount, location
  - Sold quantity tracking (three times per day)
- Yelp records
  - Basic information (location, phone, etc.)
  - Linking to Groupon deal(s)
  - Rating tracking (three times per day)
  - Reviews: rating, content, author, time

It should be noted that different from most deal data sets found in public for academic usage, this data set tracks the sales volume of each deal. Based on this feature, we obtain information about the competition among deals; in other words, we can answer such questions as "Which deal is the best-selling one given a set of available deals?" This also sketches out the main focus of this chapter and the CRG framework since we intend to draw on the framework to analyze and predict the competition effects in social media.

From the analysis of the data set, we have extracted some interesting characteristics of Groupon deals. New deals get put online every day in two batches. Specifically, we checked the exact online time of each deal based on the collected data since the collected data for each deal have a "startAt" tag that indicates exactly when the deal starts. The first batch contains an average of 6.73 new deals, whereas the second one contains only 4.72 deals (Figure 17.1(a)). The available duration of a deal (i.e., the number of days a deal is available for purchase on Groupon) is very diverse. The duration of a deal being available for purchase ranges from several days to months. The average duration is 9.21 days, with a standard deviation of 20.14 days. This diversity is based on the fact that there are various types of deals (marked with tags) offered on Grouopn. It is apparent that the distribution is closely matched by an exponential distribution, as is demonstrated in Figure 17.2(a).

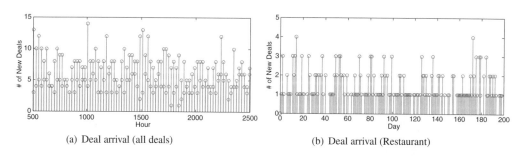

(a) Deal arrival (all deals)   (b) Deal arrival (Restaurant)

Figure 17.1 Deal arrival process.

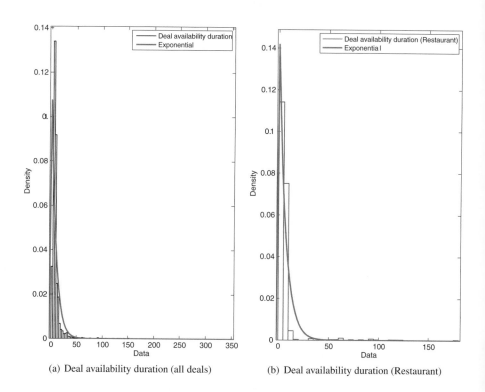

(a) Deal availability duration (all deals)   (b) Deal availability duration (Restaurant)

Figure 17.2 Deal availability duration.

The valid duration of the deal (i.e., the number of days in which a customer may utilize the deal after the deal goes online) also varies remarkably, with an average of 126.38 days and a standard deviation of 47.96 days. Note that on average the valid duration of deals is substantially larger than the average available duration of deals.

A Groupon deal may be marked by multiple tags, among which the most popular ones include (1) Beauty and Spa, (2) Restaurants, and (3) Art and Entertainment. These three tags involve more deals than any combination of other tags (Figure 17.3). In terms of a specific type of deal (e.g., Restaurants), the arrival of new deals is quite

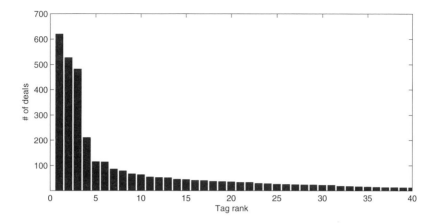

Figure 17.3 Tag distribution.

predictable. The Restaurant-type deals still arrive in batches, while the interval could be 24 or 48 hours. Each batch is composed of an average of 1.65 deals (Figure 17.1(b)).

The average available duration of the deal is exactly 7 days, with a standard deviation of 14 days. It can be seen that the distribution is closely matched by an exponential distribution, as is demonstrated in Figure 17.2(b). The valid duration, on the other hand, lasts for an average of 109.44 days, with a standard deviation of 28.31 days. In the following analysis, in an attempt to eliminate the heterogeneity among the various types of deals, we confine the targeting data set to the deals tagged as Restaurants.

The daily sales volume of deals is presented in Figure 17.4(a) and 17.4(b). On average, the sales volume of all deals amounts to 36.35, while 13.66 deals are settled for Restaurant-type deals per hour. In this case, it is assumed that each deal is purchased and utilized by exactly the same user. The purchase record then represents the arrival distribution of the effective user (users who actually purchase a deal). Note that the distributions are again closely matched by an exponential distribution, as is illustrated in Figures 17.4(a) and 17.4(b).

Additional information regarding the cross-effect of Yelp ratings and the sales volume of Groupon deals is available through linking the deal records to Yelp records. First, there are markedly more deals offered by vendors with four-star rating on Yelp, while no deals are provided by vendors with one- or two-star ratings. Moreover, the sales volume of a great number of deals amounts to 1000, which indicates that this is a general capacity that a typical vendor is able to afford (Figure 17.5(a)). New reviews are defined as all of the reviews posted within the duration from the start of a deal's availability until its expiry. By tracking the new reviews reported by customers after the deal goes online, we determine a significant but complex relation between the sales volume and rating distribution of new reviews. The relation, which can be explained with network externality, is positive when the original Yelp rating of the vendor is three stars, but it becomes negative when the original rating is five stars. The results reveal a correlation between the externality effects and the original rating

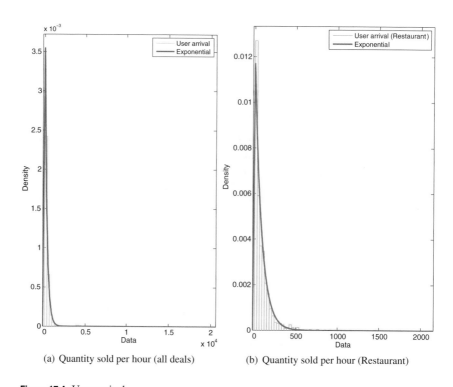

(a) Quantity sold per hour (all deals)   (b) Quantity sold per hour (Restaurant)

Figure 17.4 User arrival.

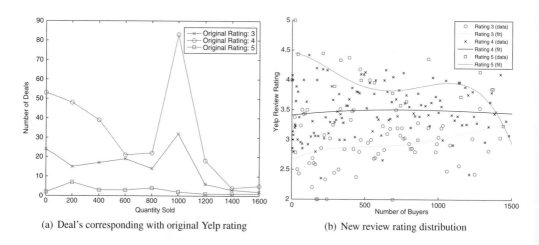

(a) Deal's corresponding with original Yelp rating   (b) New review rating distribution

Figure 17.5 Yelp review rating vs. Groupon deal.

of the vendor. A simple negative or positive assumption does not properly capture the complex externality effect. Consequently, we utilize the curve-fitting toolbox in MATLAB with the polynomial model at the degree of 5. The data have been smoothed by the application of the moving average method (Figure 17.5(b)).

17.3   System Model

The system model is formulated based on the observations from the Groupon–Yelp data set. We set a deal website providing multiple deals as the deal set $\mathcal{D}[t] = \{d_1, d_2, \ldots\} \subset \mathcal{D}^{all}$, where $\mathcal{D}^{all}$ is the universal deal set and $\mathcal{D}[t]$ is the available deal set at time t. It is assumed that the system time t is discrete. A one-to-one relation exists between the vendor and the offered deal; that is, a vendor provides exactly one deal among the universal deal set $\mathcal{D}^{all}$. Note that each deal shown in the online deal set $\mathcal{D}[t]$ belongs to the universal set. New deals arrive and are incorporated into the deal set $\mathcal{D}[t]$ following a Poisson arrival distribution with parameter $\bar{\lambda}$. Specifically, the opportunity for all offline deals to go online follows a Poisson arrival process, and each deal may go online in an independent manner in this batch with a probability of ρ_d if it is offline in the previous slot. Each deal goes offline and is removed from the deal set $\mathcal{D}[t]$ following an exponential distribution with parameter $\bar{\mu}$. The price of each deal d is p_d, which is controlled by the vendor. The quality of the deal d is r_d, of which the customers are unaware.

Customers arrive at the website stochastically following an exponential arrival process with parameter $\bar{\lambda}_u$. One customer is going to purchase exactly one deal upon their arrival at time t and browse the available deals in $\mathcal{D}[t]$. The customer may utilize the deal when the deal goes offline. This is based on the observation from the data set that the deal's validity is significantly longer than the sales duration and consequently the probability of utilizing a deal within the sales duration is negligible.

The valuation of the deal depends on the quality of the deal, which could be either known or unknown to the customer before purchase. It is also affected by the sales volume of the deal before it goes offline. This externality effect could be positive or negative: it is determined by the characteristics of the deal. Based on the observations from the data set, it is assumed that the externality is not only a function of sales volume, but also of the original quality of the deal. The utility of customers is therefore given by

$$U(r_d, n_d^*, p_d) = V(r_d, n_d^*) - \alpha p_d, \tag{17.1}$$

where r_d is the original rating of the deal d, n_d^* means the number of customers purchasing deal d before the deal goes offline, p_d denotes the price of the deal, and α represents the weight of the payment. The exact form of the valuation function $V(r_d, n_d^*)$ refers to the real data extracted from the data set (Figure 17.5(b)). In general, when $r_d \leq 3$, the valuation of the deal increases with n_d^*. In the case that $3 < r_d \leq 4$, the valuation function is slightly concave in n_d^*. When $r_d > 4$, the valuation function becomes a decreasing function.

First, note that the customers are unaware of the quality of the deal. Additional effort is required to obtain this knowledge through social learning. Furthermore, the utility of a customer is realized when the deal goes offline, which happens *after* the customer chooses the deal. It is possible that the sales volume of the deal increases before the deal goes offline and therefore exerts a positive or negative influence on the utility of the customer. It is advisable for a rational customer to consider the current

Table 17.1. Review rating distribution vs. original rating.

Original	1-star	2-star	3-star	4-star	5-star
3-star	350	322	374	397	280
4-star	480	507	736	1302	1032
5-star	27	27	45	92	154

state of the available deals and predict the increase in the sales volume of the deals so as to estimate the expected utility of certain deals that they are inclined to choose.

17.3.1   External Information from Social Media

Customers collect information about the unknown deal quality r_d from personal experience, reviews, or ratings shared on third-party social media sites such as Yelp and Facebook. Based on the observations from the data set, it is assumed that such information arrives at the system in a stochastic manner. The information is considered as signals and thus contributes to the knowledge of the customers regarding the unknown quality r_d. It is assumed that the current estimation of the expected rating of deal d at time t is denoted as $r_d[t]$, which is a random variable. New reviews w_d on the quality of deal d arrive following a Poisson arrival process with parameter $\bar{\lambda}_{w_d}$. The value of reviews w_d is a random variable with conditional probability function $Pr(w_d|r_d)$, which describes how accurately the review reflects the true quality of the deal. The reviews are independent when they are on the condition of r_d. Since the reviews arrive in a stochastic manner, customers who arrive at different times may have acquired different sets of reviews and consequently have divergent estimations of r_d.

Belief is the customer's estimation of the probabilistic distribution of $r_d[t]$ after the collection of all available reviews. A belief regarding deal d at time t is denoted by $\mathbf{b}_d[t] = \{b_{d,X}[t]|X\}$, where $b_{d,X}[t] = Pr(r_d = X|\{w_d\}[t])$, $\sum_X b_{d,X}[t] = 1$. In a stochastic system, the belief regarding deal d can be updated when new review w'_d arrives following the Bayesian updating rule as follows:

$$b_{d,X}[t] = \begin{cases} \dfrac{Pr(\{w'_d\}|r_d=X)b_{d,X}[t-1]}{\sum_{X'=1}^{5} Pr(\{w'_d\}|r_d=X')b_{d,X'}[t-1]}, & \text{new review } w'_d. \\ b_{d,X}[t-1], & \text{else.} \end{cases} \qquad (17.2)$$

We then denote $\mathbf{b}[t] = \{\mathbf{b}_d[t]\}$ as the common belief of all customers regarding all deals at time t. However, $\mathbf{b}[t]$ is intractable in terms of real data since its dimension shows exponential growth with increasing numbers of deals. An approximation is essential for its simplification. According to the observations from the collected Yelp data set, it is known that the review ratings received by a vendor generally follow Gaussian distributions (Table 17.1). The variance of the received ratings is determined by the average rating of the deal. Such an observation gives rise to the assumption that $b_{d,X}[t]$ follows a Gaussian distribution with the average rating $b_{d,avg}[t]$ and varianc $b_{d,var}$. In this case, it is necessary to track $b_{d,avg}[t]$ of each deal rather than the whole $\mathbf{b}_d[t]$, and so computation complexity is significantly reduced. Finally, we denote $\mathbf{b}_{avg}[t] = \{\mathbf{b}_{d,avg}[t]\}$ as the belief in an average sense.

17.4   Stochastic DSG

We propose a game-theoretic stochastic learning model for the deal selection problem. The structure of the model resembles that of the D-CRG [14] in state, profile, and belief. However, the original model is inapplicable to this problem for the following reasons: (1) the available deals (tables) are no longer fixed but should be depicted by a stochastic process; (2) the reviews (signals) are not always generated synchronously with the customer's arrival process; and (3) the externality could be positive, negative, or quality-dependent. It is therefore necessary to develop a new game-theoretic stochastic model to address such new characteristics in the deal selection problem.

We consider a DSG with players as the customers who arrive at the system in a stochastic manner. A customer may select exactly one deal $d \in \mathcal{D}[t]$ upon their arrival at time t. Once the deal goes offline, the customer will depart from the game and the utility is realized immediately. The utility is given by the utility function $U(r_d, n_d^*, p_d)$, which takes the number of customers choosing the same deal (n_d^*), deal quality r_d, and the price p_d as inputs. It is advisable for a rational customer to select the deal that maximizes their expected utility in the stochastic game. The objective is to determine the optimal deal selection strategy for each customer in the game.

According to the system model we formulated in the previous section, customers arrive at the system following a Poisson arrival process with parameter $\bar{\lambda}_u$. A customer's action space is represented by the available deals when they arrive at time t; put another way, a customer's action is denoted by $a \in \mathcal{D}[t]$. A customer's action will remain unchanged until their departure from the system. Customers leave the system only after the selected deals go offline. Therefore, their departure follows the deal departure process, which is assumed to be an exponential distribution with parameter $\bar{\mu}$. The utility of the customer is realized immediately upon their departure.

17.4.1   Multidimensional Markov Decision Process

A rational customer seeks the maximization of their utility in the game. Since the system is stochastic, the exact utility of each deal cannot be obtained. It is necessary for the customers to estimate the expected utility they can receive from each deal before choosing the deal based on their knowledge of the system. In this case, we take advantage of the M-MDP [15], which is also the foundation of the D-CRG [14], to estimate the expected utility of the customers.

The state in M-MDPs represents the current observations and the customers' knowledge of the deals in the game. In this case, we denote the state as

$$\mathbf{s}[t] = \{\mathcal{D}[t], \mathbf{n}[t], \mathbf{b}_{avg}[t]\} \in \mathcal{S}, \tag{17.3}$$

where $\mathcal{D}[t]$ represents the deals available for purchase and $\mathbf{n}[t] = \{n_d[t] | d \in \mathcal{D}^{all}\}$ is the number of customers choosing each deal d at time t. It is assumed that $n_d[t]$ is rounded to hundreds or even thousands. This is common practice on deal websites such as Groupon, where only rounded figures are revealed to the public. According to what was mentioned in the previous section, $\mathbf{b}_{avg}[t]$ is the belief regarding each deal d's quality. Finally, $\mathcal{S}$ is the universal set of all possible states. A rational customer takes advantage of the state information upon their arrival so as to maximize their expected utility. Consequently, the optimal deal selection strategy is expected to be connected to the arrival state of the system. Note that the state describes the customers' knowledge of the system based on their limited observations of public information. It is unlikely to achieve an accurate reflection of the hidden information of the system, such as the exact sales volume and the quality of the deals.

The strategy profile, which is denoted by a function $\pi(\mathbf{s}[t]) \in \mathcal{D}[t]$, describes the actions of each player in every possible state of the system. It can be treated as the behavior predictions of the players in a given M-MDP. In the DSG, the strategy profile describes which deal is to be selected by the next customer under the current state $\mathbf{s}[t]$. Due to the effect of externality on the utility in (17.1), it is also necessary for a rational customer to be aware of the deal selection strategies of other customers in the system.

17.4.2   State Transition

The state of the system may transition from one to another with the occurrence of certain events. The transition is likely to be determined by the viewpoint of the customer [15]. Specifically, a customer may observe that the system state changes when new customers arrive and select deals and when certain deals go online or offline. However, their utility is realized when the selected deal goes offline. What differentiates this event from others is that in the case of its occurrence, the customer also departs from the system. Consequently, no future state transition will affect the customer's utility. When the customers are in the system and choose the deal d, the observed state transition probability tends to be represented as

$$Pr(\mathbf{s}'|\mathbf{s}, \pi, d) = Pr(\{\mathbf{n}', \mathbf{b}'_{avg}, \mathcal{D}'\}|\mathbf{s}, \pi, d). \tag{17.4}$$

Note that the transition probability not only hinges on the current state $\mathbf{s}$, but also on the strategy profile π. Generally speaking, the state changes with the occurrence of specific events, for which the probability of occurrence is known. In the system, the following three independent events may change the state:

(1)   A new customer arrives.
(2)   A new review w_d on a specific deal d arrives.
(3)   A deal d' goes online or offline.

New Customer Arrives

A new customer arrives following a Poisson distribution with parameter $\bar{\lambda}_u$. When the time interval T is small enough, the probability of a customer's arrival can be denoted by $\lambda_u = T\bar{\lambda}_u$ [15]. Upon the arrival of a new customer, only the grouping state $\mathbf{n}$ will change. However, the new grouping state $\mathbf{n}'$ relies on the strategy profile π (i.e., which deal is selected by the new customer). The state transition probability conditional on the arrival of new customers is as follows:

$$Pr(\mathbf{n}'|\mathbf{n}, \pi, d, (\text{new customer})) = \begin{cases} \Lambda(\lambda_u), & \mathbf{n}' = \mathbf{n} + \mathbf{e}_{\pi(s)}; \\ 1 - \Lambda(\lambda_u), & \mathbf{n}' = \mathbf{n}; \\ 0, & \text{else,} \end{cases} \quad (17.5)$$

where $\mathbf{e}_x$ is the unit vector in dimension x and $\Lambda(\lambda_u)$ is the probability that (rounded) n_d increased by 1 (e.g., 100 more amounts are sold) after this purchase.

New Review Arrives

Recall that a new review w_d on the quality of deal d arrives following a Poisson arrival process with parameter $\bar{\lambda}_{w_d}$. Based on the assumption that the time slot is so short that a maximum of one review can be generated within a slot, the review arrival probability can be represented as $\sum_{d \in \mathcal{D}_{all}} \lambda_{w_d}$, where $\lambda_{w_d} = T \bar{\lambda}_{w_d}$. The belief state regarding a specific deal will change with the new review. Based on the fact that the belief follows a Gaussian distribution with a known variance, we may transform the average belief $\mathbf{b}_{avg}$ recorded in the state back to the exact belief $\mathbf{b}$ and then utilize the Bayesian updating function (17.2) to update the belief to $\mathbf{b}'$. The updated average belief can be transformed back into the average belief $\mathbf{b}'_{avg}$ in the new state $\mathbf{s}'$. The state transition probability conditional on this event is as follows:

$$Pr(\mathbf{b}'|\mathbf{b}, \pi, d, \text{new review } w_{d'} \in \{1, 2, 3, 4, 5\}) \quad (17.6)$$

$$= \begin{cases} \dfrac{\lambda_{w_{d'}} \sum_X Pr(w_{d'}|r_{d'}=X)b_{d',X}}{\sum_{d \in \mathcal{D}_{all}} \lambda_{w_d}}, & \text{updated by } w_{d'}; \\ 0, & \text{else.} \end{cases}$$

Deal Online or Offline

Finally, the state also changes when a new deal goes online or an available deal goes offline. Based on the batch arrival property we observed in the data set, it is assumed that the opportunity for deals to go online follows a Poisson arrival process with parameter $\bar{\lambda}$. When the assumption of the short slot time holds, we have the deal arrival probability per slot as $\lambda = T\bar{\lambda}$. Each deal may go online independently when the opportunity arises. Specifically, let ρ_d be the probability that deal d go online at this slot if it is offline in the previous slot during this batch. The state transition probability conditional on the arrival of a set of deals δ is as follows:

$$Pr(\mathbf{s}'|\mathbf{s}, \pi, d, \text{new deal set } \delta) \quad (17.7)$$

$$= \begin{cases} \prod_{d' \in \delta} \rho_{d'} \prod_{d'' \in \mathcal{D}^{all} \setminus (\delta \cup \mathcal{D})} (1 - \rho_{d''}), & \mathcal{D}' = \mathcal{D} \cup \delta, \mathcal{D} \cap \delta = \emptyset; \\ 0, & \text{else.} \end{cases}$$

This formulation is inspired by two observations from the Groupon data set: deals arrive in batches periodically and the repeated availability of popular deals. These special patterns in the data set reduce the complex calibration of the model to a data set. Specifically, the arrival rate of batches can be estimated through the measurement of the average period of the batches in the data set. The probability that deal d goes online in each batch can then be approximated through the calculation of the average number of times deal d goes online in all batches in the collected data set.

Recall that a deal may go offline following the deal departure process, which is assumed to be an exponential distribution with parameter $\bar{\mu}$. Consequently, the per-slot deal departure probability can be denoted by $\mu = T\bar{\mu}$. The corresponding state transition is as follows:

$$Pr(\mathbf{s'}|\mathbf{s}, \pi, d, \text{remove deal } d') = \begin{cases} 1, & \mathcal{D'} = \mathcal{D} \setminus \{d'\}; \\ 0, & \text{else.} \end{cases} \quad (17.8)$$

State Transition Probability

By combining all of the aforementioned events with the corresponding probability, we are in a position to grasp the state transition probability given the current state. The state changes with the occurrence of any of the previously discussed events. Thus a complete form of the state transition probability will be as follows:

$$Pr(\mathbf{s'}|\mathbf{s}, \pi, d) = (\text{Prob. of Customer Arrival from } s \text{ to } s')$$

$$(\text{Prob. of Review Arrival from } s \text{ to } s')$$

$$(\text{Prob. of Deal Arrival/Departure from } s \text{ to } s') \quad (17.9)$$

To improve the tractability of the model and present it in a simpler form, it is assumed that the interval T of the discrete system time t is small enough that each time slot t admits of the occurrence of only one event. This assumption is based on the fact that the probability of multiple independent events occurring within the same time slot t will reduce to zero provided there is a decrease in the probability of each event, in accordance with the Taylor expansion of (17.9). The individual occurrence probabilities of each type of event are proportional to the interval T when T is small enough [15], and they tend to decrease when the interval T diminishes. Based on this assumption, it is sufficient for us to merely take into account the state transitions involving single event occurrences.[1]

The probability that the state remains constant is as follows:

$$Pr(\mathbf{s}|\mathbf{s}, \pi, d) = (1 - Pr(\text{Customer Arrival}))$$

$$(1 - Pr(\text{Review Arrival}))(1 - Pr(\text{Deal Arrival/Departure}))$$

$$= 1 - Pr(\text{Customer Arrival}) - Pr(\text{Review Arrival}) - Pr(\text{Deal Changes}) + \delta(T),$$

in accordance with the Taylor expansion. When T is small enough, the $\delta(T)$ will diminish to zero due to the decrease in the multiple event occurrence probability within a time slot.

---

[1] Note that this assumption can be easily relaxed without changing any of the insights we have obtained in this chapter.

In total, the overall state transition probability observed by a customer that selects deal d is shown in (17.10).

$$
Pr(s'|s,\pi,d) = \begin{cases} \lambda_u \Lambda(\lambda_u), & n'_d = n_d + 1; \\ \lambda_{w_j} \sum_X Pr(w_j | r_j = X) b_{j,X}, & \mathbf{b}'_j \text{ is updated with } w_j; \\ \lambda \prod_{d' \in \delta} p_{d'} \prod_{d'' \in \mathcal{D}^{all} \setminus (\delta \cup \mathcal{D})} (1 - p_{d''}), & \mathcal{D}' = \mathcal{D} \cup \delta, \mathcal{D} \cap \delta = \emptyset; \\ \mu, & \mathcal{D}' = \mathcal{D} \setminus \{d'\}, d' \neq d; \\ 1 - \lambda_u \Lambda(\lambda_u) - \lambda - \sum_{j \in \mathcal{D}_{all}} \lambda_{w_j} - |D|\mu, & s' = s; \\ 0, & \text{else.} \end{cases}
$$
(17.10)

It is noticeable that the transition probability from s to $s' \in \mathcal{S}$ in (17.10) totals $1 - \mu$. This is due to the fact that we ignore the event that the deal d that is selected by the customer goes offline (the fourth case in (17.10)). We will demonstrate that this formation is instrumental in the following analysis.

17.4.3   Expected Utility and Strategy Profile

A rational customer will select the deal with the highest expected utility conditional on the state $s[t^a]$ that they observe at the arrival time t^a. The expected utility is affected by not only the initially observed state of the system, but also all of the future states until the deal they select goes offline. Given a specific strategy profile $\pi(s)$, the state transition probability $Pr(s'|s,\pi,d)$ is known. Based on the assumption that customer i arrives at the system at state $s[t^e]$ and selectes deal d_i, their utility will be realized when the deal d_i goes offline. The expected utility of customer i hinges on the entering state $s[t^e]$, which is denoted as $E[u(d_i)|s[t^e]]$ and is given by

$$
E[u(d_i)|s[t^e],\pi] = \sum_{t=t^e}^{\inf} (1-\mu)^{t-t^e} \mu E[U(r_{d_i}, n_{d_i}[t], p_{d_i})|s[t],\pi]
$$
(17.11)

Note that the exactly realized state at each time slot is stochastic, whereas the state transition probability is described by (17.10) and is determined by the applied strategy profile π.

The expected utility of each deal can be acquired in a closed form through the Bellman equations. We present $W(s,d)$ as the expected utility that a customer is likely to receive if they choose deal d at state s, which is the total of the expected utilities when the deal d goes offline at this moment (with probability μ) and remains online (with probability $1 - \mu$), respectively. When deal d goes offline, the expected utility is calculated in accordance with the number of customers choosing the same deal n_d, with the deal price p_d and the belief regarding the quality of the deal $b_{d,avg}$ at the state. In the case in which the deal remains online, the state may transition following the state transition probability observed by the customer who selects this specific deal d based on the fact that deal d stays online. The Bellman equation of $W(s,d)$ on the condition of a given strategy profile π can then be given as follows:

$$W(s,d) = E[u(d)|s, \pi] = \mu E[U(r_d, n_d, p_d)|s] + (1 - \mu) \sum_{s' \in S} \frac{Pr(s'|s, \pi, d)}{(1 - \mu)} W(s', d).$$

(17.12)

The first part of (17.12) is the utility that a customer will receive when the deal d they select goes offline. The second part of (17.12) shows the expected utility in the future if the deal d remains online in the next slot. This second part is based on the fact that deal d remains online so that the conditional probability takes effect. Note that the state transition probability $Pr(s'|s, \pi, d)$ that we introduced in (17.10) had already removed the event in which deal d goes online; consequently, it is directly applicable here after normalization.

17.4.4   Nash Equilibrium and Value Iteration Algorithm

We now analyze the necessary and sufficient conditions for a Nash equilibrium in the DSG. A Nash equilibrium represents the rational outcome of a game in which each player has applied their optimal strategy in response to the strategies applied by others. From the perspective of mathematics, a Nash equilibrium is a strategy profile π^* denoted as follows.

DEFINITION 17.1   (Nash equilibrium) A strategy profile π^* is a Nash equilibrium if and only if

$$E[u(\pi^*(s))|s, \pi^*] \geq E[u(d')|s, \pi^*], \forall d' \in \mathcal{D}, \forall s \in \mathcal{S}.$$

On the other hand, the best response for each customer who arrives at a certain state s is supposed to hinge on the expected utility of each deal at that state, which is given by $W(s, d)$. It is advisable for all customers to select the deal that offers them the highest utility from all available deals. Consequently, the optimal strategy profile π^* given the currently applied strategy profile π is given as follows:

$$\pi^*(s[t]) \in \arg \max_{d \in \mathcal{D}[t]} E[u(d|s[t], \pi) = \max_{d \in \mathcal{D}[t]} W(s[t], d).$$

(17.13)

Apparently, the Nash equilibrium of the DSG is achieved when the expected utility (17.12) and optimal strategy profile (17.13) match with each other, which are known as equilibrium conditions.

LEMMA 17.2 (Equilibrium condition)   *The strategy profile π^* is a Nash equilibrium in the DSG if and only if*

$$W^*(s,d) = \mu E[U(X, n_d, p_d)|s] + (1 - \mu) \sum_{s'} \in S \frac{Pr(s'|s, \pi^*, d)}{1 - \mu} W^*(s', d). \quad (17.14)$$

$$\pi^*(s) \in \arg \max_{d \in \mathcal{D}} W^*(s, d).$$

(17.15)

Proof   For a customer who arrives at state **s** assuming all other customers follow the strategy profile π^*, their expected utility if they select deal d is given by $W^*(\mathbf{s}, d)$ described in the lemma and from (17.12). According to (17.15), we have

$$W^*(\mathbf{s}, \pi^*(s)) \geq W^*(\mathbf{s}, d), \forall d \in \mathcal{D}.$$

Thus Definition 17.1 is satisfied and π^* is a Nash equilibrium.

Given the satisfaction of the equilibrium conditions, no customer is motivated to deviate from the strategy profile π since all customers seek to maximize their expected utilities, which are acquired on the condition of π. The equilibrium conditions represent the necessary conditions for the rational outcome of the DSG. We may identify and predict the outcome of the game by checking the equilibrium conditions iteratively. However, the constant existence of a fixed-strategy Nash equilibrium may not be ensured since customers interact with each other in a complex way in the D-CRG model [15]. In view of this, we derive an ϵ-optimal Nash equilibrium: a relaxed version of a Nash equilibrium denoted as follows.

DEFINITION 17.3   (ϵ-optimal Nash equilibrium) A strategy profile π^* is an ϵ-optimal Nash equilibrium if and only if

$$E[u(\pi^*(\mathbf{s}))|\mathbf{s}, \pi^*] \geq E[u(d')|\mathbf{s}, \pi^*] - \epsilon, \ \forall d' \in \mathcal{D}, \forall \mathbf{s} \in \mathcal{S}.$$

The ϵ-optimal Nash equilibrium of the DSG can be obtained through a multi-dimensional version of the value iteration algorithm [16], which is illustrated in Algorithm 14.

Fundamentally, Algorithm 14 is an improved value iteration algorithm for the D-CRG. The π^o and W^o are the original policy and expected rewards before the updating process in Steps (4) and (5), and π^n and W^n are the updated values. Specifically, Steps (4) and (5) in Algorithm 14 utilize (17.12) and (17.13) to update

---

Algorithm 14: Multidimensional value iteration.

(1) Initialize π^o, W^o.
(2) **while** 1 **do**
(3)   **for all** s, d **do**
(4) $\pi^n \leftarrow$ (17.13).
(5) $W^n \leftarrow$ (17.12).
(6)   **end for**
(7) $W^d \leftarrow W^n - W^o$
(8)   **if** max W^d − min $W^d < \epsilon$ **then**
(9)   Break.
(10) **else**
(11) $W^o \leftarrow W^n$
(12) **end if**
(13) **end while**
(14) Output π^n and W^n.

---

the policy and expected rewards. The exact form of (17.13) is determined by the choice of utility functions, whereas the exact form of (17.12) hinges on (17.13). W^d is the difference in expected rewards before and after the updates. When the difference in expected rewards is lower than the threshold ϵ, the algorithm terminates.

THEOREM 17.4   *When Algorithm 14 terminates at round n, the ϵ-optimal Nash equilibrium of the DSG is given by π^n.*

Proof   When Algorithm 14 terminates at round n, we have $W^d = W^n - W^o$ and $\max W^d - \min W^d < \epsilon$. We also have

$$\pi^n(\mathbf{s}) = \arg \max_{d \in \mathcal{D}} W^o(\mathbf{s}, d).$$

Given that $\max W^d - \min W^d < \epsilon$, we have

$$W^n(\mathbf{s}, \pi^n(s)) \geq W^n(\mathbf{s}, d) - \epsilon, \forall d \in \mathcal{D},$$

which satisfies Definition 17.3. Therefore, π^n is an ϵ-optimal Nash equilibrium.

It is still possible to have the absence of an ϵ-optimal Nash equilibrium policy when ϵ is small enough. This phenomenon is triggered by the competitive nature of deal selection in this problem. A larger ϵ can ensure the existence of an equilibrium policy but may lead to instability since some choices are suboptimal for certain customers. A smaller ϵ also indicates a longer convergence time. ϵ is determined by the choices of the system administrator in line with their priorities regarding stability or convergence.

17.5   Simulation Results

We first conduct simulations to evaluate the performance of the game-theoretic model by drawing on the Groupon and Yelp data set we constructed in Section 17.2. Specifically, all deals tagged as "Restaurant" and the corresponding Yelp records in the data set are utilized to extract the necessary parameters for the simulations, including user arrival rate, deal online distribution, and the utility function. We model a deal website with four potential vendors. The prices of the deals are $10, $10, $60, and $60, respectively. The maximum sales volume of each deal is 1500, while the sales volume revealed to customers is rounded by 250. The rating of each deal is randomly drawn from $\{3, 4, 5\}$. Based on the aforementioned probability density function, the review w_d of each deal d takes shape as follows:

$$Pr(w_d|r_d) = \begin{cases} p, & w_d = r_d; \\ \frac{1-p}{4}, & \text{else,} \end{cases} \tag{17.16}$$

where p is the accuracy of the review. A higher p indicates a higher probability for the review to represent the real rating of the deal.

The utility function $U(\cdot)$ applied in the simulations is as follows:

$$U(d) = U(r_d, n_d^*, p_d) = f(r_d, n_d^*) - \alpha \cdot p_d, \tag{17.17}$$

Table 17.2. Simulation settings.

Parameter	Value
Maximum # of deals	4
Maximum available deals	2
Maximum quantity of each deal	1500
Average customer arrival rate	13.66 per hour
Average deal online duration	168 hours
Price factor α	0.05

where $f(r_d, n_d^*)$ is the expected rating when the sales volume of deal d amounts to n_d^* and α represents the adjustable price factor. The exact function of $f(\cdot)$ is regressed from the Yelp data set we introduced in Section 17.2. All other parameters, such as the deal arrival process, departure process, and customer arrival process, are also regressed from the data set by calculating the average and variance of the targeting process. The detailed parameter settings are listed in Table 17.2.

In all simulations, the DSG strategy is compared with four other strategies: Random, Minimum Price, Maximum Rating, and Social Optimal. The first three strategies are naive and are regarded as baselines. Customers who apply the Random strategy randomly choose one deal from the available deals upon their arrival, irrespective of the state. For the Minimum Price and Maximum Rating strategies, customers always select the deal with the lowest price and the highest rating, respectively.

$$\pi^{maximum\_rating}(\mathbf{s}[t]) = \arg \max_{d \in \mathcal{D}[t]} E[r_d | \mathbf{s}[t]),$$

$$\pi^{minimum\_price}(\mathbf{s}[t]) = \arg \min_{d \in \mathcal{D}[t]} p_d.$$

The Social Optimal strategy represents the optimal strategy that maximizes overall social welfare, which is defined as the total of the expected utilities of all customers. The Social Optimal strategy can be obtained through solution of the following Bellman equation and strategy profile equation sets:

$$W^{social}(\mathbf{s}) = \sum_{d \in \mathcal{D}} \mu E[U(X, n_d, p_d) | \mathbf{s}] + (1 - \mu) \sum_{\mathbf{s}' \in \mathcal{S}} \frac{Pr(\mathbf{s}' | \mathbf{s}, \pi^{social})}{(1 - \mu)} W^{social}(\mathbf{s}').$$

(17.18)

$$\pi^{social}(\mathbf{s}[t]) \in \arg \max_{d \in \mathcal{D}[t]} Pr(\mathbf{s}' | \mathbf{s}, \pi^{social}) W^{social}|_{n_d' = n_d + 1}.$$

(17.19)

Traditional MDP algorithms will generate this sort of strategy with the reward of social welfare at each state [16]. This strategy represents the optimal strategy preferred by a society that maximizes the sum of utilities of all customers. This strategy is based on the assumption that all customers will follow the strategy irrespective of whether they will be sacrificed for a better social utility. This suggests that certain customers may refrain from following the Social Optimal strategy since they are selfish. Implementation of this strategy requires certain external effects, such as penalties.

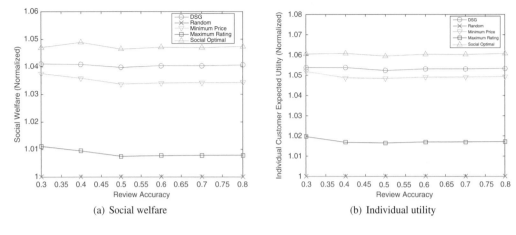

Figure 17.6 Influence of review accuracy.

We will present the performance of the two strategies. The performance gap between the Nash equilibrium and Social Optimal strategies represents the price of anarchy, or the performance degradation caused by the selfish players in the system.

17.5.1   Review Accuracy

We evaluate the social welfare of the system with various deal selection strategies. We adjust the review accuracy from 0.2 to 0.9 in the simulations, and the results are presented in Figure 17.6. Note that the values of each strategy are normalized to those of the Random strategy.

It is shown in Figure 17.6(a) that the DSG strategy remarkably outperforms all other naive strategies, including Random, Minimum Price, and Maximum Rating. The underlying reason for this improvement is that the DSG strategy takes into account the externality effect and the potential state transition. However, compared with the Social Optimal strategy, there is a minor welfare degradation in the DSG strategy, which is the price of anarchy resulting from the noncooperative nature in the DSG.

We evaluate the performance of all strategies in terms of individual customer utility, and the results are presented in Figure 17.6(b). The trend is much the same as that for social welfare, in which the DSG strategy significantly outperforms all naive strategies. Note that customers can obtain clear benefits from the fully rational strategy provided by the DSG.

17.5.2   Arrival Rate

We then evaluate the social welfare of the system under different arrival rates. The arrival rate is adjusted from 10 to 50 customers per hour. The review accuracy is set as 0.8 in this simulation. The results are shown in Figure 17.7. Note that the values of each strategy again are normalized to those of the Random strategy.

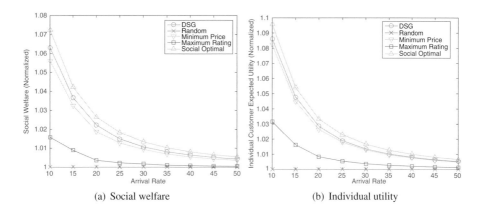

Figure 17.7 Influence of arrival rate.

The trend in Figure 17.7 suggests that the improvements of different strategies over the Random strategy diminish with the increment to the arrival rate. This is due to the limited quantities of all deals. A higher arrival rate indicates that customers are more likely to have fewer deals available for purchase when they arrive at the website. In this case, the difference among strategies diminishes. However, the DSG strategy still outperforms all other naive strategies and has a similar performance to the Social Optimal strategy under all arrival rates.

17.6   Experiments: Are Customers Rational?

Ultimately, we would like to determine whether customers in the real world behave in a fully rational way in the deal selection problem. Several deal selection strategies are applied to each snapshot of the available deals tagged as Restaurant in the Groupon data set. When a snapshot is available, the applied strategy selects a deal from the available ones correspondingly. The prediction is treated as correct when the strategy makes a correct prediction about the deal with the highest sales volume at the next snapshot. When the DSG strategy is applied, we adopt a pairwise comparison method to determine the best deal among all of the available ones. We first randomly divide the deals into pairs. For each pair, one deal is selected in accordance with the trained deal selection model, while the other deal is removed from the set. The process repeats until exactly one deal remains. In this experiment, an interesting case of the rationality of customers – the myopic cases – is also involved. For the deal selection strategy with limited rationality, the myopic strategy serves as a variant. When this strategy is adopted, customers select the deal that maximizes their myopic utilities (i.e., the utility when the deal goes offline as soon as the customer selects it). This strategy represents the case in which customers are aware of their utilities but lack the capability of estimating their impact on the externality in the future.

Table 17.3. Deal selection prediction.

Strategy	Accuracy
Random	0.2777
Maximum Rating	0.2789
Minimum Price	0.3147
Social Optimal	0.3240
Myopic	0.2867
DSG	0.3273

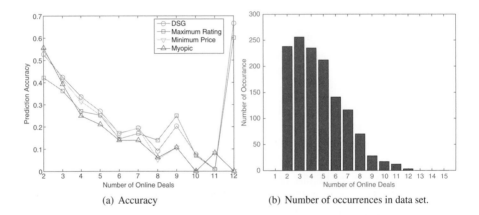

(a) Accuracy   (b) Number of occurrences in data set.

Figure 17.8 Accuracy of predictions.

We compare the prediction accuracy of the DSG strategy – both the myopic and fully rational versions – with those under the Random, Maximum Rating, and Minimum Price strategies. The results are shown in Table 17.3. It can be seen that the DSG strategy has the highest accuracy among all of the strategies, which indicates that it is more likely for customers to select the deals in a fully rational way compared with naive strategies. In addition, the Minimum Price strategy has the highest accuracy among all naive strategies, which implies that customers acquire more knowledge from the prices of the deals than the ratings on other websites.

Figure 17.8(a) presents a detailed analysis of the prediction accuracy given various numbers of deals online simultaneously. It is shown that the DSG strategy outperforms all other strategies in the majority of cases. Furthermore, the Minimum Pricing strategy performs in a similar manner to the DSG strategy when the number of simultaneously available deals is below eight. Note that according to the data set it is also quite common to have fewer than eight Restaurant-type deals available online, as is illustrated in Figure 17.8(b). However, the Maximum Rating strategy outperforms the Minimum Pricing strategy with increasing numbers of online deals. This may indicate that when the number of online deals increases, users may be inclined to seek more information so as to compare the quality of the deals. In contrast, when there is a limited number of deals available, customers may prefer to select a deal simply according to the price. The DSG strategy can take advantage of both naive strategies and predictions about the externality of the deals and performs best on average as a result.

However, the DSG strategy is still inaccurate to some extent, which also indicates that there is plenty of room for customers to optimize their decisions with the proper assistance. The DSG deal selection strategy may serve as a deal suggestion tool for assisting customers with the correct identification of the price, rating, and externality effects on the experienced quality of the deal. Such assistance will improve the utility of the customer as well as overall social welfare. In addition, the DSG strategy represents a Nash equilibrium, which is compatible with the selfish nature of the customers who seek to maximize their utility. A Nash equilibrium is considered to be a desirable outcome since it represents a predicted outcome when all customers show selfish behavior, given the maximization of all customers' utility. This indicates that a customer, even though they may be selfish, will embrace this strategy. Put another way, it requires less effort to guide the customers to follow such a strategy.

Owing to the lack of corresponding Yelp records, this experiment had to exclude many deals from the data set, which is one of its limitations. This may have led to bias in the experimental results since those deals with valid Yelp records suggest that the vendors have made some effort in terms of their promotion. Including more information sources is likely to be helpful, such as reviews on Google Maps or discussions on Twitter. However, some deals may still have no records on any third-party websites if the vendors are newcomers. In this case, we lack objective information sources for analyzing the ways in which customers gather information and their experiences regarding the deal. Analyzing customers' reactions to deals when no public reviews are available remains an unsolved problem.

17.7   Conclusion

In this chapter, a game-theoretic social learning framework was proposed to model the rational deal selection behavior in Groupon with external information from Yelp. A stochastic learning model based on the CRG was utilized to understand how rational customers select a deal according to their knowledge of external reviews and their concerns regarding the externality caused by other customers. A social media experiment that lasted for a year was conducted to trace the competition among deals on Groupon and the impact on the corresponding ratings in Yelp records. On the basis of the learning model and the social media data set, we analyzed the DSG on a deal website in a realistic setting. Simulations were conducted to evaluate the performance of the DSG framework. It was shown that compared with naive strategies, the DSG framework significantly improved social welfare and customer utility. A further discussion was carried out on the rationality of customers in deal selection based on the comparison of the simulation results with real data. According to the results, customer do make rational decisions instead of following naive strategies, but there is still room for the enhancement of the accuracy of their decisions with the help of the DSG framework.

17.8   Literature Review

The information cascade in a social network is a popular topic in social learning. More often than not, users in a social network lack global knowledge of the system state, but they may draw on some local and noisy signals to gain information. In order to reach a consensus on the state/opinion/decision, the users may exchange their information or observe the signals or actions revealed by others. Information cascade occurs when some locally revealed signals, perhaps only consisting of a small portion of the total number of signals, are sufficiently strong to dominate any other unrevealed signals. In this scenario, the global consensus will be determined by a minority of signals revealed, and these signals are likely to be biased since the majority of signals are excluded. Social learning refers to the research on how agents reach a consensus (or not) through social learning in sequential decision processes. A significant part of the existing research in this area [10,12,13,17] is based on the assumption that network externality is excluded; put another way, the actions of subsequent agents do not alter the payoffs of previous agents. In this case, agents will make their decisions purely on the basis of their own beliefs regardless of the actions of subsequent agents.

In the case in which externality does play a part in the payoffs of the users, information cascade is confronted with a more serious challenge since users' decision-making is susceptible to the impacts of others. An extreme case arises when the effect of negative externality is so strong that all users would radically abandon the potential choices and even prevent others from choosing. An application of this is the ad-free websites in which all companies may pay the website not to release any advertisements of their rivals [18].

One significant research orientation in this field is to determine the scheduling (i.e., the sequence urging the nodes to make decisions) so as to guard against undesired information cascade [19]. According to an updated study, an opinion that is expected to be popular is usually difficult to be reversed in information cascade, even though the scheduling can be determined in advance [20]. Most relevant works in this field take myopic users into account, which follow a simple myopic strategy irrespective of the expected future outcomes and externalities from subsequent users. When strategic users are involved (i.e., the users are now aware of the expected outcome in the final stage), then the outcome of the network could be either better or worse than that of the myopic user case, depending on the graph structure [21]. For the case of a dynamic state, further effort is required in order to ensure that the network will reach the correct consensus. Discussions can be found in [22] on how users cooperate to actively trace the changing state in an incomplete graph. In the case in which it is difficult for the graph to maintain the correct consensus, users achieve error reduction by incorporating new links or relationships into the graph. There are also various approaches to information cascade in machine learning. For instance, active learning is also applicable to the system from a global viewpoint. A trainer first defines an objective function or the goals of all users. Users in the network pass on their information collaboratively to maximize the objective function. A practical application of this approach is intruder detection in sensor networks, where it is essential for sensors in an incomplete graph to reach a consensus on whether an intruder is detected or not [23].

It remains a serious challenge to understand how rational human beings in the real world make decisions or respond to external issues. Game theory gives shape to a well-established mathematical framework, but it is usually too difficult to grasp all of the important characteristics in the real world. Machine learning plays a useful role in capturing the hidden relations between strategic decisions and inputs based on relatively simple decision-making models through training. The received models can assist in the verification of whether human beings do behave rationally in line with the assumptions in game theory. In addition, trained models can also provide game-theoretic models with certain feedback, such as a refinement to the original utility function. Some empirical studies have been conducted in this field. It has been shown that human beings may behave more cooperatively when they are in a repeated game and have previous experience in similar scenarios. However, they may also show selfish behavior if they have experienced betrayal previously [24]. It has also been shown that normal people have very limited memory and are unable to conduct complex strategic planning. Such limitations result in suboptimal decisions [25]. Such limited memory is also confirmed by another experiment in which it was found that human beings tend to ignore old signals in decision-making [26]. Nevertheless, when it comes to a large-scale system such as the Taobao shopping system, accuracy for predicting the decisions made by real humans is still low if only traditional machine learning algorithms are applied [27].

References

[1] U. Dholakia, "How effective are Groupon promotions for businesses?" Technical Report, Mimeo, Rice University, 2010.

[2] F. Chen, D. Joshi, Y. Miura, and T. Ohkuma, "Social media-based profiling of business locations," in *Proc. 3rd ACM MM Workshop on Geotagging and Its Applications in Multimedia*, 2014.

[3] M. Katz and C. Shapiro, "Technology adoption in the presence of network externalities," *Journal of Political Economy*, vol. 94, pp. 822–841, 1986.

[4] W. Sandholm, "Negative externalities and evolutionary implementation," *Review of Economic Studies*, vol. 72, pp. 885–915, 2005.

[5] G. Fagiolo, "Endogenous neighborhood formation in a local coordination model with negative network externalities," *Journal of Economic Dynamics and Control*, vol. 29, pp. 297–319, 2005.

[6] D. Oppenheimer, A. Ganapathi, and D. A. Patterson, "Why do Internet services fail, and what can be done about it?" in *Proc. 4th Conference on USENIX Symposium on Internet Technologies and Systems – Volume 4*, 2003.

[7] J. W. Byers, M. Mitzenmacher, and G. Zervas, "Daily deals: prediction, social diffusion, and reputational ramifications," in *Proc. fifth ACM International Conference on Web Search and Data Mining*, 2012.

[8] J. W. Byers, M. Mitzenmacher, and G. Zervas, "The Groupon effect on Yelp ratings: A root cause analysis," in *Proc. 13th ACM Conference on Electronic commerce (EC)*, 2012.

[9] T. A. Hosaka, "Groupon CEO apologizes to Japanese customers," https://phys.org/news/2011-01-groupon-ceo-japanese-customers.html.

[10] V. Bala and S. Goyal, "Learning from neighbours," *Review of Economic Studies*, vol. 65, pp. 595–621, 1998.

[11] B. Golub and M. O. Jackson, "Naive learning in social networks: convergence, influence, and the wisdom of crowds," https://web.stanford.edu/~jacksonm/naivelearning.pdf.

[12] D. Acemoglu, M. Dahleh, I. Lobel, and A. Ozdaglar, "Bayesian learning in social networks," *Review of Economic Studies*, vol. 78, pp. 1201–1236, 2011.

[13] D. Acemoglu and A. Ozdaglar, "Opinion dynamics and learning in social networks," *Dynamic Games and Applications*, vol. 1, pp. 3–49, 2011.

[14] C. Jiang, Y. Chen, Y.-H. Yang, C.-Y. Wang, and K. J. R. Liu, "Dynamic Chinese restaurant game: theory and application to cognitive radio networks," *IEEE Transactions on Wireless Communications*, vol. 13, pp. 1960–1973, 2014.

[15] Y.-H. Yang, Y. Chen, C. Jiang, C.-Y. Wang, and K. J. R. Liu, "Wireless access network selection game with negative network externality," *IEEE Transactions on Wireless Communications*, vol. 12, pp. 5048–5060, 2013.

[16] C. Y. Wang, Y. Chen, H. Y. Wei, and K. J. R. Liu, "Scalable video multicasting: A stochastic game approach with optimal pricing," *IEEE Transactions on Wireless Communications*, vol. 14, pp. 2353–2367, 2015.

[17] B. Golub and M. O. Jackson, "Naive learning in social networks and the wisdom of crowds," *American Economic Journal: Microeconomics*, vol. 2, pp. 112–149, 2010.

[18] C. Deng and S. Pekec, "Money for nothing: exploiting negative externalities," in *Proc. 12th ACM Conference on Electronic Commerce (EC)*, 2011.

[19] F. Chierichetti, J. Kleinberg, and A. Panconesi, "How to schedule a cascade in an arbitrary graph," in *Proc. 13th ACM Conference on Electronic Commerce (EC)*, 2012.

[20] M. Hajiaghayi, H. Mahini, and D. Malec, "The polarizing effect of network influences," in *Proc. 15th ACM Conference on Economics and Computation (EC)*, 2014.

[21] T. Martin, G. Schoenebeck, and M. Wellman, "Characterizing strategic cascades on networks," in *Proc. 15th ACM Conference on Economics and Computation (EC)*, 2014.

[22] S. Shahrampour, A. Jadbabaie, and A. Rakhlin, "Online learning of dynamic parameters in social networks," in *Advances in Neural Information Processing Systems (NIPS)*, 2013.

[23] M.-F. F. Balcan, C. Berlind, A. Blum, E. Cohen, K. Patnaik, and L. Song, "Active learning and best-response dynamics," in *Advances in Neural Information Processing Systems (NIPS)*, 2014.

[24] W. Mason, S. Suri, and D. J. Watts, "Long-run learning in games of cooperation," in *Proc. 15th ACM Conference on Economics and Computation (EC)*, 2014.

[25] D. Fudenberg and A. Peysakhovich, "Recency, records and recaps: learning and non-equilibrium behavior in a simple decision problem," in *Proc. 15th ACM Conference on Economics and Computation (EC)*, 2014.

[26] S. Zhang and A. J. Yu, "Forgetful Bayes and myopic planning: human learning and decision-making in a bandit setting," in *Advances in Neural Information Processing Systems (NIPS)*, 2013.

[27] S. Guo, M. Wang, and J. Leskovec, "The role of social networks in online shopping: information passing, price of trust, and consumer choice," in *Proc. 12th ACM Conference on Electronic Commerce (EC)*, 2011.

18 Social Computing

Answer vs. Vote

It is of great importance to understand how users participate in social computing systems since their values are determined by the contributions of users. In many social computing systems, users make sequential decisions on participation or non-participation and, if they decide to participate, whether to offer a piece of content in a straightforward way (i.e., answering) or to rate the existing content contributed by previous users (i.e., voting). Furthermore, there exists an answering–voting externality due to the fact that a user's utility for answering hinges on votes received in the subsequent period. In this chapter, we introduce a game-theoretic model that formulates the sequential decision-making of strategic users in the presence of this answering–voting externality. We present the theoretical proof of the existence and uniqueness of a pure-strategy equilibrium. To deepen the understandings of the equilibrium participation of users, we show that users who have greater abilities and offer their answers earlier can enjoy certain advantages. Consequently, the equilibrium displays a threshold structure and the threshold for answering gradually increases along with the accumulation of answers. We further extend the results to a more general setting in which users can choose endogenously their efforts for answering. To show the effectiveness of the game-theoretic model, we analyze users' behaviors with data gathered from a popular Q&A site Stack Overflow and show that the major qualitative predictions of the game-theoretic model match up with observations based on the data. Finally, we formulate the system designer's problem and derive from numerical simulations several design principles that offer potential guidance to the design of incentive mechanisms for social computing systems in practice.

18.1   Introduction

Social computing systems refer to online applications in which voluntary users contribute to their value. Today, the rapid advancement of social media has facilitated people's participation in online activities and their contribution to online content, which has led to a proliferation of social computing systems on the Web. Successful illustrations can be found in a wide range of domains, from question-and-answer (Q&A) sites such as Yahoo! Answers, Stack Overflow, or Quora where users solve questions asked by other users; to online reviews such as the product reviews on Amazon, restaurant reviews on Yelp, or movie reviews on Rotten Tomatoes; to social news sites such as Digg or Reddit, where online users post and promote stories under a variety of categories. These applications contribute to the usefulness of the Web by enabling large-scale high-quality user-generated content (UGC) and by providing easy access to UGC. Due to the fact that the value of social computing systems comes mostly from user contributions, it is of great importance for such system designers to acquire knowledge of the ways in which users participate in and interact with their sites.

User participation in social computing systems can take various forms. In addition to creating UGC directly by, for example, answering a question on Stack Overflow or writing a product review on Amazon, an increasingly large portion of social computing systems now allow users to participate by rating existing contributions on the site. For instance, instead of answering a question, users on Stack Overflow have the alternative of either voting up or down the answers posted by other users. Similarly, users on Amazon have the alternative of marking other users' reviews as useful or not. Such an indirect form of user participation plays multiple roles in social computing systems. First, voting offers essential information concerning the quality and popularity of contributions from users. Many social computing systems such as Stack Overflow, Quora, and Reddit rank and display users' contributions based on their received votes. What is more, the mechanism of voting also strongly motivates users to participate in a direct way and generate high-quality UGC. There are two sorts of incentives for users: the expectation of peer recognition and the virtual points offered by the system as a reward for every positive vote they receive. For instance, it is known that received votes is the main source of reputation points for the majority of users on Stack Overflow [1]. This chapter focuses on such incentive effects of voting mechanisms on user contributions. In particular, we investigate how the voting behavior of users might affect the quantity and quality of UGC in social computing systems. More generally, we will adopt Q&A terminology and refer to the action of creating UGC directly as "answering" hereinafter.

In terms of the simulation and analysis of the close interaction between answering and voting, it is essential to be aware that users participate in social computing systems sequentially rather than simultaneously. We may imagine, for instance, a question to be answered on a Q&A site. Potential contributors view the question in sequence and decide whether to participate based on observations of the history of the question. If users decide to participate, they can further choose to answer the question in a straightforward manner with potentially different levels of effort or to vote on existing answers contributed by previous users. Furthermore, the actions of future users strongly influence a current user's payoff since the payoff for answering the question is determined by the votes that the answer is to receive. What can we know in this sequential setting about the externality incurred by the voting choices made by future users on the current user's answering action? And given the presence of this sort of externality, how can we model and analyze sequential user behavior in social computing systems? Finally, how should designers of social computing systems adjust their incentive mechanisms to steer user behavior toward achieving different system objectives?

We address these questions from a game-theoretic perspective. We propose a sequential game model that captures the strategic decision-making of users who arrive sequentially and choose endogenously whether to participate or not, and if they choose to participate, whether to answer the question or to vote on existing answers. Users who choose voting are allowed to either vote up or vote down on an answer according to the quality of the answer. Users who answer the question will receive a certain amount of virtual points for each upvote their answers receive and lose virtual points for every downvote received, which constitutes a kind of externality among users known as the answering–voting externality. We further incorporate into the sequential game model two typical scenarios in social computing. In the first scenario, involving questions on focused Q&A sites such as Stack Overflow, the quality of an answer depends primarily on the domain knowledge and the professional level of a user. Therefore, we consider a homogeneous effort model in which the quality of an answer is a function of a user's ability and the cost incurred by answering is assumed to be uniform among users. The second scenario corresponds to a more general setting in which users can significantly upgrade their answers with greater effort. In this case, it is assumed that if the users decide to answer the question, they can also determine endogenously the amount of effort they are willing to exert. As a result, the quality of an answer is shaped into a function that comprises two elements: a user's ability and the effort they exert. The cost incurred by answering is also modeled as a function of a user's effort. This model is defined as the endogenous effort model.

We then analyze the sequential user behavior based on equilibrium analysis of the sequential game. We start with the homogeneous effort model. The solution concept of a symmetric subgame-perfect equilibrium (SSPE) is adopted, and it is shown that there is always a unique pure-strategy SSPE for the sequential game. To further investigate the equilibrium user behavior, it is essential to understand the answering–voting externality, which is represented by the long-term expected reward for answering. We show that such a reward increases with greater answer quality and directly contributes to a threshold structure of the equilibrium. This sort of threshold structure significantly reduces the action space of users at the equilibrium and enables us to develop a dynamic programming algorithm to calculate the equilibrium with efficiency. Furthermore, the reward for answering is also found to decrease with increasing numbers of previous answers, which demonstrates an advantage of posting an early answer. Consequently, with the accumulation of answers, answering the question becomes increasingly competitive, which is reflected in the gradually increasing thresholds of users' ability to answer. We then shift our attention to the endogenous effort model, in which we show that the results from the homogeneous effort model grasp the essence of the sequential game and can be extended naturally to the incorporation of a more general setting.

Third, after developing a sequential game-theoretic model and analyzing user behavior based on equilibrium analysis, we investigate how qualitative predictions are derived from the game-theoretic model in comparison with aggregated user behavior on a large-scale social computing site. To this end, we draw on user behavior data from Stack Overflow, one of the most popular Q&A sites, to evaluate the game-theoretic model. We find that the main qualitative predictions about the game-theoretic model are in line with the observations based on the real-world data, which represents a validation of the model.

Finally, we study how system designers can utilize the game-theoretic model to assist them in designing incentive mechanisms (i.e., the allocation of virtual points) in practice. The system designer's problem is formalized by a general utility function that can be designed to integrate multiple typical use case scenarios. From numerical simulations, we extract several design principles that can offer guidance to system designers on the way to steer user behavior to achieve a great variety of system objectives. Studies are also carried out on other influencing factors, such as the effects of user distributions on a system designer's utility.

18.2   System Model

Let us consider a single task that solicits contributions from users on a social computing site. This sort of task can take a variety of forms, such as, a question on an online Q&A forum, a product/restaurant on Amazon/Yelp for which users can post their reviews, or a tourist site on Tripadvisor where users can share their experience. In the subsequent sections of the chapter, we will adopt the terminology of Q&A scenarios such as questions and answers for ease of discussion, while the results are equally applicable to other social computing systems as well.

It is assumed that there is a countable infinite set of potential users, presented as $\mathcal{N} = \{1, 2, 3, \ldots\}$, who browse and are likely to contribute to the question. Users arrive in sequence and choose strategically to either answer the question, vote on an existing solution, or not to participate. This is denoted by $\Theta = \{A, V, N\}$, the action set where A refers to answering, V to voting, and N to not participating.

Users belong to different types, which influence their choices of actions. We represent the type of a user as a tuple of two elements: $\sigma = (\sigma_A, \sigma_V)$. The first element, $\sigma_A \in [0, 1]$, indicates the ability or professional level of a user with regard to the question. A user with a higher value of σ_A is endowed with greater capability of answering the question than a user with a lower value. The second element, $\sigma_V \in [V_{min}, V_{max}]$, models the degree to which a user would like to express their opinions through voting, known as the voting preference. σ_V can have either positive or negative values; the larger the value of σ_V a user has, the more they favor voting.

User types σ are independent and identically distributed according to a distribution with a cumulative distribution function $F(\sigma_A, \sigma_V)$. Such a distribution is assumed to be known by the general public, whereas the instantiation of type is kept only to a user themself. We further assume F is atomless on its support.

Action N is the most straightforward one among the three possible actions. A user who chooses action N will simply evade the question silently without exerting any impact on the state of the question. Users who incur no cost by choosing action N will not receive any reward from the system either. We now give a full description of the other two actions.

The answering action: Users who choose action A will submit answers of varying quality. We present the quality of an answer as $q \in [0, 1]$, which stands for the probability of an answer being favored by a future user.

For the answering action, we consider two typical scenarios in social computing. In the first scenario, involving questions on focused Q&A sites such as Stack Overflow, the quality of an answer depends primarily on the domain knowledge and the professional level of a user. The cost of answer creation is incurred mainly by the transcription of a user's knowledge and is therefore uniform among users. In the second scenario, on the other hand, users can improve their answers with greater effort, which results in a higher cost. For instance, by exerting a considerable deal of effort, most users can report desirable reviews on Amazon or interesting travel notes on Tripadvisor. We formally capture these two scenarios through the homogeneous effort and endogenous effort models as follows:

(1) *Homogeneous effort model:* In the homogeneous effort model, the quality of an answer is determined purely by a user's ability σ_A. Without loss of generality, we assume that $q = \sigma_A$. All users spend the same cost on answering but the cost is likely to be determined by the number of existing answers m. $c(m)$ is applied to symbolize the cost, and assume

  (i) $c(m)$ is nondecreasing in m (i.e., it may be harder to provide a novel answer to a question that has more answers than one that has fewer answers); and

  (ii) $c(0) > 0$ (i.e., answering a question, even when there are no existing answers, incurs some cost).

  A simple example is $c(m) = c > 0$ (i.e., there is a constant cost for answering the question).

(2) *Endogenous effort model:* In the endogenous effort model, conditional on choosing action A, a user will also decide the amount of effort $e \in [0, 1]$ that they will exert to create the answer. The quality of an answer becomes a function of two elements: a user's ability σ_A and their effort e, which we write as $q = \phi(\sigma_A, e)$. ϕ is assumed to show a monotonic increase in both σ_A and e. The cost incurred by answering is denoted by $c(m, e)$, which is assume to be strictly greater than 0 and nondecreasing in m and e.

In the following, we will initially focus on the homogeneous effort model, which improves our understanding of the essence of the game. In other words, we assume $q = \sigma_A$ and regard $c(m)$ as the cost of answering. Then in Section 18.4 we extend the results to the endogenous effort case. The gain for answering a question is generated by the reward available in the system, which is connected with the voting actions of future users and will be discussed later in this section.

The voting action: Users can choose action V if there is at least one existing answer to the question (i.e., $m > 0$). It is assumed that once a user decides to vote, they tend to choose a random answer with equal probability upon which to cast their vote. Users can choose either to vote up or to vote down an answer according to the answer quality.

In particular, if the chosen answer has quality q, then for the user the probability of voting up is q and that of voting down is $1 - q$. The utility of a user with type σ who chooses action V can be presented as $\sigma_V + R_V - C_V$. Recall that σ_V is the internal preference of a user toward voting. When $\sigma_V < 0$ it indicates that the user dislikes voting and more incentives are required to stimulate their voting. R_V stands for the reward offered by the system. More generally, it is assumed that it is possible for R_V to have a negative values which models the case in which the system discourages voting by charging users for voting. $C_V > 0$ denotes the cost incurred by users for casting a vote (e.g., the effort of evaluating the quality of an answer).

The answering action and the voting action are connected through an incentive mechanism that is established with virtual points. In particular, if a user chooses action A, they will receive R_u points for every upvote received by their answer and lose R_d points for every downvote received. Consequently, R_u and R_d, together with R_V give a definition of the mechanism in the model, which connects the answering with the voting actions of users, determines the equilibrium of the game, and offers the system designer a tool for incentivizing desired user behavior.

Action rule and utility: An action rule describes how a user will play when any possible situation is provided in the game. We utilize the number of existing answers m to symbolize the state of the game, which serves as a summary of the history of the question. When a user is confronted with the question, they first observe the state of the question and then choose their action according to the state as well as their own type σ. More generally, our assumption includes mixed actions. In other words, a user will choose a probability distribution over the action set Θ instead of a single action item. As a consequence, a user's action rule in the game is a mapping from m and σ to a probability distribution over Θ. The action rule in the model is denoted by

$$\pi(m, \sigma) = [\pi_A(m, \sigma), \pi_V(m, \sigma), \pi_N(m, \sigma)],$$

where $\pi_\theta(m, \sigma)$ with $\theta \in \Theta$ represents the probability of choosing action θ and thus $\pi_A(m, \sigma) + \pi_V(m, \sigma) + \pi_N(m, \sigma) = 1$.

Given an action rule π, the probability of a random user choosing action A at state m can be calculated as $P_\pi^A(m) = \mathbb{E}_\sigma[\pi_A(m, \sigma)]$, where the expectation is taken over the distribution of user types. Similarly, the probability of voting can be represented as $P_\pi^V(m) = \mathbb{E}_\sigma[\pi_V(m, \sigma)]$. Figure 18.1 shows the state transitions of the game given an action rule π.

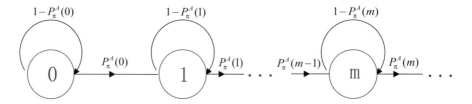

Figure 18.1 The state transition of the game.

Users are assumed to be impatient and prefer to receive their reward as soon as possible, which is modeled by discounting the future with a constant factor $\delta \in (0,1)$. Such a modeling approach is a standard practice that enjoys extensive application in the economics literature [2]. Initially, we determine the reward a user can receive by answering the question, which is generated by future users' votes, so that we are in a position to understand the utility of users. Let $g_\pi(m,q)$ denote the long-term expected reward of a user who produces the mth answer with quality q given that the action rule π will be adopted by future users. This sort of function will be referred to as the reward function for answering or simply as the reward function hereinafter. Note that $g_\pi(m,q)$ is defined only for $m \geq 1$. An expression for $g_\pi(m,q)$ can be denoted as follows:

$$g_\pi(m,q) = \frac{P_\pi^V(m)}{m}[(R_u + R_d)q - R_d]$$

$$+ \delta[P_\pi^A(m)g_\pi(m+1,q) + (1 - P_\pi^A(m))g_\pi(m,q)]. \qquad (18.1)$$

The first term in (18.1) corresponds to the immediate reward, where $\frac{P_\pi^V(m)}{m}$ represents the probability of receiving a vote and $(R_u + R_d)q - R_d = R_u q - R_d(1 - q)$ is the expected reward for receiving a vote. The second term stands for the future reward, which is determined by the state transitions of the game.

On the grounds that the reward for answering is generated by future votes, the utility of a user hinges not only on the number of existing answers, their own type, and their action, but also on the action rule adopted by future users. Such a dependence triggers an answering–voting externality among users and encourages users to condition their decision-making on other users' action rules. Evaluation of the utility of a user is conducted based on the assumption that other users adopt a uniform action rule, which is adequate for the analysis of symmetric outcomes. In particular, we present $u(m,\sigma,\theta,\tilde{\pi})$ as the utility of a user who has type σ and who chooses the pure action $\theta \in \Theta$ when there are m existing answers and other users adopt $\tilde{\pi}$ as their action rule. We have

$$u(m,\sigma,\theta,\tilde{\pi}) = \begin{cases} -c(m) + \delta g_{\tilde{\pi}}(m+1,\sigma_A) & \text{if } \theta = A \\ \sigma_V + R_V - C_V & \text{if } \theta = V \text{ and } m > 0 \\ 0 & \text{if } \theta = N. \end{cases} \qquad (18.2)$$

Note that we need to multiply the reward for answering by δ since the current user will receive their reward at the beginning of the next time slot.

Modifying the notations to a certain extent, we write $u(m,\sigma,\pi,\tilde{\pi})$ as the utility of a user who adopts the action rule π. In accordance with the definition of action rule, we have

$$u(m,\sigma,\pi,\tilde{\pi}) = \sum_{\theta \in \Theta} \pi_\theta(m,\sigma) \cdot u(m,\sigma,\theta,\tilde{\pi}).$$

Solution concept: In the social computing game, users arrive and make decisions in a sequential manner. Based on the fact that there is a countable infinite set of potential users, the social computing game is a sequential game with an infinite horizon. Studies will be conducted on the game with the solution concept of an SSPE. A subgame-perfect equilibrium is a common refinement of the Nash equilibrium in sequential games. It ensures that all players choose strategies in a rational way in every possible subgame. A subgame is a part of the original game. In social computing settings, a subgame can be formally defined as follows:

DEFINITION 18.1   A subgame in the social computing game starts with a state m and consists of all of the remaining parts of the original game.

An SSPE is an action rule such that if all other users adopt it, then no single user will have an incentive to deviate from it in any subgame. We formally define the SSPE for the social computing game as follows:

DEFINITION 18.2   An action rule $\hat{\pi}$ is a SSPE of the social computing game if and only if

$$\hat{\pi} \in \arg\max_{\pi} u(m, \sigma, \pi, \hat{\pi}) \quad \forall m \geq 0, \sigma \in [0,1] \times [V_{min}, V_{max}]. \tag{18.3}$$

Although it is well known that every finite sequential game with perfect information has at least one subgame-perfect equilibrium [3], the existence of an SSPE is not a certainty for sequential games with an infinite horizon, which is the case discussed here. To show the definite validity of an SSPE as a solution concept for social computing settings, we prove in the next section that there is always a unique SSPE for the social computing game that has a threshold structure at every state and is therefore easy for users to follow.

18.3   Equilibrium Analysis

In this section, we conduct an equilibrium analysis of the social computing game to understand the ways in which users participate sequentially in the presence of answering–voting externality. In particular, the answering–voting externality is denoted by the reward function for answering, which is key to the analysis of the social computing game. Consequently, we will first investigate certain properties of the reward function for answering. These properties enable us to establish the existence and uniqueness as well as the threshold structure of the SSPE. We will then propose a dynamic programming algorithm that is applicable to obtaining the SSPE in an efficient way and conduct further discussions of the properties of the SSPE.

Initially, we show that for any action rule π, the reward function g_π can be upper bounded by a decreasing function of m, as illustrated in Proposition 18.3.

PROPOSITION 18.3   For any action rule π, we have

$$g_\pi(m, q) \leq \frac{(R_u + R_d)q - R_d}{(1 - \delta)m} \quad \forall m \geq 1, q \in [0,1]. \tag{18.4}$$

Proof We prove Proposition 18.3 by invoking another equivalent expression of $g_\pi(m,q)$ that follows its definition directly as

$$g_\pi(m,q) = \mathbb{E}\left\{\sum_{t=0}^{\infty} \delta^t \frac{P_\pi^V(Y_t)}{Y_t}[(R_u + R_d)q - R_d]\,\middle|\, m, \pi\right\},\qquad (18.5)$$

where the expectation is taken over the randomness of user types and action rules. The time slot is indexed by t and $t = 0$ stands for the current time slot. We denote by $\{Y_t\}_{t=0}^{\infty}$ the discrete random process of the state. Conditional on the current state m, we have $Y_0 = m$. By relaxing (18.5) we have

$$g_\pi(m,q) \le \mathbb{E}\left\{\sum_{t=0}^{\infty} \delta^t \frac{1}{Y_t}[(R_u + R_d)q - R_d]\,\middle|\, m, \pi\right\}.\qquad (18.6)$$

Note that in (18.6), the term inside the expectation decreases in terms of the value of Y_t. Consequently, given the current state m, $\{Y_t = m\}_{t=0}^{\infty}$ achieves the highest value among all realizations of $\{Y_t\}_{t=0}^{\infty}$. Therefore, we have

$$g_\pi(m,q) \le \left\{\sum_{t=0}^{\infty} \delta^t \frac{1}{m}[(R_u + R_d)q - R_d]\right\} = \frac{(R_u + R_d)q - R_d}{(1 - \delta)m}.\qquad (18.7)$$

Based on the results of Proposition 18.3, we show in Lemma 18.4 that no user will choose to answer the question if the number of existing answers is sufficiently large.

LEMMA 18.4 *Upon arrival at a certain state, no users will be motivated to choose action A, irrespective of other users' action rules.*

Proof Let us consider a user's utility of choosing action A. For any action rule $\tilde{\pi}$, we have

$$u(m, \sigma, A, \tilde{\pi}) \le -c(m) + \delta \frac{(R_u + R_d)\sigma_A - R_d}{(1 - \delta)(m + 1)}\qquad (18.8)$$

$$\le -c(m) + \frac{\delta R_u}{(1 - \delta)(m + 1)}.\qquad (18.9)$$

The inequality in (18.8) follows from Proposition 18.3. Note that the right-hand expression in (18.9) is strictly decreasing in m and

$$\lim_{m \to \infty}\left\{-c(m) + \frac{\delta R_u}{(1 - \delta)(m + 1)}\right\} \le -c(0) < 0.\qquad (18.10)$$

Consequently, there exists $\tilde{m} \ge 0$ such that $\forall m \ge \tilde{m}$, and we have

$$u(m, \sigma, A, \tilde{\pi}) < 0 = u(m, \sigma, N, \tilde{\pi}),$$

which implies that action A is strictly dominated by action N and thus users will have no incentive to choose action A.

Lemma 18.4 shows that the state in the social computing game will stop its growth after a certain value. As a result, the last state becomes an absorbing state, which represents the maximum number of answers that a question can possibly have. On account of the existence of such an absorbing state, we can then establish the existence of an SSPE, as is demonstrated in Theorem 18.5.

THEOREM 18.5   *There always exists an SSPE for the social computing game with homogeneous effort.*

Proof   We explicitly construct an SSPE action rule $\hat{\pi}$ to present the existence result. From Lemma 18.4, we know that there exists $\tilde{m} \geq 0$ such that $\forall m \geq \tilde{m}$, and we have $u(m, \sigma, A, \tilde{\pi}) < 0 = u(m, \sigma, N, \tilde{\pi})$

For $m \geq \tilde{m}$, we choose $\hat{\pi}$ such that $\pi_V(m, \sigma) = \mathbf{1}(\sigma_V + R_V - C_V \geq 0)$, $\pi_N(m, \sigma) = 1 - \pi_V(m, \sigma)$, and $\pi_A(m, \sigma) = 0$. We can validate that this particular choice of $\hat{\pi}$ is the best response of users for state $m \geq \tilde{m}$ independent of other users' action rules. For $m < \tilde{m}$, we construct $\hat{\pi}$ using backward induction. Recall from (18.2) that a user's utility at state m depends on other users' action rules only for states starting from $m + 1$. Put another way, the modification of other users' action rules for states $m' \leq m$ exerts no impact on a user's best response at state m. On the basis of this observation, we iteratively set $\hat{\pi}$ from $m = \tilde{m} - 1$ to 0 as the best response of users given by

$$\hat{\pi}(m, \sigma) \in \arg\max_{\pi} u(m, \sigma, \pi, \hat{\pi}). \tag{18.11}$$

We can verify that the constructed action rule $\hat{\pi}$ satisfies (18.3) and is therefore a valid SSPE, which proves the existence of an SSPE.

Upon the establishment of the existence of an SSPE, we can derive a tighter bound on $g_{\hat{\pi}}$ and the absorbing state for SSPE action rules, as demonstrated in Corollary 18.6.

COROLLARY 18.6   *If $\hat{\pi}$ is an SSPE action rule, then*

$$g_{\pi}(m, q) \leq \frac{P_V[(R_u + R_d)q - R_d]}{(1 - \delta)m} \quad \forall m \geq 1, q \in [0, 1], \tag{18.12}$$

where $P_V = \mathbb{E}_{\sigma}[\mathbf{1}(\sigma_V + R_V - C_V \geq 0)]$.

Proof   Corollary 18.6 can be proved in a similar way to Proposition 18.3. The only necessary modification is to apply a tighter bound to $P_{\hat{\pi}}^V$ (i.e., $P_{\hat{\pi}}^V \leq P_V$), since in an SSPE users will choose action V only if their utility for voting is above 0.

COROLLARY 18.7   *If $\hat{\pi}$ is an SSPE action rule, then $\hat{\pi}_A(m, \sigma) = 0$, $\forall m \geq \overline{m}, \sigma \in [0, 1] \times [V_{min}, V_{max}]$, where $\overline{m} = \lceil m^* \rceil$ such that $c(m^*) = \frac{\delta P_V R_u}{(1-\delta)(m^*+1)}$.*

Proof   Corollary 18.7 can be proved following the same steps as those in Lemma 18.4 and applying the tighter bound of $g_{\hat{\pi}}$ given by Corollary 18.6.

Next, we show that given an arbitrary action rule π (not necessarily an SSPE), the reward received by a higher-quality answer almost always turns out to be larger than that of a lower-quality answer. Proposition 18.8 presents a summary of the results.

PROPOSITION 18.8   Given an action rule π and $m \geq 1$, $g_{\pi}(m, q)$ is a continuous function of q. Moreover, $g_{\pi}(m, q)$ either equals 0 for all $q \in [0, 1]$ or is strictly increasing in q.

Proof Let us consider the time series expression of $g_\pi(m,q)$ in (18.5). Since the expectation is irrelevant to q, we have

$$g_\pi(m,q) = \mathbb{E}\left\{ \sum_{t=0}^{\infty} \delta^t \frac{P_\pi^V(Y_t)}{Y_t} \middle| m, \pi \right\} [(R_u + R_d)q - R_d], \qquad (18.13)$$

which is linear in q and thus a continuous function of q. Moreover, we have

$$\mathbb{E}\left\{ \sum_{t=0}^{\infty} \delta^t \frac{P_\pi^V(Y_t)}{Y_t} \middle| m, \pi \right\} \geq 0. \qquad (18.14)$$

If the equality holds, then $g_\pi(m,q) = 0$, $\forall q \in [0,1]$. On the other hand, since $R_u > 0$ and $R_d > 0$, it follows that $g_\pi(m,q)$ is strictly increasing in q.

Proposition 18.8 shows that the reward function $g_\pi(m,q)$ is strictly increasing in answer quality q, apart from the extreme case in which no users are willing to vote. This indicates that users with greater abilities will have an advantage for answering the question. Such a property is applicable to an apparent simplification of the SSPE, which is presented in Theorem 18.9.

THEOREM 18.9 *There exists a pure-strategy SSPE with a threshold structure in each state; in other words $\forall m \geq 0$, $\sigma_V \in [V_{min}, V_{max}]$, $\exists \hat{a}(m, \sigma_V) \in [0,1]$, and $\hat{\sigma}_V = C_V - R_V$ such that*

$$\begin{cases} [\hat{\pi}_A(m,\sigma),\, \hat{\pi}_V(m,\sigma),\, \hat{\pi}_N(m,\sigma)] = [1,\, 0,\, 0] \text{ if } \sigma_A > \hat{a}(m,\sigma_V) \\ [\hat{\pi}_A(m,\sigma),\, \hat{\pi}_V(m,\sigma),\, \hat{\pi}_N(m,\sigma)] = [0,\, 1,\, 0] \text{ if } \sigma_A \leq \hat{a}(m,\sigma_V) \text{ and } \sigma_V ge \hat{\sigma}_V \text{ and } m \geq 1 \\ [\hat{\pi}_A(m,\sigma),\, \hat{\pi}_V(m,\sigma),\, \hat{\pi}_N(m,\sigma)] = [0,\, 0,\, 1] \text{ otherwise.} \end{cases}$$
$$\qquad (18.15)$$

The above action rule is a unique SSPE in the sense that other possible SSPEs differ from it in actions only for 0 mass of users.

Proof Define $U(m,\sigma_V)$ as the maximum utility that a user with voting preference σ_V can receive at state m other than choosing action A, i.e.,

$$U(m,\sigma_V) \triangleq \max\{\sigma_V + R_V - C_V, 0\} \cdot \mathbf{1}(m \geq 1). \qquad (18.16)$$

Note that $U(0,\sigma_V) = 0$ since action V is not an option when $m = 0$.

Let us consider an arbitrary SSPE $\hat{\pi}$. We first show that there exists a threshold $\hat{a}(m,\sigma_V)$ so that users will choose action A in $\hat{\pi}$ only if their abilities are above the threshold. We know from Proposition 18.3 that

$$u(m,\sigma,A,\hat{\pi})|_{\sigma_A=0} = -c(m) + \delta g_{\hat{\pi}}(m+1,0) \leq -c(m) < 0 \leq U(m,\sigma_V). \quad (18.17)$$

If the following inequality holds:

$$u(m,\sigma,A,\hat{\pi})|_{\sigma_A=1} = -c(m) + \delta g_{\hat{\pi}}(m+1,1) \geq U(m,\sigma_V), \qquad (18.18)$$

since $g_{\hat{\pi}}(m,\sigma_A)$ is a continuous function of σ_A, there exists a solution $\sigma_A^* \in [0,1]$ to

$$-c(m) + \delta g_{\hat{\pi}}(m+1,\sigma_A^*) = U(m,\sigma_V). \qquad (18.19)$$

We set $\hat{a}(m, \sigma_V) = \sigma_A^*$. Furthermore, according to Proposition 18.8, (18.18) also implies that $g_{\hat{\pi}}(m, \sigma_A)$ is strictly increasing in σ_A since $g_{\hat{\pi}}(m + 1, 1) > 0$. On the other hand, if (18.18) does not hold, we set $\hat{a}(m, \sigma_V) = 1$, indicating that users can by no means have ability that is above the threshold.

Let us consider a user with type $\sigma = (\sigma_A, \sigma_V)$. When $\sigma_A > \hat{a}(m, \sigma_V)$, this implies that (18.18) holds and therefore we have

$$u(m, \sigma, A, \hat{\pi}) = -c(m) + \delta g_{\hat{\pi}}(m + 1, \sigma_A) > -c(m) + \delta g_{\hat{\pi}}(m + 1, \sigma_A^*) = U(m, \sigma_V),$$
$$(18.20)$$

which shows that it is optimal to choose action A with probability 1 (i.e., $\hat{\pi}_A(m, \sigma) = 1$). Similarly, when $\sigma_A < \hat{a}(m, \sigma_V)$, we have

$$u(m, \sigma, A, \hat{\pi}) < U(m, \sigma_V), \qquad (18.21)$$

which shows that action A is strictly dominated by the other two actions and thus $\hat{\pi}_A(m, \sigma) = 0$. When $\sigma_A = \hat{a}(m, \sigma_V)$, there exists at least one action from $\{V, N\}$ that has the same utility as that of the choice of action A; therefore, $\hat{\pi}_A(m, \sigma) = 0$ is optimal.

Afterwards, for cases in which action A is dominated (i.e., $\sigma_A \leq \hat{a}(m, \sigma_V)$), users will only take action V and action N into account. It can be seen that the best responses for users to choose are $\hat{\pi}_V(m, \sigma) = \mathbf{1}(\sigma_V \geq C_V - R_V) \cdot \mathbf{1}(m \geq 1)$ and $\hat{\pi}_N(m, \sigma) = 1 - \hat{\pi}_V(m, \sigma)$.

Consequently, the action rule given in (18.15) characterizes an SSPE. Furthermore, such an action rule is essentially a pure-strategy action rule in which users will choose the action with probability 1 in all situations.

To prove Theorem 18.9, further endeavor is required to show that the action rule given in (18.15) is also a unique SSPE. Based on the fact that when (18.18) holds, $g_{\hat{\pi}}(m, \sigma_A)$ must be strictly increasing in σ_A, the solution to (18.19) and thus the threshold $\hat{a}(m, \sigma_V)$ are unique. Consequently, all possible SSPEs will differ from the action rule in (18.15) only in boundary cases (i.e., users with $\sigma_A = \hat{a}(m, \sigma_V)$ or $\sigma_V = C_V - R_V$). Since the type distribution F is atomless on its support, these users add up to having 0 mass, which finalizes the proof.

From Theorem 18.9, the SSPE of the social computing game not only exists, but is also unique as a pure strategy. Furthermore, such a unique pure-strategy SSPE has a threshold structure in each state: users will choose to answer only if their ability σ_A is greater than a threshold function $\hat{a}(m, \sigma_V)$; otherwise, users will choose either to vote or not to participate according to a constant threshold $\hat{\sigma}_V$ on their voting preferences. Thanks to this sort of threshold structure, the action space of users is markedly simplified. Consequently, the SSPE can be represented equivalently by a threshold function $\hat{a}$ together with a constant $\hat{\sigma}_V$. We show in Corollary 18.10 that this equivalent form of the SSPE can be obtained through a dynamic programming algorithm in an efficient way.

COROLLARY 18.10   *The unique pure-strategy SSPE of the social computing game can be obtained through a dynamic programming algorithm as is shown in Algorithm 15.*

Algorithm 15: A dynamic programming algorithm to find the unique SSPE.

(1) $\hat{\sigma}_V \leftarrow C_V - R_V$

(2) $\hat{a}(m, \sigma_V) \leftarrow 1$ for $m \geq \bar{m}, \sigma_V \in [V_{min}, V_{max}]$

(3) $g_{\hat{\pi}}(\bar{m}, q) \leftarrow \frac{P_V[(R_u + R_d)q - R_d]}{(1-\delta)\bar{(m)}}$

(4) **for** $m = \bar{m} - 1 : 0$ **do**

(5) $U(m, \sigma_V) \leftarrow \max\{0, \sigma_V + R_V - C_V\} \cdot \mathbf{1}(m \geq 1)$

(6)   **if** $\delta g_{\hat{\pi}}(m+1, 1) - c(m) \leq U(m, \sigma_V)$ **then**

(7) $\hat{a}(m, \sigma_V) \leftarrow 1$

(8)   **else**

(9) $\hat{a}(m, \sigma_V) \leftarrow a$ where $\delta g_{\hat{\pi}}(m+1, a) - c(m) = U(m, \sigma_V)$

(10)   **end if**

(11)   **if** $m \geq 1$ **then**

(12) $P_{\hat{\pi}}^A(m) \leftarrow \int \mathbf{1}(\sigma_A \leq \hat{a}(m, \sigma_V)) dF(\sigma)$

(13) $P_{\hat{\pi}}^V(m) \leftarrow \int \left[\mathbf{1}(\sigma_A \leq \hat{a}(m, \sigma_V)) \cdot \mathbf{1}(\sigma_V \geq \hat{\sigma}_V) \right] dF(\sigma)$

(14) $g_{\hat{\pi}}(m, q) \leftarrow \dfrac{\left\{ \frac{P_{\hat{\pi}}^V(m)}{m}[(R_u + R_d)q - R_d] + \delta P_{\hat{\pi}}^A(m)g_{\hat{\pi}}(m+1, q) \right\}}{1 - \delta(1 - P_{\hat{\pi}}^A(m))}$

(15)   **end if**

(16) **end for**

(17) Output $(\hat{a}, \hat{\sigma}_V)$

Proof From Corollary 18.7, we know that for $m \geq \bar{m}$, no users will choose action A in an SSPE. Consequently, we can set $\hat{a}(m, \sigma_V) = 1$ for $m \geq \bar{m}$ and $\sigma_V \in [V_{min}, V_{max}]$. Furthermore, as $P_{\hat{\pi}}^A(\bar{m}) = 0$, we can derive from (18.1) the expression of $g_{\hat{\pi}}(\bar{m}, q)$ as is given by Algorithm 15. Afterwards, based on $g_{\hat{\pi}}(\bar{m}, q)$, we can iteratively calculate the threshold from $m = \bar{m} - 1$ to 0, following the steps outlined in the proof of Theorem 18.9.

The essence of an SSPE rests with the threshold function $\hat{a}(m, \sigma_V)$, which determines the portion of users who will answer the question at each stage. How will this threshold vary according to different m and σ_V? In particular, how do the voting preferences of users influence their decisions on whether or not to answer the question? Does a user have an advantage if they post an early answer? In addition, with the accumulation of answers, will users become more selective in answering the questions? In the following, we will show the properties of the threshold function that help us to answer these questions. Propositions 18.11 and 18.12 present a summary of the results.

PROPOSITION 18.11   In an SSPE, at any state $m \geq 0$, the threshold of user ability for answering (i.e., $\hat{a}(m, \sigma_V)$) increases with users' voting preference σ_V. Moreover, there exists a lower bound on the threshold as

$$\hat{a}(m, \sigma_V) \geq \frac{R_d}{R_u + R_d}, \quad \forall m \geq 0, \sigma_V \in [V_{min}, V_{max}]. \tag{18.22}$$

Proof For any $m \geq 0$, it is sufficient to prove the results for the case where $g_{\hat{\pi}}(m + 1, q)$ is strictly increasing in q. Otherwise, we have $g_{\hat{\pi}}(m+1, q) = 0, \forall q \in [0, 1]$, which implies $\hat{a}(m, \sigma_V) = 1$ and Proposition 18.11 holds.

Let us consider two voting preferences σ_{V1} and σ_{V2} such that $1 \geq \sigma_{V1} \geq \sigma_{V2} \geq 0$. If $-c(m) + \delta g_{\hat{\pi}}(m + 1, 1) \leq \max\{0, \sigma_{V1} + R_V - C_V\}$, then according to Algorithm 15, we have $\hat{a}(m, \sigma_{V1}) = 1 \geq \hat{a}(m, \sigma_{V2})$. Otherwise, we have

$$-c(m) + \delta g_{\hat{\pi}}(m + 1, \hat{a}(m, \sigma_{V1})) = \max\{0, \sigma_{V1} + R_V - C_V\}$$

$$\geq \max\{0, \sigma_{V2} + R_V - C_V\}$$

$$= -c(m) + \delta g_{\hat{\pi}}(m + 1, \hat{a}(m, \sigma_{V2})).$$

Since $g_{\hat{\pi}}$ is strictly increasing in answer quality, we can conclude that $\hat{a}(m, \sigma_{V1}) \geq \hat{a}(m, \sigma_{V2})$. Therefore, $\hat{a}(m, \sigma_V)$ is increasing in σ_V.

To show the lower bound, note from the expression of $g_{\hat{\pi}}$ in (18.5) that

$$g_{\hat{\pi}}\left(m, \frac{R_d}{R_u + R_d}\right) = 0 \leq g_{\hat{\pi}}(m, \hat{a}(m, \sigma_V)), \quad \forall m \geq 0, \sigma_V \in [V_{min}, V_{max}], \quad (18.23)$$

which implies that $\hat{a}(m, \sigma_V) \geq \frac{R_d}{R_u + R_d}$ due to the monotonicity of $g_{\hat{\pi}}$.

PROPOSITION 18.12 In the SSPE $\hat{\pi}$, $\forall q \in [0, 1]$, $g_{\hat{\pi}}(m, q)$ is decreasing in m. In addition, the threshold of user ability for answering (i.e., $\hat{a}(m, \sigma_V)$) is increasing in m for any given $\sigma_V \in [V_{min}, V_{max}]$.

Proof We first show that $g_{\hat{\pi}}(m, q)$ is a decreasing function of m based on mathematical induction. According to Corollary 18.7, users will not choose action A at the absorbing state $\overline{m}$ in an SSPE. Therefore, we have $P_{\hat{\pi}}^A(\overline{m}) = 0$ and

$$g_{\hat{\pi}}(\overline{m}, q) = \frac{P_{\hat{\pi}}^V(\overline{m})[(R_u + R_d)q - R_d]}{(1 - \delta)\overline{m}}. \quad (18.24)$$

Then, $\forall m$ such that $1 \geq m \geq \overline{m} - 1$, we show in the following that if

$$g_{\hat{\pi}}(m + 1, q) \leq \frac{P_{\hat{\pi}}^V(m + 1)[(R_u + R_d)q - R_d]}{(1 - \delta)(m + 1)}, \quad (18.25)$$

we can derive $g_{\hat{\pi}}(m, q) \geq g_{\hat{\pi}}(m + 1, q)$, and as a result

$$g_{\hat{\pi}}(m, q) \leq \frac{P_{\hat{\pi}}^V(m)[(R_u + R_d)q - R_d]}{(1 - \delta)m}. \quad (18.26)$$

Assume that the above conclusion does not hold (i.e., $g_{\hat{\pi}}(m, q) < g_{\hat{\pi}}(m + 1, q)$). Then, according to the monotonicity of $g_{\hat{\pi}}$ with respect to answer quality q, we have $\hat{a}(m, \sigma_V) \geq \hat{a}(m + 1, \sigma_V)$, which implies $P_{\hat{\pi}}^V(m) \geq P_{\hat{\pi}}^V(m + 1)$. Moreover, from the optimality-form expression of $g_{\hat{\pi}}$ in (18.1), we have

$$g_{\hat{\pi}}(m, q) - g_{\hat{\pi}}(m + 1, q) = \frac{\frac{P_{\hat{\pi}}^V(m)}{m}[(R_u + R_d)q - R_d] - (1 - \delta)g_{\hat{\pi}}(m + 1, q)}{1 - \delta(1 - P_{\hat{\pi}}^A(m))}$$

$$\qquad (18.27)$$

$$\geq \frac{\left\{\frac{P_{\hat{\pi}}^V(m)}{m} - \frac{P_{\hat{\pi}}^V(m+1)}{m+1}\right\}[(R_u + R_d)q - R_d]}{1 - \delta(1 - P_{\hat{\pi}}^A(m))} \geq 0,$$

which contradicts the assumption. Therefore, $g_{\hat{\pi}}(m,q) \geq g_{\hat{\pi}}(m+1,q)$ must hold. Furthermore, based on (18.27), it is known that

$$g_{\hat{\pi}}(m+1,q) \leq \frac{P_{\hat{\pi}}^V(m)[(R_u + R_d)q - R_d]}{(1-\delta)m}. \tag{18.28}$$

By substituting (18.28) into (18.1), we can then derive (18.26).

Therefore, it can be concluded that $g_{\hat{\pi}}(m,q)$ is an increasing function of m for any given $q \in [0,1]$, which proves the first part of Theorem 18.9. The second part of Theorem 18.9 is then subject to easy verification based on this result and the monotonicity property of $g_{\hat{\pi}}$ in terms of answer quality q.

It is shown in Proposition 18.12 that there is an advantage to providing an early answer to the question, as the answers that are posted earlier will receive more rewards than those posted later. Furthermore, since it is more profitable to answer the question when there are fewer answers, more users are inclined to answer at the earlier stages of the game. With the accumulation of answers, answering the question becomes increasingly competitive; users are gradually discouraged from answering the question, which is left to a select group of users with high ability, until the question reaches the absorbing state where no more answers will be posted.

18.4   Extensions to Endogenous Effort

In the previous section, we analyzed sequential user behavior in social computing systems under the homogeneous effort model based on the assumption that the quality of an answer corresponds to the user's ability and all users incur identical cost for answer creation. Such a model is in line with cases in which domain knowledge and the expertise of users play crucial roles in answering the question, as in focused Q&A sites such as Stack Overflow. A more general setting would be that users, in addition to making strategic decisions on whether to answer the question or not, can also decide endogenously how much effort to exert in answer creation. In this section, we study the social computing game under such an endogenous effort model and show that the previous results can be extended naturally to the incorporation of such a more general setting.

The main actions are defined as actions in the action set Θ. Under the endogenous effort model, in addition to the main actions, users will choose another action $e \in [0,1]$, which denotes the amount of effort they are willing to exert in answer creation. Similarly, in analogy to the homogeneous effort case, we consider mixed strategies for main actions and present the corresponding action rule as π. Let $u_E(m, \sigma, \theta, e, \tilde{\pi})$ represent the utility that a user with type σ who arrives at state m and chooses action $\theta \in \Theta$ and $e \in [0,1]$ will receive provided that other users adopt the main action rule $\tilde{\pi}$. We have

$$u_E(m,\sigma,\theta,e,\tilde{\pi}) = \begin{cases} -c(m,e) + \delta g_{\tilde{\pi}}(m+1, \phi(\sigma_A, e)) & \text{if } \theta = A \\ \sigma_V + R_V - C_V & \text{if } \theta = V \text{ and } m > 0 \\ 0 & \text{if } \theta = N. \end{cases}$$

$$\tag{18.29}$$

The utility of a user choosing action rule π is $u_E(m, \sigma, \pi, e, \tilde{\pi}) = \sum_{\theta \in \Theta} \pi_\theta(m, \sigma) \cdot u_E(m, \sigma, \theta, e, \tilde{\pi})$.

It can be seen in (18.29) that the effort of a user influences their utility for choosing action A and therefore their optimal action rule. However, the choice of effort only has a local impact to the extent that, given the state m and other users' main action rule $\tilde{\pi}$, a user's utility will be independent of other users' efforts. Furthermore, we note that the properties of the reward function for answering in Propositions 18.3 and 18.8 are derived in terms of the answer quality q, which will still hold for the endogenous effort case with $q = \phi(\sigma_A, e)$.

In the endogenous effort case, the SSPE is formally defined as follows:

DEFINITION 18.13   An action rule pair $(\hat{\pi}, \hat{e})$ is an SSPE for the social computing game with endogenous effort if and only if

$$(\hat{\pi}, \hat{e}) \in \arg\max_{\pi, e} u_E(m, \sigma, \pi, e, \hat{\pi}) \quad \forall m \geq 0, \sigma \in [0, 1] \times [V_{min}, V_{max}]. \quad (18.30)$$

As mentioned previously, we wish to determine whether there exists an SSPE for the social computing game with endogenous effort, and if so, what the structure of such an SSPE is. We answer these questions in Theorem 18.14.

THEOREM 18.14   *There exists a pure-strategy SSPE for the social computing game with endogenous effort. In this equilibrium, users choose their main actions in accordance with the following threshold structure:*

$$\begin{cases} [\hat{\pi}_A(m, \sigma), \hat{\pi}_V(m, \sigma), \hat{\pi}_N(m, \sigma)] = [1, 0, 0] & \text{if } \sigma_A > \hat{a}(m, \sigma_V) \\ [\hat{\pi}_A(m, \sigma), \hat{\pi}_V(m, \sigma), \hat{\pi}_N(m, \sigma)] = [0, 1, 0] & \text{if } \sigma_A \leq \hat{a}(m, \sigma_V) \text{ and } \sigma_V \geq \hat{\sigma}_V \text{ and } m \geq 1 \\ [\hat{\pi}_A(m, \sigma), \hat{\pi}_V(m, \sigma), \hat{\pi}_N(m, \sigma)] = [0, 0, 1] & \text{otherwise.} \end{cases}$$

$$(18.31)$$

Moreover, conditional on choosing action A, each user chooses an effort $\hat{e}(m, \sigma_A)$ based on the state m and their ability σ_A.

Proof   Initially, we demonstrate that there must be an absorbing state in the SSPE. From Proposition 18.3 and the monotonicity of $c(m, e)$ in e, we have

$$u_E(m, \sigma, A, e, \hat{\pi}) \leq -c(m, 0) + \frac{\delta R_u}{(1 - \delta)(m + 1)}, \quad (18.32)$$

where the right-hand expression is strictly decreasing in m and goes to negative infinity as $m \to \infty$. Consequently, there exists $\tilde{m} \geq 0$ such that $\forall m \geq \tilde{m}$ and the utility of choosing action A is strictly less than 0, which indicates that action A is strictly dominated by action N.

Afterwards, we construct a pair of action rules $(\hat{\pi}, \hat{e})$ that satisfy the conditions sketched out in Theorem 18.14 and prove them to be an SSPE. For $m \geq \tilde{m}$, since the probability of choosing action A is 0 for all user types, we can set $\hat{a}(m, \sigma_V) = 1$. The choice of effort is irrelevant in this case. Furthermore, let $\hat{\sigma}_V = C_V - R_V$. It can be shown that the main action rule in (18.31) is the best response for all users independent of other users' main action rules and thus is an SSPE for state $m \geq \tilde{m}$.

For $m < \tilde{m}$, $(\hat{\pi}, \hat{e})$ can be constructed by iteratively picking the best response backward from $m = \tilde{m} - 1$ to 0. At each state m, let

$$\hat{e}(m, \sigma_A) \in \arg\max_{e\in[0,1]} \{-c(m,e) + \delta g_{\hat{\pi}}(m+1, \phi(\sigma_A, e))\}. \tag{18.33}$$

The best response of users at this state is to choose action A with probability 1 and to exert effort $\hat{e}(m, \sigma_A)$ if

$$-c(m, \hat{e}(m,\sigma_A)) + \delta g_{\hat{\pi}}(m+1, \phi(\sigma_A, \hat{e}(m,\sigma_A))) > \max\{0, \sigma_V + R_V - C_V\}. \tag{18.34}$$

Otherwise, it is optimal to choose action V with probability 1 if $m \geq 1$ and $\sigma_V + R_V - C_V > 0$ and to choose action N in all the other cases.

According to the above procedure, we have constructed $(\hat{\pi}, \hat{e})$ for state $m < \tilde{m}$ such that it is the best response for users given that the same main action rule is adopted by others. Consequently, the action pair $(\hat{\pi}, \hat{e})$ is also an SSPE for state $m < \tilde{m}$.

Further effort is required to show that $\hat{\pi}$ satisfies (18.31) for state $m < \tilde{m}$. The key is to show that the utility of answering with optimal effort increases with user's ability. Consider $0 \leq \sigma_{A1} \leq \sigma_{A2} \leq 1$. We have

$$- c(m, \hat{e}(m, \sigma_{A1})) + \delta g_{\hat{\pi}}(m+1, \phi(\sigma_{A1}, \hat{e}(m, \sigma_{A1})))$$

$$\leq -c(m, \hat{e}(m, \sigma_{A1})) + \delta g_{\hat{\pi}}(m+1, \phi(\sigma_{A2}, \hat{e}(m, \sigma_{A1}))) \tag{18.35}$$

$$\leq -c(m, \hat{e}(m, \sigma_{A2})) + \delta g_{\hat{\pi}}(m+1, \phi(\sigma_{A2}, \hat{e}(m, \sigma_{A2}))). \tag{18.36}$$

The inequality in (18.35) is based on the fact that $g_{\hat{\pi}}$ is increasing in answer quality q and that $q = \phi(\sigma_A, e)$ is an increasing function of σ_A. The inequality in (18.36) is derived from the definition of $\hat{e}$ in (18.33). Consequently, a user with greater ability can obtain a higher utility from answering than a user with lesser ability. Based on the condition in (18.34), such a monotonicity property leads directly to the threshold structure for answering where the threshold $\hat{a}(m, \sigma_V)$ can be set as the solution $a \in [0, 1]$ to the following equation:

$$-c(m, \hat{e}(m,a)) + \delta g_{\hat{\pi}}(m+1, \phi(a, \hat{e}(m,a))) = \max\{0, \sigma_V + R_V - C_V\}. \tag{18.37}$$

When there is no solution to (18.37) within $[0, 1]$, $\hat{a}(m, \sigma_V)$ can be set as 0 if the left-hand side is greater or 1 otherwise. Furthermore, the threshold structure for voting can be verified with $\hat{\sigma}_V = C_V - R_V$.

It can be seen from Theorem 18.14 that there is an SSPE for the social computing game with endogenous effort that has a quite similar structure to the unique SSPE for the homogeneous effort model. The difference here is that the calculation of the threshold function for answering now requires consideration of different possible efforts. Put another way, in order to decide whether or not to answer the question, a user has to determine their optimal effort first and then evaluate their utility for answering with such optimal effort. Furthermore, note that the SSPE characterized in Theorem 18.14 may not be unique since there are probably multiple optimal efforts and the quality function ϕ may not be strictly increasing.

Table 18.1. (a) Reputation updating rule and (b) statistics of the data set.

(a)			(b)	
Action	Reputation change		Questions	430K
Answer is upvoted	+10		Answers	731K
Answer is downvoted	−2 (−1 to voter)		Votes	1.32M
Answer is accepted	+15 (+2 to accepter)			

18.5   Empirical Evaluations

In this section, we draw on real-world data from a popular Q&A site, Stack Overflow, to validate the model. In particular, we investigate how qualitative observations derived from the data compare with the predictions of the model. We will first introduce the data set and then present the evaluation results.

18.5.1   Data Set Description

Stack Overflow is one of the most popular and active Q&A sites, where questions are under the strict restriction of being factual and programming-related. Questions in Stack Overflow are generally difficult and therefore usually entail strong domain knowledge and expertise to answer, which makes it highly suitable for the homogeneous effort model. In addition to raising and answering questions, voting is another popular type of user activity on Stack Overflow, which is designed to provide supplementary information concerning the quality of answers as well as long-lasting incentives for users to answer questions. The model of Stack Overflow has proved successful and has been adopted by over 100 other focused Q&A websites under Stack Exchange [4].

Various types of user activities in Stack Overflow are linked through an incentive mechanism that is established with reputation points. Table 18.1(a) shows how reputation points are gained and lost by actions regarding the discussions. Note that, to guard against abuse, downvotes are discouraged to a certain extent in that the voter will lose 1 reputation point by casting a downvote. Furthermore, in Stack Overflow, the user who raises a question can choose an answer as the selected answer, which brings slightly more reputation points to the contributor than a regular upvote does. In addition to the listed actions, the reputation of a user can change through many other means, such as offering or winning a bounty associated with a question. On the whole, a user's reputation summarizes their activities on Stack Overflow since registration and offers a rough measurement of the amount of expertise the user has, as well as the level of respect they have received from their peers.

The user activity data on Stack Overflow is available to the public through the Stack Exchange Data Explorer [5]. We gather questions that were posted in the first quarter

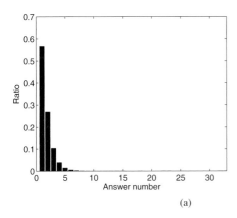 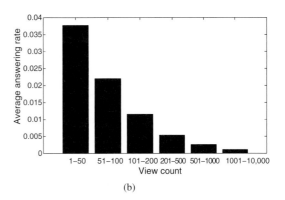

(a)   (b)

Figure 18.2 (a) The distribution of answer counts. (b) The average answering rate by different view count intervals.

of 2013 (i.e., from January 1, 2013, to March 31, 2013). We incorporate all of the answers and votes concerning these questions (as of March 2014) into the data set. Note that we only impose time restrictions on questions rather than on the related answers and votes. We account for questions that received at least one answer and further exclude questions that are closed for various reasons, such as being marked as subjective or duplicates. In addition, to adapt the data to the model, we consider the action of accepting an answer simply as a regular upvote. In other words, we treat the user who raises the question in the same way as other users in terms of voting. Table 18.1(b) displays the statistics of the data set.

18.5.2   Observations and Validations

The saturation phenomenon: In the analysis, the existence of an SSPE is based on the observation that the number of answers to a question stops increasing after a certain value, which represents a finite sequential game. For a verification of this observation, we present in Figure 18.2(a) the distribution of answer counts for questions in the data set. The maximum answer count is 33 and it can be seen that the distribution is concentrated around the lower end. Further investigation is conducted on the ways in which the answering rate varies according to the view counts of a question. The answering rate is defined as the number of answers to a question divided by the number of users who view this question. The results are shown in Figure 18.2(b). It is found that the answering rate drops rapidly with increasing view counts. This serves as an illustration that as users continue to arrive at the question and with the accumulation of answers it becomes increasingly difficult for the question to obtain new answers. Consequently, there exists a saturation phenomenon for answers to a question, which serves as the justification for the observation.

The advantage of greater ability: A key prediction derived from the model is that the reward function for answering registers monotonic growth in answer quality,

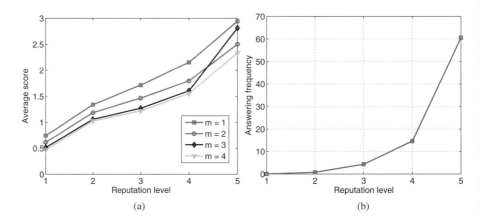

Figure 18.3 (a) The average score of answers versus the reputation level of users by different time ranks. (b) The relative frequency of answering versus reputation level.

as is stated in Proposition 18.8. In homogeneous effort settings, this suggests that a user with greater ability can receive a higher reward for answering a question than a user with lesser ability. Such a prediction plays a fundamental role in the equilibrium analysis and leads straightforwardly to the threshold structure of the equilibrium. The justification for such a prediction should be preceded by an investigation into how the average scores of answers vary with contributors' abilities. The answer score is defined as the number of positive votes of an answer minus the number of negative votes, which is indicative of the reward a user can receive for their answer. Since user ability defies direct observation from the data, we treat reputation as a rough approximation of a user's ability. In particular, we quantize the reputation with a set of logarithmic boundary values as $\{0, 100, 1000, 5000, 20,000, 1e7\}$. On the whole, a user with a higher reputation level is more likely to have greater ability for answering the question. Figure 18.3(a) presents the results for answers with various time ranks that correspond to different states in the model. It is shown in Figure 18.3(a) that at any state users with greater ability can receive more rewards for answering a question. As a result, the observations from the data are consistent with the predictions of the model.

Further investigation is conducted on the relative frequency of answering for users with varying levels of ability. In particular, we present the numbers of answers contributed by users from different reputation levels normalized by the population size of the corresponding reputation level. The results are shown in Figure 18.3(b). It can be seen that the frequency of answering increases drastically with increasing user ability, which serves as evidence for threshold structures in users' decision-making. According to threshold structures, users with greater ability are more inclined to answer questions. Since various types of questions may have different thresholds, the average frequency of answering therefore registers a monotonic increase with user ability.

The advantage of answering earlier: Another important prediction derived from the model is that the reward for an answer decreases in terms of its time rank, as is

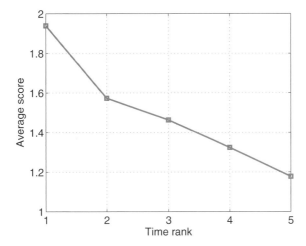

Figure 18.4 The average score versus time rank.

stated in Proposition 18.12. In other words, there is an advantage to providing an early answer. To compare such a prediction with observations from the real-world data, we can first infer from Figure 18.3(a) that, for most reputation levels, the score of answer decreases in m. We present in Figure 18.4 the curve of the average score of answers versus the answer time rank. It can be seen that answers that are posted earlier receive higher scores on average, which corresponds to the prediction.

18.6 Numerical Simulations

In this section, we conduct numerical simulations of how the model can contribute to insights into the design of incentive mechanisms for a great variety of social computing systems.

18.6.1 Simulation Settings

Recall that a mechanism in the model is defined as a set of three parameters $\{R_V, R_u, R_d\}$, which specify how the system should reward voting and answering, respectively. The system designer adjusts these parameters to steer user behavior on the site. Based on the characteristics of the applications, system designers are likely to be interested in the optimization of different metrics. Consequently, we regard a general function as the system designer's utility that covers many typical use-case scenarios in social computing. We denote q_k and t_k as the quality and arrival time of the kth answer and K as the number of received answers. The system designer's utility function can be written as

$$U^s(K, q_1, t_1, \ldots, q_K, t_K) = K^{-\alpha} \sum_{k=1}^{K} \beta^{t_k} q_k, \tag{18.38}$$

where $0 \leq \alpha \leq 1$ and $0 \leq \beta \leq 1$. We show three typical use-case scenarios that can be captured by (18.38) with different choices of α and β as follows:

(1) Use Case 1: $\alpha = 0$ and $\beta = 1$, where the objective function becomes the sum of qualities. In this case, the diversity of answers is valuable since the system designer prefers a majority of rational answers over a minority of near-perfect ones. Furthermore, answers have long-lasting values that can withstand the test of time.

(2) Use Case 2: $\alpha = 0$ and $\beta < 1$. In this case, a diversity of answers is valuable but the question is time sensitive since the system designer expects answers to arrive earlier rather than later.

(3) Use Case 3: $\alpha = 1$ and $\beta = 1$, where the objective function serves as the average quality of answers. In this case, individual answer quality instead of diversity is valuable to the system designer. Moreover, answers have long-lasting values in this case.

It is assumed that user types are drawn identically and independently according to the probability density function $f(\sigma_A, \sigma_V) = \frac{\lambda e^{-\lambda \sigma_A}}{2(1-e^{-1})}$ over $[0, 1] \times [-1, 1]$. In other words, we assume σ_A and σ_V to be independently distributed; σ_V follows a uniform distribution and σ_A follows a truncated exponential distribution with parameter λ. Note that the larger λ is, the rarer the users with high ability are. Unless otherwise stated, we set by default $\lambda = 1$. We assume $C_V = 0.2$ and set the discounting factor $\delta = 0.9$.

In terms of the homogeneous effort model, we choose $c(m) = 1 + 0.1m$. For the endogenous effort model, we assume $c(m, e) = 0.1m + 5e^2$. We adopt $\phi(\sigma_A, e) = \left(\frac{\gamma + \sigma_A}{\gamma + 1}\right) e$ as the quality function, where $\gamma \geq 0$ is a parameter that controls the degree to which the answer quality depends on a user's ability. The larger γ is, the less dependent the answer quality is on a user's ability and thus the more it is on the amount of the user's effort.

18.6.2   Simulation Results for Homogeneous Effort

In the first simulation, we investigate the influence of R_V on the system designer's utility. The results for all three use cases are presented in Figure 18.5, where we set $R_u = 2$ and $R_d = 1$. In all cases, when R_V is small, the system designer's utility increases quickly with increasing R_V. This is due to the fact that a greater reward for voting motivates more users to vote rather than to leave without participation, which contributes to a stronger incentive for answering. However, as the value of R_V increases, it starts to discourage users from answering since voting turns out to be more profitable. When diversity is valuable for the system designer such as in Use Cases 1 and 2, the system designer's utility will decrease when R_V exceeds an optimal value. It can be further noted that the optimal value is around 1.2, which is just enough to make voting preferable over no participation for all users. In terms of Use Case 3, since the average quality of answers is less sensitive to R_V when R_V is large, the

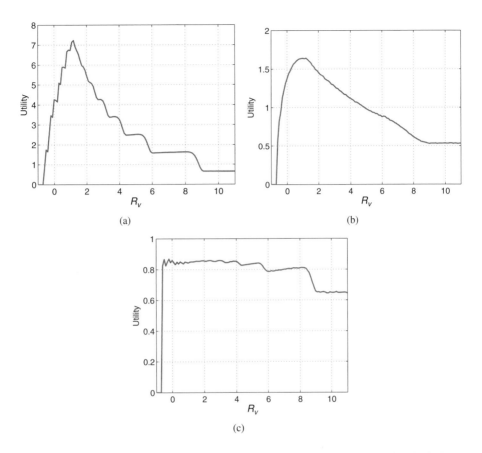

Figure 18.5 The system designer's utility versus R_V: (a) Use Case 1: $\alpha = 0$ and $\beta = 1$; (b) Use Case 2: $\alpha = 0$ and $\beta = 0.9$; (c) Use Case 3: $\alpha = 1$ and $\beta = 1$.

system designer's utility fluctuates within a small range until R_V is large enough so that no users will be motivated to answer the question when voting is an alternative.

An essential principle for the design of incentive mechanisms can be obtained through the above simulation: voting should be encouraged, but in moderation! Practically, the reward for voting is supposed to be designed to be large enough to make voting preferable over no participation for the majority of users, but to be relatively small compared with the reward for answering. Furthermore, when the system designer is uncertain about the optimal value, it would be advisable to overestimate this value rather than underestimating it, especially for cases in which a few desired near-perfect answers are available.

We now study how the system designer's utility depends on R_u and R_d. Recall that a user will receive R_u points for receiving an upvote and lose R_d points for receiving a downvote. We show the simulation results in Figure 18.6 where we set R_V as 1. In terms of Use Case 1, R_u plays a primary role in the impact on the system designer's utility. Since diversity is valuable in this case, a larger R_u will motivate more users to provide their answers, and therefore it contributes to a higher utility for

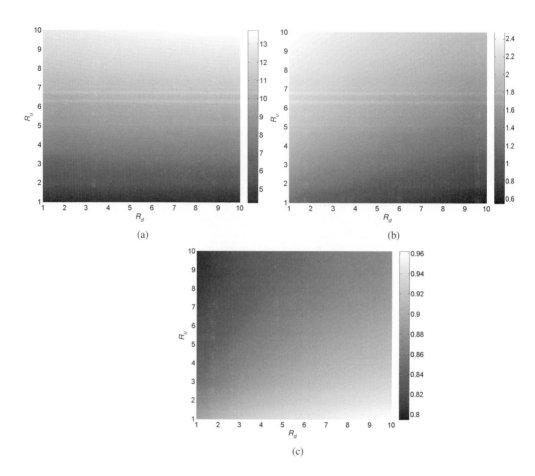

Figure 18.6 The system designer's utility versus R_u and R_d: (a) Use Case 1: $\alpha = 0$ and $\beta = 1$; (b) Use Case 2: $\alpha = 0$ and $\beta = 0.9$; (c) Use Case 3: $\alpha = 1$ and $\beta = 1$.

the system designer. The influence of R_d is more apparent in Use Cases 2 and 3. To our surprise, it is found that the value of R_d influences the system designer's utility in two divergent directions for these two cases. In particular, with increasing R_d, the utility decreases in Use Case 2, while it increases in Use Case 3. An explanation for this is as follows: recall from Proposition 18.11 that $\frac{R_d}{R_u+R_d}$ sets a lower bound on a user's ability for answering. Therefore, roughly speaking, the thresholds of user ability for answering will increase along with increasing R_d. Higher thresholds will reduce the system designer's utility in Use Case 2, since the accumulation of answers is more time-consuming. On the other hand, higher thresholds contribute to higher quality, which enhances the system designer's utility in Use Case 3. Furthermore, since the diversity of answers is valueless in Use Case 3, the ratio of R_u to R_d serves as the primary factor influencing the system designer's utility.

In summary, we can derive another principle that offers potential assistance to the design of incentive mechanisms in practice: when a diversity of answers is desired,

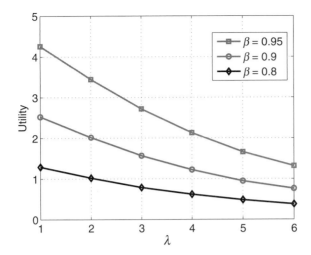

Figure 18.7 The system designer's utility versus λ for $\alpha = 0$ and different values of β.

a high reward should be assigned to users for each upvote they receive. Based on the relative value of the answer quality and the answer timeliness, different strategies should be adopted so as to formulate the penalty for receiving downvotes.

In the third simulation, we studied the influence of λ on the system designer's utility. Recall that λ controls the shape of the user-type distribution; the larger λ is, the rarer are users with high ability. We present the system designer's utility versus λ in Figure 18.7. It can be seen that the system designer's utility decreases with increasing λ, which illustrates the value of high-ability users for social computing systems. Consequently, for applications that depend heavily on users' domain knowledge and expertise, it is of great importance to develop and maintain an active community of elite members.

18.6.3 Simulation Results for Endogenous Effort

Finally, we consider the endogenous effort model in the simulation. We are particularly interested in how the sensitivity of answer quality in terms of effort influences the system designer's utility. We present curves of utility versus γ for all the three use cases in Figure 18.8. We set $R_V = 1$ and $R_d = 2$ in the simulations. It is clear that in Use Cases 1 and 3, the utility decreases with increasing γ, whereas in Use Case 2, the utility increases before decreasing.

Since a larger value of γ indicates that the answer quality will be more independent of the user's ability, low-ability users will gain an advantage for answering with large γ values. As a consequence, the threshold of user ability for answering will decrease with increasing γ. Lower thresholds result in lower quality on average, which explains the decrease of utility in all three use cases. In addition, lower thresholds imply that answers will be posted earlier, which leads to the nonmonotonic behavior of utility in Use Case 2.

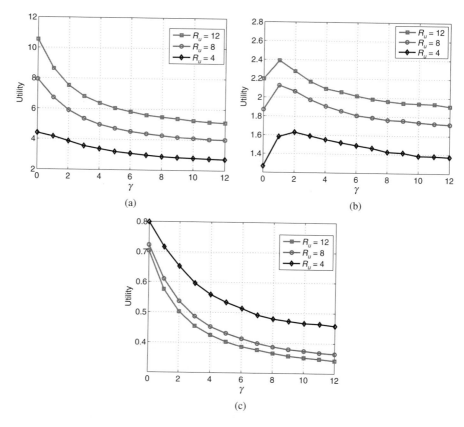

Figure 18.8 The system designer's utility versus γ: (a) Use Case 1: $\alpha = 0$ and $\beta = 1$; (b) Use Case 2: $\alpha = 0$ and $\beta = 0.9$; (c) Use Case 3: $\alpha = 1$ and $\beta = 1$.

18.7   Conclusion

In this chapter, we studied sequential user behavior in social computing systems from a game-theoretic perspective. The game-theoretic model explicitly involves the answering–voting externality, which is common in social computing systems. We started with a homogeneous effort model and proved the existence and uniqueness of a pure-strategy SSPE. To deepen our understanding of the equilibrium user participation, we demonstrated the existence of advantages for users with greater ability and for those providing an early answer. Consequently, the equilibrium displayed a threshold structure where the threshold for answering increased with increasing numbers of answers. The results derived for the homogeneous effort model demonstrated the essence of the game and could be extended naturally to the more general setting in which users endogenously decide on the effort they will exert for answering. The game-theoretic model was verified through evaluations of user behavior data gathered from Stack Overflow. In particular, we showed that the main qualitative predictions of the game-theoretic model were in line with observations from the data. Finally, we studied the system designer's problem through numerical simulations and derived several design principles that could offer potential guidance for the design of incentive mechanisms for social computing systems in practice.

18.8   Literature Review

There is a growing body of literature that studies user contributions to social computing sites with game-theoretic approaches. Various forms of incentives have been taken into account so as to stimulate user participation, including badges [6,7], monetary rewards or virtual points [8–11], and attention [12]. Badges are utilized by social computing sites to recognize users for their various types and degrees of overall contribution to the site. In [6], Anderson et al. proposed a model for user behavior on social media sites in the presence of badges. Based on the analysis of the best strategy of users, they found that users were influenced by badges, which was in line with the aggregated user behavior they observed from Stack Overflow. In [7], Easley and Ghosh analyzed equilibrium existence and equilibrium user participation for two widely adopted badge mechanisms: badges with absolute standards and those with relative standards. The major difference between the work in this chapter and that of [6,7] is that we regard virtual points as the incentive for users and study user behavior within a single task such as a question instead of the overall contributions of users on a site.

The work in this chapter has a closer relation to studies applying monetary rewards or virtual points as the incentive for user contributions [8–11]. Gao et al. studied cost-effective incentive mechanisms for microtask crowdsourcing in [9], where a novel mechanism for quality-aware worker training is proposed to reduce the requester's cost for stimulating high-quality solutions from self-interested workers. In [10], Ghosh and Hummel studied the issue of whether, in the presence of strategic users, the optimal outcome can be implemented through a set of mechanisms that are based on virtual points. The game-theoretic model shares several common characteristics with [10], including the assumption of voluntary participation and the consideration of both homogeneous effort and endogenous effort. The incentive mechanism design problem for online Q&A sites was analyzed in [11], in which the objective was to motivate users to contribute their answers more rapidly. Similarly to the studies in [11], we utilize the number of answers in the game-theoretic model in order to summarize the history of a question without further differentiating answer quality.

The difference between the work in this chapter and that of [8–10] mainly consists in the following two respects: first, we consider that users participate sequentially rather than simultaneously. In many social computing systems, users act sequentially and will make divergent decisions in various situations. For instance, a user is inclined to answer a question if there are few answers, or they are inclined not to participate if the question has already received a large number of answers. The sequential game model we considered enables us to study the strategic decision-making of users in various states and therefore better characterize the dynamics of user behavior on social computing sites. Second, we explicitly incorporate the answering–voting externality into the game-theoretic model, whereas in previous research the voting action was either excluded [8,9,11], had no influence on other users' utility [10], or was assumed to be performed by another group of nonstrategic users [12].

Another popular research topic for user participation in the context of social computing is based on the analysis of empirical data from the perspective of social psychological [13–16]. User behavior on Taskcn, a crowdsourcing site, was investigated in [15]. The authors showed that users who remain on the site learn to take strategic approaches in order to optimize their desired payoffs. In [16], by using surveys and user behavior data, Tausczik and Pennebaker found that earning a reputation (i.e., accumulating virtual reputation points) served as a crucial incentive for users on Q&A sites. These studies provided evidence for strategic user behavior in social computing systems and thus motivated the search for a more systematic understanding of user participation in such environments with game-theoretic models.

References

[1] A. Anderson, D. Huttenlocher, J. Kleinberg, and J. Leskovec, "Discovering value from community activity on focused question answering sites: A case study of stack overflow," in *Proc. 18th ACM SIGKDD International Conference on Knowledge Discovery and Data Mining*, 2012.

[2] P. A. Samuelson, "A note on measurement of utility," *Review of Economic Studies*, vol. 4, pp. 155–161, 1937.

[3] M. J. Osborne and A. Rubinste, *A Course in Game Theory*. MIT Press, 1994.

[4] "StackExchange." http://stackexchange.com.

[5] "Stack Exchange Data Explorer." http://data.stackexchange.com/help.

[6] A. Anderson, D. Huttenlocher, J. Kleinberg, and J. Leskovec, "Steering user behavior with badges," in *Proc. 22nd International Conference on World Wide Web*, 2013.

[7] D. Easley and A. Ghosh, "Incentives, gamification, and game theory: An economic approach to badge design," *ACM Transactions on Economics and Computation*, vol. 4, pp. 16:1–16:26, 2016.

[8] D. DiPalantino and M. Vojnovic, "Crowdsourcing and all-pay auctions," in *Proc. 10th ACM Conference on Electronic Commerce*, 2009.

[9] Y. Gao, Y. Chen, and K. J. R. Liu, "On cost-effective incentive mechanisms in microtask crowdsourcing," *IEEE Transactions on Computational Intelligence and AI in Games*, vol. 7, pp. 3–15, 2015.

[10] A. Ghosh and P. Hummel, "Implementing optimal outcomes in social computing: A game-theoretic approach," in *Proc. 21st International Conference on World Wide Web*, 2012.

[11] S. Jain, Y. Chen, and D. C. Parkes, "Designing incentives for online question and answer forums," in *Proc. 10th ACM Conference on Electronic Commerce*, 2009.

[12] A. Ghosh and P. McAfee, "Incentivizing high-quality user-generated content," in *Proc. 20th International Conference on World Wide Web*, 2011.

[13] M. Burke, C. Marlow, and T. Lento, "Feed me: motivating newcomer contribution in social network sites," in *Proc. SIGCHI Conference on Human Factors in Computing Systems*, 2009.

[14] K. Ling, G. Beenen, P. Ludford, X. Wang, K. Chang, X. Li et al., "Using social psychology to motivate contributions to online communities," *Journal of Computer-Mediated Communication*, vol. 10, p. JCMC10411, 2005.

[15] J. Yang, L. A. Adamic, and M. S. Ackerman, "Crowdsourcing and knowledge sharing: strategic user behavior on taskcn," in *Proc. 9th ACM Conference on Electronic Commerce*, 2008.

[16] Y. R. Tausczik and J. W. Pennebaker, "Participation in an online mathematics community: differentiating motivations to add," in *Proc. ACM 2012 Conference on Computer Supported Cooperative Work*, 2012.

Index